ECONOMICS OF DEVELOPMENT

ECONOMICS OF DEVELOPMENT
WITH SPECIAL REFERENCE TO INDIA

D. BRIGHT SINGH, M.A., PH.D.
Professor of Economics, University of Madras

ASIA PUBLISHING HOUSE

BOMBAY - CALCUTTA - NEW DELHI - MADRAS
LUCKNOW - BANGALORE - LONDON - NEW YORK

ISBN 0. 210. 33780. X

PRINTED IN INDIA
BY AJANTA OFFSET AND PACKAGINGS LTD., DELHI-7, AND
PUBLISHED BY P. S. JAYASINGHE, ASIA PUBLISHING HOUSE. BOMBAY-1

To

CHITRA, RAJU AND RANJI

who kept me going

PREFACE

ALTHOUGH THE problems of growth, stagnation and decline of national economies have engaged the attention of economists since the days of Adam Smith, yet at no time was so much attention, time and talents devoted to the understanding of economic development and the analysis of its different aspects as in recent years. A study of the processes and problems of economic expansion involves a happy blending of theory and practice, of economic science and applied economics. The intricacies of the subject and the wide scope of analysis which it provides have fascinated the theorist while the vast vista of research opened out on the empirical side, has attracted many scholars into the field of investigation and collection of primary data. At the same time, economic planners and policy makers in their quest for scientific knowledge on which programmes of development can be based. turn with increasing avidity to the findings and conclusions of the economists.

The labours of the economists and statisticians have resulted in the accumulation of a large fund of knowledge relating to economic growth and development. The spate of literature on this subject has been so rapid. that it is hard indeed for anyone to acquaint himself fully with all or even the more important of the current writings. Apart from the theoretical analyses of outstanding modern economists, a considerable amount of factual and statistical information about national income, savings and investment. population, employment, trade, transport, commerce, industrial and agricultural production, etc., has been furnished by specialists working under the auspices of national governments and public bodies as well as of International Institutions like the World Bank and the United Nations Organization. Besides. in recent years, sociologists have also entered the field and have made important contributions towards widening our knowledge of the social and institutional factors that stand in the way of the economic progress of the poorer countries of the world.

Undoubtedly, the phenomenal growth of theoretical knowledge on the subject of economic development and the availability of abundant statistical materials relating to the many underdeveloped regions of the world have enabled the specialist to be better informed and better equipped to analyze the problems of growth of the country in which he is primarily interested. He is in a much more advantageous position today than his counterpart could have been about fifteen years ago, to have an over-all view of the problem and is more competent to sift the issues involved, to examine them in their true perspective and explain the real causes of economic backwardness and also to suggest ways and means by which a country can get out of a state of economic stagnation. However, the large number of educated people who either as students or as public spirited citizens are desirous of knowing more about the economic problems of their country and the policies which are enunciated for its economic betterment would neither have the time nor inclination to wade through the mass of published material that is available. It is to meet the requirements of such people that the present book is designed. I have drawn largely from the writings of modern authors who have specialized in the subject, but as far as possible I have tried to examine their observations and conclusions against the background of the Indian economy. Although there is a certain amount of uniqueness in the economic problems of particular countries, yet there is a great deal of similarity as regards some fundamental issues and objectives. Wherever relevant, I have made a comparative assessment of the problems of development confronting other underdeveloped countries and of the methods which they have adopted to tackle these problems.

The book falls into four divisions. The first two chapters are of an introductory nature: Chapter I deals with the main points of difference between what are called developed and underdeveloped economies and Chapter II contains a summary account of the theories of growth. Chapters III to VII are concerned with certain important problems of economic development— the social and institutional obstacles, population pressure, and the problems of capital formation, savings and the choice of investment techniques. The third section deals mostly with policy matters—monetary and tax policy, foreign trade policy, deficit financing and the role of foreign capital. Chapters XIV and XV discuss the importance of agriculture and the nature and causes of instability in a growing economy. The last three chapters forming the fourth section examine the role of the government in economic development and the need for economic planning to facilitate rapid economic growth. The concluding chapter is a brief review of planned development in India in which attention is focussed on the extent to which the Indian economy has progressed towards the stage of self-sustained growth.

In writing this book, I have received much help from some of my friends and colleagues. I am grateful to Prof. V. Shanmugasundaram for the trouble which he took to make available to me some valuable reading material and statistical data. Similar help I received from Sri V. K. Narasimhan, Assistant Editor of *The Hindu*, Madras. Dr. M. Venkataraman, Professor of Mathematics, Madras University, spared some of his time to help me to spell out the quasi-mathematical language of a few important articles on economic growth. I benefited much also by discussions with a former colleague of mine Dr. P. G. K. Panikkar, now of the Department of Economics, University of Kerala, on the importance of agricultural improvement in economic development. Apart from these friends to all of whom I am greatly indebted, I am thankful also to the Librarian of the Madras University Extension Library at Madurai and his assistants˙ for their excellent and courteous service.

I thank the Madras University for permission to publish this work.

D. BRIGHT SINGH

University of Madras
8 July 1963

CONTENTS

LIST OF TABLES

ECONOMICS OF DEVELOPMENT

Chapter I

THE NATURE AND MEANING OF
ECONOMIC UNDERDEVELOPMENT

PRIMITIVE MAN acquired the necessary things of life directly from land, but as his skill and intelligence developed, he devised new methods and techniques by which he was able to get more from land with relatively less effort. Increase in population and the organization of society into communities and nations limited the availability of natural resources for each individual or group of individuals so that it became a necessity to adopt better and more efficient methods of utilizing land. This resulted in the formation of capital which increased the productivity of labour. Viewed in this manner, economic progress is the advancement of a community along the line of evolving new and better methods of production, and raising of the levels of output through development of human skill and energy, better organization and the acquisition of capital resources. The richer and economically advanced countries are those which have progressed far in this direction, while those which have made limited progress or stagnated are the poor and economically backward countries.

Economic advancement brings in its wake important social, institutional and organizational changes. A rise in national and per capita output is implicit in economic growth. This improvement in income helps and in turn is facilitated by larger savings, increased capital formation and technological development. Rise in the per capita availability of capital resources, improvement in the skill, efficiency and earning power of labour, better organization of production, development of means of transport and communications, growth of financial institutions, urbanization, rise in the standards of health and education and expectation of life, greater leisure and increased recreation facilities and the widening of the mental horizon of the people, all these characterize economic growth. The high levels reached in these directions mark an economically developed community. Some of these factors like income and capital per head, labour productivity etc. can be assessed in quantitative terms, while some others which are equally important are of a qualitative nature and as such their significance to the countries to which they relate cannot be directly estimated. However, no study of the forces which help the economic advancement of a nation or a community over a period of time or in comparison with other countries is possible unless we make use of some reliable indicators which help quantitative assessment.

1

Thus statistical data relating to incomes, capital equipment per head, natural resources, productivity of labour, the rate of savings, distribution of national income, rate of population growth etc. constitute the basic material for analysing the causes and nature of economic growth.

MEASURING ECONOMIC GROWTH—USE OF INCOME DATA

One indicator of the standard of economic well-being attained by a country is the amount of productive assets it has acquired. As an economy advances, new productive resources are discovered, existing resources are better utilized and the stock of national and human capital assets is augmented. The more of these resources a country has, the better is its economic position. But an estimate of the size of this stock is difficult because of the lack of a common base for aggregating the different types of resources into one category. Even in respect of capital accumulation, calculation is not easy because of the restricted sense in which the term ' Capital ' is used in national accounts. In the wider economic sense capital should include both durable and non-durable items of investment as also various forms of social or human capital which add to the productive capacity of the economy. A more common criterion of economic development is aggregate flow of output in the form of national products or national incomes. Here the question arises as to whether total income or per capita income is to be considered as the correct indicator. In so far as structural change in the productive sector of the economy is an important feature of economic progress, the former would appear to be a better measure of growth than per capita output figures.[1] According to Meier and Baldwin net national product is preferable to per capita incomes as an indicator of economic growth because a larger real national income is normally a prerequisite for an increase in real per capita income. Besides, output per head may be misleading in some cases. Thus as between two countries of the same size resources and population at the beginning of a period, if population in one increases at a much faster rate, but at the same time output also increases at a similar high rate so that per capita output remains constant, while in the other per capita output increases because of a very low rate of population increase and a slightly higher rate of growth of output, it cannot be said that economic growth is more rapid in the latter. In fact, if at the beginning of the period the former country was already over populated, the maintenance of the per capita output and the attainment of a high rate of income increase should be considered as a greater achievement.[2]

But in so far as economic growth has little meaning unless it improves the material well-being of the members of the community, it is proper to consider

[1]Kuznets, Simon and others (Eds.), *Economic Growth of Brazil, India and Japan.* Duke University Press, Durham, N. C., 1955, p. 13.

[2]Meier, Gerald M., and Robert E. Baldwin, *Economic Development*, Asia Publishing House, Bombay, 1960, p. 5.

change in per capita income as the better indicator of growth. In using per capita output figures for purposes of comparison, emphasis may be laid on the production aspect of income or its consumption aspect. If the production effort of the community is the major consideration and the idea is to focus attention on the increase in the contribution per head of the people to total output, a division of the national product by the work force or better still, an index of the productivity per man hour would be a more reliable means of correctly estimating economic progress. But in the economically backward countries of the world, statistical data relating to labour force or man hours worked are even less reliable than population figures and as such, calculations of this kind would be subject to a large margin of error. On the other hand, if the emphasis is on the improvement in the standard of living of the people and a better distribution of incomes is visualized as a consequence of economic growth, data relating to consumption per head are to be made use of.

LIMITATIONS OF INCOME DATA

It is however, important to bear in mind the limitations of national income figures, especially when they are used for purposes of comparison between different countries. Apart from the basic difficulty involved in the definition of income and in the question of its components, i.e. what items are to be included and what are not to be included, national income figures are to be used with care in estimating the relative achievements of different countries or of the same country over time. Many things evade monetary computation such as improvement of the health of the people, dietary habits etc. The extent to which government service—military defence and national security— adds to national income cannot be estimated. While the contribution of private capital to national output can be calculated with reference to profit returns or interest earned, a similar calculation is not possible in respect of government capital investment such as hydroelectric projects, roads or irrigation works in so far as there is no correspondence between the size of government debt and the quantity of government capital.[3] Besides, the statistical data available in low income countries are meagre and unreliable. This is due to the lack of resources which can be spared for the collection of statistical information and the social conditions prevailing in these countries. The value of time is not properly appreciated and records of production, sales or consumption are not kept. Units of weights, volume etc. are not accurately or firmly fixed. National income data include only recorded incomes. Many unpaid social services and intra-family services such as the service of housewives, although they add to the real income of the community, are not included in national income computations. In poor or low income countries in which agriculture predominates, and a large subsistence sector exists along with a monetized sector, a good part of the output does not enter into the circle of exchange

[3]Villard, Henry H., *Economic Development*, Rinehart, New York, 1959, p. 24.

and as such are excluded from national income calculations. To this extent national income figures of these countries tend to be underestimates. And for the same reason, the shrinking of the subsistence sector swells up national income statistics to a greater extent than what actual increase in physical output would warrant. On the other hand, in the economically advanced countries, national income data tend to be exaggerated as compared with the poorer countries. The very fact that statistical details are more adequate and comprehensive tends to swell up the aggregate figures. Increased commercialization, the tendency for money incomes to rise at a faster rate than real incomes and the decline in the importance of goods gratuitously provided within the family, all these create an upward bias in the income data.

Another difficulty in national income computations arises out of differences in the methods of valuing certain special items. Valuation of some articles differs according as factor cost, wholesale or retail price or export price is taken into account. Besides, in a large country like India with inadequate means of communication and transport, prices of the same commodities may differ considerably from region to region. Professor Kindleberger draws attention to the difference between net geographical product and national product. Income produced by factors of production located in the country but owned abroad is part of the former but not of the latter. This may be misleading because output includes exports but not imports. If the two happen to be equal there is no mistake in the calculation of income. But if balance of payments departs from zero as it normally does, there is an error.[4]

Whether aggregate or per capita output is taken as a measure of economic growth, a mere rise in the levels need not be an unmistakable sign of progress. National income data do not take into account the cost and the benefit side of the income account fully. Increase in money income involves certain social costs which have to be taken into account if a correct assessment is to be made of the addition to real income of the community. In any estimate of economic improvement of a country over a period of time or in a comparison of the rates of growth of different countries, the welfare aspect of income increase cannot altogether be ignored. A rise in money income alone is not a measure of economic improvement because it is likely that in the process of securing higher incomes, the community would have been subjected to social costs like overcrowding in urban areas, disruption of social habits, increasing disagreeableness of work, restriction of access to country side etc. It is also possible that higher incomes are attained at the cost of depletion of valuable natural resources so that while income increases immediately, it affects seriously the potentiality of growth of the economy. The exploitation of oil resources in some small countries of Western Asia swells up national incomes, but this rise does not reflect the well-being of the people at large. Nor can the social and economic effects of redistribution of incomes brought about by income growth be lightly glossed over. It is possible that rise in per capita income is attended

[4]Kindleberger, Charles F., *Economic Development*, McGraw-Hill, New York, 1958. p. 6 (f.n.).

with greater disparity in income and wealth so that while economic progress boosts up the income of a few privileged persons inordinately, the proportion of low income and poor people may also simultaneously increase. Repeal of the Corn Laws in England in 1846 helped in an increase in national income, but the rise in income involved also a shifting in the distribution of income in favour of the industrial and manufacturing classes and to the disadvantage of land owners. It is difficult to gauge the net result of such distribution by weighing the disadvantages of one class against the advantages of the other.[5] Obviously in instances such as this, when rise in income takes place along with increasing destitution of many, it is against commonsense to say that there is economic progress. Hence Viner points out that a rise in aggregate national output can be considered as an indication of progress, only if it helps in at least maintaining the standard of life of an increasing number of people at existing levels or in raising the standards of life and income of the existing number of people.[6] Moreover, the composition of goods produced in the country may change. The quantity and the money value of production may go up but the type of goods that are produced and their quality may deteriorate. The tastes, likes and dislikes of the consumers may alter. It is therefore not possible to say that merely because output has increased, real income also has increased to a corresponding extent. Economic growth is a multi-dimensional phenomenon; it involves not only increase in money incomes, but also improvement in social habits, education, public health, greater leisure and in fact all the social and economic circumstances that make for a fuller and happier life. As Kuznets has remarked, the social aggregates dealt with by statistical methods are " only results *engros* and cannot reveal the underlying motivations and aspirations of the human agents and of the institutional factors at play ".[7] National income data can therefore only indicate the trend of aggregate earnings of the community but do not correctly measure the economic standard attained. Furthermore, a rise in incomes may be attended with considerable fluctuations which dislocate economic life and bring about serious hardship to many. Hence figures of national output can be said to reflect economic growth only if the rise is steady and sustained and is at a faster rate than the growth of population so that there is on the whole a continuous improvement in per capita incomes and in the standard of living of the people.

[5]Youngson, A. J., *Possibilities of Economic Progress*, The University Press, Cambridge, 1959, p. 10.

[6]Viner, J., *International Trade and Economic Development*, Oxford University Press, London, 1957, p. 98.

[7]Kuznets, S., *Income and Wealth of the United States: Trends and Structure*, The International Association for Research in Income and Wealth, New York, 1952, p. 15. A similar observation is made by Herbert Frankel, " Incomes have meaning only in relation to the social context in which they are imbedded. It is fallacious therefore to assume that aggregate (or average) incomes are a measure of development." ' United Nations Primer for Development,' *Quarterly Journal of Economics*, August, 1952, p. 309.

For purposes of comparing the relative rates of growth of output in different countries we should have either an international unit of account or various indices of income, employment, output etc. In the first edition of his well known work Colin Clark introduced the concept of International Unit or I.U. which he defined as " the amount of goods and services which could be purchased for one dollar in the U.S.A. over the average of the decade 1925–34 or an amount interchangeable with them ". Later, realizing the fact that while the I.U. served reasonably satisfactorily in comparing economically advanced countries, it was less so as a unit of measurement in respect of low income countries, Colin Clark introduced the Oriental Unit or O.U. defined as " the quantity of goods or services exchangeable directly or indirectly for one rupee in India in 1948–49.[8] Commonly however, international comparisons of income changes are made on the basis of index numbers relating to the respective countries. But the index number has serious defects which bewilder every student of economic growth. A production index assumes that the quality and nature of the goods produced do not vary over time and that opportunity costs remain constant. A new product may be produced, or the quality of the same product may be changed, but these changes will not be taken into account in so far as the production index is based on a fixed list of products. This obviously leads to considerable difficulties in comparisons of output between two countries when the economic significance of the commodities in the list varies widely between one country and another. Thus when a comparison of the rates of growth in two countries is made in terms of index numbers, as for instance when it is said that in one country the rate of growth of income is 2 per cent higher than in another, there is little meaning unless due notice is taken of changes in the structure of production. Austerity measures may raise growth rate in one country but the index number does not in any manner indicate the strain involved in the economy. Nevertheless the index number is helpful in so far as its movement up or down indicates at worst the direction of growth; the changes in movement indicate at best whether there is acceleration or retardation of growth. Moreover, the defects of the index number can be reduced if a large number of separate indices are used, e.g. for manufacturing, agriculture, mining, services and so on.[9] However, economic growth cannot be compared between two countries in terms of index number alone. Rise in values is estimated with reference to prices prevailing in the base period. The usual method employed is to compare prices in period 2 multiplied by the amount of goods produced in that period with the amount of goods produced in period 1 multiplied by prices of period 2. The base period chosen is therefore of considerable significance. The choice of a base period covering a year or years when prices

[8]Clark, Colin, *The Conditions of Economic Progress*, 3rd edition, Macmillan, London, 1957, p. 20.

[9]Nutter, Warren G., ' On Measuring Economic Growth,' *Journal of Political Economy*, February, 1957, pp. 51–63.

are rising or falling rapidly would give a distorted view of the trend in the subsequent years. There is again the vexed problem of aggregation. Weighting of different categories of goods is done in order to incorporate the relative significance of the different commodities, but this in turn creates a difficulty in so far as fundamental changes in the composition of national product, such as the introduction of new commodities, would make the earlier weighting useless. The discrepancy may not be great when relatively short period comparisons are made, but since economic growth is concerned with the attainments over longer time periods, this would create a real problem.

The limitations of national income figures appear particularly pronounced when they are used for comparing the levels or rates of growth of income between the rich and the poor countries. In order to make such comparisons, incomes estimated in national currencies are converted into some international currency such as the U.S.A. dollar at the official exchange rates. This leads to some distortion. Because of various restrictions on international trade such as quotas, tariffs and exchange control, the official exchange rate seldom reflects the true parity values of the currencies. Incomes of low income countries converted at foreign exchange rates appear lower than what they really are. In fact the more economically backward is the country concerned, the greater is this sort of underestimation. Findings of Gilbert and Kravis relating to some OEEC countries show that in comparisons of their per capita national product with that of the U.S.A., the disparity is substantially much less when the value of the per capita product is computed on the basis of domestic prices or American prices than when exchange rates are used for conversion.[10] M. F. Millikan mentions that the real income of Asian Countries (excluding the Middle East) in 1950 calculated in local currencies and converted at the official exchange rates was $ 58 but it would be three and a half times higher than this if allowance were made for bias in estimation.[11] In view of this distortion Prof. E. E. Hagen feels that if per capita incomes below $ 100 in the United Nations International Statistics are multiplied by 3, $ 100 to 300 by $2\frac{1}{2}$, $ 300 to 600 by 2 and $ 600 to 1,200 by $1\frac{1}{3}$, we would get a more realistic picture of the relative per capita income position of the different countries.[12]

Hagen points out that this underestimation arises from the fact that the export goods of low income countries are less labour intensive than domestically consumed goods. The latter are therefore much cheaper. Foreign exchange rates reflect the relative prices of goods and services of internationally traded goods. This means that a large volume of goods which are produced and

[10]Quoted in Villard, Henry H., *Economic Development*, Rinehart, New York, 1959. p. 27.

[11]Statement of M. F. Millikan before the Sub-committee on Foreign Economic Policy of the Joint Committee on the Economic Report: 84th Congress of the U.S.A.; 1st session 1955, pp. 21–28, quoted in C. F. Kindleberger, *Economic Development*, McGraw-Hill, New York, 1958, pp. 7 and 8.

[12]Hagen, E. Everett, 'Some Facts about Income Levels and Economic Growth,' *Review of Economics and Statistics*, February, 1960, pp. 62–67.

consumed in the poorer countries and which do not enter into foreign trade are not given as high a price as the export and import goods. Hence the larger proportionately is the volume of such goods, the greater will be the underestimation. From another point of view, understatement of the income of low income countries and overstatement in the case of high income countries spring from the disparity in the productivity of labour and hence in the level of wages. Differences in wage levels between countries correspond to inter-country productivity differentials in the production of traded goods (manu- factured and agricultural products). In the matter of services (which constitute the tertiary sector) the productivity difference is much less between countries of different standards of economic development. Wage increases in the tertiary sector follow wage movements in materials production, especially in industry. But since services are non-traded (internationally) and the wage level in the agricultural and industrial sector is much lower in low income countries than in the richer countries, the price of such services will tend to be low in the former. As an economy develops, the tertiary sector tends to expand in relation to the other sectors. Hence in the high income countries as economic development proceeds, non-traded goods i.e. services will become more and more expensive because the prices of such goods will rise along with prices of manufactured and agricultural goods. Thus increased productivity differentials will be accompanied by an increasing degree of overvaluation of per capita incomes of richer countries.[13]

Despite these limitations, per capita income figures do indicate at least roughly the standard of economic development attained by different countries. If real national income increases at a faster rate than the growth of population so that per capita income rises steadily, it is undoubtedly a mark of economic improvement, taking the country or community as a whole. The great disparity in per capita income figures of the various countries of the world as given in the national income accounts may be to some extent less if corrections are made for statistical or other bias in calculation. But the difference will still be considerable and shows the extent to which some countries have lagged far behind others. Similarly, the annual rate of increase in incomes is a rough but reliable indication of the speed of economic growth. While it is true that in so far as economic growth is a multi-dimensional process, a uni-dimensional means of measurement such as national or per capita income cannot be alto-gether satisfactory, yet for gauging the relative performance of different countries in any period of time, or for estimating the achievements of any one country over a period of time, national income statistics constitute an important source of evidence. It has also to be added that for any proper assessment of the motive forces behind growth and to measure the extent to which structural and organizational changes have taken place in the process of economic growth, other aspects of progress of a non-economic kind,

[13]Bela Balassa, ' Patterns of Industrial Growth: Comment,' *American Economic Review*, June, 1961. p. 395.

such as standards of health and education, expectation of life, social amenities available etc. are also to be taken into account. However, in any ordinal ranking of individual countries with reference to their standard of economic development, per capita income figures are useful.

DEVELOPED AND UNDERDEVELOPED COUNTRIES

On the basis of a careful study of income statistics pertaining to the various countries of the world, Prof. Everett E. Hagen makes the following grouping of countries with reference to their per capita incomes. The income figures relate to the year 1957. Per capita incomes in national currencies have been converted to U.S. dollars by use of foreign exchange rates.[14]

Table 1

PER CAPITA GNP THROUGHOUT THE WORLD

Group of countries	Population (thousands)	GNP ($ million)	Average GNP per capita ($)
1. PER CAPITA GNP UP TO $ 100			
America: Falkland islands and Bolivia	3,277	324	99
Greenland	27	3	100
Asia and the Middle East: (includes Afghanistan, Burma, China, India, Nepal, Pakistan, Thailand, Viet Nam and some other small countries)	1,226,763	88,557	72
Oceania: (excluding Australia and New Zealand)	2,790	124	45
Africa: (includes Eritrea and Ethiopia, Kenya, Liberia, Libya, Madagascar, Nigeria etc.)	154,467	11,589	75
Sub Total or Average	1,387,324	100,597	73
Per cent of World Total	49·7%	8·7%	
2. PER CAPITA GNP of $ 101—$ 300			
Latin America: (includes Brazil, British Guiana, Colombia, Dominican Republic, Ecuador, Guatemala, Haiti, Mexico, Nicaragua, Paraguay, Peru, Surinam and some other countries)	138,115	35,428	257
Asia and the Middle East: [includes Aden, Ceylon, China (Taiwan), Indonesia, Iran, Iraq, Jordan, Turkey, U.A.R. and others]	241,320	37,277	155
Europe: (Albania, Andorra, Faeroe Islands, Portugal, Spain, Yugoslavia)	57,848	15,668	271
Africa: (Algeria, Ghana, Mauritius, Morocco, Rhodesia and Nyasaland, Tunisia)	40,060	6,215	155
Sub Total or Average	477,343	94,588	198
Per cent of World Total	17·1%	8·2%	

[14]Hagen, Everett E., ' Some Facts about Income Levels and Economic Growth,' *Review of Economics and Statistics*, February, 1960, pp. 62–67.

PER CAPITA GNP THROUGHOUT THE WORLD—(contd.)

Group of countries	Population (thousands)	GNP ($ million)	Average GNP per capita ($)
3. PER CAPITA GNP OF $ 301—$ 600			
Latin America: (includes Argentina, Chile, Costa Rica, Cuba, Panama, Puerto Rico, Uruguay)	43,472	19,447	447
Asia and the Middle East: (Japan, Malaya, Singapore, Lebanon, Cyprus)	100,803	31,504	313
Europe and U.S.S.R.: (includes Bulgaria, East Germany, Gibraltor, Greece, Hungary, Iceland, Ireland, Italy, Malta, Poland, Rumania, San Marino and U.S.S.R.)	343,199	188,889	550
Union of South Africa	14,167	5,606	395
Sub Total or Average	501,641	245,446	489
Per cent of World Total	18%	21·3%	
4. PER CAPITA GNP OF $ 601—$ 1,200			
Latin America: Venezuela	6,191	4,013	648
Europe: (Austria, Belgium, Czechoslovakia, Denmark, Finland, France, West Germany, Netherlands, Norway, United Kingdom, Lichtenstein, Monaco.)	202,119	198,757	983
Asia and the Middle East: (Israel)	1,937	1,407	726
Sub Total or Average	210,247	204,177	971
Per cent of World Total	7·5%	17·7%	
5. PER CAPITA GNP OF $ 1,201 AND ABOVE			
America: U.S.A. and Canada	189,609	475,561	2,521
Europe: Luxembourg, Sweden, Switzerland	12,800	17,910	1,399
Asia: Kuwait and Qatar	248	675	2,722
Oceania : Australia and New Zealand	11,921	15,673	1,315
Sub Total or Average	213,578	509,819	2,387
Per cent of World Total	7·7%	44·2%	
World Totals or Average	2,790,133	1,154,628	414

The figures in the above table show the wide disparity in per capita incomes between different countries and also a great deal of concentration of incomes internationally. Thus nearly 50 per cent of the world's population share only 8·7 per cent of the world's income, while 7·7 per cent of the population have 44·2 per cent of the total income of the world. The annual per capita income in the first group is $ 73 while in the latter it is $ 2,387. Of the world's total population of 2,790 million, about 2,000 million or more than 70 per cent, get a per capita income which is below the world's average of $ 414. Income data relating to the year 1953 and published in *The Year Book of National Accounts Statistics*, U.N., 1958, show that only 7 countries—U.S.A., New Zealand, Canada, U.K., Australia, Sweden and Switzerland—had a per capita income of above $ 1,000. Among the countries getting below $ 100 are Thailand, Philippines, Bolivia, Belgian Congo, China, India, Pakistan, Indonesia and Burma. India with $ 57 per head, Pakistan $ 51 and Burma $ 48 come at the bottom of the list. It is worth adding that all the high income countries of the world today are in the temperate region, while most of the poor or low income countries are in the tropical or subtropical region.

Not only do the existing levels of incomes show such wide disparity, but there is also considerable difference in the rate of growth of output per head in recent years. The annual rate of increase in total product in the richer countries has been about 2·5 per cent to 3 per cent, as compared with about 1·5 per cent in the low income countries. Per capita output in the U.S.A., Japan, Australia, Sweden and Norway has increased at the rate of more than 20 per cent per decade while in the poorer countries with rapid increase in population and slow increase in output, per capita income has either not increased, or increased only to a negligible extent.[15] Since the per capita incomes of many of the low income countries are at subsistence level now, it is not possible that these would have been much lower some hundred years ago. It would therefore mean that there was little growth of income per head over these years. Similarly, extrapolating the present rates of growth of richer countries backwards from 1952–54 it would be found that a low of about $ 100 is reached by the late 18th or early 19th century. In actual fact per capita income of countries like the U.K. and U.S.A. was not that low at the end of the 18th century. Professor Simon Kuznets therefore concludes that the present rates of growth in these countries could not have persisted over long periods in the past but must have been concentrated in relatively recent years.[16]

It is possible to have a clearer idea of the relative position of low income countries by examining in some detail the four aspects of income—production, distribution, consumption and the socio-economic aspect.

(1) Income—the Production Aspect

The major cause of the low per capita income and output of labour in the poorer countries is the scarcity of co-operant factors—land, natural resources

[15]According to Dr. K. Mukerji of the Gokhale Institute of Politics and Economics, Poona, the per capita income of India stagnated at about Rs. 270 (at 1948–49 constant prices) for thirty years from 1921–22 till national planning movement started. *Papers on National Income and Allied Topics*, Vol. II, Edited by Dr. V. K. R. V. Rao and others, Indian Conference on Research in National Income, Asia Publishing House, Bombay, 1962, p. 24.

[16]Kuznets, Simon, *Six Lectures on Economic Growth*, Free Press, Illinois, 1959, pp. 25–28. Data relating to the U.S.A. illustrate the rapid growth of income in that country since the last quarter of the 19th century. U.S.A. in 1875 had a population of 46 million and an annual income of about $ 16 billion which works out to a per capita income of $ 350. In 1950 population increased to 150 million, annual income to $ 240 billion and income per head to $ 1600, i.e. in 75 years per capita income increased by four and a half times—Villard, Henry H., *Economic Development*, Rinehart, New York, 1959, p. 7.

and capital. Of the 35·7 billion acres of the earth's surface only 2·6 billion acres or about 7 per cent is believed to be suitable for cultivation purposes. Most of the low income countries of Asia and the Far East are overpopulated and the per capita availability of land suited for cultivation is very limited. It has been estimated that Asia has only 0·52 acre of cultivable land per head while in North America it is 3·10 acres or about six times higher. Further, most of the land available for cultivation in the poorer countries of the world have already been in use and they do not have any large unused but potentially cultivable land areas. On the other hand, in some of the richer countries like Australia, Canada and the U.S.A. and also in some low income countries of Latin America, the resources available in the form of unused land which can be brought under cultivation are quite extensive. Scarcity of land is thus undoubtedly one of the important factors hindering economic expansion. It is clear that there is very limited scope for increasing output by making land available in countries where the people are most in need of it. Thus for increasing output, these countries have to depend on better utilization of existing land resources, but the economic backwardness of these countries prevents any full use being made of the potential productivity of their best land or any modification or overcoming of the deficiencies of their poorer land.[17]

Statistical data relating to mineral and other resources available in the low income countries are meagre. In many of these countries no scientific survey has been made of the potentialities in mineral or water resources. To a large extent economic backwardness is due not so much to the lack of resources as to the failure to exploit these resources. Technological development in the richer countries helps in the discovery of new resources whose commercial value could not have been thought of at an earlier time. It is also to be observed that much of the resources with which some low income countries have been endowed by nature, remains unused. It is estimated that in the advanced European countries, 60 per cent of the available water power is utilized while in Asia only 13 per cent, in Middle America 5 per cent, in South America 3 per cent and in Africa a little more than 0·1 per cent has been harnessed into use.[18] The relative position of some countries of the world in the matter of production of coal, petroleum and iron ore which constitute the key materials of industrialization is shown in Table 2.

Of the world's supply of coal, petroleum and iron ore, U.S.A. has 30·2 per cent, 42·1 per cent and 27·3 per cent respectively. U.S.S.R. has 19·2 per cent of coal, 9·9 per cent of petroleum and 24·1 per cent of iron ore. India's supply of coal forms 2·5 per cent of world production, petroleum 0·03 per cent and iron ore 1·5 per cent. Japan's position in respect of coal and

[17]Buchanan, Norman S. and S. Ellis Howard, *Approaches to Economic Development,* Twentieth Century Fund, New York, 1958, pp. 33–37.

[18]Banks, A.L. (Ed.), *The Development of Tropical and Subtropical Countries,* Edward Arnold Ltd., London, 1954, p. xiv, 70: quoted in Meier, G.M. and R. E. Baldwin, *Economic Development,* Asia Publishing House, Bombay, 1957, p. 293.

Table 2

PRODUCTION OF COAL, PETROLEUM AND IRON ORE IN SOME COUNTRIES
(Output in thousand metric tons)

Country	Coal	Petroleum (Crude)	Iron Ore
Canada	11,407	23,051	11,240
	(0·7)	(2·7)	(6·0)
Mexico	1,408	12,972	489
	(0·09)	(1·5)	(0·26)
U.S.A.	476,842	353,718	51,171
	(30·2)	(42·1)	(27·3)
Brazil	2,233	524	2,073
	(0·14)	(0·06)	(1·1)
Chile	2,278	462	1,663
	(0·14)	(0·05)	(0·9)
India	40,067	253*	2,935
	(2·54)	(0·03)	(1·5)
Japan	46,555	345	1,099
	(2·95)	(0·04)	(0·5)
France	55,129	1,264	17,120
	(3·5)	(0·16)	(9·1)
U.K.	225,568	146	4,558
	(14·3)	(0·02)	(2·4)
U.S.S R.	303,700	83,800	45,200
	(19·2)	(9·9)	(24·1)
WORLD TOTAL	1,579,700	839,800	187,400

Percentage in world production given in brackets.
*1949.
SOURCE: *Statistical Year Book*, U.N. 1957.

petroleum is similar to that of India, while in the matter of iron ore, her production is about one third that of India. But considering the size of the country, the output of these basic industrial materials in India is quite meagre and inadequate.

Low per capita incomes account for low rate of savings and capital formation. Net capital formation amounts to 12 to 15 per cent or more of national income in economically advanced countries. But the corresponding rate for backward economies is about 5 per cent or less. A body of experts of the United Nations estimated it at 6 per cent of the national income in the Middle East in 1949 and 4·4 per cent in the Asian and African countries.[19] Although there has been some improvement in recent years, the disparity is still wide.

Scarcity of capital is reflected in the very low capital-labour ratio in low income countries as compared with countries which have advanced far in

[19]*Measures for the Economic Development of Underdeveloped Countries*, United Nations, 1951, pp. 35 and 76.

industrialization. Estimates made by Prof. Colin Clark of capital per occupied
person in manufacturing industries in some countries are illustrative of the
relative position of the different countries in this respect.

Table 3

CAPITAL PER OCCUPIED PERSON IN
MANUFACTURING INDUSTRY ABOUT 1939

Country	Year	Amount of Capital (Sterling)	Country	Year	Amount of Capital (Sterling)
U.S.A.	1939	1,250	Australia	1936–'37	330
Canada	1936	1,107	Venezuela	1936	330
Denmark	1928	703	Palestine	1936	293
Germany	1936	513	Brazil	1945	283
India	1938–'39	507	Rumania	1937	248

SOURCE: Colin Clark, *Conditions of Economic Progress*, 3rd edn., Macmillan & Co.,
London, 1957, pp. 582-83.

According to a calculation made by the United Nations Department of
Economic Affairs in 1949, real capital per worker in Asia and the Far East
excluding Japan was only 10 per cent of that of the U.S.A.[20] The consumption
of commercial sources of energy is a rough measure of the disparity in capital
equipment per worker in different countries. In 1956 the estimated consumption of commercial sources of energy expressed in terms of coal (metric tons)
was 8·25 in Canada, 8·58 in the U.S.A., 5·03 in the U.K., 5·66 in Norway, 4·59
in Sweden, and 3·6 in West Germany; while in the mainland of China it was
0·18, Pakistan 0·05, India 0·12, Ceylon 0·08 and in Burma 0·04; the average
for North America was 6·59 while for South America and Asia it was 0·59
and 0·23 respectively.

Lack of capital combined with overpopulation has seriously narrowed down
the employment opportunities in low income countries with the result that
too large a proportion of the working force is dependent on agriculture and
other extractive industries. The rigidity or flexibility of the structure of production and the distribution of the working force in the primary, secondary and
tertiary sectors constitute an unmistakable indication of the level of economic
development attained by a country. With the progress of industrialization
and economic advancement, there is a transfer of population from agriculture
to industry. Simultaneously, there is a rise in the proportion of people
engaged in the tertiary services. The position of the low income countries in
this respect in comparison with economically advanced countries is illustrated
in Table 4.

[20]U.N. Department of Economic Affairs, *Economic Survey of Asia and the Far East, 1949*, New
York, 1950, p. 296.

Table 4

DISTRIBUTION OF LABOUR IN DIFFERENT INDUSTRIES AND OCCUPATIONS

Country and Year	Agriculture, Fishing and Forestry	Distribution of Labour as Percentage of Total				
		Mining	Manufacture	Transport and Communication	Commerce and Finance	Profession and other Services
Turkey (1950)	75·6	0·3	13·0	1·6	3·3	8·1
India (1951)	69·4	←— 10·7 —→		1·6	6·1	12·2
Burma (1931)	69·0	1·0	13·0	←— 14·0 —→		3·0
Indonesia, Java (1930)	65·4	...	15·4	2·0	9·4	7·3
Egypt (1947)	61·1	0·2	13·7	3·4	10·4	11·2
Philippines (1948)	60·1	0·4	12·4	2·9	7·2	17·1
Brazil (1950)	56·0	3·0	13·7	4·3	6·6	16·5
Spain (1940)	50·6	1·1	23·6	3·5	6·6	...
Ceylon (1946)	43·9	0·4	12·7	←— 25·1 —→		17·9
Chile (1940)	34·1	5·7	20·9	4·4	9·6	25·4
Japan (1950)	32·6	2·0	←— 32·6 —→		15·5	17·3
Argentine (1947)	25·7	0·5	30·0	6·5	14·3	23·0
Norway (1950)	24·6	0·7	36·7	10·4	11·2	16·6
France (1951)	20·2	←— 41·4 —→		6·0	16·4	16·0
New Zealand (1945)	20·1	1·3	30·9	12·3	16·8	18·6
Switzerland (1941)	19·9	0·4	44·5	4·0	10·3	20·9
Sweden (1950)	19·3	0·5	41·2	8·2	13·1	17·7
Denmark (1952)	19·0	...	38·4	6·7	14·7	21·1
Canada (1951)	18·7	2·0	34·0	7·8	16·5	20·8
Australia (1947)	16·8	1·8	35·8	10·0	16·1	19·3
Germany (1950)	11·8	←— 49·0 —→		←— 18·8 —→		20·3
U.S.A. (1950)	11·6	1·7	35·7	7·8	19·2	23·8
Great Britain (1951)	4·5	3·9	45·8	7·8	14·2	24·1

SOURCE: Colin Clark, *Conditions of Economic Progress*, 3rd edn., Macmillan & Co., London, 1957, pp. 510–19.

While in the countries with less than $ 100 of per capita income, more than 60 per cent of the labour force is engaged in agriculture, fishing and forestry and less than 15 per cent in manufacturing industries, the position is reversed in the rich countries with per capita income of $ 600 and above. In the latter group of countries, about 40 per cent of labour is engaged in manufacture and 15 per cent or less in agriculture. In general, the proportion of people engaged in tertiary services seems to vary with the standard of economic advancement. It is estimated that about 60 per cent of the world's population or about 1·3 billion of people depend upon agriculture. Of this, over 1 billion or 77 per cent live in Asia, Africa, Central and South America. Historical studies as well as the recent findings of Simon Kuznets, L. H. Bean and Colin Clark[21] show considerable uniformity in the rise of industry as economic growth proceeds. Hollis B. Chenery observes that the share of industrial output in national income rises from 17 per cent at a per capita income level of $ 100 to 38 per cent at a level of $ 1,000. The share of transportation and communication also doubles over this range while primary production declines from 45 per cent to 15 per cent. There is simultaneously a change in the composition of manufactured goods. As income rises, the proportion of investment and related products rises while that of consumer goods falls. Higher rates of growth of industries according to Chenery is due not only to conditions of demand (i.e. as income increases, demand for food and agricultural commodities increases at a slower rate than for manufactured commodities) but also due to conditions of supply.[22]

The very fact that there has been too much of concentration on land use, and capital per head is very low, explains the low productivity of labour in this sector of the economy. With nearly 70 per cent of the working population engaged in agriculture and allied occupations, the income from agriculture, fishing and forestry formed 48·7 per cent of the aggregate income of India in 1954. The low level of productivity of labour in primary industry in the poorer countries as compared with that of advanced countries in the same industry is seen in the table below.

Table 5

LABOUR PRODUCTIVITY IN PRIMARY INDUSTRY

Country and Year		Output per Man in I.U.
Thailand	1947	101
Turkey	1952	127
Ceylon	1950	206
Brazil	1950	288
Malaya	1949	292
Switzerland	1950	535
Belgium	1950	925
Argentine	1947	985
Netherlands	1950	992
Canada	1951	1595

SOURCE: Colin Clark, *Conditions of Economic Progress*, 3rd edn., Macmillan & Co., London, 1957, p. 276.

[21]Kuznets, S., ' Quantitative Aspects of the Economic Growth of Nations,' *Economic Development and Cultural Change*, July, 1957, Supplement.

Bean, L. H., ' International Industrialization and per capita Income,' *Studies in Income and Wealth*, Vol. 8, National Bureau of Economic Research, New York, 1946.

Clark, C., *Conditions of Economic Progress*, 3rd edn., Macmillan, London. 1957.

[22]Chenery, B. Hollis, ' Problems of Industrial Growth,' *American Economic Review*, September, 1960, pp. 624–54.

Output per man does not measure the difference in the productivity of labour when comparison is made between densely populated low income countries and rich countries where the land-labour ratio is high such as Canada. The availability of land as well as capital per head explains largely the difference in output per head. But even comparisons between densely populated high income countries like Netherlands and Belgium and low income countries like Turkey, Ceylon and Thailand show the wide disparity in output per head in the primary industry. That a poor country with a predominantly agricultural economy tends to be unprogressive even in agriculture is illustrated by the great difference in the yield of rice per acre in some countries of the world.

Table 6

RICE PRODUCTION IN DIFFERENT COUNTRIES

Country	Output per hectare in 1955 (in 100 Kilograms)
Philippines	11·9
Viet-Nam	12·3
India	12·6
Thailand	14·3
Burma	14·8
Brazil	15·0
U.S.A.	34·3
Australia	45·9
Japan	48·1
Italy	51·0

SOURCE : Benjamin Higgins, *Economic Development: Principles, Problems and Policies*, Constable, London, 1959, p. 16.

It may be noted that the output of rice in Thailand and Burma which are major rice producing countries in the East is about one fourth of that in Japan, Italy and Australia.

A similar disparity is observable in manufacturing industry also (Table 7).

Normally as a country advances economically, the proportion of labour engaged in the tertiary industry or service sector and the proportion of income generated in that sector to total income tend to increase. The supply of services per head of population is thus a broad indicator of the standard of development attained by a country. It is generally presumed that productivity in services is not likely to differ much between countries, but the figures in Table 8 show that both the supply of services per head of population and the real product per man-hour in service industries are closely correlated to the income level of the country.

Table 7

NET INCOME PRODUCED PER MAN-HOUR IN MANUFACTURING IN 1950 (IN I.Us)

Country	I.Us	Country	I.Us
U.S.A.	1·404	U.K.	0·412
Canada	1·231	Chile	0·403
Sweden	0·879	Germany	0·395
New Zealand	0·806	Belgium	0·381
Australia	0·594	Israel	0·346
Denmark	0·575	Argentine	0·317
Brazil (1948)	0·547	Philippines (1948)	0·300
Norway	0·497	France	0·296
Netherlands	0·459	Japan	0·236
Turkey	0·416	India	0·174

SOURCE : Colin Clark, *Conditions of Economic Progress*, Macmillan, London, 3rd edn., pp. 336–37.

Table 8

PRODUCTIVITY AND SUPPLY OF SERVICES PER HEAD IN DIFFERENT COUNTRIES

Country and Year	Real Product per Man-Hour in Service Industries in I.Us	Supply of Services per head of Population per Annum in I.Us
U.S.A. 1950–52	1·477	721
Canada 1950–52	1·442	637
New Zealand 1950	1·214	627
Australia 1951–52	0·850	412
France 1950–52	0·781	372
U.K. 1950–52	0·697	423
Ireland 1950–51	0·667	308
Union of S. Africa 1950	0·555	192
Argentine 1951	0·475	225
Chile 1950	0·409	190
Japan 1950–52	0·391	147
Italy 1935–38	0·347	98
Peru 1950–51	0·247	100
Colombia 1944–45	0·156	50

SOURCE : Colin Clark, *Conditions of Economic Progress*, Macmillan, London, 3rd edn., 1957 p. 377.

To some extent, differences in productivity has to be explained in terms of the differences in the quality of labour. Low standards of health and vitality and literacy and lack of mobility partly explain the poor performance of labour in some countries. But these low standards are as much the cause as the effect of low incomes. By far the major factor responsible for the disparity in manufacturing industry is the differences in capital equipment per worker and also the rapid advance of technology in the high income countries and the lack of it in the poorer countries of the world. As for productivity in agriculture, superiority in agricultural techniques employed in advanced countries and the fact that owing to pressure of population cultivation is pushed further and further in the direction of poorer land in the economically backward countries provide the chief explanation. Since labour is cheap, the tendency in low income countries is to work more intensively the available land even when it is of a poor quality. Harvey Leibenstein remarks: " As long as industrial capital remains relatively scarce and as long as the vast majority of the labour force is engaged in agriculture, it would appear to be reasonably safe to postulate that under these circumstances and at least for the early stages of development the system is operating under diminishing returns with respect to labour."[23] Low land-labour and capital-labour ratios also account for under-employment and disguised unemployment in agriculture which is another characteristic of low income countries.

One important feature of the economies of some of the low income countries particularly of countries of South America as well as Malaya and Ceylon in the East, is that their production is very much foreign trade oriented. In some of these countries exports constitute more than 30 per cent of the Gross National Product. In Ceylon it exceeds 40 per cent. The exports are mostly raw materials or agricultural products and are concentrated on one or a few articles. For example tin ore exports from Bolivia, cotton from Egypt, copper from Chile, coffee from El Salvador and sugar from Cuba. The national income of these countries is thus highly susceptible to fluctuations resulting from varying trends in the foreign markets for their products. The tendency for terms of trade to turn against agricultural materials and the establishment of foreign enterprises on monopolistic lines for the exploitation of the resources have prevented these countries from making good use of their natural resources.

(2) Income: the Distribution Aspect

The much lower income of poor countries is more inequitably distributed than in the richer countries. In the early stages of development disparity in income and wealth tends to increase because of large profits earned by the entrepreneur class. In general, wage earnings appear to form a lower proportion of total national income in low income countries than in the economically advanced ones. According to Colin Clark's estimates labour's share of net income in high income countries like the U.S.A., U.K., Canada, Australia,

[23]Leibenstein, Harvey, *Economic Backwardness and Economic Growth*, Wiley, New York, 1960, p. 56.

New Zealand and Switzerland was more than 70 per cent about 1950, while in Chile and Mexico it was below 60 per cent.[24] On the other hand, unearned income of land owners in the shape of land rent forms a relatively very high proportion in poorer countries. According to one estimate the share of rent formed 52 per cent of the value of agricultural output in Egypt in 1939–40 or one-fifth of the total national income.[25] With the rise in the prices of agricultural commodities at a faster rate than rental rates, this proportion must have come down to some extent, but still the share remains quite high. Professor Bonné feels that this must be true of other low income countries of the Middle East and also South and South-East Asia. He considers that rent claims would constitute about one-third to one half of the gross output of non-irrigated land and approximately one-third of the irrigated crops.[26] Although no categorical statement can be made in this connection, there are statistical evidences to show that the disparity in income distribution is less in countries like the U.S.A. and Canada than in the poorer countries. In the years 1946–50, the richest 10 per cent of the income earners in the U.S.A., Canada and Sweden, received less than 30 per cent of the aggregate income while in Italy and Ceylon the proportion was about 35 per cent and in El Salvador about 45 per cent.[27]

In the economically advanced countries there is a tendency for the share of the incomes of the highest income groups to decline because of the reduction in the share of property income payments. The share of property income comes down because of increased retention of earnings by corporations and also because of the decline in productivity differentials (and therefore in the variance of profit rates) as between firms in a given industry and between industries. Recent studies show that there has been a significant decline in wealth inequality in the U.S.A. as well as in the United Kingdom.[28] With the spread of mass production techniques and the decline in the prices of consumer durables purchased by the lower income groups, the disparity in the distribution of real incomes in these countries has also been reduced possibly to a greater extent than in the case of money incomes. Findings of Solomon Fabricant and John Kendrick in respect of the U.S.A. lend support to the view that with the decline in the share of income from property that of wages in national income has risen.

[24]Clark, Colin, Conditions of Economic Progress, 3rd edn., Macmillan, London, 1957, pp. 618–19. According to a recent estimate, the share of wages and income of the self employed persons in India is 24 per cent of total national income. Moni Mukherji, Papers on National Income and Allied Topics, Vol. II, Ed. by Dr. V. K. R. V. Rao and others, Asia Publishing House, Bombay, 1962.

[25]Mahmoud, Anis, National Income of Egypt, Cairo, 1950, p. 752, quoted in Alfred Bonné Studies in Economic Development, Routledge and Kegan Paul, London, 1957, p. 40.

[26]Bonné Alfred, ibid., p. 41.

[27]Kindleberger, C. F., Economic Development, McGraw-Hill, New York, 1958, p. 8.

[28]Oshima, Harry T., ' Consumer Asset Formation and the Future of Capitalism,' Economic Journal, March, 1961, pp. 23-24.

The disparity in income distribution in the low income countries has not however helped in increasing the savings ratio. This is obviously due to the fact that though there is a great deal of concentration of incomes in a few hands, the amount of such incomes in absolute terms is small in relation to the needs of the economy. Besides, such incomes tend to be diverted normally into non-economic investments or dissipated in unproductive forms of expenditure and do not help in adding to the real resources of the economy.

(3) *Income: the Consumption Aspect*

The low level of earnings in the poor countries is naturally reflected in the low level of spendings. By far the greater proportion of the expenditure of these countries is on necessaries, particularly food. On the average, expenditure on food forms more than 50 per cent of the total expenditure of families in the low income countries, while in the rich countries the proportion is well below 50 per cent. In Sweden, Israel and Norway it is less than 40 per cent while in China, India and Pakistan it is above 60 per cent. Also, there is considerable difference in the quality of food consumed. In the poorer countries cereals predominate, while in the industrial and advanced countries there is not only greater variety, but the consumption of nourishing items like fruits, meat, milk, fats and sugar very much exceeds that in low income countries. In terms of supply of calories per person per day, the variation is from more than 3,000 in the high income countries to 2,000 or even less in some of the economically backward countries. These differences are shown in Table 9.

It is possible that the actual food consumption in the low income countries may be a little more than what the figures indicate. On the other hand, food thrown away or wasted in some of the richer countries like the U.S.A. has to be deducted in order to show the actual consumption.[29] It is important to consider also certain special circumstances obtaining in the poorer countries. In view of the fact that the proportion of children in these countries is larger, the average requirement of food on a per capita basis must be correspondingly smaller. Climatic differences and the differences in physique also reduce the minimum requirement for the maintenance of health. An additional point to be considered is that in many low income countries which are predominantly agricultural, many items of food are consumed at the farm itself where they are produced, and as such escape valuation and measurement. But even allowing for all these points, the fact still remains that the consumption of food in the poorer countries is very much below that of developed ones. The plain fact that emerges is that in countries where the average per capita supply of calories is about 2,000 (which is only a little above the life sustaining minimum of 1,800 calories), the per capita income is $ 100 or less. Since

[29]Bonné, Alfred, *Studies in Economic Development*, Routledge and Kegan Paul, London, 1957, p. 44.

2,000 calories is only the average per capita supply, it means that quite a
large number of people in the backward countries would be getting very
much less food than the barest minimum requirement.

Table 9

CONSUMPTION OF FOOD IN DIFFERENT COUNTRIES OF THE WORLD
NET FOOD SUPPLIES PER CAPITA
(Kilograms per year)

Country and Year	Cereals as flour	Sugar refined	Meat	Milk		Calories per day
				Fat	Protein	
U.K. 1959–60	84	50	71	7	7	3290
Australia 1959–60	88	50	114	7	7	3260
Canada 1959–60	71	45	82	8	9	3150
U.S.A. 1960	66	41	95	8	9	3120
Argentina 1957–59	115	34	109	4	4	3090
Switzerland 1959–60	83	41	54	10	10	2980
Netherlands 1959–60	86	40	44	8	9	2970
France 1959–60	107	32	74	6	7	2940
Germany: Fed. Rep. 1960–61	83	29	57	6	7	2940
Turkey 1958–59	199	10	13	3	3	2850
Israel 1957–59	123	29	29	4	5	2780
Italy 1960–61	142	21	27	4	4	2740
Brazil 1957	106	31	29	2	2	2640
S. Africa 1959	140	41	43	3	3	2580
Chile 1957	129	37	31	3	3	2570
Japan 1959	151	14	6	1	1	2210
Ceylon 1960	138	19	3	1	1	2150
Philippines 1958	127	13	10	...	1	2100
India 1958–59	136	14	2	3	2	1980
Pakistan 1957–59	153	15	4	2	2	1970

SOURCE: *Statistical Year Book 1961*, U.N.

The large proportion of expenditure on food of low calorific value would
only mean that by far the major part of the earnings of an average family
is devoted to the purpose of just keeping body and soul together. Expenditure
on other necessary things and ordinary comforts of life has to be cut short
considerably or avoided altogether. The proportion of expenditure on housing
and clothing is about 20 per cent in the poorer countries as compared with
40 per cent or more in countries like Norway, Sweden and the U.S.A. Here
climatic conditions obviously play a predominant part in deciding what is
necessary and what is not in the different countries. Nevertheless, the very
low standard of housing conditions in these countries cannot be explained
away in terms of climate alone, but bespeaks the woeful lack of means. The
appalling living conditions of workers in the plantations, and of the factory

workers in the cities of India, described in the Report of the Labour Investigation Committee (1946) and the Census Reports are indicative only of economic and social backwardness. General poverty is also reflected in the very low standards of consumption of industrial goods and services. Citing from a publication of the League of Nations in 1945, Professor Bonne shows that in the period 1926-29 the value of the annual per capita supply of finished factory products was $ 254 in the U.S.A., between $ 100 and $ 164 in the U.K., Germany and some other industrial countries, $ 28 in Japan and $ 3 in China and India.[30] Although some improvements since then must have taken place, the difference between rich and poor countries in this respect could not appreciably have been reduced. The purchase of dwellings and consumer durables by households in the U.S.A. in 1953–57 was 120 per cent of the purchase of construction and equipment by business, while in Japan in 1955 it was only 35 per cent.[31] In countries like India, which are far below Japan in point of economic development, this percentage must be much less than 35. The consumption of newsprint and the owning of luxury or quasi-luxury consumer durables like radios and passenger cars broadly indicate the standards of life attained by a country. The marked difference in this respect between rich and poor countries is shown in Table 10.

The annual consumption of newsprint exceeds 20 kilograms per head in the economically advanced countries excepting France in the list on p. 24 while in India it is 0·2 and in Pakistan 0·1. There is one passenger car for every three persons in the U.S.A. and for every four persons in Canada. The ratio of the number of people to the number of cars is 1,545 in India and 1,783 in Pakistan.

(4) *Income: Socio-Economic Aspect*

Low standards of living go along with certain demographic and social characteristics typical of poor countries. Many of these countries are beset with the problem of overpopulation. The density per square kilometre is quite low in the Central and South American countries, but in most of the other underdeveloped countries although the density is not so great as in some of the industrialized countries of Europe like Belgium, Germany, Netherlands and U.K., yet considering the resources and the employment opportunities available, overpopulation does stand in the way of rapid economic progress. Among the Asiatic countries density is the highest in Japan with 252 people per square kilometre ; Ceylon and India come next with 151 and 136 respectively. In contrast to this the average density in five countries of South America–Argentina, Brazil, Chile, Colombia and Venezuela—is only 9 per square kilometre. Also, land-labour

[30] *Industrialization and Foreign Trade*, League of Nations, 1945, p. 22, quoted in Alfred Bonné *Economic Development*, Routledge and Kegan Paul, London, 1957, p. 50.

[31] Oshima, Harry T., ' Consumer Asset Formation and the Future of Capitalism ,' *Economic Journal*, March, 1961, p. 20.

Table 10

CONSUMPTION OF NEWSPRINT AND THE NUMBER OF RADIOS AND PASSENGER CARS IN SOME COUNTRIES*

Country	Population in thousands	Newsprint Consumption Kilograms per Capita	Radio Receivers in thousands	Ratio of Population to Number of Radios	Number of Passenger cars in use (thousands)	Ratio of Population to Number of Passenger cars
U.S.A.	180,676	36·6	170,000	1·1	61,431	2·9
Canada	17,814	27·9	8,050	2·2	4,104	4·3
Australia	10,275	30·2	2,284	4·5	1,924	5·3
Sweden	7,480	26·0	2,744	3·1	1,088	6·9
France	45,542	10·4	10,981	4·2	5,550	8·2
U.K.	52,383	24·9	15,163	3·5	5,542	9·5
Argentina	20,006	7·5	3,350	5·9	402	49·8
Ceylon	98,96	1·0	279	35·5	83	119·2
Japan	93,200	7·7	14,635	6·4	420	221·9
Turkey	27,829	0·8	1,341	20·7	46	604·9
Burma	20,662	0·5	115	179·9	18	1,147·9
India	432,567	0·2	2,148	201·4	280	1,544·9
Pakistan	92,727	0·1	250	370·9	52	1,783·2

*Data relate mostly to 1960. SOURCE: *Statistical Year Book 1961*, U.N.

ratio is very high in some of the richest countries of the world. Thus in the U.S.A. population density per square kilometre is 19; New Zealand 9; Canada 2 and Australia 1.[32] In recent years the rise in the rate of growth of population in some of the economically backward countries of the world has aggravated their demographic problem. In many of these countries, population increases at more than 3 per cent per year compared with less than 2 per cent rise in the advanced countries. A higher proportion of the people in the age group 0—15 and a lower proportion in the working age group 20—60 than in the richer countries is another demographic characteristic of low income countries. In other words, the number of dependents per member of the working age group is higher in the poorer countries.[33] Another aspect of the problem of population in these countries is the higher rate of growth of population in urban areas as compared with the rural areas. Such an unbalanced increase is a feature of the early stages of industrialization. In advanced countries this process of expansion of the urban sector has lost its momentum. Thus in the first half of the 20th century, the proportion of urban population more than doubled in Egypt, Puerto Rico and Japan, while in countries like U.K. and France, the increase in the proportion has been very negligible. This

[32] *Statistical Year Book 1961*, U.N.
[33] This aspect of the problem is discussed at some length in Chapter IV.

trend in population and increasing concentration in urban centres have created many social and economic evils such as insanitary conditions of living, unemployment, ill health and destitution.

These cumulative factors—low incomes, poor nourishment, inadequate housing, and bad conditions of living—have helped in keeping down the standards of health at a very low level. Figures relating to infant mortality and expectation of life broadly indicate the standard of health of the people in different countries. (Table 11.)

Table 11

EXPECTATION OF LIFE, INFANT MORTALITY RATES AND PER CAPITA INCOMES IN DIFFERENT COUNTRIES

Countries	Expectation of Life-years at Birth	Infant Mortality Rate (1956)*	Per Capita Income†
U.S.A.	70·5 (1955) Whites	26·0	1855·5
New Zealand	70·4 (1950–52)	23·2	1322·0
Canada	68·5 (1950–52)	31·9	1299·2
U.K.	70·3 (1955)	24·5	1121·5
Australia	68·4 (1946–48)	21·7	1071·7
Sweden	72·0 (1951–55)	17·0	1045·8
France	66·5 (1950–51)	35·9	685·6
Germany (Fed. Republic)	66·6 (1949–51)	38·6	603·2
Chile	52·0 (1952)	112·3	359·1
Spain	50·1 (1940)	51·7	335·6
Italy	56·4 (1935–37)	48·4	309·8
Mexico	38·9 (1940)	83·3 (1955)	230·1
Japan	66·1 (1955)	40·7	181·0
Portugal	61·3 (1955–56)	87·8	172·3
Ceylon	59·8 (1954)	66·5	112·1
India	32·0 (1941–50)	99·9 (1955)	57·1

*Death of infants under one year of age per 1,000 live births. †Income figures relate to the year 1953.

SOURCE: *Statistical Year Book 1961*, U.N., and Irma Adelman, *Theories of Economic Growth and Development*, Stanford, California, 1961, pp. 4 and 5.

The close positive relation between per capita income and expectation of life and the inverse relation between income and infant mortality rate are obvious from the figures. Among the countries listed above, those with per capita incomes of more than $ 1,000 per year have an expectation of life of above 68 years and infant mortality rate below 32 per 1,000. Sweden tops the list with the highest life expectation of 72 years and the lowest infant mortality rate of 17·0. As against this, in countries with less than $ 100 per capita income, expectation of life is 50 years or less, and infant mortality rate exceeds 70 per 1,000. Tuberculosis death rate per 100,000 population was estimated at 64 for countries with over $ 200 per capita income in 1939, and 333 in the case of countries with per capita income of less than $ 100 per year.

Low income accounts for poor medical and public health and educational facilities. In 1945–54 the percentage of illiterate population below the age of 10 was less than 5 in Australia, Canada, U.K. and the U.S.A., while it was as high as 62 in Mexico, 75 in Egypt, 82 in India and 92 in Indonesia. In 1951–53 the number of inhabitants per physician was 770 in the U.S.A., 950 in Canada, 1,000 in Australia and 1,200 in the U.K. As for the low income countries there was one physician for every 3,000 people in Brazil, 3,600 in Egypt, 5,700 in India and 71,000 in Indonesia.[34]

The socio-economic conditions which are characteristic of low income countries may now be summarized. Low aggregate and per capita incomes; limited availability of land, natural and capital resources per head; hence low productivity of labour which explains the low earnings of the workers, the meagreness of savings and capital formation; the dependence of the major part of the population on agriculture and the extractive industries for earning a living, poor yield of agriculture per capita as well as per unit of land; great disparity in the distribution of income and wealth, and concentration of large rental incomes in the hands of a few property owners; low levels of consumption expenditure and predominance of the outlay on food items; very unsatisfactory housing conditions and negligible spending on the ordinary comforts of life; great density of population and its high rate of growth; high infant mortality rate, uneconomic distribution of population in the different age groups, heavy dependency load, concentration of population in urban centres; low standards of literacy, inadequate medical facilities, poor health standards and short expectation of life—all these are the common economic and social characteristics of the poor and backward countries of the world today. It is important to note that all these features tend to exist together and operate cumulatively in maintaining the economic status quo of the poorer countries at a low level. On the other hand, in advanced countries exactly opposite features work conjointly and help in a steady rise in the level of economic activity. From this it follows, that economic growth would mean the escape of a country from the vicious grip of these adverse factors and its advance towards higher levels of living. The very fact that an economy has succeeded in overcoming some of the obstacles to growth would enable it to throw off the dead weight of the other deterrent factors. Thus an increased rate of investment made possible by better mobilization of the scarce domestic resources or massive foreign aid would raise the levels of productivity, increase total and per capita incomes and facilitate further rise in investment. A rise in earning and income per head would increase physical efficiency, improve educational standards, help in the use of better technology, bring down birth rates and thus cumulatively assist in maintaining the upward momentum of the economy. It is therefore clear that so long as an economy is moving within

[34]Higgins, Benjamin, *Economic Development*, Norton, New York, 1959, p. 20.

the vicious circle set by the above-mentioned adverse social and economic factors, it will continue to be poor; and its economic salvation depends on its success in breaking this vicious circle and getting over the initial obstacles to progress.

Countries whose economic advancement has been held down by the obstacles indicated above are called underdeveloped, while others which have got over these difficulties and have created circumstances favourable to the maintenance of a high and steady rate of growth are called developed economies. Although the terms 'developed' and 'underdeveloped' are not free from ambiguity and do not enable us to make any rigid classification of the different countries of the world, yet they broadly indicate the relative economic status of the countries concerned. It is however, necessary to point out certain basic features of underdevelopment which would clarify our notion of the difference in the economic position of the countries categorized in this manner. In the first place, underdeveloped countries have generally low per capita incomes—only generally, because there may be exceptions as for instance Kuwait with a very high per capita income. The United Nations experts use the term ' underdeveloped ' to mean " Countries in which per capita real income is low when compared with the per capita real incomes of the U.S.A., Canada, Australia and Western Europe."[35] Low level of real incomes would mean that the economy has failed to provide acceptable levels of living to a large proportion of the population. For analytical purposes it may be advantageous to designate countries which are getting a per capita income below a certain level as underdeveloped, and those above it as developed. Thus Professor Higgins fixes the income limit of $ 500 per head per annum to differentiate the two categories of countries. It is however not proper to make a strict classification of countries on the basis of per capita income alone. We should rather concentrate on the top few countries which are decidedly developed and the bottom few which are decidedly underdeveloped if the idea is to understand the distinguishing characteristics of the two groups. The rise from the bottom category is gradual and invariably slow and the changes that come over the economy in the course of transformation mark a lengthy intermediate stage. But undoubtedly a rise in per capita real incomes is on the whole a true indication of economic improvement.

The second aspect of underdevelopment is that the term suggests that the countries which are so designated have potentialities for development and expansion. In other words, underdevelopment would mean failure to make good use of the economic potentialities of the country. The failure to make full use of the resources with the help of existing technological knowledge may be due to social institutions or political factors. However, this aspect of the problem has to be interpreted in a relative sense. Thus it cannot be said that the most economically advanced countries of the world today such as the U.S.A. have been utilizing their economic potentialities to the fullest extent

[35] *Measures for the Economic Development of Underdeveloped Countries*, U.N., New York, 1951, p. 3.

possible. Viewed in this manner, it is possible to conceive of a gap of under-development. The potentialities of countries differ considerably. Given this difference, the maximum to which one may reach may be very much below that of another. We have of course to leave out regions which because of climatic or geographical factors cannot develop under the present standards of technological knowledge. But assuming a fair amount of natural resources which may enable a country to raise its economic standards, if such higher standards are not actually attained because of failure to utilize the resources, then that country should be called an underdeveloped one. Thus Japan with a very much lower per capita income as compared with Australia or Canada should be called economically developed. As Niculescu points out, " There is little meaning in saying that an adult rabbit is underdeveloped because a baby elephant is so much bigger ".[36] On this basis, it would be possible to grade different countries in degrees of underdevelopment.

Thirdly, underdeveloped countries are backward in the level and character of economic performance compared with other countries.[37] Such countries are not using the best techniques of production available in other countries which are economically better off. When economic development takes place, more goods and services become available per head of population. But the economic benefit accruing to the community as a result of increased production can be assessed correctly only by balancing against this benefit the increased real cost in the form of greater efforts, sacrifices and the larger number of workers employed in productive activity. If more goods and services are produced by employing more workers for longer hours and under more adverse working conditions, there is no real economic improvement. But if more is produced with less effort and sacrifice then we are justified in saying that there has been economic development.[38] Increased production with less effort and lower cost per unit of output implies that the technique of production is efficient. In fact the level of technology attained in the production of both industrial and agricultural goods is a reliable indicator of the standard of economic development. The employment of advanced technology goes along with larger capital resources, high attainments in the field of scientific research, greater availability of entrepreneurial skill and a good supply of efficient and skilled labour.

Finally it should be remembered that the term ' Underdeveloped ' denotes only one aspect of a country's or community's life. It only means that performance in the economic sphere is poor. A country with a low level of economic development may yet have great achievements in art, religion, literature and

[36]Niculescu, B. M., ' Underdeveloped, Backward or Low Income,' *Economic Journal*, September, 1955, p. 547.

[37]Kuznets, Simon, Underdeveloped Countries and the Pre-industrial Phase in the Advanced Countries—An Attempt at Comparison,' *Proceedings of the World Population Conference Papers*, Volume V. Reprinted in Agarwala, A. N. and S. P. Singh, *India 1958*, Oxford. pp. 135–53.

[38]Villard, Henry H., *Economic Development*, Rinehart, New York, 1957, pp. 15–16

philosophy to its credit. Nor should we forget the fact that economic development would not by itself improve human welfare and happiness and raise the standard of social well being. General conditions of living, social attitudes of the people, their psychology and mental make up, decide whether they are happy and contented when their income rises. It is quite possible that rise in incomes may affect the capacity of the people for enjoyment, destroy peace and quiet and add to the strain of life. In short, it is wrong to equate economic prosperity with human happiness and enjoyment. Nevertheless the fact remains that the satisfaction of the basic requirements of life and better living conditions made possible by increased production are necessary preconditions for developing the full potentialities of the human race.

Economic growth therefore means the transformation of a society or a country from a state of underdevelopment to a high level of economic achievement. It involves the adoption of better and improved techniques of production, better organization and utilization of the means of production and the removal of institutional and social obstacles that stand in the way of material progress. It results in the attainment of higher standards of life and improved social well being. This transformation is reflected in the main in a sustained and steady rise in the per capita real incomes. The rise in the per capita product implies the application of scientific knowledge to production, increased productivity of labour and hence more leisure, change in the techniques of production and patterns of life as well as in international relations.[39]

[39]Kuznets, Simon, *Six Lectures on Economic Growth*, The Free Press of Glencoe, Illinois, 1959, p. 13.

Chapter II

THEORIES OF ECONOMIC GROWTH AND DEVELOPMENT

THE DEFINITION of economic growth as the process of transformation of low income countries into high income ones raises the question as to how and under what conditions such a transformation takes place. If the underdeveloped countries are moving in a vicious circle of low levels of productivity and per capita incomes, low rate of savings and capital formation and absence of technological innovations, how is this vicious circle broken and the energies of sustained growth released? A theory of economic growth should answer this question. It should explain the phenomenon of change, mention the conditions which favour as well as hamper economic growth, and indicate the requisites for maintaining a steady rate of growth when once it has started. Such a theory should give us a better insight into the reasons why some countries of the world continue to remain poor while others have experienced a rapid rise in incomes. The phenomenon of vigorous economic growth in some of the Western countries as well as in Japan, Australia and New Zealand is a comparatively recent one. The development of the modern economy of England started in the 18th century and was ushered in by the Agricultural and Industrial revolution. Countries of Western Europe followed Britain. Rapid economic growth commenced in the U.S.A. about a century later, and in Japan towards the close of the 19th century. How was it that this great change took place only in some countries and passed by others which continue to remain underdeveloped and poor? The countries which are economically advanced today were at one time less developed than others which have now sunk to a much lower position. From the 9th to the 13th century A.D. the Italian cities were far ahead of the West European countries in the matter of economic attainment but they in turn lagged behind most of the countries of Western and Eastern Asia. Before the discovery of the sea route to India at the close of the 15th century, many of the cities in Western Asia situated on the great land routes between the two continents had enriched themselves considerably by trade. China was then economically prosperous. Since the level of economic attainment is determined by a complex of conditions we cannot say that the economic condition of England and other European countries in the 13th or 14th centuries was similar to that of the underdeveloped countries of today. Political and social conditions and demographic features would have been different but that these countries then had many of the characteristics of economic backwardness cannot be disputed.

In the early stages of its evolution political economy was concerned with the analysis of the wealth getting and wealth using activities of the community or the nation. It dealt with what is today called macro economic or aggregate economic problems. Adam Smith called his great work *An Enquiry into the Nature and Causes of the Wealth of Nations* and devoted much attention to the analysis of the difference in the progress of opulence in different nations. The problem of economic growth and the development of capitalism engaged the attention of the classical writers particularly Smith, Ricardo and Malthus. Later, Karl Marx developed his theory of the decay of capitalism based to a large extent on the premises of the classical writers. Equally important to an understanding of the problems of growth under the capitalist system are the ideas of Schumpeter relating to the role of the entrepreneur. The classical economists lived and wrote at a time when England had established her industrial leadership of the world. The impressive achievements in the industrial field, accumulation of savings, rapid growth of capital and increased productivity, naturally attracted the attention of these writers. These obviously are the primary features of a growing economy and as such, the views of the classical writers on these matters should help in clarifying the issues involved in the economic growth of contemporary underdeveloped countries.

The basic ideas of these writers in the matter of economic growth relate to the following: (*a*) Savings and capital accumulation; (*b*) development of technology; (*c*) the role of entrepreneurship; (*d*) the importance of demand and an expanding market; (*e*) institutional factors; (*f*) the decline of capitalism. These may now be briefly examined.

SAVINGS AND CAPITAL ACCUMULATION

According to the classical economists the main factor that helped economic development was the accumulation of capital. Capital accumulation results from savings and the main source of savings is profits. Profits are the rewards or the earnings of businessmen who utilize land and employ labour in productive work. Out of the total earnings of the community a part is paid as wages to the labourers and another part to the land lords in the form of rent. Hence the size of profit depends on the size of payments on account of rent and wages. These economists did not worry about excess of labour or the deficiency of it. They believed that supply of labour would adjust itself to the demand for it. Higher wages would increase the supply of labour, while lower wages would reduce it. Population growth according to them was a composite of a biological urge and a rational calculation of the value of children.[1] Wage rate was supposed to be fixed by the subsistence level, and a rise in the level of wages would bring about an increase in the supply of labour. This means that when wage is at the subsistence level, there is full employment of labour. Profits

[1]Lowe, Adolph, ' The Classical Theory of Economic Growth, ' *Social Research*, 1954, Vol. 21, No. 2, p. 134.

earned by the businessmen constituted the major part of the savings of the community. What was saved was assumed to be invested. Thus so long as profits are rising, investment will also rise and the economy will grow and when profits decline capital accumulation is slowed down and growth stops.

It is thus clear that the main proposition of the classical model of economic growth is the trend in profits. Adam Smith laid much emphasis on the virtues of saving. It was according to him the secret of economic betterment of a community or country. In his chapter on the accumulation of capital[2] he extols frugality and parsimony without which economic growth is not possible. In his words: " Capitals are increased by parsimony and diminished by prodigality and misconduct . . . parsimony and not industry is the immediate cause of the increase of capital. Industry indeed provides the subject which parsimony accumulates. But whatever industry might acquire, if parsimony did not save and store up, the capital would never be greater."[3] Undoubtedly, in the early stages of development of Britain, saving by the profit earners and their converting of the savings into investment played the major role in the building up of industries in the country. Thus Keynes observed about the 19th century: " Europe was so organized socially and economically as to secure the maximum accumulation of capital. While there was some continuous improvement in the daily conditions of life of the mass of the population, society was so framed as to throw a great part of the increased income into the control of the class least likely to consume it."[4]

Marx stressed the dependence of profits on the level of technology and of consumption. The use of improved technology increases the productivity of labour and causes its displacement. With a reserve army of unemployed, it is not possible for the employed part of labour to raise its wage level. Hence the surplus value or profit which the capitalist employer earns, would rise. Marx made some refinements in the analysis of savings and capital. In the first place, while Smith and Ricardo considered the level of profits as determining capital accumulation and investment, Marx pointed out that it was the rate of profit and not the absolute level of profits that influenced accumulation and investment. A decline in the rate of profit would reduce accumulation of capital and therefore of investment. Secondly, Marx also made a distinction between constant and variable capital, the former denoting capital goods and inventions currently used, and the latter denoting working capital or pay rolls.

The classical economists felt that savings and investment get automatically adjusted to each other. Whatever was saved was invested and there is no possibility of any increase in investment unless it is preceded by increase in savings. Later, Schumpeter showed that investment can and does exceed

[2]*Wealth of Nations*, Book II, Chapter III.
[3]*Wealth of Nations*, Everyman's Library, London, Vol. I, p. 301.
[4]Keynes, J. M., *The Economic Consequences of the Peace*, London, 1919, p. 16.

voluntary savings through credit creation by the banking system. This increased investment makes possible a rise in gross output in money terms while a deficiency in investment in relation to savings would reduce national income. Schumpeter also made an important contribution by making a distinction between an increase in investment brought about by the large sales or profits experienced by the businessmen in the previous period, and also rise in investment brought about by long run factors like technological change, discovery of new resources, etc.

DEVELOPMENT OF TECHNOLOGY

Capital accumulation helps growth of output because it facilitates technological improvements which raise labour productivity. The striking feature of capitalist growth in Adam Smith's time was increasing division of labour which facilitated increased use of machinery. Apart from natural resources and a country's geographical position, the main factor promoting economic development according to Smith was division of labour. This was the true dynamic force. Both increased mechanization and division of labour were facilitated by increase in labour supply but machine was considered as a complement of labour rather than a substitute for it.[5] Smith also stressed the fact that steady economic expansion is possible only if there is steady expansion of market which in turn is possible only if technology is of a type that is labour attracting.[6] It was however, Ricardo who visualized the development of capitalist economies as a race between technological progress and population growth. Specifically, in the matter of cultivation of land, increasing population necessitates extension of cultivation to infra marginal or poorer quality land or to more intensive cultivation of better type lands. In either case, output per unit of labour declines and this could be prevented only by technological improvements or better arts of production.

The great importance of technological improvement in capitalist development was recognized by Marx also. He emphasized two aspects of technological development which are worth noticing. Firstly, he brought out clearly the inter-relation between investment and technology. Surplus value is the source of capital formation. To the extent technological improvement increases labour productivity, surplus value or profit of the capitalist is increased. An increase in the gross rate of addition to the capital stock of the country makes it easier to bring about further innovations. The other aspect of technology

[5]Adam Smith observed: "The invention of all those machines by which labour is so much facilitated and abridged seems to have been originally owing to the division of labour. Men are much more likely to discover easier and readier methods of attaining any object when the whole attention of their minds is directed towards that single object than when it is dissipated among a great variety of things." *The Wealth of Nations*, Everyman's Library, London, Vol. I, p. 9.

[6]Lowe, Adolph, ' The Classical Theory of Economic Growth,' *Social Research*, 1954, Vol. 21, No. 2, p. 139.

which Marx emphasized was its Janus-faced nature. On the one hand, by increasing labour productivity and by increasing the surplus value, technology helps expansion of the economy and further increases output; on the other hand, adoption of improved technology brings about a displacement of labour which reduces consumption levels and thereby affects profits and slows down economic growth. However, despite this adverse effect of technology, capitalists continue to make innovations because of three reasons—firstly, since technology improves productivity, it has the effect of reducing the relative value of the fixed capital stock even when there is a physical increase in it. Since rate of profit is the ratio of surplus value to the value of fixed capital, this would raise the profit rate; besides, the secondary effect of displacement of labour would be a lowering of the cost of labour or fall in real wages which also widens the profit margin. Secondly, innovations bring in temporary profits to the pioneering enterpriser. Thirdly, it is possible that even while the rate of profits declines, it would raise the total volume of profits.

ROLE OF ENTREPRENEURSHIP

Although the classical economists recognized the importance of the organizer of industry as the agent responsible for bringing together the other factors of production in any productive enterprise, they did not assign to him any dynamic role in economic growth. Marx however, stressed the fact that the entrepreneur's aim of widening the profit margin through adoption of new technology and improved means of production provided an important element in economic development. But it was Schumpeter who assigned to the entrepreneur the key role in economic development. He conceived of the circular organization of production in which the value of a final product would be the sum of the cost of the means of production. That is to say, the various factors which combine in production are remunerated out of the value of the final product. When the circular flow is functioning normally, the sum of the remuneration to the factors or the value of the means of production will be exactly equal to the value of the end product. If the final value of the product exceeds the value of the means of production, there emerges a surplus which is the profit of the entrepreneur. The greater this surplus or profit, the greater will be entrepreneurial activity and the faster will the economy grow. On the other hand, if there is a deficiency in the surplus, growth will slacken. The extent to which the difference between the value of the product and the value of the means of production can be widened depends on the activities of the entrepreneur. He achieves this by making innovations which involve, producing a new commodity, finding out a new market for the final product, finding out new sources of raw materials, and adopting new combinations of production. By this activity the entrepreneur causes a discontinuous disturbance in the circular flow of the economy. It is the disequilibrium caused in this manner that is the source of monopoly profit.

Three conditions are necessary in a free enterprise capitalist economy if entrepreneurial activity is to flourish. In the first place, there should be an ample supply of technological knowledge and information. Secondly, the entrepreneur should have the power of disposal over means of production. The entrepreneur's own financial resources may be limited or nil. He can therefore have control over the means of production if purchasing power is made available through the expansion of bank credit. When bank credit becomes available in this manner and is made use of by the entrepreneur, investment exceeds current savings. This would have an initial inflationary effect. But since the entrepreneur's activity results in an increased output which would match the increase in purchasing power, prices will after some-time, tend to come down. The third important requisite for the emergence of the entrepreneurial class is the existence of a favourable socio-cultural environment. By this Schumpeter means the economic or tax policy of the state, and institutional factors which affect the prospects of the entrepreneurs. If trade unions are strong and labourers are able to demand and secure higher wages, if the state's tax policy affects profit earnings or the state adopts a policy of restricting profit incomes or distributing national income in a manner that will affect the chances of making large profits, the entrepreneur's incentive will be lost. In short, social climate is favourable when there is free scope for the entrepreneurs making larger profits.

If these conditions are favourable, entrepreneurial activity is encouraged. However, the entrepreneur is not swayed primarily by the profit motive. He is a leader in society and wants distinction and success for the sake of success. His aggressive policy results in the production of new commodities or adoption of better methods of production, discovery of new resources, new markets etc. all of which conduce to the general advancement of the economy. When once one entrepreneur shows the way in a particular direction, the large monopoly profit which he earns draws in others into the same field. Thus innovations tend to appear in clusters. The result is expansion of credit and the widening of the spread between savings and investment. The tendency of innovations to appear in swarms is due to the fact that initial difficulties are removed by the pioneer so that lesser individuals can enter the field and also because innovations in one industry and the expansion of that industry help innovation and expansion in other industries also. Expansion however, cannot continue for long because the limits of credit expansion will soon be reached. Moreover, increased production will result in a glut in the market and consequent fall in prices and losses for businessmen. Decline in economic activity sets in, and will continue until the process is repeated. Schumpeter's theory thus not only explains the process of growth in a capitalist economy but also brings out the true nature of the growth—its tendency to proceed by fits and starts.

EXPANSION OF MARKETS AND DEMAND

The author of the *Wealth of Nations* showed clearly that division of labour, use of machinery and increased production are made possible and facilitated by the expansion of the market. Without a steady rise in demand, external economies cannot be realised. The securing of overseas markets by a country helps in its continued economic expansion even after the limits of its domestic markets are reached. In this respect Malthus and Marx very much anticipated the recent emphasis on the demand factor as a condition for sustained rise in income. Malthus emphasised the demand aspect of capital accumulation and growth and correctly indicated the possibility of excess savings leading to retardation of economic growth. According to him the virtues of frugality and parsimony operated both ways. While Smith made much of savings and frugality as the corner stone of economic development, Malthus drew attention to the fact that since aggregate consumption is the sum of the consumption of workers as well as of capitalists, any reduction in the consumption level of the capitalists would mean lowering the level of aggregate demand. So long as investment opportunities are available investment would be increased and savings would increase correspondingly. But if the limits of investment opportunities are reached, and if savings continue beyond this point, it would reduce consumption to such an extent that investment will be discouraged. Thus Malthus questioned Say's Law of Demand and anticipated later Keynesian reasoning about the role of savings and investment in the determination of the level of economic activity and income.

Marx believed that the aggregate level of consumption was determined primarily by the behaviour of labour. Consumption by capitalists forms a negligible proportion of total consumption, so that as a determinant of aggregate demand it is the spending by the labourers that matters. Consumption of labourers depends on the size of the wage bill. If growth is to continue, wage bills should rise in proportion to aggregate income. The idea of Marx that colonization and the securing of foreign markets helps the colonizing country not only in meeting the growing need of resources and industrial materials but also in maintaining or augmenting the demand for the country's manufactured products was later elaborated by Rosa Luxembourg. According to the latter, colonization was vitally necessary for the maintaining of the capitalist economy. The securing of one colony helps in boosting up demand for a while but when that is saturated, another colony has to be found. Thus the process of expansion of capitalist economy is linked up with the process of colonization. When colonization stops, expansion of the capitalist economy will have to stop.[7] The scope for a rise in the level of demand through better distribution of incomes and rise in the standard of living of the masses in a free enterprise economy was thus underestimated by Marx and the Marxian economists. Nevertheless they made a contribution to the theory of economic growth in

[7]Robinson, (Mrs.) Joan, *The Rate of Interest and Other Essays*, Macmillan, London, 1954, pp. 157–58.

drawing pointed attention to the importance of the demand factor as a determinant of income.

INSTITUTIONAL FACTORS

Another important point which the classical economists stressed and in which they anticipated modern thinking on the subject of growth, is the significance of social and institutional factors. A sound administrative system, a stable government, well organized financial agencies, a legal system which is capable of ensuring the security of person and property, efficient organization of the means of production, a simple and well defined system of land-holding and inheritance and a favourable social attitude are prime requisites of economic improvement. According to Adam Smith: " Little else is requisite to carry a state to the highest degree of opulence from the lowest barbarism, but peace, easy taxes and a tolerable administration of justice, all the rest being brought about by the natural course of things ". Malthus added the principle of population and thus brought into the picture social and institutional factors and attitudes of people which determine the size of population. He also stressed the security of property which depends on the political constitution of the country and " the excellence of the laws and the manner of administering them which help to determine the important habits most favourable to regular exertions ". Besides these he added, " general rectitude of character of the inhabitants " as a factor in economic development. In his discussion of the causes and remedy for backwardness of Asiatic peoples J. S. Mill drew attention to the inefficiency in administration, lack of a stable government, heavy taxation and foolish customs and superstition of the people as the cause of economic backwardness of the countries of this region. Hence according to him better government, lower taxes, improved land tenure, improvement in public intelligence, the expansion of consumers' wants and the freeing of the community from the bonds of old customs and superstitions should be considered as the institutional changes necessary to prepare the ground for the economic development of these countries.

DECAY AND DECLINE OF CAPITALISM

All classical economists and also Marx and Schumpeter prophesied the ultimate decay of capitalism. But there is difference in their views regarding the manner in which this decay would be brought about. Adam Smith assumed constant returns to scale and saw in increasing competition among capitalists and the exhaustion of resources the seeds of capitalist decline. He felt that increased savings and capital accumulation would bring down the rate of interest if prospects of profits are bleak. Interest should cover the risk of loss of money spent as well as provide an incentive for accumulation. So long as the profit rate covers at least the risk part, there will be accumulation of savings. But when it falls below this level, it is no longer worthwhile for the accumulators of savings to increase accumulation and lend capital. Hence as in Holland of his time which Smith mentions as an illustration, owners of capital start their own business and become investors. It should be noted that Smith distinguishes between two classes of people, the savers or accumulators of capital and the investors or the profit earners. Thus demand for capital falls, because of increasing competition and the narrowing scope for profits; interest rate falls because of lack of demand for savings; and savings and accumulation decrease because of fall in the rate of interest. When savings and accumulation cease, the prospects for future growth are blighted. And the economy will drift steadily and gradually towards the stationary state.

By assuming the Law of Diminishing Returns in the place of constant returns, Ricardo built up a more logical theory of capitalist decline. Aggregate income which is the product of land, labour and capital is distributed among these factors in the form of rent, wages and profits. As population increases, land will have to be cultivated more intensively or cultivation has to be extended to poorer quality of land. The returns per unit of labour input decline but since labour supply increases with increasing population and wage per head cannot decline below the subsistence level, the aggregate wage bill will rise. Simultaneously, the rent of land would also go up. Thus a larger share of income would go to the landlords in the form of rent and with the rise in wage bill, the two would squeeze out profits. Technological progress such as better methods of cultivation would increase labour productivity and thus raise profits or arrest its decline, but in the long run as the economy reaches the state of maturity, diminishing returns to land and the consequent rise in labour costs would outweigh the advantage of technological progress if any. As profits decline, investment would drop, technological progress itself is retarded, the size of the wages fund would reduce and population would cease to grow and thus the stationary state will be reached. The stationary state conceived by Ricardo is not one of inactivity or extreme poverty but it will be one in which there is no growth or expansion. In the theory of Smith as well as of Ricardo, it is what happens to profits that determines the course of the economy. So long as profits increase, growth continues, and decline sets in because of fall in profits. But while according to Smith it was increasing competition among capitalists that brought down profits and capital accumulation, Ricardo felt that it was the rise in the earnings of the other agents of production that lowered profits. Further, Smith viewed the trend towards the stationary state as steady and gradual but Ricardo believed it to be unsteady because of the possibility of outbursts of technological changes reversing the down trend temporarily.

The Marxian analysis of economic expansion under capitalism envisages two aspects of the decline of the capitalist system—the social aspect and the economic aspect. Like the classical economists, Marx stressed the importance of technological advancement and profits in the process of expansion. Profits of the capitalist entrepreneur he designated as surplus value i.e. the excess of total earnings over wage payment. The ratio of the surplus value to the total stock of capital is the rate of profit. Capital is of two forms—variable capital out of which wage payments are made and constant capital or fixed capital representing investment in plant machinery etc. Thus the rate of profit may be represented as

$$R = \frac{O - W}{V + Q}$$

where R is the rate of profit, O is output, W is wage bill or pay rolls, V is variable capital and Q is constant capital. The social aspect of the decline of capitalism is explained in terms of the conflict between the capitalist class and the labouring class. Marx makes a distinction between the mode of production and the relations of production. The first denotes the economic side of the organization of production, the technique of production employed, the organization and the division of labour, the method of distribution of output among the factors of production, etc. Relations of productions refer to the social and institutional counterpart of the nature of economic life such as class structure and ownership of property which constitute the institutional frame work within which the economy functions. A particular pattern of economic life goes with a particular pattern of social and institutional order. Thus under feudalism the mode of production is made to fit in with a particular institutional set up. But society is dynamic and the mode of production changes which brings it into conflict with the existing institutional order. The latter is broken up and a new institutional order is established. Once again as the nature of economic life changes, calling for a new relation of production the old order is changed, as for example, capitalist methods of production necessitating the break up of feudalism.

According to this analysis, capitalism also will collapse because of the growing conflict between the owners of capital and the workers. Capital formation in a capitalist economy is made possible by the emergence of surplus value. Technological improvements necessitate additions to Q or constant capital. There is what is called capital deepening. This increases labour productivity. Additions to capital would increase the demand for labour but since productivity of labour is also rising, the demand for labour would increase less than proportionately to the stock of capital. Hence wage rate cannot rise but surplus value would for that reason go up, facilitating further capital intensification or deepening of capital. The relative decline in the demand for labour would swell up the reserve army of unemployed and increase the scope for the exploitation of labour. The progressive immiseration of the working class and the widening and deepening of the·gulf between the capitalists and the workers, the haves and the have-nots would lead to organization of labour. " Centralization of the means of production and socialization of labour at last reach a point when they become incompatible with their capitalist integument. This integument is burst as under "[8] and a new social and economic order will be established.

On economic grounds also, capitalism would break up and decay. The availability of large surplus value would add to the stock of capital in both forms. Capital intensification and technological improvements would increase the average amount of capital per firm and at the same time reduce the number of these firms. Competition among the decreasing number of firms becomes fiercer as their number declines and brings about their ruin. Besides, in so far as technological improvements increase labour productivity, labour requirement will be reduced and any rise in wages will be prevented. Since rise in productivity increases the supply of output, the failure of wages to rise would result in the lagging of consumption behind supply. Underconsumption would bring about a decline in prices and profits and lead to the decay of capitalism. The growing tension between the capitalist and labour classes of society, cut throat competition among capitalist firms and the tendency for the level of consumption to fall as the capitalist economy expands, would all combine to bring about the crash of capitalism. Thus according to Marx, capitalism carries within itself the forces of destruction ; it cannot endure because of its basic inherent defects.

Schumpeter thought that capitalism would end because the climate for entrepreneurship would become increasingly unfavourable. So long as the social and political conditions permit free scope for the entrepreneur, economic growth is possible. With the development of new forms of productive organization such as the joint stock company, the scope of the entrepreneur in the heroic sense of the term progressively gets restricted. The spread of liberalist ideas, increasing taxation, control of profits by the State, rise in wages resulting from labour organization and the growing interest taken by Governments in the wage earning class, the rise of the intellectuals and their criticism of the existing social order, would bring about the collapse of capitalism and the emergence of socialism. Thus Schumpeter visualized the end of the capitalist system as a consequence of institutional rather than economic changes.

RELEVANCE TO UNDERDEVELOPED ECONOMIES

These gloomy forebodings of the classical economists have not, however, materialized. The vigorous growth of capitalist economies in many parts of the world in recent years, the steady improvement in the conditions of life of the workers and the fact that the gulf between the capitalists and labourers has narrowed rather than widened, all go contrary to the views of these economists regarding the future of capitalism. Nevertheless, what they have said about the basic determinants of economic progress is as valid today as when it was first expressed more than two hundred years ago. The classical writers

[8]*Das Kapital*, Vol. I, Chapter 32.

assigned to capital accumulation and technology the key role in economic development. Thriftiness, the saving habit, hardwork and discipline, a favourable social and institutional order, stable government and entrepreneurial talents and skill were the other factors on which they laid great emphasis. Undoubtedly, it is the deficiency of these factors in the low income countries of today that explains their poor economic performance. Development policy in these countries should therefore aim at bringing about changes along these lines. Some of the classical economists, particularly Adam Smith, Malthus, J. S. Mill and Marx, illustrated the causes of economic backwardness, with reference to conditions prevailing in Asiatic countries like India and China. Economic stagnation in India according to Marx was due to the vastness of the country, the dispersal of its population and the peculiar village system which was brought into existence by the union of agricultural and manufacturing pursuits. This institutional structure hampered development of technology. Although the end of capitalism was considered as inevitable, Marx thought that that system was necessary to bring about material progress. The failure of capitalism to emerge before the advent of British enterprise in India was in the view of Marx the cause for the stagnation of the social and economic systems in the country.[9]

However, the classical economists were influenced in their thinking and writing by circumstances nearer home. But the economic and social conditions of England and Western Europe at the time of their industrialization were not the same as those which exist in underdeveloped countries like India today. There was no problem of overpopulation and as such the economic significance of an increasing population did not engage the serious attention of any of these economists except Malthus. They assumed that population would rise and fall in response to the demand for it. Their conception of the entrepreneur particularly of the Schumpeterian type has also been criticized on the ground that it is of little relevance to present day underdeveloped countries. Thus Henry C. Wallich[10] and H. W. Singer[11] have argued that while the entrepreneur in advanced countries had to be an innovator in the early stages of development, it is not true of the contemporary pre-industrial countries. Businessmen in these countries can adopt the technology and methods of production which have already been tried and used in the developed countries. But the adaptation of technology itself requires a certain amount of pioneering spirit and entrepreneurial skill, in so far as it is new to the country in which it is adapted. And the risks of introducing such a technology in an economically backward country will be quite large, so that the entrepreneur in these

[9]Adelman, Irma, *Theories of Economic Growth and Development*, Stanford, California, 1962, pp. 90–91.

[10]Wallich, Henry C., ' Some Notes Towards a Theory of Derived Development,' reprinted in Agarwala, A. N. and S. P. Singh, *The Economics of Underdevelopment*, Oxford, Bombay, 1958, pp. 189–204.

[11]Singer, H. W., 'Obstacles to Economic Development,' *Social Research*, Vol. XX, 1953, pp. 19–31.

countries should have some at least of the qualities of the Schumpeterian entrepreneur.[12]

THE HARROD-DOMAR MODELS OF ECONOMIC GROWTH

The phenomenal development of technology in the course of the 19th century and the rapid growth of output in many rapidly developing economies dispelled any fear of stagnation or prospective decline of capitalism which the 18th century analysis had foreboded. The trend in economic change was away from the stationary state rather than towards it. Profits did not decline and wages rose above the subsistence level. In many countries, a steady long run uptrend was almost taken for granted and consequently economic analysis shifted its emphasis from aggregate economic problems to problems of a micro economic nature such as the determination of prices and the allocation of resources. Analysis of the nature and causes of the wealth of nations, which dominated economic thinking for two centuries gave place to a study of the relations between output and prices of particular commodities. This, as has been pointed out by Mrs. Joan Robinson, was an unfortunate trend for two reasons. Firstly, it meant a departure from reality. Secondly, it ruled out discussions of problems which are actually interesting and more fruitful.[13]

In recent years however, there has been a spectacular veering back of interest towards matters concerning economic expansion and growth. The output of literature on these problems since the close of the Second World War has been enormous and as a goal of economic policy, growth has absorbed some of the public attention previously enjoyed by full employment.[14]

There are many reasons for this change. In the years after the Second World War, many countries secured their political freedom and this awakened in them the consciousness about their economic backwardness and created an urge for rapid economic development. The developed economies on their part, have viewed with sympathy this popular upsurge. There is increased realization of the fact that the rapid development of these countries is a necessity for a better international social order and peace. Poverty anywhere is recognized as a source of danger to prosperity everywhere and hence the developed countries themselves have adopted an organized policy on an international scale to help the underdeveloped countries to achieve their ambitions. The loss sustained by many European countries and Japan in the War and the disruption caused in the economic life of many more countries which did not suffer in the direct ravages of War, presented an urgent and immediate problem of national economic reconstruction and development. The growing competition between the developed countries, particularly between the

[12]Rimmer, Douglas, ' Schumpeter and the Under-Developed Countries,' *Quarterly Journal of Economics*, August, 1961, pp. 422–50.

[13]Robinson, (Mrs.) Joan, *The Accumulation of Capital*, Macmillan, London, 1956, p. v.

[14]Domar, Evsey, *Essays in the Theory of Economic Growth*, Oxford, New York, 1957, p. 14.

rigidly planned authoritarian economies and the free enterprise economies has necessitated concentration of attention on national economic development. The fear of political and warlike conflict and the realization of the fact that military strength depends directly on economic strength have also drawn attention to the need for better utilization of economic resources. It has also been observed that the great importance attached to material well-being and the great efforts directed towards attaining higher levels of living form a part of the culture of the people of Western countries who consider material well-being as a desirable goal of life for mankind.[15] Another important factor which has contributed to the great interest in problems of economic growth is the bitter experience of many countries in the 'thirtees. The inherent unsteadiness in the progress of capitalist economies, the fear of a slip back to the conditions of the 'thirtees and also the worry about the possibility of secular stagnation in mature economies, have compelled the economists to devote themselves more and more to the study of the structure and functioning of the capitalist economic system, with a view to a better understanding of its behaviour and to find out ways of ensuring growth with stability. It has been increasingly realized that in order to ensure full employment of human and material resources, economic growth is necessary.

In this shift of emphasis Keynes' *magnum opus* has played an important part. Keynes' General Theory represents a departure from the trend in economic analysis observable in the 19th century. He revived the interest in aggregate problems like the level of demand and employment, growth of income etc. The tools of economic analysis which he forged have been made full use of by later writers in better diagnosing the ills of the capitalist economy and in suggesting ways of controlling the ills. It is on the basis of Keynesian concepts that modern models of economic growth are constructed and it is with the help of Keynesian tools of analysis that the process of change and growth is explained.

Since economic growth involves changes of some fundamental variables in the economic system, the explanation of the process of growth and its nature has to be done in terms of economic dynamics. The terms 'statics' and 'dynamics' used in modern economic analysis are borrowed from theoretical mechanics. The former suggests a state of rest while the latter denotes motion or movement and change. Hence economic theory which is based on the assumption of a stationary position may be called 'economic statics'. According to Kuznets: "Static economics deals with relations and processes on the assumption of uniformity and persistence of either the absolute or relative economic quantities involved".[16] Nineteenth century economics was concerned with the analysis of micro economic problems on static assumptions. Although economics deals with social phenomena, traditional economic theory considered

[15]Clough, Shepard B., 'Strategic Factors in Economic Growth,' *Political Science Quarterly*, New York, March, 1955, p. 20.

[16]Kuznets, Simon, *Economic Change*, Norton, New York, 1954, p. 32.

it possible (and necessary for purposes of investigation) to reduce social phenomena to individual actions such as activities of individual firms and individual
human beings. The analysis was simplified by assuming static conditions and
it was presumed that since individual activities are interconnected and possess
persistent characteristics which are typical of the whole, principles derived
from a study of individual activities would have general validity. In so far
as traditional economic theory assumed static conditions and concentrated on
individual activities it is characterized as micro economic statics.

But change and variation are the essential features of the subject matter
of economic study. Hence if it is to be fruitful, the approach to the study of
economic phenomena has to be dynamic. The fundamental variables of
the economic system are manpower, quantity of capital and the output or
income per head, and the economics of growth has to study the inter-relations
between these variables and analyse and examine the behaviour of these
variables and the consequences of such variations over time. When there is
no change in data, i.e. even when capital, labour and resources are given,
there is possibility of movement in so far as the intensity or the way in which
each factor is used may alter because of entrepreneurial skill or technological
improvement.[17] Economic theory which seeks to explain the phenomenon of
economic change, the implications of such changes, and to examine the factors
at work in bringing about a given change and trace the process of that change
and the consequences of succeeding movements step by step is called economic
dynamics. And since analysis has to be done in terms of aggregates it is called
macro economic dynamics. The essential feature of dynamic theory is that
it traces the sequences over time both backward and forward. Thus according
to Harrod ' once over ' changes cannot be the subject of economic dynamics.
In dynamics the fundamental conditions will themselves be changing; it is not
concerned with rates of output but with variations in the rates of output. A
rise in the rate of savings is a change but if it is a once over change it is not
dynamic; but if a given rise in savings leads to rise in investment and output
which helps further rise in savings, in short if a sequence of interdependent
events is set in motion, then it is a dynamic concept.

Static analysis is not without uses. It provides as it were a still picture of
the economic phenomena and helps in getting a clearer view of the forces at
work. As Zeuthen points out, it has an introductory pedagogical value. " If
one wants to study the propeller of an airplane it is practical also to examine
it thoroughly before it starts moving ".[18] But its obvious defect is that it is
unrealistic and as such its analytical content would be of little use in a system
of dynamic economics. Since it disregards the effect of time, it can provide
only a limited treatment of the problems of real life. On the other hand,
dynamic analysis provides a better knowledge of the actual functioning of
the economic system and facilitates an understanding of the manner in which

[17]Tinbergen. Jan and J. J. Polak, *The Dynamics of Business Cycles*, Chicago, 1950, p. 102.
[18]Zeuthen, F., *Economic Theory and Method*, Harvard, Cambridge, Mass., 1955, p. 144.

forces of change work themselves out. In growth economics, the analysis has perforce to be in dynamic terms because it has to deal with the changes in the fundamental variables, population, capital, income, technology, etc. Thus the rate of growth of output depends on the rate of growth of capital and the capital co-efficient. Increase in output per head depends on the two rates— rate of increase in aggregate output and in population. A change in per capita output affects savings and capital formation and therefore future savings rate etc. By means of a study of such changes over time and the causes and effects of such changes it is possible to forecast future trends and suggest ways and means of directing the trend along required lines. As Kuznets observes : " The task of dynamic economics is first and foremost that of ascertaining the exact course of social changes and of distilling if possible some general characteristics of these changes either in a given social phenomenon in the course of time or in the relations among various social phenomena ".[19]

The subject matter of Keynes' analysis is aggregate problems like output, employment, savings and investment; but excepting his emphasis on savings and the role of expectations, the method is static. But though the form is static it has opened the way for a great outburst of analysis of dynamic problems.[20] The Keynesian concepts of the multiplier and the accelerator form the corner stones of modern economic growth models. Keynesian explanation of the possibilities of equality between savings and investment in under-employment equilibrium has provided the starting point to estimate the effect on income of the discrepancy between the rates of increase of these two factors. Similarly, the explanation by Keynes of investment as a demand generating factor and of savings as a demand reducing factor has been made use of to examine the role of these forces as the agency for increasing income on the one hand and for supplying resources for capital formation on the other. Thus while Keynes concentrated only on the negative aspect of savings as reducing effective demand, recent writers have analysed the positive aspect namely, savings adding to capital resources, thereby facilitating larger investment. In fact, the foundations of modern growth analysis lie in the ideas and concepts contained in the General Theory.

A brief review of the well-known Harrod-Domar Models would bring out clearly the extent to which Keynesian economics has helped in the modern analysis of growth problems.

(i) Harrod's Model

Harrod's important article ' An Essay in Dynamic Theory ' was published in the *Economic Journal*, March, 1939. This topic formed the subject of a course of lectures which he delivered at the University of London in 1947 and which

[19]Kuznets, Simon, *Economic Change*, Norton, New York, 1954, p. 37.
[20]Robinson, (Mrs.) Joan, *The Rate of Interest and Other Essays*, Macmillan, London, p. v.

were later published (1948) under the title *Towards a Dynamic Economics*. Lecture three on ' Fundamental Dynamic Theorems ' contains the core of Harrod's dynamic model.

Harrod makes two important assumptions. The first is that net saving at any period of time is a constant proportion s of the income received during that period. This net saving is actual saving and not intended saving. Hence it is equal to actual or realized investment. There may be discrepancy between intended saving and intended investment, but actual saving has necessarily to be equal to investment. Thus if actual savings exceed planned savings then actual investment also increases in the form of accumulation of inventories which is unintended investment. It should be noted that s is a proportion. Hence savings in absolute terms will be the proportion s times the income i.e. $S=sY$.

The second assumption is that the entrepreneurs who are responsible for making investment decisions and thus determine the proportion of income invested are influenced by the rate of increase in output in the previous period. The total stock of capital in a community forms a given proportion of the aggregate output. Hence when income or output increases, the stock of capital also would increase. Investment means an addition to the stock of capital. The demand for capital represents the aggregate volume of capital required given the size of output. The larger the size of output, the larger the amount of capital required. That is investment or the demand for additional capital depends on the rate of increase in income or the speed with which production is growing.

On the basis of these two assumptions the behaviour of income as a response to entrepreneurial decisions relating to investment is derived. Since actual savings or investment form a fixed proportion of income and since increase in investment depends on the rate of increase in income, it follows that entrepreneurs will be satisfied with actual investment only if income is increasing correspondingly. Thus if the rate of increase in income is too high the entrepreneurs will find actual investment less than what is desirable while if increase in income is not high enough, actual investment will be found excessive. If income growth rate is just so much as to make entrepreneurs satisfied with the actual investment, then that rate of growth of income is the ' warranted rate of growth '. Since the proportion of investment to income is fixed, an increase in income means that both income and investment will be higher in the next period. And if entrepreneurs are to accept this higher investment as a desirable one income will have to grow even faster than before. This will lead to a further increase in income, investment and so on. Investment and income will be chasing one another up a spiral. On the other hand, if there is a decrease in income, investment also would fall. But if the entrepreneurs are to be satisfied with this lower investment income should further fall. This would then mean that given the fixed relationship between income and investment and the entrepreneurial behaviour, a rise in output will necessitate further rise because

investment demand will be rising correspondingly, while decrease in output
will cause a further fall because demand for investment also will be declining.

This cumulative movement of income in the upward or downward direction
is illustrated by means of some simple equations.

$$(1) \quad GC = S$$

G stands for actual growth rate of income i.e. increment of production in a
given period expressed as a fraction of total production. Thus if the annual
rate of increase in income is 2 per cent i.e. if income of 100 increases to 102
then the value of G is $1/50$. C stands for capital and represents net capital
accumulation in the period (i.e. additions of new capital goods plus the goods
in process and stocks) divided by the increase in output in the period. Roughly
it is the ratio of increase in capital to increase in production. S is the fraction
of income saved. Change in S expressed as a fraction of income should be
small by comparison with changes in G. G may increase from say 2 to 6 per
cent i.e. three times rise in the rate of increase in income, but since S is not the
proportionate increase but a given proportion of total income S will not be
trebled say from 10 per cent of national income to 30 per cent of national
income.[21] Thus if income at a point of time is 1,000 crores, G is $1/50$ and C
is $4/1$ then $S = 80$ crores.

$$(2) \quad GwCr = S$$

Harrod defines Gw or warranted growth rate as " that over all rate of advance
which if executed will leave entrepreneurs in a state of mind in which they
are prepared to carry on a similar advance " i.e. given the level of investment
Gw represents that rate of growth of income which will make entrepreneurs
satisfied with the actual investment or putting it the other way, if Gw is the
rate of growth of income Cr is the capital required to ensure the warranted
growth rate. This will not rule out involuntary unemployment but the
entrepreneurs will be satisfied with their decision. Hence we have,

$$GC = S$$
$$GwCr = S$$

Since S does not change, if G is greater than Gw i.e. if the actual rate of
growth of output exceeds the warranted rate C must be less than Cr i.e.
equipment and stocks in the pipeline will be insufficient to sustain the existing
turnover. Hence orders for equipment will be increased but this will automatically increase G which in turn requires more of C and so on, bringing about
continuous expansion. On the other hand, if Gw exceeds G i.e. actual growth
rate falls short of warranted increase, then Cr will be less than C i.e. desired
capital will be less than actual capital equipment; hence orders for equipment
will be reduced. This will push G further down which in turn further
depresses C and so on.

Expansion and contraction however, cannot go on indefinitely. The upper
limit is set by the availability of labour and natural resources.

[21]Income increases from 100 to 106 instead of 102. If at 102 savings are $1/10$ or $10\cdot2$ it will
not be $10\cdot6 \times 3$ or $31\cdot8$ when income rises to 106.

$$(3) \quad GnCr = \text{ or } \Rightarrow S$$

Gn represents the upper limit to growth of output determined by the availability of labour, natural resources and technological improvements. It is the natural growth rate which excludes involuntary unemployment. Harrod points out that in the years after a recession *G* may be higher than *Gn* for a considerable period of time but it will not continue to be higher indefinitely. When *G* or actual growth rate is higher than *Gw* or warranted growth rate there is continuous expansion until *Gn* is reached. The limitations fixed by labour and natural resources prevent further rise. The economy cannot remain at the ceiling level; it has either to rise or fall. When *G* touches *Gn*, *Gw* catches up with it. But since the rate of rise of *G* cannot be maintained, *Gw* tends to exceed *G* and then the down trend starts. This in turn cannot continue indefinitely. In the downward phase circulating capital will be reduced. But fixed capital cannot fall since orders cannot be reduced below zero. This combined with the confidence of the entrepreneurs born out of their knowledge of the actual resources position will revive growth. Thus the course of the capitalist economy will be unsteady because of its inherent characteristics. A steady rise in income is not possible because " around the line of advance, which if adhered to, would alone give satisfaction, centrifugal forces are at work causing the system to depart farther and farther from the required line of advance ".[22] This makes it clear that the phenomenon of cyclical fluctuations is implicit in the phenomenon of growth of capitalist economies.

(ii) The Domar Model [23]

Domar points out that the preservation of full employment in a capitalist economy requires a growing income. When there is full employment equilibrium, the productive capacity of the economy is equal to its national income. Domar discusses the question as to the rate of growth of the economy which would help to maintain a continuous state of full employment. A given rate of savings and investment may be assumed to provide full employment at a certain aggregate income level. If this rate of investment is maintained in period 2 income will be at the same level as it was in period 1. But while in period 1 the given rate of investment and income level ensured full employment, it will not ensure full employment (i.e. full employment of capital and labour resources) in period 2. This is so because investment in period one would have expanded productive capacity and unless real income has increased correspondingly, the full capacity output will not be demanded and hence capital equipment and other resources will not be fully utilized. By productive

[22]Harrod, R. F., *Towards a Dynamic Economics*, Macmillan, London, 1954, p. 86.

[23]Domar, Evsey, ' Capital Expansion, Rate of Growth and Employment,' *Econometrica*, April 1946. ' Expansion and Employment ', *American Economic Review*, March, 1947. ' Theoretical Analysis of Economic Growth,' *American Economic Review*, Papers and Proceedings, May, 1952. All reprinted in *Essays in the Theory of Economic Growth*, Oxford, New York, 1957.

capacity, Domar means the total output of the economy at what is usually called full employment.[24] Supposing the amounts of investment and income are the same in money terms in period 2 as in period 1, real income can increase only with a fall in prices. But if we assume constant level of prices— and this is implicit in stability conditions—then for the attainment of full employment in period 2 both real income and money income should have to increase at the same rate.

The essence of Domar's theory consists in two important points, namely, that an act of investment increases the productive capacity of the economy and also at the same time generates income. Hence it follows that there will be stable growth only if the rate of investment is such that the additional income generated is just enough to take care of the increased productive capacity resulting from increased investment. The productive capacity may be represented as the supply side and the income generating capacity as the demand side because it is income that is created that causes demand for productive capacity to be maintained.

The supply side of capital obviously depends on the rate of investment which in turn depends on the rate of savings. Let I stand for investment. How much it would add to productive capacity depends on what Domar calls the ' potential social average productivity of investment '. This term Domar uses in order to distinguish it from marginal productivity of capital where increase in output can be attributed to the increase in capital. Domar uses the term to indicate the increase in productive capacity which *accompanies* rather than which is caused by each unit of money invested. Secondly, the term used in Domar's model deals not with an increase in national income but with that of the productive potential of the economy. Let σ represent this potential productive capacity resulting from a given investment. Then the supply side of the system can be expressed as $I\sigma$ which shows that the amount of investment multiplied by the productive capacity of each unit of investment will give the extent to which total productive capacity of the economy has increased. If I is the rate of investment then $I\sigma$ would of course be the rate of increase in the productive capacity.

Demand for the additional output comes from additional investment itself because investment generates income. Thus the demand side represented by increase in incomes is also dependent on I which comes on the supply side also. Investment generates income via the multiplier which in turn is dependent on the propensity to consume and to save. Thus if increase in income is ΔY and the propensity to save is a and the increase in investment ΔI, then the relation between change in investment and the resulting change in income can be expressed as $\Delta Y = (\Delta I)1/a$ i.e. change in investment multiplied by the multiplier gives increase in income. If the starting point is full employment equilibrium, and full employment is to be maintained as income grows, the condition is that the demand for output is equal to the supply of output.

[24]Domar, Evsey, *Essays in the Theory of Economic Growth*, Oxford, New York, 1957, p. 87.

4

Since the increase in productive capacity is $I\sigma$ and increase in income is (ΔI) $1/a$, the condition for stable growth is $(\Delta I)1/a=I\sigma$. The equation is simplified by multiplying both sides by a and dividing both sides by I. Then we have $\Delta I/I=a\sigma$. $\Delta I/I$ is the ratio of increase in investment to total investment i.e. it is the annual relative rate of growth of investment. This would mean that the "maintenance of a continuous state of full employment requires that *investment and income grow at a constant annual relative (or compound interest) rate* equal to the product of the propensity to save and the average (to put it briefly) productivity of investment ".[25]

Domar gives a numerical example to make the above result clear. Let σ or productive capacity be 25 per cent per year; savings or a 12 per cent and Y or income 150 billions per year. Investment of 12 per cent of income is necessary to maintain full employment i.e. investment required is $150\times12/100=$ 18 billions. This investment would increase productive capacity by the amount invested, by σ times i.e. $150\times12/100\times25/100$, or 18 billions $\times25/100=4\frac{1}{2}$ billions and hence national income will also have to rise by the same amount. In the example, the relative rise in income i.e. ratio of increase in income to initial income is $\dfrac{4\frac{1}{2}\text{ billions}}{150\text{ billions}}$ or 3 per cent and the value of $a\sigma$ is also 3 per cent $\left(\dfrac{12}{100}\times\dfrac{25}{100}\right)=3$ per cent i.e. increase in income is equal to the increase in productive capacity.

The model shows the inherent instability of economic growth under the capitalist system. Any slight deviation from the stability conditions in the upward or downward direction would operate cumulatively and remove the economy further away from the stability rate of growth. Thus if investment is such as to bring about a higher increase in income than in productive capacity, there will be a relative shortage of productive equipment, investment will be increased which will further push up income and so on. On the other hand, if increase in income is less than in productive capacity, it would set in motion the forces of down trend. A rise in the rate of increase in income necessitates further rise in income while a relative fall in the rate of increase will further bring down the income level. In other words, when income increases there is relative shortage, while when it falls there is relative plenty.

The close similarity between the models of Harrod and Domar is thus clear. In Harrod's model the value of saving depends on the level of income and the volume of investment depends on the rate of growth of income. If there is to be stability, intended saving must be matched by intended investment. But if this intended investment is to be forthcoming from businessmen, income must be growing. And rise in incomes generates more savings, and more investment will be made if there is further rise in income. Hence, only if there is continuous growth of income can intended savings and intended investment stay equal at prosperity levels. Similarly, in Domar's version,

[25]Domar, Evsey, *Essays in the Theory of Economic Growth*, Oxford, New York, 1957, pp. 91–92.

the level of income determines the level of intended saving. If intended investment is equal to intended saving, it increases productive capacity and this
increased productive capacity will be absorbed only if there is increase in
income. A rise in income would call for more savings and more investment
which would further push up income and productive capacity. Thus in
Domar's model also continued equilibrium requires steady growth.[26]

This brief outline of the Harrod-Domar models shows the extent to which
Keynesian economics has helped and influenced modern growth analysis.
The concept of the acceleration principle introduced in 1917 by J. M. Clark
who applied it to micro economic problems and which was later extended to
aggregate problems and popularized by Keynes plays a key role in the analysis
of growth problems by Harrod, Domar and others. The basic ingredients of
these models are the accelerator and the multiplier. The essentially dynamic
nature of these concepts has been made good use of by later writers in constructing models of economic growth. The classical economists laid emphasis on
savings and accumulation and the role of investment and technological
improvements in economic growth. They concentrated on the supply side of
the problem and took for granted the demand for capital. In a rapidly growing
economy this assumption is realistic in so far as development and growth are
quite often held up by the lack of savings and capital. On the other hand, in a
mature economy investment tends to lose its momentum while capital accumulates. Thus it was the problem of demand for capital or investment opportunities that engaged the attention of Keynes. Harrod and Domar on the other
hand observed the dynamic nature of investment and demand and directed
their attention to the analysis of the variations in capital and variation in
demand as causes of instability in economic growth. While static analysis
explains the conditions of equilibrium in terms of equality between savings
and investment, modern dynamic economics lays emphasis on equality between
rate of growth of savings and rate of growth of investment as a necessary
condition of dynamic equilibrium.

APPLICABILITY OF THE MODELS TO UNDERDEVELOPED COUNTRIES

From the point of view of underdeveloped countries, however, the Harrod-
Domar models have little significance. They relate to problems concerning
developed capitalist economies whose major ill is instability and cyclical
fluctuations in employment and income. The problem of underdeveloped
countries is not instability in growth, but growth itself. The Harrod-Domar
models attempt to explain secular stagnation which is supposed by some economists to face developed economies. Such a phenomenon, however, has not
happened, in the low income countries. Although the problem of employment
is common to both rich and poor countries, the causes of unemployment

[26]Yeager, Leland B., ' Some Questions about Growth Economics,' *American Economic Review*,
March, 1954, p. 53.

are very much different in the underdeveloped countries from that in developed countries; hence the remedial measures likely to be successful and effective in the latter would have no meaning in the former. In the advanced economies where capital is plentiful, lack of effective demand causes idleness of capital which results in unemployment of labour. Therefore, the major issue is to maintain the level of effective demand in such countries. In the backward economies on the other hand, unemployment of labour results from the lack of capital, the co-operant factor. Solution of their problem therefore lies in capital formation. Hirschman points out that the constancy of the capital-output ratio assumed in the growth models may be true of developed countries but in the backward economies where normal productivity is held back by various obstacles, it is altogether unrealistic and therefore of little use.[27] Moreover, since the variables refer only to aggregates for the economy as a whole, a model constructed on the basis of such aggregates cannot show the inter-relations between the sectors and is therefore not meant for demonstrating the structural changes which are a very important aspect of the economic development of underdeveloped countries.[28]

Apart from this, the dynamic models of growth have come in for much criticism on theoretical grounds. The major objection is that the models are based on much abstraction and rigid assumptions and are far removed from reality. Production function is assumed to be fixed; hence there is no allowance for substitution between factors. But such substitution is constantly taking place and is in fact an essential feature of growth. Technological changes and improvements on the organizational side of production bring about a shift in the pattern of production. Hence it is incorrect to make use of a fixed production function as a means to explain long term growth.[29] The models are therefore of little use in matters of policy. The capital-output ratio and the accelerator also are not constant in the real world. In fact, the contribution of capital to production is not clearly known. Lundberg mentions that recent statistical findings relating to Norway and U.S.A. show that contribution of capital accumulation to the growth rate of these economies has been small compared with the contribution of shifts in the production function, technical research, administration and investment in education.[30] The variables in the models are real magnitudes. Hence the influence of monetary and price factors in investment, savings, and demand is ruled out.[31] In reality, however, the accelerator is

[27]Hirschman, Albert O., *The Strategy of Economic Development*, Yale, New Haven, 1958, p. 35.
[28]*Economic Bulletin for Asia and the Far East*, U.N., November, 1955, pp. 34–40.
[29]It is the assumption of rigid production function in which no substitution of factors is possible that makes the economic system balanced on a knife edge of equilibrium growth. If this assumption is removed the knife edge notion of unstable balance goes along with it. Solow, R., 'A Contribution to the Theory of Economic Growth,' *Quarterly Journal of Economics*, February, 1956, p. 65.
[30]Lundberg, Erik, 'The Profitability of Investment,' *Economic Journal*, December, 1959, pp. 653–77.
[31]Tobin, James, 'Complementary and Long-range Projections,' *Econometrica*, October, 1956, pp. 429–50.

not a non-monetary element in the business cycle. Price expectations, interest rates, credit policies and conditions of the stock market affect businessmen's willingness and ability to invest. If these factors influence savings and invest- ment, it is possible that changes in them would bring about equilibrating adjustments in savings and investment when there is a deviation, and thus prevent the cumulative working of the forces of deviation. It is in fact argued that instability is very much exaggerated in the growth models. Slight devia- tions from the equilibrium path need not and do not carry the economy headlong in either direction. The real cause of instability is entrepreneurial behaviour and the lag between investment decisions and capital outlays.[32] Yeager questions the use of the concept of natural growth rate in Harrod's model. He points out that the upper limit to growth is not rigidly fixed by labour and natural resources. Even assuming that labour and natural resources are fixed, the output possible with the resources would vary according to the method of utilizing the resources. Organizational and technological changes would increase the productivity of both capital and labour so that the maximum output possible with a given supply of resources can be increased.[33] Another criticism of Yeager is that the cumulative upward and downward movements supposed to describe the real world are only a theoretical derivation from certain basic assumptions and have not been substantiated by empirical evidence. He criticizes the models also on the ground that many of the defini- tions like warranted rate of growth in Harrod's model are fuzzy and incapable of being assessed objectively.[34]

That the modern dynamic models of economic growth carry analysis to a high level of abstraction cannot be disputed. In defence of them however, it may be said that such abstractions are necessary in order to simplify the reasoning and to direct attention on the basic factors involved in the growth of advanced capitalist economies. Although they are little relevant to under- developed countries and do not help in clarifying the issues involved in the growth of such economies, they are useful in providing a better understanding of the inter-relationship between the overall targets of income, investment and saving and for checking the consistency of such targets.[35] The models are also helpful in so far as they suggest the easy susceptibility of low income

[32]Rose, H., 'The Possibility of Warranted Growth,' *Economic Journal*, June, 1959, pp. 313–32.

[33]Yeager, Leland B., 'Some Questions about Growth Economics,' *American Economic Review*, March, 1954, pp. 53–63.

[34]What is called warranted growth rate actually depends on the expectations and behaviour of individual firms. If the existing growth rate is the warranted one, it can continue only if each investor assumed that the other investors " naively projected the present rate into the future and acted accordingly ". But this is not possible because investment decisions are made by numerous firms and there is little reason to expect investors as a whole to project the current rate of growth into the future with such confidence as to guide their decisions by that criterion alone. And if this equilibrium is highly unstable and shifting, it is virtually irrelevant and cannot be assigned any great role in the economic process. Schelling, T. C., ' Capital Growth and Equilibrium,' *American Economic Review*, December, 1947, pp. 864–76.

[35]*Economic Bulletin for Asia and the Far East*, U.N., November, 1955, p. 40.

countries to inflation. A small rise in investment will have larger effects in these countries because initial investment rate and growth rate are low.

NEO-CLASSICAL MODELS OF ECONOMIC GROWTH

The theoretical models discussed above are theories of economic growth and relate to the problems of developed economies. Underdeveloped countries require a theory of development. A clear distinction between ' growth ' and ' development ' is not possible. One view is that the term ' growth ' is applicable to economically advanced countries where most of the resources are already known and developed while ' development ' should relate to backward countries where there is possibility of developing and using hitherto unused resources.[36] Professor Bonné emphasizes the spontaneous nature of growth which characterizes advanced free enterprise economies in contrast to development which requires and involves some sort of direction, regulation and guidance to generate the forces of expansion and maintain them. This is true of most of the underdeveloped countries.[37] Schumpeter makes a special interpretation of the meaning of the two terms. Development according to him takes place because of forces working within the system when other factors are given. Development is a spontaneous and discontinuous change set in motion by an impelling spirit of expansion. Growth on the other hand, is gradual and steady in the long run and is brought about by a general increase in the resources such as population and savings.[38] Since economic expansion is more or less spontaneous and automatic in the high income capitalist countries, but requires some external stimulus and direction from the Government in backward countries, we may consider the term ' growth ' in relation to developed countries, and ' development ' in relation to backward economies.

In so far as the problem of economic growth in advanced economies differs considerably from that in economically backward countries it is necessary to evolve a principle or theory of development which will be true of and applicable to underdeveloped countries. In general, such a theory of development should recognize the significance of the population factor in economic growth—its effect on income, distribution and savings; should stress the supply aspect of capital rather than its demand aspect; incorporate technological factors as an important determinant of development; and also give importance to institutional factors and agriculture in bringing about increases in output and income.

A number of theories and models of economic development have come out in recent years which attempt to incorporate the above factors in the theoretical structure. It should be remembered that in all the classical theories of economic

[36]Hicks, Ursula K., ' Learning about Economic Development,' *Oxford Economic Papers*, February, 1957, p. 1.

[37]Bonné, Alfred, *Studies in Economic Development*, Routledge and Kegan Paul, London, 1957, p. 7.

[38]Schumpeter, J. A., *The Theory of Economic Development*, Harvard, Cambridge, Mass., 1934, pp. 65–66.

growth, beginning from that of Adam Smith, considerable attention was devoted to an analysis of the part played by population, savings, technology and institutions in the growth of the capitalist system of economy. The neo-classical theories of economic growth are to a large extent influenced by these views of classical writers on the problem. But being equipped with better analytical tools the modern theorists are able to formulate more scientific and logically consistent principles relating to underdevelopment. Their contribution to the literature on this subject consists in the presentation of classical theories in a modern garb—a restatement of the ' magnificent dynamics ' of Ricardo, Marx and Schumpeter—by using the modern Keynesian and Harrod-Domar terminology.[39] A reinterpretation of classical doctrines with the help of Keynesian concepts and techniques helps in viewing the basic forces of growth in a better perspective and in getting a clearer understanding of the manner in which they function.

One important feature of the neo-classical models is that they incorporate the population factor and the supply of labour in their explanation of growth. In so far as overpopulation has been an obstacle to the rapid development of the low income countries, it is only proper that the problem of growth in such countries is approached from the point of view of labour. The appropriate rate of growth of income then would be such as would ensure equality between the rate of growth of population and the rate of capital formation.[40] Hamberg puts this equilibrium rate in the form $G=E/U$ where G is the ratio of full employment growth rate E to full utilization of capacity growth rate U ; if the value of G is greater than one it means that the growth of capital is not sufficient enough to fully employ the growing labour force whereas if G is less than one, it means that savings are too much in relation to the country's capacity to absorb them; or putting it in another way, there is insufficiency of labour to fully utilize capital. In the latter case, the remedy is to lower the savings function and increase consumption and in the former the solution is to increase savings and raise the full capacity rate of growth so as to absorb the labour force and/or adopt techniques of production which are labour using and capital saving.[41]

[39]Among theoretical models of this type are:

    (a) Robinson, (Mrs.) Joan, The Accumulation of Capital, Macmillan, London, 1956.

    (b) Little, I. M. D., ' Classical Growth,' Oxford Economic Papers, June, 1957, pp. 152–77.

    (c) Solow, Robert, ' A Contribution to the Theory of Economic Growth,' Quarterly Journal of Economics, February, 1956.

    (d) Kaldor, N., ' A Model of Economic Growth,' Economic Journal, December, 1957.

    (e) Butt, Bensusan, On Economic Growth, Oxford, London, 1960.

    (f) Meade, J. E., A Neo-classical Theory of Economic Growth, George Allen and Unwin, London, 1961.

[40]Bruton, Henry J., ' Growth Models and Underdeveloped Economies,' Journal of Political Economy, August, 1955, pp. 322–36.

[41]Hamberg, D., ' Full Capacity vs. Full Employment Growth,' Quarterly Journal of Economics, August, 1952, p. 444.

The problem of population in a growing economy and its effect on the rate of capital accumulation and growth of output are brought out clearly in Mrs. Joan Robinson's model of economic growth. Her thesis is built on two fundamental factors: first, capital formation depends on the way in which income is distributed and second, the rate of utilization of labour is a function of the supply of capital and the supply of labour. She makes the following assumptions: Total income in real terms is divided between wage earners and profit earners; the former spend their entire income on consumption; the latter spend their entire income on investment or capital formation. Capital and labour are combined in fixed proportions and there is no technological change. Total wage bill is the real wage rate times the number of labourers and total profits the profit rate multiplied by the amount of capital and hence total income is the sum of the above two.

$$Y = wN + xK$$

where Y is aggregate income, w wage rate, x profit rate and K capital, all in real terms, and N the number of labourers. Profit rate is therefore

$$r = \frac{Y - wN}{K}$$

i.e. profit rate is the ratio of total income minus wage bill to amount of capital. Since profit per labourer employed is the difference between the output per labourer and the real wage, profit rate would depend on labour productivity, the real wage rate and the amount of capital per worker or the capital-labour ratio. Hence profit rate can increase if wage rate is constant and income increases; if income is constant and wage rate decreases and if the ratio of capital to labour decreases.

The demand for labour depends on the capital available in the economy. Additions to capital depend on the rate of profit which in turn is determined by labour productivity and wage rate. Total expenditure which is the same as total income is divided between consumption and investment i.e. $Y = C + I$, and savings are equal to investment $S = I$. Consumption is equal to total wage income, and investment is equal to savings which are equal to total profits. Since all profits are invested, increase in total capital stock in a given period is equal to capital multiplied by the profit rate. And since profit rate depends on the relationship between the income that remains after wage payment and capital-labour ratio, it follows that if capital-labour ratio is high and income minus wages is constant, then profit rate will be low and therefore the rate of capital formation will be low. An increase in population and in labour force without an increase in capital would reduce labour productivity, and if real wages are constant, lower the margin of profit and thus widen the difference between capital and labour supply. It would also cause unemployment. Hence full employment is possible only if the growth rate of population is matched by the growth rate of capital i.e. if

$$\frac{\Delta N}{N} = \frac{\Delta K}{K}$$

there will be full employment of both labour and capital. And Mrs. Robinson calls this the ' golden age '.

If an economy goes off the golden age, there is possibility of its coming back to this position under certain conditions. Thus if $\dfrac{\Delta N}{N} > \dfrac{\Delta K}{K}$ or the rate of increase in population is higher than that of capital, a return to the golden age equilibrium is possible only if the profit wage relation behaves in an equilibrating manner. Thus excess of labour supply would lower the wage rate and if prices are unchanged, will reduce the real wages, and by increasing the amount of profits may increase the rate of growth of capital so that it would catch up with the increase in population. But if the real wages do not fall either because of the rigidity of money wage rates or because prices fall in the same proportion as the money wage rate, the effect would be only progressive underemployment. In general, rise in prices helps capital forma-tion so long as there is not a corresponding rise in wages. Increasing un-employment, while prices and wages are rising is quite a common feature in underdeveloped countries. On the other hand, if $\dfrac{\Delta K}{K} > \dfrac{\Delta N}{N}$ i.e. if capital growth is greater than population growth there is the possibility of equilibrium being restored through technological improvements and the shifting of the whole production function so that the economy will get itself adjusted to a higher capital-labour ratio. It should be observed that the golden age is not an ideal. It only represents a state of equilibrium growth at any conceivable rate so that each rate of growth will have its appropriate golden age.[42]

The extent to which this theory of capital accumulation and growth draws upon classical writers particularly Ricardo and Marx is obvious. But it is this influence which brings the analysis closer to the realities of an underdeveloped economy.

A similar analysis of the relation between income growth and population growth has been made by J. E. Meade.[43] Net output produced by an economy depends on four factors; net stock of capital in the form of instruments of production, the labour force, land and natural resources and technical knowledge. These factors are expressed in the production function,

$$Y = F(K, L, N, t)$$

where Y is net national income, K stock of machines, L labour, N natural resources and t technology. Natural resources can be considered as fixed. Increase in net output that may take place in any one year is the sum of the contribution of L, K and t, which are increasing i.e. $\Delta Y = V \Delta K + W \Delta L + \Delta Y^1$. V and W are marginal products of capital and labour and ΔY^1 is the increase in the rate of annual output due to technical progress. The propor-

[42]Kahn, R. F., ' Exercises in the Analysis of Growth,' *Oxford Economic Papers*, No. 2, June, 1959, pp. 143–56.

[43]Meade, J. E., *A Neo-classical Theory of Economic Growth*, George Allen and Unwin, London, 1961.

tionate rate of growth of output i.e. the ratio of increase to initial amount is therefore,

$$\frac{\Delta Y}{Y} = \frac{VK}{Y} \cdot \frac{\Delta K}{K} + \frac{WL}{Y} \cdot \frac{\Delta L}{L} + \frac{\Delta Y^1}{Y}$$

Let these four proportionate rates of growth be expressed as y, k, l and r respectively. The proportion of national income going to each factor by way of remuneration is the ratio of the marginal product of the factor times the factor to total income. Thus the amount of income paid as profits is VK/Y. Let this be called the proportional marginal product of capital (to be distinguished from net marginal product) and expressed as U. Similarly Q stands for the proportional marginal product of labour. Then the basic relationship is

$$y = Uk + Ql + r$$

The growth of the economy is indicated by the rise in the per capita real income i.e. $y - l$. Thus if y or total income increases by 10 per cent per annum and l or population increases by 8 per cent per annum income per head will increase by about 2 per cent per annum. The growth rate of real income per head will therefore be,

$$y - l = Uk - (1 - Q)l + r$$

The middle term on the right hand side indicates the tendency for diminishing returns to labour as the supply of labour is increased. The equation therefore shows that the rate of growth of income per head would be raised by an increase in real capital weighted by its proportional marginal product and also by technical progress, r, and will be depressed by the growth rate of labour weighted by one minus the proportional marginal product of labour. Savings are assumed to be invested so that capital stock K is increased as a result of savings. Savings S, constitute a proportion of income, Y. Hence the rate of growth of capital is the ratio of the proportion of income saved to initial stock of capital i.e. $k = \frac{SY}{K}$. Since U is $\frac{VK}{Y}$, $Uk = \frac{VK}{Y} \cdot \frac{SY}{K} = SV$. Hence

$$y - l = SV - (1 - Q)l + r$$

Thus if savings form 10 per cent of national income and the marginal product of real capital goods is 5 per cent per annum i.e. V is 5 per cent then the contribution of capital growth to increase in output will be 1/10 of 5 per cent per annum i.e. $\frac{1}{2}$ per cent per annum.

If growth of population and development of technology i.e. l and r are constant, the change in output per head depends on the change in the values of V, S, and Q over time. If population and technology are unchanged but savings rise, capital per head would increase and the marginal product of capital would fall. But this fall may be slowed down if there is possibility of substituting capital for other factors. Also, if we allow for improvement in technology or change in r the decline in the marginal product of capital will be offset. In other words, if population alone is assumed to be constant, then increase in income will depend on productivity of capital, the amount of savings and the state of technology i.e. $y = Vs + r$. V or the marginal product of capital will be higher, the greater the rate of technical progress, the more machine using the nature of technical progress, the lower the initial proportion of income saved, but the higher it rises with increasing income, and the more readily machinery is substituted for land and labour. S would rise because of rise in income per head and because of a shift of income towards profits.[44]

Next Prof. Meade examines the conditions of a state of steady economic growth, where population is growing at a constant proportionate rate while the rate of technical progress is constant. It is obvious that income per head will be constant under these conditions only if the rate of growth of total output is constant. But what conditions would ensure a constant growth rate in total output? This question is examined under the assumption that all elasticities of substitution between the various factors are equal to unity; that technical progress is neutral towards all factors and that the proportions of profits, wages and rent saved are all constant.

Let the proportion of national income saved out of profits, wages and rents be Sv, Sw and Sg respectively. Then S or total savings $= SvU + SwQ + SgZ$. Since l and r are assumed to be constant, the proportional marginal products U and Q will be constant. Since U, Q and Z are constant, and Sv, Sw and Sg are also constant, S as a ratio of Y will be constant. Therefore y or the rate of growth of income will be constant only if k or the rate of growth of capital is constant. This can be easily shown. k the growth rate of capital is the ratio of the proportion of income saved to capital stock i.e. $k = \dfrac{SY}{K}$. Since S is constant k will be constant only if Y/K is constant. Y/K will be constant if the rate of increase in Y is the same as the rate of increase in K i.e. $k = y$. The conclusion is thus reached that if the growth rate of the capital stock is equal to the growth rate of income, then the rate of growth of income will be constant and hence given a constant proportionate rate of growth of population, the per capita growth of income will be constant and steady.

This of course is an equilibrium position. A deviation from it is indicated by the excess or deficiency of actual savings and capital accumulation above or below the rate which is equal to the income growth rate. This is illustrated by a numerical example:

If $r = 1$ per cent per annum, $l = 2$ per cent per annum, $Q\frac{1}{2}$ and $U\frac{1}{4}$ then Y will increase by 1 per cent because of r or technical progress, and by another 1 per cent because of population growth $(Ql = \frac{1}{2} \times 2 = 1)$ i.e. by 2 per cent by the two factors combined. If capital stock increases by 1 per cent then

[44]Meade, J. E., *A Neo-classical Theory of Economic Growth*, George Allen and Unwin, London, 1961, p. 28.

the increase of capital stock would add to production by $\frac{1}{4}$ per cent. Thus total increase will be $2\frac{1}{4}$ per cent. In other words, given the productivity of the other factors, an increase in capital stock by 1 per cent will add to total output by $2\frac{1}{4}$ per cent. If capital stock were growing very fast at 100 per cent with productivity of other factors as above, total increase in output will be 27 per cent (i.e. 2 per cent because of r and l and 25 per cent because of addition to capital). In the former case, an addition of capital by 1 per cent increases output by $2\frac{1}{4}$ per cent; in the latter case, an addition of capital by 100 per cent adds to output by only 27 per cent. Hence there must be an equilibrium rate of growth of capital between these extremes which would be equal to the rate of growth of income. In the above numerical example a growth rate in capital stock of $2\frac{2}{3}$ per cent per annum will have this result since the effect of a $2\frac{2}{3}$ per cent addition to capital on income growth will be $2\frac{2}{3} \times \frac{1}{4} + \frac{1}{2} \times 2 + 1 = 2\frac{2}{3}$. This is algebraically expressed as follows:

$$a = Ua + Ql + r, \text{ i.e. } a = \frac{Ql + r}{1 - U}$$

Thus if Q is 1, l is 2 and r is 1 and U is $\frac{1}{2}$ then $a = \frac{(1 \times 2) + 1}{1 - \frac{1}{2}} = 6$

Growth of capital depends on S. Suppose SY/K is greater than the critical or equilibrium level i.e. $\frac{SY}{K} > \frac{Ql + r}{1 - U}$. This will make capital growth greater than income growth. With income growth falling, S will also be falling i.e. addition to capital stock SY/K will be falling and become equal to income growth rate. If SY/K is less than the critical level, income would grow more quickly than capital, savings would grow, capital growth would increase and thus reach equality with income growth. Thus under the assumptions made above, growth rate of real income and of the stock of real capital would both tend towards a constant rate.

Meade's analysis of economic growth thus draws attention to the role of population growth, capital increase and technology in determining the increase of income per head (which is the criterion of economic development) and also to the conditions under which a stable growth of per capita income is possible when population is increasing along with the other determinants.

Kaldor gives great prominence to technological improvements as a determinant of economic growth. He incorporates technical change in capital accumulation. The prime mover in the process of economic growth is, according to him, the capacity and readiness of the economy to absorb technical change and to invest capital in business ventures. As the share of profits in the national income increases, savings ratio also would rise. There is equilibrium rate of growth when the profit rate is such as to equate savings and investment.[45] In the case of young and relatively underpopulated countries, proportionate increases in labour and capital would maintain output per

[45]Kennedy, Charles, ' A Static Interpretation of Some Recent Theories of Growth and Distribution,' *Oxford Economic Papers*, June, 1960, p. 197.

head constant. But in the case of overpopulated countries with given techniques and capital per head, the output per unit of labour employed would tend to decrease because of the fixity of land and the operation of the law of diminishing returns. For this reason the maintenance of an equilibrium rate of growth is more precarious in such countries. It is possible to conceive of a " particular rate of growth of population, which enables the rate of growth of income to be equal to it; at any lesser rate productivity per head will rise and the growth of income will exceed the growth of population (causing the latter to increase and income per head to cease rising); at any higher rate, productivity will fall and the growth of income will fall short of the growth in population (causing the latter to contract and income per head to cease falling) ".[46] Hence, long run economic growth and rise in standard of living are possible only if there is a check to the rate of population growth before population growth rate reaches the maximum which is equal to the maximum rate of growth of income.

In his recent article ' Second Essay in Dynamic Theory '[47] Harrod emphasizes the need for elaborating the supply side of his growth equation so as to make it more relevant to underdeveloped countries. In particular, he examines the role of interest rate in determining the availability of savings and the demand for savings for carrying out plans of investment. In his original essay Cr denotes the optimum amount of capital required at the warranted growth rate of income. But the amount of savings available and therefore the amount of investment that is possible would both be affected by the rate of interest. Similarly, the natural growth rate of income requires a certain volume of savings. Given the other resources in the economy such as labour and natural resources, actual growth rate can reach the level of natural rate only if a corresponding amount of savings is forthcoming. Moreover, the natural growth rate itself will be indeterminate unless the rate of interest is specified.

Hence Harrod conceives of the natural rate of interest which he defines as the one which conforms to the natural growth of income and is determined by the natural rate of growth of per capita output Pc, and e or the elasticity of the schedule of the diminishing utility of income. Thus if e is large it means that the utility of income declines rapidly when income grows. The natural rate of interest rn is therefore:

$$rn = \frac{PcGn}{e}$$

Given the values of Pc and Gn the natural rate of interest will be low if e is large and vice versa. e is supposed on general grounds to be less than one. The capital intensity of the methods of production used by the entrepreneurs

[46]Kaldor, N., 'A Model of Economic Growth.' Economic Journal, December, 1957. Reprinted in Essays on Economic Stability and Growth, Duckworth, London, 1960. p. 293.

[47]Harrod, R. F., 'Second Essay in Dynamic Theory,' Economic Journal, June, 1960, pp. 277-93.

and therefore the value of capital required would depend on the rate of interest. Normally Cr or the capital requirements would be a decreasing function of rn, i.e. $Cr = f (rn)$. Corresponding to the natural rate of growth of output there will be the required rate of savings and also the natural rate of interest. The fraction of income actually saved s need not necessarily tend to approximate to Sr the social requirement. $\overset{.}{S}$ may be greater or less than Sr. But if S is greater than Sr then warranted growth rate will be above the natural growth rate i.e. entrepreneurs will desire to increase their investment because of the availability of larger savings. There is however, an important difference in the manner in which the natural growth rate and the warranted growth rate are determined. The natural growth rate is determined by the labour and technological resources. Given these resources the level of natural growth rate would require a certain rate of savings. But the warranted rate of growth of income is taken to be determined by the actual rate of S or savings.

What happens if S is greater than or less than Sr. If $S > Sr$ the warranted growth rate would exceed natural rate. Since the natural rate is the highest that can be achieved in the long run, the excess of warranted rate cannot continue. The actual growth rate would then hit the full employment ceiling and then it will have to fall below the warranted growth rate and a depression will set in. On the other hand, if $S < Sr$ investment will be higher than savings and hence there will be a chronic tendency to inflation—characteristic of developing economies. Excess of investment over savings, may be financed by expansion of bank credit and also by the automatic investment of inflationary profits through the capital markets. Organized capital markets are not available in the underdeveloped countries; hence if bank credit is prevented from expanding, " inflationary finance will not be generated, investments will not be undertaken and growth which would have been otherwise possible will not take place ". If growth rate is low because of deficiency of savings, it causes underemployment and unemployment. Hence it may be expedient to raise S towards the level of Sr by a budget surplus or compulsory levy. However, Harrod underlines the need for social and institutional changes to bring about growth in underdeveloped countries. Savings may not be the limiting factor to growth. Shortages of technically skilled personnel and institutional and social obstacles may account for low growth rate rather than any deficiency of S compared with Sr. For these reasons, the required rate of savings will be low in economically backward countries and the actual level of savings may not fall short of it.

Much emphasis is laid on social and institutional factors in recent writings on economic development. On the basis of a study of the ideas of classical writers about economic growth, Irma Adelman concludes that the difference between developed and underdeveloped countries has to be explained in terms of the initial endowment of natural resources and favourable social and institutional changes over time.[48] Thus in China and India in spite

[48]Adelman, Irma, *Theories of Economic Growth and Development*, Stanford, California, 1961, p. 40.

of the advantage in the form of natural resources, growth did not take place because of defective laws and unhelpful institutional and social factors. According to William Fellner, once certain initial conditions of growth have been satisfied, a rise in the rate of investment and income depends on: (a) the continued ability of the economic system to bring forth a sufficient flow of technological and organizational improvements by which all or much of the tendency towards diminishing returns from investment can be offset; (b) sufficient mobility of resources; (c) the proper flexibility of the money and credit mechanism and its adjustability to the requirements of a reasonably stable price level.[49] He lays much stress on the spread of a materialist market economy outlook among the people. Growth in the industrial economies is to a large extent helped by the existence of certain strategic social groups consisting of people who are willing to finance risky ventures, to make risky business decisions for others, scientific and technological experts and a large group of disciplined workers. Undoubtedly, the emergence of such social groups is as much helping as helped by economic development. But in low income countries where these are lacking, a social and political climate necessary for their emergence has to be created. Baumol holds a similar view. Among the institutions in advanced economies which have helped growth one of the most important is the joint stock form of business organization which has facilitated the emergence of big business firms. A corporate form of business is in a better position to undertake risks and bear risks than small establishments under individual entrepreneurship. The joint stock company is compelled to improve its efficiency because of competition and to forge ahead in order to maintain itself. The stock holder ownership, is conducive to growth because a stock holder gains only when his company pulls ahead at a rate faster than others.[50]

Institutional and social factors however, cannot be incorporated in a neat mathematical model. But they are vitally important to economic progress and no explanation of the process of economic expansion can be adequate unless a detailed analysis is made of the non-economic forces operating in the economy. The only attempt to incorporate these factors in a theory of growth and to explain economic advancement in terms of the social and institutional set up and the attitude of the people is that made by Prof. W. W. Rostow.

Rostow links up social and institutional factors with the economic forces of growth through certain observable propensities of the community. These propensities are: (a) propensity to develop fundamental science; (b) propensity to apply science to economic ends; (c) propensity to accept innovations; (d) propensity to seek material advance; (e) propensity to consume and (f) propensity to have children. These propensities are based on the attitudes, motives and aspirations of the people which in turn are dependent on the previous political, economic and social factors. The prime movers in a process

[49]Fellner, W., *Trends and Cycles in Economic Activity*, Henry Holt, New York, 1956, p. 118.
[50]Baumol, William J., *Business Behaviour, Value and Growth*, Macmillan, New York, 1959, p. 145.

of economic growth are the total working force and the size and productivity of the capital available in the economy. The size of the working force and its ability to contribute to output are determined by birth rate and prior and current death rate which give the rate of growth of population and therefore the rate of growth of the working population, and also by the role of women and children i.e. whether women accept employment in factories and fields and whether children are employed or not. The skill of the working force and the degree of effort put forward by the working force depend on its quality and standard of efficiency. The size and productivity of capital depend on (a) the proportion of income saved and invested which of course is determined by the propensity to consume and (b) the technological level attained by the economy. The latter is determined by the volume of resources devoted to the pursuit of fundamental science, as well as applied science and also the proportion of the flow and pool of potential innovations accepted for commercial and economic purposes. The use of these propensities to explain the quantity and quality of labour and capital available in an economy " involves a frank abandonment of the effort to make economic behaviour solely a function of what are conventionally regarded as economic motives. The propensities exhibit the extent to which the actual economic activities of a society deviate from those which would obtain if ' economic ' motives alone were operative ".[51]

The actual process of growth of the economy is explained in terms of the development of particular sectors. Since natural resources are relatively fixed, diminishing returns may set in in particular sectors. The price of the commodities produced in such sectors would rise relative to that of others. This necessitates the application of science and technology and stimulates the search for innovations in order to counteract the tendency to diminishing returns. In the earlier stages of economic development such obstacles fixed by natural limitations led to the search for more fertile lands, mines, sheep grazing land and so forth. In more recent times the application of science and technology to attain this end has taken the form of scientific and technological research, for example research in timber substitutes when timber prices go very high or research in synthetic textiles because of high prices of natural textile fibres and so on. Engineering efforts to harness natural resources in productive employment, labour saving and efficiency increasing inventions, innovations in transportation, all belong to this category. The important point to notice in this connection is that such possibilities of offsetting the tendency to diminishing returns and increasing output through alternative and more productive methods of employing resources spring from the motives and attitudes of the people, particularly their propensity to make use of science and technical knowledge for this purpose. If these motives are lacking, it is obvious that

[51]Rostow, W. W., *The Process of Economic Growth*, Second Edition, Oxford, London, 1960, p. 35.

such innovations are not possible and the economy would have to stagnate.

Analysis of growth taking place in particular sectors and then spreading to the other sectors and thus to the whole economy is carried further by classifying the sectors into three broad categories—Primary growth sectors, Supplementary growth sectors and Derived growth sectors. In the primary growth sectors, the " possibilities for innovation or for the exploitation of newly profitable or hitherto unexplored resources yield a growth rate.markedly higher than the average for the economy ". Thus development of the Cotton textile industry which constituted the leading sector in Britain's industrial development in the late 18th century and early 19th century helped development of the engineering and chemical industries. In the supplementary growth sectors " rapid advance occurs in direct response to— or as a requirement of—advance in the primary growth sectors ". Derived growth sectors are those " where advance occurs in some fairly steady relation to the growth of total real income, population, industrial production, or some other overall modestly increasing parameter ".[52] The increase in food output and provision of housing and other amenities when population and income go up belong to this category.

When the expansion of a particular sector has such a detonating effect and takes up the other sectors along with it in its course of expansion, the structure of the economy gets transformed. This transformation is significant in so far as it lifts the economy from a state of stagnation into one of self-sustaining growth. Rostow introduced the now well-known concept of ' take off ' to indicate this crucial stage in the economic evolution of a community. The ' take off ' is defined " as the interval during which the rate of investment increases in such a way that real output per capita rises and this initial increase carries with it radical changes in production techniques and the disposition of income flows which perpetuate the new scale of investment and perpetuate thereby the rising trend in per capita output ".[53] The take off stage according to Rostow is indicated by: (a) a rise in the rate of productive investment from about 5 per cent or less to over 10 per cent of national income or net national product; (b) the development of one or more substantial manufacturing sectors with a high rate of growth; (c) the existence or quick emergence of a political, social and institutional frame work which exploits the impulses to expansion in the modern sector and the potential external economy effects of the take off, and gives to growth an ongoing character.[54] An allied factor which helps the transformation is the increased supply of loanable funds. This results from shifts in the control over income flows including transfer of capital from landlords and others to the state or to the investing business classes through capital markets, redistribution through inflation, increased

[52]Rostow, W. W., *The Process of Economic Growth*, Second Edition, Oxford, London, 1960, p. 265.
[53]*ibid.*, p. 274   [54]*ibid.*. p. 284.

inflow of foreign capital, large export earnings, in short a shift of income flows into more productive hands. Besides this transfer of incomes, another agency that facilitates the take off is an adequate supply of entrepreneurship—the emergence of a social group which is actuated by the profit making and acquisitive motive.

The pre-take off period in an economy is marked by a low rate of investment and a rate of growth of income that is just sufficient to meet the needs of population growth. Since per capita income tends to remain low and constant, it is impossible for the economy to raise its standard. Any marginal increase in investment involves considerable strain. But if conditions favourable to the take off occur, and the opportunities are made use of properly, income would go up, rate of savings and investment would rise so that further increases in income and investment would be easier and automatic. Growth then becomes self-sustained. Rostow gives historical illustrations of the occurrence of take off in several countries. In Great Britain, France, Belgium and the U.S.A. the take off occurred in the period covering the last quarter of the 18th century and the first half of the 19th century. In Germany, Sweden and Japan it took place in the latter part of the 19th century; in Russia and Canada in the 20 or 25 years preceding the outbreak of the First World War; while India and China seem to have entered the period of the take off about the middle of the present century. The initial momentum for development came from different sectors of the economy in the different countries. In Britain cotton textiles played the leading role. The introduction of the railroad initiated take offs in the United States, Germany and Russia. The enlargement and modernization of the armed forces was an important factor in the Russian, Japanese and German take offs. The timber industry, followed shortly by the pulp industry, set in motion the process of industrial development in Sweden; while in Denmark meat and dairy products and in Japan the silk thread industry which provided a major source of foreign exchange facilitated economic transformation. The domestic manufacture of consumption goods replacing imports helped in accelerating development in Australia and the Argentine.

The take off covers a period of about two or three decades. The economic sequence of a country before the take off occurs is divided into two stages by Rostow—first the traditional society, covering the whole pre-Newtonian era and characterized by limited production functions and a hierarchical social structure with little scope for vertical mobility, and second, the transitional society in which the initial preconditions for the take off are created. The major changes in this stage are evolution of modern science, and the modern scientific attitude, development of technology, widening of the market and expansion of trade, the building up of social overhead capital particularly transport, and increased productivity in agriculture. These conditions are necessary to bring about take off in the next or third stage. The take off period is succeeded by two stages—the drive to maturity and the age of high mass consumption. The former relates primarily to technological maturity. The leading sectors of the take off are supplanted by new leading sectors; significant social changes are brought about; the proportion of people engaged in agricultural operations decreases; the number of white collar workers increases relatively; society gets a bit bored with industrialization and high incomes and starts searching for other objectives—increased welfare, social security or leisure. The economy seeks to provide enlarged private consumption and turns out durable consumer goods and services on a mass basis. Western Europe and the United States according to Rostow should have reached this stage even about the beginning of the present century.

Rostow's analysis of the factors of economic growth thus represents a deviation from the neo-classical models. Although the importance of institutional and social factors in economic growth has been recognized by nearly all writers who showed interest in the subject of economic development, yet it was Rostow who made an attempt to incorporate these factors as basic elements in the theory of growth. As has been observed already, the models of Mrs. Robinson, Kaldor and Meade mark an improvement over the Harrod-Domar models in so far as they have taken into account the supply side of capital and labour resources and the role of technology and population growth in economic development. But they have the limitations of abstract theoretical structures based on simple assumptions which seriously detract from their applicability to the real world. Economic development is a complex phenomena and it is not possible to grasp the true nature of the problem of growth unless attention is devoted to an understanding of the significance of the non-economic factors. The growth models concentrate on the factors that help capital accumulation and its influence on the rate of growth of income, but capital accumulation is more an effect, almost a symptom of economic growth than its primary cause. As Domar observes: " The use of growth models as a practical guide to economic development is enticing but the pitfalls are deep indeed. The rate of growth of output is expressed in our models essentially as a function of the propensity to save and the capital coefficient (in one form or another). Given only slightly optimistic, but plausible magnitudes of these two parameters, economic development seems assured—on paper of course. Both are most heroic abstractions implying a long list of assumptions about the actual working of the economy which these parameters, in their simple innocence, conceal."[55] The same point is underlined by Harrod. He writes: " The theory of economic growth would have a wider ambit including dynamic theory in the narrow sense. It would comprise also such matters as the sociological effects of the impact of economic progress, the contribution of the social pattern to it, the contribution of education both general and technological, the need for political security, the usefulness of greater or less Governmental intervention in successive phases, the development of moral codes etc."[56] In fact, a theory of economic growth which should explain the

[55]Domar, Evsey, *Essays in the Theory of Economic Growth*, Oxford. New York, 1957, p. 13.

[56]Harrod, R. F., ' Second Essay in Dynamic Theory,' *Economic Journal*. June, 1960, p. 277.

causes of economic expansion and provide an answer to the basic question
why development takes place in one country but not in another, and why the
rate of growth differs from one country to another and from one period to
another in the same country and lay down general postulates regarding the
conditions of steady growth requires a mass of empirical work and the collection
and synthesis of data and ideas from all social sciences.

WHAT REALLY BRINGS ABOUT ECONOMIC GROWTH

From the foregoing brief review of the theories of economic growth and
development it would be clear that the following factors are the basic determinants of economic progress: (a) Natural resources or the original endowment
of an economy including not only land but also mineral, water, forest and
other resources; climate of the country, its geographical position and features,
natural harbours etc.; (b) the quantity and quality of its population, the
size of the working population, the health and intelligence of the people,
their sense of discipline and spirit of co-operation, willingness to work, diligence,
character etc.; (c) entrepreneurial skill; (d) social and institutional factors
that are conducive to economic effort; (e) a stable and helpful government,
an efficient system of administration, and high sense of responsibility of the
administrative personnel; (f) favourable external circumstances involving
attitude of neighbouring countries, prospects of foreign trade, the stimuli of
external contacts, inflow of foreign capital etc.

This however, does not mean that economic development is not possible
in a country which does not have all these features in full measure. There are
some regions of the world like the Sahara or Greenland where climate or the
absence of natural resources which can be exploited with the technological
and scientific knowledge now available, rules out the possibility of any economic
development. But meagreness of natural resources has not prevented Switzerland from developing into one of the high income countries of the world.
It is however, fair to add that limitation of resources does place a handicap
in the efforts of a country towards the attainment of the highest standards of
economic efficiency. Certainly, given the other factors, the availability of
abundant natural facilities makes it easier for a country to go further ahead
in the economic race than one which is relatively deficient in natural endowments. Thus Japanese economic advancement would have been much greater
if natural endowment were more favourable. Undoubtedly, a fair share of
natural resources is essential for economic prosperity and well being.

A healthy, intelligent and hard working population is an obvious asset.
Where the people in general are hard working, thrifty and enterprising, entrepreneurial skill will not be lacking. Similarly, political conditions, the stability
of the government, the legal system and administrative efficiency, affect the
economic prospects of a community. The loss of political freedom and foreign
domination has ruined the economy of many a country. South India which

was once economically advanced with many industries and a flourishing external trade lost both its political freedom and its economic prosperity in the course of the 13th and 14th centuries. Social institutions, customs and tradition may foster or hamper economic growth. But social institutions reflect the character and attitudes of the people; and they are not unchangeable. In fact outmoded social institutions which may be a serious obstacle to economic growth in the initial stages of development get altered in the course of, and because of material progress and become helpful to productive efforts of the people when once economic growth gets under way. Lastly, the economic history of many countries illustrates to what extent geographical position and external factors have helped trade and commerce and industrial development. The prosperity of the Mediterranean cities and of some regions in Western Asia in the middle ages was primarily due to their geographical location— either because they had good harbours and had easy access to foreign markets or because they were on the big land routes of trade. The discovery of sea route to India spelt the ruin of many of the trading centres in Western Asia.

In the ultimate analysis, the three fundamental factors of progress are labour, capital and technology. Of these the first is the active agent and provides the motive force. Capital is man-made and technological attainments are due to human intelligence and ingenuity. The availability of an abundant supply of capital resources and a high standard of technological development characterize all economically advanced countries. Capital and technological knowledge are applied in a much greater measure not only in the industrial sector but in agriculture as well, in the high income countries as compared with the underdeveloped countries. Since capital accumulation and the achievements in technology which are of basic importance in increasing productivity and income are dependent on the human factor, the origin of economic growth has to be traced to this source—the motives, the natural talents and aptitudes of the people. Capital formation depends on increased production and savings. Thus capacity for hard work, diligence, frugality, thought for the morrow and the keen desire to improve materially, account for increased savings and the accumulation of capital. Enterprise, ambition and the competitive spirit help in converting the savings into productive investment. A scientific bent of mind and the propensity to apply science to material ends help development of technology. Application of the mental powers to invention and science and the keenness to make use of scientific knowledge to improve methods of production, so that material needs can be better satisfied with lesser effort, spring from a particular frame of mind. The mental qualities or the texture of the mind of a shrewd money making businessman or a talented technician are different from that of a poet or artist. Reason dominates the first, emotion and imagination dominate the latter. But there is no denying the fact that the first is important in economic life and welfare. Men of learning and intelligence were not lacking in India in the 18th century. But their mental powers had a slant towards religion, philosophy, ethics, art and poetry.

Their proficiency in mathematical calculations and knowledge of astronomy were used in the construction of temples and palaces and in fixing the date and time of religious rites and festivals rather than in devising means for improving the yield of agriculture or in inventing gadgets to increase the production of industrial goods for consumption. On the other hand, in the 18th century in Western Europe the remarkable progress in industry and agriculture was precisely due to the application of science to material ends. Human intelligence and enterprise are behind all economic progress. But given a stock of human intelligence and enterprise in a community, there will not be economic progress if these are directed to non-economic purposes.

Assuming then a community of people who are capable of and prepared to do hard work and who have the urge to improve materially and the index of whose expansion effort[57] is fairly high, economic growth takes place if the other set of factors that influence progress are on the whole favourable. If these circumstances are adverse—such as unstable and weak government, lack of natural resources, and adverse external circumstances—then human spirit by itself can achieve little. In such a set up, the urge and motive for economic betterment is lost, and the community becomes passive with regard to material advancement. The social and institutional pattern itself will be modified and adjusted to a condition of stagnation and would in course of time become an obstacle to healthy economic effort. The community's attitude to work changes adversely, ambition is curbed, and poverty and lack of urge for economic improvement would work cumulatively to keep the country economically stunted. It is however, not necessary that all the factors indicated above should be sufficient enough to induce growth. Particular advantage may lie in one or two directions and this may offset the deficiency in others. Thus natural resources may be lacking, but this may be counterbalanced by the existence of a helpful government or favourable external circumstances or the deficiency in the latter may be offset by advantageous geographical conditions and resource position. That country succeeds in coming up to a high level in the economic struggle which is favourably placed with regard to the entire set of circumstances. There is in this respect a close similarity between the material progress of individuals and of nations. Character, integrity, health, intelligence, learning, capacity for work, ambition and the will to improve, ability to get on well with others, inherited wealth, all these help advancement of an individual in economic and social life. Individuals possessing all these qualities and facilities in an abundant measure are very rare. On the other hand, those who lack all these requisites cannot succeed in life. Successful men are those who have a right combination of these qualities. Thus character and intelligence may offset the deficiency in inherited wealth and a man endowed in this manner rises up in spite of certain adverse factors. In the same manner in nations also, it is a right combination of the requisites

[57]Baumol, William J., *Business Behaviour, Value and Growth*, Macmillan, New York, 1959, p. 145.

for economic growth that helps development. In short, economic growth takes place when there is a convergence of several strategic factors in the right proportions and with a propitious timing.[58]

[58]Clough, Shepard B., 'Strategic Factors in Economic Growth,' *Political Science Quarterly*, Columbia University, New York, March, 1955, p. 21.

Chapter III

SOCIAL AND INSTITUTIONAL FACTORS

THE PRIMARY importance of human effort in any productive enterprise is obvious. Natural resources are free gifts while capital resources are man-made. The manner in which the latter two factors are combined in any scheme of production and the extent to which output is increased by such a combination depends upon human ingenuity, skill, diligence, effort and enterprise. In economic activity, human effort takes two forms—physical labour and the enterprise of the organizer. If these two forms of effort are of a high order, economic growth is possible. It is therefore not surprising to find that in any country which is economically advanced, the labour force is efficient, hard working, well disciplined and well organized, while the entrepreneurial class possesses the necessary drive, energy and initiative to launch forth new ventures and new schemes of production.

THE HUMAN FACTOR IN ECONOMIC DEVELOPMENT

Intensive study of the problems of underdeveloped countries and analysis of the causes which make for disparity in the standards of economic development of different countries have brought into greater prominence the significance of the human factor. In the opinion of Kaldor: " A study of the dynamics of economic growth leads beyond the analysis of economic factors to a study of psychological and sociological determinants of these factors. It was the emergence of the outlook typical of the capitalist entrepreneur which gave rise to modern capitalism rather than the other way round; and in countries where capitalist development lags, the explanation is to be sought in the persistence of attitudes incompatible with such development notably in the traditional attitude of the peasantry."[1]

Since human effort, the attitudes and aspirations of the people and their will to work are such important factors in determining economic growth, it follows that any outlay on building up the physical and mental efficiency of labour which would help in changing favourably human attitudes, should be an eminently worthwhile investment from the development point of view. It has been shown that in Puerto Rico in the decade 1930–1940 large-scale social investment resulted in a significant speeding up of the process of economic development. While previously labour was unattractive from the point of view

[1]Kaldor, N., *An Expenditure Tax*, George Allen and Unwin, London, 1955, p. 180 f.n.

72

of the employer because of its inefficiency, the improvement in the quality of labour, which resulted from the large social investments created an increase in the demand for labour.[2] It has also been increasingly realized in recent years, that the mere transfer of capital equipment from advanced countries to the non-industrial countries does not ensure growth, so long as the complementary resources in the form of technical and organizational skill, and an efficient labour supply are not forthcoming. Greater attention is therefore devoted to the building up of human capital. Thus the recent United Nations Technical Assistance Administration Missions to underdeveloped countries include not only economists, engineers and technicians to assist in drafting plans for the allocation of resources and in building up the physical assets, but also specialists in education, social welfare and cultural anthropology whose attention will be directed towards minimizing the evils of social friction that will arise in the wake of economic transformation, besides devising measures to mould and shape the social factors that would help economic advancement. Also, much current thinking on the subject of economic growth is devoted to the analysis of the institutional factors that hamper or facilitate material progress. In his Presidential address at the Annual meeting of the American Economic Association in 1960, Prof. T. W. Schultz, emphasized the role of investments in human capital in increasing productivity, and pointed out that this was one of the major factors responsible for the remarkable increase in productivity in the U.S.A. The fact that with the growth of national income the capital-output ratio in the U.S.A. has tended to decline or at best to remain constant, should be explained primarily in terms of investments in human capital formation which are not included in the statistical computation of annual investment outlays. He also cited the example of the economic recovery of some of the war devastated countries in Europe which was out of proportion to the investments in non-human capital. Investments in human capital formation take the forms of health facilities and services, on the job training, formally organized education at the elementary, secondary, and higher levels, study programmes for adults and means to promote the mobility of labour.[3]

SOCIAL CHARACTERISTICS OF DEVELOPED AND UNDERDEVELOPED ECONOMIES

Sociologists make a distinction between certain characteristics of the social attitudes and behaviour of people in advanced countries which are conducive to material advancement, and those of the people in less developed countries which explain their economic backwardness. Thus according to Talcott Parsons, the principle of ' achievement ' predominates in the distribution of economic goods in developed countries, while that of ' ascription ' predominates

[2]Nurkse, R., *Patterns of Trade and Development*, Stockholm, 1959, p. 38.
[3]Schultz, Theodore W., ' Investment in Human Capital,' *American Economic Review*, March, 1961, pp. 1–16.

in backward countries i.e. while in advanced countries the assignment of
economic objects to individuals is based on their achievements or their performance, in the backward countries it is done with reference to the individual's
social status, kinship relations, etc. Secondly, in the distribution of economic-
cally relevant tasks among members of society, different principles are adopted
which are designated as universalism and particularism. This means that in
materially advanced countries, assignment of tasks is done in an objective
manner with reference exclusively to the individual's qualities and ability,
while in the poorer countries, the principle is particularistic, in the sense that
consideration is given mostly to the individual's family connections, social
status, etc. Thirdly, in the less developed countries, the performance of economically relevant tasks is diffuse or general, based on no objectively accepted
principle while in contrast, in the high income industrial countries there is
greater specificity.[4] This is reflected in the low levels of production and limited
division of labour in underdeveloped countries. Lastly, in the less advanced
societies, there predominates an attitude of self-orientation or ego centredness,
while this is less prominent in advanced societies. In reality, these four traits
of social character and behaviour are inter-dependent. Thus principles of
ascription, particularism and diffuseness tend to co-exist in so far as in all
these there is a common factor, namely, the entry of a personal, family or
class motive in economic decisions. On the other hand, the co-existence of
achievement, universalism and specificity would only indicate that the society
is better evolved so that it can take up an objective attitude or apply a common
norm in the determination of economic issues.[5] In short, the personal or clan-
note predominates in the economic issues of underdeveloped countries, while
in economically advanced countries, the general or social note predominates.
In a sense this analysis is only an elaboration of what Henry Maine said a
long time ago about the social transformation of a backward society into an
advanced one, namely, the evolution from status to contract.

These traits of character of societies belonging to different levels of economic
development are mostly inherent and reflect broadly the difference in race,
religion, climate and political conditions. The relationship between character
and attitudes on the one hand, and social institutions on the other, are so
close that it is difficult or impossible to isolate the one from the other, or
point out the extent to which the character and values of a society influence
the texture of their social institutions. Nor is it possible to attribute to social
institutions alone the particular behaviour pattern of members in society. It
is however plausible to assume that given some basic traits of character which
may be due to racial qualities or conditions of living, the goals and values
in life which spring from that character background tend to get institutiona-

---

[4]Parsons, T. and E. A. Shils (Eds.), *Toward a General Theory of Action*, Harvard University
Press, Cambridge, Mass., 1951, pp. 81–84.

[5]Hoselitz, Bert F., *Sociological Aspects of Economic Growth*, Free Press, Glencoe, Illinois, 1960,
pp. 31–45.

lized which lead to the evolution of particular patterns of social relationship and ways of doing things. These social institutions, like forms of religion, social classification, law, custom, etc. thus represent a crystallization of human attitudes and values. But when such a development takes place, the institutions themselves would affect the social behaviour of the people. Thus attitude and behaviour on the one hand, and institutions on the other, act and react upon one another with the result that the institutional structure becomes more and more rigid. When institutions get thus fossilized, it would appear that the society becomes a slave to custom and tradition; and if such institutions are inimical to any improvement in material well being, it would not be possible for society to make any economic progress unless by some means of social revolution this institutional straitjacket is thrown out. For, in such a situation the economic actor's behaviour is oriented to the institutional system in which he acts and aspires. His behaviour and action will have meaning only if looked at from the angle of the institutional fabric which binds him.[6]

The manner in which institutions interpreted in a broad manner (i.e. organizations and policies, both governmental and private) would affect economic activity can be easily illustrated. The tax and commercial policies of the state directly affect the calculations of costs and profits in business. Distribution of economic goods is affected by the system of land tenures, while social institutions like the caste system or joint family system in India affect division of labour, the incentive for effort and industrialization. Lack of proper educational facilities and means to communicate knowledge has a bearing on economic activity in so far as it restricts the supply of skilled and efficient labour and entrepreneurship; and religious beliefs and social customs directly influence a man's attitude towards material welfare and may foster or hinder a spirit of aggressiveness in economic activities.[7] Apart from this, there are ample historical illustrations to show the impact of social institutions on economic development. Thus in France, the slow growth of the economy as compared with the neighbouring countries has been attributed to social rigidities which hampered the free flow of men and resources into productive enterprises, the social prestige attached to professions and services as against business, and to the tradition-bound modes of living which restricted labour mobility. Inherited consumption patterns emphasize leisure and personal service, while in agriculture, resistance to new techniques and large-scale operations explain the low productivity of the primary sector.[8] Hoseltiz

[6]Sawyer, John E., 'Social Structure and Economic Progress: General Propositions and some French Examples,' *American Economic Review*, Proceedings Number, May, 1951, pp. 322–23.

[7]Wolf, Charles, 'Institutions and Economic Development,' *American Economic Review*, December, 1955, pp. 868–81.

[8]Sawyer, John E., 'Social Structure and Economic Progress: General Proposition and some French Examples,' *American Economic Review*, Proceedings Number, May, 1951, pp. 325–29.

explains the disparity in economic advance between Anglo-Saxon and Spanish America by the difference in the social values of the people who colonized Anglo-Saxon America as against the Latin American traditions and values of life which were implanted in Spanish America. The tenacious clinging to the social and cultural system introduced by Spain some four hundred years ago, has been a deterrent to rapid economic progress in most of the Latin American countries, while a progressive spirit and outlook on life characterizes the former.[9] In a recent study of the growth of capitalism in two East Asian Countries—China and Japan—Prof. Norman Jacobs contrasts the social institutions of the two countries and attributes the vast difference in economic development of these two countries to the fact that while the social set up in Japan has been helpful to material advancement, in China institutional factors have obstructed economic progress. The dominating position of the ruler in China and his right of interference in private property and economic activity, the low estimation in which business was placed, social stratification and immobility, the system of dividing property equally among all sons, and the dogmatic orthodoxy of religion, all these hampered economic development in China. In Japan, the sharply contrasting social institutions like an independent peasantry, freedom in external and internal trade activities, the social respect attached to commerce and industry, constant shifting in the status hierarchy, the law of primogeniture, the individualistic attitude to religion and the appreciation of labour as man power, were all factors conducive to economic growth along Western lines.[10] It is therefore possible to conceive of a type of socio-economic low level equilibrium in most of the present day underdeveloped countries where the economies have got stagnated owing to traditional patterns of life and modes of behaviour which are unfavourable to economic progress. The absence of any explosive forces of economic progress and the tendency of the economy to move on traditional lines reinforce the existing institutional pattern making it less amenable to change.

Marx emphasized the inter-relationship between institutional factors and economic change. His thesis was that economic change would take the lead and bring about an institutional modification that would fit in with the new economic set up. In underdeveloped countries such as India, the institutional frame work has become rigid and inelastic as a result of age-long tradition, custom and superstition. Religious factors have also contributed to the inflexibility of the social institutions. This institutional frame work has undoubtedly, hampered economic expansion. Consequently, if the necessary social change is to be brought about by economic change, the latter should be sharp and spectacular enough. It is not possible to visualize an economic transformation of that order. Hence the sensible policy would be to direct attention on the removal of these social obstacles and at the same time, take steps towards

[9]Hoselitz, Bert F., ' Social Implications of Economic Growth,' *The Economic Weekly*, Annual Number, Bombay, January, 1959, pp. 185–87.

[10]Jacobs, Norman, *The Origin of Modern Capitalism and Eastern Asia*, Oxford, London, 1958.

building up the economy which would help in bringing about social changes as well.

From this brief outline of the close relationship between social institutions and economic development, it becomes clear that a satisfactory explanation of the process of economic growth would be possible only if due consideration is given to non-economic factors also. Although the classical economists were aware of the significance of social institutions and attitudes of the people, they did not give these factors the prominence which they deserve. Everett Hagen points out that the classical economists treated sociological factors as parameters, but progress in growth theory is possible only if these are treated as variables.[11] What Rostow has attempted in this direction has already been indicated in the previous chapter. But further light on the problem of growth can be thrown only if a deeper analysis is made of the human response to material opportunities and an explanation is given as to why in certain countries and under certain conditions this response is favourable while in others it is altogether absent. Obviously, the response to the stimuli in the form of economic opportunities depends on the psychological attitude of the people, the extent to which they are alive to the situation and the keenness of their desire to make use of the opportunities. In an enquiry of this nature the province of the economist borders on that of the psychologist, the sociologist and the anthropologist. This underlines the need for a co-operative effort on the part of scholars trained in these various disciplines to clarify and understand the different facets of the problem of economic growth. Much progress has been made in this direction by writers like Yale Brozen, Joseph Spengler, W. W., Rostow, Alexander Gershenkron, Marion Levy and Sol Tax. Also sociologists and anthropologists like Godfrey, Monica Wilson and Daniel Lerner have by their investigations widened our knowledge relating to the economic aspects of certain social factors. Such enquiries by economists and sociologists would help in clarifying some basic socio-economic issues, like the emergence of creative individuals in the field of business, the factors affecting the different value systems of different communities, the appearance of creative ability in clusters in particular groups, and the bursts of creative and restless energy at certain times, etc.

While the formulation of an acceptable theory of economic growth has to await further investigation in the field of sociology, it is possible to make some observations about the manner in which social factors affect economic activity. These may be brought under the following heads: (a) Productivity of labour and general attitude to economic effort; (b) Savings and capital formation, (c) Entrepreneurship and (d) Technology.

---

[11]Hagen, Everett, 'Turning Parameters into Variables in the Theory of Economic Growth,' *American Economic Review*. Proceedings Number, May, 1960, p. 623.

LABOUR PRODUCTIVITY AND GENERAL ATTITUDE TO WORK

The low productivity of labour in underdeveloped countries is to a large extent due to adverse social and institutional factors. Also institutions like religion, caste and joint family system and political circumstances have affected the general attitude of the people to hard work and sustained economic effort.

(i) Labour Productivity

The contribution of labour to national output depends on the size of the labour force and its quality, its organization and also the extent to which it is assisted by capital equipment. Social customs like early marriage affect population growth rate and thus influence the size of the labour force. Where there is no social legislation to prevent the employment of children in factories or in the fields, both the quantity and quality of labour are affected. The employment of children directly increases the number of workers at a cheap wage rate. Forces of competition bring down the average wage level. Apart from this, a serious social harm is done in so far as the children who are drawn into employment at a tender age are deprived of the opportunity for better equipping themselves by education, and training. This combined with adverse effects on health, prevents them from earning as much as they otherwise could when they grow up. On the other hand, social customs which prevent womenfolk of the middle and upper income classes from engaging themselves in occupations outside their homes reduce the quantity of labour available in an economy.

From the point of view of its contribution to economic growth, the quality of labour is as important as its size. Labour in most of the underdeveloped countries is characterized by its lack of enterprise and inefficiency. Enterprise will not be forthcoming unless there is a strong urge on the part of the workers to improve their material well-being and unless such an urge is reinforced by the willingness to do hard work. Their attitude to life should be active and not passive. It is a well-known fact that workers in low income countries are not willing to make use of opportunities for earning more even if they are aware of the opportunities. This attitude springs from an inherent inertia and unwillingness to exert oneself. It is true that markets in underdeveloped countries are limited in size because of the low income of the people and the consequent lack of variety in consumption. But the fact is that even this limited demand is not taken advantage of by the producers. It is mentioned that the demand for bush knives, hoes and other iron implements in some of the backward regions of the upper Volta River in Africa is much greater than the local supply, yet the local producers do not take up this as a whole time job, and do not concentrate on the production of these goods.[12]

[12]Herskovits, Melwille J., ‘The Problem of Adapting Societies to New Tastes,’ *The Progress of Underdeveloped Areas*, Ed. by Bert F. Hoselitz, Chicago, 1952, p. 94.

Disguised unemployment and underemployment are common features in most of the underdeveloped economies. This is obviously due to the super-abundance of labour in relation to the complementary factors of production. Marginal productivity of labour therefore tends to be zero. In the industrially advanced Western countries the problem of relative scarcity of labour and excess of capital resources has directed attention to the need for examining why capital tends to remain idle and what conditions would be needed to keep it fully employed. If in an underdeveloped country like India the problem is one of excess labour, can it be said that a really earnest effort is made to understand the true nature of the problem and find out ways by which labour can be made to yield, even under the existing factor supply situation, as much as it could? The fact that marginal productivity of labour is zero does not mean that increased effort of existing labour will not yield any marginal product. On the other hand, it will increase the output per head. This underlines the need for greater effort on the part of labour.[13] In an address to the Indian legislature at Delhi a few years ago, Prof. Gunnar Myrdal drew pointed attention to the need for harder and more sustained and efficient work on the part of ordinary labour. More labourers are engaged in doing a given piece of work in India than in an advanced economy. Labour is cheap in the sense that more labourers can be obtained at a low wage rate but it is not cheap when the wage rate is compared with the contribution of the average worker. If Sweden, a small industrial country with 2 per cent of India's population, produces a national income of 50 per cent more than that of India, and if the average Swedish worker earns twenty to twenty-five times as much as the Indian labourer earns, the explanation should be found to some extent in the availability of greater per capita capital equipment in the former country, but to a large extent in the fact that the average worker in Sweden works for longer hours with greater diligence and more efficiency than the average Indian labourer. Lack of work in a poor country like India is an excuse for laziness. Precisely because a country is underdeveloped, much work awaits to be done—industrial plants to be constructed and equipped, lands to be made to yield more than they do, houses to be built and repaired, latrines, drains and sanitary wells to be dug, trees to be planted, books to be printed and books to be read, floors and streets to be swept and cleaned, children to be washed and educated, sick and old people to be cared for, etc., etc. All this work adds to the nation's income and raises the level of savings and investments on the basis of which more intensive work can then be done. The result is economic development.

To some extent labour inefficiency in underdeveloped countries is due to the low standard of health and literacy. Employment in modern industrial establishments requires not only a certain degree of skill on the part of workers but also a certain standard of education. Without literacy the employees

[13]Smithies, Arthur, ' Rising Expectations and Economic Development', *Economic Journal*, June, 1961, p. 258.

would find it difficult to adjust themselves to factory work and to assimilate urban ways of life. Physical fitness is also important. Poor health directly affects the efficiency of workers and results in high rates of absenteeism. Diseases and illnesses are obviously detrimental to all kinds of productive activity, but their adverse effect is felt particularly in industrial employment which requires continuous and co-operative effort from labour. Climate also is undoubtedly a contributory factor to the efficiency or inefficiency of labour. It is no accident that practically all the economically advanced nations of today are found in the temperate regions of the world where climate is not only favourable to sustained physical and mental effort, but also compels people in a way, to be physically active. On the other hand, a good number of the underdeveloped countries are in the tropical regions where nine months of the year are hot, and three months hotter. Health and vitality of the people are sapped, and they fall an easy prey to the many tropical diseases. Moreover, the physical requirements of the people living in the tropics, in the form of food and clothing and shelter are much less than what are necessary in the temperate and cold regions, and the impulse to greater effort is for that matter less. Modernization of factory construction and air conditioning of offices may to some extent obviate the rigors of climate but the number of workers who benefit by such arrangements would be no more than an infinitesimal fraction of the total working population.[14]

The lack of an efficient industrial labour force constitutes another problem in the pre-industrial economies. The psychological attitudes and mental characteristics that make for an efficient industrial labour force are different from that required in field or agricultural labour. What is required of the former is diligent application, punctuality, discipline and capacity to work in co-operation with others. Experience has shown that manual labourers in some of the backward regions of the world, such as parts of Africa, even when they are little educated, are quick to learn simple mechanical skills and are able to acquit themselves well in operations requiring skill and deftness of hand. But their real difficulty is to adjust themselves to the routine, order and discipline necessary in industrial employment. Industrial establishments are concentrated in urban areas and the labour force in the factories are drawn mostly from the neighbouring villages. The difficulties which the workers in industries experience in adjusting themselves in the industrial set up, spring from two main factors. In the first place, the pattern of work in the towns is quite different from that to which the labourer is accustomed in the villages ; secondly, they fail to get assimilated easily in the new social environment and seldom become part of a regular source of labour supply in the industrial areas. The freedom and the leisurely ways of life and work to which the labourer is accustomed in the rural areas stand in sharp contrast to the regularity, restriction and monotony of factory labour. In the villages, periods of activity and

[14]Lee, Douglas H. K., *Climate and Economic Development in the Tropics*, Harper and Brothers, New York, 1957.

leisure are determined by seasonal factors, while in the factories the schedule of operations is fixed without any reference to the will and inclination of the labourer to work or not. In fact one of the basic problems in the industrialization of a backward economy is to train the labourer to the monotony of work and to hold the labourers on to the job continuously. The only factor which impels the worker to accept employment is the wage that he gets, but this by itself does not ensure regularity on the part of the worker. It is not surprising if wage incentives have little appeal to people who are familiar with an economic organization of a non-monetary nature, and accustomed to payments of remuneration in kind. Even when the recruit from the village attracted by the money wage, holds on for some time, he invariably leaves the town and goes back to his village when he has earned some money.

The high rate of labour turnover in the pre-industrial countries resulting from this unfavourable attitude of labour to the type of work in industries necessitates frequent fresh recruitment and training and constitutes a significant drain on the efficiency and earnings of industry. In Turkey, peasants show a reluctance to enter permanent employment off the land. Instability of the labour force has appreciably raised costs in South African factories; and in Ceylon in recent years, difficulty in obtaining local replacements for Indian immigrants in estates and in other enterprises has led to a reduction in output and in some cases the prospect of having to close down.[15] Attempts to stabilize labour force by various measures such as the establishment of factories near the village homes of the workers as in South Africa by the South African Social and Economic Planning Commission, wage incentives tried by the Firestone Plantation in Liberia, provision of hospital, schools and other facilities, imposition of taxes on labourers payable only in currency, holidays with pay contingent upon a record of steady work, wage increases for those who stay on the job, etc., have been attended with only very limited success.

In fact such incentives cannot be helpful in attracting and maintaining labour in industries so long as the social attitudes and prejudices of the workers remain unchanged. The basic problem is one of not only drawing labour into the towns but also enabling them to get assimilated in town life, and making them feel at home in the new surroundings. And this is not an easy one, in view of the low standard of literacy of the workers and their age long adherence to particular modes of life. The labour force in the industrial cities of India are drawn from the villages all over the country. Speaking different languages and belonging to various religious faiths, castes and communities, and differing in customs and manners, they find it difficult to mingle freely and fail to develop a feeling of oneness. Most of the workers are not pulled in by the cities but pushed out of the villages by a combination of adverse factors like unemployment, poverty, famine, pestilence, etc. They drift in the towns for some time, seeking employment and seldom take roots there.

[15]*Processes and Problems of Industrialization in Underdeveloped Countries*, U.N., 1955, p. 21.

6

Since invariably they leave their families in the villages, their attachment is to their rural homes. They regard their stay in the towns as only transient and make use of every opportunity to go home and visit their relatives. As such it is difficult to train these people to be a disciplined, stable and effective set of factory workers. As Hoselitz puts it, they do not constitute an industrial 'reserve army' but a demoralized, unhealthy and pitiful 'lumpen proletariat '.[16] It is therefore clear, that measures to improve the quality and efficiency of labour in industries can be successful only if they are directed to bringing about a change in their social attitudes and to weaning them away from the traditional patterns of village life. Decentralization of industries, improvement in means of communication and mass education would bring about this social transformation, but the process of change is bound to be slow.

(ii) General Attitude to Economic Effort

Apart from the harmful effect on the quality and efficiency of labour, social and institutional factors have affected the enterprise and general attitude of the people to productive effort and their desire for material improvement. Instability of political conditions is one cause of the lack of enterprise. If a society is not keenly desirous of improving its economic conditions, the attitude can be traced to a series of past failures and frustrations as for instance, the case of Red Indians in America. This applies in a large measure to the colonies of metropolitan countries. Political domination of one country by another and economic exploitation create an attitude of disinterestedness towards work and enterprise in the indigenous population. Also, when there is no stable government in a country and no assurance of safety and security of personal property, the impulse to work hard and accumulate wealth is destroyed. Within a country exploitation of the weaker social groups by the strong, and the lack of an institutional arrangement by which the worker is assured of the fruits of his labour have a demoralizing effect and if this state of affairs continues for generations, it is no wonder that productive effort of the community is seriously impaired and in course of time laziness and apathy become 'natural' social characteristics. As an extreme case may be mentioned the system of slavery which has a disastrous effect on both the masters and the slaves in respect of their productive efficiency and practically destroys all elements of social character that are conducive to economic growth.[17]

Religion can help or hinder economic growth. If a religion does not proscribe acquisitiveness or enjoin poverty as a virtue upon its believers; if it does not

[16]Hoselitz, Bert F., 'The City, the Factory and Economic Growth,' *American Economic Review*, Proceedings Number, May 1955, p. 178.

[17]Lewis, Arthur W., *Theory of Economic Growth*, George Allen and Unwin, London, 1955, pp. 107–13.

prevent people from bending their minds to increase production; if it en-courages a spirit of experimentation and promotes impersonal economic relations, it may be considered helpful to economic advancement. It is Max Weber's thesis that the Protestant ethic played a large part in the economic growth of Western countries. According to a recent writer, Protestantism helped economic growth by providing a cheap form of religion which made it possible to release labour and capital for economic development; by pro-moting sectarian groups and fostering a questioning spirit that weakened the traditional social class structure of society; by relaxing the bureaucratic controls of the state; by promoting a close group cohesion and by encouraging a rational approach to problems of life including problems of an economic character.[18] While no categorical statement can be made in this matter, it has to be admitted that the spirit of questioning traditional values and order, and the rational individualistic approach to the fundamental problems of life, which are associated with Protestantism, did create an intellectual atmosphere that was conducive to industrialization and material advancement. Any religion which fosters such a spirit or attitude should be deemed as favourable to economic progress. Although rapid capital formation in Japan was certainly not caused by Weber's Protestant ethics,[19] the fact that the religious order and principles in Japan in a large measure conform to these requirements, substantiates the fundamental notion involved in Weber's thesis. Thus while Confucianism in China strongly emphasized dogmatic orthodoxy, in Japan concern with the problems of man's personal adjustment evoked a number of different solutions. Also, while in China the inter-relationship of political authority with orthodox religion equated heterodoxy with political error, in Japan in contrast there were frequent and violent sectarian battles.[20] In other words, the principles and practice of religion in Japan from the point of view of their impact on economic activity were more or less the same as that of Protestantism in the Western countries in the 18th and 19th centuries.

But, if the basic tenets of religion discourage wordly pursuits, or give little positive inducement to thrift, hard work and the accumulation of wealth, economic advancement is likely to be halted or slowed down. It is said that in the Western countries there is no necessary conflict between wealth and piety.[21] But Confucianism in China lays great emphasis on simple living and contemplation, while Hinduism favours asceticism and other-worldliness. Obviously, the merits of a religion cannot be related to its effect on accumulation of wealth and prosperity. But the fact that certain forms and

[18]Clark, S. D., ' Religion and Economic Backwardness,' *American Economic Review*, Proceedings Number, May, 1951, pp. 261–63.

[19]Aubrey, H. G., ' The Role of the State in Economic Development,' *American Economic Review*, Proceedings Number, May, 1951, p. 271.

[20]Jacobs, Norman, *The Origin of Modern Capitalism and Eastern Asia*, Oxford, London, 1958, pp. 161–85.

[21]Belshaw, Horace, *Population Growth and Levels of Consumption*, George Allen and Unwin, London, 1956, p. 161.

principles of religion, in so far as they vitally affect the individual's attitude to life and beaviour in society, do foster or hinder economic advancement cannot be disputed. Much of the religious precepts form the basis on which social and legal institutions are organized, as for instance disapproval of usury in Islam. The doctrine of *karma* according to which a man's status and well being in the present life are determined by his deeds in the previous life, and the attitude of other-worldliness which Hinduism fosters are cited as instances to show how religion can have an unhealthy influence on economic activity. It has however to be added that while a religion may be divinely inspired, there has grown around the hard core of the faith a body of dogmas, principles, rites and ceremonies which affect the attitudes and social behaviour of the followers. These institutional frills of a religion may be a deterrent to economic growth while the religious faith as such may not be. Much of these is man made, and made quite often to suit the particular customs and traits and ways of life of the society. Thus the doctrine of *karma* may lead to a negative or defeatist attitude to life on grounds of predetermination, or may play a dynamic role in impelling people to right action on the ground that such action would determine the pattern of their future life. In the same manner, the attitude of other-worldliness may be inspired by a conscious disinterestedness in a transient life or only an escape from the realities of life. And if the latter is the case, it may be due as much to religion as to the defeatist attitude of the individuals which in turn may be caused by a traditional sense of frustration and despair.

Another social institution which has operated as a drag on economic advancement in underdeveloped countries is the family structure. The term family has a wider connotation in underdeveloped countries than in the industrial ones. It covers a large number of both close and distant relatives who become dependants of the earning members. Such extended family relationship naturally acts as a burden on the enterprising members. In fact it may be said that as the earnings of an individual increase, there is a corresponding increase in the number of dependants who look up to him for support. Thus on the production or earning side, the pattern of the economy may be based on individual initiative, but on the consumption side it is dictated by the traditions of a collective system.[22] In a recent sample survey in East Pakistan, it was found that 78 per cent of the workers have extended families with dependants other than wife and children.[23] Where a regular joint family system exists as in some parts of India, the evils of extended family relationship become more pronounced. It may be that in the joint family system in which the earnings of members are pooled together and shared according to needs, there is some sort of a social security arrangement, the family as a unit taking the responsibility for supporting the weaker members. In some instances,

[22]Heskovits, Melville, ' The Problem of Adapting Societies to New Tastes,' *The Progress of Underdeveloped Areas*, Ed. by Bert F. Hoselitz, Chicago, 1952, p. 102.

[23]*Economic Bulletin for Asia and the Far East*, U.N., December, 1959, p. 17.

the pooling of the resources by the earning members and the availability of a number of reliable and competent members connected by close ties of blood, have helped in the emergence of big businesses. But the defects of such a social organization outweigh its merits. Leadership being vested in the eldest member, tends to be conservative. Since consumption is related not to production but to needs, the incentive on the part of active members to produce more and to accumulate is seriously affected. There is little scope for individual initiative and drive. The system reduces incentives to personal saving and restricts mobility of labour. It promotes nepotism and minimizes the right to bequeath which otherwise might serve as a powerful spur to greater effort and enterprise.[24] In India as a result of industrialization and spread of education, the joint family system has already shown signs of disintegration. This is inevitable. As the opportunities for making individual economic profit increase, the ties of extended kinship are bound to weaken. In Japan, the restriction which the joint family system places on commercial or manufacturing enterprises has been eased by the common practice adopted by the families controlling large enterprises of marrying their daughters to promising employees who then take the family name.[25]

Agriculture predominates in the economic structure of most of the under-developed countries. But agricultural productivity is low because of inefficient and traditional techniques of production and also because of a faulty system of land holding. Ownership of land has a prestige value and quite often, the big landlord while being keenly alive to the significance of extensive landed property as a mark of his social power and status, exerts himself little in properly utilizing it as a source of production and earnings. The disinterestedness in land as a means of production is exemplified in absentee landlordism. Certainty of title and security of tenure are basic requisites for the efficient utilization of land. These however, are unsatisfactory in many under-developed countries. In India, the law of inheritance which entitles each of the sons and daughters to a share of the paternal property has led to the evils of fragmentation and subdivision of holdings. Mechanization and large-scale operations in agriculture become impossible with the result that agriculture far from being a dynamic sector of the economy, generating forces of growth and expansion, has come to be of a subsistence nature and a way of life.

SOCIAL FACTORS AND SAVINGS

Social institutions in underdeveloped countries which reflect their economic backwardness affect also the patterns of consumption and thereby influence savings and capital formation. The level of savings and the rate of capital

[24]ibid.

[25]Linton, Ralph, ' Cultural and Personality Factors Affecting Economic Growth,' Ed. by Bert F. Hoselitz, *Progress of Underdeveloped Areas*, Chicago, 1952.

formation play a crucial role in economic growth. In the underdeveloped countries these are very low compared with advanced economies. The major reason is of course, the low level of per capita incomes. But the fact that even the meagre savings are not properly mobilized and canalized into investment point to the need for examining the causes of this condition. No doubt in all countries irrespective of their standard of economic achievement, a part of the national output which could have been utilized for adding to capital assets is wasted. In the present context, we have to examine how far this wastage is caused by social factors and habits of the people. Obviously, the attitudes, habits and customs of the people have much to do with the pattern of their consumption. Economic habits like thrift, frugality, thought for the morrow, interest in the security of the family, and desire for improving the economic status of the family may be promoted by favourable social institutions or destroyed by an uncongenial social set-up. Economic historians have laid much stress on the social characteristics of the people in European countries in the early stages of industrialization which played a decisive part in the accumulation of wealth and formation of capital. Herbert Frankel mentions that the great growth of capital in the 18th and 19th centuries in Europe was due not to mechanical forces but to the evolution of new patterns in social relationships. " It was due to the emergence of new types of social activity . . . . To repair and maintain; to think of tomorrow, not only of today; to educate and train one's children; to prepare oneself for new activities; to acquire new skills; to search out new contacts; to widen the horizon of individual experience; to invent, to improve, to question the dead hand of custom and heritage of the past, in all these and not in mechanical calculations, or mechanical regimentation lay the causes of capital accumulation." [26]

This however cannot be said of the present day underdeveloped countries. In so far as any addition to the capital stock of the economy raises incomes at a given rate, the very fact that the incomes are low makes it important that what little margin is available over consumption should be turned into productive capital and not frittered away in consumption or in the formation of non-productive capital. Admittedly, since the consumption levels are very much depressed, the scope for further lowering of this level is very much restricted. But where however, social customs and practices are responsible for indulgence in costly rites and ceremonies and sumptuous weddings there is scope for augmenting savings through educating the people and helping them to grow out of their non-economic and wasteful social practices. But primarily, wastage of investible resources arises in the consumption patterns of the rich few. The disparity in the distribution of income and wealth in underdeveloped countries is much sharper than in developed countries. To the extent wealth is concentrated in a small number of hands, there is an obvious potential for

[26]Frankel, Herbert, S., *The Economic Impact on Underdeveloped Societies*, Oxford, London, 1953, p. 69.

increased savings especially when it happens that a large part of this concentrated wealth is not profitably employed.

In underdeveloped countries like India, land has not only an economic value but also a basic and important social value involving deep sentimental attachment. When the social esteem of a man with extensive landed property is great, it is natural that there is a strong preference for investment in land. The economic loss involved consists in the fact that the rich man who invests his resources in this manner is not concerned with whether the property is productively employed or not, but values only the social prestige which such property brings to him. Also, quite a high proportion of the capital available in the community tends to remain in circulation in the real estate market. Another way in which capital gets dissipated is investment in ' hard ' goods such as jewels and precious metals. At one time, investments in such indestructible and easily transportable goods might have been a good insurance against the consequences of political insecurity or periodical economic disasters like drought or famine. Today such investment has outlived its economic justification. But the practice of adorning women and children with costly jewellery has got imbedded in social customs and institutions so that it is impossible to remove it by an appeal to mere economic reason. What is required is again a change on the social front, a change in the attitudes and prejudices of both educated and uneducated people.

Much has been said and written in recent times about conspicuous consumption in poor countries. Such conspicuous consumption takes the form of heavy and needless outlays on grand feasts and ceremonies, on palatial buildings and costly luxury goods which are more a means of displaying wealth and satisfying the sense of vanity than of meeting economic needs. This trait has been observed among all classes of people. The imitation of American ways of living is an instance that illustrates the manner in which levels of consumption tend to outpace the levels of production. This is unmistakably a sign of social immaturity and thoughtlessness on the part of large sections of people. It is an indication of immaturity in the sense that people who are attracted by such modes of living do not stop to think that higher standards of living in the Western countries have been made possible only by the hard work of the people. In the developed countries, rise in standards of living and real consumption follow from improvements in supply conditions. On the other hand, in the pre-industrial countries of today, there is impatience to attain high levels of consumption without waiting for supply to increase, or making an effort to reach a certain level in production which would justify that higher level of consumption. Little is done to emulate the hard work, diligence and effort behind the end products of Western civilization which catch the eye.[27]

Parallel to conspicuous consumption, there is what is called ' conspicuous industrialization '—the passion for grand schemes of industrialization regard-

[27]Singer, H. W., ' Obstacles to Economic Development,' *Social Research*, Vol. 20, 1953, pp. 27-31.

less of whether the preconditions for such expansion exist or not. There is no dispute about the need for industrial development in the primary producing countries. But over-ambitious projects to satisfy national vanity rather than the real economic needs of the country hamper growth in so far as they tend to take away attention from other more urgent investment requirements which are less impressive but more important from the long-term point of view of the economy. To the same category of conspicuous spending at the state level may be mentioned the inordinate outlays on embassies and international representations. Such expenditures of capital in the name of nationalism with a view to attain international prestige may result as a reaction to long years of political dependence. The tendency to equate such spendings with international status is indicative of an inability to realize sufficiently well how actually such international prestige and status are acquired. At any rate, the fact that such heavy expenditures by poor countries are a waste from the point of view of productive capital accumulation cannot be disputed.[28]

It is clear that a change in the consumption savings pattern that would promote economic growth is possible only if a significant modification is brought about in the social environment and the system of values. There is to be a specific development-minded attitude on the part of the leading sections of the society, and preparedness to cut adrift from vested interests and old habits. It might also call for new social and economic institutions designed to foster savings. And since the scope for the classical means of maximizing savings through maximizing profits is limited, the state has to assume some responsibility for generating and mobilizing savings through taxation and loans, through the establishment of savings institutions and by attempting to bring about the necessary improvement in the social structure.[29]

SOCIAL FACTORS AND ENTREPRENEURSHIP

The history of industrialization in the Western countries is in the main a record of the drive, enthusiasm and hard work of a small body of business leaders, who made economic progress possible. Since the entrepreneur is the agent who combines the other factors of production in any scheme of productive enterprise, it is only natural that this agent should play the predominant part in the economic advancement of a country. This is stressed by all modern economists. Thus Prof. Kaldor writes: " In my view the greatly accelerated economic development of the last 200 years—the rise of modern capitalism—can only be explained in terms of changing human attitudes to risk taking and profit making. It was the result of the displacement of production units governed by a traditionist outlook—the peasant and the

[28]Levy, Marion, J. (Jr.), 'Some Obstacles to Capital Formation in Underdeveloped Areas,' *Capital Formation and Economic Growth*, National Bureau of Economic Research, Princeton, 1955, p. 483.

[29]*Economic Bulletin for Asia and the Far East*, U.N., December, 1959, p. 20.

artisan—by business enterprises led by men who found risk taking and money making their chief interest in life; by men who were out to make a fortune, rather than just a living. The emergence of the business enterprise characteristic of modern capitalism was thus the cause rather than the result, of the change in the modes of production; and it was the product of social forces that cannot in turn be accounted for by economic or technical factors."[30]

Schumpeter considers the entrepreneur as primarily the innovator who breaks the normal circular flow of consumption and production by combining the materials and forces of production differently from what has come to be normal. His economic activity represents a departure from the accepted patterns of production, and generates forces of growth and helps in a general and all round expansion. The true entrepreneur according to Schumpeter should therefore have the characteristics of a born leader—the imagination to dream and the will to found a private kingdom in business, the will to conquer, the impulse to fight and to prove oneself superior to others and the capacity to find joy in creating and getting things done.[31]

This is the entrepreneur in the heroic sense of the term. Certainly some of the outstanding men of business like Rockefeller, Henry Ford, Krupp or Lord Beaver-Brook who have built up a kingdom in business and accumulated large fortunes and helped in the economic development of their countries possessed in a great measure some of the characteristics mentioned by Schumpeter. But with the emergence of the new forms of business organization and the increasing role played by modern Governments in the economic and business sphere, the scope for the Schumpeterian entrepreneur is getting very much restricted. For the spontaneous growth of entrepreneurship, certain social and institutional conditions are necessary. Successful businessmen should have a social standing equal to that of outstanding military men or distinguished scientists or political leaders. Men of ability and talents would enter business only if entrepreneurial activity would enable them to achieve distinction and social esteem. Business should have free access to capital and labour supplies. It is mentioned that while inventions are made in France, the commercialization of such inventions takes place in other countries because of the lack of an adequate supply of capital in the former. The inability to recruit labour has also led to the shifting of entrepreneurship from one country to another. Artificial restrictions on entrance to industry, such as licensing of certain pioneering enterprises, have a dampening effect on innovating entrepreneurial talent. Also, there should be a pool of promotable people from which new supplies of managers and entrepreneurs can be drawn.[32] This is possible only if the people are materially minded and imbued with a zeal for economic improvement, and the educational system is of the type

[30]Kaldor, N., *Essays on Economic Stability and Growth*, Duckworth, London, 1960, p. 236.

[31]Schumpeter, Joseph, A., *Theory of Economic Development*, Harvard, 1934, pp. 66–70.

[32]Brozen, Yale, ' Entrepreneurship and Technological Change,' *Economic Development— Principles and Patterns*, Ed. by Williamson and Buttrick, Prentice-Hall, 1954, pp. 214–21.

that is biassed towards engineering, technology and science. Equally important is the presence of a sound legal and administrative system and political
organization that provides free scope for private enterprise, sufficient incentives
for the accumulation of wealth, and an assurance of adequate pecuniary reward
for the assumption of risks and personal effort.

Many of these conditions are absent in the underdeveloped countries. On
the other hand, the rigid social and institutional set up which is characteristic
of economic backwardness stands in the way of the emergence of a pioneering
entrepreneurial class. Institutional factors like the family and caste system
which have had a restrictive effect on the supply of an enterprising and hard
working labour force have also adversely affected the coming up of entrepreneurial talents. The joint family system affects individual initiative. Where
caste or class feeling is strong, loyalty is confined to members of the group and
wider loyalties which are necessary for the organization of large enterprises
get weakened. Nepotism, graft and squeeze which are characteristic of economic underdevelopment and social backwardness are attributable to the pressure
of responsibility towards the family or class.[33] The ascriptive and particularistic
traits in social behaviour also spring from group or communal feelings. When
honesty is confined to the family or caste, appointments to responsible positions
tend to go to members of particular groups or communities; and where there
is a regime of family control in business, management is generally selected
from within the controlling family, and family bonds also determine to a large
extent, advancement in the hierarchy. Moreover, because of the greatly
centralized nature of management in a family concern, there is less scope for
younger men to acquire experience in leadership and decision making.[34]
The manner in which the rigid stratification of occupations under the caste
system in India affects industrialization is well summarized by a United Nations
study as follows: " The hereditary principle governing the division of labour
barred low caste persons from the attainment of higher roles and required
them to follow occupations prescribed by their caste status. A powerful factor
in the stabilisation of the system was a deep rooted belief that the achievement
of a higher status, possible in the next life through the transmigration of
souls, required perfection in the performance of the hereditary caste roles, and
that non-conformist behaviour resulted in corresponding degradation to inferior
caste positions. Such value orientations in so far as they still exert influence,
obviously inhibit individual initiative in penetrating new fields of economic
activity preventing in particular, those who might be well fitted for leadership
from turning their talents to industrial entrepreneurship."[35] However, quite
often economic development has taken place through the enterprise of particular classes of people who do not get properly integrated in the accepted social

[33]Belshaw, Horace, *Population Growth and Levels of Consumption*, George Allen and Unwin,
London, 1956, p. 154.
[34]*Management of Industrial Enterprises in Underdeveloped Countries*, U.N., 1958, pp. 8 and 9.
[35]*Processes and Problems of Industrialization*, U.N., 1955, p. 19.

order and who react against it by diverting their skill and talents to business lines. Thus the Quakers in Britain who carried individual self-determination of faith to an extreme, also contributed outstanding men of business who were responsible for the foundation of some of the well-known industrial and financial establishments. To the same order would belong the Parsees of India.

Among other factors which have hampered entrepreneurship in the underdeveloped countries may be mentioned, social conservatism, the low standard of urbanization, the conservative system of education and the absence of any great social prestige attached to business achievements. In the West, urbanization and industrialization have favourably reacted on each other. The cities are the centres in which the adaptation to new ways, new technologies, new consumption and production patterns and new social institutions is achieved. The faster tempo of movement in urban areas attracts men of a venturesome spirit. Other facilities like education, higher levels of income and demand of the city dweller, better contacts, etc., have encouraged business to come up in them. In the Asian countries many cities are cultural importations from abroad. Industrial cities of the Western type are relatively few. The cultural pattern of them are in many ways very remote from traditional native culture.[36] Moreover, the number of people living in cities is a very small proportion of the total as compared with the position in the economically advanced countries of the West. The predominance of villages and the fact that agriculture is the main occupation also explain the characteristic conservative attitude of the people and the lack of a competitive spirit. This has also resulted in a carry over to industry of attitudes and practices associated with patterns of management in rural areas. Thus the arbitrary landlord's attitude observable in the managers of businesses in cities has been cited as one of the causes for labour management difficulties. The slowness to introduce new techniques of production in industry has also been the effect of this influence of the ideas and outlook associated with agrarian economies on the industrial sector. It is also a fact that business talents and achievements are not an object of so much social acclaim in the pre-industrial countries, as in the advanced ones. Low social status of business turns talents to the traditional honorific careers. Shrewdness and intelligence in business are in fact suspect; and quite often business skill is equated with double dealing and lack of integrity. This derogatory conception of businessmen is due as much to the known practices among the businessmen as to the popular prejudice against the entrepreneurial class. The low standard of education and the type of education that has become popular in some of the poorer countries like India have also something to do with the slow emergence of entrepreneurship. In the Asian countries learning and education are biassed towards religion. The usual criticism that was raised against the educational system in India until recently, was that it gave undue importance to arts as against science.

[36]Hoselitz, Bert F., *Sociological Aspects of Economic Growth*, Free Press, Glencoe, Illinois, 1960, p. 225.

In a large measure this was due to the encouragement given under the British regime for the training and supply of qualified civil servants. Also, the absence of industrialization itself limits the opportunities for men of science and technology. Allowing for this deficiency in the system of education, the fact remains that in India it did not contribute even the little that it could, to the development of entrepreneurial talents. The main reason for this is the tendency on the part of the educated classes to have their centre of gravity in the West and to be out of touch with the masses and their problems. Edward Shils points out that this ' social scotoma ' is a product of a hierarchical society in which the higher castes and classes had little feelings for those beneath them and also of the religious tradition of non-attachment.[37]

These difficulties account for two important features of business in underdeveloped countries. Firstly, the starting of industrial ventures by foreigners who bring with them not only the capital, but also the business spirit and improved technology. Instances are, the Scotch and English in India, Syrians, Armenians, Jews, Greeks and other Europeans in Egypt, Lebanese and Syrians in Brazil and Columbia, Spanish and French investors in Mexico and Indians and Chinese in Malaya and Burma. Secondly, lack of capital and the consequent incapacity and unpreparedness to take risks, combined with the particular traits of character among the people in underdeveloped countries, have diverted investments away from industry into real estate, and also into commerce and trade. Such undertakings do not require the ability to handle a large number of workers or mechanical skill or knowledge of technology. They also fit in with the usual mental prejudice against forms of physical labour which necessitate a man soiling his hands. What is more important in such investments is that risks are less than in industry and the turnover of money is much quicker.[38] Even when industries are started, the tendency is normally towards safe undertakings. Concentration of investment on a few export products in Chile and Brazil and on sugar production in Cuba illustrates this point.

There is, however, one advantage to the economically backward nations of today which needs to be mentioned. Being late comers in the field of industry, they are in a position to learn from the experience of industrially advanced countries and introduce types and patterns of industries which have been tried and found to be successful elsewhere. Further more, it is possible today for the businessman of the underdeveloped countries to visit the industrial

[37]Shils, Edward, ' The Intellectual, Public Opinion and Economic Development,' *Problems of Economic Growth*, Office for Asian Affairs, Delhi, 1960, p. 55.

[38]There is in addition the fact that the rate of profits for such commercial undertakings is substantially greater than in industries. Money-lending yields 18 to 60 per cent interest while inventory speculation brings in 70 per cent. As a result, money will not be forthcoming into industries unless expected profits are very high. This is said to be a feature of early stages of industrialization as in the U.S.A. in the 19th century.

Aubrey, Henry G., ' Investment Decisions in Underdeveloped Countries,' *Capital Formation and Economic Growth*, National Bureau of Economic Research, Princeton, 1955, pp. 412–13.

centres in other countries and acquire on the spot information about matters relating to the starting, operation and management of industries and also to get an insight into the secrets of successful and efficient business management. He can function with much limited resources in so far as he has no need to risk huge amounts of money in experimentation and trial. His contribution to economic development consists therefore in introducing those techniques of production which have been tried in other countries or adapting them to suit the different economic circumstances and factor supply situation in his own country.

But as against this advantage, there are certain difficulties of an institutional and economic nature which have to be surmounted. While heavy expenditures involved in experimentation and innovation can be avoided, the fact that the underdeveloped countries have to make up a large leeway in capital formation, necessitates large initial investments even when the state assumes the responsibility for providing the overheads. Costly capital equipment has to be imported from foreign countries, large payments have to be made for foreign advice and for the services of middlemen; at times industrialists would have to provide their own power and transport facilities. Inventories of accessories and machine parts have to be built up and raw materials in large quantities have to be stocked, the latter because of the absence of a regular net work of industrial and raw materials supplies. All these add up to the large size of investment required. Apart from this financial commitment, the businessman in a pre-industrial economy has to face other difficulties springing mainly from some uncertainties which are peculiar to countries of a low standard of economic development. A correct estimate of the returns of an investment can be made only if reliable information on a number of factors like various items of cost, size of the market and demand conditions, the degree of competition, overhead facilities, etc., is available. In advanced countries, market research programmes conducted by big businesses, and information regularly published by research organizations of the Government and by the banking and other financial institutions, provide the necessary data on which the businessman can base his estimates. Also, in the making of these forecasts he can have the services of specialists. But in the economically backward countries, these data are quite inadequate and defective so that the element of risk involved in business undertakings tends to be large. Even when the degree of risks is known, the possibility of adequately covering these risks is limited in the low income countries. Furthermore, it has been pointed out that in an underdeveloped country the effect of even small changes tends to be magnified. A slight increase in the inflow of particular imports or in the rate of new investment may make a large difference in the local producer's potential market. This clearly is one of the major reasons why businessmen are likely to be more timid and less venturesome in these countries, than their counterparts in advanced countries. New ventures are therefore rare; instead, businessmen prefer to take as a model another firm which is found to be successful and fix the size of plant and equipment and scale of operations with reference to the model. Thus the proneness to imitate on the part of businessmen in the less developed countries has partly at least to be attributed to these adverse circumstances in which he has to operate.

These obstacles and difficulties arising out of social, institutional and economic factors explain why entrepreneurship remains a scarce factor in the less developed countries. They also suggest the broad lines along which improvement has to take place. In the main, measures to foster individual initiative and business enterprise would involve provision of better educational facilities and change in the pattern of education, improvement of the quality and standard of skill of workers, reducing the rigidity of social customs and habits, organization of financial institutions, provision of economic and social overhead facilities, supply of information and statistical data relating to business and the national economy, improvement of the legal system and administrative machinery, etc. The magnitudes involved underline the great need for state action. In the matter of reform of the legal system and of the administrative machinery, the state is under an obligation to itself. In the sphere of industrialization, the lack of private entrepreneurship on an adequate scale, the huge initial outlays involved in some of the essential investment schemes such as public utilities and key industries, and the unattractiveness of such ventures from the commercial point of view, point to the need for state enterprise supplementing private enterprise. Also, as has been stressed by the Government of India, the state would have to assume the responsibility for undertaking new industrial enterprises which serve as a model to private business. In the present economic and social set-up in many of the under-developed countries, such public programmes would be necessary to get private operations under way.

Apart from direct participation in the entrepreneurial field, the state can create the social and economic conditions favourable to growth through the following administrative and fiscal measures: (i) The social and institutional set-up can be attuned to economic advancement through the extension of education and by giving a new orientation in education to technological improvement and to the provision of the necessary skills and aptitude for industrial employment and management; (ii) the state can also ease the problem of financial resources by improving financial liquidity by encouragement of banking in rural areas and by the establishment of financial corporations through which the financial resources collected by the state can be canalized into private investment; (iii) the uncertainties of private business can be reduced by the state furnishing statistical information and market data collected by its own agents, by sponsoring research institutes and by providing other information to business relating to exports, imports, foreign markets, internal market conditions, etc. To the extent the state's tax and fiscal policy add to the uncertainties of private business, this can be lessened by the simplification of the tax and fiscal system; (iv) the entrepreneurial requirements can be met if the state can take measures to encourage the drafting of management personnel from the professions, army, the civil service, etc.; provide adequate training facilities in business management, by offering common production facilities and repair and maintenance facilities to smaller firms on the lines of industrial estates; organize or start technological institutes to improve the quality of output and popularize new methods of efficient production; (*v*) the quality of labour can be improved by starting vocational schools, by minimum wage legislation, by efficient organization of labour and by devising means to establish better labour-management relationship. Also, it would be possible to increase the supply of capable managers of business as well as skilled labourers if care is taken to train up those categories of workers who are employed in large Government undertakings like multipurpose projects, and industrial undertakings.

Recently, an American economist has drawn attention to the entrepreneurial potentiality found in the large number of businessmen in small undertakings in underdeveloped countries.[39] Some of the few indigenous ' islands of entrepreneurship ' are an occasional modern large farm, bicycle shop, lorry transport, brick kilned potter's shop, small brick factory and the like. The owners of such establishments although they do their business on a small scale do possess certain entrepreneurial skill and the question is whether they do not constitute a class of promotable people. It is therefore worthwhile to investigate the economies of their business, the problems of management which they have to tackle and the factors which stand against their emergence as large-scale operators. Such entrepreneurship is found scattered all over the country and an understanding of their difficulties and problems would help in taking measures to augment the supply of skilled and enterprising businessmen who constitute the mainstay of any free enterprise economic structure.

THE PROBLEM OF TECHNOLOGY

The application of science to methods of production results in the emergence of new techniques which increase productive efficiency. Improvements in technology are preceded by the accumulation of scientific knowledge, development of both fundamental and applied science, mastery of scientific techniques and a spread of scientific attitude through society. This brings about also a simultaneous change in social relationships and in institutions and a weakening of the hold of traditions and social prejudices on the people. Herbert Frankel points out that technological change is not a mere improvement in the technical know how. It means much more than this. It should be preceded by sociological change also, a willingness and desire on the part of the community to modify their social, political and administrative institutions so as to make them fit in with the new techniques of production and the faster tempo of

[39]Wolf, Charles and Sydney C. Sufrin, *Capital Formation and Foreign Investment in Underdeveloped Areas*, Syracuse, 1958, p. 29.

economic activity.[40] It thus follows that the social set-up of the backward pre-industrial economies is not conducive to technological improvements on any significant scale.

It is possible to identify a distinct pattern in the evolution of technology. First, advancement of fundamental and applied science, resulting in a scientific discovery or an addition to scientific knowledge; secondly, an invention or the making use of existing knowledge for a useful end; thirdly, an innovation or the application of the invention to economic production, and finally, the improvement and extension of the new techniques on a commercial scale which brings about the expansion of an industry and directly or indirectly helps other industries to grow, resulting in all round economic progress.[41] Thus innovation in the economic field represents commercialization of an invention which springs from scientific advancement; while invention is a scientific fact, innovation is an economic fact.[42] For successful technological development of this nature to take place, three conditions are necessary. It requires large capital investments at every stage; it needs not only a scientific attitude and bent on the part of the community but also entrepreneurial skill of a high order with the ability to understand the possibilities of using scientific inventions for commercial purposes. Lastly, commercialization is possible only if the new product can find an expanding market i.e. only if the public take to the product without hesitation so that demand rises even as production expands. This again shows clearly why technological progress on a marked scale is possible only in advanced economies. Apart from resulting in increased and efficient production, technological development, necessitates fresh investment and accelerates the growth of national income. Important innovations will make a few firms grow faster than the growth of national income while other firms may be lagging behind. But if innovations take place in capital intensive industries as it quite often happens, there will be a tendency for aggregate business investment to exceed aggregate business savings. The ideal economic set-up for innovations to take place is competition among big firms in which price cutting is not possible so that sales can be increased only through product variation, thus making the end product more attractive to the consumer. The industry as a whole consisting of independent firms will expand and this expansion itself fosters further advancement in technology. A typical example is the American automobile industry. On the other hand, if the industries are highly competitive and organized on a small scale like cottage industries, the scope for innovation is considerably restricted.[43] Since at any rate, improvement in methods of production would be beneficial whether the industry is organized on a small or large scale, either such small units

[40]Frankel, Herbert S., *Economic Impact on Underdeveloped Countries*, Oxford, London, 1953, pp. 22–23.

[41]Keirstead, B. S., *Theory of Economic Change*, Macmillan, Toronto, 1948, p. 133.

[42]Kuznets, Simon, *Six Lectures on Economic Growth*, Free Press, Glencoe. Illinois, 1959, pp. 30–31.

[43]Villard, Henry H., *Economic Development*, Rinehart, New York, 1959, pp. 82–97.

have to organize research in new techniques on a co-operative basis or the state should take the responsibility for doing it.

For the underdeveloped countries beset with the problems of low per capita incomes, increasing pressure of population, low levels of consumption and low savings margin, the major objective should be to increase labour productivity. Since the labour-capital and labour-land ratios are high, it would be difficult to find capital resources on a scale necessary to increase output through securing better combination of the factors of production. The only possibility of increasing output with the capital resources available for these economies consists in increasing labour productivity by adopting improved techniques of production that do not require capital on a large scale. However, as has been indicated above, it has not been possible for backward economies to make any progress in this line. In the main, limited resources and the abundance of labour supply have stood in the way of technological advancement. Lack of resources explains the paucity of organized research institutions, the scarcity of large economic units and the low level of effective demand. To these should be added the absence of specialization, labour immobility, and an adverse socio-political environment, which fosters inertia and conservatism and hampers initiative, enterprise and inventiveness.[44]

This lag in industrialization and the failure to adopt modern technology have placed the pre-industrial economies in an unenviable situation. In the present day industrial economies technological advancement proceeded along with economic progress in conformity with the factor supply situation. The shift from coal to fuel power in the late 18th and early 19th centuries to the electricity era of the late 19th century and the atomic energy era of the mid-20th century, corresponds with a similar pattern of industrial production and economic activity. Economic development and technological improvement reacted on each other favourably. While technology helped economic advancement, the latter in turn facilitated the inflow of increasing resources into research and scientific learning and thereby fostered invention and innovation. In contrast, the main problem in this respect in underdeveloped countries is that they awoke to the need for economic development at a time when both technology and economic development had advanced far in other countries. The techniques they have to adopt have been evolved in advanced countries with a different economic set-up and different factor supply situation. Modern technical knowledge thus gets superimposed on a retrograde economic and social system. In the absence of complementary factors like trained personnel, entrepreneurial ability and an adequate supply of financial resources, adoption of advanced technology tends not only to be less productive and more expensive, but also causes a dislocation in the economy. The abundance of capital, scarcity of labour and high wage rates have necessitated technical

[44] Vakil, C. N. and P. R. Brahmananda, 'Technical Knowledge and Managerial Capacity as Limiting Factors on Industrial Expansion in Underdeveloped Countries,' *International Social Science Bulletin*, Vol. VI, No. 2, 1954, UNESCO, pp. 212–17.

innovations in the West to be of the capital intensive and labour saving type. Moreover, steady expansion in demand and increased variety of consumption made possible by rising national incomes induce a constant change in technology, and the rapid scrapping of capital goods. What is more important, the use of advanced technology requires high levels of training, scientific skill and understanding which are rare in countries importing these technologies. It is therefore not surprising when we are told of " instances of production equipment which is well suited to the needs of industrialised countries but whose performance fails to measure up to expectations in the industrial environment of underdeveloped countries ".[45] As Brozen remarks: " A technology developed for an Oil-coal-iron-water-power-broadleaf-forest complex of resources is not easily transferable to tropical rain forest or semi arid regions in which the primary source of power is wind and sun ".[46] Labour saving advances in technology such as the attempts to evolve a device in the U.S.A. of combining mechanical picking and mechanical weeding in cotton production or conversion of coal into gas by underground igniting of coal are of little relevance to a country like India with an over-abundant supply of agricultural labour. It would thus appear that technology which was suited to present day developed countries some years, say a century ago, would be suitable for underdeveloped countries of today. But machines representing that stage of technology are only in the industrial museums of the developed countries and it would not be possible to induce any big firms to take up the large-scale production of out-dated machines. Perhaps techniques practised in a country which has not advanced to the level of highly industrialized countries of the West and where small scale production still continues to occupy a prominent place in the nation's economy, such as Japan, would be in a better position to meet the particular needs of pre-industrial economies. But as it is, the businessman has seldom the choice; if he has to organize an industry he does it on the model of Western countries and has to import advanced mechanical devices which are designed and manufactured there. Engineers to whom the task of preparing blue prints for industries is entrusted, and who have a good text book knowledge of advanced industrial technology " adopt the same technology as in the West, considering the production function as a single process line with only scale variability ".[47]

Besides being a misfit in the economic circumstances of the underdeveloped countries Western technology causes also some economic wastes. The high initial investment required creates a severe strain on the financial resources. The fact that the machines needed have to be imported from advanced countries involves a large draft on foreign exchange. The maintenance of such machinery

[45]*Management of Industrial Enterprises in Underdeveloped Countries*, 1958, U.N., New York, p. 17.

[46]Brozen, Yale, 'Invention, Innovation and Imitation,' *American Economic Review*, Proceedings Number, May, 1951, p. 255.

[47]Wolf, Charles, and Sydney C. Sufrin, *Capital Formation and Foreign Investment in Underdeveloped Areas*, Syracuse, 1958, p. 42.

necessitates recurring foreign exchange expenditure for which an export surplus has to be built up which becomes difficult because of the distortion in internal price structure. From a wider point of view, industrialization with costly imported technology would affect international specialization on rational lines in so far as the backward economies would find it difficult to maintain their balance of payments unless by encouraging exports by means of subsidies or by restricting imports by means of tariffs. The pressure on local savings which importation of capital equipment and investment and the maintenance of such equipment involve would reduce the possibility of investing the meagre resources in a manner and in lines of production which would be more economical and more appropriate to local conditions. Concentration on capital intensive lines of industrialization in poor agricultural countries would lead to the displacement of labour for whom alternative employment opportunities are lacking. Another aspect of the wastage involved in the use of advanced technology is that the effective life of the imported expensive equipment in underdeveloped countries is often much shorter because of inexperience in handling the machinery, lack of technical skill and lack of care and proper maintenance. Moreover, most of the machinery is manufactured in temperate climates and are unsuited to tropical climates.[48]

On the ground of the difficulties mentioned above, it is not fair to take the line that industrialization or adoption of improved technology is not advisable in underdeveloped countries. There is no denying the fact that only by building up heavy industries can economic growth forces be generated in the underdeveloped countries. But the difficulties in the way of importing advanced technology and the problems involved in it underline the need for discretion and caution in the using of modern techniques. As regards the large industrial operations, the problem of choice of technology is not a serious one in so far as technical processes including plant design are fairly standardized in this type of operation so that the patterns of organization and scale that are advantageous in the West would be so in the underdeveloped countries as well. Even here, a certain flexibility exists in the design of equipment for some ancillary operations, for example, materials handling. By this means the operations can be made more capital saving and labour intensive. The real conflict arises only in respect of small industries which are important from the point of view of employment but in which a high degree of mechanization or adoption of high level of technology is not possible. For such industries few prototype plants are available in industrialized countries. This provides great scope for the application of the ingenuity and skill of engineers and technicians of underdeveloped countries. It should be the task and concern of such trained and qualified men to evolve new techniques of production or adapt technology to suit the requirements of their countries. It is also impor-

48Singer, H. W., 'Obstacles to Economic Development,' *Social Research*, Vol. 20, 1953, pp. 19–31, also Baster, James, 'A Second Look at Point Four,' *American Economic Review*, Proceedings Number, May, 1951, pp. 399–406.

tant that businessmen and entrepreneurs are well informed of the variety of plants and machines available in particular lines of production, their sources of supply, cost, etc. In certain cases, if small industries concentrate in particular localities it would be possible to carry out a particular stage in productive operation on a large scale. This would be beyond the means of a single plant but a possible solution is the establishment of common facility services on the lines adopted in industrial estates in India and other underdeveloped countries. Since capital is scarce in underdeveloped countries it is also necessary to see to it that when once a machinery is installed, the rate of its utilization is kept high.[49] This is a capital saving device, and the way of achieving it is by means of first assessing the extent of under-utilization through the use of methods of work study and then by increasing the application of labour to a given unit of capital through use of overtime or by the device of multiple shifts. These measures however, are not substitutes for the major means of solving the problem of technology in underdeveloped countries, namely, the development of new, simpler and inexpensive techniques appropriate to the factor endowments of the countries which would help in increasing productivity more than proportionately to the costs involved.

THE CONFLICT BETWEEN ECONOMIC AND SOCIAL PROGRESS: NEED FOR INTEGRATION

Planned development in the economically backward countries, mostly sponsored and engineered by governments has meant the superimposition of an advanced form of economic structure on a social foundation which is ill fitted to bear the burden. In these countries the social organization has remained quite rigid and inflexible for ages; the customs and social habits of the people, their religious dogmas, laws of inheritance and property, and social stratification, all these are different from what are common in the economically advanced countries. Although in countries like England, the industrial revolution caused considerable social dislocation which manifested itself in the form of exploitation of labour and all the evils of congested city life, society was able to adjust itself rapidly to the requirements of the modern economy. At any rate, economic advancement was not squeezed into so short a span of time as is envisaged in many of the present day developing economies. Moreover, the attitudes and values of the people and their social organization even at the time of industrial revolution were different from those of the people in the modern pre-industrial economies. Such comparatively smooth social and economic adjustments seem to be difficult in countries like India. The fundamental reason is that the cultural patterns and values of the people are not what would go in well with an acquisitive temperament and a passionate desire for material improvement. We therefore find a dichotomy between sectors and regions of the economy which have developed

[49] *Management of Industrial Enterprises in Underdeveloped Countries*, U.N., 1958, pp. 17-19.

economically along Western lines and other sectors which are lagging far behind. There is in short, a conflict between social progress and economic progress. There are three reasons why this conflict is of much greater magnitude than what confronted the Western nations in a corresponding stage of their economic evolution. In the first place, the size of the community affected by the spread of the factory system in the initial stages of industrialization in the West was of far smaller dimensions than in contemporary Asia, Latin America and Africa. At the beginning of the 19th century, the population of Great Britain was three per cent of the present Indian population. The mere magnitude of the number of people who are drifting to the towns from the rural areas poses serious social problems the like of which the industrializing countries of Western Europe in the 19th century had not to face. Secondly, in the Western countries industrial revolution was preceded and accompanied by revolutions in agriculture, commerce, political systems and values, science, art and religion. On the other hand, there is no corresponding change in the non-economic sphere in contemporary underdeveloped areas. To some extent this is due to the fact that economic growth in the West was spontaneous in the sense that industrial development was brought about by an awakening on the part of the entrepreneurial classes, who saw opportunities of profitable investments and made use of those opportunities; while in the backward countries of the present century economic growth is a sponsored one, in which the pattern of development and schemes of implementing the development policy are conceived and drafted by an official class. The social and political changes, and changes in the attitudes and values of the people corresponded to the spontaneity in economic changes and therefore fitted in well with the new scheme of things in the West. Thirdly, the spirit behind modern industrial economy and the pattern of organization on which it is based are alien to the underdeveloped countries. The adoption of modern technology, the higher tempo of activity and the hurried pace of life which go with it, represent the imposition of a form of foreign culture distinct from the one to which the people in the agricultural countries have been traditionally accustomed. The difficulty of getting this foreign culture integrated with the traditional patterns of life presents many social problems.

The impact of industrialization on social life has different aspects. The growth of cities and the concentration of industries in urban areas cause a movement of rural population towards the cities. The security of village life is lost and the rural areas are exposed to the influence of urban development. This in itself is advantageous in the long run in so far as the patterns of life in the village would undergo a welcome change. In the initial stages however, it creates difficult social problems. City life requires adoption of new ways of life and the development of new social relations. Older men from villages with high family or class status may have to be subordinate to younger men in factories or offices. Such new relations have a disruptive effect on the age-long social structures which are not given up without much psychological strain. Again, the introduction of new techniques of production dislocates old patterns of social life. New skills are to be learned, much different from the skills of the traditional craftsman. The worker accustomed to a free and leisurely sort of life in the villages has to be under the strain of discipline and restriction of movement and has to adjust his movements to the speed and regularity of the machine. All these factors affect the morale of the workers and their feeling of security.

Some of the results of this economic impact on social structure are advantageous and help economic progress. The shake up of the customary patterns of social life is as inevitable as it is beneficial. Thus in India old social systems like the joint family have already shown signs of giving way to the demands of economic progress. Under the influence of industrialization the caste system is losing its rigidity. And the system of education with its traditional bias to the arts, religion, and philosophy shows a perceptible shift in emphasis in favour of the sciences and technology. But beneficial though these changes are, they create in the early stages difficulties of adjustment. Sharp socio-economic changes bring about a form of psychological conflict in the minds of people of the older generation steeped in traditional patterns of life and customs and the younger generation who show an unnecessary haste towards social reform in the direction of Western ways of living. The economic effects of such social tensions are not easily known but that they are not always favourable to steady progress in material advancement leaves little room for doubt.

But it is in the sphere of industrial and urban employment that these social evils have become most glaring. The drift of population from the rural to the urban areas is of an order of magnitude not justified by the extent of industrialization or the increase in the employment opportunities. If size of population is an index of urbanization, there is no mistake in saying that urbanization in some of the underdeveloped countries like India and China has outrun industrialization. As a result, while the number of labourers who constitute a steady, regular and dependable force is relatively small, those who are seeking employment exceed the possibilities of absorption and are very much beyond the capacity of all existing social amenities. To provide these in an adequate measure is not within the financial means of even the richest of cities. That urbanization has grown considerably faster than industrial employment is borne out by statistical data relating to India. While the proportion of labour force employed in industries increased from 11 to 13 per cent between 1911 and 1951, the percentage of population living in localities of 20,000 or more inhabitants increased from 4 per cent to 12 per cent.[50] Over-crowding in cities is thus not a measure of industrial expansion. Nevertheless, such a trend aggravates the social evils of city life. Unemployment affects the morale of the immigrants, while bad housing conditions, the disruption of family life and the disappearance of old patterns of authority and control promote delinquency, beggary or destitution and crime. It has been remarked

[50] *Economic Bulletin for Asia and the Far East*, U.N., December, 1959, p. 21 f.n.

that the first generation youth who repudiate their parents as peasants and already consciously reject traditional authority, but who have not yet acquired the new kinds of values and controls appropriate to the new environment are particularly apt to show a propensity to criminal and anti-social behaviour.[51] To these evils should be added all the bad social characteristics of city life in the early stages of industrialization such as, bad employer-employee relations, long hours of work, low levels of wages inadequate to maintain family life, industrial home work, sweat shop methods and child labour. Protective social and labour legislation and humanitarian policies adopted by some employers have eased the problem to some extent in the more advanced among the backward countries but in others it persists.

The social evils of industrialization are not confined to the cities but extend to the rural community as well. While rapid industrialization in some of the underdeveloped countries is significant enough to be called something of an industrial revolution, there has not been any parallel agrarian revolution to make villages a better place to live in. Rapid growth of population and disappearance of old handicraft industries have swelled the volume of rural unemployment. The break up of the extended family system and the uprooting of the workers from their traditional communities as a consequence of industrialization have also hastened the decay of those devices of self help and mutual aid which provide a measure of security to the weaker and handicapped members of the rural community and stability to the village economy. Thus many of the social security functions performed by the family in the pre-industrial societies have tended to fall increasingly upon the state.

Most of the social and economic evils mentioned above are the inevitable consequences of rapid industrialization on a large scale and should be considered as the social costs of economic growth. Although in view of the nature of the situation in contemporary pre-industrial countries these evils are of a larger dimension than what some of the Western countries had to face at a corresponding stage in their economic development, yet there is one advantage in so far as knowledge about the true nature of these evils and of the means to control them is greater today than before. But it would be unwise to leave the problem to be solved in the natural process of social evolution. The fact that in these countries economic growth is not spontaneous but is predominantly an induced process under the guidance of the state, invests the governments with the responsibility of controlling the evils and smoothening the transformation of the economies. Moreover these social problems are so extensive, complicated and deep that only through efforts on a national scale backed by vast resources can the problem be properly tackled. The importance and urgency of the matter have been adequately recognized by the governments of several underdeveloped countries and they have incorporated in their development plans schemes to improve the social conditions and bring about an integration of economic advancement with social progress. Thus, the First Five-Year

[51]*Processes and Problems of Industrialization*, U.N., 1955, p. 123.

Plan of Pakistan (1955–56 to 1959–60) states that the government's policy " is to develop the resources of the country as rapidly as possible so as to promote the welfare of the people, provide adequate living standards and social services, secure social justice and equality of opportunity, and aim at the widest and most equitable distribution of income and property".[52] The Second Five-Year Plan of India made it clear that " the task before an underdeveloped country is not merely to get better results within the existing frame work of economic and social institutions, but to mould and refashion these so that they contribute effectively to the realization of wider and deeper social values.[53] Similar objectives have been laid down in the development plans of other countries like the Philippines, Burma and Ceylon.

This emphasis on social reforms as part of the programme of economic development is necessary because planned development under the leadership of the state is characterized by a desire to achieve certain results more quickly than would be possible under free enterprise. Since industrialization is sought to be concentrated into a shorter time span, the social evils are also likely to appear in larger proportions and more suddenly. Hence planning should be for social amelioration as much as for economic betterment. A well thought out scheme of integration between the two sides of progress will therefore facilitate transformation of the economy with minimum adverse effects.

Such an integrated programme would be possible if the approach is made along the following lines. In the first place, planning for development should give as much consideration to the problems of the villages as to those of the urban areas, to agriculture as much as to industry. Many of the investment projects of India under the Five-Year Plans directly benefit both the rural areas and the industrialized regions of the country as for instance hydro-electric projects. Dispersal of industries in villages, establishment of industrial estates, rural electrification, improvements of means of communications and the opening of rural banking institutions and schools and the extension of medical and puplic health facilities would help in the economic and social betterment of the rural parts, infuse a spirit of enterprise among the people, improve their morale and thereby facilitate a more balanced development of the agricultural and industrial sectors of the economy. Secondly, where social reform is attempted, the change should be brought about in easy stages with due regard to the prevailing attitudes and prejudices of the people. Grafting of improvements to the existing patterns of life is necessary in view of the fact that habits and prejudices have deeper roots in non-industrial regions than in urban areas. Any sharp transition would upset the existing modes of life and cause avoidable social tension. The premium on the arts, the classics and theology which characterize the curriculum of education

[52]*The First Five-Year Plan*, The National Planning Board, Government of Pakistan, December, 1957, p. 1.

[53]*The Second Five-Year Plan*, Planning Commission, Government of India, New Delhi, 1956, p. 22.

in Asian countries should give place to greater emphasis on science and technology. But the transition can be made smooth if more people can be attracted to technical training and certain specialized technological courses by giving an academic flavour to such training. As Maurice Zinkin remarks: " The model of education in the Asian countries must be 19th century Germany or 20th Century America with their courses in everything from journalism to carpentry, not England or France with their belief that the academic must be really academic".[54]

The third method of reducing the social evils involved in rapid industrialization is to integrate social and economic advancement by attempting to bring about social changes through economic projects and economic changes through social projects. Thus encouragement of small industries has the economic objective of increased production and higher incomes but it is productive of social good in the form of higher levels of employment. Community Development Projects give as much importance to the improvement of social conditions and attainment of certain social objectives like enthusiasm for work, spirit of co-operation, self help, discipline and leadership, as to the economic advantages arising from productive employment of villagers. Similarly, economic programmes for depressed classes, tribal groups and nomadic tribes have a large social welfare component in their immediate purpose.[55] On the other hand, social programmes can be made to cover economic purposes. All forms of ' human investment ' i.e. outlay on education, public health, etc. improve the social conditions and material well-being of the community as well as improve their efficiency as productive workers. Various social programmes that aim at promoting the spirit of self help, build up character and contribute to economic activity. Measures taken to ameliorate the conditions of life of industrial employees, such as higher wages and bonuses, assistance in child care, education, health, recreation, etc. represent expenditure on social objectives which have a beneficial effect on economic activity in so far as such outlays would reduce instability of labour, cut down the higher cost of labour turnover, promote labour employee co-operation and encourage labour to put forth greater effort.

[54]Zinkin, Maurice, *Development for Free Asia*, Collins, 1958, pp. 150-51.
[55]*Economic Bulletin for Asia and the Far East*, U.N., December, 1959, p. 29.

Chapter IV

POPULATION AS A FACTOR IN ECONOMIC GROWTH

THE ECONOMIC significance of labour as a factor of production consists in its dual aspect—its role as a consumer as well as a producer. In combination with the other factors labour contributes to total product. But unlike the other factors labour is also the consumer of the product. And the amount of consumption requirements does not vary to any noticeable extent whether labour is fully employed or not. In other words, when there is full employment of labour, given the supply of other resources and the standards of organization and technology, total product is maximized, but when the level of employment falls, consumption level is not reduced. Thus cost of labour has to be incurred by society whether labour is used or not. It is true that some cost is involved in maintaining the quality of land and capital even when they are unused. But this cost incurred on these two factors is much less when they are idle than when they are employed. It is this aspect of labour which makes a high level of employment of labour and the avoidance of unemployment very much necessary from the economic point of view. The contribution of population or labour to economic growth is therefore determined by its impact on the consumption side as well as the production side.

Clearly when the number of people increases, consumption requirements increase in a corresponding determinable proportion. But the extent to which growth in the number of people contributes to output depends not only on the extent of increase in the number, but also on its organization, the availability of complementary resources, the techniques of production adopted, etc. Since the area of land or natural resources is fixed, given the rate of growth of population, the prospects of economic growth depend on the extent to which current output exceeds current consumption in so for as this excess determines the possible rate of capital accumulation in the economy. Hence in examining the role of population in economic growth we have to keep in mind these two major factors namely, the increase in total output brought about by population increase and the rise in total consumption requirements of the economy. We have to see how far the growth of population would help in maximizing this difference.

Before we examine the various factors that determine the contribution of population to output it would be useful to have a broad view of the more important characteristics of the population of low income countries as compared with that of the economically advanced countries.

DEMOGRAPHIC CHARACTERISTICS OF DEVELOPED AND UNDERDEVELOPED COUNTRIES

An examination of the distribution of population among the different regions and countries of the world and its rate of increase would bring into relief the economic significance of the size and trends of population in the more advanced countries as compared with the low income countries of the world. In 1950, 55·2 per cent of the world's population was concentrated in Asia and 23 per cent in Europe including U.S.S.R.; while, countries of Africa, Northern America, Latin America and Oceania (Australia, New Zealand and the Pacific Islands) accounted for 8 per cent, 6·7 per cent, 6·5 per cent and 0·5 per cent respectively. If the world is divided into two broad areas—the technologically developed areas which are the high income countries—Northern America, Temperate South America, most of Europe, Australia, New Zealand and the U.S.S.R. and technologically underdeveloped areas which are the low income countries comprising Africa, Central America, the Caribbean, Tropical South America, Asia excluding Japan and the Pacific Islands, it is found that in 1950, the population of the former group amounted to 863 millions or about ⅓ of the total (34·5 per cent) and that of the latter amounted to 1,637 millions or about ⅔ (65·5 per cent) of the total. Making use of another geographic division, the countries of Asia and the Far East including Japan contained 53·4 per cent of the world's population in 1956 while the rest of the world contained the remaining 46·6 per cent. Among the countries in the former group the population of China was 621·2 million or 42·5 per cent and that of India was 387·3 million or 26·5 per cent. The rest of the countries of the region carried 454 million or 31 per cent.

Variation in the density of population in the different countries is shown in Table 12.

Since total area refers to total land area and inland water and includes arid deserts, swamps and forests in which human habitation in any civilized form is well nigh impossible, the density per square kilometer of total area has not much significance. Arable land includes fields with crops, land temporarily fallow, temporary meadows used for pasture, gardenland and areas under fruit trees and plantations. There is considerable variation in density per square kilometer of arable land. The world average in 1956 was 198 and in the East Asian regions it was 375. Among the latter, population density per square kilometer of arable land was very high in some countries; Japan 1,783, China (Mainland) 568, Ceylon 586, India 245, Pakistan 343, Philippines 347 and Viet Nam 591. Only in Afghanistan, Iran and Laos was density less than 150 per square kilometer.

On the basis of density of population and standards of economic achievement, countries are classified into four groups: (a) Developed and thickly populated areas—Japan, Switzerland and Italy; (b) Developed and thinly populated areas—U.S.A., Canada, U.S.S.R.; (c) Underdeveloped and thinly populated areas—Brazil, Gold Coast and Burma; and (d) Underdeveloped

ECONOMICS OF DEVELOPMENT

Table 12

ESTIMATED POPULATION DENSITY IN
DIFFERENT COUNTRIES IN 1956

Country	No. of persons per sq. kilometer of	
	Total area	Arable land
Africa	7	95
North America	9	81
Latin America	9	185
Europe	84	273
Oceania	2	60
U.S.S.R.	9	91
Burma	29	232
Ceylon	136	586
China (Mainland)	64	568
India	118	245
Japan	243	1,783
Pakistan	88	348
Philippines	74	347
Thailand	40	265

SOURCE: *Economic Bulletin for Asia and the Far East*, U.N., June, 1958, p. 5.

and thickly populated areas—Egypt, Java, India and China. From the point of view of rate of growth of population another fourfold classification is made: (*a*) Low density and moderate growth—Northern America, Temperate South America, Australia and New Zealand and the Soviet Union; (*b*) Low density and rapid growth—parts of Africa, Central America, Tropical South America, South-West Asia and the Pacific islands; (*c*) High density and moderate growth —most of Europe and Japan and (*d*) High density and rapid growth—the Caribbean, Central South Asia, South-East Asia and East Asia (excluding Japan). The first two groups (areas of low density) occupy about 80 per cent of the world's land surface and contained in 1950 about 31 per cent of the world's population; in the remaining 20 per cent of the land area nearly 70 per cent of the population is concentrated. It is estimated that disparity in density of the four regions will be widening in the course of years. In the present densely populated and high growth areas which are economically backward the pressure of population tends to become more and more acute. Thus one half of the world's people live in monsoon Asia. Concentration in particular areas of this region is already outstandingly great. Future rapid increase in this area which seems assured, constitutes therefore a world problem of the first order.[1]

The rate of growth of population is directly determined by the birth rate and death rate. In a country which is socially and economically very backward,

[1]*The Future Growth of World Population*, U.N., 1958, pp. 27–29: also Spengler, J. J., ' The Population Problem : Dimensions, Potentialities, Limitations,' *American Economic Review, Papers and Proceedings*, May, 1956, p. 346.

the poverty of the people, ill health, illiteracy and lack of medical facilities account for high mortality and fertility rates. Hence rate of growth of population tends to be low because of a high turnover of population. Population growth rate remains at a fairly constant low level in the high income countries also. With industrialization, growth of towns, improvement in education, increased medical facilities and rise in the standard of life, birth rate tends to come down but a corresponding decline in death rate also follows it, so that rate of growth of population remains moderate. This is the stage reached by many of the advanced countries today. In the intermediate stage which normally covers the early period of industrialization, the position is different. Death rate comes down sharply but birth rate continues to be high with the result that the annual rate of growth of population rises appreciably. Many of the contemporary underdeveloped countries are in this stage. Data relating to the years 1954–56 show that the birth rate in most of the Asiatic countries was 40–50 per 1,000 population per year. This is true of some of the Latin American countries also. On the other hand, in some of the developed countries it is about 20 per 1,000 population. In France in the above-mentioned period, it was 18·6 and in the United Kingdom 15·7. In only one country of the East, Japan, was the rate lower than 20 (19·2). (*See* Table 13.)

Table 13

CRUDE BIRTH RATES IN DIFFERENT COUNTRIES 1954–56

(Per 1,000 Population Per Year)

Burma	44
Ceylon	42
China	37
Fedn. of Malaya	44·1
India	40–43
Indonesia	43
Japan	19·2
Pakistan	50
Philippines	49
Brazil	45
Chile	40
Mexico	46·5
Venezuela	46·9
Australia	22·5
France	18·6
U.K.	15·7
U.S.A.	24·8

SOURCE: *Economic Bulletin for Asia and the Far East*, June, 1959, p. 6.

The Gross Reproduction Rate " which indicates the average number of daughters borne by each woman during the reproductive period at prevailing age specific fertility rates " is above 2 for underdeveloped countries, while for countries like France, U.K. and U.S.A., it is well below 2. This rate is a more or less reliable indicator of population trends. In the three developed countries above-mentioned, it is observable that this rate tended to decline in the 1940s but has in recent years shown a significant rise. On the other hand, there is a sharp and steady decline of this rate in Japan from 2·30 in 1930 to 2·12 in 1940, 1·76 in 1950 and 1·08 in 1956. The birth rate in this country in 1945–49, was 30 per 1,000 population ; it came down to 24 in 1950–54 and to 18·5 in 1956.

A high level of fertility is connected with the marriage rate, age at marriage and other social and economic factors. In economically backward countries 97 to 99 per cent of women of 45–49 years are or have been married, while in the developed countries this proportion varies from 85 to 92 per cent. The age at marriage is also much lower in the countries of the former group. 82·5 per cent of the girls of the age 15–19 years, are married in India (1951). In Pakistan also (1951) the corresponding figure is very high (72·7 per cent), whereas in Australia it is 5·7 (1947), in France 3·9 (1954), in U.K. 4·4 (1951) and in the U.S.A. 17·4 (1950). According to the National Sample Survey of India (fourth round) the average age at marriage (1946–51) was only 14·6 years in rural areas and 16·4 years in urban areas. Social and cultural factors like the high social value attached to family in countries like China and India, early marriage, joint family system and limited urbanization, all these have helped to maintain high birth rates. On the other hand, customs like the one of forbidding widows to remarry and the poor health of women would have to some extent exerted a pull in the downward direction.

Mortality rate in underdeveloped countries has also remained quite high compared with advanced countries. For the years 1954–56 crude death rate per 1,000 population was 29 in Burma, 27–31 in India, 30 in Pakistan, 24 in Indonesia and 21 in the Philippines. Among the Latin American countries, it was about 13 in Chile and Mexico and 20 in Brazil and Venezuela. In the high income countries this rate is much lower—9 in Australia, 12·2 in France, 11·6 in U.K. and 9·3 in the U.S.A. It is however important to notice that while fertility rate shows no appreciable signs of declining, the death rate in many underdeveloped countries has come down quite sharply in recent years. Thus in China it declined from 20 before the Second World War to 11 in 1950 and 8 in 1956. In Ceylon the death rate in the late 1930s was around 25 per 1,000 but was only 13 in 1950 and 10 in 1956. The 1951 Census Report of India shows that population growth rate was very slow up to about 1921 because of high death rates due to plague, famine, cholera, malaria, etc. but since then, there has been a marked decrease in death rates as a result of improvement in public health and medical facilities.[2]

The relative trends in the fertility and mortality rates in underdeveloped

[2]The World Health Organization said on 17 September, 1962, in Geneva, that deaths from some of the most dreaded quarantinable diseases dropped spectacularly between 1950 and 1960. World deaths from small-pox dropped from 358,456 in 1950 to 59,950 in 1960, deaths from cholera dropped from 212,092 to 32,857 and from plague from 41,796 to only 443 in 1960. *The Hindu*, Madras, 19 September, 1962.

countries explain the acceleration in the rate of growth of population in recent years. Annual increase in world population remained at about 1·1 per cent between 1920 and 1950. But in the years 1950–56 this rate went up to 1·6 per cent. In the less developed countries of Asia, Africa and Latin America, the annual rate of growth has steadily risen over the years 1920–56. In the advanced countries however, we find a decline or slow rise in the period 1930–50 and an appreciable rise since 1950.

Table 14

RATE OF POPULATION GROWTH BY REGIONS 1920–56
(Per cent)

Region	Years			
	1920–30	1930–40	1940–50	1950–56
World Total	1·1	1·1	1·1	1·6
ECAFE Region	1·1	1·2	1·3	1·5
S.W. Asia	0·9	1·1	1·6	2·3
Africa	1·0	1·0	1·5	1·7
North America	1·4	0·8	1·4	1·7
Latin America	1·8	1·9	2·2	2·5
Europe	0·8	0·7	0·3	0·8
Oceania	1·1	1·0	1·7	2·3
U.S.S.R.	1·1	0·9		

SOURCE: *Demographic Year Book*, U.N., 1957, Table 2.

While in most of the underdeveloped countries there has been a marked increase in population in the last thirty years or so, there is among them considerable disparity in the rate of increase. In the years 1954–56 it exceeded 3 per cent per year in the case of Malaya and Singapore (in the former 3·2 per cent and in the latter 3·9 per cent); in India it was 1·2 to 1·3 per cent, Pakistan 2 per cent, Philippines 2·8 per cent, Burma 1·5 per cent and Ceylon 2·4 per cent. Among the Latin American countries, the rate of growth in these years was 3·3 per cent in Mexico, 2·8 per cent in Chile, 2·7 per cent in Venezuela and 2·5 per cent in Brazil. Among the high income countries, in France and U.K. the rate was 0·6 per cent and 0·4 per cent respectively, in U.S.A. 1·6 per cent, in Australia 2·4 per cent. More recent figures show further rise in the rate of increase in the low income countries. Thus in India the present annual rate of growth of population is found to exceed 2 per cent per year.[3]

On the basis of available data relating to trends in birth and death rates and gross reproduction rates estimates have been made about future trends in population by standard methods of population projection. Thus a recent

[3]Thus according to the Census of 1961 the rate of growth of population in the decade 1951–61 was 2·15 per cent per year.

United Nations Study makes the following projection of world population by the medium assumption.

Table 15

WORLD POPULATION 1900–2000

Year	Population in millions	Increase per cent
1900	1550	
1925	1907	23
1950	2497	31
1975	3828	53
2000	6267	64

SOURCE: *The Future Growth of World Population*, U.N., 1958.

The figures show a steady rise in the rate of growth of population over the years 1900–2000. In the first two quarters of the present century, world's population increased by 23 per cent and 31 per cent and it is estimated that in the third quarter the rise will be by 53 per cent and in the last quarter population is expected to go up by 64 per cent. Between 1900 and 2000 population would have increased by more than four times. Such projections into the future lead to some pessimistic conclusions. Thus Professor Villard observes that if world population continues to grow at the present rate of $1\frac{1}{2}$ per cent per annum the weight of population in A.D. 4250 will be equal to the estimated weight of the world.[4] And Professor Arthur Lewis cites the computation of statisticians that at the present rate of increase, world's population will reach 10,000 million in just over a century. While with technological improvements and augmentation of capital resources, production may increase possibly in proportion to growth of numbers, the total land area cannot be increased so that even if population increases at one per cent per year there will be only standing room for each inhabitant of the earth in 1120 years (if each person requires one square yard of standing room).[5] It is however not possible to make any guess about the earth's carrying capacity or the maximum number of individuals who can draw their sustenance from the earth's resources. Scientific discoveries would help in a more intensive use of the gifts of nature and increase the supply of things to meet human needs out of resources which are today unused, while no categoric assertion is possible in the matter of a continuance of the present rate of growth of population.

An important feature of the world's population trends in the present century is that the rate of growth is much sharper in the low income countries as compared with the richer countries. Thus as between the first and last quarters

[4]Villard, Henry H., 'Some Notes on Population and Living Levels,' *Review of Economics and Statistics*, Vol. XXXVII, 1955, p. 189.

[5]Lewis, Arthur, W., *Theory of Economic Growth*, George Allen and Unwin, London, 1955, p. 309.

of the century the rates of increase are 22 and 71 per cent for Africa, 57 and 95 per cent for Latin America and 19 and 75 per cent for Asia. In Europe including U.S.S.R., the increase is moderate with 19 and 26 per cent respectively, while in North America and Oceania there is a decline from 56 per cent and 57 per cent in the first quarter to 30 and 40 per cent in the last quarter. Correspondingly, there is a change in the percentage of world population contained in the different countries. Between 1950 and 2000 the percentage of population in Africa to total world population slightly increases from 8 to 8·2; in Latin America from 6·5 to 9·4; in Asia from 55·2 to 61·8, while in Europe including U.S.S.R. it declines from 23 to 15·1 and in Northern America from 6·7 to 5·0. Viewed in another way, for every 100 people in 1950 there will be more than 400 in the year A.D. 2000 in Central America and tropical South America, more than 300 in Northern and Southern Africa and South West Asia, nearly 300 in Asia, about 200 in temperate South America, Australia and New Zealand, 186 in Northern America, about 150 in Southern and Central Europe and 135 in Northern and Western Europe. Obviously this discrepancy in the rates of increase in the various regions of the world is due to differences in the birth and death rate trends. The world's birth rate is expected to fall from 39 per 1,000 in 1950 to 37 in 1960 and remain at that level in 1975. But death rate is expected to come down from 33 to 31 and 29. No great fall is expected in birth rate for most of the countries. Death rate however is expected to fall more significantly in the underdeveloped countries. Thus as between 1950 and 1975 death rate would rise slightly from 9 to 10 per thousand in the case of Europe, while in North America and U.S.S.R. it is expected to remain constant at 9 and 7 respectively. On the other hand, a marked decline is anticipated in respect of underdeveloped countries, from 33 to 29 in Africa, 19 to 12 in Latin America and 33 to 20 in Asia. As a result, the natural rate of growth of population between these two points of time will decline from 13 per thousand to 12 in North America, 11 to 8 in Europe and 18 to 15 in U.S.S.R., while in Africa it will rise from 14 to 17, in Latin America from 21 to 28 and in Asia from 13 to 23.

Recently, Coale and Hoover have estimated future population trends in India on three alternative assumptions:[6] firstly, as an upper limit to population growth, the assumption is made that fertility will remain unchanged from 1951 to 1986. The second assumption used as a lower limit is that fertility remains unchanged until 1956 and then declines to half its current value by 1981 but remains constant after that. The third assumption is that decline in fertility would set in only in 1966. At this date, a precipitous linear decline commences as in the second case and reaches one half the current level by 1981. The projected population of India according to these three assumptions is shown in Table 16.

The growth of population in India according to this projection exceeds

[6]Coale, Ansley J. and Edgar M. Hoover, *Population Growth and Economic Development in Low Income Countries*, Oxford, India, 1959.

8

Table 16

INDIA'S POPULATION 1951–1986
(In millions)

	1951	1956	1961	1966	1971	1976	1981	1986
First assumption	357	384	424	473	532	601	682	775
Second assumption	357	384	420	458	496	531	562	589
Third assumption	357	384	424	473	524	569	603	634

SOURCE: Coale, Ansley J. and Edgar M. Hoover, *Population Growth and Economic Development in Low Income Countries*, Oxford, India, 1959, pp. 34–37.

the rate of growth assumed in the Census Report of India 1951, and also by the Planning Commission in the Second Five-Year Plan. The final census figures of 1961, however, show that the present population of India is 439·235 million which represents a decennial increase of 21·5 per cent in the decade 1951–61. For the two decades 1901–21 the growth rate was only 5·35 per cent. In the next twenty years 1921–41, the growth rate was 26·79 per cent. It thus appears that even at the current decennial rate, India will possibly double her 1901 population before 1971.[7] The trends in birth and death rates per 1,000 population and the rate of growth of population according to the three assumptions of Coale and Hoover in the years 1951 to 1986 are shown in Table 17.

Table 17

BIRTH, DEATH AND POPULATION GROWTH RATE IN INDIA 1951–1986
UNDER THREE ASSUMPTIONS*

Year	Birth rate per 1,000 population			Death rate per 1,000 population			Growth rate per cent		
	(1)	(2)	(3)	(1)	(2)	(3)	(1)	(2)	(3)
1951	43·2	43·2	43·2	31·0	31·0	31·0	1·2	1·2	1·2
1956	42·8	42·8	42·8	25·6	25·6	25·6	1·7	1·7	1·7
1961	41·9	41·9	38·0	21·0	21·0	20·4	2·1	2·1	1·8
1966	40·9	40·9	33·8	18·1	18·1	17·1	2·3	2·3	1·7
1971	40·2	34·0	30·2	16·3	15·7	15·4	2·4	1·8	1·5
1976	40·0	28·2	26·8	15·2	14·2	14·4	2·5	1·4	1·2
1981	40·0	22·6	23·0	14·6	11·7	12·8	2·5	1·1	1·0
1986	40·0	24·0	23·4	14·3	13·9	14·3	2·6	1·0	0·9

SOURCE: Coale, A. J. and E. M. Hoover, *ibid.*, Table 6, p. 38.
*1. Fertility unchanged.   2. Fertility declining by 50 per cent from 1966.
3. Fertility declining by 50 per cent from 1956.

It may be expected that there would be a steady decline in death rates although birth rate may not show any change for some time. According to

[7]Report in *The Hindu*, Madras, 11 September, 1962.

the estimates made by Coale and Hoover, crude death rate which has already declined from about 31 per thousand in 1951 to 25·6 per thousand in 1956 will further fall to 21 by 1961 and to 15 or less by about 1975. On the assumption that birth rate would start declining about 1966 which appears more realistic, the rate of growth of population would reach the maximum of about 2·3 per cent per year about 1966 but decline steadily thereafter to 1 per cent by 1986. Also, the above-mentioned authorities estimate that the expectation of life at birth of males would improve from 31·5 years in 1951 to 51·5 years in 1986 and of females from 32·8 to 53·1 years.

In fine, the statistical data given in the foregoing few pages relating to the distribution of population and its trends in the low income countries bring into prominence some salient features which have a close bearing on their prospects of economic advancement. In the first place, there is a concentration of population in the world's underdeveloped regions. In view of capital shortage and the low land-labour ratio, the pressure of population in these regions is already great. Secondly, the composition of population in these areas is such that the contribution of population to production is lower than what it could be, even with the techniques and resources at present available because of the relatively smaller number of people in the productive age group as compared with the high income countries.[8] Thirdly, statistical evidences show that the pressure of population in the economically backward countries of the world would increase in the next few years and the disparity in the distribution of population between the developed and underdeveloped countries would widen. In short, the burden of population would increase particularly in those areas which are already weighed down by it, and which are least capable of bearing it.

POPULATION GROWTH AND ECONOMIC GROWTH

Population growth as an obstacle to economic growth has come in for close examination only in quite recent years. At the time of Malthus and Ricardo, the fear of an inadequate response of agricultural production to meet the requirements of a growing population was quite real and this explains why the problem of the disparity in the two rates of growth evoked so much discussion by economists and publicists. The revolutionizing of the methods of agriculture, the remarkable growth of industries and the expansion of world trade laid at rest the bogey of overpopulation. In the 19th century economic advancement in the Western countries was more rapid than the growth of population so that the problem came to be one of relative scarcity of labour supply. Hansen's thesis of economic maturity and the stress he laid on a high rate of growth of population as one of the conditions for economic expansion is illustrative of the complete shift in the nature of the population problem. The fact that the population growth rate which showed ominous signs of

[8] This aspect of the problem is explained in some detail on pp. 125–30.

rapid slackening in the 1930s has revived significantly in recent years in some of the Western industrial countries like the U.S.A. and U.K. has created the feeling that in advanced high income countries, population is not an extraneous factor which impinges on the economy by a too rapid or too slow rate of increase, but something which favourably responds to the requirements of the economy. It is therefore not surprising that in the writings of Western economists since Malthus' time the problem of population received scant attention.

Of late, increasing awareness of the growth problems of underdeveloped economies some of which are decidedly overpopulated, has revived interest in the study of population trends and their consequences on economic progress. But the fact that in their early days of industrialization, the advanced countries were never faced with the threat of population growth outrunning economic growth seems still to influence the views of some modern writers who are inclined to minimize the dangers of overpopulation or even extol the advantages of a rapid growth in the number of people. In an important article Prof. Arthur Lewis shows with the help of the model of an economy with a capitalist sector and a subsistence sector, how the former expands and thereby promotes over-all development of the economy by drawing more and more labour from the subsistence sector at a wage rate slightly higher than what prevails in the latter sector. The limits to the expansion of the capitalist sector in this model are set by the availability of cheap labour from the subsistence sector.[9] Colin Clark feels that the neo-Malthusian fear is very much exaggerated. In support of his view that the density per square mile of 400 in Pakistan and India need not cause any anxiety, he makes a comparison between Italy and India. In countries like Denmark and Italy where density of population is as high as in India, agricultural returns are much greater which according to him suggests the possibility of improving agricultural yield in India and Pakistan with the present density of population. However, he concludes that the underdeveloped countries can support a larger population only if there is free emigration; if there is no restriction on the imports of the products of underdeveloped countries into developed countries and if external assistance is forthcoming easily.[10] Opportunities opened up by international trade and emigration according to another writer have a mitigating effect on the population pressure of underdeveloped countries. And if underdeveloped countries can " find a place in the immensely complicated channels of world trade " they can have a good chance of successful economic development because it will enable them to obtain the productive agents and equipment in which they are lacking.[11] Hirschman holds the view that the pressure of population will be a

[9]Lewis, Arthur W., 'Economic Development with Unlimited Supplies of Labour,' *The Manchester School*, May, 1954, Reprinted in Agarwala, A. N. and S. P. Singh, *The Economics of Underdevelopment*, Oxford, India, 1958, pp. 400–49.

[10]Clark, Colin, 'Population Growth and Living Standards,' *International Labour Review*, August, 1953, Reprinted in Agarwala, A. N. and S. P. Singh, *ibid*, pp. 32–53.

stimulant to economic growth. According to him the activity undertaken by a community in resisting a decline in its standard of living when there is rapid growth in numbers causes an increase in its ability to control its environment and organize itself for development.[12] At the World Population Conference at Rome in 1954, Prof. Alfred Bonné mentioned that the recent trends of economic growth in a number of middle Eastern countries contradict the gloomy views on the development prospects of this area. This in his opinion points to the fact that the bogey of overpopulation should not be exaggerated. At the same Conference, the Russian economist, Ryabushkin, stressed the need for considering the dynamics of population along with the dynamics of production or the possibilities of increasing production when population grows. He pointed out that the neo-Malthusian use of India as an example of too rapid population growth is fallacious. Economic growth can keep up with and proceed more rapidly than population growth.

Many of these views are one-sided and, as will be shown presently, reveal a lack of understanding of the realities of the situation in the underdeveloped countries. It is sufficient at this stage to remark that if a rapid growth of population is to be taken full advantage of, some preconditions are required which are absolutely lacking in the underdeveloped countries. Thus population growth can be a stimulus to increased activity only if the social attitudes and values of the people are conducive to a favourable reaction. The will and preparedness to face and surmount economic difficulties and turn seeming obstacles into opportunities for advancement are characteristic of people in a progressive economy. And the absence of such qualities among people in a backward economy is precisely what keeps them backward. In the same way, the activity to make use of the possibilities opened up by international trade depends on the extent to which the country is already developed. The better organized an economy and the more industrialized it is, the greater is its competitive strength in the field of international trade and the greater its chances of benefiting by it.

Labour has to be combined with the other factors of production in any productive enterprise. So long as the size of population is small and the supply of labour is inadequate in relation to the availability of capital and land resources under a given state of technology, an increase in the number of people will be beneficial. Thus where land resources are abundant in relation to population, population growth assists rapid industrialization. In such a situation a rapid uptrend in population would increase per capita output through its favourable effects on economic organization and technical progress. Thus growth of population would lead to an extension of division of labour and increased specialization; would bring about economies of scale and

[11]Penrose, E. F., ' Malthus and the Underdeveloped Areas,' *Economic Journal*, June, 1957, pp. 238–39.

[12]Hirschman, Albert O., *The Strategy of Economic Development*, Yale, New Haven. 1958, p. 181.

would also foster technological progress and organizational improvements. It is therefore possible to conceive of a most advantageous size of population in a country, given the supply of other factors and the state of technology, which would bring about maximum returns per head of population. This concept of an optimum size of population of a country is an extension of the principle of optimum combination of factors of production in an industry which makes labour productivity reach its maximum. This is obviously a static concept but optimum as such cannot remain constant because of changes in technology which make it possible to increase the yield of labour as well as of other factors by new combinations. In view of the variability of the factors of production it would be advantageous to consider the benefit or otherwise of a given rate of change in population in relation to the other factors. In this sense, an optimum rate of growth of population may be defined as that rate of growth which is most conducive to the maintenance of a high level of employment and a rapid rate of economic progress (where economic progress is defined as an increase in output per capita). A more rapid growth of population in so far as it involves higher consumption would reduce the rate of savings and amount of capital investment and thereby slow down the rate of economic progress. On the other hand, a slower rate of growth of population might induce less capital investment and thus be less favourable to both the maintenance of a high level of employment and the rate of economic progress.[13] In so far as change in the population growth rate itself affects the rate of the investment and capital formation, it is difficult to say what an optimum rate of increase in population is in any country at any particular point of time. However, trends in per capita output, the degree of unemployment and underemployment, and the presence or absence of diminishing returns in the economy indicate broadly whether the growth of population in a period of time exceeds or falls short of the optimum rate. These indices in respect of India suggest that the present rate of growth of population in the country has definitely passed the optimum rate. Thus Kingsley Davis thinks that although in the three decades 1921–1951 a 44 per cent increase of population in India was attended with a similar increase in national product also, the latter could not have been totally due to population growth. With a lower rate of population growth increase in per capita output would have been greater. According to him population in India would have passed the optimum earlier than 1921 and growth of population since then contributed little to national product.[14] And Professor Villard feels that in underdeveloped countries such as India, it is quite possible that a drop in population growth all the way to zero would speed up the rate of increase of total income.[15]

[13]Barber, Clarence, L., ' Population Growth and the Demand for Capital,' *American Economic Review*, March, 1953, pp. 136–37.

[14]Davis, Kingsley, ' Social and Demographic Aspects of Economic Development in India,' Kuznets, S. *et al*, (Ed.), *Economic Growth*: *Brazil, India, Japan*, Duke, Durham, 1955, p. 278.

[15]Villard, Henry H., ' Some Notes on Population and Living Levels,' *Review of Economics*

POPULATION GROWTH AND CAPITAL FORMATION

In a primitive economy having little or no capital resources, output per head of labour depends on the quantity and nature of land available for each worker. As population grows, land and natural resources are more and more fully worked and in that very process capital is being formed. Hence productivity will not be affected adversely, but may actually be increased if the loss in the amount of natural resources per worker resulting from growth of population is offset by the increasing availability of capital resources. It is therefore possible to conceive of a certain stage in the course of the development of a nation when the land-labour ratio is such as to facilitate the laying of a foundation for capital structure. Therefore if for some reason or other, this opportunity for building up capital is missed, labour productivity should necessarily decline and capital accumulation becomes very difficult. Most of the developed and economically advanced countries of today are those that, as their population grew and the natural resources per head became less and less, were able to build up capital which, unlike land, is of an expanding nature and is therefore capable of taking care of an increasing population. And most of the underdeveloped countries are those which have missed this opportunity, so that in such countries the limited per capita availability of land is paralleled by the limited capital resources per head, with the result that their economies have got stagnated at a very low level of development. The crux of the problem thus appears to be the constancy of the factor land, which means that in the absence of a proportionate increase in capital, the productivity of labour must fall steadily—the faster the rate of growth of population the more rapid will be the decline in per capita output, and the more difficult becomes capital accumulation. Capital formation thus becomes synonymous with economic development. In reality, the fact that capital resources are meagre while labour resources are abundant, constitutes the major development problem in underdeveloped countries. This problem has two aspects. Firstly, since these economies have got stagnated at a low level and are overburdened with heavy population, the initial capital resources required to ensure growth are very large. Secondly, the combination of low capital with great density of population and high rate of growth makes it extremely difficult for these countries even to maintain the existing standards of the economy, let alone increasing the stock of capital. These two aspects of the problem may now be examined in some detail.

(a) Capital Requirements of Underdeveloped Economies

Capital is required not only for making investments in agriculture and industry so as to increase their returns but also on economic overheads like roads, railways, harbours and also for what is called human investment such as investments in schools, hospitals, sanitary installations, etc. all of which provide the necessary basis for economic development to take place. It is therefore difficult to make any correct estimate of the capital requirements of a country which is in the early stages of development. Uncertainty and inadequacy of statistics and differences in definition add to the difficulties. Apart from this, capital requirement per worker varies considerably in the same industries in different countries because of differences in technology, organization, etc. Thus capital per occupied person in the chemical industry ranges from £ 373 in Hungary (1937) to £ 5,430 in the U.S. (1939). For electric light and power, it ranges from £ 1,740 in India (1938–39) to £ 6,250 in Denmark (1928). Even in the textile industry which is more homogeneous it ranges from £ 123 in Brazil (1945) to £ 813 in Canada (1936). As for variations in different industries in the same country, it is seen that in the U.S.A. capital per occupied person ranges from £ 435 in textiles and clothing to £ 5,430 in chemicals. For the average of all manufacturing industries it ranges from £ 192 in Hungary (1937) to £ 1,250 in the U.S.A.[16] Furthermore, it is not proper to calculate capital needs in static terms. In the initial stages of industrialization it will be difficult to utilize all the capital resources that may be available unless other production factors have also been utilized. In the process of economic growth new combinations of the factors and changes in organization would be possible which would affect the capital requirements for particular enterprises.

In a growing economy the needs of capital increase continuously overtime because of the growth of population and because of the need for ensuring an increase in the rate of growth of national income. On this ground, economists make a distinction between 'demographic' investments and 'economic' investments; the first relates to the investment required to maintain a constant living standard as population grows, and the second relates to investments for bringing about a rate of growth of national income higher than the rate of growth of population so that per capita income rises and a higher standard of living is attained. Obviously, the first is determined by the rate of growth of population while the second has to be related not only to increase in population, but also to the required rate of increase in per capita income. In an underdeveloped country in which population is growing rapidly and per capita income is low, the demographic rate of investment alone would absorb the savings available in the economy. To find the capital necessary in order to support a population growing at the rate of 1 per cent per year at existing levels of per capita income the required savings are estimated at 2 to 5 per cent of the national income. Hence if population increases at the rate of 2·5 per cent per year which is common in many underdeveloped countries,

[16]Mandelbaum, K., *Industrialization of Backward Areas*, Oxford Institute of Statistics, p. 59; and Clark, Colin, *Conditions of Economic Progress*, Macmillan, London, 3rd Edn., 1957, pp. 582–83. Quoted in *Economic Bulletin for Asia and the Far East*, June, 1959, p. 34 f.n.

5 to 12·5 per cent of national income would be absorbed by demographic investments alone with no rise in living standard.[17]

In view of the above-mentioned difficulties, estimates which have been made about capital requirements of underdeveloped countries should be considered as only rough indications of the magnitudes involved. One arbitrary method is to make use of the value of capital available per worker in developed countries as a measure to calculate the capital requirement of workers in similar industries in the less developed countries. Thus in 1951 Spengler postulated $ 1,500 as the capital required per worker for underdeveloped countries. The U.N. experts in the same year estimated the amount at $ 2,500.[18] On the basis of the 1954 Census of Manufactures in India the total fixed and working capital per worker in 29 industries was found to average Rs. 5,100 or $ 1,100. According to the Six-Year Programme of Investment of Ceylon (1954–55 to 1959–60) the capital required per worker directly engaged in the work indicated in the programme equals about Rs. 11,500 or $ 2,415. In a hypothetical development programme for Ceylon, Joan Robinson estimated a capital requirement of Rs. 13,000 million so as to increase employment by 1·5 million persons over 10 years. This amounts to Rs. 8,700 or $ 1,800 per worker.[19] The Second Five-Year Plan of India (1951–52 to 1955–56) envisaged a total investment of Rs. 62,000 million in the public and private sectors combined, over the five years, which it was hoped would provide additional employment to about 8 million people. This gives an investment of Rs. 7,750 or $ 1,600 per additional worker. Similar calculations for other countries based on the estimates in the National Development Programmes work out to $ 1,730 in the case of Philippines, $ 5,500 for China and $ 6,000 for Japan. The figure is high in China because of the emphasis on heavy industry and the exclusion of self-employed workers; and in Japan the high figure of $ 6,000 is indicative of the relatively high standards of industrialization and economic advancement of the country. As a rough approximation therefore $ 1,500 may be taken as the amount of capital per additional worker required for a more balanced development in Asian countries other than Japan.[20] Since economic development aims at and involves the employment of the additional labour supply resulting from growth of population, the total investment requirements may be calculated by multiplying the net annual increase in the labour force by the amount required per head. It is estimated that in the ECAFE region excluding Japan, the annual increase in labour force amounts to about 9 million and hence the annual capital requirements of the region would be of the order of $ 13,500 million or 14 per cent of the aggregate national income of these countries. Since this works out to about $ 10 per head of the total population, the requirements in India will

[17] *The Determinants and Consequences of Population Trends*, U.N., 1953, p. 278.

[18] *Measures for the Economic Development of Underdeveloped Countries*, U.N., 1951, p. 77.

[19] *Economic Bulletin for Asia and the Far East*, U.N., June, 1959, p. 34.

[20] *Ibid.*, p. 35.

be about 4,000 million dollars or 2,000 crores rupees.

Another method of estimating capital requirements is based on the relationship between increase in capital and increase in income. Since investment of a certain amount per year results in an increment of income, it is possible to make use of the ratio of these two as a guide to determine what rate of investment would be needed to ensure a desired rate of growth of income. Thus if R is this ratio, p the rate of increase in population and y the desired rate of increase in per capita income, the required rate of capital investment K, per year as a proportion of national income may be expressed in the form

$$K=R(p+y).$$

Thus if $R=3:1$, $p=1$ per cent and $y=0$, so that per capita income would be constant then K or investment required is 3 per cent of national income. But if per capita income is to increase at 1 per cent per annum, the investment required is 6 per cent of national income. The application of this method for purposes of estimating capital requirements can be illustrated as follows: excluding Japan the ECAFE region had in 1956 a total population of 1,370 million increasing at 1·7 per cent a year. If an investment of 3 per cent of national income leads to an increase in income of 1 per cent and if per capita income is assumed to be $ 65 in this region, in order to increase per capita income by 3 per cent per year, the capital required annually would be 14·1 per cent of national income or $ 12,700 million. It is obvious that if the yield of a unit of investment is greater than what is assumed above, a smaller amount of investment would be sufficient to get the same rate of increase in per capita income.[21]

Making use of this principle some writers have attempted to calculate the capital requirements of underdeveloped countries on certain assumptions. Thus H. W. Singer takes the hypothetical case of an underdeveloped community of 1,000 members of whom 70 per cent are engaged in agriculture and 30 per cent in the non-agricultural sector. The per capita income of the community is $ 100 with $ 57 per head of the 700 people in agriculture and $ 200 per head of the people in the non-agricultural sector. Annual rate of growth of population is assumed to be 1·25 per cent. Economic development involves the transfer of the entire net addition to the population in the agricultural sector to the non-agricultural sector. This would be 8·75 persons per year. If to this is added the natural increase in the latter sector of 3·75 persons, additional employment to be found in the non-agricultural sector would be for 12·5 persons. Capital required for equipping each of the people transferred from the agricultural sector at $ 1,600 per head would be $ 14,000 annually (8·75 × 1,600 = 14,000). On the assumption of a capital-income ratio of 6 : 1 for this investment, the annual increase in income from this source would be $ 2,333. In the agricultural sector an increase in productivity of 3 per cent annually is needed to provide a moderate rise in consumption for the whole

[21]*Economic Bulletin for Asia and the Far East*, U.N., June, 1959, pp. 39-40.

community. This means an increase in income of $ 1,200 per year from this sector. Assuming for this sector a capital-income ratio of 4 : 1, investment required is $ 4,800. Lastly, to provide capital for the natural increase in the non-agricultural sector of 3·75 persons per year so that they would produce $ 200 per head annually, investment required is $ 800 per head on the assumption of a capital-income ratio of 4 : 1. Total investment on this account is therefore $ 3,000. The aggregate cost of the programme will then be $ 21,800 (i.e. 14,000+4,800+3,000) and the increase in national income will be $ 4,283 (i.e. 2,333+1,200+750) which gives an annual rate of increase in income of 4·3 per cent (i.e. 4,283/100,000) and a per capita rise in income of 3 per cent. The investment of $ 21,800 represents 22 per cent of the assumed national income of $ 100,000. Since in countries with a per capita income as low as $ 100, the proportion of savings cannot be more than 6 per cent, it means that domestic resources available will be only $ 6,000 leaving a gap of $ 15,800 or 70 per cent. It also means that if investment is limited to the existing rate of savings of 6 per cent of national income and the population growth rate is 1·25 per cent per year, no economic development is possible.[22]

A similar calculation has been made by Spengler about capital requirements for developing an underdeveloped community in a period of 25 years. This involves reducing the number of agricultural workers, transferring them to the industrial sector, providing necessary capital equipment for all new workers and for those transferred from agriculture and raising the equipment of all other workers. On the basis of different assumptions he found that in order to raise per capita income by 3·2 per cent per year and from $ 100 to $ 220 in 25 years, the capital required would be 13·8 per cent of national income if population increased at 1 per cent per year and 19·5 per cent if population increased at 2 per cent annually. He concludes that even the 13·8 per cent investment rate cannot be reached unless there is substantial foreign investment.

These estimates rough as they are, indicate the extent to which resources are to be increased in underdeveloped countries either from domestic savings or from foreign assistance in order to reach that level of capital formation which would ensure a fairly high rate of income growth. A United Nations study on the relationship between population changes and economic and social conditions underlines the need for an inflow of a large volume of foreign capital into low income countries if capital formation in them is to make any progress. Assuming that the capital per worker in Asia should amount to $ 1,000 to $ 2,000, the total needs can be estimated to be in the range of $ 425,000 to $ 850,000 million, an amount from one and a half to three times in excess of the national income of the U.S.A. Eugene Staley in his *World*

[22]Singer, H. W., ' The Mechanics of Economic Development,' *The Indian Economic Review*, August, 1952, Reprinted in Agarwala, A. N. and S. P. Singh, (eds.), *The Economics of Under-development*, Oxford, India, 1958, pp. 381–99.

Economic Development notes that in the course of four decades $ 270,000 million would be required to raise the standard of living in the major part of Asia to the level reached in Japan in the late 1930s.[23] Making an allowance for the fall in the purchasing power of the dollar since Staley wrote, the amount should be equivalent to $ 540,000 million at current value of the dollar.

(b) Population Growth as an Obstacle to Capital Formation

While capital requirements are of this large order, the structure of population in underdeveloped countries is such that it seriously hampers capital formation. Broadly speaking, the contribution of a growing population to economic growth consists in what it adds to production minus what it takes away from the national product in the form of consumption. In overpopulated, low income countries like India, the savings margin is low because what is contributed by population to the national product is small in relation to the size of population; on the other hand what is absorbed by way of consumption is high in relation to the volume of national product. The extent to which population can help in an increase in output depends upon: (*i*) the amount of income producing equipment per worker and the state of technology; (*ii*) the qualitative composition of the labour force and (*iii*) the size of the labour force. It is observed that in advanced industrial countries if an investment of 10 per cent of national income increases national product by about 2·5 per cent, and population and labour force increase by 1 per cent per year, the contribution of capital to income increase would be 0·6 to 0·75 per cent, increase in labour force would account for 0·7 per cent and technical progress for 1 per cent. In non-industrial countries the very low capital equipment per worker is both the cause and effect of low productivity of labour. The inadequacy of reproducible resources affects labour productivity and per capita earnings. Low income accounts for low savings which in turn makes it difficult or impossible to furnish labour with adequate capital equipment. Inadequate capital resources and low standards of education account for the slow development of technology. Apart from these, productivity of labour remains much lower than that in advanced countries because of its poor quality. According to Spengler, the qualitative composition of the labour force depends on its genetical composition, i.e. inherited mental and physical characteristics which affect its capacity to develop and exercise skills; its health composition which determines the number of people who can be enrolled in the labour force and their capacity and effort in work; and its educational composition the degree of which influences the character, discipline, alertness and diligence of the worker.[24] The qualitative composition of the labour force in under-

[23]Staley, Eugene, *World Economic Development*, International Labour Office, Montreal, 1944, Ch. 4.

[24]Spengler, Joseph J., *Economic Development: Principles and Patterns*, Williamson, Harold F., and John A. Buttrick, (eds.), Prentice Hall, New York, 1954, pp. 76–78.

developed countries is a definite limiting factor in economic progress. The low standard of health, lack of mobility of labour and the scarcity of technical skill reduce the level of efficiency, keep down productivity and make the economic contribution of the total labour force much less than what limitations in capital equipment per worker alone would warrant. It has been pointed out that if the age composition of population and its state of health in underdeveloped countries improve to the level in developed countries, per capita income may rise by 20 to 30 per cent, other circumstances remaining unchanged.[25]

Given the size of population, the strength of the labour force depends on the age composition of the population and on a social factor, namely, whether custom permits the free entry of women into the labour force or confines them to domestic work. In India according to the Census of 1951, 58·6 per cent of the population was aged 15–64; but the labour force forms only 40 per cent; the bulk of the remaining 18 per cent are of course women. The age structure of the population affects the ratio of labour force to total population, its flexibility and mobility as well as its skill and efficiency. Population between the ages 15 and 59 constitutes the productive age group. While the proportion of people between these ages is 61 per cent of the total in Northern America and 62 per cent in Europe, it is only 55 per cent in Asia. In countries where population growth rate remains constant because of high mortality and high fertility rates, this ratio of the economically active to total population tends to remain lower than in countries where the constancy in the rate of growth of population is due to low mortality and low fertility rates. Also, when population growth rate rises because of fall in mortality rate while fertility rate remains high, this ratio falls appreciably. Thus in India it is estimated that the ratio of population in the age group 15–59 which was 56·1 per cent in 1955 would fall to 53·4 per cent in 1970 and to 52·3 per cent in 1980.[26] The future estimated trend of this ratio in the different regions of the world is shown in Table 18.

It is obvious that when in one country the number of people in the working age group is larger than in another, there is a favourable ratio of producers to consumers in the former. In the latter, savings are found to be lower not only because the number of producers is relatively smaller but also because the smaller productive group has to satisfy its own consumption needs and those of its dependants before it can put by anything for purposes of investment. As between two countries with the same population and same labour productivity, but with difference in age composition, the one with the higher percentage of workers can provide not only a larger aggregate savings, but also a higher percentage of savings in relation to income. Assuming a community with a population of 1,000, minimum consumption per capita of $ 50,

[25]Spengler, Joseph J., 'The Population Obstacle to Economic Betterment,' *American Economic Review, Papers and Proceedings*, May, 1951, p. 344.

[26]*Economic Bulletin for Asia and the Far East*, U.N., June, 1959, p. 22, Table 20.

ECONOMICS OF DEVELOPMENT

Table 18

ESTIMATED PROPORTION OF POPULATION IN THE AGE GROUP 15-59

(As a percentage of total population)

Continent	1950	1975
World	56	54
Africa	54	54
North America	61	56
Latin America	54	52
Asia	55	54
Europe	62	59
Oceania	59	55
U.S.S.R.	59	59

SOURCE: *Future Growth of World Population*, U.N., 1958.

production per worker of $ 200 and marginal propensity to consume of 70 per cent, it would be found that if 30 per cent of the population are working, savings would be 5 per cent of its income, but with 40 per cent of its population working, the savings rate would be 11·2 per cent. The investment of these savings and the resulting increase in income would widen the disparity in the rate of savings in the process of time. Thus in the above model assuming that an investment of 3 per cent of income increases income by 1 per cent, if 30 per cent of the population are working, per capita income would rise to $ 203·3 in the next income period and savings to 5·4 per cent whereas if 40 per cent of the population are working, the rise in income will be $ 207·5 and savings 11·9 per cent of the total income of the community.[27]

AGE COMPOSITION AND CONSUMPTION REQUIREMENTS

This adverse effect of the age composition of population on savings and capital formation springs from the fact that it raises the consumption requirements in the economy and increases the dependency load of the productive workers. The proportion of income spent on the consumption of food and other necessary articles is inversely related to the size of income. This is true of individuals and families as well as of nations. In low income countries there is a tendency for marginal propensity to consume to rise with increase in per capita incomes. Normally, people cling to existing patterns of consumption when income is reduced but when there is a rise in incomes it quite often happens that the proportion of expenditure is increased because of the shift in demand from inferior to superior goods and because of demand for a wider variety of goods. The demonstration effect following from rise in incomes and standard of life of the people, and change in consumption habits in consequence of the

[27] *Economic Bulletin for Asia and the Far East*, U.N., June, 1959, p. 41.

movement from rural to urban areas are reflected in increasing expenditure on the consumption of luxury and quasi-luxury commodities. The age composition of the population also has much to do with the levels of consumption. A country with a rapidly growing population is typically ' young ' that is to say, there will be a larger proportion of population in the lower age groups than in a country where population growth rate is stationary. And a population which is relatively young will spend a larger share of its income on food than an older population with the same per capita income. In other words, increase in the number of people in the lower age groups distorts the proportion of total population against production and in favour of consumption. On the other hand, the view has sometimes been put forward that an increase in the proportion of aged people although they are dependants on the productive age group, does not counteract, but supplements or reinforces the tendency towards increased savings. This, however, is a hypothesis and statistical information in support of it is not complete.[28]

While the demand for basic consumption goods is high in underdeveloped countries, the means to satisfy this demand are scarce. The supply of domestic food production indicates roughly the carrying capacity of a country in respect of population. Data relating to the year 1955–56 show that the low income countries are decidedly in a disadvantageous position in this respect. The United States and Canada have 6·8 per cent of the world's population but produce 18·3 per cent of the total agricultural output of the world. The corresponding figures for Australia and New Zealand are 0·4 and 2·6 per cent and for Western Europe 11·0 and 14·6 per cent respectively. In contrast, the Far East and Western Asia support 54·7 per cent of the world's population with 34·3 per cent of the world's agricultural production. India which was a net exporter of food until about 1920 has now become a net importer of food. It is significant to note that the rate of growth of population in India has accelerated since that date. The regular import of about 3 million tons of food annually has taken up a considerable amount of the country's foreign exchange earnings which otherwise could have been utilized for the purchasing of much needed capital goods from foreign countries. The need for making the country self sufficient in the matter of food is well realized, but increases in food production have not been commensurate with the efforts taken or the expenditure incurred. And the problem is likely to become more serious in the near future. In a country like India the average income elasticity of demand for food is 0·7 or 0·8 which is high in comparison with economically advanced countries. Increasing population, urbanization and rise in per capita incomes would help to maintain if not aggravate the pressure on the food front. Assuming a constant fertility rate and an annual income increase of 1 per cent, it is estimated that by the year 1980 the population of India would increase by 78 per cent and food demand by 118 per cent. If a 3 per cent income increase per year is assumed, the demand for food would go up by

[28]*Determinants and Consequences of Population Trends*, U.N., 1953, p. 218.

238 per cent.[29] India's food problem is therefore, as the Planning Commission points out, not a temporary disequilibrium between supply and demand but a manifestation of the continually growing pressure of population on food supply.[30]

From the point of view of economic growth, " a high food drain economy " like India faces another difficulty which arises from the concentration of labour on agriculture, the income generating capacity of which is limited as compared with manufacturing industry. Since consumption requirements are great in underdeveloped countries and at the same time labour productivity is low, a larger proportion of the population is devoted to the production of food and agricultural commodities than in advanced economies. But then the very fact that a large part of the material and labour resources of a country is devoted to the production of food and other agricultural products indicates that the economy can support proportionately a smaller population than another where a larger proportion of the income is spent on non-food and non-agricultural goods.

Over-population and the increase in the proportion of people in the non-working age groups add to the drain on the resources of the economy in another manner. A rapidly growing population involves also increased spendings on social items which do not add to the physical capital assets of the country. Expenditure on house construction, on public health and education, undoubtedly adds to the productivity of the economy by improving the health, skill and quality of the labour force but it does not add directly to the stock of reproducible resources. It is true that in advanced countries the proportion of expenditure on these items is much greater than in low income countries, but the point to note here is, that the latter have to divert for this purpose a larger proportion of their meagre investible resources, which can be otherwise utilized for capital formation in the narrower sense of the term. Besides, the long leeway which the underdeveloped countries have to make in respect of education and social welfare facilities, and the fact that they have to set apart large funds for these purposes even when they are just making a start in industrialization programmes, have made the problem one of much larger dimensions than in advanced economies. An idea of the magnitude of the outlays on this account in India can be had from the estimate made by Coale and Hoover.[31] The Government of India have a programme of 100 per cent coverage of all persons in the age group 6–13 in an eight year basic education system by 1981. The population in this age group is estimated to rise to 43 million in 1981 and 67 million in 1986 and the expenditure on compulsory education will amount to Rs. 20 to 25 billion. As for housing, the urban

[29]*Economic Bulletin for Asia and the Far East*, U.N., June, 1959, p. 30, Table 26.
[30]*The First Five-Year Plan* 1951, Planning Commission, Government of India, New Delhi, pp. 78–81.
[31]Coale, Ansley J., and Edgar M. Hoover, *Population Growth and Economic Development in Low Income Countries*, Oxford, India, 1959, pp. 248–54.

population is estimated to rise from 18·6 per cent to over 30 per cent of total population between 1956 and 1986 and the expenditure on housing which this trend would necessitate would be of the order of Rs. 40·7 billion in the thirty years 1956–1986. According to these writers, even under conservative assumptions, the expenditure on education and housing would increase to Rs. 6 billion per annum in the five-year period 1981–86, i.e. more than 2 per cent of national income, two and a half times as great as that of 1956 and perhaps 15 to 20 per cent of total investment.

AGE COMPOSITION AND DEPENDENCY LOAD

The existence of a relatively larger proportion of population in the lower age group and a smaller proportion in the economically effective group, 15–59 years, in underdeveloped countries as compared with developed countries constitutes a drag on the productive effort of the economy. Persons below the age of 15 and above 60 do not normally contribute to production but are dependent on the rest of the population. The proportion of people below 15 is higher in underdeveloped countries than in developed countries while the position is reversed in respect of population above the age of 60. Thus it is estimated that in Great Britain population above 65 years of age will rise from 11 per cent of the total in 1952 to about 16 per cent in 1982. In 1952 in that country the ratio of people in the productive age group (15–65) to those above 65 was 6 : 1 but it will decline to 4 : 1 by 1982. Since the proportion of persons below the age of 15 is likely to remain constant in that country the number of producers in relation to the number of consumers would decline by 2·9 per cent which is expected to reduce living standards by 3 to 4 per cent.[32] However, the addition to dependency load caused by an aging population is negligible compared with that caused by an increase in the number of persons below 15 years for the simple reason that the total number in this group will be much larger while the expenses incurred per head of children is not likely to be much lower than on aged peoples. The dependency load is calculated with reference to the contribution to production of a population as compared with its consumption. Thus if we count the consumption needs of an adult of productive age as one, that of a child as one-third and an aged person as one-half, we find that in an underdeveloped country, the population of which on the average is composed of 42 per cent children, 3 per cent aged and 55 per cent adults of productive age, there is a ratio of 128 consumer equivalents per 100 adults of productive age. In an advanced country where the age composition is more favourable to production (23 per cent children, 67 per cent adults and 10 per cent aged) the corresponding ratio is 119 per 100.[33] Looked at in another way, while in the industrialized countries in West Europe there are two dependents for every three workers, in most of the countries of

[32]Hopkins, W. A. B., 'The Economics of an Aging Population,' *Lloyds Bank Review*, January, 1953, p. 33.

9

Asia, the ratio is 3 : 4. Roughly then, the age composition of population in underdeveloped countries may be said to be one-sixth less favourable than in a high income country like the U.S.A.[34] In a country like India the fact that even people of working age are less fully employed than in the developed countries adds to the burden. The combined effect of a larger proportion of children to adults and the existence of underemployment more than offsets the fact that the proportion of the people in the highest age group, 65 and above, (who are also dependants) is greater in advanced than in underdeveloped countries. It appears that there is a progressive worsening of the situation in this respect. In the East Asian underdeveloped countries there has been a tendency for the average age of population to decline, which means that the proportion of population in the working age group will decrease. The increase in labour supply will therefore be slower than increase in population or in other words consumption would rise faster than production.

From what has been stated above it may be seen that a large part of the resources of underdeveloped countries is diverted from the formation of capital to the formation of population. But since mortality rate among children in low income countries is much higher than in industrial countries it means not only a diversion of resources but a wastage of resources as well. It has been estimated that the cost of maintaining children who die before reaching the age of 15 is 3 per cent of the national income in India as against 0·1 per cent in the case of England. If this proportion of national income were devoted to investment, capital formation would rise by nearly 50 per cent.[35] But though the proportion of total national income spent on this group is large, yet in view of the low per capita income, the expenditure per head of children is meagre and as such children are very much handicapped in the matter of preparation for life as compared with children in advanced countries. What is worse, the dependency load represented by the large proportion of children is sought to be relieved by employing them at an early age and making them contribute what little they can to the family income. As a result, there is underemployment in the economy as a whole and lower per capita output. A more serious social and economic consequence following from this fact is that the premature employment of young persons by denying them opportunities to build up their mental and physical equipment amounts to wasteful exploitation of the oncoming generation of workers. The U.N. study on population makes the telling remark: " The position is rather like that of peasants compelled by hunger to harvest their wheat every year before it has ripened ".[36]

[33]*Determinants and Consequences of Population Trends*, U.N., 1953, p. 265 f.n.
[34]Spengler, J. J., ' The Population Obstacle to Economic Betterment,' *American Economic Review, Papers and Proceedings*, May, 1951, pp. 343–54.
[35]Villard, Henry H., *Economic Development*, Rinehart, New York, 1959, p. 196.
[36]*Determinants and Consequences of Population Trends*, U.N., 1953, p. 265.

POPULATION GROWTH AND UNEMPLOYMENT

The demographic problem of many of the underdeveloped countries is not only an excess of population in relation to the existing land and capital resources but also one of a high rate of growth of numbers coming on top of it. In view of the difficulties mentioned above in increasing reproducible resources of the economy, population pressure has manifested itself in the form of a growing volume of unemployment, both overt and disguised. Paradoxically enough, unemployment has tended to increase along with an increase in national incomes. In India according to the National Sample Survey conducted towards the end of 1953, total urban unemployment in the country at the time was of the order of five million. The total labour force constituted about 35 per cent of the population comprising of a little more than 32 per cent gainfully employed and a little less than 3 per cent unemployed. Less than three-fourths among the gainfully employed persons were fully employed and the rest more than one-fourth underemployed to various degrees. If seriously underemployed persons may be considered as virtually unemployed, we get 5·8 per cent of the population either unemployed or badly under-employed. It is estimated that over the years covered by the First and Second Five-Year Plans, additional employment to the extent of three million was provided in the agricultural sector and twelve million in the non-agricultural sector. On the basis of the estimated annual increase in population it is calculated that the total labour force by 1981 would rise to 238·3 million against 139·6 million in 1951, i.e. an addition to the labour force by about 3·3 million a year. The increase in total labour force that would occur in the thirty years 1951 to 1981 is twice the present population of the United Kingdom or more than one and a half times the total number of currently employed people in the U.S.A. The backlog of unemployment at the end of the Second Plan period is estimated at about 8 million. If this is added to the expected natural increase in labour force it would mean that the additional employment that will have to be created in the period 1951–1981 would be 106·8 million. Dr. V. K. R. V. Rao is of the opinion that of this 107 million people, 67 million will have to be absorbed in industries and 40 million in agriculture.[37]

Unemployment of this magnitude in an underdeveloped country is of a structural kind and differs from unemployment in advanced industrial countries. While in the latter, deficiency in effective demand is the main cause of unemployment, in the former, unemployment and disguised unemployment are brought about by inadequacy of complementary resources to labour. By definition, underdeveloped countries are those which lack adequate capital and whose incomes are so low that annual savings and investment constitute a much smaller proportion of national income than in advanced countries.

[37]Rao, V. K. R. V., ' Population Growth and its Relation to Employment in India ' in *India's Population*, Ed. by Agarwala, S. N., Asia Publishing House, Bombay, 1960, p. 98.

Added to this, is the significant fact that in most countries of this category, population is excessive and tends to grow at a faster rate than in economically well developed countries. As a result, when people of these countries have become conscious of the need for rapid economic development and are prepared to make the effort to attain this end, they find themselves face to face even at the very outset, with large numbers of unemployed. This backlog of unemployment is due by and large to historical causes. It is conceivable that in India at a time when her indigenous industries flourished and when the death rate was as high as the birth rate, there was a proper adjustment between capital formation and population growth. The decay of these industries in the face of foreign competition seriously hampered domestic capital formation while the decline in the death rate with the establishment of peace and order and the provision of better medical and health facilities, favoured an inconveniently high rate of population growth.

In order to provide full employment when labour supply is increasing a proportionate increase in the stock of reproducible resources is necessary. This however is possible only if per capita income is high enough to have a sufficient margin between production and consumption. But increase in income is dependent in turn on the rate of investment or capital formation. The existence of unemployment of the Marxian type and also of underemployment and disguised unemployment in underdeveloped countries should be explained in terms of inadequacy of capital and income. In other words, the full employment growth rate of income or the rate at which income should grow in order to build up annually an amount of capital necessary to keep labour fully employed, is greater than what it actually is. But at the same time since the existing stock of capital is scarce in relation to labour supply, capital would be fully utilized but the per capita output of labour would be small. This means that any further addition to capital and income can be effected only with greater and greater strain. At the same time, growing labour supply pushes up the rate at which income *should be* increasing in order to ensure full employment of labour. Thus the difference between full employment growth rate of income and the actual growth rate becomes wider and wider. The growing inadequacy of capital and income results in increasing unemployment of labour. In this manner the inadequacy of capital not only causes unemployment, but also causes unemployment to grow. Since to begin with there is a backlog of unemployment and any moderate increase in the rate of investment will not absorb this idle labour, and since population is steadily increasing, it follows that unless the annual rate of investment increases at a much faster rate than population growth, the scarcity of capital in relation to labour will become more and more acute. But in a low income country in the early stages of development it is well nigh impossible for the economy—if it is left to its own resources—to raise the rate of investment to the required high level.

COMPARISON WITH DEVELOPED COUNTRIES

The foregoing analysis makes it clear that population pressure constitutes the major obstacle to economic growth in the underdeveloped countries of today. Hence the arguments that density of population in the underdeveloped countries is not so high as in some industrial countries and that the latter benefited by a rapid increase in population in their early stages of development and that therefore the problem of overpopulation in underdeveloped countries is much exaggerated, are quite unconvincing. It is true that in recent years a few countries like Argentina, Australia, Canada and the Union of South Africa have developed rapidly because of the growth of population.[38] Among underdeveloped countries, Brazil, Burma and the Gold Coast in Africa are sparsely populated, with abundant natural resources and their growth potential is great. Population per square mile is 17 in Brazil, 49 in the Gold Coast and 73 in Burma. Increase in numbers in these countries is likely to produce certain advantageous results made much of by writers like Sauvy, Toynbee and Dupreel, such as better organization and technological advancement, social mobility, greater frequency of personal contacts, intellectual stimuli and changes in values conducive to material advancement. But even here, while increase in population is on the whole beneficial, differences in the rate of growth of population are likely to have an effect on the rate of growth of the economy. At present, population in the Gold Coast and Burma is estimated to increase at the rate of 1·5 per cent and 1·2 per cent per annum respectively, whereas in Brazil it is between 2·2 per cent and 2·6 per cent, so that despite her vast natural resources, it appears that in the last mentioned country, the rate of economic advancement would have been greater still, had population increased less rapidly.[39]

But most of the underdeveloped countries of the world have not only an excess of population but are also experiencing a rise in the rate of increase in numbers. Many of these countries have recently emerged from a colonial status and have awakened to the need for quickly building up their economies. They are aware of their potentialities and are proceeding ahead with ambitious schemes of planned economic development. But precisely at this eventful time of their economic history there has been a significant uptrend in population which threatens to be a formidable drag on their attempts at expansion. The more important countries falling in this category are Egypt with a population density per square mile of 1,500, Java with 1,009, India with 293 and China with 156. The annual percentage rate of increase is about 2 or exceeds 2 in these countries. The cause of this significant rise in the growth of population is well-known—the rapid fall in death rate against a constant or even increasing

[38]*Processes and Problems of Industrialisation in Underdeveloped Countries*, U.N., 1953, pp. 15–18.
[39]*World Population and Resources*, (PEP, 1955), pp. 141–48.

birth rate. The phenomenal decline in death rate in many of the under-developed countries of the world in recent years has been attributed to the application of modern medical and sanitary knowledge at a very low cost to control some widespread diseases on a mass basis. In the decade 1940–50 death rate declined in Puerto Rico by 46 per cent,[40] in Formosa by 43 per cent and in Jamaica by 23 per cent. In the same period in Ceylon death rate per 1,000 a year declined from 21·0 to 12·6. In a remarkably short time of two or three years, the death rate in this country fell to the low levels attained in Western countries. But since birth rate has not shown any signs of decline, the annual rate of growth of population has gone up so high as 2·7 per cent. In Taiwan under Japanese administration crude death rate declined from 33·4 per 1,000 on the average in the years 1906–1910 to 18·5 in the years 1941–43.[41] It has been pointed out that many of the present day poorer countries show death rates of developed countries but birth rates of underdeveloped countries.[42] In many of these countries which have experienced this change, the position is more or less the same as in Ceylon. It appears that this lag between birth and death rates will continue for some time so that it is not possible to expect any notable fall in the rate of population increase in the immediate future unless there is some significant change in the socio-economic conditions in these areas. What is important to remember in this connection is that this trend in population in most of the underdeveloped countries has been due fundamentally to the fact that while these countries benefited much and quickly from the adoption of death control techniques, they have not experienced any change in their cultural patterns or social conditions which would help in restricting the growth in numbers or in the size of the families.[43]

While the density of population per square mile and its annual growth rate are quite high in the majority of underdeveloped countries, yet they are not so high as in some of the advanced countries. But it should not be forgotten that there is a great difference in the position of these two groups of countries. In both, growing population has obviously meant a decline in per capita extent of land available. Thus in India, area of cultivated land per

[40]Puerto Rico however experienced in this decade remarkable economic development—per capita income rising from $ 122 in 1939 to $ 399 in 1952. But she was helped by favourable external factors. That country was permitted to pour its excess population into the U.S.A. and in return attracted large investments of American capital—Slesinger, Reuben E., ' Some Comments on Non-agricultural Possibilities for Raising the Levels of Living of Underdeveloped Nations,' *American Economic Review, Papers and Proceedings*, May, 1956, pp. 334-35.

[41]Coale, Ansley J., and Edgar, M. Hoover. *Population Growth and Economic Development in Low Income Countries*, Oxford, India, 1959, p. 14.

[42]Slesinger, Reuben E., ' Some Comments on Non-agricultural Possibilities for Raising the Levels of Living of Underdeveloped Nations,' *American Economic Review, Papers and Proceedings*, May, 1956, p. 328.

[43]Davis, Kingsley, ' The Amazing Decline of Mortality in Underdeveloped Areas,' *American Economic Review, Papers and Proceedings*, May, 1956, p. 314.

capita steadily declined from 1·11 acres in 1921 to 1·04 in 1931 and 0·84 in 1951.[44] But while in the developed countries the decline in the area of cultivated land per head of the population has been more than offset by an increase in the amount of capital, a similar shift in labour-resources ratio has not occurred in the underdeveloped areas of the world. This constitutes the major source of trouble in their attempts at development.

Moreover, there is no comparison between the economic conditions and the demographic situation in the underdeveloped countries of today with those prevailing in the developed countries at a corresponding stage in their economic evolution in the past. The decline in death rate that has taken place in recent years in some of the underdeveloped countries is much greater than what it was in the early 20th Century in the present advanced countries. In the latter, the decline was steady and gradual, extending over decades and resulting directly from advancement in science. In the former, death control techniques have been imported in their advanced and well tried form and made cheap and available even to the poorest through government and international agencies. On the other hand, the birth rate in the European countries in their pre-industrial stage was not so high as it is in some of the countries in Asia, North Africa and Latin America. Kingsley Davis points out that the excess of births over deaths in most of the underdeveloped countries has been in recent years four to ten times what it was in North-West Europe prior to 1,800.[45] While in the low income countries birth rate ranges from 40 to 60 per 1,000, the highest rate recorded in the 18th Century in some of the countries of North-West Europe was less than 40 per 1,000. It was 34 in Denmark in 1780, 39 in Sweden in 1751 and 38 in Norway in 1751. In the U.S.A. in the 100 years preceding 1870, demographic transition was rapid. Fertility rate declined more rapidly than mortality rate as a result of growing industrialization and urbanization and late marriages; and all groups, urban, rural, industrial and agricultural shared in the decline in fertility.[46] Furthermore, the pressure of population on land was less in some of the European countries. India in 1950 had 293 people per square mile. France and England had 105 and 115 at the end of the 18th Century. Growth of population in America benefited by geographical expansion towards the West. When population grew most rapidly, the West always had some room for yet another farm. Long before the land frontier was gone, other resources were being developed and industry had grown sufficiently to provide opportunities for the population not needed in agriculture.[47] It should also be remembered that in the course of the 18th and 19th Centuries the modern advanced countries were already well on the way to industrial leadership and enjoyed a per capita income several times higher than what it is today in the underdeveloped countries.

[44]*Census of India*, 1951, Vol. I, Part I-A Report, p. 141.

[45]Davis, Kingsley, ' The Amazing Decline of Mortality in Underdeveloped Areas,' *American Economic Review, Papers and Proceedings*, May, 1956, p. 305.

[46] & [47] *Proceedings of the World Population Conference*, U.N., 1954, Summary of Report, pp. 128–29.

Besides, while then the problem of excess population could be solved easily in European countries by emigration, such possibilities are not available now for the overpopulated low income countries.

The conclusion can therefore be made that the economic and political conditions in which the underdeveloped countries find themselves today are not such as would make an increase in population a favourable factor in economic growth. A demographic situation and trend which would have been advantageous to the present developed countries in their early stages of industrialization is not only not favourable but inimical to growth in the underdeveloped countries of today which are in different circumstances. The real solution for the present pre-industrial countries can be found only in increasing capital stock so as to make a large amount of capital resources available per head of the population. But while increase in numbers necessitates the acquisition of larger amount of capital, the very fact of rapid growth in population makes capital accumulation more difficult.

THE WAY OUT OF THE POPULATION BARRIER

Most economists are however agreed on the point that many underdeveloped countries are overpopulated, that population pressure is the main obstacle to economic progress and that unless this barrier is broken, all efforts at stepping up capital formation would be futile. There is nevertheless, some division of opinion regarding the means by which this end is to be attained. There is one school of thought which firmly believes that if income is sufficiently raised, fertility rate will decline and when that stage is reached further growth of income would be easier. Professor Harvey Leibenstein has argued that under-developed countries, whose per capita income is low and population growth rate is constant because of high birth and high death rates, are in a Malthusian underemployment equilibrium position based on a subsistence structure.[48] He bases his argument on the observed relationship between per capita income and fertility rate and quotes approvingly Dupont's capillarity thesis according to which the recognition by a community of the fact that the chances of rising socially are greater with lesser number of children, brings about with a rise in per capita incomes, a change in social attitudes and a strong motivation for family restriction. Leibenstein proceeds on the assumption that population is an increasing function of income up to a certain level of income, but beyond that point it is a decreasing function of income. When income is very low the costs compared with utility of a large number of children are low. Since at this stage mortality rate is high, a large number of children are necessary to maintain the existing strength of population. Also, since children are sent for employment at a tender age, and they become economically useful members early, the burden of rearing children is not felt much. At the next stage, when mortality rate falls there is a lag in fertility rate because it takes time for

[48]Leibenstein, Harvey, *A Theory of Economic Demographic Development*, Princeton, 1954.

social attitudes to be changed. Since more children survive to the productive age, the contribution of children to production as a proportion of the costs of maintaining them will increase. However, as the income increases further, the significance of children as contributors to production and income is reduced but at the same time the advantage of having fewer children in rising in social and economic status creates a social attitude favourable to restriction of family size. At this stage per capita income will be high and both birth and death rates will be low and the rate of growth of population will fall or remain constant.[49]

The underemployment equilibrium which characterizes the overpopulated low income countries pertains to the first and second stages above mentioned. Displacement from this equilibrium is possible by securing an initial per capita income gain through the importation of a large amount of foreign capital, or technological innovations or migration of labour out of the country. This initial income gain sets in motion two forces—an annual increase in total income through rise in the level of investment, and a rise in the rate of population growth. As a result of the latter trend, per capita income does not rise to the extent that it otherwise would. It is however stressed—and this is the crux of the whole theory—that if the per capita income rises sufficiently high, that itself would bring down the rate of growth of population so that after a certain stage is reached, further increase in investment and per capita income becomes easier. The time that would be taken for this stage to be reached depends on : (a) the magnitude of the initial income gain which displaces the equilibrium ; (b) the initial capital-labour situation, i.e. their relative magnitudes and (c) the rate at which population is growing. It follows then that the larger the initial income gain and the slower the rate of growth of population the more quickly would the point be attained after which further growth becomes less and less difficult. Hence, in underdeveloped countries faced with the problem of overpopulation, economic development is possible only if a very strenuous effort is made in the initial period to start large income generating investment schemes. Such a strenuous effort is twice blessed in that it helps to reduce the rate of growth of population itself and also makes further development easier. The fact that there is a biologically determined maximum rate of population growth between 3 and 4 per cent makes it possible to break the obstacle of numbers by sufficiently raising the level of investment. Thus Leibenstein conceives of a critical minimum in respect of this initial income gain. If the effort fails below this level, economic growth is not only not possible but actually becomes more difficult because of increasing population so that the economy would find itself further behind the position from which it started. On this ground it is argued that backward economies continue to be backward because the " efforts to escape from economic backwardness, be they spontaneous or forced, are below the critical minimum required for

[49]Leibenstein, Harvey, *Economic Backwardness and Economic Growth*, John Wiley, New York, 1957, pp. 164–67.

persistent growth ".[50] Given the population growth rate, the critical minimum effort in the form of investment should therefore be of such an order as to break the population barrier to economic expansion.[51]

Leibenstein's thesis is logically attractive, but it has only limited practical significance. Let us examine what its practical implications are. It should be remembered that in the absence of foreign capital, emigration and technological innovations, the initial rise in income can be obtained only by lowering consumption and by increasing domestic savings and investment via the multiplier. The problem then boils down to making a much larger investment out of current domestic resources. We have in particular to find out on the basis of our knowledge relating to population and its rate of growth, capital stock, income and the rate of savings and investment, the extent to which the last-mentioned factor should increase in order to bring about a much higher rate of increase in per capita income. This can be done with reference to the production functions of the factors of production. The figures made use of in this connection by economists like Paul Douglas and Tinbergen relate to industrialized countries.[52] For India the co-efficients for labour obtained by different writers range from 0·40 to 0·77 and those for capital from 0·23 to 0·60. In a recent study of this kind made by the Secretariat of the United Nations Economic Commission for Asia and the Far East relating to under-developed areas of this region, the figures 0·7 and 0·3 are made use of for labour and capital respectively.[53] According to this calculation, if population is assumed to increase at the rate of 1·5 per cent per year, employment is 30 per cent of the population and savings and investment are 7 per cent of the national income and there is no improvement in operation efficiency, total income increases by only 78 per cent in 30 years and per capita income by 14 per cent. This obviously is very low. On the other hand, if we assume that income growth would have any perceptible effect on population growth only when the per capita income in a country like ours is doubled, and that it is desirable to bring about this effect in a shorter period than 30 years, say in 20 years, then it is clear that a much greater investment effort than indicated in the above illustration is necessary. If to this is added the consideration that the assumed population growth rate and the capital-output ratio are under-estimated, the required investment proportion becomes higher still. If we assume a population growth rate of 1·7 per cent per year and per capita income of $ 65 (which were the average rates in the ECAFE region excluding Japan

[50]Leibenstein, Harvey, *Economic Backwardness and Economic Growth*, John Wiley, New York, 1960, p. 95.

[51]Galenson, W., and H. Leibenstein, 'Investment Criteria, Productivity and Economic Development,' *Quarterly Journal of Economics*, August, 1955, pp. 343-70.

[52]Paul Douglas arrived at the figures 0·75 and 0·25 as representing the elasticity of production of labour and capital on the basis of the performance of manufacturing industries in the U.S.A. in the years 1799-1922—*The Theory of Wages*, Macmillan, New York, 1934, pp. 124-29, 155-58. Tinbergen gives the following figures: 0·7 for labour, 0·2 for capital and 0·1 for land—*The Dynamics of Business Cycles*, Chicago, 1950, pp. 122-23.

[53]*Economic Bulletin for Asia and the Far East*, U.N., June, 1958, pp. 17-31.

in 1956) and capital-output ratio of 3 : 1, the investment required to increase per capita income by 3 per cent a year would be 14·1 per cent of national income.[54] But if per capita income increases only at the rate of 3 per cent per year it would take 24 years for income per head to double. A doubling of income in a shorter period of, say 10 years, which means a rise by 7 per cent of per capita income every year, is possible (under the above assumptions with regard to population increase and capital-output ratio) only if investment is 26·1 per cent of national income. It does not appear possible to reach such high targets of savings and investment in a country like India, where the consumption level is very low and where, in spite of considerable attempts at raising the tax revenues in the last few years, there has not been any great improvement. Attempts at further reducing consumption are bound to react adversely on the already low level of labour efficiency.

Further, the theory assumes that the rate of growth of population would come down if per capita income rises fast enough. Leibenstein himself gives the examples of Western countries and Japan where decline in the rate of increase in population has synchronized with an acceleration in economic growth. The implication here is that a mere rise in incomes has a direct bearing on population trends. What is more, it assumes that a moderate rise in incomes increases the rate of growth of population (in conformity with the Malthusian assumption), but a rise in income which is above a certain level brings it down. But in actual fact, the population problem in a low income country is not a simple problem of arithmetic, but an intricate social one influenced by custom and tradition and the social attitudes and prejudices of the people. As such, changes in social attitudes and cultural patterns will have a more direct bearing on population trends than mere increase in incomes. The sudden drop in the rate of growth of population in Japan in recent years has been due largely to family planning and to the permissive legislation in respect of birth control and not to economic growth.[55] Improvement in economic conditions may create social attitudes favourable to family restriction, but this need not necessarily happen. Rate of growth of population in urban areas is lower than in villages not because income is higher but because the social conditions are different. Rise in the income of a family living in a village is likely to lead to an increase in numbers rather than to any restriction in the expansion of the size of the family. The Indian Census data of 1951 show that in the Southern zone, which is not economically the most advanced part of the country, the age of marriage is higher and the birth rate is lower than in any other region in the country.[56] It would thus appear that the desired end can

[54]*Economic Bulletin for Asia and the Far East*, U.N., June, 1959, p. 39.

[55]Family planning in Japan has brought down the birth rate by one half in the last ten years. *Economic Bulletin for Asia and the Far East*, U.N., June, 1959, p. 3.

[56]The percentage of females aged 15 and over who remain unmarried is 10·1 in the South against 6·5 in West India and 4 in North and Central India. There is a corresponding difference in respect of males. Birth rate in South India is 36 or 37 per thousand per year compared with 42 in West India and 44 in Central India. On the other hand, death rate in the South is 21 or 22 per thousand, while in Central India it is 34, East India 26 to 28 and West India 26—*Census of India,* 1951, Vol. I, Part I-A, Ch. 11.

be reached more easily by concentrating on the social front than on the economic front.

This, however, does not mean that economic development can be neglected. What is stressed here is, that by educating the people and by effecting a favourable change in their attitudes through well planned propaganda, it would be possible to bring down population growth rate considerably. It is idle to wait for economic development to do the trick. If by such measures a new sense of values is created among the people and they are enabled to develop a materialistic attitude towards life instead of being other-worldly, it is quite possible that the birth rate would start declining rapidly and in as spectacular a manner as death rate in recent years has come down. People in rural areas of backward countries even when they are not literate, have commonsense enough to understand the simple fact that the chances of economic betterment of their families are greater when the size of the family is smaller. The need for family planning is realized by the rural folk in India and the experience of social workers in this field shows that the view that motivational resistence to fertility control is strong in underdeveloped countries is very much exaggerated. But it is obvious that contraception if it is to be really effective among the rural masses, should be cheap and simple. Effort along these lines would yield significant results. Here it is worth pointing out that the major factors responsible for the decline in death rate, new drugs and other medical means are fast reaching the end of their possibilities so that the extent to which death rate would further fall on account of these techniques becomes less and less. This would mean that even a small gain in the way of controlling birth rates would have a proportionately larger effect on the natural rate of increase of population. Undoubtedly, this would involve a huge responsibility on the state and necessitate large expenditure. But the steps taken in this line in Japan and China recently, contain a lesson for us and show us the possibilities of this programme of action.

At the present rate of growth, India's population in about 215 years would be 7 billion and the land area available per Indian will be 5,000 sq. feet. Sheer numbers of people will have stifled economic development so that unless the birth rate is reduced, India would be unable to achieve an economic breakthrough from its state of underdevelopment and unemployment to a better life envisaged by her Five-Year Plans. This is a matter of great importance and urgency deserving an extremely high priority in all our Plans for economic development. It is now taken for granted that much sacrifice has to be borne by the present generation in the form of restricted consumption and other limitations in the interests of a future of plenty and prosperity. But if no earnest and serious attempt is made at reducing birth rate even now, all the efforts taken and sacrifices borne by the present generation would only succeed in bequeathing a lower level of real incomes to a much larger number of people. From a purely economic standpoint therefore expenditure on population control is one of the most profitable forms of investment for

India. With reference to the technical aid which the U.S.A. is extending to India Professor Villard remarks : " I venture the guess that if the $ 80 million we are currently spending each year in India together with the funds which the Indian Government is contributing to development were instead devoted to making birth control generally available, the reduction in population increase would be greater than the enlargement of income that the funds are currently achieving. It would appear then that making birth control devices available would be the most economic way of raising Indian living levels and the most important type of technical assistance that we could possibly make available under the Point IV Programme."[57]

The decline in birth rate would improve the capital-labour ratio and thereby help increased productivity of labour and a rise in per capita incomes. But the other aspect of the problem, namely, the scope for increasing incomes even in the existing factor supply situation needs to be considered. There is a depressing parallelism (depressing from the point of view of underdeveloped countries) between advanced countries which are beset with the problem of over-expansion or under-utilization of capital and the underdeveloped countries which are tormented with the problem of population growth outrunning capital growth. Under-utilization of capital which threatens to land the developed economies into stagnation is sought to be met by the creation of money incomes sufficient to produce that order of effective demand which would keep capital fully employed. In underdeveloped economies unemployment and underemployment of labour are due to inadequacy of capital as well as income. But both capital and income are the product of employment of labour. Hence the vicious circle. This vicious circle can be broken only if labour is made to create an excess income with techniques and capital supply as they are. Herein lies the importance of finding out ways not merely of increasing the employment of labour, but what is of greater significance, increasing the per capita yield of labour. The crucial question is therefore whether the best use is made of the labour resources. It may be argued that full and efficient employment of labour is not possible because of the inadequacy of complementary factors. But if complementary factors themselves are dependent on labour productivity there is no way out, short of importing capital, except to increase labour productivity with the existing equipment.

Logically, this would mean the lowering of the capital-output ratio, by devising capital-saving technological improvements, by better and more economical utilization of existing capital assets and by avoiding the wasteful use of plants and equipment. This points to the need for resisting labour-saving devices and for adopting labour-intensive methods where feasible. However, choice of labour-intensive techniques would, while providing large employment opportunities, fail to accelerate the rate of economic progress, as heavy investments in capital intensive projects

[57]Villard, Henry H., ' Some Notes on Population and Living Levels,' *Review of Economics and Statistics*, Vol. XXXVII, 1955, p. 190.

would. But in the present situation a proper balancing between the two schemes of investment is necessary. To the extent that there is shortage of technically skilled labour and relatively greater scarcity of this factor in particular regions of the country, better employment of labour can be secured by training and by improving mobility of labour. Capital resources which remain unutilized to whatever extent, are a potential source of employment. There is besides ample scope for increasing the productivity of labour by improving the efficiency of labourers and by creating a greater zest for work. Also attention is to be devoted to the organization side of labour. Such measures would bring in increased incomes without involving any great additional investments and the resources made available by enlarged incomes can be mobilized and utilized for investment by proper fiscal and foreign trade policies.

Chapter V

CAPITAL FORMATION

CAPITAL IS defined as produced means of production. According to Colin Clark, capital goods " are reproducible wealth used for purposes of production ".[1] A United Nations Study defines capital " as those goods resulting from economic activity which are used for the future production of other goods ".[2] The basic feature of capital is therefore that unlike land and natural resources it is man-made and the stock of it can be increased by human effort. The aggregate capital stock of a country or the total national capital at any point of time is made up of, all construction and improvements attached to the land; machinery and equipment in the hands of producers, private and public; inventories in the hands of business enterprises; and net balance of claims against foreign countries. All these above items minus the last one, namely, net balance of claims against foreign countries, constitute total domestic capital. Total domestic capital is made up of (a) fixed domestic capital—construction and improvement attached to the land together with machinery and equipment, and (b) working capital, i.e. inventories and producers' stocks available for future production.

The accretion to the capital stock defined in this way in a given period of time represents capital formation in that period. Production of capital goods thus involves three stages. Firstly, there should be a sufficient margin of savings in the economy, that is to say, aggregate production in a given period of time should exceed aggregate consumption; secondly, financing of these savings or mobilization and canalization of these savings through financial agencies or institutions; and lastly, investment or conversion of the savings into investment goods. Investment would thus consist of all additions to capital goods. And since investment is made possible by savings, it may be defined as the process whereby part of the goods available to a community in a given period is withdrawn from final consumption and incorporated into the productive capacity.[3]

[1]Clark, Colin, The Conditions of Economic Progress, Macmillan, 3rd edn., London, 1957, p. 566.
[2]Analyses and Projections of Economic Development, U.N., 1955, p. 20.
[3]Analyses and Projections of Economic Development, U.N., 1955, p. 20. The supply of capital goods is augmented by reducing the production of consumption goods and making available the resources for the production of the former or by increasing the total output of the economy by adding to capital goods only. In the former case, the release of resources as a result of reduced consumption obviously represents savings; in the latter case, to the extent total output is increased, income rises, but since consumption does not rise with income, the savings margin is widened. It is however, possible for planned investment to exceed savings in so far as industries, besides collecting funds from the public by loans, drawing from Insurance Companies and Savings Banks and making use of profits earned by them for reinvestment, can also borrow from Commercial Banks— Clemence, Richard V., Income Analysis, Wesley, 1951, p. 97.

According to the purpose for which the concept is used, the term capital formation can be given a broad or narrow connotation. Thus if long-term overall economic growth is the object of analysis, capital formation should be made use of in the wider sense of the term so as to cover not only all uses of current product that contribute to a rise in national income, that is, additions to construction, equipment and inventions but also outlays on education, technical training, public health, recreation, etc. which add to the efficiency and productivity of labour and raise the level of economic welfare of the community. That is to say, capital formation should denote investment in physical or material capital as well as personal or intangible capital. The latter is as much important to economic growth as the former. Normally, however, the term capital formation considered as a factor responsible for increasing national output, is given a narrower meaning. In this sense, capital formation includes (a) additions to construction (including residential) and to producers' durable machinery and equipment and (b) accumulation of inventories in the form of stocks of raw materials, finished goods and work in progress and also stores like tools, implements, spares, oil, coal, etc.[4]

Capital formation defined thus excludes the following important items :[5]

(a) Durable goods purchased by households excepting dwellings. The expenditure on these is treated as current outlays on consumption.

(b) Inventories of museums, works of art and other collectors' items.

(c) Discovery of sub-soil resources such as petroleum or minerals. However, in some cases expenditure involved in the creation of structures to exploit such resources is considered as part of capital formation.

(d) Net changes in foreign investment. The exclusion of this item is justified on the ground that " the concept of capital formation is designed to measure changes in the physical capacity of a country's economy ".

A distinction is drawn between gross capital formation and net capital formation. The former includes all expenditure incurred in increasing the capital stock while the latter is measured after allowances are made for depreciation, obsolescence and accidental damage to fixed capital. The rate of gross capital formation in a given year is the ratio of gross capital formation to the Gross National Product while the rate of net capital formation is the ratio of net capital formation to the net national product or national income. Although the latter is made use of mostly for analytical purposes, the former is a more reliable measurement in so far as it avoids all difficulties of making estimates of consumption of capital goods and the special problem involved in the computation of costs of replacement when the capital goods that is

[4]It has been estimated that stocks in existence or inventories form normally one-third to one-half of national income and the increase in stocks constitutes about 15 to 20 per cent of the increase in net fixed investment and 1 to 2 per cent of increase in national income—Dutta, Uma ' Increase in Inventories in Relation to Fixed Capital Formation and National Income,' *Papers on National Income and Allied Topics*, Vol. I, Indian Conference on Research in National Income, Asia Publishing House, Bombay, 1960, pp. 135–40.

[5]*Concepts and Measurement of Capital Formation*, U.N., 1953, p. 8.

replaced is not the same in quality as the one which replaces it. It has also been observed that variation in the rate of gross capital formation as between developed and underdeveloped countries is less than in net capital formation, since the expenditures on replacement form a larger fraction in under-developed countries than in developed countries.[6]

CAPITAL FORMATION: MEASUREMENT

Measurement of the size of capital resources available in an economy and the rate at which it is increasing, has assumed considerable importance in recent years. To a large extent this has been due to a shift in emphasis from micro economic to macro economic studies. Analysis of aggregate economic problems has made it necessary to assess quantitatively the variables involved. The close relation between real net capital formation and the growth of national income is obvious, and any measures aiming at achieving a higher rate of increase in national output should have to take into account the level of savings and the extent to which investment can be accelerated in the economy. Precise measurement of national income requires measurement of capital also, because present level of income can be maintained only if capital is maintained and increase in national income is made possible by increasing the stock of capital goods. Hence not only the size of present capital but also the extent to which it can be augmented is to be estimated. Unless a society is able to keep its capital intact, it will have to suffer economic retrogression. And whether there is a net accretion to capital or there is capital consumption, can be known only if the quantity of the existing stock of capital is known. Moreover, the figures relating to capital formation of a country over a period of time constitute a record of its economic history and reflect the developing pattern of the economy and its vicissitudes over time. As such, a study of these figures helps in an understanding of the factors which promoted or hampered economic growth. The dependence of the growth of national income and therefore of the economy on the rate of capital formation makes measurement of capital of particular significance to backward economies in the early stages of growth. Planning for economic development in these countries is possible only if data regarding the size of capital in the economy and the scope for increasing it are available. The basic question which these countries have to consider is the amount of capital resources required to ensure a given rate of growth in income. They have therefore to find out not only the magnitude of the existing capital stock and the overall capital requirements of the economy but also the capital needed in each sector and industry of the economy in order to achieve the particular targets in these sectors in conformity with the overall programmes of development.

[6]Kuznets, Simon, 'International Differences in Capital Formation and Financing,' *Capital Formation and Economic Growth*, National Bureau of Economic Research, Princeton, 1955, pp. 19–106.

10

However, the measurement of capital formation is beset with many statistical difficulties. Usually four methods are made use of for measuring capital formation.[7] The first is the estimate of the accumulation of funds in a given period, say a year. An estimate is made of savings or the difference between production and consumption and this difference is equated to investment on the obvious assumption that savings are equal to·investment. The defect of this method is that it deals only with the flow of funds and is not directly related to production. Moreover, in an underdeveloped country like India this method has only limited·practical value in so far as adequate and satisfactory accounts of savings and spendings are not available and the existence of a large non-monetized sector makes calculations difficult. The second method is to calculate the expenditures for machinery, equipment, buildings and other construction and works incurred by enterprises. Capital expenditure covers apart from the purchase price of fixed assets, expenses incurred in the transportation of equipment, installation, engineering, architects' legal and other services and indirect taxes as well as losses on account of brokerage, etc. The expenditure method generally implies acceptance of the accountants' definition of capital expenditures. There is the possibility of a lack of uniformity in the definition of capital as between firms, industries and countries. Understatement of capital formation is also likely since in general, business practice tends to charge to current expense, items of relatively small cost even though the expected lifetime may considerably exceed one year. Another method is to estimate the value of capital assets at the beginning and the end of the year. Any addition to this value after deductions are made for depreciation, obsolescence and changes in prices is assumed to represent net fixed capital formation. Here again there is a difficulty, particularly in underdeveloped countries. It is the market value of capital goods that is taken for comparison at different points of time. In underdeveloped countries markets are not developed and as such, reliable market value cannot be known. The fourth method is the commodity flow approach according to which capital formation is measured in terms of domestic production plus imports of capital goods less those other than dwellings sold to households or exported. Although valuation of the assets presents a formidable difficulty, this method is of some value in underdeveloped countries which depend on imports for their capital equipment. The value of the imported capital goods in a period represents approximately the additions made to capital stock. Thus an estimate is made by Hawkins of capital formation in Nigeria and Ghana in the years 1946–55 on the basis of import statistics. In respect of buildings constructed in this period, the value of imported cement is calculated and the cost of building is presumed to be ten times the cost of cement. This, however, is a crude method and provides no means to measure investment expenditures

[7]*Concepts and Measurement of Capital Formation*, U.N., 1953, p. 10, also K. S. Rao, ' Capital Formation in Farm Business,' *Papers on National Income and Allied Topics*, Vol. I, Indian Conference on Research in National Income, Asia Publishing House, Bombay, 1960, p. 70.

of small enterprises which use little or no imported materials and also investments in the agricultural sector.[8] Apart from these difficulties, the commodity flow approach can lead to a satisfactory estimate of capital formation only if adjustments are made on account of changes in the inventories of capital goods used by their producers or distributors so that the actual flow of capital goods to the ultimate users of such goods can be known.

.In addition to these general defects of the usual methods of estimating capital formation, we have to mention certain special problems involved in any such valuation. Firstly, there is the problem of quality change. The deflated money value of a particular capital item may be the same at two points of time but the new machine that replaces the old one may be superior in quality. The fact that the number of machines and their money value are unaltered cannot be interpreted to mean that there is no net addition to capital formation because the stock of capital available at the second period may be more productive. The output per unit of labour therefore rises and as such, the same stock of goods can be produced with lesser number of labourers. The workers thus released may be employed in other enterprises and the added output of labour in these enterprises should also be attributed to the improved quality of capital. This makes it difficult to measure the volume of capital with reference to its value and quantity alone. A second problem arises in the matter of allocating capital consumption over time. If a building loses 20 per cent of its value in 10 years, the average capital consumption is 2 per cent per year but the actual depreciation and loss in value in any particular year may fall short of or exceed the arithmetic average.[9] The basic difficulties in measuring capital formation spring from the fact that we are dealing with groups of different categories of goods which cannot be reduced to a standard unit of measurement. The very definition of capital lacks precision. Changes in prices, differences in quality, shifts in ownership and use, the degree of depreciation, all these make it impossible to measure exactly the extent to which capital has increased over time. Hence there is need for caution and care in the interpretation and use of statistical data relating to capital. The estimates have to be accepted as only rough indications of the changes in magnitude.

THE ROLE OF CAPITAL FORMATION IN ECONOMIC GROWTH

The process of investment or the creation of investment goods results in capital formation. Investment comes about because of the action of demand

[8]Hawkins, E. K., ' Capital Formation in Nigeria and Ghana 1946–55,' *Bulletin of the Oxford University Institute of Statistics*, February, 1959, pp. 40–42.

[9]Denison, Edward F., ' Theoretical Aspects of Quality Change, Capital Consumption and Net Capital Formation,' *Problems of Capital Formation*, National Bureau of Economic Research, Princeton, 1957, pp. 215–86.

factors or supply factors or both.[10] Investment undertaken in response to the known trend of demand for consumers or producers goods may be called demand investment. The normal replacement investment is caused by a continuation in the demand for consumer goods which these capital goods help to produce. If the demand price for the consumer goods rises, there is the likelihood of increased investment which makes an addition to the existing capital capacity. On the other hand, supply investment is defined as additions to capital equipment resulting from the initiative of the producers of capital goods. Thus the entrepreneurs of the Schumpeterian type would desire to bring a new commodity or an improved and cheapened one to the market. The production of such goods requires investment in new capital equipment. Such investments are made by the pioneering enterprises with the hope of making profits and on the calculation that the finished product will have large sales.

Capital formation plays a decisive part in determining the level and rate of growth of national income. The vital role of capital in this respect depends on the fact that among the different factors of production capital has the unique characteristic of unlimited expansibility. The extent of land and natural resources is fixed and the growth of labour force is limited by physiological factors. But, capital which is man-made and is fabricated by human ingenuity and skill with the financial and natural resources available, is capable of increasing in quantity as well as improving in quality. Given the availability of land and other natural resources, and assuming labour supply to be constant, any increase in the productive capacity of the economy is possible only if the quantity of its capital is increased. Capital formation data relating to countries which have attained different stages of economic development show that the ratio of gross domestic capital formation is positively associated with income per capita. A similar relation is observable in the ratio of gross national capital formation to gross national product.[11] It is clear that the capacity of an economy to increase its output depends upon the proportion of its current income devoted to capital formation as well as on the quality or efficiency of the capital stock to produce output. This close relationship between capital growth and income growth makes the concept of capital formation of vital significance in any programme of planned development.

Specifically, accumulation of capital promotes economic growth because in the first place it permits more roundabout methods of productions. The roundaboutness of production is typically capitalistic and the fact that such methods increase considerably the productiveness of any enterprise has been stressed by classical economists particularly the Austrian economist Bohm Bawerk.[12] Secondly, increase in the capital stock is manifested in both capital

---

[10] 'Youngson, A. J., 'The Disaggregation of Investment in the Study of Economic Growth,' *Economic Journal*, June. 1956, pp. 236–43.

[11] Kuznets, Simon, *Six Lectures on Economic Growth*, Free Press, Illinois, 1959, pp. 71–73.

[12] Bohm Bawerk, von Eugen, *Capital and Interest*, Vol. II, Libertarian Press, Illinois, 1959, pp. 83–85.

deepening as well as capital widening. The latter makes an economy broad-based and diversified and is characteristic of economic expansion. Thirdly, capital formation plays a strategic role in economic development. A rise in the levels of investment makes all the difference between economic stagnation and progress. When this rate rises sufficiently, it exerts an interacting and cumulative effect on the whole economy so that with every accretion to capital stock, further accumulation becomes easier and a higher rate of increase in national income less difficult to achieve. And lastly, perhaps most important, additional capital is required to bring about technical progress. Although in some cases a parti-cular innovation may not require much capital, yet to prepare the ground that makes it possible for technological improvements to take place, the application of large amounts of capital is necessary.

The contribution of capital to economic growth should not however, be exaggerated. The creation of capital is made possible by the effort of labour applied to natural resources. When once capital is formed, it functions in co-operation with the other factors of production and the output that emerges is as much the contribution of capital as of the other factors. Hence, in exami-ning the role of capital formation in economic growth the significance of the other agents should not be underestimated. Productivity of capital is to be distinguished from what a given rate of capital formation contributes to total output. The actual contribution of capital alone will be equivalent roughly to the prevailing rate of interest. Thus Alec Cairncross points out that if there is no innovation and capital gives a return of 5 per cent, an investment of 10 per cent of national income will increase total output by about $\frac{1}{2}$ per cent per year. And since in developed countries, the annual rate of growth of income averages 2 to 3 per cent, the contribution of capital is only $\frac{1}{4}$ of the re-corded economic progress.[13] In reviewing the rates of capital formation in developed and underdeveloped countries Simon Kuznets observes, that the difference in the proportion of capital formation as between advanced and poorer countries is comparatively small. Capital formation in these countries ranges from 15 to 7·5 or 5 per cent of national income. If the productivity of capital is the same in both these groups of countries their disparity in capital formation ratios does not explain the wide difference in their national and per capita incomes. The rate of growth of population in underdeveloped countries was quite low some 20 or 30 years ago. Even if we assume that population growth rate was the same in underdeveloped countries as in deve-loped countries, the actual investments made in these countries should have helped national income to grow at the rate of 6 per cent per annum resulting in 80 per cent increase over a century.[14] This, however, has not occurred and hence according to Kuznets, the explanation of the growing disparity in income growth should be found elsewhere.

[13]Cairncross, A. K., ' The Place of Capital in Economic Progress,' *International Social Science Bulletin*, Vol. VI, No. 2, UNESCO, 1954, p. 232.

[14]Kuznets, Simon, *Six Lectures on Economic Growth*, Free Press, Illinois, 1959, pp. 74–77.

One of the major factors responsible for making income grow at a faster rate than what investment figures-alone would indicate, is obviously technological innovations. Data relating to capital formation in some of the advanced countries of today show that the proportion of national income invested has shown a tendency to rise till a high level is reached, and then to decline slightly or remain constant. Thus in the U.S.A. the rate of investment rose from about 15 per cent of the national income in 1869–78 to 19·5 per cent at the end of the century. In the 20th century, the proportion declined gradually to about 15 per cent but has tended to rise in recent years. Between 1937 and 1948 excepting the war years the rate of capital formation remained at about 15 to 16 per cent in the U.S.S.R.[15] Similarly, a study relating to capital formation in Britain in the years 1870–1914 shows that total gross investment (home and foreign investment) as a proportion of gross national income ranged between roughly 15 and 20 per cent.[16] On the other hand, national income in the U.K. increased by about 70 per cent and in the U.S.A. by 140 per cent over the last quarter of the 19th century; between 1900 and 1950 national income at market prices rose by more than six times in the U.K. and by nearly thirteen times in the U.S.A. The explanation has to be found in the vast improvements in technology and the increased efficiency of labour. Technological improvement is no doubt possible only if financial resources are available and substantial investments are made. Changes in technology are obviously embodied in capital goods and the rate of technological advance is influenced by the rate of capital formation. However, such investments tend to be heavy only in the initial stages. And the point to note here is, that when the initial step towards technological innovations is taken, technology becomes the dominant factor in economic growth. Since the quality of capital equipment is improved and there is even the possibility that technical progress is of a capital saving nature, the rate of growth of output will not be related to the amount of the nation's resources utilized for investment purposes. The rate of investment may remain constant or even fall, but the rate of growth of national income would continue to rise.

Of equal significance is the human factor. The major capital stock according to Kuznets is the training, character and skill of the people. Investments in education both general and technical and in public health, etc. add to the standard of efficiency of labour, but such expenditures are not included in any computation of capital formation. In fact economic growth is fostered by many factors of which capital is only one. This would mean that given a certain increase in total national output, only a part of it can be attributed to the net addition to the stock of capital interpreted in the narrower accounting sense of the term.

[15]Kaplan, Norman M., ' Capital Formation and Allocation,' *Soviet Economic Growth*, Ed. by Bergson, Abram, Row and Peterson, New York, 1953, pp. 37–87.

[16]Lenfant, J. H., ' Great Britain's Capital Formation, 1865–1914,' *Economica*, May, 1951, pp. 151-68.

THE CAPITAL-OUTPUT RATIO

The close relationship between capital formation and income growth has suggested a quantitative assessment of the ratios between the two. This ratio —the capital co-efficient or capital-output ratio—as it is called, has assumed much prominence in discussions of the possibilities of income increase resulting from investment, and has been made use of increasingly in theoretical analysis as well as in policy formulation. In simple terms, " the capital output ratio may be defined as the relationship of investment in a given economy or industry for a given time period to the output of that economy or industry for a similar time period " [17] At the outset, this concept has to be distinguished from the concept of marginal productivity of capital. The latter indicates the contribution of capital alone—other factors being assumed to be constant—to total output while the former assumes increase in the other inputs as well. Thus while marginal productivity of capital ranges from about 5 to 10 per cent, the contribution of capital in combination with other factors which are also varied is bound to be much higher—25 to 40 per cent—normally. In other words, capital-output ratio can be the same as the marginal product of capital only if the contribution of the other factors, land and labour, is zero.

The difference between average and incremental or marginal capital-output ratios is also to be noted. The first is the quantitative relationship between the stock of capital available in a period of time and the output of that time period. On the other hand, the more widely used concept of incremental capital-output ratio is the relationship between the net capital formation of a certain time period and the additional net output that results in the first subsequent time period in which the effects of that capital formation can be fully felt.[18] This of course is based on the logical assumption that capital formation causes an increase in output, that is, capital formation has to precede the increment in output that results from it. What period of time should elapse before the effect of investment is felt, depends obviously on the nature of the investment. Some writers recommend allowing a period of two or three years for the evaluation of the direct and indirect results of the investment.[19] However, because of the practical difficulties in a calculation of this sort, the incremental capital-output ratio is usually interpreted as the relationship between the increment of capital and increment of output both in the same time period.[20]

[17]Rosen, George, *Industrial Change in India*, Asia Publishing House, Bombay, 1959, p. 37.

[18]*Economic Bulletin for Asia and the Far East*, U.N., November, 1955, p. 26 f.n.

[19]*Analyses and Projections of Economic Development*, U.N., 1955, p. 21.

[20]Harvey Leibenstein makes a distinction between Net Incremental Capital-Output Ratio (NICOR) in which other factors are assumed to be unchanged (this amounts to marginal product of capital) and the Adjusted Incremental Capital-Output Ratio (AICOR) when a given change is assumed in the other factors, say 1 per cent increase—*Economic Backwardness and Economic Growth*, John Wiley, New York, 1960, p. 178.

Another distinction is between gross capital co-efficient and net capital co-efficient. The former refers to the relationship between fixed capital in the economy and the gross value of output while the latter relates to the fixed capital and net output that is, after deductions are made for the value of goods, raw materials, fuel, light, power, etc. used in the process of production and depreciation charges. Also, since the investment and output in the economy cover investments and outputs in different sectors and industries, it is possible to make use of capital co-efficients of particular sectors and industries in investment decisions pertaining to individual industries. The capital-output ratio for the economy as a whole is the average of the sectoral ones weighted by the output increase in the different sectors. Obviously the overall ratio depends on the weights given to the separate units and the relative degree of capital intensity in the different sectors.

Features of Capital-Output Ratio

Normally, the value of capital in developed economies is estimated to be about two to three times the national product. In any particular economy however, the ratio depends on various factors. To the extent inventories as working capital are included on the side of capital, the proportion of output will vary inversely to the size of inventories, fixed capital remaining constant. It is also obvious that the ratio of output to capital depends directly on the extent to which existing capital is utilized. Capital in the form of machines is better and more fully utilized if instead of one shift, double shift is introduced; this would of course increase the depreciation of the capital equipment, but even if capital depreciates twice as fast as when there is a single shift, the productivity flow will be greater than the rate of depreciation. Thus in a period of depression when there is under utilization of capital because of lack of effective demand, the ratio of capital to output rises.

Since the overall capital-output ratio of the economy depends on the ratios of the individual sectors, any shift in the relative importance of the different sectors or the introduction of capital saving or capital intensive techniques in particular enterprises or sectors will directly affect the overall ratio. Thus a shift in emphasis from agriculture and light industries to capital goods and heavy industries raises the ratio. In the same manner, the ratio of capital to output rises if in particular sectors the technique of production is changed involving increased use of capital. Apart from capital structure, the ratio is affected also by the time taken by investments to mature. If the investment takes a long time to mature, the capital-output ratio will tend to be high.

Even when the techniques and capital structure remain unchanged, the ratio of capital to output will change and fluctuate because of price variations. Capital-output ratio rises and falls with variations in the cost of the inputs— the wage rate, rate of interest and prices of raw materials. Where capital equipment is imported, a rise in the cost of the equipment raises the ratio.

On the other hand, if import restrictions are severe, it is likely that the existing equipment will be used to its maximum capacity in which case the ratio will decline. Lastly, the availability of external economies and the utilization of by-products would lower the ratio. Thus the development of social overheads and public utilities increases the yield of capital in the other sectors of the economy which benefit by such facilities. It is also possible that the expansion of one industry would have a favourable effect on other industries and help in bringing down the ratio of capital to output of these industries.

It has been observed that while the capital-output ratios of particular industries or particular sectors of an economy have fluctuated considerably over time, there is a fair degree of constancy in the overall ratio of the entire economy. In a country like the U.S.A. the capital co-efficients range from 0·07 in clothing to 3·2 in railroads, 3·6 in communications and 2·7 in public utilities.[21] What is significant to note is that not only is there great disparity in the co-efficients of different industries at any point of time but that for a particular industry the ratios vary considerably over time. This is inevitable in so far as improvements in techniques of production alter the degree of capital intensity of particular industries. As against this, the overall ratio in some of the developed countries has remained fairly constant over a long period of time. According to a calculation made by Simon Kuznets, the ratio of net fixed capital and inventories to net national product in the U.S.A. was around 3·5 : 1 in the years 1889 to 1944, the range of variation being 2·99 : 1 in 1889 to 4·03 in 1934. The latter figure however has no great significance as it relates to the depression period. Excepting this, the maximum was 3·86 in 1929.[22] This constancy must be due to various interacting forces. Thus the gradual decline in interest rates over this period and diminishing returns operating in the advanced countries should have tended to pull the ratio in the upward direction, while technological improvements, improvements in labour skill and external economies would have operated in the opposite direction.[23] Apart from this, inter industrial shifts would have also contributed to this stability. While the ratio tended to rise in agriculture, mining and manufacturing, it declined in the transportation and public utility sectors. Another factor is that the annual increments to capital would be too small to have any appreciable effect on the ratio. Domar points out that if capital growth is at the rate of 3 per cent per year and if output is assumed to be completely constant it would take 23 years for the aggregate capital co-efficient to double.[24] But since income is also increasing at the same rate and increase in income

[21]Domar, Evsey, ' Interrelation between Capital and Output in the American Economy,' *International Social Science Bulletin*, Vol. VI, No. 2, 1954, UNESCO, p. 241.

[22]*ibid.*, p. 238.

[23]Bruton, H. J., 'Growth Models and Underdeveloped Economies,' *Journal of Political Economy*, August, 1955. Reprinted in Agarwala, A. N. and S. P. Singh, (Eds.) *Economics of Underdevelopment*, Oxford, India, 1958, pp. 224 & 225.

[24]Domar, Evsey, ' Interrelation between Capital and Output in the American Economy,' *International Social Science Bulletin*, Vol. VI, No. 2, 1954, UNESCO, p. 241.

necessitates a corresponding increase in the demand for capital, the capital-output ratio is bound to be stable.

A review of the trend in the capital output figures of U.K. and U.S.A. reveals a great similarity in pattern. In both the countries the ratio shows a very gradual rise since the last quarter of the 19th century to the 20's of the present century. With the exception of a sharp rise in the depression period (1930s) which, however, is due to special circumstances, the ratios in the two countries show a general downward trend up to about the middle of the century. Since then, there has been an appreciable movement upward. In the U.K. over the years 1870 to 1900 capital increased at the same rate as income; per capita real income and capital per head increased by about 40 per cent in 25 years; in 1895 to 1913 capital per head continued to rise while real output per head remained more or less constant; between 1924 and 1938 real output rose substantially more than the stock of capital thus bringing down the capital-output ratio.[25] It would therefore appear that in both these countries· there was a considerable step up in investment in capital intensive enterprises in the first quarter of the present century. Since then, and up to recent times, a relatively low rate of capital accumulation was accompanied by the adoption of new techniques of production, the scope for the full utilization of which increased in the course of years. Investments in heavy capital-intensive enterprises such as public utilities, transport and railways, tend to be lumpy at certain periods. At such stages the capital-output ratio rises. But with the passage of time, as they come to be fully and better utilized, the ratio of capital to output tends to decline. Adoption of capital-saving inventions in later years, external economies, improvement in organization, skill and knowledge of labour also helped in an increase in output without a corresponding demand on capital. The rise in the ratio in recent years should be attributed to the large investments for building up the economies after the ravages of war and for the replacement of equipment worn out by overstrained working during the war and also to the new drive to increase productivity with a view to improve the economic and political strength of the nation.

Statistical data do not fully bear out the assumption that the ratio of capital to output is likely to be higher in the developed than in the underdeveloped countries. At any rate, the variation of the capital co-efficients between countries which have attained different standards of economic advancement is not very systematic. Nor is there any correlation between the marginal capital-output ratio and the rate of growth of the economy. Estimated ratios for some of the underdeveloped countries are higher than that for advanced economies while in the same industry there are instances where the ratio is lower in the developed countries. In reality, the overall ratio for the economy depends on the mix of industries in the economy rather than the capital intensity of each individual industry. In underdeveloped countries the factor

[25]Phelps Brown, E. H., and Bernard Weber, ' Accumulation, Productivity and Distribution in the British Economy 1870-1938,' *Economic Journal*, June, 1953, pp. 263-88.

supply situation is generally such that more labour would be available for operating a unit of capital. The capital-labour ratio in them is low but in so far as the productivity of labour is also low, the capital-output ratio tends to be high.[26] But the abundance of labour power would encourage the adoption of capital light techniques of production in which case capital-output ratio will fall. It would thus appear that the differences in the capital-output ratios between advanced and low income countries have to be explained in terms of the different factor endowments of the countries concerned. In general, to the extent developed economies have larger shares of economic activity conducted by industries with relatively high capital-output ratios, the overall capital co-efficient of such economies will be higher than in poorer countries.

LIMITATIONS OF THE CONCEPT

The quantitative relationship between investment and output which the capital-output ratio suggests is, however, deceptive. In fact no precise calculation of the ratio for an economy or even for an industry is possible, and as such, no exact estimate can be made of the capital requirements in an economy on the basis of an assumed capital co-efficient so as to bring about a certain rate of growth of income. The limitations of the concept partly spring from the fact that it is not possible to measure the two sides of the ratio with any degree of exactness. On the one hand, the concept of capital is nebulous and any attempt to make a quantitative assessment of it is beset with formidable difficulties. Apart from the index number problem, no clear demarcation between capital goods and non-capital goods is possible. A substantial part of the savings gets invested in land and labour which adds to the productive efficiency of these agents, but the magnitude of capital formation that takes place in this manner is not known. Besides, some durable consumption goods are productively employed but they do not enter into any computation of the capital stock of society. On the other hand, the calculation of output is also not based on any clear cut definition and is subject to a considerable margin of error. Given the capital cost, the choice of gross output instead of net output, to calculate the ratio, results in substantial divergence between the two. As between two industries in which the same investment is made but the durability of capital in the two varies, the capital-output ratio calculated on a net output basis will be the same for both but if the calculation is on the basis of gross output the ratio will be higher for the investment which has a longer life. This is so because depreciation charges which are included in gross output will be greater for the short lived equipment.[27] Again in the case of investment in social overheads which account for a good part of capital formation in growing economies, there is no possibility of estimating the returns in so far

[26]Gross, R. N., ' A Note on Capital-Output Ratios,' *The Review of Economics and Statistics*, August, 1955, p. 305.

[27]Kindleberger, Charles P., *Economic Development*, McGraw-Hill, New York, 1958, p. 43.

as they spread over a long period of time and confer both direct and indirect benefits on the various enterprises in the economy. The time pattern of investments or the lag between investment and yield presents another problem in measurement. Investment in retail trade for example has a quick turnover and the relationship between capital invested and returns is easily known, but in the case of other investments in which the gestation period is long and the yield spreads over a long period of time, as in rubber plantation, it is impossible to estimate the annual returns on the investment.

Another factor which contributes to the limited reliability of the capital co-efficient is that it is affected by many variables which cannot be measured. Technological improvements, better utilization of equipment, improvement in organization, labour skill and methods of production, changes in demand and price, climatic conditions, all these affect the size of output. The experience in India in the First Plan period is illustrative of this uncertainty. The overall ratio for the economy in the plan period was assumed to be 3 : 1 but the large yield of agriculture which was due in a great measure to favourable climatic conditions brought down this ratio to 2 : 1. The variables involved are not only not measurable, but their behaviour also cannot be foreseen.

Capital-output ratio has only a limited practical significance in so far as it does not indicate what the actual contribution of capital alone will be in a given scheme of investment. In making a decision with regard to investment in any enterprise, the planner or the entrepreneur has to weigh the cost against the returns. The cost of capital or the interest to be paid will be found worth incurring only if the contribution of capital is known. It is the marginal product of capital that is equated with interest. In so far as the capital co-efficient indicates the extent to which returns would increase if the supply of capital *along with* other factors is increased, it does not help in making any decision with regard to the scale of investment. Further, the capital-output ratio does not indicate the extent to which other resources are to be increased in combination with capital. Given the technique of production, it assumes that when the amount of capital is varied, the other factors are also to be varied proportionately. The requirement of other factors can be known only if the production function is known. And if the elasticity of supply of the other factors is limited, greater weight will be given to the relative cost of these factors than to capital in investment decisions. In other words, the attractiveness of a low capital-output ratio cannot by itself influence investment decisions; nor would a high capital-output ratio shift investment from capital intensive to capital light enterprises. The choice of techniques in such cases would have to be made on other considerations.[28]

It is therefore not surprising that the capital-output ratios for particular countries estimated by different authorities show considerable variations. An expert Committee of the United Nations estimated in 1951, that in the under-developed countries in Latin America, Africa, Middle East, South Central

[28]Rosen, George, *Industrial Change in India*, Asia Publishing House, Bombay, 1959, p. 38.

Asia and the Far East excluding Japan with a population of about 1,500 millions growing at the average annual rate of 1·25 per cent, an investment of $ 19 billion per year or 20 per cent of their incomes, would secure an increase in their national incomes by 2½ per cent per year.[29] This gives a capital-output ratio of 8 : 1. But, Colin Clark suggests a ratio of 4 : 1 for countries belonging to this category. The same ratio, 4 : 1, was assumed for Ceylon by the International Bank for Reconstruction and Development in 1953. Differences in the estimates are to some extent due to the components on the capital side as for instance, whether inventories or working capital are included or excluded, but they are due largely to the assumptions on which the estimates are based. But it must be observed that even a small change in the ratios will have a magnified effect on capital requirements and the incremental output resulting from investments. Thus Rosen points out that if a ratio of 3 : 1 is computed with a margin of error of ⅓ on either side of the ratio, then the range within which the ratio actually falls may be 2 : 1 and 4 : 1. This means that the rate of return of capital as measured by the ratio falls between 25 per cent and 50 per cent. And this is a difference of 100 per cent in the rate of return.[30] Again, if a figure of 3·0 for the capital-output ratio is used when 4·0 proves to be the correct one, the rise in output comes to be overestimated by 32 per cent after one year and by rising percentages thereafter, if the rate of the investment depends on the increments in output.[31]

Because of the limitations mentioned above, estimates of capital requirements based on capital co-efficient figures tend to be less reliable than what they appear to be. Such estimates are made with reference to the actual growth rate of population and a desired rate of per capita income increase. Thus if population increases at 1 per cent a year, and the capital-output ratio is 4 : 1 then an increase in per capita income by 1 per cent per year would necessitate an investment of 8 per cent of national income. One writer has calculated that in South-East Asian countries with a per capita income of $ 50 and an annual rate of growth of population of 1·33 per cent and average savings of about 4 per cent of national income, if a capital-output ratio of 4 : 1 is assumed, per capita income would decline to $ 47·01 in 1970. Given the population growth rate of 1·33 per cent and capital co-efficient of 4 : 1 per capita income of $ 50 can be maintained only if 5·32 per cent of national income is invested annually. On the same assumptions regarding population growth and capital co-efficient, per capita income can be raised by $ 1 a year or by 2 per cent only if 20 per cent of national income is invested. Investment requirements rise to 40 per cent of national income if per capita income increase is to be 5 per cent a year. Also, if two million people in this region are to be transferred from agriculture to industries so that after twenty years the proportion of

[29] Measures for the Economic Development of Underdeveloped Countries, U.N., 1951, p. 78.

[30] Rosen, George, Industrial Change in India, Asia Publishing House, Bombay, 1959, p. 40 f.n.

[31] Eckstein, Otto, ' Capital Theory and Some Theoretical Problems in Development Planning,' American Economic Review, Papers and Proceedings, May, 1961, p. 96.

industrial to agricultural population will increase from 30 : 70 to 60 : 40, investment required will be 43 per cent of national income which would gradually decline to 26·3 per cent after 15 years and then to 21·3 per cent. This would also raise per capita income from $ 50 in 1950 to $ 96 in 1970.[32] It is obvious that these arithmetical calculations which appear to have a great degree of certainty can be correct only if the assumed capital-output ratio is exact and is not influenced by factors like the intensity of use of capital, technological improvements, etc.

These limitations of the capital-output ratio underline the need for extreme caution in making use of it in the formulation of investment policy. It is worth repeating that this concept as distinct from the concept of marginal productivity of capital does not establish that a given rise in the level of investment would inevitably result in a certain increase in output. The ratio does not imply a causal theory; it indicates only a statistical association between investment and output.[33] However, it indicates broadly the social productivity of capital. The ratios relating to particular industries or sectors of the economy give an idea of the degree of capital intensity required in different enterprises and enable a preliminary estimate to be made of the investment required to obtain a given income. As such, in the absence of other reliable data, it is indispensable if some notion is to be found of the possibilities of putting the various alternatives into practice.[34] Given the supply of capital resources in an economy, even a rough measure of the capital requirements of different industries helps in allotting priorities to the different lines of investment. Moreover, the trends in capital-output ratios pertaining to particular sectors and to the economy as a whole over time provide an insight into the trends in the factor combinations.[35] This helps in an assessment of the extent to which particular resources or factors are to be increased to maintain a given rate of growth of the economy.[36]

[32]Abbas, S. A., *Capital Requirements for the Development of South and South-East Asia*, Wolters, 1956, pp. 114–27.

[33]*Economic Bulletin for Asia and the Far East*, U.N., November, 1955, p. 26 f.n.

[34]*Analyses and Projections of Economic Development*, U.N., 1955, p. 22.

[35]Rosen, George, *Industrial Change in India*, Asia Publishing House, Bombay, 1959, p. 42.

[36]The limitations of the capital-output ratio have led, of late, to a reaction in favour of the production function as a better means of measuring the capital requirements of growing economies. According to the Cobb Douglas Production Formula, product is the function of labour and capital: $p = f(L, C) = bL^k C^{1-k}$: In this formula constant returns are assumed. k and $1-k$ are the labour and capital co-efficients and b is a constant. For the period 1914–22 in the U.S.A. b is given a value of 1·01 and k is assumed to be 0·75. Hence $p = 1·01L^{0·75} C^{0·25}$. Thus according to this formula increase in the supply of capital by 1, raises output by 0·25 and a similar increase in labour raises output by 0·75. Similar estimates have been made for India; Divatia and Trivedi calculated the values for Indian manufacturing industry in the year 1938–39 as $p = 12·17, I^{0·402} C^{0·598}$ and for 1948, Bhatia estimated the figures at 0·67 for labour and 0·26 for capital. (*See* Colin Clark, *Conditions of Economic Progress*, Macmillan, London, III edn., 1957, pp. 589–91.) Tinbergen points out that capital per head figures are better than capital-output ratios in certain cases in so far as for a given country the number of

Capital-Output Ratios in Developed and Underdeveloped Countries

Whether the capital-output ratio in underdeveloped countries would be high or low is a matter about which there is difference of opinion. In this respect the average ratios pertaining to developed economies or to particular industries in such countries do not provide any definite guide. The variation in the ratio as between low income countries themselves is as marked as that between developed and underdeveloped countries. Furthermore, even in respect of the same industries the ratio differs considerably from country to country. A recent estimate of incremental capital-output ratios in some of the advanced and underdeveloped countries relating to the year 1950–59 is illustrative of this point. Among the developed countries it ranges from 3 : 1 in the case of Germany (Federal Republic) to 6·7 : 1 in the case of Denmark. For U.S.A. it is 5·3 : 1 and for the U.K. 6·1 : 1. Some of the smaller but industrially advanced countries have higher ratios than the bigger industrialized countries. The capital co-efficient is as high as 8·9 in Norway, 7·8 in New Zealand, 7·0 in Finland and 6·4 in Sweden. On the other hand, it is 4 in Austria and 3 in Japan. As for the less developed and poorer economies, the capital co-efficient figures are as high as 12 in Argentina and Morocco and as low as 1 in Philippines and Thailand. In most of these countries however, the capital-output ratio is below 4 : 1. In India, Jamaica, Israel, Iraq, Brazil, Panama, Guatemala, it is 2 : 1 and in China, Burma, Mexico, Turkey, Malta, Spain and Chile, it is 3 : 1. In Ceylon, Colombia, Costa Rica, Puerto Rico and Portugal the capital co-efficient is 4. There is besides no correlation between the rate of growth of national income and capital output figures. In Jamaica and Israel where the annual rate of growth of gross domestic product is as high as 12 and 11 per cent, the incremental capital-output ratios are as low as 2 : 1, while in Argentina and Morocco with the highest capital co-efficients of 12 and 11 the rate of growth of gross national product is only 2 per cent per year.[37] Defects in statistical computations apart, the disparity has to be explained by the difference in factor endowments, the ease or difficulty with which capital equipment can be imported, the nature of economic activity, the rate of growth of population, etc.

Capital co-efficients of particular industries also show similar variation

persons to be employed is known whereas the quantity of product is not known before hand but has to be made as high as possible (Tinbergen, Jan, *The Design of Development*, John Hopkins, Baltimore, 1958, p. 72). Prof. Eckstein remarks that " statistically these functions explain the historical changes in output with astounding precision and unless the economic structure changes, the aggregate production functions should do very well better than the incremental capital output ratios "—' Capital Theory and some Theoretical Problems in Development Planning,' *American Economic Review, Papers and Proceedings*, May, 1961, p. 97. However, a correct estimate of the production function in low income countries is as difficult as it is to calculate the capital-output ratios, and unless the production function is worked out with greater precision it cannot be used extensively in investment programming.

[37] *The Eastern Economist*, Annual Number, Delhi, 1962, pp. 48 and 65.

between countries. An estimate relating to the year 1946–47 shows that the capital-output ratios in some of the agro-industries in India were much higher than that in an industrialized country like Canada. The capital co-efficient in the case of wheat flour was 1·83 in India and 1·31 in Australia but 0·35 in Canada; fruits and vegetable processing 1·44 in India but 0·85 in Canada and 0·74 in Australia; sugar 1·49 in India and 0·86 in Canada. But in some small manufacturing industries the ratio is lower in India. Thus in paints and varnishes, it is 0·38 in India as against 0·52 in Australia, 0·74 in Canada and 0·89 in New Zealand. In cement manufacturing the co-efficient is 1·75 for India but 3·97 for Canada while it is as low as 0·87 in New Zealand; for cotton textiles the ratio is 0·58 in India as compared with 0·67 in Canada. But in a heavy industry like iron and steel the ratio seems to be relatively high in India—1·30 against 1·04 in Canada. It may be plausible to argue that in respect of bigger manufacturing industries the ratio tends to be high in the initial stages in poorer countries because of the costliness of imported equipment, lack of adequately trained personnel to operate the machines, lack of proper maintenance of equipment and probably underutilization of capital equipment. However, in course of time, as the industry gets well established, many of these difficulties would disappear, capital will be fully exploited and the ratio would tend to come down even below that of richer countries because of cheapness of labour, availability of materials, etc. This possibly explains the lower ratio for cotton and woollen textiles and some other small manufactures in a low income country like India.

In the last few years the overall capital-output ratio of India has shown some marked fluctuations. Divatia and Trivedi estimated the capital co-efficients of Indian manufacturing industries in 1938–39 at 2·045. According to a recent estimate[38] the average capital-output ratio of manufacturing industries in India during the period 1946–55 was 1·976. It reached the maximum of 2·31 in 1952 and the minimum of 1·51 in 1948. The rise in the years 1946–50 was due to the large industrial investments made after the war on account of new industries and replacement of worn out machinery and rehabilitation of existing industries. The slight decline of the ratio to 2·05 in 1951 must have been caused by the better utilization of capacity necessitated by the Korean War boom. Since then, with the commencement of the First Five-Year Plan and large investment schemes in the public and private sectors, the ratio has remained above 2 : 1. The overall capital-output ratio for the economy shows a rise from the First to the Second Plan and since the end of the Second Plan period a decline. This is shown in Table 19.

As has been observed already, while the First Five-Year Plan estimated the ratio at 3 : 1 the actual figure turned out to be lower because of increased production, particularly in the agricultural sector. The availability of un-

[38]Mukherjee, B. N., 'The Capital-Output Ratios in Indian Manufacturing Industries, 1946–55,' *Arthaniti*, Calcutta, May, 1959, pp. 153–60.

Table 19

CAPITAL OUTPUT RATIOS IN INDIA
(In the three Plan periods Rs. million)

	First Plan	Second Plan	Third Plan
	at		*at*
	1948–49 prices		*1960–61 prices*
National Income at the beginning of the Plan	88,500	104,800	145,000
National Income at the end of the Plan	104,800	125,300	190,000
Absolute increase in National Income (output)	16,300	20,500	45,000
Net investment (input)	33,600	67,500	104,000
Investment: Output	2·06 : 1	3·29 : 1	2·31 : 1

SOURCE: *Eastern Economist*, Annual Number, Delhi, 1962, p. 51.

utilized capacity over the First Plan years would also have contributed to the decline in the ratio. On the other hand, during the Second Plan period when no unutilized capacity was available and the monsoons were not favourable, the ratio rose to a little above 3 : 1. The stress laid on heavy industries and the large investments in the Second Plan period should also be mentioned as a factor contributing to a higher capital co-efficient. As for the period to be covered by the Third Plan, if the investment and increase in national income turn out to be the same as expected, the capital co-efficient would fall below 2·5 : 1. This however, is not unlikely, in view of the scope for better utilization of capacity installed in the Second Plan period, and the possibility of increased agricultural output resulting from the investments which have already been made in this sector.

What the actual capital-output ratio would be in underdeveloped countries in the early stages of growth, and what its trend would be as the economy progresses, appear to be, by and large, a matter of guess work. Among the forces which tend to push up the ratio may be mentioned the following. Firstly, economic development of present day underdeveloped countries which have stagnated for centuries in a state of under-employment equilibrium is possible only if very heavy 'lumpy' investments are made for the provision of social overhead facilities—improvement of means of communications, construction of roads and railways, hydro-electric schemes, establishment of financial and banking institutions, development of ports and harbours, etc. To the extent such large investments have to precede industrial expansion, and in so far as the external economies from such development projects would take much time to fructify, the capital-output ratio in the initial stages is bound to be high. Secondly, (and this also emerges from the fact that underdeveloped countries are late in the race for economic development) the low income countries have to import technology and capital equipment from

11

industrially advanced countries. With scarcity of labour and abundance of capital, the technology and capital goods developed in the advanced countries are generally always of the capital-intensive type. In so far as the poorer countries are incapable of developing a technology suited to their own factor endowments, they have to import such costly equipment. Since skilled labour is lacking, management is unsatisfactory and the maintenance of capital goods defective, it would not be possible to operate the capital goods efficiently. All these would make the ratio of output to cost of capital, small. It has also been mentioned that in the early stages of growth, when the income of the people rises and conditions of life improve, there will be a tendency on the part of the people to demand costlier manufactured consumption goods which are the products of capital intensive industries. Fuller exploitation and possible exhaustion of non-reproducible wealth such as mineral and other subsoil resources, would necessitate importing of materials from abroad or the production of synthetic substitutes all of which add to the investment and costs of production and raise the capital-output ratio. Lastly, urbanization which goes hand in hand with industrialization would necessitate large investments in urban house construction and the provision of other amenities and add to the cost side of capital.

The experience of present day developed countries in a corresponding stage of their economic growth lends support to the view that capital-output ratio will rise in the early stages of development. Over the twenty years of the United States economic development, from 1879 to 1899, the overall capital co-efficient steadily rose from 2·98 in 1879 to 3·01 in 1884, 3·21 in 1889, 3·59 in 1894 and 3·85 in 1899. On this ground it is estimated that in the underdeveloped countries of the South and South-East Asian region the ratio of investment to income would go up from the level of about 4 : 1 in the mid-twentieth century to over 5: 1 about 1970.[39] Large investments in social overheads and in heavy industries have to be concentrated in this period of two decades, so as to prepare the ground for self-sustained growth at a later stage.

On the other hand, some valid points are brought out to substantiate the view that in the backward economies, even if the ratio is high to begin with, it would rapidly come down. Available statistical data relating to many of these countries show that with few exceptions the capital co-efficients are lower than in developed countries. A recent study of the United Nations estimated the capital-output ratio for Brazil at 4·8 : 1 in 1925; this high ratio was due to accumulation of capital in agriculture and building, and low technical level. But as a result of investment in industry, transport and electricity and overall development of the economy, the ratio rapidly fell to less than 3 : 1 in 1945 and to 2·5 : 1 in 1954.[40] It should be noted that in this calculation there is to some extent an underestimation on the capital side

[39] Abbas, S. A., *Capital Requirements for the Development of South and South-East Asia*, Wolters, 1956, p. 119.

[40] *Analyses and Projections of Economic Development*, U.N., 1955, p. 22.

because of the non-inclusion of inventories. Also, favourable economic factors in the Latin American countries would have helped in an efficient utilization of capital, labour and natural resources. Nevertheless, the findings indicate the possibility of the ratio coming down rapidly in underdeveloped countries. Although the initial investments may be heavy, in process of time the capital stock would be better utilized. There would be improvement in the skill of labour as well as of management, better experience in the handling and maintenance of machines, and as a result the output per unit of capital invested will rise. Further, their lateness in economic development helps the pre-industrial countries in so far as they can import up-to-date technology from the advanced countries and skip the long period of costly experiments and research in technological innovations. It is also not too much to hope that the poorer countries of today with factor endowments different from that of the industrial countries would be able to adapt technology to suit their resources position and they would be able to produce capital goods of a cheaper variety requiring greater quantity of labour to work with. Such a process will be facilitated by the increasing scope for closer contacts with richer countries, greater ease in the communication of ideas and the dispersal of technical knowledge and skill. Perhaps the easier flow of technical information and knowledge from developed to underdeveloped countries is the most decisive factor in not only accelerating the pace of economic growth in the latter, but also in enabling them to evolve techniques of their own, and stand on their own legs. The increasing attention devoted to public health, education and technical training would raise the productivity of labour and thereby help in a great measure to increase national output without any proportionate increase in fixed capital. Also, when development gets underway, various external economies would arise and industries in which no additional investment is made would benefit by the expansion of some key major industries and public utilities. Colin Clark mentions the point that economic growth would involve the expansion of the tertiary sector which is relatively capital-scarce as compared with the secondary or industrial sector and as such with every increase in the proportion of labour engaged in the tertiary industries, capital requirements will decline relatively.

It would thus appear that the forces tending to raise the capital co-efficient in underdeveloped countries are balanced by opposite forces which would reduce it. Hence it would be hazardous to make any definite conclusion regarding the behaviour of capital co-efficient in developing economies. The actual trend depends upon the specific forces at work in any particular country, its factor supply situation, the economic conditions under which growth takes place, the pattern of economic and industrial development which the country adopts, its contact with advanced economies, the skill, efficiency and aptitudes of its people, etc. In respect of India, after reviewing the factors affecting the capital co-efficient, Coale and Hoover make the cautious remark that " there appears no ground to expect an unusually high ratio and a fair presumption for expecting the ratio to be rather on the low side in the near term future

as compared with the ratios of 3 : 1 and higher in developed countries ".
They however add that as development proceeds the ratio is likely to rise.[41]
As the economy develops, there will be need for increased investment in housing
and other welfare categories. But while the need for greater housing facilities
is great in India, the fact that cost of construction and standards are lower
would prevent the capital co-efficient rising higher because of this factor.
On the other hand, investment in transport, communication and other economic
and social overheads requires a large amount of capital. And although unlike
in many other low income countries much of these overheads is already available
in India, they are strained to their capacity and there is need for fresh investments on a substantial scale. Against this, the possibility of importing capital-
saving technology from the advanced countries and the fact that there is great
scope for the economizing of capital in the agricultural sector and in handicrafts and small industries would lower the ratio. This possibility is particularly
great in agriculture which constitutes an important segment of the economy
and accounts for about 25 to 30 per cent of the total growth of output in the
country. The present ratio in agriculture is supposed to be about 1 : 1 and
the scope for expanding agricultural output through labour-intensive methods
would be a major factor in keeping the overall capital-output ratio low.

But on the whole it appears that the forces tending to raise the capital
ratio in India are stronger than those working in the opposite direction. In
general, so long as emphasis is laid on industrialization, hydro-electric projects
and the development of social overheads, investment is bound to rise rapidly
without, in the initial period, yielding any corresponding increase in output.
It would take a fairly long period of time before this preliminary phase of
preparing the ground for growth can be completed. To this should be added
the tendency towards greater capital intensity in Indian industries observed
by Rosen. His view is that the effect of government policy in recent times has
been both to raise labour costs directly in terms of higher wages and amenity
costs and to reduce greatly the area of manageability of labour. This rise in
labour costs combined with the competition of government plants has forced
the private firms to introduce more capital intensive and labour saving equipment.[42] It would thus be seen that the chances for the capital-output ratio
in India to come down in the next two or three decades are very limited. The
decline observed in the early stages of the Third Plan period may well prove
to be a very temporary phenomenon.

Low Level of Capital Formation in Underdeveloped Countries

The additions made to the stock of capital of an economy directly increase its

[41]Coale, A. J. and E. M. Hoover, *Population Growth and Economic Development in Low Income
Countries*, Oxford, India, 1959, p. 233.

[42]Rosen, George, ' Capital-Output Ratios in Indian Industry,' *Indian Economic Journal*,
October, 1956, pp. 107-21.

productive capacity. There is a much closer positive correlation between the rate of capital formation and per capita incomes than between the capital-output ratio and the level of income of a country. Arranging different countries in seven groups in the order of their per capita incomes, Simon Kuznets finds the variation in the average rate of capital formation as follows:

Table 20

PER CAPITA INCOME STATUS AND RATE OF CAPITAL FORMATION
(The data relate to the years 1950–55)

Groups of Countries according to Product per capita	Ratio of Gross Domestic Capital Formation to Gross Domestic Product
1	21·3%
2	23·3%
3	17·2%
4	15·7%
5	18·2%
6	
7	17·1%

SOURCE: Simon Kuznets, Six Lectures on Economic Growth, Table 8, pp. 72 and 73.

In groups 1 and 2 taken together the ratio of gross domestic capital formation to gross domestic product is 22·2 per cent; in 3, 4 and 5 it is 16·3 per cent and in 5, 6 and 7 it is 16·2 per cent. The fact that in general, the rate of capital formation is higher in richer countries than in low income countries is further illustrated by figures relating to particular countries. (Table 21.)

Table 21

GROSS DOMESTIC CAPITAL FORMATION AS A PERCENTAGE OF GNP
IN SOME COUNTRIES

Countries Group A	Year	Gross Domestic Capital Formation	Countries Group B	Year	Gross Domestic Capital Formation
Norway	1959	29%	Burma	1960	17%
Austria	1960	24%	Portugal	1959	17%
Netherlands	1960	24%	Ceylon	1960	13%
Canada	1960	23%	Ireland	1959	13%
Switzerland	1959	23%	Chile	1959	11%
Sweden	1960	22%	Philippines	1959	8%
U.K.	1960	16%	India	1959	8%
U.S.A.	1960	16%			

SOURCE: Statistical Year Book. U.N., 1961.

The average rate of capital formation works out to 22 per cent in the case of high income countries which are in Group A, and to 12 per cent in Group B countries whose per capita incomes are well below the world's average. Obviously enough, in countries with a high rate of capital formation, the amount of capital per employed person is greater than in the low income countries in similar industries. This disparity is shown in Table 22.[43]

Table 22

CAPITAL PER PERSON EMPLOYED IN SOME INDUSTRIES IN THE U.S.A., MEXICO AND INDIA
(Thousands of U.S. Dollars, 1950 prices)

Industry	U.S.A. 1950	Mexico 1945	India 1950
Bread and bakery products	5·0	1·7	3·5
Cotton yarn and cloth	8·7	2·1	1·8
Flour and grist mill products	39·1	10·4	5·6
Iron and steel industries	32·1	10·8	5·7
Sugar refining	26·8	8·2	2·6
Wood pulp, paper and paper products	10·2	8·9	6·6

SOURCE: Tinbergen, Jan, *The Design of Development*, Johns Hopkins, Baltimore, 1958, p. 73.

The annual rate of capital formation in India is about one-third of that attained in some advanced countries like Canada, Germany and Japan. Similarly, in respect of capital per head of employed labour, India ranks much below Mexico and as compared with the U.S.A., the capital available per head of worker is about one-fifth. Apart from the statistical data, scarcity of capital is reflected in the methods of production usually adopted in under-developed countries. Much of the work that is done by mechanical power in advanced countries is performed by manual labour in the underdeveloped countries. This is basically due to the difference in the factor endowments of the countries concerned. But this disparity in factor supply in a large measure accounts for economic stagnation in so far as productivity of labour will be much lower when capital available per head is very limited; as a result, a vicious circle is created in which low capital formation accounts for low productivity per head which in turn keeps down savings and prevents a rise in the level of investment.

The obvious explanation of the scarcity of capital in underdeveloped countries is therefore to be found in low level of productivity and savings. Given the low level of savings the only possibility of accelerating capital formation is by the proper and careful utilization of the meagre savings for investment purposes. It is necessary here to emphasize the obvious fact that

[43]See also Table 3 on p. 14.

savings and investment represent a real cost in the form of consumption fore-gone. Interest is the compensation paid for the sacrifice involved in postpone-ment of consumption and accumulation of savings. On the other hand, investment is undertaken with a view to make a profit which represents the earnings out of investment. Thus any investment undertaken will be dependent on the rate of interest to be paid which is the cost of the marginal productivity of capital that determines the return on investment. It is thus clear that the lower is the interest rate and the higher the rate of returns on capital, the larger will be investment, other conditions remaining the same. In developed coun-tries both these factors are favourable to a high level of investment. Large savings and adequate institutional facilities for mobilizing savings and cana-lizing them into investment keep down the rate of interest, while improvement in technical skill and efficiency of labour, discoveries of new raw materials and the availability of expanding markets raise the marginal potential revenue of investment. In contrast, in underdeveloped countries savings are meagre, difficult to mobilize and interest rate is high. And the lack of demand for a variety of goods, rigidities in factor supply and the fact that " the future typically appears very uncertain in these countries " account for a rapid decline in the marginal potential revenue of capital. Level of investment is therefore much lower.[44]

This theoretical explanation of the low level of investment stresses two important factors affecting capital formation in underdeveloped countries: firstly, lack of savings and proper institutional agencies to mobilize even the meagre savings; and secondly, lack of an expanding market. In poorer economies the propensity to consume is high. But this refers to goods which are required to meet the primary needs of society and as such, a disproportio-nately large number of people are engaged in the production of things that meet elementary needs. Production of such commodities requires relatively smaller investment but at the same time since productivity of labour and earnings in these occupations are low, there is little scope for the generation of savings large enough to promote investment and capital formation. Low earnings also prevent expansion of demand. The demand for a wide variety of goods is an incentive for larger investments. Hence the importance of foreign trade in these countries. The role of expansion of foreign markets in promoting economic growth in some of the present day developed countries in the early stages of growth is a matter of history. The possibilities of such a development in contemporary underdeveloped countries are however, limited.

On the other hand, even the meagre savings that are available are not properly canalized into investment because of the lack of organized financial institutions. This accounts for the great disparity in interest rates from region to region in the same country. These two factors constitute the major deterrents to the emergence of entrepreneurship in many of the low income countries.

[44]Williamson, H. F. and A. J. Buttrick (Eds.), *Economic Development: Principles and Paterns*, New York. 1954, pp. 150-55.

True entrepreneurship is not forthcoming because the avenues of productive employment of capital are limited. It is this factor that explains the common phenomenon of investment in land, in real estate speculation, in consumer durables and foreign exchange, inordinate expenditure on palatial buildings and luxury goods, foreign tours, etc.

Undoubtedly, such expenditures are possible only because of a previous act of saving. Hence the magnitude of expenditures of this nature measures the potential savings of the economy which are dissipated. The hoarding of cash balances does not absorb real resources but releases them from consumption uses. But productive investment materializes only if two steps are taken— savings and the acquisition of capital goods. The accumulation of cash balances implies savings but to the extent they remain in that form, the supply of financial resources to potential productive borrowers is restricted and the chances of savings being turned into investment are denied. The same can be said of investment in land. The purchase of land makes available financial resources to the seller and here again whether the transaction promotes investment or not depends on the manner in which the financial resources acquired by the seller are utilized. There is capital formation if the seller invests in capital goods or in business and there is wastage if he dissipates it by indulging in conspicuous consumption or other uneconomic spending. On the part of the purchaser of land, if he uses it productively for better and more intensive cultivation or for other productive purposes, his expenditure results in increased output. But if he buys land for merely holding it, an opportunity for productive employment of savings is lost. The holding of land does not use up society's real resources, but there is a social loss in so far as an opportunity to direct resources from consumption to productive asset creation is missed. Quite often, such investments are made for speculative purposes. The craze for holding of land for this purpose itself pushes up the value of land and this brings capital gains to the holder. But these gains are not the result of any productive effort and do not represent any contribution to total output. Besides, the springing up of a host of middle men and administrators causes a wastage of human effort.[45] Furthermore, when land is used as a highly liquid asset, and money is borrowed by using land as a collateral, and the borrowed money is not productively employed, aggregate potential saving of the economy will be reduced. If the speculative demand for land is high, and purchases are made out of borrowed funds, the rate of interest on such loans would rise which would in turn push up the general interest rate and make it difficult for prospective industrialists to borrow. Also, if the rate of return on money lending on the basis of land which is hypothecated, is high, it will result in turning business energy more and more into such channels and lower the natural level of investment in industrial enterprises.[46]

[45]Baumol, W. J., *Business Behaviour, Value and Growth*, Macmillan, New York, 1959, p. 115.

[46]Rosenberg, Nathan, 'Capital Formation in Underdeveloped Countries,' *American Economic Review*, September, 1960, pp. 706-15.

It is thus clear that low capital formation in underdeveloped countries is to some extent due to the underdeveloped nature of the investment mechanism and other institutional deficiencies which weaken the inducement to invest. The restricted flow of savings into investment, the acquisition of non-productive assets, the lack of entrepreneurial skill, the unattractiveness of investment in business and industry are all representative of behaviour patterns common in most of the underdeveloped countries. These may disappear with economic progress but the knowledge of these limitations should help in directing government's economic policy towards removing them. This would promote the emergence of the true entrepreneur class and accelerate capital formation and economic progress.

CAPITAL FORMATION IN INDIA

Estimates about capital formation in India show that the growth of investment in the Indian economy has been slow and halting and does not stand comparison with the levels attained in the developed countries and even in some of the underdeveloped countries. Capital formation in the three years preceding the commencement of the First Plan period was as follows:

Table 23

NATIONAL INCOME AND CAPITAL FORMATION IN INDIA 1948-1951
(Rs. Millions)

Year	National Income	Domestic Fixed Capital Formation (net)	Ratio of 2 to 1 (per cent)
	(1)	(2)	(3)
1948–49	86,500	3,410	4·0
1949–50	90,100	4,150	4·6
1950–51	95,300	4,530	4·7

SOURCE: Rangnekar, D. K., *Poverty and Capital Development in India*, Oxford, London, 1959. p. 212.

Inventory accumulation in these three years has been estimated at Rs. 1,610, Rs. 710 and Rs. 960 million for 1948–49, 1949–50 and 1950–51 respectively. If these are added to the figures in column 2, the ratio of total domestic investment would form 5·8 per cent of national income in 1948–49, 5·4 per cent in 1949–50 and 5·7 per cent in 1950–51.

The trend in capital formation in the First Plan years is shown in Table 23.

Table 24

CAPITAL FORMATION IN INDIA 1951–56
(Rs. Millions)

Year	National Income	Domestic Fixed Capital Formation (net)	Ratio of 2 : 1 (per cent)*
1951–52	99,700	4,880	4·9
1952–53	98,200	4,630	4·7
1953–54	104,800	4,980	4·7
1954–55	96,100	5,430	5·4
1955–56	99,800	6,000	6·0

It is estimated that inventory accumulation amounted to the quite high figure of Rs. 2,390 million in 1951–52. If this is included, total domestic capital formation in 1951–52, the first year of the First Five-Year Plan, would amount to Rs. 7,270 million or 7·3 per cent of the national income. The sharp rise in inventories in 1951–52 was due to speculative hoarding and involuntary stock piling. Stocks were drawn down in the next two years but in the last two years of the First Plan, 1954–55 and 1955–56, accumulation of inventories again went up. Thus if inventories are included capital formation would have risen to about 7½ per cent at the close of the Plan and the average rate over the five years would have been about 6 to 6½ per cent of national income.[47]

Some investment takes place in the rural sector outside the money economy. This takes the form of rural construction performed by unpaid family service with free local materials and also such works as road building, sinking of wells and improvement of farms done under the Community Development Schemes.

In the three years preceding the commencement of the First Plan, aggregate investment was running at a rate of about 5½ per cent of national income. Of the total, inventories accounted for 32 per cent in 1948–49, 14·7 per cent in 1949–50 and 17·4 per cent in 1950–51. Investment in transport and communications was more or less constant over the three years at about 15 per cent. Industry and mining absorbed about 28 per cent in the first and third years but rose to above 33 per cent in 1949–50. There was however, substantial rise under agriculture and irrigation and power. Investment under the former head rose from 0·7 per cent in 1948–49 to 6·2 per cent in 1950–51 and that under irrigation and power increased from 1·9 per cent to 12·6 per cent in the same years. As regards later years, the following estimate made by the Indian Taxation Enquiry Commission illustrates the relative trend.

[47]Rangnekar, D. K., *Poverty and Capital Development in India*, Oxford, London, 1959, pp. 230–32.

Table 25

DISTRIBUTION OF INVESTMENT IN INDIA IN 1950–51 AND 1953–54

(*Millions of Rupees*)

	1950–51	1953–54
Public Investment	1,850	3,050
Private Investment		
(a). Organized enterprises : Public Ltd. & Private Ltd. Cos.	550	550
(b) Urban housing	900	1,200
(c) Rural investment	1,400	1,600
(d) Transport other than Railways	250	200
Investment abroad (net)	600	700
Aggregate net investment	5,550	7,300

SOURCE : *Report of the Taxation Enquiry Commission*, Government of India, 1953–54, Vol. I, p. 138.

There is a marked increase in the proportion of public investment in the total investment from about 33 per cent in the pre-plan year to 42 per cent in 1953–54. In the private sector there is some absolute rise under urban housing and rural investment but the relative share of the sector has been pulled down by an absolute decline under transport and a relative decline under organized enterprises. In the last two years of the First Plan however, along with the general rise in the tempo of investment in the economy, investment position in the private sector also appears to have improved.[48] But on the whole, over these years there was slackness in private investment owing to various factors like lack of an adequate supply of investible funds, higher taxation, government controls and regulations and the general uncertainty about government policy towards the private sector. It should also be remembered that taking the public and private sectors together, against the rough target set by the Planning Commission of increasing aggregate investment by about 40 per cent, the actual achievement was only an increase to the extent of about 16 or 17 per cent. Investment at the end of the Plan was only about Rs. 17 per head of population as against Rs. 15 in 1950–51, representing an increase of only 13 per cent.[49]

[48]For the entire corporate sector including public and private limited companies and branches of foreign companies, but excluding financial companies, net total capital formation amounted to Rs. 441 crores in the period 1951–55. The average capital formation in these companies in the four years 1951–54 was about Rs. 680 million but it rose to Rs. 1,680 million in 1955, and to Rs. 3,560 million in 1956—Sastry, N. S. R., and K. A. Antony, ' Capital Formation in the Corporate Business Sector in India,' *Papers on National Income and Allied Topics*, Vol. I, Indian Conference on Research in National Income, Asia Publishing House, Bombay, 1960, pp. 159–71.

[49]Rangnekar, D. K., *Poverty and Capital Development in India*, Oxford, London, 1959, pp. 233–34.

The Second Five-Year Plan estimated an investment of Rs. 62,000 million—Rs. 38,000 million in the public sector and Rs. 24,000 million in the private sector—over the five years (1956–61); and the rate of investment was expected to increase from about 7 per cent to about 11 per cent of national income. Actual aggregate investment in both the sectors in the Second Plan was Rs. 67,500 million. National income nearly reached the level originally expected to be attained at the end of the Second Plan (about Rs. 145,000 million at current prices). It is estimated that over the 10 years covered by the First and Second Plans total investment in the private and public sectors increased from over Rs. 5,000 million per annum at the beginning of the First Plan to about Rs. 16,000 million at the end of the Second Plan. The share of public investment rose from about Rs. 2,000 million per annum to Rs. 8,000 million. The aggregate investment in the 10 years at current prices has been estimated at Rs. 101,100 million, Rs. 52,100 million being in the public sector and Rs. 49,000 million in the private sector. It is expected that national income would rise to Rs. 190,000 million at the end of the Third Plan. With population growing at the rate of 2 per cent per annum, per capita income would rise from about Rs. 330 at the end of 1960–61 to about Rs. 385 at the end of 1965–66. This will require a rise in investment rate from 11 per cent of the national income to about 14–15 per cent of national income by the end of the Third Plan. Correspondingly, domestic savings should rise from 8·5 per cent of national income to 11·5 per cent.[50]

However, compared with the capital formation figures of the developed countries and even some of the underdeveloped countries and the availability of capital per head in these countries, the above estimates relating to India appear to be very modest. They indicate only the extent to which further progress has to be made in the line of investment in order to attain a moderate increase in national and per capita incomes. The target of investment to be attained at the end of the Third Plan in India is 14 to 15 per cent of national income. But the current level of gross domestic capital formation is nearly 30 per cent in Japan, Australia and Norway and above 20 per cent in most of the West European countries. Even among underdeveloped countries high rates of 21 per cent to 26 per cent have been attained in Jamaica and Israel. In some of the other underdeveloped countries in Asia the rate is higher than in India, Ceylon 11 per cent, Thailand 16 per cent, China (Taiwan) 17 per cent, Burma 16 per cent. In fact India ranks among the lowest of the underdeveloped countries in this respect.

Measures to Promote Capital Formation in Underdeveloped Countries

A Committee of the United Nations estimated in 1949 that in order to ensure a steady growth of per capita incomes in underdeveloped countries an annual

[50]*Third Five-Year Plan*, Planning Commission, Government of India, 1961, pp. 32, 75, 76, 91.

investment of 13 per cent of the national income would be required.[51] Since population growth is quite high in most of these countries, aggregate consumption level would rise so much as to absorb any improvement in production brought about by a small rise in the rate of investment. Only if there is an appreciable increase in capital formation and the rise in output per capita is substantial, can, the savings margin widen sufficiently as to make further increase in investment easy. This view of the situation brings into prominence not only the true nature of the problem of capital formation in underdeveloped countries but also the urgency of it.

It is possible to widen the savings margin and step up the rate of capital formation by lowering the level of consumption, raising the level of production with available resources and by making use of foreign capital. By severe austerity measures and by cutting down consumption to the bone, Russia and Japan were able, in the second and third decades of the present century, to raise the level of savings and investment to about 30 per cent of the national income.[52] This, however, is not possible in most of the underdeveloped countries of today. Consumption level is already very low in these countries and the political faith and form of government and the government's objective of improving economic welfare through economic planning, rule out the possibility of any severe restrictive or austerity measures. As for foreign capital, the larger part of it is in the form of loans which have to be repaid—apart from the annual interest payments to be made. Its flow moreover, is conditioned by many economic and political considerations and it cannot be very much relied upon to bring about the necessary economic transformation. Underdeveloped countries therefore have to depend mostly on their own resources to bring about their economic salvation.

There is, however, great scope for raising the level of investment even with the available resources. To the extent the flow of finance into investment is hampered by institutional factors, it is possible to facilitate this flow by institutional changes involving the development of banking, insurance and other financial institutions and by creating special financial agencies of the government to canalize the savings. Apart from this, there are other measures which would help capital formation in underdeveloped countries.

(a) Better Utilization of Existing Capital

Since higher level of investment is possible only by raising the level of per capita income it is worthwhile to examine how far production per head can

---

[51]*Methods of Financing Economic Development in Underdeveloped Countries.* U. N., 1949, p. 61.

[52]If capital-output ratio is 2: 1, investment 10 per cent of national income, and if income increases by 5 per cent a year and consumption by 2·5 per cent, then in five years net national product will rise from 100 to 130·9, consumption from 90·0 to 99·34 and investment from 10 to 31·56; but if consumption increases at the same rate as net product, then the rate of growth at the end of five years will be the same as in the first year—Celso Furtado, ' Capital Formation and Economic Development,' *International Economic Papers*, No. 4, p. 137.

be increased by better and more efficient application of the capital equipment available. Since one of the major problems of underdeveloped countries is capital scarcity, it is necessary to utilize the existing capacity to the maximum extent possible. This would in addition to saving internal capital resources, help also in the saving of foreign exchange which may be utilized for the importing of additional and necessary capital equipment. Fuller utilization of capital involves the optimal utilization of managerial skill. which also is a scarce factor in the poorer economies. If total output is increased without increasing the stock of capital, by the application of more labour units, both the capital-output ratio and the capital-labour ratio fall.

But it appears paradoxical that in countries where there is scarcity of capital, there is also under-utilization of capital. In reality, there is unemployment of capital in many low income countries. This situation arises quite often as a result of the inadequacy of complementary resources such as the skilled labour required for the operation and maintenance of the machinery. Business fluctuations either domestic or of the imported kind, or domestic shifts in market structure, or the falling off of the demand for particular products also lead to idleness of capital.[53]

A recent study of the problem of utilization of capital in India shows that there was in 1951–59 and particularly in the latter half of the decade, a marked rise in the utilization of capacity in the industries in the organized sector. This has been attributed to government policy and efforts, rising demand for capital goods and foreign exchange difficulties which considerably restricted the flow of capital equipment from abroad. It is found that as between infra-structure industries, i.e., social and economic overheads establishments, and producer and consumer goods industries, there was a persistent tendency towards a nearly full utilization of capacity in the first category, exemplified by the adoption of three shifts in all the industries belonging to this group. The producer goods industries do not reflect the same intensive use of capital equipment. On the other hand, the last category, namely, consumer goods industries expanded too fast with the result that expanded capacity could not be utilized. To some extent this was due to shortage of raw materials; partly it was also due to the inadequate expansion of the infra-structure industries. The conclusion is therefore drawn that an acceleration of the general growth of the economy can occur only if the existing structural imbalance is removed by restricting fresh investments in the consumer goods industries and by making increased investments in the infra-structure sector. These findings lend support to the emphasis laid by the government in the Third Plan on heavy industry and on the expansion of social overhead facilities.[54]

[53]Sturmthal, Adolf, 'Economic Development, Income Distribution and Capital Formation in Mexico,' *Journal of Political Economy*, June, 1955, p. 191.

[54]Budin, Morris and Samuel Paul, 'The Utilization of Indian Industrial Capacity,' *The Indian Economic Journal*, July, 1961, pp. 19–47.

The experience of Japan in the last quarter of the nineteenth century is a classic illustration of the possibilities of fuller utilization of capacity as a means to accelerate capital formation. A rough estimate of the trends in the overall capital-output ratio in that country shows a steady decline from 2·50 in 1883–92 to 1·29 in 1893–1902. This was the result of maximum utilization of capital capacity in the secondary and tertiary sectors by means of multiple shifts and greater application of labour and by new methods of rice cultivation, double cropping, seed and fertilizer improvement, etc., which reduced agricultural population with very little investment activity in agriculture and pushed up agricultural labour productivity by 76 per cent in the two decades before 1900. Thus by careful husbanding of the available resources and by utilizing existing capacity to the straining point, Japanese economy was able to lift itself by its bootstraps. The remarkable achievement at the end of the nineteenth century paved the way for Japan's take off in the third decade of the twentieth century. In the first quarter of this century, inflow of foreign capital and increased domestic savings raised the capital-output ratio of the Japanese economy and a strong base for the industrial future of the country was laid in the years after the Russo-Japanese War and First World War. This austere preparation enabled Japan to escape her low level equilibrium trap and enter the Harrodian World of developed economies.[55] It thus becomes clear that if existing capital is fully utilized as it is done actually in wartime, it could serve as a starting point for rapid economic growth.

(b) Improvement and Adaptation of Technology

Modern technology is to a large extent capital saving but it increases labour productivity and helps in achieving a larger outturn with relatively lesser use of real resources. Looked at in this manner, it is clear that underdeveloped countries can benefit by recent technological advances. It is mentioned that in the 1930s as a result of improvements in technology in the U.S.A., important rises in production occurred while total capital was even declining. Recent economic history of the West European countries provides further evidence in support of this view. In 1950–57 the Gross National Product of Germany rose by 70 per cent. Much of this rise was due to increased labour productivity. In Norway, Sweden, Belgium and Luxembourg, improvement in productivity was even higher than in Germany. And this was largely due to automation and rationalization. There is undoubtedly great scope in at least the more advanced among the poorer countries such as India, for the adaptation of technology to suit their needs and factor endowments. In the field of agriculture as well as in industry, it would be possible to devise improved and cheap techniques of production, which without absorbing much of capital would be able to secure substantial improvements in labour productivity. Increased earnings per head would be one of the major factors contributing to accelerated

[55]Ranis, G., 'The Capital-Output Ratio in Japanese Economic Development,' *The Review of Economic Studies*, October, 1958, pp. 23–32.

capital formation. Without any exaggeration it may be said that economic growth is a function of technological expansion of the right type.

(c) Making the Best Use of Labour Resources

In order to increase production and investment it is necessary to make better and more efficient use of not only the scarce factor namely capital, but also the abundant factor, labour. Although much of the disparity in labour productivity between underdeveloped countries and developed countries is due to the larger capital equipment and better technology available in the latter, the fact cannot be disputed that there is considerable difference in the skill, willingness to work and application of labour. According to an estimate made by Solomon Fabricant, per capita output in the U.S.A. increased in the eight decades 1869–73 to 1949–53 at the annual rate of 1·9 per cent. Only about 1/10 of this growth is attributed by Fabricant to a rise in the stock of tangible capital. The main cause for this improvement in output was, that the people of America had learned to produce with a given amount of capital and labour, a larger and larger volume of goods. In other words, as much as 9/10 of the growth was due to improvement in the quality of labour and the efficiency of the productive arts.[56] In no economically advanced country of the world today is labour inefficient, indolent or lacks the willingness to do hard work. And there is no reason why any country should remain economically backward if its people are diligent, enterprising and hardworking. The manner in which the economies of Germany and Japan have been built up so quickly and so efficiently in recent years after the ravages of the most destructive of wars, shows convincingly what human capital is capable of achieving. It is true that in order to build up such human capital, large investment in social services, in public health, education and in scientific and technological research is necessary. But the fact is that even with the equipment now available in the low income countries there is scope for increasing output by better utilization of labour power. The underdeveloped countries which are worried over the problem of scarcity of capital would better ask themselves the question whether they are making the maximum use of their labour power which is abundant. The argument that labour cannot be fully employed because of inadequacy of capital bespeaks a defeatist attitude and an unpreparedness to face the task ahead. In agriculture, in many of the smaller industries as well as in many construction works, the output, and therefore the earnings of labour can be increased substantially if labour is prepared to do a little more hard and honest work. On the other hand, the

[56]Shultz, Theodore W., 'The Role of the Government in Promoting Economic Growth,' *State of the Social Sciences*, Ed., White, Leonard D., Chicago, 1956, p. 372; also Massel, Benton F., ' Capital Formation and Technological Change in U. S. Manufacture,' *The Review of Economics and Statistics*, May, 1960, p. 186; Solow, R., ' Technical Change and the Aggregate Production Function,' *The Review of Economics* and *Statistics*, August, 1957, pp. 312–20; Abramovitz, Moses, ' Resources and Output Trends in the U.S.A. since 1870,' *American Economic Review*, *Papers and Proceedings*, May, 1956, pp. 5–23.

tendency on the part of labour to give precedence to rights and privileges over duty and responsibility makes one despair of any contribution of labour to capital formation. In the ultimate analysis it is the human factor that really counts in capital formation and economic progress.

(d) The State and Private Entrepreneurship

Given the capital and other resources, the State can without incurring any heavy investment expenditure contribute to capital formation in two ways. Firstly, to the extent shortage of financial capital is due to inadequate mobilization of savings, the State can help by proper organization of savings institutions and agencies to canalize savings into investment. If savings especially in the rural areas hide themselves in hoards, it only indicates that a part of the current income of the community is not properly utilized but is for all practical purposes wasted. There is no denying the fact that a vicious circle is here involved in the form of economic backwardness causing underdevelopment of financial institutions and the lack of the latter in turn hampering capital formation. But like other vicious circles common in an underdeveloped economy, this can be broken only by attacking the problem at both ends. Secondly, by means of a suitable and well defined economic policy, the State can make private enterprise contribute more to national production. In the economic circumstances obtaining in the poorer countries today, large investment by the State in social overheads and public utilities and perhaps in some key industries is necessary and desirable. But the field of public enterprise is to be well demarcated and at any rate, uncertainties about the limits of the public sector should not deter the private sector from contributing its best to economic development. Thus if a suitable tax or fiscal policy would provide sufficient incentives to the private sector it would facilitate capital formation. If investment incentive in the private sector is lacking because of inadequate demand for mass production goods, a tax policy of redistribution of income in favour of the wage earning class would be helpful. But this would have a negative effect on savings. It is therefore possible to conceive of an ideal pattern of income distribution in which the loss in savings resulting from taxation of higher incomes is more than offset by increase in investment resulting from higher demand for manufactured consumption goods because of increased incomes of the mass of income earners. That is to say, by maintaining a proper balance between the two forces it would be possible to raise the level of investment.[57] To the extent uncertainties are created by the nationalization, fiscal and import and export policies of the government and its system of taxation, it is clear that by removing these difficulties, the contribution of private enterprise to national output can be increased. It is also important to make a study of the contribution of capital to production in comparable industries under State management and under private manage-

[57]Sturmthal, Adolf, ' Economic Development, Income Distribution and Capital Formation in Mexico,' *Journal of Political Economy*, June, 1955, p. 196.

ment; and if it is found that the yield of capital is greater in the latter—and this is possible if there is more efficient and better utilization in private enterprise—economic logic requires that government enterprise is wound up and handed over to the private sector. But where, however, private enterprise is not forthcoming and it is felt that the sponsoring of an industry by the State would show the way to private entrepreneurship and thereby promote industrialization, investment of public funds is justifiable.

(e) Disguised Unemployment as a Potential Source of Capital Formation

A review of the possibilities of promoting capital formation in underdeveloped countries by making more efficient use of the available resources will not be complete unless an examination is made of the suggestion that by productive employment of surplus labour, additional capital can be ˙ created at no great cost. A characteristic feature of most of the underdeveloped countries is an excess of population and the dependence of the majority of the population on agriculture. In fact, more people are apparently engaged in agricultural activity than would be warranted by the extent of land and capital available and the techniques of agricultural production. As a result, the removal of a certain portion of the population would not reduce agricultural production but may perhaps to some extent increase it. Duesenberry pointed out that such surplus labour can be made use of for producing capital like roads, irrigation works, etc. which are labour intensive. He called this effect on production as the unit multiplier.[58] It was, however, Nurkse who elaborated this idea further and suggested that such surplus labour in underdeveloped countries constitutes a potential source of capital formation. He mentions the following characteristics of disguised unemployment. In the first place, the marginal productivity of the disguisedly unemployed labour is zero. This is another way of saying that the transfer of such labour will not cause any decrease in total output. Secondly, it is usually associated with family employment and does not cover wage labour. Thirdly, no personal identification of the disguisedly unemployed is possible. Such unemployment is not shown in unemployment statistics. Fourthly, it is to be distinguished from seasonal unemployment which arises because of climatic factors. Lastly, disguised unemployment in underdeveloped countries is different from industrial underemployment in advanced countries. The important point of difference is that in developed countries unemployment of this nature is observable in the form of industrial labour taking up minor jobs for a temporary period of time because of lack of demand; while, in underdeveloped countries this is more or less a permanent feature arising out of the excess of labour and the scarcity of capital and not because of any deficiency of demand.

Rough estimates of the magnitude of disguised unemployment in underdeveloped countries show that it is about 25 per cent of the total labour force.

[58]Belshaw, Horace, *Population Growth and Levels of Consumption*, George Allen and Unwin, London, 1956, Appendix 1, pp. 208–10.

A study made by the Royal Institute of International Affairs in 1943 estimated disguised unemployment at the lowest at 20 to 25 per cent for the Eastern European region. Another estimate by Doreen Warriner placed the surplus in Egypt in 1937 at about one half of the farm population. A body of U.N. experts feel that " for many regions of India and Pakistan and for parts of the Philippines and Indonesia, the surplus cannot be less than the pre-war average for the East European region ".[59] Nurkse himself is of the view that in many countries ranging from South-Eastern Europe to South-Eastern Asia, the magnitude of disguised unemployment may be 15 per cent, 20 per cent, or as much as 30 per cent. On the basis of a recent Test Study of 9 selected villages in the Bombay Karnatak region, it is stated that 71 per cent of the farmers have less than normal employment and 52 per cent have less than half the normal employment. If it is assumed that 52 per cent had about half the normal employment, then 26 per cent may be deemed to be unutilized or surplus labour. If the remaining 19 per cent had about ¾ of normal employment then the surplus among that 19 per cent will be about 5 per cent. This however is only a very rough estimate of the order of magnitude involved.[60]

According to Nurkse the excess of labour in the village communities constitutes a source of disguised saving potential as well. If the total number apparently employed is 100, and excess labour is 25, it means that what is produced by 100 can be produced as well by 75. Let us assume that the 100 workers consume all the food that they produce. Now if 25 people are removed and given some work on capital projects and if the level of consumption of people remaining in agriculture is the same per head, then the amount of output consumed by the 25 people can be transferred and used to feed them in their new occupation and so what they produce now in the form of capital works becomes a net contribution to capital, made possible by the lowering of the aggregate level of consumption in the village. This of course has not involved any lowering of per capita consumption. Hence Nurkse argues that while the classical economists stressed the need for restricting consumption so that the level of savings could be raised to support a higher level of investment, and Keynes pointed out that by raising the level of consumption and spendings, income level and thereby the level of investment can be raised, the method which he has suggested would raise investment without lowering consumption.

The full effect of capital contribution from the transfer of excess labour from agriculture would follow only if the consumption level does not rise. However, if the level of consumption of the people remaining in the village as well as of those transferred rises, and if the transfer of labour to construction works involves some cost in providing equipment for them to work with, the savings and investment potential will be reduced to that extent. The cost

[59] *Measures for the Economic Development of Underdeveloped Countries*, U. N., May, 1951, pp. 8 & 9.

[60] Majumdar, N. A., ' Some Aspects of Underemployment,' *Indian Economic Journal*, July, 1957, pp. 13–15.

involved in transferring labour from the village and in transporting food from the village to the area where construction work takes place, also constitutes another leakage. But such cost would amount to only a fraction of the contribution to capital formation. If these costs can be met by getting funds from outside, or from domestic savings in the non-agricultural sector, the amount thus becoming available and used in the manner indicated above will have a magnifying effect or multiplier effect on the total rate of capital formation.

Hence the major problem involved in getting the maximum benefit out of this potential source of capital formation in underdeveloped countries is to prevent consumption level from rising. This has to be done by means of indirect or direct taxation of peasants or by a stiff land tax as was done in Japan or other measures to restrain consumption. In addition, the problem of finding out finance to supply the investment workers with food and simple tools and capital equipment has also to be faced.

While this proposition to make use of labour surplus as a source of capital formation appears sound in theory, it has certain practical limitations which needs to be mentioned. In the first place, the cost involved in putting this scheme into practice can be higher than what it is made out to be. To start with, the State should have some financial resources at its disposal in order to transport labour and food and also to provide the investment workers with some capital equipment. Unless the investment projects are in the vicinity of villages, the transport costs will be quite high. And if the projects are chosen purposely near the village without reference to their economic utility, the cost on the projects would be out of proportion to the prospective returns. It is also possible that labour cannot be dislodged from its native villages and moved to other areas unless higher wages are paid. This would add to the aggregate cost of new investments. Besides, population in underdeveloped countries is not only large but is increasing rapidly. This aggravates the problem. Secondly, implementation of the scheme would involve additional administrative burden on the State. Belshaw points out[61] that the levying of taxes just sufficient to pay for the construction and to keep down consumption would prove difficult in underdeveloped countries where the tax administration is not efficient and the tax system is defective. On the state would also devolve the responsibility of finding competent people to supervise and organize the work. Where transfer of labour is difficult because of social and institutional factors, the state's action may lead to adverse reaction on the part of the village community. Thirdly, it is questioned whether the potential savings which can be realized in this manner are as great as they are supposed to be. Since in many villages the people are bound to their place of birth by sentimental attachment, it would be possible to remove only a part of them with the best of intentions. It is likely that the class of villagers who can thus be removed

[61]Belshaw, Horace, *Population Growth and Levels of Consumption*, George Allen and Unwin, London, 1956, p. 209.

is the most backward and poor. And hence the wage goods released will not be a multiple of the average consumption of the disguisedly unemployed but of the lowest consumption classes.[62] Correspondingly, the savings raised in this manner would be low. Further, it is possible that the output in the villages may fall because of the transfer of ' excess ' labour, unless consumption level is raised. This is likely because consumption level is already very low. Also when surplus labour from the villages is transferred to urban areas, the propensity to consume of the transferred labour will rise. The leakage in the savings potential will thus be substantial. Besides, it has been pointed out, that disguised unemployment in some countries has certain special characteristics which are significant in this context. For example in some parts of Africa what is called disguised unemployment is periodical. A part of the labour force mostly of the adult male population is engaged in the clearing of land and other works which keep them employed for about a year in every two or three years, so that in the rest of the period alone can they be considered as disguisedly unemployed. As such, a low wage cannot attract labour from the villages; nor can they be kept for long in the new work.[63] Fourthly, the contribution of the transferred labour to production is not likely to be large. The quality of the labour which is easily transferable from the villages will be below the average which is low. Supervision cost of such labour will be high, while outturn of labour will be small. It is mentioned that in Latin America, absenteeism is great in the case of disguisedly unemployed labour drafted into work in urban areas.[64] Moreover the type of work on which the labourers will be engaged has necessarily to be those in which no great capital is required such as swamp clearing, construction of mud roads, etc. (if the work is to be near the villages). Such constructive works provide employment but do not add to the type of capital that is really required for rapid economic development.[65]

Although these limitations are quite real, it cannot be denied that disguised unemployment in over-populated low income countries as made out by Duesenberry and Nurkse does constitute a possible means of increasing capital formation without involving any great strain on the economy. The fact has to be stressed that in underdeveloped countries in the initial stages of growth, a start in capital formation has to be made with the existing resources. And the scheme indicated above is undoubtedly a good method of best utilizing a factor of production which is abundant in most of the underdeveloped countries. The central idea of the scheme namely, the avoiding of wastage of resources and employing them for productive purposes, and the shifting of

[62]Deshpande, S. H., ' Labour Surpluses and Saving Potential in Underdeveloped Countries,' *Indian Economic Journal*, January, 1959, p. 388.

[63]Barber, William J., ' Disguised Unemployment in Underdeveloped Economies,' *Oxford Economic Papers*, February, 1961, pp. 108–15.

[64]Kurihara, K. K., *The Keynesian Theory of Economic Development*, George Allen and Unwin, London, 1959, p. 118 f.n.

[65]Kurihara, K. K., *ibid.*, p. 119,

the factor of production which is in excess, so long as there is a possibility of increasing net output thereby, is based on sound economic logic. In fact, the Community Development Project which is becoming increasingly popular in the underdeveloped countries is substantially a measure to put this idea into practice.

Chapter VI

SAVINGS AND THE FINANCING OF INVESTMENT

THE NATURE OF SAVINGS

THE TERM 'Savings' is defined as the accounting difference between current income and consumption. It is at once clear that the savings margin can be widened either by raising the level of production or by lowering the level of consumption or by both. Saving constitutes the first of the three stages in the process of capital formation, the next two stages being the mobilization of savings and the conversion of savings into productive equipment or investment. If a high rate of capital formation is necessary for ensuring a high rate of increase in national income, it follows that the rate of savings should also be correspondingly high. However, the volume of domestic savings and the amount of investment need not necessarily be identical. Investment can exceed domestic savings to the extent the latter is supplemented by savings from abroad. The total investible resources available at any period of time are the sum of domestic savings and foreign resources which flow into the economy in the form of external capital.

Aggregate savings are the sum of savings made by the three sectors of an economy—the government, the business sector and the households. The savings of households is the difference between disposable income (i.e. income after payment of taxes) and consumption expenditures; that of the business sector is the difference between income and the dividends and taxes paid, while government saving is equal to tax revenues minus current expenditure (i.e. non-investment expenditures). Government savings constitute public savings while that of the business and household sectors form private savings. Personal savings or the savings of the household sector constitute the most important component of total savings. Thus in the U.S.A. in 1951 personal savings accounted for 52 per cent of the total savings while the corporate and government sectors contributed 25 per cent and 23 per cent respectively.[1] And in India in 1958–59 savings of the government sector accounted for 10·6 per cent of total savings, domestic corporate sector 3·5 per cent and the household sector as much as 85·9 per cent.[2] While the aggregate savings of all the

[1]Garvy, George, ' Savings and the Problem of Inflation in the United States,' *Savings in the Modern Economy*, Heller, W. W. and others (Eds.), University of Minnesota, Minneapolis, 1953, p. 327.

[2]Reserve Bank of India, *Monthly Bulletin*, August, 1961, p. 1204.

three sources plus net receipts from abroad are equal to aggregate investment, there is bound to be obviously some disparity between savings and investment of the individual sectors. The deficiency of savings in relation to investment in any sector is met by the excess of saving over investment in the other sectors. Thus it is possible to conceive of the economy as made up of spending units with balanced budgets, with surplus budgets and with deficit budgets. The spending units with deficit budgets demand loanable funds and in return issue debt or release financial assets. These assets are acquired by the spending units with surplus budgets and their holding of financial assets and debt equals the increase of net financial liabilities for the deficit spending units.[3]

As indicated above, personal savings or savings of individuals may be defined as the " difference between their current income and their current expenses, the latter including personal tax payments as well as consumption expenditures ".[4]   The difference between these two will be equal to the increase in private non-corporate assets less the increase in liabilities exclusive of gains or losses from revaluation of assets. Capital gains are excluded from income and therefore from saving as well. Although personal savings or savings of the household contribute to the bulk of national savings, there will be among individuals both dissavers and savers. Hence net individuals' saving of the community is the difference between total savings and total dissavings, i.e. the balance between the addition to assets (or reduction of debt) made by the savers and the reduction of assets (or increase in debt) made by the dissavers.

Savings of individuals may be broken up into : (1) Contractual savings represented by Life Insurance payments, mortgage payments, contributions to provident fund, etc. In a way such savings are of an obligatory nature and are therefore relatively stable. (2) Increase in liquid assets held by individuals such as holdings of currency, bank deposits, (both time and demand) shares in savings and loan associations and purchase of private securities. (3) Direct investments in farms, businesses and houses. These constitute a good proportion of rural savings and take the form of land improvements and construction. Savings in this case take place simultaneously with investment. In fact, the savers are the investors as well and no intermediaries between the two parties are involved. (4) Liquidation of debt by private individuals also represents savings. Of these four items numbers 1 and 2 are of greater importance in advanced countries where banking and financial institutions are well developed and people are accustomed to invest their savings in such institutions. Savings made in this manner are available to others while that under 3 above, are not. Thus given the same magnitude of savings in two countries, the one in which the first two categories predominate is in a better position to finance investment in new businesses and industry than the one where savings get directly invested.

[3]Gurley, J. G. and E. S. Shaw, ' Financial Aspects of Economic Development,' *American Economic Review*, September, 1955, p. 516.

[4]Friend, Irwin. *Individuals' Saving*, Wiley, New York, 1954, p. 2.

Among the income groups contributing to personal savings, business owners and farmers predominate. Thus in the U.S.A. in 1949, business owners who constituted 10 per cent of the spending units accounted for nearly half of the aggregate personal savings. A savings survey conducted by the National Council of Applied Economic Research in Delhi in January–March 1959 disclosed that 51 per cent of the households in Delhi had positive savings. Self-employed business households constituting about a quarter of the Delhi population accounted for nearly 56 per cent of the aggregate saving. This class along with the professional households and the managerial and executive class of households constituting about 37 per cent of the households in Delhi contributed nearly 86 per cent of total savings.[5] It should be remembered that these findings relate to an urban area. Obviously, in rural areas, savings of the bigger agriculturists and farmers would account for a substantial part of personal savings. Much of the investment by smaller farmers takes place in a non-monetized form. It has been estimated by Coale and Hoover that direct non-monetized investments in the rural areas of India in the form of land improvements, irrigation works, construction of dwellings, etc., would amount to about 1½ per cent of the national income in the years 1950–53 or a little less than one-fifth of the aggregate investment.[6]

DETERMINANTS OF PERSONAL SAVINGS

Various factors determine the rate and volume of personal savings. Of these, the size of income and its variation and distribution constitute the most important. Although no proportional relationship can be established between the size of income and savings, statistical evidence supports the view that disposable income is easily the most important single variable which determines the amount of saving.[7] The consumer survey data relating to the post-World War II and pre-war years in the U.S.A. indicate that individuals' saving bears a close relationship to the level of disposable personal income—a rise in income being associated with a rise in both consumption and savings. Also the Delhi Survey referred to earlier, finds that the saving-income ratio rose consistently with income, indicating a higher marginal propensity to save with increasing incomes.[8] But more important than the absolute amount of income at any point of time is the variation in its size. There is normally a lag between income change and the levels of consumption. This lag is greater when the change in income is in the downward direction than when it is in the upward direction.

[5]*Delhi Savings Survey*, National Council of Applied Economic Research, Delhi, Asia Publishing House, Bombay, 1960, p. 12.

[6]Coale, A. J. and E. M. Hoover, *Population Growth and Economic Development in Low Income Countries*, Oxford, India, 1959, p. 149.

[7]Garvy, George, ' Savings and the Problem of Inflation in the United States,' *Savings in the Modern Economy*, Heller, W. W. and others (Eds.), University of Minnesota, Minneapolis, 1953, p. 343.

[8]*Delhi Savings Survey*, p. 10.

Thus when a family's income rises, consumption expenditure rises haltingly, so that the savings margin is to some extent widened. On the other hand, when income declines, consumption expenditure tends to remain at the existing level for sometime or declines only slightly so that there is an appreciable decline in the savings of the family. Hence the view is put forward that consumption depends only on the permanent income of an individual or family and is invariant for temporary changes. This hypothesis seems to be borne out by statistical evidences relating to the U.S.A. Post-World War II surveys in that country show that " within a given income class, consumer units with a decrease in income from the previous years were more prone to dissave and less likely to save than units with stable income or increased income, whereas there was no pronounced, consistent difference between the latter two groups in this respect ".[9] Klein also finds an appreciable stimulating influence of an increase in income on the proportion of income saved.[10] The findings of Ruth Mack in 1948 also lend support to the view that people whose income has recently fallen to a certain level will spend relatively more than people whose income has been stable at that level.

The degree of concentration of income or the disparity in the distribution of income and wealth is sometimes mentioned as a factor which affects the rate of savings. It is presumed that given the size of income, the greater this disparity, the larger will be the volume of savings. Since in any economy there are classes of income earners who have a high propensity to save and others with a high propensity to consume, any change in the pattern of income distribution favouring the former will help to increase savings. However, the propensity to save is determined not merely by the size of an individual's income but also by the nature of his employment. Normally a farmer is capable of making larger savings than an urban dweller with the same income. Hence it is not so much the distribution of income at a particular point of time that determines the level of savings as the movement of population between different income groups and between different employments. Such shifts of population add to or decrease the number of savers against dissavers and the change in the volume of savings will be the net effect of this increase and decrease.

Some writers hold the view that it is not the absolute level of income of a family but its relative income position that determines the pattern and size of savings. This notion is based on the premise that a family's consumption expenditure is to a large extent determined by the standards of living of its neighbours. What is important is not whether a family earns a large or a small income but whether it makes half or twice the average income of the community to which it attunes its spending pattern. Hence a proportional

[9]Friend, Irwin, *Individuals' Saving*, Wiley, New York, 1954, p. 122.

[10]Klein, Lawrence, ' Assets, Debt and Economic Behaviour,' *Studies in Income and Wealth*, Vol. 14. National Bureau of Economic Research quoted in Friend, Irwin, *Individuals' Saving*, Wiley, New York, 1954, p. 123.

increase in everybody's income will not result in an increase in the saving's ratio.[11]

Apart from the size and changes in income, some demographic and social factors also affect the rate of personal savings. The age composition of the population has a bearing on the rate of savings. The saving class in a community mostly belongs to the age group 35 to 55 or 60. Those in the age group, 18 to 34 and above 60 are dissavers. In advanced countries, the proportion of people above 60 years of age is increasing and this is said to have a depressing effect on saving. This trend however is compensated by an increase in the proportion of people of the age 35–55 and a decrease in the proportion of people below 15 years. However, the Survey of Savings in Delhi shows that in that city the saving-income ratio tended to increase with increasing age of the head of the household. This difference has to be explained by the fact that the proportion of people above 65 is much smaller in India than in advanced countries and the aging of population in India in recent years has meant a proportionate increase in the number of people between 35 and 60 who are in the productive age group and whose propensity to save is higher than that of the other groups. This may also be partly explained by the fact that the expenditure on consumer durables by people aged 18 to 35 is not relatively so great as that of the same group in richer countries. The joint family system and the dowry system provide means for the acquisition of durable consumer goods at the start of married life. Hence the rise in savings between the age groups 25–35 and 35–60, will not be so sharp. On the other hand, the commitments of expenditure on education, dowries, wedding expenses, etc. on elderly people provide strong incentives for saving by people who are fairly advanced in age. To some extent the rate of savings is dependent on the size of the family also. For the obvious reason that consumption expenditure of larger families is greater than that of the smaller ones, savings margin for the first will be narrower. This is of particular significance in a country like India where the average income is very low and hence propensity to consume on the average is high. This would mean that the deterrent effect of larger families on savings will be all the greater. The Delhi Survey data do not show any clear effect of family size on saving although there is some evidence of decline in the saving-income ratio with increasing family size.[12] It may be presumed that for the country as a whole, saving-income ratio is inversely correlated to the size of families.

As mentioned earlier, the incomes of farmers along with that of business entrepreneurs constitute an important source of personal savings. To the extent cost of living is lower in the villages than in the urban areas, the drift of population to the towns and the decrease in the proportionate strength of

[11]Brady, Dorothy S, and Rose D. Friedman, ' Savings and the Income Distribution,' *Studies in Income and Wealth*, Vol. X, 1947, quoted in *Savings in the Modern Economy*, Heller, W. W. and others (Eds.), University of Minnesota, Minneapolis, 1953, p. 231 *f.n.*

[12]*Delhi Savings Survey*, p. 17.

the farming class should contribute to lower savings. The relative decline in the number of primary producers and therefore of rural communities as against increase in the number of urban dwellers is a common feature of industrialization and economic advancement. Thus in the U.S.A. the ratio of rural to urban population declined from 2·89 in 1870 to 1·19 in 1910, 0·95 in 1920, 0·78 in 1930, 0·77 in 1940 and 0·57 in 1950. Such a trend in the population is observable in India also in recent years although not so marked as in the U.S.A. Urbanization brings about significant changes in the social attitudes and spending patterns of individuals and of families. The chances of spending more are greater and although the avenues for productive investment of savings also increase, the vast majority of the new entrants into the towns do not have the means to save.

Another determinant of personal savings is the asset position of individuals and families. The possession of a large volume of liquid assets has a deterrent effect on savings in so far as families which have accumulated such assets can use them to supplement current income for consumption. Thus obviously, holdings of cash tend to be dissipated easily on consumption when current income is not found to be adequate enough to meet current consumption expenditure. Further, people holding such liquid assets are not likely to have the same urge to save as in the case of those who do not have, or have only small amounts of such assets. On the other hand, it is presumed that a high level of consumer and mortgage debt would have the opposite effect on saving by discouraging rather than stimulating consumption.[13]

Other economic and social factors affect the long term trend in the personal savings of a community. Among these may be mentioned political conditions, price level in the country, expectations of a rise or fall in the price level, the existence of savings institutions, the general attitude of the people to the acquisition of wealth and to work and effort, the capacity and willingness to provide for the future, the desire to maintain or improve the standard of life of the family, birth and death rates and the rate of growth of population, the age of marriage, social customs like dowry, joint family, etc., increase or decrease in the availability of consumer credit as well as of consumption goods, extent of monetization of the economy and other institutional changes.

The complexity of the forces that affect savings of a community thus makes it difficult to formulate any savings function. The assumption that the rate of savings is an increasing or decreasing function of income thus appears to be too sweeping and mechanical. Savings at any point of time are the net effect of the various forces that increase or decrease the desire of the community to save, and its capacity to save. The balancing of gross saving against dissaving is sensitive to changes in the structure of the economy and the motives of the members of the community and their thrift or improvidence. Changes in motives can affect, and do affect the volume of savings irrespective of changes in the volume of disposable income. Broadly speaking, therefore, savings may

[13]Friend, Irwin, *Individuals' Saving*, Wiley, New York, 1954, p. 134.

be said to be determined by the rate and pattern of growth of the economy and the institutional and social changes that are brought about in the process of growth. The expectations of consumers are as important in the determination of the level of consumption expenditure and savings as the expectations of entrepreneurs are important in determining the level of investment. Such an inference has the defect of being vague, but has the merit of being based on a recognition of the multitude of forces that affect the problem and therefore of being more realistic.[14]

SAVINGS, INVESTMENT AND NATIONAL INCOME

For capital formation to take place, there must not only be the necessary savings in the economy but also the agencies through which these resources can be mobilized and canalized into investment. Resources available in an economy are used for the production of consumption goods as well as producers goods. Aggregate income is the value of both these categories of goods. Hence if at any time the supply of producers goods is to be increased, part of the resources used for the production of consumption goods is to be released and directed into the making of producers goods. Since savings are the difference between income and consumption, the extent to which the supply of consumption goods is restricted measures the addition to savings of the economy.

In a monetized exchange economy, the transfer of real resources from the consumption goods sector to the producers goods sector is effected through the operation of the monetary mechanism. Since the consumers get their incomes in money, any restriction of the demand for consumption products would leave with the consumers a large volume of money. It is by securing these money balances that the investors get command over real resources which can be utilized for the production of capital goods. Money balances are transferred to the investors through the selling of securities by them. A payment is made by the business classes to the saving classes in order to persuade the latter to part with their money balances. The business classes are prepared to pay this charge which is interest, because they can productively employ the real resources which they secure with the help of the additional amount of money released by the savers. Thus on the one hand, real resources are made available because of non-consumption, and on the other, money balances are released with which the real resources can be procured. And the rate of interest plays the part of price which helps in allocating resources to those businessmen who are capable of putting the resources to the best use. Given the rate of interest, those investments alone are undertaken which are capable of yielding an adequate return, while those enterprises or lines of investment which cannot stand this test go without the funds and are thus weeded out. In this manner in a free enterprise capitalist economy, the operation of the market mechanism

[14]Farrell, M. J., ' The New Theories of Consumption Function,' *Economic Journal*, December, 1959, p. 694.

helps in the mobilization of savings and in the utilization of these savings for investment purposes. But whether the economy is a free enterprise one or a centrally planned one, the principle underlying savings and investment is the same, namely, additional investment or the increased production of producers goods is possible only by reducing consumption or the demand for resources for producing consumption products.

The foregoing explanation of the process of savings and investment is true only of a simple economy consisting of two sectors—one demanding consumption goods (the households) and the other demanding investment goods (the business class). However, in a modern economy there are some other factors to be considered which affect the smooth and simple operation of the mechanism. In the first place, modern businesses are able to make fresh investments or add to their existing stock of capital goods without resorting to the capital market. This is possible because a successful business concern can make use of a part of its profits for reinvestment. In fact, in modern countries the plough-ing back of profits constitutes one of the main methods by which businesses expand their scale of operations. To the extent businesses can depend on their own earnings to finance investment, they can bypass the capital market. Secondly, modern governments, particularly of underdeveloped countries, are playing an increasingly important part in the investment field and as a result of this activity, governments can directly affect the allocation of resources between consumption and investment uses. By increasing taxation the state can lower the level of consumption, and the money balances which come into the hands of the government can be utilized for augmenting the supply of consumption goods or of producers goods. When the consumers restrict their demand for consumption goods either of their own accord or when they are compelled to restrict consumption because of taxation, the savings of the economy are increased ; but in the first case saving is voluntary, in the latter case it is compulsory ; also, investment which is made possible through increased taxation is determined by the will of the state and not by the free play of market forces. Thirdly, the ability of the banks to create and destroy money affects the distribution of real resources between consumption and investment. When banks expand credit the money balances available in the community are increased. Assuming full employment, this activity of the banks would mean that more money can be placed in the hands of the investors even when there is no corresponding reduction in consumption demand. But in such a situation when the banking system expands credit in favour of the government or of private business, excess demand would result in inflation which would reduce the volume of consumption. Inflation thus causes forced savings in the economy to match the increased demand for investment. Lastly, foreign trade of a country affects its level of savings and investment. Thus net imports would add to the supply of consumption goods and thereby release real resources for investment purposes. The effect of such net imports would then be the same as additional savings. On the other hand, when exports are in excess of imports, the country having such a favourable balance of trade would be accumulating claims against foreign countries which in effect would be the same as adding to investment.[15]

Although the operation of the four factors mentioned above makes the adjustment between savings and investment a little more complicated, yet equality between these is brought about by the operation of certain economic forces. By definition, savings *ex post* have necessarily to be equal to investment *ex post*. The difference between the current income of the three components of the economy—the government, the business sector and the households—and their current expenditure constitutes the current savings of the economy. Net investment of an economy in a given period of time is gross additions made to the capital stock in the period minus depreciation. Net output of an economy is the same as net income; output is made up of consumption goods and production goods. Net output minus consumption is equal to investment. Net income minus consumption expenditure is equal to savings. Since saving and investment are defined alike, they must obviously be identical in amount.[16]

While realized savings are necessarily equal to realized investment, there need not be, and usually there is not, any equality between anticipated savings and investment. In a period of boom and optimism, anticipated investment or *ex ante* investment tends to exceed *ex ante* savings. But the excess or deficiency of one or the other brings into play certain forces which bring about the necessary adjustment making them equal at the end of the period. Suppose an individual decides to save Rs. 100 more. Savings of the economy are increased to this extent. But the individual's decision not to spend Rs. 100 reduces the demand for consumption by Rs. 100. The producers therefore would be able to either sell goods worth Rs. 100 less, or be able to sell the same quantity of goods at a lower price per unit so that their earnings fall by Rs. 100. If price falls and the earnings of the business class decline by Rs. 100, the increase in the savings of the individual is offset by the decrease in the savings of the business sector. On the other hand, if the individual's decision to save reduces the volume of sales, the stock of goods remaining unsold will increase by Rs. 100, i.e. inventories accumulation increases to this extent, and since inventories constitute an item of investment, the volume of investment would have risen to the same extent as the volume of savings has increased.

Government's activity in spending and saving complicates the problem but does not affect the basic principle of equality between saving and investment. Government's saving is the difference between tax revenues and current expenditures. If by taxation government collects additional revenues, the savings of individuals are correspondingly reduced. If the additional revenues add up to the cash balances of the government, then increase in government savings will be equal to decrease in the savings of the private sector and there

[15]Weiler, E. T., *The Economic System*, Macmillan, New York, 1952, pp. 591–603.

[16]Shoup, Carl S., *Principles of National Income Analysis*, Houghton Mifflin, New York, 1947, p. 289.

is no change in the level of investment. If, however, government uses the additional tax proceeds for investment purposes, there will be decreased saving and lower investment in the private sector but this decrease will be matched by higher saving and higher investment in the government sector. Aggregate saving and investment will therefore be equal ; that is to say, for the total economy, saving by individuals, plus saving by corporations plus saving by government will be equal to aggregate investment.

Since per capita incomes are very low in underdeveloped countries, while propensity to consume is high, savings are meagre and the investment rate and the rate of growth of income are correspondingly low. Added to this is the pressure of a high rate of growth of population which tends to depress per capita incomes further down. Hence, the major problem of the low income countries is to step up the level of savings and thereby accelerate the rate of growth of income. The importance of a high margin of savings in economic development was much emphasized by the economists of the eighteenth and nineteenth centuries. In the twentieth century, however, the advantage of large savings in an advanced economy has come to be questioned. The great depression of the 1930s and Keynes' analysis of the problem of unemployment, directed attention to the fact that in certain circumstances the habit of thrift and abstinence far from being a virtue, may be a vice. Since the level of employment depends on the demand for output, any reduction in the demand for consumption goods which is implicit in the savings activity of private individuals, would create unemployment unless the decline in the demand for final goods is offset by increased demand for investment goods. According to this analysis, the level of output and of employment can be raised only by raising the level of spendings of the community. Since one man's expenditure is another man's income, savings or the abstinence from spending on consumer goods would do a positive harm to the economy. Such a development can be avoided if the spending on producers goods is increased correspondingly through, if necessary, deficit spending by the government.

In recent years war expenditure, large spendings by the government and inflation, have brought into prominence another aspect of savings, viz. its role in controlling price rise. If inflation is due to excess spendings in the economy and this excess spending is facilitated by the expansion of bank credit and increase in money supply, the logical means of controlling it would be to reduce the level of spendings. If investment demand cannot be lowered, then the alternative available is to lower consumption demand. It is possible to reduce the level of consumption by taxation, by compulsory borrowing and by direct control of the production and distribution of consumption goods. Thus stress is laid in the present context of inflation in most countries of the world, on increased savings as a means to keep under control the price level.

The views of the classical economists regarding savings are of great relevance to the present day underdeveloped countries. The problem in these countries is not one of regulating the level of savings so as to maintain effective demand in the economy but one of creating and promoting savings. So long as these economies are backward and the investment requirements far exceed the savings available, there cannot be any possibility of a failure of demand to keep resources fully employed. Unemployment arises not because of excess of savings or fall in demand for consumption goods, but because of the inadequacy of savings and therefore of capital equipment necessary for keeping labour engaged. Abstinence, restriction of consumption and a tightening of the belts are as important in present day underdeveloped countries in order to ensure economic progress as they were in the eighteenth or nineteenth century West European countries. In short, the problem of saving in the poorer countries of today is one of enlarging it, and properly utilizing it for productive investment.

Economic transformation of these countries would involve the breaking of the vicious circle of low income, low savings and low level of capital formation. When once the rate of savings and investment is raised sufficiently high, national income and per capita income would rise and the savings margin will be widened. The rise in national income by itself facilitates further increase in savings. Savings become then automatic involving no strain on the economy. Professor Weiler mentions the following ways in which increase in national income would necessitate as well as help in larger savings.[17] Firstly, growth of per capita income increases the power to save. When income is stationary, savings can be increased only by giving up products which form part of an accustomed way of living. But when income increases, savings can be effected with a lesser sense of loss or sacrifice because the individual has only to abstain from the consumption of goods which would have become possible by the rise of income. Secondly, economic growth increases the desire to save. As real income rises, people require more and more money for transaction and liquidity purposes. People will desire to keep larger cash balances and as such, would save a part of the money incomes which they get. Thirdly, as an economy grows, people would require more non-money assets also, like bonds, industrial securities, etc. There will be greater demand for life insurance, retirement annuities, pension and provident funds. All these represent savings and the increasing use of these means of saving reflects the economic advancement of a country. Economic growth itself increases these avenues of saving and provides not only an incentive for saving but also facilitates larger savings by the community. Lastly, the competitive accumulation of wealth which is characteristic of a free enterprise economy creates a desire to save. Accumulation of wealth has a prestige value and the drive for earning more and saving more, springs from the desire to distinguish oneself. With economic growth this competition becomes keener, and the satisfaction arising from the accumulation of additional assets is greater. Saving is thus promoted not because the individual concerned would benefit by investing the resources, but because the competitive thrill involved in making money and accumulating

[17]Weiler, E. T., *The Economic System*, Macmillan, New York, 1952, pp. 597–603.

13

wealth constitutes a source of satisfaction. All these factors are characteristic of an advanced economy. They indicate a change in the economic circumstances as well as in the social attitude of the people which in turn is a product of economic advancement. Thus economic growth not only provides the means by which more savings can be accumulated but also furnishes the human motives that are conducive to capital accumulation.

SAVINGS IN DEVELOPED AND UNDERDEVELOPED COUNTRIES

Savings in developed countries have certain characteristics which differ from those in underdeveloped countries. Firstly, the level of savings in the former countries is invariably much higher than in the poorer economies; secondly, there is a significant constancy in the rate of savings; thirdly, a major problem connected with savings in advanced countries is one of economic instability.

(a) High Level of Savings in Developed Economies

The figures in the following table show the disparity in the rate of savings between developed and underdeveloped countries.

Table 26

LEVELS OF GROSS AND NET DOMESTIC SAVINGS 1950–59
(per cent of gross domestic product)

High Income Countries			Low Income Countries		
Country	Gross Domestic Saving	Net Domestic Saving	Country	Gross Domestic Saving	Net Domestic Saving
Japan	28·7	21·1	Rhodesia and Nyasaland	20	14
Norway	27·1	17·2	Venezuela	24	16
Finland	26·7	21·7	Congo	24	16
Germany (Fed. Republic)	26·3	17·2	Jamaica	12	5
Australia	26·1	20·2	Puerto Rico	2	-4
Netherlands	25·7	15·9	Argentina	18	8
Canada	22·5	11·4	Burma	20	14
New Zealand	22·5	15·9	Spain	15	8
Austria	20·4	13·3	Colombia	18	9
Italy	19·5	10·6	Greece	9	4
U.S.A.	18·6	9·9	Brazil	15	10
Denmark	18·5	12·4	Iraq	17	13
France	18·4	9·1	Turkey	12	8
Belgium	17·6	8·0	Ceylon	11	9
U.K.	15·2	7·2	Chile	8	1
			Philippines	7	2
			Indonesia	5	2
			India	...	7

SOURCE: *World Economic Survey 1960*, U.N., pp. 21 and 61.

Among underdeveloped countries, the high rate of savings in Rhodesia and Nyasaland, Venezuela and Congo is exceptional, and is due to the reinvestment of earnings in some of the foreign-owned industrial establishments. Export earnings of some commodities like oil also account for large savings. But in the majority of low income countries savings are much less than 10 per cent of national income as compared with about 20 per cent or more in economically advanced countries. In the three years 1948–50, the ratio of gross savings to Gross National Product exceeded 15 per cent in the U.S.A. and was about 21 per cent in Canada. This was made up of personal savings to the extent of 4 to 6 per cent, savings of corporate enterprises 5 to 8 per cent and surpluses in the governmental accounts, increase in the social security reserves and other funds, about 6 per cent. In Japan, in the years 1950–59, gross domestic savings amounted to 28·7 per cent of Gross National Product per year. And in 1957, 18 per cent of the disposable personal income was saved and total savings reached the high rate of 32·1 per cent of Gross National Product. This high level is primarily due to the internationally known strong saving habit of the people of Japan. The rapid growth of the national economy and the significant rise in per capita incomes have also been obvious contributory factors. In advanced Western countries, the maintenance of a high level of savings and investment is, to a large extent, due to the reinvestment of undistributed profits by business enterprises. In the post-World War II years accumulation of this kind was greatly helped by a series of favourable factors such as, inflation, the prevalence of a sellers' market and rapid rise in business earnings ; limitation of dividend distributions; and favourable fiscal treatment by government of that part of business earnings which gets reinvested. While company profits were taxed heavily, large allowances were granted for replacement expenditure. Slow expansion of the capital markets and their inability to meet the growing capital requirements of industry and trade, also contributed to the increase in reinvestment of profits. In Britain, the relative decline in personal and company savings in recent years has been more than offset by increase in public savings, budget surpluses and national insurance contributions. By and large, the high level of savings in advanced countries has to be attributed to the large per capita incomes and the facilities for saving.

(b) Constancy in the Rate of Savings

A second feature of savings in economically advanced countries is that although national and per capita incomes have increased rapidly over a long period, the proportion of savings to national income has tended to remain, on the whole, constant. This is borne out by the findings of Simon Kuznets for the U.S.A. and of Modigliani for Canada and Sweden. Thus in the U.S.A. over the years 1897–1949, the proportion of savings remained at about 15 per cent of national income. Goldsmith points out that although saving in the U.S.A. has shown considerable short-term cyclical fluctuations and the saving-income ratio has risen sharply in periods of boom and fallen precipitously during depression, the saving-income ratio has been on the whole constant over the last 60 years or so.[18] Savings in that country increased at the rate of 1¾ per cent per year which is slightly less than the rate of growth of Gross National Product. Different explanations have been given for the steadiness of the saving-income ratio in advanced countries. Professor Arthur Lewis thinks that one of the factors responsible for this phenomenon is the tendency for the proportion of profits to rise rapidly in the early stages of development and then to become constant or even to fall. The tendency for profits rate to remain constant or fall after a stage, is according to him due to the rapid rise of real wages in the later stages of economic development.[19] Arthur Smithies holds the view that the savings function has been dropping secularly as a result of the trend towards urbanization and more equal distribution of income. And Modigliani has argued that increments to income are absorbed by expenditures on new types of product which become available with economic growth and technological improvements.[20] Professor Duesenberry puts forward the thesis that as a family's income improves, its outlay also rises because of the ' demonstration effect ' and the indulgence in what is called ' Conspicuous Consumption '. That is to say, people try to imitate the ways of living of others who are socially and economically better off, so that when there is a rise in personal income it does not add much to savings, but is expended on luxury products or other items which would show off the family's improved economic position. In fine, it may be said that the proportion of income saved does not increase as income rises (and this is against what family budget studies would indicate) because of certain opposite forces at work. A rise in per capita income should according to the family budget studies lead to a larger proportion of the income being saved. But this is offset by other factors, such as urbanization, more equitable distribution of incomes, availability of new and a wider variety of products and the change in the age composition of the population, i.e., a relative increase in the number of the aged who are dissavers.

(c) The Problem of Adjustment between Savings and Investment

A high level of savings is almost automatic in advanced economies. But a high level of self-generated savings creates the problem of adjusting the level to investment demand so as to avoid economic instability. In a free enterprise capitalist economy, the people who make decisions with regard to the scale of

[18]Goldsmith, Raymond W., ' Trends and Structural Changes in Savings in the Twentieth Century,' *Savings in the Modern Economy*, Heller, W. W. and others (Eds.), University of Minnesota, Minneapolis, 1953, pp. 133–34.

[19]Lewis, Arthur W., *Theory of Economic Growth*, Allen and Unwin, London 1955, p. 238.

[20]Modigliani, F., ' Fluctuations in the Saving-Income Ratio—A problem in Forecasting,' *Studies in Income and Wealth*, Vol. XI, New York, 1949, pp. 384 & 385, quoted in Abramovitz Moses, ' The Economics of Growth,' *Survey of Contemporary Economics*, Vol. II, Haley, B.F. (Ed.), Irwin, Homewood, Illinois, 1952, p. 149.

investment in different lines of enterprise are different from those who make the savings. Hence equality between planned investment and planned savings can be only a matter of rare chance. Traditionally, it was believed that adjustment between savings and investment could be brought about through the working of the market forces and the interest rate. An excess of savings in relation to investment demand would lower the interest rate and raise the demand for savings while an excess of investment would, by raising the interest rate call forth greater savings. This smooth adjustment between savings and investment has, however, been questioned on both theoretical and statistical grounds. Recent analysis shows that while the level of savings at any point of time is determined by the level of income, the rate of investment is determined by the rate of growth of income. Demand for savings comes from businessmen whose investment decisions are influenced by their expectations of future demand for their products. A lag between savings and investment is therefore likely, and this lag creates economic instability. In general, excess of savings over investment has a deflationary effect while excess of investment over savings has an inflationary effect. The tendency for the volume of savings in absolute terms to rise rapidly in developed countries has created the problem of finding an outlet for such savings into investment. If investment opportunities fail to increase as savings increase (and this is likely in developed countries according to the stagnation theorists) the result will be a fall in income and increasing unemployment. In view of the large opportunities of investment presented by the advancement of science and technology in recent years, the rise in the standard of life of the people and the growing demand for a wider variety of products, the stagnation thesis cannot be taken seriously; nevertheless, it focuses attention on a problem of vital concern to developed countries, namely, to maintain the balance between savings and investment.

Aside from the possibility of economic instability being created by maladjustment between savings and investment, variations in the level of savings would have international repercussions as well through foreign trade. If domestic savings in one country are excessive, it would lead to unemployment, and a favourable balance of trade. And other countries which have trade relations with the first country would have to face a balance of payments deficit unless the latter is prepared to make large overseas investments to compensate for the decline in its offtake of foreign products. This effect on international trade position depends of course on the size and importance of the country concerned, in world trade. Excess or deficiency of domestic savings in a small country will have little effect on world trade. But such fluctuations in bigger countries will have a sharp international effect as was illustrated by the rise of domestic savings in the U.S.A. in 1951.

In contrast to economically advanced countries, the problem of savings is of a different nature in low income countries. The level of their domestic savings is low, in some cases lower than what is required to maintain existing standards of life. What is worse, the rate of savings in most of the under-developed countries does not show any appreciable rise in recent years. Thirdly, allied to the problem of low level of savings is the one of inadequate mobilization of the savings available in the economy.

(a) Low level of Savings in Underdeveloped Countries

Figures given in Table 26 illustrate the position of underdeveloped countries in respect of domestic savings as compared with developed countries. In 1930 the Central Banking Enquiry Committee of India pointed out that " the surplus left with the agriculturists who constitute the bulk of the popula-tion is very little even in normal years ".[21] And a Report prepared by a Reserve Bank official at the instance of the International Monetary Fund in 1952 mentioned: " There has never been much saving in the rural sector which for many years has probably been a deficit sector ".[22] The low level of investment and capital formation in India and other underdeveloped countries is itself evidence of the inadequacy of domestic savings in these countries. In 1950–51 net savings in India formed about 5 per cent of national income as compared with 15 per cent in the U.S.A.   Among underdeveloped countries some of the Latin American countries show a better record. In 1946–48 savings formed 14·6 per cent of Gross National Product in Cuba, 12·2 per cent in Colombia, 11·2 per cent in Brazil, 10·8 per cent in Mexico and 10·0 per cent in Chile. According to an estimate made by the United Nations experts,[23] domestic savings in underdeveloped countries throughout the world amounted to $ 5,240 million in 1949 or 5½ per cent of the estimated national income ($ 97,000 million) of these countries. For Asiatic countries excluding Japan but including Egypt, the same source estimated savings at $ 2,530 million or 4·3 per cent of the national income of $ 59,400 million. On the average, according to these estimates, annual savings per head in Asia are a little over $ 2 per head. Personal savings accounted for only about 1½ per cent of the national income in India in 1948–51. Reinvested profits of businesses which constitute a large part of domestic savings in economically advanced countries form only about 10 per cent of national income in low income countries.[24] The comparison drawn by Professor Belshaw between these countries and a small but rich country like New Zealand brings out the great disparity in this matter. In 1949–50 the net savings of New Zealand amounted to $ 250 million or a little under 19 per cent of the national income

[21-22]Quoted in Rangnekar, D. G., Poverty and Capital Development in India, Oxford, London, 1959, pp. 52–53.

[23]Measures for the Economic Development of Underdeveloped Countries, U.N., 1951, p. 76.

[24]In some underdeveloped countries like Brazil 1946–49 and Cuba 1945–48 personal savings were higher than in India. Personal savings formed about 4 per cent of national income in Brazil and 2·3 per cent in Cuba—Bernstein, E.M., ' Financing Economic Growth in Under-developed Economies,' Savings in the Modern Economy, Heller, W. W. and others (Eds.), Univer-sity of Minnesota, Minneapolis, 1953, pp. 271–73.

of $ 1,344 million. The per capita savings of this country, $ 125, far exceeded the per capita total income in India (about $ 70). Looking at the position in another way, in New Zealand with a population of $\frac{1}{600}$ of Asia, domestic savings were about $\frac{1}{10}$ of that of Asia. In other words, savings in under-developed countries are a much smaller percentage of a much smaller income per head.[25]

The deficiency of savings in poorer countries becomes all the more glaring when viewed against their capital requirements. Rapid industrialization calls for increased investment in costly capital intensive schemes. Moreover, for comparable industrial establishments, capital requirements are greater in the low income countries because of the higher cost of acquiring the capital equipment from foreign countries and installing them. The need to provide ancillary services and to carry larger stocks of stores and raw materials also swells up the financial requirements. Quite often, wrong estimates about capital requirements are made, and in the face of scarcity of internal resources and the lack of organized capital markets, underestimation of the financial needs lands the industrial ventures into disaster. This is one of the reasons why private domestic capital tends to shy away from such investments. Also, lack of necessary funds drives the entrepreneurs to choose capital light schemes, when economic development would better be served by capital intensive projects. Thus scarcity of savings combined with the lack of institutional facilities hampers entrepreneurship and industrialization of the economy.

(b) Stagnation in Savings

Not only are savings very low in underdeveloped countries as compared with developed countries, but the saving-income ratio in these countries does not show any increase in the last few years in spite of the fact that strenuous efforts have been made to accelerate the rate of economic progress. Data relating to savings in underdeveloped countries prepared by the United Nations bear out this point.

The figures in Table 27, show the variations (increase or decrease) in savings of different sectors expressed as a percentage of Gross Domestic Product. It is seen that of the 24 countries listed, there was increase in domestic savings in only seven in the years 1950–59. In nearly all the others, there was a decline. Decline of domestic savings is particularly marked in the case of Congo (19 per cent of the Gross National Product) and in Puerto Rico and Ceylon (7 per cent each). The components of domestic savings—the government, corporate and household sectors—show considerable variations in the different countries. Only in three countries (Jamaica, Equador and Trinidad) did government savings increase by 2 per cent or more of the gross product. In another five countries the increase was only about 1 per cent

[25]Belshaw, Horace, *Population Growth and Levels of Consumption*, Allen and Unwin, London 1956, p. 114.

Table 27

INCREASE OR DECREASE (−) IN THE LEVEL OF SAVINGS IN UNDERDEVELOPED COUNTRIES 1950–52 TO 1957–59, AS PERCENTAGE OF GROSS DOMESTIC PRODUCT

Country	Total net Saving	Foreign Saving	Domestic Saving	Government Saving	Private Saving Total	Corporate rate	House- hold
Jamaica	10	2	8	2	6	2	4
Burma	7	10	−3	−3	...	...	...
India	5	3	2	...	2	...	...
Panama	4	2	2	...	2	3	−1
Greece	4	2	3	...	3	...	...
Ecuador	4	2	2	4	−2	−1	−1
Chile	4	2	2	1	1	...	...
Rhodesia and Nyasaland	3	7	−4	...	−4	−5	1
Philippines	2	1	1	1	...	1	−1
Puerto Rico	1	8	−7	...	...	1	...
Korea (Republic)	1	2	−2	...	−2	...	...
Spain	...	1	−1	...	−1	...	−1
Trinidad and Tobago	...	...	...	2	−1	4	−5
China (Taiwan)	...	...	...	...	...	...	...
Costa Rica	...	1	−1	−2	1	−1	2
Brazil	...	−1	...	...	1	1	...
Colombia	−1	−1	...	1	−1	1	−2
Portugal	−1	2	−3	1	−3	...	...
Venezuela	−1	4	−5	1	−6	1	−7
Ceylon	−2	5	−7	−3	−4	−2	−2
Honduras	−2	2	−3	−2	−2	1	−2
Union of South Africa	−4	−3	...	...	...	1	−1
Congo	−10	9	−19	−5	−14	−14	...
Morocco	−14	−9	−5	−2	−3	1	−2

SOURCE : *World Economic Survey 1960*, U.N., p. 75, Table 2·13.

while in the remaining countries the volume of government savings has remained roughly stable or even declined. Countries in which government savings declined are Burma, Costa Rica, Ceylon, Honduras, Congo and Morocco. The decline or stagnation in government savings in many of the underdeveloped countries is understandable in view of the large financial commitments of the state in connection with economic development. Increase in population and higher costs of economic and social services. have combined with non-resilient tax resources to bring about a decline in government savings. Efforts to increase tax income have met with only very limited success in these countries. However, the fall in the level of private savings (corporate and household sectors) is seen to be of a greater magnitude than the decrease in government savings. Private savings increased by 2 or more than 2 per cent of Gross National Product in Jamaica, India, Panama and Greece and by 1 per cent in Chile, Costa Rica and Brazil. All the others registered a decline. It may be noted that in most countries, household savings have fallen significantly. Only in three countries, Jamaica, Rhodesia and Nyasaland and in Costa Rica, do household savings show any rise. Eleven countries show a fall—in Venezuela the decline is as much as 7 per cent of Gross National Product—while in the remaining ten, domestic savings seem to have remained constant. In Congo, while household savings did not fall or rise, corporate savings declined by 14 per cent of the Gross National Product. The major factors responsible for the fall in household savings have been the low level of per capita income and the shifts in the distribution of income. The tendency for the number of wage earners and the wage rates to rise and the transfer of income to income groups with low saving capacity have prevented any increase in household savings. Also, unfavourable export experience and the adverse effects on unincorporated enterprise which is a significant constituent of household savings, have played a part in bringing down the total of savings of this category in many countries.

Foreign savings have contributed to offset the deficiency of domestic savings in many of the underdeveloped countries, particularly in Burma, Puerto Rico, Rhodesia and Nyasaland and in India.[26] Thus in Burma, while domestic savings declined by 3 per cent of Gross National Product, foreign savings increased by 10 per cent so that total net savings increased by 7 per cent of Gross National Product. And in Rhodesia the total net increase in saving of 3 per cent is the result of 7 per cent addition to foreign saving and 4 per cent decline in domestic saving. In Congo, a decline in domestic saving to the extent of 19 per cent of Gross National Product is partly compensated by an increase in foreign savings of 9 per cent. In over one-third of the countries, increases in foreign saving have amounted to 2 to 3 per cent of the gross product. In one-fourth of the countries, such increases have been even larger, while in the case of Congo and Burma it was 9 and 10 per cent respectively. On the whole, the flow of official capital has been larger than the flow of private capital. A large part of foreign official capital in the form of loans and grants has gone into the countries with lower per capita incomes. During the period 1950–59 nearly 22 per cent of the total flow of external public funds went to countries with per capita incomes of less than 100 dollars. On the other hand, private foreign capital has gravitated to countries with higher per capita income levels.

On the whole, in spite of foreign savings, the aggregate net savings available in the underdeveloped countries for capital formation have remained quite small in amount. Among the underdeveloped countries, there are exceptional cases like Rhodesia and Nyasaland, Venezuela, Israel and Congo where the

[26]Foreign saving is equal to payments for imports of goods and services, minus receipts from exports of goods and services. A positive foreign saving reflects an excess of such payments over receipts and a negative foreign saving an excess of receipts over payments.

rate of savings has exceeded 25 per cent and has thus approximated or even exceeded the levels in developed countries. This, however, has been due to the different structure of the economies of these countries. In export-oriented countries, foreign investments made on a large scale for the exploitation of the natural resources and large reinvestments by foreign companies, have contributed to the high rate. But in the majority of the underdeveloped countries savings have remained low because of the low levels of production and income and the lack of institutional facilities to mobilize the savings.

Recent studies in India also show that in spite of some appreciable rise in national income the proportion of savings has failed to respond to the requirements. Data relating to savings in India in the last one decade or so are the following : (i) Professor Rangnekar has made a calculation of India's net savings in the years 1948–49 to 1951–52.[27] (ii) The Indian Conference on Research in National Income, Delhi, has made an estimate for the years 1949–50 to 1954–55. (iii) The National Council of Applied Economic Research, Delhi, has estimated savings in India in the years 1950–51 to 1957–58. (iv) Recently, the Reserve Bank of India has published data of savings in India in the period 1950–51 to 1958–59.[28] These data are presented in Table 28. In view of the differences in the methods of computation and items included under the different heads and the scarcity of reliable sources of information, the disparity in the different findings is understandable. The figures, however, help us in getting a general idea of the trend in savings in the Indian Union since 1950–51.

The national income of India in the year 1948–49 was Rs. 86,500 million. The savings of that year as worked out by Professor Rangnekar amounted to about Rs. 3,000 million or 3·6 per cent of the national income of that year. Estimates of savings for the years 1955–56 and 1957–58 made by the National Council of Applied Economic Research are higher than the Reserve Bank of India figures. The Reserve Bank estimates do not include the household sectors, savings in the form of inventories in agriculture and trade, non-monetized investment and consumer durables. It is also pointed out that saving in the form of urban non-corporate investment is probably underestimated and the suggestion is made that the aggregate saving-income ratio may be about two percentage points higher than that estimated in the study if these items of saving are also fully taken into account.[29]

The Reserve Bank study shows that the saving-income ratio varied between 5·1 per cent, the lowest in 1951–52 to 9·1 per cent the highest in 1955–56. Over the years 1951–52 to 1958–59 the average saving-income ratio was 7·2 per cent. From the peak of 9·1 per cent reached in 1955–56 the ratio declined rather sharply in the year 1957–58. If the entire nine-year period is broken up into three sub-periods of three years each, it will be found that the saving-

[27]Rangnekar, D. G., *Poverty and Capital Development in India*, Oxford, London, 1959, pp. 227–28.
[28]*Reserve Bank of India Bulletin*, August, 1961.
[29]*Reserve Bank of India Bulletin*, August, 1961, p. 1200.

Table 28

SAVINGS IN INDIA 1948–49—1958–59

(Rupees in Millions)

Year	Source			
	(a)	*(b)*	*(c)*	*(d)*
1948–49	2,980	...	...	...
1949–50	4,410	5,100	...	...
1950–51	5,960	5,910	6,240	6,360
1951–52	5,770	4,680	...	5,040
1952–53	...	5,180	...	5,850
1953–54	...	6,690	...	5,990
1954–55	...	8,000	...	6,830
1955–56	...	...	11,350	9,100
1956–57	...	...	...	9,930
1957–58	...	...	12,110	8,180
1958–59	...	...	...	9,750

SOURCE: (a) Rangnekar, D. G., *Poverty and Capital Formation in India*, Oxford, London, 1959.

(b) Indian Conference on Research in National Income, Delhi, *Papers on National Income and Allied Topics*, Vol. I, Asia Publishing House, Bombay, 1960.

(c) National Council of Applied Economic Research, Delhi.

(d) *Reserve Bank of India Bulletin*, August, 1961.

income ratio was 5·9 per cent in the first period (1950–51 to 1952–53), 7·3 per cent in the second period (1953–54 to 1955–56) and 7·9 per cent in the third period (1956–57 to 1958–59). In the First Plan period, 1951–52 to 1955–56, the ratio was 6·6 per cent and in the first three years of the Second Plan, it was 7·9 per cent. While looked at in this manner the savings ratio seems encouraging, it is to be noted that the aggregate marginal saving-income ratio declined from 19·1 per cent in period II to 14·2 per cent in period III.

The contribution of each sector to total savings in these years is shown in Table 29.

It may be observed that government savings which accounted for 38·2 per cent of aggregate savings in 1951–52 declined sharply in the next few years and reached 7·6 per cent in 1955–56. Since then it revived but only slightly. Increasing costs of government administration and lack of response in tax revenues explain this trend in government savings. There is a perceptible decline in the contribution of the corporate sector also; and this was due to higher costs of production, increasing wages, higher taxes, export difficulties, etc. The household sector has been the mainstay of savings in the economy contributing on the average more than 80 per cent of total savings. There is however, a steady decline in the share of rural household sector in aggregate savings while that of the urban sector has appreciably increased. Comparing the proportion of savings to total income of the different sectors, it is see

ECONOMICS OF DEVELOPMENT

Table 29

CONTRIBUTION OF DIFFERENT SECTORS TO TOTAL SAVINGS IN INDIA
(Percentage figures)

Year	Government Sector	Averages of Three-Year Periods	Domestic Corporate Sector	Averages of Three-Year Periods	Household Sector					
					Rural	Averages of Three-Year Periods	Urban	Averages of Three-Year Periods	Total	Averages of Three-Year Periods
1950–51	14·7		5·1		29·9		50·3		80·2	
1951–52	38·2	21·6	11·1	5·2	38·7	33·1	12·0	40·1	50·7	73·2
1952–53	15·1		0·7		31·9		52·3		84·2	
1953–54	11·9		3·8		34·4		49·9		84·3	
1954–55	12·0	10·1	5·7	5·3	24·8	25·0	57·5	59·6	82·3	84·6
1955–56	7·6		6·0		19·3		67·1		86·4	
1956–57	12·9		5·4		21·6		60·1		81·7	
1957–58	13·9	12·5	2·2	3·7	25·1	23·8	58·8	60·0	83·9	83·8
1958–59	10·6		3·5		24·8		61·1		85·9	

SOURCE : *Reserve Bank of India Bulletin*, August, 1961.

that while the savings-income ratio of the government sector declined from 10·3 per cent in the First Five-Year Plan period to 8·2 per cent in the first three years of the Second Plan, and that of the domestic corporate sector from 37·0 per cent to 32·4 per cent, the ratio of savings to income of the household sector rose from 5·3 per cent to 6·7 per cent. This was made up of a rise in the savings-income ratio of the rural household sector from 2·5 per cent to 2·7 per cent and that of the urban household sector from 12·6 per cent to 16·9 per cent. On the whole in the years 1950–51 to 1958–59 the government sector contributed on an annual average 13·9 per cent of total savings, domestic corporate sector 4·7 per cent and household sector 81·4 per cent.

What is really disturbing in the above data is that savings in India have not increased to any appreciable extent since 1950–51. In relation to the large needs arising from schemes of planned development, the rise in absolute savings from Rs. 6,360 million in 1950–51 to Rs. 9,750 million in 1958–59 or from Rs. 18 per head of the population to about Rs. 24 per head is far from encouraging. The extent of deficiency is seen when the actual figures of savings are set against the Plan targets. An investment of more than Rs. 100 billion in the Third Plan period means stepping up the rate of investment from the existing level of about 11 per cent of national income to about 14 per cent. The Planning Commission assumes that the current level of savings is about 8·5 per cent of national income. To realize the target of investment in the

Plan, the rate of savings will have to be raised to about 11·5 per cent of the national income at the end of the Third Plan.[30]

(c) Disparity between Actual and Potential Savings

Another aspect of the problem of savings in low income countries is that even the meagre savings are not properly mobilized. It is the opinion of some economists that inadequacy of savings in these countries is much exaggerated. The problem in them according to this view is that a substantial part of what is not consumed in the economy is not available for investment. A good part of the surplus over consumption goes into the form of ' passive capital '—in the purchase of land, residential construction and in the acquisition of gold and jewels. It is pointed out by Malenbaum that in India during the First Plan years, nearly 45 per cent of the investible resources available in the economy would have gone into passive forms of capital and only 55 per cent of the savings were invested for productive purposes. There is also much wastage of savings. It is estimated that in India over 7 per cent of national income is used for ceremonial purposes and another 6 per cent spent on tobacco, intoxicants, refreshments, amusements, etc.[31] In the oil countries of the Middle East, a large part of the earnings arising from the exploitation of their mineral wealth is used up for the construction of palatial buildings and the purchase of luxury goods from foreign countries. This is true of some of the Latin American countries also. In these countries a considerable amount of savings is diverted into holding dollar currency deposits and securities. The governments of these countries also indulge in such wasteful use of domestic savings. Large expenses on foreign embassies, construction of imposing buildings for official purposes and expenditure on various forms of conspicuous production are illustrative of this point. Also, governments are responsible for hoarding of foreign currencies where the law requires that the local currency or savings banks deposits must be backed to the extent of 100 per cent by foreign exchange. This involves practically the sterilization of foreign exchange equal to that part of the money supply which the government will never be required to redeem in foreign exchange.[32]

Hoarding of gold and silver constitutes another important drain on the savings of the economy. The United Nations experts pointed out that a part

[30]Dr. Lokanathan, Director of the National Council of Applied Economic Research, Delhi, holds a less pessimistic view regarding future savings in the country. On the basis of a survey of urban households conducted by the National Council of Applied Economic Research in thirty towns and cities of India, it is found that urban households save about 14 per cent of their income. The average rate of saving for the whole economy is presumed to be well over 10 per cent. According to Dr. Lokanathan, the rate would reach 18 to 20 per cent of national income by about 1975. *The Hindu*, Madras, dated January 21, 1962.

[31]Wolf, Charles (Jr.) and S. C. Sufrin, *Capital Formation and Foreign Investment in Underdeveloped Areas*, Syracuse University Press, 1958, p. 11.

[32]*Measures for the Economic Development of Underdeveloped Countries*, U.N., 1951, p. 36.

of the required capital investment could be financed not by increasing savings but by using the gold and foreign exchange which lie in the hoards of some private individuals in the underdeveloped countries. They have estimated that in some countries of South and South-East Asia and Middle East, private gold hoards are as large as 10 per cent of the national income. If these hoards could be mobilized, they would contribute 2 per cent of the national income to capital formation over a period of five years.[33] Social custom in India requires the granting of dowry, partly in jewels, by parents to their daughters at the time of marriage. Current earnings have therefore to be used up for the acquisition of this necessary stock of wealth. In addition, a sizeable portion of gold is also held in the form of plates and bullion by the richest classes. The production of gold and silver in India accounts for only 1·4 per cent and 0·5 per cent respectively of world output, but she possesses 6·8 per cent and 26 per cent of the world's stock of these metals. The present stock of gold in the country is made up of current production and a large amount smuggled into the country from outside. The *Annual Report of the Bank for International Settlement* for 1934–35 estimated the gold hoarded in India from 1493 to 1936 at Rs. 14,500 million or £ 1,095 million.[34] According to an estimate made by Kitchin in his evidence before the Royal Commission on Indian Currency and Finance in 1926, India had in 1834 roughly £ 60 million worth of gold and 1,350 fine oz. of silver which were approximately 10 per cent and 30 per cent of the world's total production. Recently, an attempt has been made to estimate the stock of gold at present in India by adding up the annual amounts of smuggled gold to the estimated amount available in the country in 1834 after making allowance for exports and imports, changes in the political boundary of the country and losses due to different uses and abrasion. The estimated annual value of smuggled gold into India is $ 72 million or Rs. 340 million according to Franz Picks' 1953 *World Black Market Year Book*. This agrees closely with Dr. Shenoy's estimate of an annual average of contraband gold in the eight years ending 1955 at 1·23 million oz. valued at Rs. 360 million. Hence the total value of gold smuggled into the country in the ten years since 1947 would be of the order of Rs. 3,400 million. On this basis it is estimated that the value of gold stock in India as on 31st March, 1957 would be about Rs. 29,630 million at current prices. Thus gold stock in India is about 2½ times the foreign exchange gap in the Second Plan period and nearly three times the annual investments in recent years.[35] It is observed that India's share of the world's stock of gold was more or less stable for the hundred years ending 1935, but since then has

[33]*ibid.*, p. 35.

[34]Quoted in Bonné, Alfred, *Studies in Economic Development*, Routledge and Kegan Paul, London, 1957, p. 196.

[35]Prakash Vinod, ' An Estimate of the Stock of Precious Metals in India,' *Papers on National Income and Allied Topics*, Indian Conference of Research in National Income, Vol. I, Asia Publishing House, Bombay, 1960, pp. 272–98.

declined. This fall may be attributed to change in social attitudes, spread of education, greater banking and credit facilities, conferment of legal rights on women in inherited property and greater security of life and property all of which are the attendant effects of material advancement.

The acquisition and stocking of precious metals undoubtedly represent savings. But these savings are not productively employed and the question naturally arises as to how these passive investments can be drawn into productive investments and capital formation. The possibilities in this line are, however, limited. Firstly, the stock is not as large as is often supposed and there are evidences to show that the amount of gold hoarded is decreasing. Since it is a fixed stock its use for capital formation will be only an once for all use. Or if the stock is used over a period of 5 years or so, the annual addition to national investment will not be large. Secondly, there is the difficulty of diverting this passive investment. It is to be borne in mind that in countries like India, the desire to acquire gold jewels is based on social custom and there is a sentimental attachment to precious metals. It is sometimes supposed that gold hoarding is really a function of income and any rise in interest rates or the prices of these metals is likely to result in a conversion of these assets into money.[36] The possibility of such shifting assumes that in keeping gold stocks or silver stocks, the individual is influenced by commercial or speculative motives which is not true in a country like India. Perhaps to some extent the offer of very attractive prices, which have necessarily to be higher than international prices, would bring about dishoarding. But such a measure would also encourage illicit imports. The transfer of gold from one party to another by means of purchase and sale obviously does not raise the savings of the community. The right method would be the acquisition of these stocks by the government in return for gold or silver certificates. Thereby it would be possible to make use of past savings for current investment and the gold and silver acquired in this manner could be used for the importing of capital equipment. But this again cannot be expected to work satisfactorily in countries where hoarding of precious metals is done not on commercial or business considerations but is influenced by more intractable motives.

While the hoarding of gold and other precious metals is to a large extent part of social custom or practice, this cannot be said of other types of passive investment. It may be said that investment in land or in foreign exchange or luxury construction is largely due to lack of better alternative investment opportunities and also to some extent as a safeguard against monetary and economic instability. Investment of this nature represents potential savings of the economy which are not productively employed. It is observed that savings are low in underdeveloped countries because the demand for savings is low. This is an exaggeration of a truth. And the truth is that since financial

---

[36]Chandavarkar, A. G., 'The Nature and Effects of Gold Hoarding in Underdeveloped Economies,' *Oxford Economic Papers*, June, 1961, pp. 137-48.

facilities are lacking and investment opportunities are limited, much of the savings get dissipated. All these point to the fact that the difference between potential savings and actual savings is great in underdeveloped countries. This margin of difference can be narrowed only with economic progress which would involve expansion of markets and widening of the investment opportunities. The problem of wastage of savings and malinvestment is real in underdeveloped countries. It underlines the need for finding out satisfactory measures of mobilizing the savings of the economy. But this should not divert attention from the major problem, which is the scarcity of savings.

THE PROBLEM IN UNDERDEVELOPED COUNTRIES

The problem of savings in underdeveloped countries is threefold: first they have to generate larger savings; second, they have to mobilize savings to the maximum extent possible; third, provision is to be made for the canalization of savings into productive investment.

(a) Generating Savings

The primary requirement for accelerating capital formation in underdeveloped countries is to widen the savings margin. In any economy, whether it is developed or undeveloped, it is possible to conceive of an upper and lower limit of savings.[37] The maximum level of savings is determined by the extent to which consumption can be lowered and production can be raised. Consumption requirements depend on social factors, the size and composition of population and the standard of life to which the community is accustomed. In times of acute necessity, as for example during war, the level of consumption is lowered appreciably but in normal times the minimum level of consumption is more or less fixed. In poor countries the level of consumption approximates to the minimum determined by physiological considerations. On the production side also, there is a maximum point beyond which output cannot be increased in the short period. This maximum depends on the organization and techniques of production, size and efficiency of labour force, capital equipment available, etc. Thus the minimum consumption requirements and the maximum production level possible under given conditions constitute the limits above which savings cannot rise. It is obvious that in normal times the maximum limit of savings is not reached. The minimum level of savings in an economy relates to the savings necessary to maintain capital equipment, so that the level of production can be kept constant. If savings fall below this point, it would necessitate capital consumption and bring about decline in output. In an underdeveloped economy the range between the upper and lower limits of savings is narrow. This is because consumption level is already

[37]Sen, Amartya Kumar, ' Optimising the Rate of Saving,' *Economic Journal*, September. 1961, pp. 491–95.

low and it cannot be depressed further; and production cannot be increased much unless techniques and organization of production are improved. On the other hand, even to maintain the existing level of production, investment of nearly the whole of the possible surplus over minimum consumption is necessary. As the economy grows, the limits of savings are extended. While the minimum level of consumption rises, the maximum level of production rises further and the savings margin widens; also, as the stock of capital increases, the strain on existing productive capacity to maintain the levels of production will be eased, that is to say, the economy will have sufficient capital resources to produce more output than is necessary to maintain existing standards of consumption.

Underdeveloped economies, therefore, have to find out the means of widening the savings margin. To the extent the economy indulges in unnecessary consumption, that is, consumption the denial of which will not affect productive efficiency, there is scope for increasing savings. On the other side, if by better organization and by devising better techniques of production output can be increased with the existing resources, there is possibility of widening the savings margin. The scope for such expansion of savings may be briefly examined. Arthur Lewis[38] lays great emphasis on a well-organized capitalist sector—this would mean private as well as public capitalist sectors—as the agency which would not only increase production but also promote savings. According to him poor countries are poor because their capitalist sectors are small. Much national savings cannot arise out of rent incomes and wages and salaries. In India, 1 per cent of the non-agricultural population which is subject to income-tax, and shares about 5 to 7 per cent of the national income is probably responsible for as much as 40 to 50 per cent of the total personal savings in the country.[39] The capitalist or business class does not indulge in conspicuous consumption as the land owning class, and is swayed primarily by the profit motive which prompts it to make larger and larger investments and build up bigger enterprises. Hence the growth of the capitalist sector would insure not only increased production and profits but also the reinvestment of large profits. Such a capitalist sector is fostered under conditions which ensure security of capital investments and provide profitable opportunities for investments. Heavy taxes on profits have a disincentive effect on private business and hamper reinvestment of profits and expansion of the private capitalist sector.[40] This also implies that a transfer of income to the capitalist sector as happens during inflation promotes larger savings and larger investment. A high ratio

[38]Lewis, Arthur W., *Theory of Economic Growth*, Allen and Unwin, London, 1955, pp. 225–44; also *Aspects of Industrialization*, National Bank of Egypt, Cairo, 1953, p. 15.

[39]'Mobilization of Domestic Capital,' *Report and Documents of the Second Party of Experts*, U.N., 1953, p. 83.

[40]A study of the urban savings in India by the National Council of Applied Economic Research, Delhi, shows that in the case of the corporate enterprises in the country retained earnings accounted for as much as 40 per cent of income after taxes—Summary reported in *The Hindu*, Madras, January 21, 1962.

14

of profits to rent and wages is therefore a factor conducive to larger savings.[41]
A more equitable distribution of wealth and income undoubtedly satisfies
our sense of social justice but in a free enterprise economy it is generally accepted
that it would raise the level of spendings and lower the level of savings.[42]
Prof. Ellis points out that egalitarian tax policies of the state and other measures
to bring about better distribution of wealth do not contribute to larger
savings. Since the poor are in the vast majority, such distribution of income
cannot very much increase productivity either.[43] For this reason, and
in so far as the primary and urgent concern of the underdeveloped countries
is increased production and larger savings, egalitarian measures as have
been adopted in many of the underdeveloped countries appear a little premature. According to Geoffrey Tyson this redistribution of current income has
affected investment adversely because it has taken away from those who are
the traditional savers to give to those who are not, and given their conditions
of life, probably cannot be savers. At the same time, tax rates have been raised
to a point where they act as a definite deterrent to individual and corporate
saving.[44]

Since agriculture contributes to more than 50 per cent of the national
incomes of underdeveloped countries and supports a large percentage of
the population, it is necessary to examine whether the primary sector is made
to yield as much of the savings as it is capable of generating. In recent years
the agricultural sector in most of the countries has benefited by a rise in the
prices of primary commodities and its favourable terms of trade with the
industrial sector. But rural savings have on the whole stagnated. In India,
the volume of saving of the rural household sector as a proportion of its income
has remained constant at about 2·6 per cent throughout the nine years 1950–51
to 1958–59.[45] The scope for increasing rural savings through increased production and more effective taxation requires to be investigated. As compared
with the industrial sector, the savings of the rural sector are much lower in
all countries. Inequality of income is lesser in the agricultural sector; there is
lesser chance of windfall gains than in the industrial sector; many unexpected
losses have to be incurred; and there is little possibility of speculative gain;
hence the spirit of enterprise is less pronounced among farmers. To these, some
special factors are to be added in respect of the underdeveloped countries of
Asia. In these countries especially in villages the family system is such that it
provides security for its members against ill health and old age so that no

[41]According to a recent Reserve Bank study of savings in India, the decline of savings in
1957–58 was due, among other factors, to the fall in the profits-wages ratio, additional taxation
and decline in the profits of some manufacturing industries, particularly cotton textiles—
Reserve Bank of India Bulletin, March, 1960, p. 327.

[42]*Measures for the Economic Development of Underdeveloped Countries*, U.N., 1951, p. 36.

[43]Ellis, Howard S., ' The Financing of Economic Development in Underdeveloped Areas,'
Indian Economic Journal, January, 1956, p. 264.

[44] ' Saving and Planning in Asia,' *Lloyds Bank Review*, October, 1953, pp. 26–27.

[45] *Reserve Bank of India Bulletin*, August, 1961, p. 1208.

great provision is needed for old age; there is little hope of improvement and a deep rooted fatalism has destroyed all incentive to earn more wealth and save more.[46] On the other hand, improvements in communication and the increasing contact with urban areas are rapidly changing the consumption pattern of the villagers and have exerted an adverse influence on rural savings. It would therefore appear that rural savings can be increased substantially by improving agricultural production through better organization and by creating the necessary enthusiasm among villagers and by a properly designed tax policy which would restrain conspicuous consumption and the frittering away of income on non-productive investments. Mention should also be made of the possibility of increasing agricultural output and therefore income of the rural areas by putting both land and labour to better uses. It is estimated that full employment of India's labour would increase the national income by 15 to 20 per cent.[47]

Foreign trade constitutes another source of additional savings. A high ratio of foreign trade to national income is helpful to realize large savings. This is because foreign trade is easily subject to state control for revenue and other purposes. But though export earnings form a substantial portion of the national income of many underdeveloped countries, they have not been able to exploit fully this source of savings and capital formation. Their inability in this respect is due largely to their undeveloped nature, the type of goods they export and their inferior bargaining power. By suitable export and import measures government can help in bettering the terms of trade which would increase the export earnings of each unit of goods delivered in foreign markets. What is equally important is to adopt suitable measures by which export earnings can be profitably used for the importing of capital goods and other materials necessary for domestic investment. The possibilities of increasing savings through foreign trade by means of selective import controls and multiple exchange rates are also to be exploited.

Taxation can be used not only for increasing production through the offer of incentives to greater effort but also for inducing savings and investment especially in the form of reinvestment of profits. There is considerable unanimity of opinion among economists about the usefulness of tax and fiscal measures for widening the savings margin in underdeveloped countries in the early stages of development. When development acquires momentum, voluntary savings by individuals and firms will rise sufficiently high to meet the capital requirements. But in the early phases of expansion some amount of compulsion to save via the power of the state becomes necessary.[48] Particularly

[46] Liang, C. C., 'Mobilization of Rural Savings with Special Reference to the Far East'; 'Mobilization of Domestic Capital,' *Report and Documents of the First Working Party of Experts*, U.N., 1952, p. 145.

[47] Wolf, Charles (Jr.) and S. C. Sufrin, *Capital Formation and Foreign Investment in Underdeveloped Areas*, Syracuse University Press, 1958, p. 14.

[48] Ellis, Howard S., 'The Financing of Economic Development in Underdeveloped Areas,' *Indian Economic Journal*, January, 1956, p. 266.

taxation can be made use of to mop up a substantial part of the increase in incomes resulting from economic improvement. Egbert de Vries and Elmer Starch point out that in rural areas in Turkey and Indonesia, marginal propensity to save in some cases is as high as 60 per cent.[49] In drawing attention to the continued scarcity of savings in underdeveloped economies the United Nations World Economic Survey of 1960 stresses the need for increased government saving by economy in expenditure and by absorbing the larger part of the increase in national income through taxation.

A high rate of savings is possible if people are prepared to put forth effort to maximize output even with the resources available and are willing to keep down their expenditure within reasonable limits. If Japan in the last decade was able to register a record annual rate of growth of output of 6·5 per cent with a saving level well over 25 per cent of the national income, it was due to the traditional saving habits of the people supported by the wide propagation of education. But even in countries where such will and attitude are deficient, it would be possible to increase savings through acting on the basic human motives for saving. By drawing the attention of the people to the importance of saving, by means of community action for promoting the attitude of the people to work and effort, and by publicity work, the savings habit can be fostered.

(b) Mobilizing Savings

The fact that savings are meagre in underdeveloped countries underlines the need for arrangements for effectively mobilizing all the savings that the economy is capable of generating. Adequate facilities for this purpose would not only help to prevent the dissipation of savings on conspicuous consumption and unproductive investments but also serve as inducement to the people to save more. In other words, the success of a scheme for the proper mobilization of savings is measured by the extent to which it is capable of reducing the difference between actual and potential savings of the economy.

Obviously, the prime requisite for the satisfactory mopping up of existing savings resources is the availability of suitable agencies and institutions. Given the adverse social conditions and backwardness of the countries in most parts of Asia and the Far East, provisions for the satisfactory mobilization of domestic savings should take into account the following criteria: safety of investment, yield, liquidity, accessibility, simplicity, divisibility, transferability, standardization, privacy and personal relations.[50] Security of money deposited with savings institutions is attained through many standard practices such as deposits insurance, guarantee of savings by government, as well as the general

[49] Quoted in Wolf, Charles (Jr.) and S. C. Sufrin, *Capital Formation and Foreign Investment in Underdeveloped Areas*, Syracuse University Press, 1958, p. 13.

[50] Liang, C. C., ' Mobilization of Rural Savings with Special Reference to the Far East '; ' Mobilization of Domestic Capital,' *Report and Documents of the First Working Party of Experts*, U.N., 1952, pp. 152–53.

regulation of banks to insure solvency. The yield on the savings should be sufficiently attractive. Liquidity is an important consideration in so far as rural incomes are highly unstable and hence the small saver should be enabled to make use of his saved amount in times of emergency. This is necessary to prevent savings flowing into hoards in the form of non-productive assets. Wide dispersal of savings agencies in the villages so that they would be within easy reach of the people, simplicity of procedure in making as well as withdrawing deposits, avoidance of delay in the transaction of such businesses, the grading of bonds or certificates in low denominations suitable to the pockets of the savers, a certain degree of privacy in the matter of savings accounts maintained by the savers and what is more important, establishment of personal relations, are equally important points to be observed if the rural savings are to be properly mobilized in these countries.

In the urban areas institutional facilities for savings are greater and the savings habit among the income classes who can afford to save, is quite well developed. Thus according to the recent survey of savings in Delhi, it is found that 51 per cent of the households had positive saving and of the total number of persons who saved, 44 per cent saved contractually largely through life insurance and to some extent through purchase of liquid assets.[51] Measures to improve mobilization of savings have therefore to concentrate on rural areas. Such measures can be summarized as follows :

(i) Promotion of Small Savings

In recent years, many of the countries in the East started vigorous campaigns to induce small savings. Ceylon started the National Savings Campaign in 1950–51 and the Colombo Plan Savings Campaign in 1951–52. Vigorous educational campaigns have been carried out and sale of savings stamps has become a popular means of collecting small savings from school children and estate labourers. The Central Bank in Philippines started a thrift campaign in January 1951 by distributing thrift posters and pamphlets. Pakistan and India have been making increasing use of savings certificates. Japan has experimented with the opening of ' uninscribed ' term deposits by commercial banks which carry no inscription of the depositors and has found them a useful means of mobilizing domestic capital. The provincial Bank of Taiwan (China) started in March, 1950 a kind of special interest savings deposit known as preferential savings deposit which has a minimum term of one month with a higher interest rate than the usual one. In addition, Post Office Savings Bank has been increasingly made use of in most of these countries to promote savings among the low income earners.

(ii) Popularizing Government Bonds

The absorption of government bonds especially in rural areas is very much

[51] *Delhi Savings Survey*, National Council of Applied Economic Research, Delhi, Asia Publishing House, Bombay, 1960, p. 70.

limited. One factor responsible for this unpopularity is that the yield on government bonds cannot be made attractive enough, for there is the danger that higher rates of interest on these would push up the general rates of interest. The United Nations Economic Commission for Asia and the Far East, however, suggest that comparatively higher yielding bonds may be issued provided they are only available to individuals and not to institutions. It is argued that higher cost to Government is worth bearing if it results in attracting personal savings which do not ordinarily find their way to the bond market.[52] Other means of making bonds popular are, introducing lottery features, providing tax incentives, that is, tax concessions on the income derived from bonds, propaganda and appeal to local interest. Thus if special bonds are issued for development projects in particular areas, the local people may be persuaded to purchase the bonds because of their interest in the project. Public resistance to the purchase of bonds because of fear of fall in value due to inflation may be got over by the offer of inflation and deflation proof bonds based on an independent index number so that the bond holder can be insulated against changes in the value of money as reflected in this index. The issuing of a variety of bonds with different maturity dates, interest rates and redemption terms would also help in popularizing these assets.

(iii) Co-operative Agencies

Co-operative credit societies have been set up in most of the underdeveloped countries of the East. They have been remarkably successful in mobilizing small savings in Western countries especially in Germany, Czechoslovakia and Canada. In the underdeveloped countries of the East, however, co-operative credit societies have been mostly distributors of credit and have in general failed to encourage savings. Improvement in this line is possible only if a greater degree of security and higher rates of interest are offered. The F.A.O. Regional Office at Bangkok suggested in 1951 the following measures to improve co-operative institutions as agencies for collection of rural savings: the establishment of a strong advisory council and a central apex institution; attracting the relatively well-to-do farmers to the co-operative movement; adequate interest rates; government guarantees to deposit liabilities of qualified societies; better education and training of co-operative officers and agents, etc.[53] It has been noted that in many countries, co-operative credit societies, even in the matter of granting credit facilities, have to compete with the village money lenders who charge exhorbitant rates of interest. The success of the latter is due to the immediate granting of funds and easy accessibility. The suggestion has therefore been made that the underdeveloped countries should start small loan banks on the model of state-run pawn shops in Indonesia

---

[52] ' Mobilization of Domestic Capital,' *Report and Documents of the First Working Party of Experts*, U.N., 1952, p. 79.

[53] *Measures for Mobilizing Rural Savings*, F.A.O. Office, Bangkok. ' Mobilization of Domestic Capital,' *Report and Documents of the First Working Party of Experts*, U.N., 1952, pp. 138–41.

for combating usury. The principal purpose of such banks should be to make small loans against the security of movable goods without enquiry about the purpose for which the loans are wanted. These institutions are preferably to be a state monopoly run on the cost of service principle with no profit motive. The state pawn shops in Indonesia have been found to work quite efficiently. They get their funds from the state at $3\frac{1}{2}$ per cent interest and use the post office as a banker for checking account purposes. The main purpose of such banks is, however, not the mobilization of savings but bringing down the rates of interest in the villages so that they would in course of time be a means of supplanting the village money lender and supplementing the co-operative credit scoeties. It is said that the government pawn shops in Indonesia have definitely succeeded in reducing interest rates charged by money lenders.[54]

(iv) Fostering the Insurance Habit

Another means to better mobilize savings in underdeveloped countries is to popularize the insurance habit among the villagers. Insurance can gain popularity only with the education of the people. But the habit can be fostered in rural areas through well-directed propaganda. Insurance facilities have been developed in most of the underdeveloped countries but they are largely confined to the urban areas. In some of these countries the insurance business has been nationalized and attempts have also been made to extend insurance operations to the rural areas as well. In India, life insurance business was nationalized in 1956 and the Life Insurance Corporation of India was set up. There has been notable progress in insurance activity in recent years. The new business written by the Corporation increased from 567,000 policies involving a sum assured of Rs. 2,003 million in 1956 to 1,258,000 policies and Rs. 4,975 million in 1960. The resources of the Corporation have been invested in government securities and in the shares and debentures of companies. In 1960, of the total investments of insurance funds, investments in the public sector constituted about 79 per cent while investments in the private sector accounted for 21 per cent. An intensified scheme of rural insurance was introduced in Rajasthan in 1958 and the extension of the scheme to other rural areas of the country is envisaged.

(c) Canalization of Savings into Investment

The problem of financing investment relates primarily to the private business sector. To a large extent, apart from the resources made available by the state, the agricultural sector depends on its own resources for investment. Much of the investment in this sector takes place simultaneously with savings as for example in building construction, land improvements, sinking of wells,

---

[54] State pawn shops in Indonesia by ECAFE Secretariat—'Mobilization of Domestic Capital,' *Report and Documents of the First Working Party of Experts*, 1952, pp. 117–23.

etc. Also a large part of the capital formation that takes place in the villages of underdeveloped countries is non-monetized. As for the public sector, the resources are found by the state out of taxation, borrowing and inflationary finance. To some extent the state is providing financial resources to the private sector also through special financial institutions but for the major part of its financial requirements the private sector has to depend on other sources. The methods of financing adopted by a private business unit fall into three categories. To some extent it depends on its own earning as when part of the profits is not distributed as dividends but reinvested. Secondly, it can mobilize financial resources through the sale of its securities; thirdly, it can borrow directly from the surplus spending units through flotation of loans. The first constitutes internal finance, the second and third constitute external finance of a business.

External financing is facilitated by financial intermediaries or agents which specialize in collecting the resources from the surplus spending units like households and other economic units which save a large part of their current incomes and in making these resources available to the deficit spending units which are mostly business firms. The financial intermediaries in a developed free enterprise economy are banks, brokers, investment houses, insurance companies and other agencies of the credit and security markets. In a simple economy under conditions of perfect competition, the available savings of the economy flow easily and directly into investment and the net yield of assets held by the savers who are the investors as well, is equal to the effective marginal product of capital. But as the economy grows and its functioning becomes more complex, a large number of intermediaries spring up who help in the transferring of savings from one group of people who are the lenders to another who are the borrowers. While in the simple economy there is only one risk of loss of a failure of investment directly affecting the investor and saver, an additional risk is involved as a result of the coming into existence of the intermediate agencies; that is, in addition to the risk involved in the failure of the enterprise in which the investment is made, there is a second risk of the loss of the money advanced which the saver or lender has to face.

Loans are made on the basis of tangible assets. Hence it may be expected that as an economy grows, and the role of the financial intermediaries in financing investment through loan transactions increases, more and more financial claims, liabilities and evidences of ownership (equities) will be created, and the proportion of these intangible assets to the tangible assets or wealth of the economy will rise. Raymond Goldsmith calls this relation between the two types of assets as the Financial Interrelations Ratio which is expressed as

$$\frac{\text{National Assets}}{\text{National Wealth}} - 1.$$

The ratio is zero when there are no intangibles, that is, no financial interrelations so that national assets are equal to national wealth, and the higher is the

ratio the denser the net financial interrelations. Goldsmith has calculated this
ratio in the U.S.A. for the years since 1850 and finds that F.I.R. has a secular
tendency to rise. However, he points out that this ratio is not a measure of
economic advancement; it is more indicative of the change in the financial
structure of the economy and is determined by such factors as the size of
government debt and the part played by the banking system, insurance companies and other institutional agencies in the financing of economic activity.[55]
At any rate, this ratio is rarely less than one in advanced economies.

Since the close of the 19th century some significant changes in the methods
of financing of investment in developed countries have occurred. Firstly,
there has been a marked decline in recent years in the amount of resources
made available to private enterprise by the capital market. This is due partly
to the general decline in funds in the capital market, and partly to the decreasing reliance of private business on this source. Changes in the distribution
of income and egalitarian tax and fiscal measures of government have reduced
the concentration of wealth in the community and as a result, the capital
market has been denied the necessary funds to grow along with the economy
and its needs for financial resources. On the other hand, private business has
come to rely more and more on reinvestment of its earnings. Secondly, as
between loan capital and share issues, private business firms have tended to
show increasing preference for the former. Private business finds the former
cheaper and less vexatious. As against this, the tax policy of the state, and
limitation of dividends, either enforced by the state or voluntarily adopted
by the firms in order to ensure larger reinvestment of profits, explain the
declining significance of equity capital. Thirdly, the importance of commercial
banks as an agency for providing finance for private business is also declining.
Increasingly, financing is done through the agency of many other financial
intermediaries like governmental insurance and lending agencies, postal
savings, credit unions, private investment companies and others. As a result
of these developments, the financial mechanism in advanced economies has
become more complex and less amenable to control and regulation through
the traditional monetary and credit control measures.

Financial institutions grow with economic advancement. When with
industrialization national income increases, financial resources needed for
fresh investment also increase. Besides, industrial development creates confidence in investment and the surplus spending units in the economy are prepared to place their savings at the disposal of business firms directly or through
intermediaries. From the investor's point of view, investment becomes attractive if it does not make his position very illiquid. Liquidity would be increased
through the development of financial institutions like the limited liability
company and the securities market. Growth of commercial banking also

[55] Goldsmith, R., 'Financial Structure and Economic Growth in Advanced Countries,'
Capital Formation and Economic Growth, National Bureau of Economic Research, Princeton,
1955, p. 118.

promotes savings and ensures easier flow of savings into investment. But since these institutions, develop only with economic growth, underdeveloped countries find themselves in a difficult position in the early stages of development. The realization of the need for industrialization has come about rather suddenly and hence in the early stages of growth they experience a sort of institutional inertia which retards rapid industrialization.[56] Even in India where the joint stock form of business organization and the securities market are better developed than in many other underdeveloped countries, the flow of private savings into industrial investment is unsatisfactory. In the nineteenth century and in the earlier years of the twentieth century, the problem in India was similar to the one which confronts many of the underdeveloped countries of today. Commercial banking was slow to develop. Foreign capital flowed into trade and also into investments in plantation and mining industries which were assured of an export market. The inadequacy of financial institutions and the difficulty of mobilizing domestic capital led to the emergence of the commercial organization peculiar to India, the Managing Agency System. The growth of commerce and the development of other financial institutions in more recent years have reduced the usefulness of this method of financing business.

However, commercial banks have on the whole been of only very limited help to the financing of industrial development in underdeveloped countries. In many of these countries the entry of domestic capital into the banking field has been impeded by the general timidity of local capital in venturing into unexplored fields and the scarcity of trained men to handle the funds.[57] Where commercial banking has been fairly developed as in India, their organization and general policy based on the British model have not been conducive to the provision of long term capital to industry. They have strict standards of liquidity and security. At the time when they were started, they were designed primarily to provide working capital for commerce, particularly international commerce, and not to provide long term capital for industry and agriculture, and they have been reluctant to make any change in this traditional policy. Since they have been accustomed for long to particular lines of business, viz. trade and commerce, they hesitate to plunge into new and riskier types of business in which the returns, after allowance is made for the risk element, may not be attractive. Moreover, the principal depositors and shareholders of the banks who are usually importers, exporters and merchants, might object to any investments being made in new lines for fear of loss as well as for fear that such diversion of resources would affect the supply of means to businesses in which they are interested.

Therefore, if banking in underdeveloped countries is to play a part in the canalization of savings into investment in the industrial field and agriculture, a change in their traditional lending pattern is to be brought about. The

[56] *Processes and Problems of Industrialization in Underdeveloped Countries*, U.N., 1955, pp. 35–36.
[57] *Domestic Financing of Economic Development*, U.N., 1950, p. 189.

prime requirement is the liberalization of the present restrictions on long term lending. It would also be possible to make them of greater use in industrial financing if some regulatory and directional measures are adopted by the Central Banks. Upper limits may be set for the total amount of credit each bank could grant for certain specified purposes. Banks may be permitted to include certain types of loans and investments as part of their required reserves in order to give them an incentive to grant such credit. Supplementary reserve requirements may be imposed applicable to increases in certain classes of assets; and the central bank may make conditional guarantees on the servicing and repayment of certain worthwhile kinds of bank loans.[58]

Steps have been taken in some underdeveloped countries to make good this deficiency in commercial banking practice. Since the close of the Second World War, Central Banks have been set up in many countries which lacked it. The State Bank of Pakistan, the central banking authority of the country, was established in July, 1948. In India the Reserve Bank of India organized its Department of Banking Development in 1950 with the object of giving greater attention to problems of rural finance and to the extension of banking facilities in semi-urban areas. The Union Bank of Burma was strengthened and reorganized by the Union Bank of Burma Act of March 1952. In 1951, the Indonesian Government reformed its central banking system. Another step taken in the direction of promoting banking in underdeveloped countries was the establishment of development banks to cater to the needs of industrialization and also to liberalize the lending policy of commercial banks so as to enable an easier flow of bank funds into industrial ventures. With a view to develop the banking habit among the people and to provide banking facilities in rural areas, steps have been taken to open branches of bigger banks in rural areas under state guidance and control. This policy is of course based on the assumption that in view of the economic backwardness and lack of enlightenment of the rural masses, private banks in normal circumstances would not establish their branches in the rural areas. Thus in India, the State Bank of India established in 1955 by the nationalization of the Imperial Bank of India, was entrusted with the responsibility of mobilizing rural savings and providing better credit facilities for agriculture, industry, trade and commerce. In accordance with a programme of expansion of banking in rural areas, the State Bank was required to open at least 400 branches by 30 June, 1960. The target was reached before the expiry of the prescribed period. In accordance with the recommendations of a Sub-Committee, it has now been decided that the State Bank should open another 300 branches before July, 1965. The State Bank of India has been allotted about 145 Centres, while the Subsidiary banks are expected to open 155 Centres under their respective branch expansion programmes.

The failure of commercial banks to meet adequately the financial require-

[58] ' Mobilization of Domestic Capital,' *Report and Documents of the Second Working Party of Experts*, U.N., 1953, p. 133.

ments of industry, the general pattern of economic development that is evolving in the underdeveloped countries and other circumstances have necessitated the setting up of special financial agencies to provide long term credit to industries. Governments in many of the underdeveloped countries have taken upon themselves the responsibility for providing the necessary incentive for growth and for setting up the basic social overheads necessary for economic development. Large investments in research schemes and development projects have involved the governments in huge financial commitments. Along with their needs, financial resources at the disposal of the state have also increased significantly. By taking away the income of the people which could otherwise have been saved and at the same time, by forcing people to save more through deficit financing and inflation, the state has succeeded in transferring to itself a large part of the financial resources of the community. The ability of the state to raise foreign loans has also augmented the resources at its command. On the other hand, private business firms are faced with increasing difficulty in raising adequate funds from the capital market. Higher taxation and higher wage payments have also eaten into their savings which could otherwise have been possible. All these have necessitated the state taking greater interest in the financing of industries. Furthermore, in so far as economic development in underdeveloped countries is organized and regulated by the government, it would serve better the purposes of planned development if the flow of financial resources is directed into desired channels in conformity with the requirements of the Plans. Even in advanced countries the responsibility of the state in helping small businesses, which are edged out of the capital markets by bigger rivals has been recognized.[59]

These circumstances have led to the setting up of finance and development corporations in many countries. As the United Nations Experts point out " the establishment of development corporations is an indication of the wide spread recognition that economic progress in the underdeveloped countries requires concerted public action on an increasing scale ".[60] The Finance Corporation is primarily devoted to bringing together government and/or private funds and advancing them as loans to public, private or mixed corporations, co-operatives or individuals, on the security of tangible movable or immovable property for periods of not less than five years. The Finance Corporations of India and Pakistan have also powers to underwrite issues of stocks, shares or bonds as well as to make or guarantee loans or subscribe to debentures. As distinguished from Finance Corporations, the Development Corporations have more comprehensive functions. They are set up with wholly or partly government finance and are required to take the initiative

[59] Gaitskell, Hugh, ' Savings and the World Economy—A British View,' *Savings in the Modern Economy*, Heller, W. W. and others (Eds.), University of Minnesota, Minneapolis, 1953, p. 43.

[60] ' Mobilization of Domestic Capital, ' *Report and Documents of the Second Working Party of Experts*, U.N.. 1953. p. 259.

in the creation, direction or operation of individual enterprises. Such corporations supply part or all of the equity capital required for industrial enterprises rather than provide loan funds, and frequently assume responsibility for management and control. However, the objectives and activities of Development and Finance Corporations vary from country to country. The Chilean Development Corporation set up as early as 1939 is invested with wide powers. That of Ecuador includes among its objectives the establishment of new agricultural settlements. The Puerto Rico Corporation lays emphasis on educational training and provision of technical advice to industries. The Agricultural and Industrial Credit Corporation of Ceylon established in 1953 has two main objectives, to help in the development of new industrial enterprises and in the refinancing of agricultural debt. Some countries have set up special corporations to serve a variety of purposes, for meeting the requirements of industry or export trade, or agriculture, small industries, etc. Thus in India the Industrial Finance Corporation was established in July, 1948 to provide medium and long term finance to public limited companies and co-operatives engaged in manufacturing, mining and the generation and distribution of power. Since 1959, State Finance Corporations on the model of the Industrial Finance Corporation have been set up in most of the states. The National Industrial Development Corporation was established in 1954 with the object of financing industries and promoting planned industrial development. In June, 1955, the Industrial Credit and Investment Corporation of India was set up as a private limited company. The main function of this institution is to assist, expand and modernize private industrial enterprises. Earlier in the same year, the National Small Industries Corporation was started with the purpose of assisting small industries in marketing their produce and in acquiring their capital equipment through hire purchase system. Another important private limited company, the Refinance Corporation for Industry Private Ltd., was established in 1958 to provide medium term credit facilities to medium sized industrial units.

The sources of finance of the corporations also vary in different countries. The bulk of the original capital and supplementary capital is in some cases provided by governments from regular fiscal budgets or extraordinary budgets. Sometimes, the Corporations like other government establishments have resorted to borrowing or discounting at central banks. Earmarked taxes are also assigned to meet the financial requirements of the Development Corporations. The Chilean Development Corporation has depended largely on foreign loans and government contributions for its funds. The Corporations of Mexico and Turkey have borrowed substantial sums from the Export Import Bank of the U.S.A. and also from the International Bank for Reconstruction and Development. Corporations have also been empowered to receive deposits from the public and raise funds through the sale of securities or bonds or take loans from commercial banks. In Venezuela, a good part of the tax revenues obtained from the petroleum companies was made available to the Venezuelan

Development Corporation set up in 1946. In India the shares of the authorized capital of the Industrial Finance Corporation are subscribed by the Central Government, the Reserve Bank, the Scheduled banks, Insurance Companies, and the Life Insurance Corporation of India. The Corporation is also authorized to raise funds by the sale of bonds up to five times the paid-up capital and accept deposits from the public. The bonds and the debentures of the Corporation are guaranteed by the Central Government in respect of repayment of the principal and payment of interest. The State Corporations are also authorized to issue bonds and debentures. The capital of the National Industrial Development Corporation as well as of the National Small Industries Corporation is subscribed entirely by the Government of India. In contrast, the paid-up share capital of Rs. 5 crores of the Industrial Credit and Investment Corporation of India was subscribed wholly by domestic and foreign private investors. In the case of the Refinance Corporation the shares so far issued have been contributed jointly by the Reserve Bank of India, the Life Insurance Corporation and a few of the larger Scheduled Banks.

As has been indicated already, financial institutions like the Development and Finance Corporations have been found necessary in view of the special problems that have arisen in the underdeveloped countries in the early stages of their economic growth. In a sense these institutions form a link between the government and private enterprise. In some countries Development Corporations have as their objective the promotion of enterprise in the private sector. But the general idea behind such institutions in all cases is to see that the process of economic growth is not hampered by the lack of financial resources through normal channels. In the early stages of development of the present day advanced economies such a need did not arise, because financial agencies developed in these countries in step with industrial advancement. Contemporary low income countries require a faster rate of economic development and as such they cannot afford to wait for the slow emergence of financial institutions. Even as the pattern of economic development is planned and designed by the state, the agencies and intermediaries to mobilize and canalize the financial resources into investment have also to be created. However, if the new agencies for mobilization and canalization of savings are to work satisfactorily, it is important that they are run and operated efficiently. They should be able to provide funds to business, industry and agriculture at relatively low cost; they should be a dependable source from the point of view of private business; and there should also be a steady increase in the capital available through this source so as to meet the increasing needs of a growing economy. It is also important that they avoid inflationary methods of financing. Those methods of financing which rely only partially on the national government and central banks for their resources are usually least inflationary. The use of ' counterpart ' funds arising out of grants to governments under the various Mutual Aid programmes and which have become available to some countries like Japan, Indonesia, Turkey and India, provides a means of financing with least inflationary effect. In reality the test of the usefulness of Development Corporations is the extent to which they promote industrial and economic growth without affecting stability.

Chapter VII

INVESTMENT CRITERIA

THE EMERGENCE of savings in real terms and the mobilization of these savings through the agency of the market mechanism and financial institutions, facilitate investment or conversion of savings into productive assets. The level of investment in an economy depends on the amount of savings available and the absorptive capacity of the economy. The latter term is defined as the ability of individuals and society as a whole to utilize the capital assets available and make good use of the stream of output increments. Thus the skill and knowledge of the people to operate the productive equipment and their capacity to demand and absorb the products of capital assets determine the extent to which investment can increase with advantage.[1]

Since in low income countries the investible resources are very much limited in relation to the great and increasing need for them, the problem of choosing between alternative employment of these resources assumes considerable importance. This involves decision regarding the distribution of resources between industries and agriculture, between public sector and private sector, capital goods and consumer goods industries, and allocation to different geographical regions in the country. Normally the flow of real resources for investment in these different sectors is influenced by economic, political and social factors. Considerable emphasis is laid on rapid industrialization in all the underdeveloped countries. This obviously is necessary if the growth of national income is to be accelerated. But it is also realized that agricultural expansion plays a vital role in economic growth and as such it is imperative that any programme of planned development should ensure adequate investment in agriculture also. In the same manner, the allocation of investment between capital goods and consumer goods involves economic considerations. The share of investment of the public sector as compared with the private sector is determined by the role of the public sector in the national economy, the strength and vitality of private enterprise and the political philosophy and faith of the community.

As regards allocation of investment among different regions in the country, it is obvious that to a large extent, the share going to each region depends upon economic factors, the standard of economic development already attained by the region, the availability of natural resources, skilled labour and entre-

[1]Horvat, Branko, ' The Optimum Rate of Investment, ' *Economic Journal*, December, 1958, pp. 747–64.

preneurial skill, financial facilities and communication and transport system, the size of the market, the nature of the industry and the raw materials used. However, political factors also come into play here. The interest of the local community in developing their particular regions and the influence which they can bring to bear on the government affect the extent to which a central government responsible for the economic development of the entire economy would divert resources into particular regions. Moreover, government itself may be swayed by motives of bringing about a balanced development as between different regions. In that case the central government would increase the share going to economically backward regions with a view to raise them to a comparable level with the more advanced areas. Thus the tendency for the wide dispersal of industries in a country is largely the influence of political factors. Nevertheless economic facts tend to assert themselves, so that when once disparity has manifested itself, as for instance between a predominantly industrial and agricultural area, it gets perpetuated because an industrialized and high income region would be able to get larger investments out of its own income as well as by drawing capital from the less developed regions; wages tend to be higher in the industrialized regions, while scarcity of capital keeps up interest rates and prevents any improvement in the rate of capital formation in the agricultural areas. Primarily, this sort of dualism common in many underdeveloped countries is due to differences in factor endowments[2]. But as indicated above, the national government is likely to be interested in balanced development between different regions and may therefore, under certain conditions, bias its investment policy towards the less developed regions.

When the aggregate investment over a period of years in the different sectors of the economy is fixed, the question emerges as to what techniques of production are to be adopted in the matter of utilization of the available investible resources. Since the major objective is economic development or increase in national output, the question of choice of techniques boils down to one of finding out the best method to be adopted in production so as to realize the targets. The investment resources allotted to a particular industry may be concentrated on techniques involving large amounts of capital or the resources can be spread thin over a large number of productive units by adopting capital-light and labour-intensive techniques. The investment criterion in respect of this decision is thus one of choosing between capital-intensive and labour-intensive techniques. However, this problem is closely related to the other one of choosing between industries and agriculture or between different industries. Thus preference for heavy industries as against small or cottage industries or the decision in favour of industries as against agriculture implies also a decision in favour of capital-intensive methods of production.

[2]Hirschman, Albert O., ' Investment Policies and Dualism in Underdeveloped Countries,' *American Economic Review*, September, 1957, pp. 551–68.

THE NEED FOR INVESTMENT CHOICE

Under theoretically ideal conditions in a system of free enterprise when there is free and perfect competition, resources and factors of production will be employed optimally. Wages of labour and interest rate will be determined in the competitive market according to conditions of supply and demand and the employment of each factor will be carried up to the point at which its marginal product is equal in value to the price paid for it. Since an increase in the supply of any factor—labour or capital—would reduce its price, there is an incentive for larger employment of these while a shortage in supply will raise the price and lead to the substitution of it by factors whose costs have not gone up. As a result, there will be not only full employment of the resources but also their most effective utilization. In actual practice however, these results are not attained. The emergence of external economies in production and increasing or decreasing costs to scale make it impossible to attain the ideal distribution of resources and income over time. Long-term prices and interest rates are not independent of investment decisions but are influenced by the choice of projects and the scale of investment and employment in different lines of production. As such, prices " cease to be perfect signalling devices through market mechanism ".[3] Perfect competition also assumes perfect foresight about changes in the supply of factors and their prices, conditions of their demand and changes in technology. These assumptions are clearly unreal and hence optimal allocation of investment under free enterprise is not likely to be attained.

Moreover, modern technological conditions make it difficult to bring about any fine adjustment between output and cost at the margin in any long-period production process. Different techniques may be available in any line of production but each technique represents a given combination of factors—say, labour and capital—which cannot be altered. One technique may involve the combination of a larger amount of capital and a smaller amount of labour than another. When once a technique is accepted, the ratio in which the factors are combined has also to be accepted. Given the technique, it is not possible to keep capital constant and vary labour or vice versa. If a new combination is desired, then a different technique which will meet the requirement will have to be adopted. The private entrepreneur has to make his decisions regarding investment on the basis of known and unknown data such as the state of technique, labour supply, wage and price level, amount of disposable funds available to him, and the technical relation between capital and labour. His main objective is to maximize private profits, to widen the difference between costs of production and value of output as much as possible. In this there are two possibilities; the entrepreneur may set the present value of anticipated future earnings against current total costs of production and aim at maximizing the excess of the former over the latter,

[3]Eckstein, Otto, ' Investment Criteria for Economic Development and the Theory of Intertemporal Welfare Economies,' *Quarterly Journal of Economics*, February, 1957, pp. 56–85.

or he would attempt to maximize the ratio of future earnings to present value of capital i.e. raise the rates of returns on present invested capital. The choice between these two alternatives—maximization of net returns and maximization of the rate of returns of capital—depends on the present availability of disposable funds. If funds at the disposal of the entrepreneur are large and relatively easy to get, he is likely to aim at maximizing aggregate profits. Such a decision would lead to investment in capital-intensive projects. On the other hand, if there is scarcity of investible resources at present, the entrepreneur is likely to concentrate on the rate of returns on capital, in which case the investment would tend to be capital light. In so far as bigger firms are in a position to command larger resources from the capital market on attractive terms, bigger firms tend to become bigger still and more capital-intensive, while the difficulty of getting an adequate supply of investible resources by smaller firms makes capital light investments attractive for them.[4] Thus deficiency in the capital market and the lack of perfect elasticity in the supply of capital, cause the existence of small firms using old technology side by side with large firms employing the latest technology. In the former, the investment-output ratio will be low while in the latter it would be high. Such an allocation of investment and choice of technology do not warrant the optimal utilization of resources. Competition in course of time would result in the elimination of the weaker and smaller firms, but the process of this change is long drawn out and costly from the social point of view.

Investment allocation under an unregulated free enterprise system has other limitations. The private investor attempts to maximize his own profits and not the social product. In an economy where capital resources are very limited and where therefore the best utilization of resources in the best interests of the economy as a whole is the most important consideration, a better ordering of investment becomes absolutely necessary. The private investor's foresight is limited. The impact of a particular investment or a technique of production on the national economy and the effect of the starting or expansion of particular industries on other sectors of the economy, on the distribution and composition of income, on the supply of factors of production and their cost, are not and cannot be looked into when private investment decisions are made. It is obvious that an overall view of the effect of investment on the national economy can be had only by an agency which has a more comprehensive and adequate knowledge of the behaviour of the different sectors of the economy. It is mentioned that in agriculture, trades and services and even in industry, private investment will tend to duplicate existing methods rather than introduce new and improved ones.[5] The fact is that there is a substantial

[4]Barriere, Alain, ' Capital Intensity and the Combination of Factors of Production,' *The Theory of Capital*, Proceedings of a Conference held by the International Economic Association, Hague, D. C. (Ed.), Macmillan, London, 1961, pp. 143-60.

[5]Hagen, Everett E., ' The Allocation of Investment in Underdeveloped Countries—Observations Based on the Experience of Burma,' *Investment Criteria and Economic Growth*, Massachusetts Institute of Technology, Asia Publishing House, Bombay, 1961, p. 68.

difference between private profitability and profitability from the national point of view. Besides, the estimate of costs and profits made by the private investor is likely to be misleading when viewed against the interest of the community or the nation. Investment in a new enterprise may provide employment to those hitherto unemployed and would thus raise the income of such workers. This is a gain from the point of view of these workers and the community, but is not taken into account as income gain or profits by the investor. On the other hand, private profit may be over-estimated as when it does not take into account the losses sustained by competing rivals. Moreover, quite often profits are calculated by private investors on the basis of factor prices which do not correctly reflect the value of the factors used or of the products. Thus when a labour-intensive project is chosen, hitherto unemployed labour may be paid the current wage rate. This additional cost involves a sacrifice on the part of the employer, but from the point of view of the country, the sacrifice is much less in so far as little loss is involved in the transfer of these unemployed workers into the new enterprise.

These limitations of investment decisions by private enterprise justify government's participation in investment activity. Government is in a position to have a better overall and long-term view of the problems involved in the allocation of investment and choice of technology. The resources at the disposal of the government are much greater than what a private businessman can command. Government has also more detailed and correct information regarding the resources position of the entire economy, and the requirements of different sectors. It is also possible for the government to estimate the repercussions on the economy as a whole, of expansion or contraction of investment and activity in particular lines of production. The state can therefore by its investment policy and by its participation in the economic activities of the country bring about a better distribution and utilization of the nation's resources. Particularly, the state's activity in this direction is capable of generating large external economies which help overall economic growth. The major source of such external economies is economic overheads like roads and railways, irrigation works, hydro-electric projects, etc.

Further, the state can through its investment policy bring about what is called balanced growth i.e. expansion of each industry or sector of the economy in such a manner that the development of the one helps in the development of others. The growth of each sector or industry is thus made to proceed in step with one another, so that the expansion needs of one can be met by the progress of another. Such a balanced development of the economy is possible if the state has powers to control and regulate investment decisions of private enterprisers and if the state itself has ownership of the means of production to some extent which would enable it to affect or influence the allocation of investment and choice of techniques for the whole economy.

SPECIAL INVESTMENT PROBLEMS IN UNDERDEVELOPED COUNTRIES

The problem of allocation of investment and choice of techniques is more complicated in underdeveloped countries than in developed countries because of the special economic and social characteristics of the former. Inappropriate factor endowments combined with limited opportunities for technical substitution of factors present a serious difficulty in choosing suitable investment policies or techniques of production. There is in underdeveloped countries what Professor Kindleberger calls " structural disequilibrium at the factor level ". In these countries capital is scarce but labour is abundant. As a result, a large volume of unemployment and disguised unemployment exists. Taken as a whole, the marginal product of labour is very low or even zero. But the actual wage rate in these countries is not what the normal working of the forces of demand and supply would bring about. This disparity between the actual wage rate and the marginal productivity of labour is due to the existence of an organized sector along with an unorganized sector in these economies. Wage rate in the former is maintained at a high level because of labour unions, elaborate social security legislation and the welfare policy of the government. Moreover, the increased demand for products requiring capital-intensive methods of production and the restrictions on the new entry of firms which would use labour-intensive methods of production tend to isolate the organized sector from the rest of the economy. In choosing techniques of production the businessmen in the organized sector take for granted the market wage rate as against the real wage rate. And since the former is higher than the latter, the techniques of production adopted tend to be more capital-intensive than is warranted by the factor supply situation. Also, the organized sector is influenced by the methods of production used in advanced countries.

It would thus appear that there can be full employment of labour only if the wage rate is brought down and less capital-intensive methods of production are adopted. This, however, is not practicable because of the prevailing dichotomy between the organized and unorganized sectors of the economy. Possibilities of modifying the techniques with a view to make them fit in with the requirements of factor endowments are limited in the former. The nature of technology in the organized sector does not provide any chance of increasing employment of labour unless there is an increase in the availability of capital to the extent required by the prevailing technique. If we assume that the organized sector is a fixed co-efficient sector, i.e. one in which the ratio of capital and labour is fixed at different levels of output, and the unorganized sector is a variable co-efficient sector, a rise in the level of income and demand will not lead to any proportionate increase in the employment in the fixed co-efficient sector, because of the limits fixed by the scarcity of capital and technical conditions. Hence unemployed labour would have to be drawn into the unorganized or variable sector so long as the marginal product of labour is higher than the wage rate in that sector. If, however, labour supply is excessive, the result will be overt or disguised unemployment. In such a situation as Eckaus points out, the usual contra-cyclical measures to relieve unemployment will not be successful. The only solution lies in increasing the supply of capital.[6] The dualistic nature of the economy also aggravates the problem of investment allocation in so far as different techniques have to be chosen for the two sectors. So long as capital is inadequate, the dichotomy between the two sectors will continue. In short, the two sectors present distinct investment problems.

Also, because of this structural disequilibrium in underdeveloped countries, the profit maximization criterion which is based on a comparison between the market price of the factors of production and their productivity and which is applicable to developed countries becomes irrelevant to underdeveloped countries.[7]

Since labour is plentiful and capital is scarce in most of the underdeveloped countries, the natural investment choice would be the one which would involve the employment of the total labour force with backward techniques of production. The ratio of total capital stock to the value of total labour force employed (i.e. wage rate of labour multiplied by the number of labourers employed) measures capital-intensity. Given the wage rate, the lower the capital-intensity and the higher the stock of capital, the larger will be the number of people employed. However, the scarcity of capital in underdeveloped countries prevents the full employment of labour even when wage rate and capital-intensity are relatively low. Professor Lange points out that the disparity between the total labour force available in an economy and the actual employment is indicative of its economic backwardness. According to him this state of affairs in low income countries is due to certain historical factors. The feudal mode of production in these countries, the absence of any effort to improve productive efficiency, and conspicuous consumption by the feudal ruling classes prevented the formation of capital and hindered industrialization. Expensive colonial administration and wasteful expenditure by domestic monarchy and its officials also operated as a deterrent. Profit taking by foreign entrepreneurs and the removal of profits from these countries deprived them of the source of accumulating their own capital. Capital drained in this manner led to the starting of capital-intensive industries in the foreign countries while the capital that was invested in the underdeveloped countries found its way into consumers goods industries and in the production of raw materials and staple food products—leaving little scope for the development of the domestic economy.[8]

[6]Eckaus, R. S., ' The Factor Proportions Problem in Underdeveloped Areas, *The American Economic Review*, September, 1955, pp. 539–65.

[7]*Economic Bulletin for Asia and the Far East*, U.N., June, 1961, p. 30.

[8]Lange, Oskar, *Essays on Economic Planning*, Indian Statistical Institute, Calcutta, Asia Publishing House, Bombay, 1960, pp. 33–38.

Thus apart from capital shortage, the above-mentioned socio-political circumstances inherited from the past stand in the way of adoption of modern and efficient methods of production. For instance an agricultural investment programme involving conversion of small farms into large estates is bound to cause resistances in a country where ownership of landed property confers a social prestige. The sentimental attachment to inherited landed property presents a serious obstacle to the formation of large estates even when the small holding is proved to be uneconomic. Assuming that the necessary capital is found, investment in heavy industries can succeed in building up a strong industrial base and promote economic growth only if the community acquires a set of social values that are conducive to economic expansion. In many of the underdeveloped countries such motivations are lacking and to that extent investment becomes necessary in fields other than industries and agriculture so that the people may be attuned to new ways of living and imbibe a spirit of enterprise. It is therefore necessary that in drawing up an investment programme in underdeveloped countries care should be taken to see that development programmes and projects do not as far as possible violate existing social institutions or wrench the people from existing modes and values but are rather adapted to existing values and motivations. The assumption here is that with industrialization and growth, those social prejudices which are inimical to economic progress will gradually give way to attitudes which favour economic growth.[9]

Adoption of modern methods of production implies the use of modern technology. Economically advanced countries with large amounts of capital at their disposal can afford to make use of better and more improved, or the latest technology even when the adoption of more and more capital-intensive techniques reduces the output per unit of capital. This is possible because the fall in the output per unit of capital is more than offset by increased output per unit of labour which is a relatively scarce factor. From the private entrepreneur's point of view, it is advantageous to go ahead in this direction because the increased productivity of labour adds to his profits. But most of modern technology requires the application of large amounts of capital which many underdeveloped countries cannot afford. In the contemporary low income countries advanced techniques are imported, but they do not have the necessary capital to assimilate it. It has been pointed out that the per capita income in Latin America in the 1950s ($ 247) was about the same as the per capita income of the U.S.A. in the 1840s. In the last 110 years investment per head in the U.S.A. increased from $ 505 to $ 3,330. Thus when Latin America imports modern technology from the U.S.A. it would mean that that country with an income equal to what it was in the U.S.A. hundred years ago is using technology which is suited to the U.S.A. of today. This points to the extent

[9]Hagen, Everett E., 'The Allocation of Investment in Underdeveloped Countries—Observations Based on the Experience of Burma,' *Investment Criteria and Economic Growth*, Massachusetts Institute of Technology, Asia Publishing House, Bombay, 1961, pp. 60–63.

to which investment effort has to be increased in Latin America to assimilate modern technology. For instance, if underdeveloped countries adopted the road building techniques of advanced countries like the U.S.A. and U.K., the former would be unable to meet the cost necessary for maintaining and utilizing this capital asset, that is to say, such expenses on up-to-date techniques of road construction are not worth incurring unless there are costly and heavy vehicles and heavy traffic which require the service of such roads and which would ensure the full utilization of this capital asset.[10]

The way out of this difficulty would seem to be the adaptation of modern technology or the development of the type of technology that would fit in with the factor supply situation in the pre-industrial countries. But the scope for the adaptation of advanced techniques to the needs and conditions of underdeveloped countries is also very much limited. As an illustration of the difficulty in this matter is mentioned the recent Chinese attempt to use capital-saving small blast furnaces in the place of large modern furnaces. It proved to be a failure because the small furnaces were more fuel-intensive and possibly more capital-intensive if transport requirements were also taken into account.[11] Even assuming that such adaptation is possible, the cost that will have to be incurred in connection with research and experiments of new processes would be beyond the means of many underdeveloped countries. The U.N. Economic Commission of Latin America in 1952 therefore recommended the creation of an Institute of Technological Research to develop processes and techniques of production that will be suitable to the low income and capital poor countries.

Investment choice thus constitutes a vexed problem in modern underdeveloped countries. It would not be possible to make any correct approach to it unless we have a better understanding of the true nature and significance of the problem. As has been pointed out by Eckaus, a proper assessment of the factor proportions problem in low income countries is not possible unless we have more knowledge pertaining to the range of input variability, the extent to which economies of scale arise because of large-scale operations and organizational changes, the scope for input variation in the agricultural sector and also the true nature of technological change and its contribution to production.[12] It may, however, be pointed out that although the blind adoption of advanced capital-intensive techniques of production is an unwise and uneconomic investment, yet the need for such improvements in the organized sector of the economy of underdeveloped countries is undoubtedly great. Many countries have therefore attempted to combine advanced and up-to-date techniques with simpler and capital-light investments.

[10]*Analyses and Projections of Economic Development*, U.N., 1955, p. 8.

[11]Eckaus, R. S., ' The Factor Proportion Problem in Underdeveloped Areas,' *The American Economic Review, Papers and Proceedings*, May, 1960, p. 644.

[12]*ibid.*, pp. 644–45.

THE CRITERIA OF INVESTMENT IN UNDERDEVELOPED COUNTRIES

Investment decisions in underdeveloped countries are to be based on a consideration of their factor endowments, the techniques of production which are suitable to them and the choice of those methods of using the resources which would ensure a high rate of income growth without endangering social and economic stability. In recent years economists have put forward various investment criteria to attain the objective of accelerated economic development. Although in general all these criteria have as their main purpose increase in national income, yet they differ according to the emphasis they lay on the means of achieving this end. On this basis it is possible to classify the different criteria as follows:

(a) Principles of investment which accept the present factor endowment position as it is, and suggest the designing of investment policy accordingly.

(b) Criteria which aim at maximizing the rate of growth through methods which even go against the factor supply situation.

(c) Investment policies which are influenced by and which aim at controlling the special problems that arise in the wake of economic development.

(d) Investment criteria which specially emphasize the time factor involved in economic progress. The salient features of these different criteria may be briefly examined.

(a) Factor Endowment Criteria

This principle of investment stresses the need for full utilization of the available labour and capital resources. If the factor endowment of an underdeveloped country is such that labour supply is abundant while capital is scarce, its investment policy should aim at adopting those techniques of production which combine a small amount of capital with a large amount of labour. In other words, in so far as capital is in short supply while labour is abundant, it is necessary to adopt labour-intensive techniques. The available capital is to be spread thin extensively. Thus capital-intensive methods according to this analysis are suited only to countries with a factor endowment different from that of many of the present day underdeveloped countries. If this principle is accepted by all countries, it would conform to the Hekscher-Ohlin version of the comparative cost doctrine. If capital is scarce in underdeveloped countries comparative advantage can be realized by low capital-labour ratios. In favour of this thesis, it may be pointed out that it agrees with the basic economic principle of making the best use of available resources. Secondly, it implies a relatively high ratio of output to capital or in other words its implementation results in the product per unit of capital being increased.[13] It meets the requirement of the neo-classical rule that there is efficient allocation of any factor of production when marginal productivity in the different uses

[13]Polak, J. J., ' Balance of Payments Problems of Countries Reconstructing with the help of Foreign Loans,' *Quarterly Journal of Economics*, February, 1943, pp. 208–40.

is equalized. Fuller utilization of labour in the face of limited availability of capital reduces productivity of each unit of labour, but total product may be increased because of larger employment. Quick turnover of capital ensures flexibility in investment. In an underdeveloped country with scarcity of capital this is an important consideration because such countries cannot afford to have large capital investments stuck up in particular lines. Capital light investment it is argued, need not necessarily stand in the way of technological improvements. On the other hand, such methods facilitate the gradual development of types of technology that would suit the requirements of the economy. Thirdly, the principle of combining factors of production according to their availability and supply ensures the full absorption of labour into employment. Unemployment of labour in underdeveloped countries, whether disguised or otherwise, is a social evil and constitutes an economic waste. Under-utilization of any factor of production obviously implies a defect in economic organization and is indicative of an economic imbalance. It is argued by some economists that the principle of investment in underdeveloped countries should be one which aims at putting to work unemployed labour. Thus the abundant factor is to be made use of to build up the scarce factor. It is in conformity with this principle that in India and Burma in certain projects of capital formation, importance is given to labour-intensive methods by means of employing unpaid or partly paid labour.

While the factor endowment criterion appears logical, it has serious defects when looked at from the point of view of economic growth. The principle of equating the marginal productivity of any factor of production may lead to efficient allocation of resources only in the short run under static conditions. As Maurice Dobb shows, if capital-light projects are preferred because of resources position, it amounts to accepting the existing state of affairs without any desire for change or progress. If low capital-labour ratio reduces the productivity of labour, then any policy which spreads capital thin over the abundant supply of labour would only maintain labour productivity at a low level. Viewed in the dynamic setting of a growing economy, this principle is defective in so far as it fails to realize the importance of changes in the structure, organization and techniques of production as a means to promote growth. If immediate employment is the objective, this principle leads to the adoption of inefficient techniques. It is not therefore an economic objective. Economic growth is possible only if the rate of investment is increased through techniques which would raise the productivity of labour and enlarge per capita savings. The rate of capital formation is in fact not independent of the techniques of production used in an economy. For increasing investment it is not enough if aggregate output is increased. It is the surplus of production over consumption per capita that really matters. In short, the principle of organizing production in accordance with the factor endowment position of an underdeveloped country does not help in the formation of a strong capital base in the economy. It is true that a high rate of turnover of capital imparts an element of flexibility in investment but against this has to be set the possibility that a high rate of capital turnover may co-exist with a high rate of depreciation of capital equipment. In that case the rate of net output will not necessarily be high. Moreover, the distribution of a given amount of capital over an increasing quantity of labour can add to net output only if we assume that the cost of employing labour is zero.[14] But if labour costs something, we have to take into consideration not only the output per unit of capital but also the output per unit of labour. If the output per unit of labour falls below the cost of labour because of a low capital-labour ratio, it is not worthwhile employing that additional unit of labour. Since productivity of labour is dependent on the quantity of capital available per head of worker this sets a limit to the extent to which capital can be diluted among a large number of labourers.

Secondly, the assumption that capital-output ratio is reduced when capital is spread widely may be misleading. In measuring the quantity of capital employed in a particular enterprise, we have to take into account the total amount of capital employed both directly and indirectly in producing the commodity. This is necessary because the productivity of labour in one industry may rise, in consequence of additional investments in a different line for example in transport or communications. In that case, the product-capital ratio in the first industry is something different from the relationship between the actual investment made in that sector and the product of that sector. Also, capital and labour are combined with other resources—natural resources—and the efficiency of a technique of production cannot be measured correctly without reference to the availability and nature of these other resources. Moreover, while the initial allocation of capital may be relatively small, and the capital-output ratio may be low from the immediate point of view, this need not be so over a long period of time. Conversely the ratio may be initially high, but may fall over time. In many industries a low capital-output ratio may be only apparent and not real. Thus in agriculture it is generally assumed to be low. But if working capital like expenditure on fertilizers, etc. is also taken into account, the ratio may tend to be high.

The notion that the combination of factors of production in accordance with their availability conforms to the principle of comparative advantage is not true under all conditions. According to this principle a country with an abundant supply of labour and scarcity of capital should concentrate on the production of goods which can efficiently be produced by labour-intensive methods, and another country with a different factor supply position should adopt the opposite method. This arrangement would conform to the principle of comparative advantage only if we make the assumption that the ratio in which factors are to be combined is the same for the same industry in all countries or that

[14]Sen, A. K., ' Some Notes on the Choice of Capital Intensity in Development Planning.' *Quarterly Journal of Economics*, November, 1957, pp. 561–84.

capital is equally substitutable for labour in producing all the commodities traded in.[14a]

Another defect of this principle of investment is the possibility that where in the initial stages of development a labour-intensive pattern of investment is adopted, under government auspices or through prolonged government protection, vested interests will be created which would oppose any change in the techniques of production at a later stage. Thus strong trade union organizations would stand in the way of mechanization even when conditions justify or require such change. Inefficient and outmoded methods of production would thus get perpetuated. In a situation like this, the possible solution would be the organization of production in such a manner that it can be mechanized with small alterations.[15]

The employment possibility claimed in favour of capital light techniques is quite often exaggerated. It is not possible to increase employment by just reducing the quantity of capital available in each industry. The absorption of labour depends upon the flexibility and adaptability of the other factors of production. Capital employed in two industries may be the same, but in one the amount of labour that can be combined with capital may be fixed by technology and cannot be varied, while in the other variation of labour may be possible. The first industry is more productive than the second; and if labour-intensive methods of production are recommended, then more labour can be absorbed only in the second industry. But the output of the second industry may be actually less than that of the first in spite of increased employment of labour. Hence Leibenstein points out that the rigorous application of the labour absorption criterion would never permit the introduction of labour-saving technology in over-populated areas.[16] Further, employment potential of an investment cannot be judged by what happens in the initial stages. The employment potential of a capital-intensive scheme may be limited to begin with, but its secondary and tertiary effects on employment may be great, while in a labour-intensive scheme, employment potential may not increase but remain constant over time. Besides, a lower capital-labour ratio does not mean a lower amount of capital per unit of output. And if capital per unit of output remains the same, the surplus available for paying wages will be the same irrespective of variations in capital per worker.[17]

Nor is it possible to avoid capital-intensive projects altogether. The criterion of a low capital-output ratio is of limited validity when unused natural resources such as water or mineral resources can be developed only by means of heavy

[14a]Chenery, Hollis B., ' Comparative Advantage and Development Policy,' *American Economic Review*, March, 1961, p. 27.

[15]*Economic Bulletin for Asia and the Far East*, U.N., November, 1955, p. 44.

[16]Leibenstein, Harvey, *Economic Backwardness and Economic Growth*, Wiley, New York, 1960, p. 260.

[17]Bettelheim, Charles, *Studies in the Theory of Planning*, Asia Publishing House, Bombay, 1959, p. 299.

initial investment. In certain lines of production like the manufacture of steel, petroleum refineries, etc. the use of latest capital-intensive technology is definitely advantageous. Social overheads and other basic economic facilities like transport, communications, port, harbours, etc. are as necessary for promoting economic growth in a country as they require a large volume of capital investment.

A refined version of the equal marginal product theory which assumes that there is efficient allocation of capital resources when the marginal productivity of capital in different industries is the same, is what is called the Social Marginal Productivity criterion. This theory was put forward by A. E. Kahn[18] in 1951 and later elaborated by Hollis B. Chenery.[19] According to this view, the benefit of an additional unit of investment has to be estimated not with reference to what it would yield to the private investor, but by the total net contribution of the marginal unit to national product. The cost and benefit items which enter into the calculation of the private investor are different from social costs and social benefits. Thus social and economic overheads may not be productive from the point of view of the individual producer. Similarly, social costs in the form of soot produced by a factory or the bad smell or unhealthy conditions created by a tannery may not enter into the cost calculations of the producer. According to Kahn, " the correct criterion for obtaining the maximum return from limited resources is social marginal productivity, taking into account the total net contribution of the marginal unit to national product and not merely that portion of the contribution (or its costs) which may accrue to the private investor ". This principle would require equating of long run marginal social productivity of investment in different sectors or the maximization of the total net increment to the national product wherever accuring directly or indirectly.[20] The Social Marginal Productivity criterion differs from the simple capital turnover principle in so far as it takes into account both external economies and diseconomies in the computation of the contribution of an investment. Social marginal product resulting from an investment is calculated by deducting from the addition to output due to the investment, the alternative output sacrificed as a result of drawing factors of production from other fields into this one. Thus the factors are valued at their social opportunity cost, so that when the opportunity cost of labour is very close to zero the SMP criterion will approximate the capital turnover criterion.[21]

Chenery improved upon the SMP criterion by working out a formula for its quantitative determination. According to him the formulation of an optimum investment programme does not require an accurate measurement of the

[18]Kahn, A. E., ' Investment Criteria in Development Programmes,' *Quarterly Journal of Economics*, February, 1951, pp. 38–61.

[19]Chenery, Hollis B., ' The Application of Investment Criteria,' *Quarterly Journal of Economics*, February, 1953, pp. 76–96.

[20]*Economic Bulletin for Asia and the Far East*, U.N., November, 1955, p. 41.

[21]Sen, A. K., ' Some Notes on the Choice of Capital Intensity in Development Planning,' *Quarterly Journal of Economics*, November, 1957, pp. 561–84.

marginal productivity of each investment. It is possible to rank the various projects in the order of their social value, and given the amount of funds available for investment, those items beginning from the first in the list of rankings which may be financed out of the funds may be accepted. In fixing the rank of the different projects Chenery takes into consideration the effect of an investment on national income, on balance of payments and also the cost of the domestic and imported materials utilized in production.

Social marginal productivity of an investment is a function of the effect of the investment on income Y, balance of payments B, and distribution of income D, and other factors. Thus

$$SMP = f(Y\,B\,D\,\ldots)$$

Let U stand for SMP. Then increment in U or

$$\Delta U = \frac{du}{dY}\,\Delta Y + \frac{du}{dB}\,\Delta B + \frac{du}{dD}\,D + \ldots$$

that is to say, the increase in SMP is the sum of the effect of a change in income, in balance of payments position, in the distribution of income, etc. Chenery leaves out the effect of change in the distribution of income on the ground that it is difficult to assess with any degree of exactness. Change in the balance of payments position of the country is reflected in the over-valuation or under-valuation of the domestic currency at existing rate of exchange. Thus if r represents the over-valuation of domestic currency and distribution effect is left out,

$$\Delta U = \Delta Y + r\,\Delta B$$

If r is zero, then balance of payments is in equilibrium. If it is positive the domestic currency is over-valued, i.e. the country has a balance of payments deficit, and if r is negative the domestic currency is under-valued. In under-developed countries r may be appreciably greater than zero because of the relative inelasticity of imports and exports.

In any year SMP will be

$$SMP = \frac{X + E - Mi}{K} - \frac{L + Md + O}{K} + \frac{r}{K}\,(aB1 + B2)$$

where (i) K is increment to capital, i.e. investment; X is increased market value for output; E is added value of output due to external economies; Mi is cost of imported materials and (ii) L is labour cost, Md is cost of domestic materials; O is overhead cost. (iii) The effect of an investment programme on external balance is broken up into two parts; firstly, the effect of installation on balance of payments, i.e. the demand on foreign exchange necessitated by the installation of equipment. This is represented by $B1$; secondly, the effect of operation of the plant on balance of payments, i.e. draft on foreign exchange for financing the import of materials, spare parts of machines, etc. Calculation of the effect of operation cost on balance of payments for each year of the life of the equipment is possible. But installation cost is incurred in a lump sum in the first year; its effect on the balance of payments annually is to be estimated. The annual cost of installation on foreign exchange is amortization rate of this lump sum plus interest on it; a is combined amortization rate and interest on current borrowing. Thus the above statement can be summarized as follows: The effect of an investment on SMP is found by subtracting from the increase in the net value of output and external economies as a ratio of amount invested, the sum of the total cost incurred in producing the output and the adverse or favourable effect on balance of payments also expressed as a ratio of investment. The equation is simplified as follows: If V is social value added domestically (i.e. $X+E-Mi$) and C is total cost of domestic factors (i.e. $L+Md+O$) and Br is balance of payments effect or balance of payments premium per unit of investment, then

$$\text{SMP} = \frac{V}{K} - \frac{C}{K} + \frac{Br.}{K}$$

The applicability of this formula is illustrated by Chenery with reference to the production of certain commodities in Greece. Thus in the production of cement, investment (K) in thousands of dollars is 6750; capital turnover $V/K=0.93$; cost ratio $C/K=0.37$; balance of payments effect $Br/K=0.07$; $\text{SMP}=0.93-0.37+0.07=0.63$. Similarly for fertilizers, the SMP is 0.44, for sulphuric acid, 0.41 and for glass manufacture, 0.39. The ranking of the projects in this manner according to their SMP helps in their selection when the funds at disposal are not equal to cover all the projects. The projects to be selected depend on their rank and the number of projects that would be selected depends on their cost and the availability of funds.

The merit of the SMP criterion consists in its drawing attention to the overall effect of an investment programme on the national economy. While this principle has greater general applicability than the simple equal marginal productivity theory, it has many of the limitations of the latter. It presupposes the attainment of an optimal income distribution by purely fiscal means, and the possibility of making adjustments for the risks caused by imperfect forecasting, and *ex ante* co-ordination of investment decisions and so on.[22] The concept is vague; it is less definite than the private profit criterion although it is more generally applicable. Market prices do not correctly reflect social values and as such, quantitative assessment of the costs and benefits arising from investment is not possible. Chenery mentions the need for making corrections of market prices for tax, subsidy and fiscal policies, corrections for regulated cost plus prices in transportation and public utilities, and also in respect of idle resources whose market value is not known. In the case of certain items of output which are not marketable such as education and public health, price equivalents have to be imputed. The interest rate also influences the fixed cost components of the SMP. It would be difficult or impossible to calculate the costs of a large number of items which contribute to the total cost of a project. It may also be pointed out that the effect of an investment on balance of payments arises

[22]Eckstein, Otto, ' Investment Criteria for Economic Development and the Theory of Intertemporal Welfare Economics,' *Quarterly Journal of Economics*, February, 1957, p. 60.

not only from the costs incurred in connection with the installation and operation of the plant which may be balanced against the exports of the country concerned, but it also depends on the availability of foreign loans, their expected flow over time and repayment conditions as well as on the effects of successive investments on economic development. Chenery's formula also fails to take due account of structural interdependence and of the nature and value of external economies.[23] Nor is the principle based on any proper consideration of the effect of investment on the composition, distribution and flow of income over time. The contribution of an investment to economic welfare is certainly very much affected not only by the growth of income but also by its distribution. The major defect of this model however, is that it considers only the once-for-all effect of an investment. Given the volume of investment, it indicates the manner in which it can be utilized so as to maximize social product. But any development programme has necessarily to be concerned about the future. We should care not only for the immediate returns of a given investment and its short-term effect on income, but also about the extent to which it would help in the accumulation of capital which will promote long-term growth. A proper investment criterion should take into account the indirect effect of investment on future savings, consumption pattern, population growth, etc., which affect the future growth prospects of the economy. The SMP criterion in short, does not consider the multiplier effect of present investment on future income. And it fails to recognize the significance of the differences in the nature and quality of the various factors of production which are combined with capital and which contribute to total output.

(b) Criteria of Investment to Accelerate Growth

Harvey Leibenstein criticizes the SMP principle on the ground that it does not stress the need for generating the forces of economic growth in an underdeveloped country. According to him the object of economic development must be to maximize the amount of capital per worker and improve the quality of the labour force, its skill, knowledge, energy, and adaptability. In an important article published in the *Quarterly Journal of Economics*, 1955[24] Galenson and Leibenstein introduced the concept of the marginal per capita reinvestment quotient as the criterion for investment in underdeveloped countries. The reinvestment potential of an economy's output is the difference between the output per labourer produced with a given capital stock per worker on the one hand, and the consumption of the population and the wear and tear and replacement of capital equipment on the other. The proportion of this surplus to capital per labourer gives the reinvestment quotient.

[23]Lombardini, Siro, ' Quantitative Analysis in the Determination of the Efficiency of Investment in Underdeveloped Areas,' *International Economic Papers*, No. 9, pp.129–30.

[24]Galenson, W. and H. Leibenstein, ' Investment Criteria, Productivity and Economic Development,' *Quarterly Journal of Economics*, August, 1955, pp. 343–70.

Total national income is divided between two main categories, wages and profits. Little is saved out of wage income, but a good proportion of income accruing in the form of profits is saved and becomes available for investment. Thus given the same income in two countries but with profit-wages ratio higher in the one than in the other, the investment potential of the former is greater. The larger the amount of capital available per head, the greater will be the output per head. And since the stock of capital available per worker at any point of time is due to investments made in the preceding years, it follows that product per head in future can be maximized by increasing investment which in turn is possible by increasing the proportion of profits to wages. The output resulting from increased investment would flow into the accumulation of capital goods, investment in human capital and also consumption. The proper investment policy should be one which increases the flow of resources into capital proportionately to a greater extent than the flow into consumption. The building up of the total capital in the form of capital goods and human capital thus depends on the general reinvestment year by year and the increase in the size of population.[25]

If annual reinvestment is to be large, the proportion of profits to national income is to be maximized and the proportion of wage income is to be minimized. This would therefore necessitate increasing the ratio of capital to labour in production, i.e. it would lead to the adoption of capital-intensive methods of production. Since the propensity to consume of the working classes is high, the voluntary savings from wage income as well as compulsory savings extracted from the wage earners by means of taxation would be small. On the other hand, the adoption of capital-intensive methods of production will tend to concentrate income in the hands of profit earners and since big capitalists are generally accumulation-minded, the increased flow of income into their hands would lead to both larger savings and larger reinvestment. It is this reinvestment that would increase productivity and enable the economy to grow.

Stress is laid on capital-intensive methods on other grounds also. The reinvestment quotient criterion would favour long-lived capital goods which accompany capital-intensive methods of production because as Domar has shown[26] under conditions of economic growth, the ratio of replacement cost to gross investment would be considerably lower for long-lived than for short-lived capital goods and as such, other things being equal, the reinvestment quotient will be higher in the former. A more important justification for the adoption of capital-intensive methods, is the fact that the rate of growth of population in most of the underdeveloped countries is very high and unless productivity of labour is considerably increased through the application of more capital to each unit of labour, output per head would fall which would make accumulation of capital impossible. In view of the high rate of growth

[25]Leibenstein, H., *Economic Backwardness and Economic Growth*, Wiley, New York, 1960, p. 266.
[26]Domar, Evsey D., ' Depreciation, Replacement and Growth,' *The Economic Journal*, March, 1953, pp. 1–32.

16

of population and the need for providing basic economic environment in the form of overheads like railways, roads, irrigation works, etc. heavy investments become necessary. Underdeveloped countries, if they are to develop successfully, have to make a large initial effort to increase output and have to do so very early in the development attempt. Leibenstein conceives of a critical minimum in the initial investment effort;[27] if this level of investment is not reached, the country will revert to its former underdeveloped state. The initial effort should be such as to raise per capita income sufficiently high, so that the level of savings and capital accumulation can be maintained. In other words, the investment allocation or choice should be so made that there is rapid capital accumulation early in the process of development. And this is necessary for two reasons; firstly, the rate of growth of income should be high enough to overcome the population hurdle and secondly, industrialization and the urbanization that would go hand in hand with it would in turn create an environment conducive to the lowering of the birth rate and a decline in the rate of growth of population.[28]

The reinvestment quotient criterion has been subjected to many criticisms. The basic assumption that large profits would make possible correspondingly large reinvestment is questioned. A. K. Sen points out that merely by choosing that investment which gives a higher rate of reinvestible surplus per unit of capital, growth rate cannot be increased. The surplus may be large per unit of capital, but if the propensity to consume of the people engaged in that production goes up, investible surplus is adversely affected.[29] It is important to distinguish between product per unit of capital and product per worker. When there is capital deepening in any industry the proportion of labour to capital employed decreases. As a result, product per worker increases and correspondingly the investible surplus available from each worker's output also rises. But looked at from the point of view of capital, it is clear that as the volume of capital is increased, the output per unit of capital decreases. Hence reinvestment per unit of capital previously invested declines.[30] Galenson and Leibenstein accept the truth in this criticism but point out that since long-lived investment implies a lower replacement rate during the earlier periods, a greater rate of reinvestment is possible in the initial stages.[31] Further, there is no guarantee that capital deepening whenever possible would ensure the best use of available capital resources. On the other hand, it is not unlikely that there would be such an inefficient allocation of capital

---

[27]*See* also Chapter IV.

[28]Galenson, W. and H. Leibenstein, ' Investment Criteria, Productivity and Economic Development,' *Quarterly Journal of Economics*, August, 1955, pp. 343–70.

[29]Sen, A. K., ' Some Notes on the Choice of Capital Intensity in Development Planning,' *Quarterly Journal of Economics*, November, 1957, pp. 561–84.

[30]Neisser, Hans, ' Investment Criteria, Productivity and Economic Development,' comment, *Quarterly Journal of Economics*, November, 1956, p. 645.

[31]Galenson, W. and H. Leibenstein, *Quarterly Journal of Economics*, November, 1956, p. 647,

that the resultant increase in income will be smaller. It is even conceivable that maximum capital intensity would lower profits and reduce savings.[32] The application of the marginal reinvestment quotient principle would lead to the rise in the profit-wage ratio and the capital-labour ratio. If the beneficial results envisaged by Leibenstein are to follow, it is not enough if the profit-wage ratio rises; it is important that the ratio of savings to output should rise.[33] It is incorrect to assume that reinvestment will be larger in capital-intensive industries. In India and other Asian countries, textile firms yield large profits and a large part of these profits is reinvested in the business. But in the iron and steel industry which is more capital-intensive, profits per unit of capital and reinvestment appear to be smaller.[34] Further, the view that the propensity to save out of wages is zero is also not acceptable. A rise in the productivity of labour increases aggregate real output and if wages remain constant it is possible for the labourer to maintain his standard of life and save more. When total output increases, even if total wage bill exceeds the minimum consumption level, the state can through its tax and fiscal policy and other regulatory measures see to it that actual consumption does not rise and eat up the increased earnings.

Another criticism is that this principle of investment violates social welfare ideals. Adoption of capital-intensive methods of production would imply displacement of labour. At any rate, the proportion of labour employed to the volume of capital will decline. This criterion neglects the social costs of unemployment and has no regard for the well-being of the majority of the population. Increasing concentration of income in the hands of a few people which the implementation of this policy would entail, may raise production but the increased output would be shared by a smaller number of people. As one writer observes, " Coping with the population problem by withholding from the people whatever is necessary to feed their increasing numbers at the level they are accustomed to, means increasing the mortality rate now so that it may fall in the future which does not seem logical ".[35] Indifference to the depression in the standard of living or the starvation of about half the population in the interests of larger investment, and the preference for a lower aggregate income against a higher one if the former has a higher savings component do not according to some writers make economic sense.[36] It is unwise to

[32]Eckstein, Otto, ' Investment Criteria for Economic Development and the Theory of Intertemporal Welfare Economics,' *Quarterly Journal of Economics*, February, 1957, p. 66.

[33]Bator, Francis M., ' On Capital Productivity, Input Allocation and Growth,' *Quarterly Journal of Economics*, February, 1957, pp. 104–05.

[34]Oshima, Harry T., ' Investment Criteria, Saving Propensity and Economic Development,' *Indian Journal of Economics*, April, 1959, p. 400.

[35]Moes, John, ' Investment Criteria, Productivity and Economic Development,' *Quarterly Journal of Economics*, February, 1957, pp. 163–64.

[36]Chenery, Hollis B., ' Comparative Advantage and Development Policy,' *American Economic Review*, March, 1961, p. 30.

be solely concerned with making the reinvestment quotient as large as possible in each period, especially when this concern results in an insufficient supply of consumer goods throughout. In the opinion of Professor Villard, reliance on increasing income and urbanization as a means to bring down the rate of growth of population is mistaken. It would be cheaper and more effective if direct methods such as birth control measures are adopted to keep down the rate of growth of population. Against these criticisms, the authors of the reinvestment quotient principle contend that it would not be possible in under-developed countries to keep down consumption levels through taxation because of administrative deficiencies, that the real choice in underdeveloped countries is between a relatively low level of consumption now, so that it can be high later, and that what is preferred between these two alternatives will depend on the attitude of the people. As regards population control through direct measures, it is of doubtful validity. There are serious difficulties in the way. Apart from the cost involved, other obstacles like the mental attitude of the people, and their social and moral values are also to be taken into consideration.

The attachment of a premium on future income as against present income and levels of consumption has also come in for criticism. Particularly in a democratic set up, sufficient attention is to be devoted to ameliorating the living conditions of the present generation and improving their consumption standards. Much has been said about the importance of the enthusiasm and co-operation of all classes of people for successfully implementing the schemes of economic development. It would be unwise to expect such co-operation, enthusiasm and goodwill if the policy of economic development is one which patently neglects the material welfare of the present generation in order to improve the welfare of a generation in the future.[37] Leibenstein's thesis has also been criticized on the ground that it fails to take into account the balance of payments effects of an investment policy. Of two techniques of production, one relatively more capital-intensive than the other, the rate of reinvestible surplus per unit of capital may be larger in the former, but it is possible that the import content of it is also larger than that of the latter. If the balance of payments position of the country concerned is already strained, it would be unsound policy to concentrate investment on the former.

Despite these limitations, the reinvestment quotient criterion is useful in so far as it lays great emphasis on a higher rate of income growth as the main objective of investment policy. If the prime concern of an underdeveloped

[37] The need for devoting proper attention to the effect of investment on consumption is pointed out by Otto Eckstein. According to him the effect on future consumption stream of a present investment depends on the marginal productivity of capital invested, net income made possible by reinvested capital and the output of the projects which becomes available for further investment. Investment choice is to be so made as to maximize the present value of the future consumption stream. The discounted value of the future income stream resulting from an additional investment, Eckstein calls " the marginal growth contribution of the project"—' Investment Criteria for Economic Development and the Theory of Intertemporal Welfare Economics,' *Quarterly Journal of Economics*, February, 1957, pp. 56–85.

country is to generate the forces of economic growth, it is but proper that in choosing the techniques of production and in allocating the scarce resources of capital among different lines of investment, due regard is given to the growth potential of investment.

UNBALANCED VERSUS BALANCED DEVELOPMENT

Emphasis on resource allocation as a means to promote economic growth has led to two different views—as to whether growth should be balanced or unbalanced. Writers like Rosenstein Rodan and Ragnar Nurkse lay great stress on the need for simultaneous investment in many sectors. Nurkse argues that lack of markets and deficiency in demand constitute the basic factors responsible for slow growth. It is pointed out that by making investments in varied fields of enterprise it would be possible to raise the level of demand and expand internal markets. The growth of one industry helps the development of others in two ways—firstly, it may supply raw materials required by other industries; secondly, by providing employment it helps increase in demand for the products of other industries so that the starting or expansion of other industries would become worthwhile. The result will be all-round economic expansion. The effect of increased investment and expansion of one industry on others in the form of increased demand or reduced costs has been called ' dynamic external economies ' by Scitovsky. On the other hand, other writers recommend that the proper investment policy in underdeveloped countries should be to concentrate on a few sectors or industries which have great growth potentialities. Thus Paul Streeten, A. O. Hirschman and W. W. Rostow recommend unbalanced growth, i.e. increase in investment and production to be concentrated in a few sectors. At any point of time in an economy some industries may be expanding while others remain stationary or contract. The expanding industries require funds to finance their growth, while the industries which are stagnating will have with them unused resources. The former are the borrowers and the latter the lenders. If the capital intensities of both categories are the same, the excess financial needs of the one will be offset by the saving of the others. But if the capital intensity of the expanding industries is greater, aggregate business investment will exceed savings and thereby economic growth would be promoted. In so far as public utilities and transport are capital-intensive, their development would normally be a great growth-generating force as it was in the U.S.A. in the 70s and 80s of the 19th century.[38] To the same category of investment would belong the steel industry, irrigation, hydro-electric projects, etc.

In a scheme of unbalanced development precedence may be given to industries over agriculture. It is argued that investment in industries and their development without waiting for the primary sector to expand sufficiently,

[38]Duesenberry, James, ' Innovation and Growth,' *The American Economic Review—Papers and Proceedings*, May, 1956, pp. 135–40.

can be justified in so far as the growth of industries would provide an expanding market for industrial materials and would thereby promote the development of agriculture. Furthermore, development of industries necessitates the building up of economic overheads which would have a beneficial effect on the all-round expansion of the economy. Recommendations about development of this nature are obviously based on the presumption that perfect competition would not lead to the optimal allocation of resources over time.

It should however be remembered that in the historical examples which Rostow has given,[39] concentration of the development of a few industries or sectors was helpful to economic growth chiefly because of the availability of foreign markets. The imbalance implied in the higher rate of expansion of one or two industries results in excess of production in certain lines and deficiency of supply in relation to demand in other sectors which can be set aright only by means of foreign trade. To the extent international trade has been subjected to various restrictions today, the safety valve provided by foreign trade cannot be taken for granted, and a country which resorts to this technique of development should be prepared to depend on its own market for the disposal of goods as well as for the supply of materials which it requires. It should be said in favour of balanced growth, i.e. simultaneous advance on all fronts, that it helps in the avoidance of special shortages or special excess capacities and in the minimization of inflationary pressures in the economy. On the other hand, the modern argument for concentrated or unbalanced growth is based on the scope for economies of scale which such a method of development would generate. However, it is possible that the full benefit of economies of scale cannot be reaped because of insufficient effective demand for the products, or because of insufficient savings to meet the investment requirements of expansion. In such a situation it would be necessary to strike a balance between economies of scale and the requirements of balanced growth. Sacrifice of external economies would reduce the rate of growth but balanced development would ensure an element of stability in the economy. If the country is vast, with abundant natural resources and wide internal markets, it can combine balance and self-sufficiency with concentrated growth on a regional or functional basis. But if the country is small, it can resolve the conflict only by depending on foreign trade, which means that it should have to liberalize its foreign trade policies and in turn should have the benefit of a freer trade policy on the part of other countries.

UNBALANCED DEVELOPMENT: A. O. HIRSCHMAN'S THESIS

Hirschman has drawn attention to a different aspect of unbalanced development on the basis of which he recommends an investment policy for underdeveloped countries.[40] He classifies investment into Social Overhead Capital

[39]*See* Chapter II, p. 66.
[40]Hirschman, A. O., *The Strategy of Economic Development*, Yale, New Haven, 1958, pp. 76–97.

(SOC) and Direct Productivity Activities (DPA). SOC comprises those basic services without which primary, secondary and tertiary productive services cannot function, for example, transportation and power. The characteristics of these services apart from their being basic, are that they are mostly provided by public agencies, they cannot be imported and they involve heavy, lumpy initial investments. Direct productivity activities relate to investments which result in direct increase in the supply of goods and services. The question is posed as to the direction in which fresh investment should flow—in SOC or DPA, or rather the "efficient sequence" as between the two types of investment. Increase in the investment on SOC expands the productive capacity of the economy. If this is provided by the government, it would help expansion of direct productivity activity of private investors. This is so because when the productive capacity of the economy is increased in the form of SOC, the unit cost of production of final goods will fall, the private producers will have large profits and they will be encouraged to increase their productive activity. In other words, they would benefit by increasing returns resulting from the availability of excess capacity. But when the available social overhead facilities are fully employed, the expansion of DPA will stop; and it can be revived only by the further expansion of SOC. However, it is possible to conceive that since increased DPA activity would generate income, it would be easier to build up further the SOC without any great strain on the economy; that is to say SOC would expand automatically in response to the need. On the other hand, if initially investment is increased in DPA, it will strain the existing stock of SOC and compel its expansion. In fact further increase in DPA may not be possible unless SOC is increased. Thus the construction of a railway or the building of a road may encourage the establishment of new industries (here SOC precedes DPA) or a new industry may be started first and its requirements for transport, marketing etc. would necessitate the construction of roads, railways, etc. (here DPA precedes SOC). Thus DPA may be considered as a pressure-creating investment and SOC as a pressure-relieving investment.

To which of these investments preference is to be given in underdeveloped countries depends on various considerations. Hirschman points out that expansion of SOC provides opportunities for increasing direct investment, i.e. it invites increased DPA. If the private producers are enterprising and alert enough to be aware of the opportunities and are prepared to invest in DPA, it would be a sound policy for the public sector to invest in SOC. But if initiative is taken under government auspices on the DPA side, it would become obligatory to meet the requirements of growing DPA by providing more SOC, i.e. development is made possible via shortage of social overheads. According to Hirschman, in situations where motivations are deficient, it seems safer to rely on development via shortage than on development via excess capacity. In underdeveloped countries entrepreneurial skill of the type necessary to take advantage of the opportunities provided by SOC is lacking and hence the initiative has to come from the DPA sector. Nevertheless, there should not be any total neglect of public utilities. Some basic overheads are absolutely essential if development is to take place at all. In this, there is no choice. It is also possible that in an underdeveloped country there may be regions which are relatively advanced and other areas which are very backward. It would therefore be proper if DPA is made to precede SOC in the latter, while precedence in the reverse order is given in the advanced or industrialized regions.

Undoubtedly, investment in social and economic overheads in under-developed countries is of primary importance. The basic conflict in investment in these countries is between quick-yielding projects with low capital-output ratios which help in an immediate increase in real income and consumption on the one hand, and basic facilities which entail large investments and necessitate the postponement of the increase of consumption or even involve the lowering of the present levels of consumption on the other. The second alter-native while raising the income level to a smaller extent in the immediate future, will achieve a faster rate of development in the long run. Also the fact that the capital-output ratio in the latter type of investment is high is not an indicator of the real burden of such investments on the economy from the long term point of view. In so far as social overheads increase the yield of other investments and help the capital-output ratio of the latter to fall, it is necessary to take into account the overall effect of such investments in making investment choices.[41]

(c) Investment Criteria which Aim at Controlling Specific Problems

Some principles of investment have been put forward which aim not so much at promoting economic development as at promoting economic development with stability. Instability in the initial stages of growth is manifested in the form of balance of payments deficit and inflationary pressures. Balance of payments difficulties of pre-industrial countries spring from the fact that they have to depend on foreign countries for their capital equipment and also require foreign exchange for getting materials when operating the equipment. Also, the rise in money income resulting from investment and industrialization leads to the importing of foreign consumption goods. It is possible that in some cases foreign exchange may not be much required at the construction stage but needed at the operation stage or vice versa. This underlines the need for a correct estimate of the requirements and the availability of foreign exchange over time. In contrast, investment in and the development of certain industries would bring about large savings in foreign exchange. It is mentioned that in India the setting up of petroleum refineries would have resulted in a net saving of around Rs. 200 to 300 million annually in foreign

[41]See *Economic Bulletin for Asia and the Far East*, U. N., June, 1958, p. 27, Table 2, for an illustration of this effect.

exchange.[42] What J. J. Polak has stated with reference to the balance of payments effects of investments out of foreign borrowing in European countries of the post-Second World War years may not be of much relevance to underdeveloped countries of today, but it relates to a problem which the latter countries also have to face. From their effect on balance of payments Polak classifies investments into three categories:

(*i*) investment, yielding goods which add to the exports of the country or replace goods formerly imported. The net effect of this would be to create an export surplus.

(*ii*) investment, replacing goods previously sold in the country or exported from the country; the effect in this case on balance of payments is likely to be neutral.

(*iii*) investment, which would result in adding of goods to those sold in the country and in excess of demand. Here the balance of payments effect will be negative.

In the interests of minimizing any adverse effect on balance of payments of any investment policy it is important to concentrate as much as possible on the first category of investments and leave out the third category altogether. As regards the second category of investments, they are to be chosen with care and discrimination, weighing the possibilities of their adverse effect on balance of payments against the benefit which may accrue out of them to the economy.

The practical significance of Polak's classification has however, been questioned. Kahn points out that certain investments may raise real income without increasing money income which could be spent on imports; that is to say, there is fear of increased imports only when money income increases as against real incomes. Thus investment in better tools would increase production of agricultural goods which would be consumed directly. Even when money income rises along with real incomes because of an investment, it does not necessarily follow in all cases that imports will increase. Also to say that investment should be made as far as possible in those enterprises which add to the exports or replace imports is not saying much because there is no possibility of knowing *ex ante* what these enterprises are. In fact the large imports of low income countries are to a great extent due to the undiversified nature of their production. As the economy develops and more industries are started which supply additional consumption goods for the domestic sector, the propensity to import will decline. Nor is there any guarantee that if investment is concentrated on export-oriented industries, economic development would be promoted. Thus in India and other colonial countries before 1914, much of foreign capital was invested in the plantation and extraction industries which produced export goods; nevertheless, the effect of such investments on income and employment in the country was meagre and it contributed little to the economic development of these countries. In reality, the balance of payments effect

[42]*Economic Bulletin for Asia and the Far East*, U.N., November, 1955, p. 45.

of an investment cannot be assessed without reference to the overall development programme. It is not possible to isolate the balance of payment effect
of individual investments. Investment in one line may conform to Polak's
first category, but the development of the industry in which the investment is
made may foster or hamper other industries which would have an unforeseen
effect on the external balance of the country. On the other hand, balance of
payments effect in one investment may be neutral but if it helps other export-
oriented industries through a fall in the prices of the materials supplied by the
former and required by the latter, it would help increase in exports. Besides,
the effect of an investment on balance of payments depends upon other factors
also, such as the manner of financing investment and any change that it may
bring about in the distribution of income. If financing is non-inflationary,
production of goods for the home market would not by itself constitute a
threat to external balance. Similarly the distribution of income resulting
from the investment may be such as to bring about increased saving or increased
spending on foreign commodities. All these point to the fact that the " balance
of payments effect of any given investment can be estimated only by taking
into account the complicated spatial and time interdependence of all investments ". And as such the practical value of this criteria is limited.

While balance of payments difficulties reflect external disequilibrium in a
growing economy, inflationary pressures at home are indicative of internal
disequilibrium. Internal instability of this nature arises from excess of investment over domestic savings. Large expenditures are incurred in the early
stages of development on projects which have a long gestation period so that
in the early years of such development programmes, large money incomes are
generated without any corresponding increase in the supply of consumers
goods. This leads to a rise in the price level in these countries. Apart from
this, in countries like Ceylon and Malaya which are large exporters of primary
commodities, instability is brought about through fluctuations in the demand
for their export goods in the foreign markets which create boom and depression
conditions in the exporting countries. Where inflation results from excess
investment in social overheads or in large and capital-intensive projects, it
can be controlled by spreading investment in agriculture and in capital-light
consumers goods industries which yield quick returns. As for internal instability
arising from foreign trade, the solution lies mainly in the diversification of
production. Internal stability can be promoted by avoiding concentration
on the production of a few primary commodities and by making the structure
of production more flexible. Thus irrigation and mixed farming will reduce
agricultural instability. By laying greater emphasis on food production, and
on better distribution of food by developing transport and by building up
food reserves and by giving priority to the production of essential consumer
goods, inflationary pressures can be relieved. Obviously, investment policy of
this nature would be in conflict with other criteria which emphasize the importance of external economies and capital intensity. The shifting of investment

to consumer goods industries and labour-intensive methods of production may possibly slow down the rate of economic growth but it may be viewed as a sacrifice which has to be borne in the interests of stability.

(d) The Time Factor Criteria

On the cost side of an investment programme we should include not only the aggregate investment outlay, but also the time taken by the project to yield a certain amount of returns. This is because of the fact that owing to economic, social and political considerations, a country cannot afford to wait for too long a period of time for the enjoyment of the returns from the investment. Thus the time factor becomes an important determinant in the choice of techniques. This aspect of the problem of investment has been explained and illustrated by A. K. Sen. Let us assume that the economy has two alternative investment projects in view, the one capital-intensive, and the other labour-intensive. The consideration here is not the rate of returns on the capital invested, but the absolute returns which either of these projects will yield over a given period of time. Let the time at the economy's disposal be a period of ten years, and the annual returns of the two projects are as follows:

Period	I. Capital-intensive Project (returns)	II. Labour-intensive Project (returns)
1st year	4·0 Million	6·0 Million
2nd ,,	5·0 ,,	7·0 ,,
3rd ,,	6·0 ,,	8·0 ,,
4th ,,	7·5 ,,	9·0 ,,
5th ,,	9·0 ,,	10·0 ,,
6th ,,	10·5 ,,	11·0 ,,
7th ,,	12·0 ,,	11·5 ,,
8th ,,	13·5 ,,	12·0 ,,
9th ,,	15·0 ,,	12·5 ,,
10th ,,	17·5 ,,	13·0 ,,
	100·0 ,,	100·0 ,,

* Excess over 2nd 58·0—49·0=9·0.
† Excess over 1st 51·0—42·0=9·0.

Over the first six years, the returns of the capital-intensive project are less than that of the other project; but after the 6th year the yield of the former rises more rapidly so that the sharper increase in the latter part of the ten-year period offsets the deficiency in the first six years. The returns of both the projects are the same over the entire period of ten years. Thus if the time at the disposal of the economy is ten years, it will be indifferent as to which of the projects is chosen. We leave out of account employment considerations. This time span of ten years may be called the period of recovery, because it is the period of time required over which the high rise of income of the capital-intensive project in the latter period just offsets its deficiency in the earlier period. If the time at the disposal of the economy is not limited, then undoubtedly the capital-intensive project will be preferred, because after the fifth year, its yield increases steadily at a much faster rate than the other. But once the time limit is fixed, the choice between the two techniques becomes important. Thus if the time at disposal is eight years, the labour-intensive technique will be chosen because the excess of its yield over the other technique in the first six years is greater than the excess of the yield of the latter in the seventh and eighth year. Hence labour-intensive technique is attractive if either the time limit is reduced given the relative yield of the two, or given the time limit, the excess yield of the labour-intensive technique in the first period is greater than the excess yield of the other method in the latter period and vice versa.[43]

The problem can be viewed from the cost side also. A capital-intensive project by definition involves a large initial capital outlay but its operating costs may be lower than another which is less capital-intensive. Thus when a capital-intensive project is implemented, there is a saving in operating costs as compared with a labour-intensive project. It is therefore possible to visualize a period over which the higher initial capital investment is recouped through the saving in operating costs. The difference in the saving on account of operating costs of the two projects is indicated by the time taken for the recovery of the investment. Obviously, this is longer for the less capital-intensive project. Hence if the difference in initial outlay is less than the difference in the saving in operating costs as reflected in the time taken to redeem the investment, the capital-intensive project will be preferred and vice versa. Thus in Soviet investment planning, a maximum period is fixed in advance for recovery of investment, and other conditions being equal, a project is chosen in preference to others if its period of recovery is less than that of others.

The time factor is certainly an important consideration in the determination of the techniques of production in underdeveloped countries. But there is an element of arbitrariness in the fixation of the time limit in this criterion which detracts from its apparent simplicity. Moreover, the returns pattern of an investment over time or the savings in operating costs that arise over a period of years is dependent not only on the techniques, organization and operation of the particular project concerned, but also on the external economies available and the manner in which it is affected by the growth or stagnation of the other sectors of the economy. As in the case of the balance of payments criteria, it is not possible to isolate a particular project from the rest of the economy in order to estimate the effect of the time factor on its attractiveness or otherwise from the development point of view.

[43]Sen, A. K., ' Some Notes on the Choice of Capital Intensity in Development Planning,' *Quarterly Journal of Economics*, November, 1957, pp. 561–84.

PRACTICAL APPLICATION OF INVESTMENT CRITERIA

The various investment criteria mentioned above, relate to different aspects
of the investment problem. Since the problems of growth which the underdeveloped countries have to face are manifold, the practical significance of
any one of the criteria, considered in itself is limited. The limitations of the
investment criteria from the point of view of practical applicability spring
from the following factors: In the first place, the objectives of an investment
policy are not and cannot be correctly defined.[44] Or there may be a large
number of conflicting objectives, as for example, maximization of welfare;
maximization of the aggregate output stream or per capita income stream;
or raising the level of consumption. But, it is not possible to consider the
maximization of any one of these objectives independently of the rest. It
would be possible to draw up a programme for maximizing any one of these,
only subject to a number of stated constraints. Some of the objectives like
economic welfare are vague. If the social objectives are stated in very general
terms, it becomes necessary to interpret the components of these objectives
in definite economic terms, for example, standard of living to be broken up
into its various components, like money income, prices, employment, etc.
Secondly, the principles of investment recommended by the various writers
are defective as theories. It is doubtful whether a sound theory can be formulated at all in respect of the complicated problem of investment. The theory
may be ' erroneous ' in the sense that it is not in agreement with the postulate
chosen or it may be incomplete because of its failure to take into account all
the variables involved. Or again, some parts of the theory may be irrelevant
from the point of view of its practical application. Finally, the investment
criteria fail or are defective because of the various non-measurable aspects of
investment projects which affect the implementation of an investment policy.[45]
For example the effect of institutional, social or cultural factors on a certain
investment project cannot be estimated. Moreover, the implementation of certain investment programmes will set in motion a series of
consequences occurring over time and affecting the different sectors of the
economy in different ways. It is difficult to estimate the effect of such
repercussions.

However, in recent years improvements in the techniques of planning
have made it possible to make use of investment criteria in the formulation of
programmes of economic development. Thus programming which in simple
term means rational, deliberate, consistent and co-ordinated economic policy,
aims at assuring the maximum national income through time by optimizing

[44] Leibenstein, Harvey, ' Why We Disagree on Investment Policies for Development,'
Indian Economic Journal, April, 1958, pp. 369–86.

[45] Tinbergen, Jan, ' The Relevance of Theoretical Criteria in the Selection of Investment
Plans,' *Investment Criteria and Economic Growth*, Massachusetts Institute of Technology, Asia
Publishing House, Bombay, 1961, pp. 9–10.

the composition of investment.[46] It is mainly concerned with the allocation of resources in the proper way by balancing the supply and demand for different commodities and factors of production. Its central idea is to fix certain targets to be attained in a given period of time through efficient utilization of resources and to ensure consistency in the allocation of the resources. When targets of production are fixed, factors of production are allocated with reference to their estimated supply and demand. In drawing up such programmes, inter-industry analysis and input-output tables which show the inter-dependence of the different sectors of an economy in respect of the demand of each industry for the output of other industries and the demand of the latter for the products of the former are made use of.[47] An analysis of the structure and interdependence of industries in this manner helps to estimate the extent to which increased investment in one industry or sectors necessitates the expansion of the other industries. The use of investment criteria has been helped also by the method of shadow or accounting prices. Accounting prices become necessary in drawing up investment programmes because of the discrepancy between the real and market prices of the factors of production. Thus owing to the activity of trade unions and governments' minimum wage legislation, the market wage is maintained, at a higher level than the intrinsic value of the service of labour. That the equilibrium wage rate is lower than the market rate is indicated by the existence of disguised unemployment and by the fact that the marginal product of labour is low or even zero. On the other hand, the market rate of interest may be cheaper than the equilibrium interest rate. Similarly, fundamental disequilibrium in the balance of payments of low income countries creates a discrepancy between the actual rate of exchange of domestic currency and the official or legal rate. The existence of such disparity would lead to a pattern of allocation of resources different from what it would be if allocation is made on the basis of real or equilibrium prices. For instance, the fact that the market rate of interest is lower and wage rate higher than the real rate, results in the adoption of techniques of production which are more capital-intensive than would be warranted by the real rate of interest which alone reflects the availability of capital funds. Hence accounting prices or shadow prices are used in programming. These are hypothetical prices at which supply is sufficient to satisfy the demand and the use of them would assure the full use and no more than the full use of the scarce factors of production.

These techniques of programming have been adopted with advantage in Soviet investment planning. Planning in the U.S.S.R. lays emphasis on technical efficiency and full employment of resources, advanced technology and least

[46] Rosenstein, Rodan P. N., ' Programming in Theory and in Italian Practice,' *Investment Criteria and Economic Growth*, Massachusetts Institute of Technology, Asia Publishing House, Bombay, 1961, pp. 19-20.

[47] Chenery, Holis B., ' Comparative Advantage and Development Policy,' *The American Economic Review*, March, 1961, pp. 31-39; also Lombardini, Siro, ' Quantitative Analysis in the Determination of the Efficiency of Investment in Underdeveloped Areas,' *International Economic Papers*, No. 9, pp. 125-45.

average unit cost of production. The plan gives priorities " to those branches and sections of the economy, the accentuated development of which is essential for the successful accomplishment of the plan's fundamental tasks and seeks to ensure proportionality in the development of every branch and every industry so that each must furnish to the economy that amount of goods and services which the economy requires at the given stage of socialist develop-ment ".[48] As far as possible, these techniques and methodology have been made use of in the drafting of the Indian Five-Year Plans also. Investment planning in the Philippines seeks to apply the SMP criteria. The investment formula in that country is based on five principles: to direct resources towards the most productive uses; to conserve foreign exchange; to reduce unemploy-ment; to improve the distribution of real income and to promote economic growth. Priority is given to particular projects according to the ratio of benefits accruing to the economy with reference to these principles, relative to the cost in terms of scarce resources, foreign exchange and capital. Benefits are measured in terms of contribution to foreign exchange earnings, to national income and employment. However, if a project which fails to satisfy these conditions is considered essential from the point of view of the economy, its rank in the list is raised by giving it a weightage by the use of the ' essentiality multiplier '. Benjamin Higgins mentions two defects of the Philippine formula of investment: its failure to include a direct measure of the external economies and its reliance on current market prices for the allocation of scarce factors. Yet, considering the limitations under which an underdeveloped country has to operate, the investment planning in the Philippines may be said to make the best use of the techniques and data available.

CAPITAL-INTENSIVE VERSUS LABOUR-INTENSIVE TECHNIQUES

Running through all the various criteria of investment is the controversial issue as to whether capital-intensive or labour-intensive techniques are suited to an economically underdeveloped country. In general, some of the criteria, such as the reinvestment quotient principle and those which recommend invest-ment policy to be directed to the attainment of a high rate of income growth, favour capital intensiveness while others like the capital turnover criteria and the employment absorption criteria favour labour-intensive and capital-light schemes. It may be observed that in all the principles put forward regarding a sound investment policy, there is an implicit or explicit recognition of three issues—the major one of economic growth and the minor ones of employment potential and the immediate increase in the supply of consumption goods. If economic growth alone is considered without taking into account the special problems of underdeveloped countries, there cannot be any dispute

[48] Grossman, Gregory, ' Suggestions for a Theory of Soviet Investment Planning,' *Investment Criteria and Economic Growth*, Massachusetts Institute of Technology, Asia Publishing House, Bombay, 1961, pp. 96–120.

about the fact that capital-intensive schemes have a decided superiority over the opposite technique. But when the needs of growth are visualized against the background of the factor endowments situation and the unemployment position in these countries, emphasis shifts to the attainment of other objectives as well as economic development. Thus the arguments for labour-intensive measures and against capital-intensive schemes are raised by those who are influenced by short term considerations in investment policy whereas the arguments against labour-intensive measures and in favour of capital-intensive projects are put forward by those who give great prominence to economic growth.

The fundamental point in favour of capital intensity is that it helps growth. If production is divided between two sectors—the capital goods or investment sector and the consumption goods sector—Maurice Dobb points out that the growth of the economy depends on the building up of the investment sector. This is possible only by increasing production in the consumption goods sector so that a growing surplus becomes available for investment in capital goods. The productivity of labour in the consumption goods sector depends on the capital intensity or the availability of capital per worker in that sector. Different techniques involving different degrees of capital intensity or investment per worker are possible in the consumption goods sector. The investment per worker in the capital-intensive technique is high while it is low when capital light technique is adopted. But the surplus generated in this sector is indicated by the ratio of wage cost, and also investment per worker to per capita output. Though total investment in the capital-intensive technique is greater than in the capital light technique, the productivity of labour in the first may be greater still, so that the ratio of the investment per worker to the earnings per worker, or the intensity of capital in relation to wage may be lower. In that case, the surplus per unit of capital and per labour employed will both be high when a capital-intensive technique is adopted. A high level of productivity of labour employed in the consumption goods sector is of importance for two reasons. Firstly, unless productivity is increased, a sufficient surplus cannot be generated and this surplus production of consumption goods, say food, is necessary in order to support the workers employed in the investment sector. Thus aggregate employment in the investment sector and therefore the output of capital goods, depend on the number of workers employed in the consumption goods sector multiplied by the surplus of output per head. If the wage rate in the consumption goods sector is equal to the consumption per head, then the surplus available for supporting the investment sector is equal to the productivity per labourer in the consumption goods sector multiplied by the number of labourers minus the wage rate multiplied by the number of workers. The second reason why surplus creation in the consumption goods sector is important is that as more labourers are drawn into the investment goods sector which is expanding, the proportion of labour engaged in the consumption goods sector will decrease and the output in the latter sector can increase or even remain constant only if productivity per head is increased.

Adoption of a cheaper technique or capital-light technique does not mean that the capital-output ratio will be low. Strictly speaking, a technique may be called as one of low capital intensity only when it requires a relatively small amount of capital per unit of output.[49] Thus when very backward techniques are adopted, productivity of labour will remain so low that more capital will be required for producing a given amount of output than when a more advanced and more capital-intensive technique is employed. Bettelheim cites the example of certain Indian industries in which when power using techniques are used capital-output ratio is actually lower than when non-power using techniques are adopted; for example, handlooms as compared with powerlooms. Obviously then, if a technique of production involves a larger amount of capital and a larger quantity of labour per unit of output, it is completely uneconomic and there is no economic justification for investing in such techniques. It is true that cheap capital goods of low productivity will increase employment but this is a short term effect and will not last. The production of very cheap capital goods of low productivity would involve engaging a large number of workers immediately, but the low productivity of labour in the consumption goods sector would reduce the surplus and make it difficult to maintain the level of employment in the investment sector. In the extreme case, if productivity of labour in the consumption goods sector is just equal to wage rate, then there is no surplus, no employment in the investment sector is possible and growth would stop.

On the other hand, it is argued that advanced capital-intensive techniques can help to attain, in the long run, both higher levels of employment and increased consumption. Labour is required for producing the capital equipment as well as for operating the equipment which embodies the technology. From the long term point of view, employment depends on income growth. The introduction of advanced techniques in the consumption goods sector would immediately reduce employment in that sector, but the very fact that better techniques are adopted would generate sufficient amount of savings which would help expansion of the investment sector and the provision of greater employment. As Dobb points out " a course of increasing total investment at the maximum possible rate may do more within the not-so-distant future to absorb any reserve army of unemployed into employment (as Soviet experience shows; employment there having increased to between four and five times what it was twenty-five to thirty years ago) than the minimum capital intensive use of the existing investment potential at the expense of its growth rate can do in the near future. In other words, maximizing investment potential and maximizing employment may only be in conflict as policy objectives within a fairly narrow time horizon; and discussion of such matters might be less at cross purposes if the participants were careful to indicate the

[49] Bettelheim, Charles, *Studies in the Theory of Planning*, Asia Publishing House, Bombay, 1959, pp. 338–39.

17

time dimension to which their maximizing propositions referred."[50] Apart from reducing employment from the long term point of view, backward techniques would reduce aggregate consumption level also. Consumption per worker depends on productivity as well as wage rate. If the latter is constant, higher productivity would increase the supply of real goods for consumption. But if low techniques are used in the consumption goods sector and productivity falls, the consumption needs of workers using such techniques can be satisfied only by reducing the consumption of workers using better techniques or the consumption of workers in the investment sector or by reducing employment in the investment sector. In that case output of capital goods will fall and this would adversely affect production in the consumption goods sector. Besides, there is a wastage of investment in so far as the diversion of a part of the investment fund to meet the consumption requirements of workers in the consumption goods sector whose productivity has fallen, could better have been utilized for adding to investment.[51]

The foregoing arguments point to the conclusion that in the interests of economic growth, capital-intensive techniques are to be adopted in both the investment and the consumption goods sectors. This is necessary in so far as the productivity of consumption goods sector depends on and in turn affects the output of capital goods. There is more employment and more output in the investment sector, when the surplus generated in the consumption goods sector is enlarged; and the greater will be the surplus in the latter sector, the more and better capital goods it is supplied with. The expansion of the investment sector in turn is limited by the growth of the consumption goods sector. As investment in the former goes up, the demand for consumption goods will rise. But more consumption goods can be supplied only by increasing investment in the consumption goods sector. Hence, if labour-saving devices are adopted in both the sectors, the capacity for the investment sector to grow will increase. Also, if real wage is reduced, output of consumption goods can be maintained at a relatively low level and this would also help expansion of the investment sector.[52]

Most of the underdeveloped countries however, have adopted a combination of the different investment criteria involving a compromise between the opposing techniques of production in their investment policies. This appears to be a sensible policy in view of the manifold problems which they face and the competing claims of the different sectors on the financial resources of the economies. Rapid growth of population, decline in the land-labour ratio, low income of the people, the need for raising the levels of consumption and

[50] Dobb, Maurice, ' Second Thoughts on Capital Intensity of Investment,' *Review of Economic Studies*, Vol. XXIV, 1956–57, No. 1, p. 38.

[51] Bettelheim, Charles, *Studies in the Theory of Planning*, Asia Publishing House, Bombay, 1961, pp. 302–03.

[52] Dobb, Maurice, *An Essay on Economic Growth and Planning*, Routledge and Kegan Paul, London, 1960, pp. 69–70.

for providing the necessary social and economic infrastructure, inflation and balance of payments difficulties, all these press upon the limited resources of these countries. It is therefore difficult and unwise to adhere to any one of the investment criteria and go ahead with it. It is being increasingly realized that investment in social and economic overheads is to be given top priority if the economy is to be made to grow. Of equal importance is increased agricultural production so that self-sufficiency in food can be attained, level of consumption can be raised and the strain on the balance of payments may be eased. Investment in heavy industries has also been found necessary if the growth of the economy is to be accelerated. Also the pressure of population and its high rate of growth in many underdeveloped countries have drawn the attention of the planners to the need for providing more and more employment. Thus in the matter of investment choice, the above-mentioned problems of underdeveloped countries create a conflict between capital-intensive methods which are necessary for the provision of overheads and the building up of heavy industries and capital light and labour-intensive methods which can be adopted for the improvement of agriculture and for providing greater employment opportunities.

In view of these circumstances, the investment policy in underdeveloped countries has come to be influenced by the following considerations: comparative costs which stress the need for designing the investment pattern with reference to factor endowments; diversification of the economy; provision of increased employment opportunities; increased use of domestic resources; building up the industrial base for future expansion; increasing the supply of consumption goods in the short period and substitution of imports and promotion of exports to ease the pressure on the balance of payments position.[53] The major problem with regard to investment allocation in these countries is the choice of such a combination of the methods of production which would ensure a high rate of growth of income on the one hand, and a rise in the level of consumption and employment on the other.

In this matter, the United Nations experts have consistently held the view that the investment problem can be solved only by choosing in the initial stages of economic development those techniques that contribute most to production for a given cost as measured by accounting prices. To begin with, underdeveloped countries are advised to make use of less capital-intensive methods of production. This would be in accordance with the factor endowments of these countries, particularly the lack of entrepreneurial skill and shortage of capital resources. It is argued that in the early stages at least, employment opportunities and income growth should not be in conflict. According to this view, the suitable technologies for underdeveloped countries would be the simplest of alternative techniques, the sturdiest of available capital equipment, the smallest type of plant consistent with technical efficiency and the technology that makes the best use of the most plentiful factors of

[53] *Economic Bulletin for Asia and the Far East*, U.N., December, 1958, p. 62.

production.[54] It is admitted that this policy would slow down the rate of growth. However, in so far as there already exists in many of the low income countries a small organized and capital-intensive sector along with a larger, unorganized and labour-intensive sector, there is the possibility of adopting both the techniques of production. To the extent increase in productivity and in savings and investment is an important consideration, capital-intensive techniques cannot be left out. Such methods are to be adopted in those sectors where they have a decided advantage. In fact, in certain investments like the development of transport and communications, capital-intensity is unavoidable. Hence a suitable combination of the two techniques is considered as the ideal method. As the economy grows and industries are started, there should be a planned and gradual transition to better and higher techniques of production.

The plea for a combination of techniques does not however mean that small industries should be made to survive simply because they are small and provide large employment in relation to the capital used. Many of the cottage industries in India for instance, are quite inefficient, and it is good for the economy that they are weeded out. In India in 1948–49 cottage industries contributed almost twice as much to the output of domestic product as conventional, factory establishments. But since more than six times as many workers were engaged in cottage industries as in factories, the average productivity was less than one-third that of the factory employee and only 10 to 15 per cent above that of the agriculturists. Although average wages in the cottage textile industry were not much more than half those in the mills, the unit cost of production was substantially higher.[55] Hence it is important in the short run to raise productivity in the cottage industries. This can be attained by means of better organization of cottage industries, extension of co-operative facilities to this sector, by the offer of financial and technical help by the government, by providing electric power facilities, by better training of the workers and by research on improving the techniques of production.

The policy of the Government of India with regard to industrialization of the country is based on this conception of the role of both small industries and heavy industries in the transitional stage of the country's economic development. Broadly speaking, the objective of the government is to promote the growth of heavy industries in the interests of generating the growth potential of the economy and at the same time support small industries in order to provide employment opportunities. Simultaneously, steps are taken to improve the standard of efficiency of the latter. It is mentioned in the Second Five-Year Plan that conditions have to be created in which modern techniques can be adopted and introduced more and more in small industries, so that the transition from backward to the advanced techniques of production may be

[54]*Processes and Problems of Industrialization in Underdeveloped Countries*, U.N., 1954, p. 48.
[55]*Ibid.*, p. 49.

orderly and smooth.[56] But the importance of heavy industries in a growing economy has also been fully realized by the government. The Third Plan recognizes that the slow growth of agricultural production is one of the main limiting factors in the progress of the Indian economy and envisages concentrated effort in agriculture on a comprehensive scale, but it also lays stress on the fact that " the development of basic industries such as steel, fuel and power, machine building and chemical industries is fundamental to rapid economic growth ".[57] It is thus clear that the investment policy of the Indian economy continues to be one in which equal emphasis is laid on the need for raising labour productivity and incomes as well as on creating more employment opportunities. Capital-intensive techniques are to exist alongside of labour-intensive techniques, each to secure distinct objectives, the first to be confined on the whole to the capital goods sector, and the latter to the consumers' goods sector.

---

[56] *The Second Five-Year Plan*, Government of India, 1956, pp. 30–31.
[57] *The Third Five-Year Plan*, Government of India, 1961, p. 50.

Chapter VIII

MONETARY POLICY

What Monetary Policy Means

Monetary policy aims at regulating the flow of currency, credit and other money substitutes in an economy with a view to affect the total stock of such assets as well as to influence the demand of the community for such assets.[1] Obviously, measures to regulate the volume of money supply would have a direct effect on resources allocation and levels of activity in an exchange economy which functions through the mechanism of money. Real resources available at any point of time get distributed among the following three channels: private consumption, public or government expenditure, and investment both public and private. Through monetary policy, i.e. through interest rate manipulations and expansion or contraction of credit and through fiscal measures, i.e. by raising or lowering the levels of taxation, the monetary authorities or the government can reduce or increase the flow of resources into private consumption or government expenditure and thereby increase or reduce the availability of resources for investment and capital accumulation which of course will have a direct bearing on the rate of growth of the economy.[2] Also, by proper adjustment of the flow of resources along these lines, it would be possible to impart an element of stability to the growth of the economy.

The great faith placed on monetary policy in the nineteenth century as a means to regulate the functioning of the economy was largely lost in the 1920s and 1930s. One obvious reason for this significant set back was the failure of monetary policy and the usual techniques of monetary control to prevent business depression. The shift in the emphasis from manipulation of the stock of money to fiscal measures in Keynesian economics also played a part in bringing about a de-emphasis of the role of monetary measures in economic policy. However, in recent years monetary methods have come back into the foreground as a reliable means of regulating national economic activity. To some extent, this revival is due to the gradual disappearance of factors responsible for the abeyance of monetary policy in the earlier years. But the major factor that has helped in the come back of monetary policy is the

[1] Hart, A. G., ' Monetary Policy for Income Stabilization,' *Income Stabilization for a Developing Democracy*, Ed. by Max F. Millikan, Yale, 1953, p. 304.
[2] Smith, Warren L., ' Monetary Fiscal Policy and Economic Growth,' *Quarterly Journal of Economics*, February, 1957, pp. 36–55.

development of inflationary conditions in most countries of the world, both developed and underdeveloped, since the outbreak of the Korean War. This inflationary rise in prices has been due to large investment outlays, and expenditures on defence and warlike equipment. It should also be observed that although at times monetary policy sank to the background, faith in it was at no time altogether lost. Even when monetary policy was proved to be of little value in regenerating economic activity in depression conditions, it was realized that it could be used as a powerful tool for counteracting over-expansionist forces. The extent to which investment activity has expanded in recent years is indicated by the fact that between 1954 and 1956 gross fixed capital formation increased by about 20 per cent in Western Europe while output rose by only 10 per cent. In the same years in the U.S.A. Gross National Product rose by 10 per cent while output of business construction and producers' durable equipment increased by 15 per cent. In underdeveloped countries, heavy public expenditures on development schemes, and deficit financing on a large scale have created circumstances favourable to inflationary price trends.

In the advanced capitalist countries of today, the primary objective of monetary policy is the maintenance of economic stability. Recent economists who strongly advocate economic stability as the chief purpose of monetary policy have invoked the quantity theory of money in support of their views. As an economy grows, the demand for money increases and unless the monetary authorities ensure on expansion of money supply in proportion to the increase in national output, demand for goods would fall, inventories would accumulate and prices would decline. The reverse happens if supply of money is in excess of demand for it. There can be stability only if the quantity of money is increased in step with increase in national output and real income. Here stress is laid specially on the manipulation of currency supply rather than the total quantity of money comprising both currency and credit money. The logic behind this view is that credit is only a by-product or fall out of the monetary system and as such what is to be regulated is money balances and not credit. It is assumed that manipulation of the former would take care of the latter.[3] Adjustments in the quantity of money with reference to the rate of growth of the economy and the demand for money, would bring about changes in the rate of interest which in turn would mitigate excess demand (interest rate rising) or encourage (through fall in interest rate) fresh investments and thereby check the decline or promote the rise in business activity. Professor Shaw calls such a system of automatic regulation of money supply with reference to the demand for it as the " Demand Standard of Monetary Control ".

However, even in economically advanced countries, where a high rate of growth of output as compared with low income countries is more or less

[3] Shaw, E. S., ' Monetary Stability in a Growing Economy,' *The Allocation of Economic Resources*, Essays in honour of B. F. Haley, Stanford, 1954, pp. 326–27.

assured, economists have not lost sight of the role which monetary policy can be made to play in ensuring the maintenance of the growth rate or even increasing it. To the extent monetary policy achieves full employment or near-full employment, it obviously fosters economic growth. Apart from this, it has been claimed that if monetary policy succeeds in keeping prices reasonably constant, it makes its maximum contribution to economic growth and to the balance of that growth.[4] A stable increase in the volume of money, ensures efficiency of the payments mechanism, avoids inflation and the evils resulting from it, reduces the uncertainties in private and governmental economic planning and minimizes social conflict as well as the financial distractions in the growth process. In the papers submitted recently by the panel of American economists to the Joint Economic Committee on the relationship of prices to economic stability and growth, there is substantial agreement in the matter of the close relationship between money supply and price level. Milton Friedman pointed out " that the total stock of money in a country will have to grow to accommodate itself to the growth in output and in population. In addition, it has to grow to satisfy the desire of the public to increase the ratio of cash balances to income as their real income rises." He recommended in an advanced country like the U.S.A. an annual 3 to 5 per cent increase in money supply.[5] But although there is much to be said in favour of stability of price level, the point is sometimes raised that a mild rise in prices or a slight dose of inflation is conducive to the growth of national output. It is mentioned that economic growth in the U.S.A. since 1953 might have been greater if effective demand had been maintained at a rate equal to the expansion of productive capacity. And the central thesis of the above study seems to be that " growth has been sacrificed on the altar of price stabilization ".[6] Otto Eckstein, the Technical Director of the study, remarks that the amount of growth that was surrendered for what at best was a small gain toward stabilizing the price level was very large.

Critiques of monetary policy, whether the objective of such policy is economic stability or growth, are not lacking. The major objections raised against monetary policy are twofold. In the first place, it is said to be ineffective or at least incapable of attaining most of its objectives; secondly, monetary policy as conceived and practised today goes quite often against social interests.

    [4] Ellis, Howard S., ' Discussion of the Paper on Relation of Money to Economic Growth by Charles R. Whittlesey,' *The American Economic Review—Papers and Proceedings*, May, 1956, pp. 208–10.

    [5] Friedman, Milton, ' The Supply of Money and Changes in Prices and Output,' *The Relationship of Prices to Economic Stability and Growth*, Compendium of papers submitted by Panelists appearing before the Joint Economic Committee (85th Congress, Second Session, U.S.A.), March 31, 1958, p. 254.

    [6] Hoover, Calvin B., ' Staff Report on employment, growth and price levels prepared for consideration by the Joint Economic Committee, Congress of the U.S.A., December 24, 1959— A Review,' *Quarterly Journal of Economics*, August, 1960, p. 375.

According to this view, the ineffectiveness of monetary policy springs from various factors. Firstly, the objectives of monetary policy are not quite clear and definite and cannot be put down in unambiguous terms. As usually enunciated, these objectives are economic stability, full employment and economic growth. Economic stability is normally equated with price stability and those who advocate monetary policy to attain this end, point out that stability can be ensured through variations of the quantity of money in response to the demand for it which in turn is dependent on the rate of growth of national output. But as has been indicated already, a difficulty arises here when maintenance of price stability conflicts with economic growth. If it is admitted that a rise in effective demand reflected in a rise in price level is necessary for the full employment of capacity output, then monetary policy or price policy should lay greater emphasis on growth of output rather than on the maintenance of a stable level of prices. Nor is the term full employment free from any ambiguity. In the context of a dynamic economy full employment should mean not only the full utilization of existing resources but also full employment of the increasing supply of capital equipment and other resources.[7] That is to say, monetary policy should, through regulation of the flow of money and credit and manipulation of interest rates, aim at the proper absorption of expanded capacity so as to ensure a steady increase in national output. The last mentioned objective, namely, economic growth is still less certain and clear than the other two.

Another criticism of monetary policy is that it is slow operating. Many monetary influences are likely to take hold with a time lag and fail to become effective instantaneously. On the basis of a study of business cycles in which the peaks and troughs attained in money stock are compared with that in economic activity in point of time, Milton Friedman comes to the conclusion that there is a lag between monetary changes and changes in economic activity to the extent of about 16–20 months. This conclusion has been questioned;[8] but to the extent monetary policy takes time to be effective, it ceases to be a potent weapon to control business fluctuations. If through interest rate variations or credit policy, quick changes cannot be brought about in the matter of investment decisions or levels of demand, it is quite likely that economic forces which are behind such variations would gather enough momentum of their own to make any monetary measures totally ineffective.

Empirical evidence has been brought forward to substantiate the thesis that the usual monetary measures to control deflation or inflation are ineffective. The lowering of interest rates in the 1930s had no effect on investment decisions, while in the period of inflation in the 1940s, monetary measures could not hold the price line. It may be pointed out that the failure of the

[7] Whittlesey, Charles R., ' Relation of Money to Economic Growth,' *The American Economic Review, Papers and Proceedings*, May, 1956, pp. 188–210.

[8] Culbertson, J. M., ' Friedman on the Lag in effect of Monetary Policy,' *Journal of Political Economy*, December, 1960, pp. 617–21.

monetary techniques in the great depression of the 1930s was due largely to the fact that the depression was quite unprecedented and that economic as well as non-economic factors were operating to increase its severity. But the failure of monetary policy in a period of inflation brings to light another aspect of the problem which is quite important. Monetary policy has to operate through influencing the demand for liquid assets. But people's demand for holding liquid assets arises from their precautionary and speculative motives which are of a psychological nature, are highly volatile and cannot for that reason be predicted. Also, monetary policy in attempting to control the price level through changes in the quantity of money will have only limited effect in so far as it can have little influence over the velocity of circulation of money. And such changes in velocity play a preponderant part in periods of both expansion and contraction.

But the major obstacle to an effective monetary policy is the rapidly narrowing sphere within which it has to operate. Through expansion or contraction of credit the supply of investible resources is regulated and brought into equality with the demand for them. But obviously, this will have an effect on investment only to the extent investment depends upon such resources. In reality, these resources provided by the banking system are only a limited part of the total actual supply. Moreover, monetary policy can have only very limited control over the types of loans and investments that banks acquire. Similarly, there is little scope for controlling the extent or type of uses to which the money that is being created is put by the public. It has also to be remembered that banks are not the sole purveyors of credit and in modern days investible resources are secured to a large extent outside the banking system in the advanced capitalist countries. In the first place, the public hold liquid assets other than cash which can be easily converted into cash when there is need for it. Thus in the U.S.A. in 1959 commercial bank loans increased markedly through the sale of the United States government securities to non-bank holders. Increasing volume of credit was provided to finance expanding economic activity but the funds were obtained largely from the savings of the public represented by the government securities and only to a negligible extent through creation of new money by the banking system.[9] In such a situation, measures to control credit creation by banks will have little effect on the levels of investment and economic activity. Secondly, the scope of the usual techniques of monetary control has been much restricted because of the emergence of non-banking financial intermediaries. It has been explained in quite unambiguous terms by the Radcliffe Committee,[10] that the level of spendings by private business on investment and by the community on final goods depends more on the overall liquidity position of the economy than

[9]Thomas, Woodlief, ' How much can be Expected of Monetary Policy ? ' *Review of Economic and Statistics*, August, 1960, p. 274.

[10]*Report of the Committee on the Working of the Monetary System*, H.M.S.O., London, 1959, pp. 174–89.

on the liquidity position of the banking system alone. And this liquidity position depends on the activity of several agencies which provide credit, such as Insurance Companies, Finance Corporations, House Building Societies, Pension Funds, etc. As a result of the increasing competition for resources because of the emergence of these intermediaries, the commercial banks suffer losses of reserves. The banks are therefore compelled to limit the volume of credit which they can provide but this directly shifts the demand of the unsatisfied borrowers to the financial intermediaries. Thus so long as financial assets can be transferred between intermediaries, attempts of the Central Bank to control credit can be circumvented. It is thus clear that the present array of weapons at the hands of the Central Bank is inadequate to meet the new situation. Techniques are therefore to be devised which would affect the liquidity of the entire financial structure.[11]

Monetary policy of the orthodox type is found not only to be ineffective but it has also been criticized on the ground that it quite often goes against social interests. It is pointed out that monetary policy is asymmetrical in its consequences in respect of the borrowers. This arises from the fact that the elasticity of demand for bank funds differs between business institutions. Those which depend mainly on accommodation from banks are compelled to pay higher rates on the same amount which they require in a period of tight money policy. And those which have large internal resources at their disposal or can resort to borrowing outside the banking system are little affected. To the former category belong some house building societies, local governments and small businesses. Furthermore, a stringent monetary policy in a period of rising prices goes against social interests in so far as it affects long-term welfare considerations, brings about cuts in domestic investment activity and thereby hinders economic growth. Credit restriction falls heavily on investments of a social nature which are necessary for promoting economic expansion. There is therefore the possibility of the limited resources being frittered away on the production of consumption goods and diverted from investments on worthwhile purposes.[12]

Some of these criticisms of monetary policy seem exaggerated. Nevertheless, they point to the fact that in the context of current developments in the financial structure of modern advanced countries and the need for generating the forces of economic development and promoting social welfare, traditional monetary policy requires a considerable degree of modification and refining. The difficulties in the way of monetary policy spring in the main from the fact that the tools of monetary control are rapidly getting outmoded and as such fail to cope with the new problems arising in a modern economy.

[11]Hogan, Warren P., ' Monetary Policy and the Financial Intermediaries,' *The Economic Record*, December, 1960, pp. 517–29.

[12]Schlesinger, James R., ' Monetary Policy and its Critics,' *Journal of Political Economy*, December, 1960, pp. 601–16.

Monetary Policy in Underdeveloped Countries

The limitations of monetary policy listed above, appear more pronounced in relation to the needs of present day low income countries. And this for two reasons. Firstly, the problems that monetary policy is expected to tackle in underdeveloped countries are more numerous, more complicated and even less clear and unambiguous than in developed countries. Secondly, deficiencies in the monetary system, the unorganized nature of money markets and other financial problems of a special nature in underdeveloped countries, present great difficulties in the way of proper handling of the usual monetary techniques of control.

Among the objectives of monetary policy in underdeveloped countries top priority is to be given to economic development. While emphasis shifts from monetary and price stability in advanced economies to economic expansion in underdeveloped countries, the importance of economic stability is not to be ignored. Other objectives apart from growth and stability but which have a close bearing on economic expansion are the mobilization and canalization of domestic savings and the financing of investment. Since the last three items are directly or indirectly helpful in fostering economic growth, the objectives in underdeveloped countries as in developed countries can be reduced to two, viz. economic stability and economic growth.

Inflation as a Symptom of Instability in Underdeveloped Countries

While instability in economically advanced capitalistic countries involves both deflation and inflation, in contemporary underdeveloped countries it is invariably one sided. In view of large investment demands which tend to outrun the resources available, the trend is normally towards a persistent rise in price levels. Monetary policy to control instability in low income countries would therefore in general, mean a policy to control inflation. The major characteristic of inflation is a persistent and continuous rise in prices which is self-propelled, and the basic reason for such a rise is an excess of demand for real output over the available supply of such output. In an exchange economy the demand for output is represented by the offer of money for securing real goods. The aggregate money or nominal income of a community is the sum of disposable personal income, disposable public income and undistributed profits of businesses. If this money income rises faster than real income there is inflation.

Aggregate demand for goods at any point of time can be broken up into: (a) Demand for investment and consumption coming from the private sector; (b) government expenditure and (c) exports. And the supply available to meet this demand is made up of : (a) Private income and savings; (b) Public revenues i.e. government receipts from taxation and public undertakings and (c) imports. In estimating excess demand, all these three sets of supply and demand factors are to be taken into account. If the sum of the demand factors set against the sum of the supply factors is zero then there is balance in the economy. Otherwise, if the former exceeds or falls short of the latter there is imbalance in the economy which manifests itself in the form of inflation or deflation. It thus follows that even when government expenditure exceeds government receipts i.e. when there is a deficit budget, it need not be inflationary, provided the excess demand arising in the public sector is offset by an excess of savings over investment in the private sector or if imports exceed exports.

The total expenditure of the government is met normally out of tax revenues and receipts from government undertakings. And if expenditure exceeds normal revenues, then the government resorts to deficit financing i.e. borrowing from the central bank. Normally, government's current revenues from the two sources indicated above, and the consumption expenditure of the community are proportional to the national income. Hence the crucial factors that bring about an excess demand are government deficit, private investment and the surplus on current account or excess of exports over imports. The size of deficit financing by government is generally reflected in the size of government debt; excess of private investment expenditure can be roughly measured by the increase in bank credit and excess of exports over imports is shown in the foreign exchange reserves. It would thus mean that variations in government's debt, in bank credit or advances and in foreign exchange reserves of a country taken together broadly reflect the size and trend of excess demand in the economy.

Economic development implies acceleration in the rate of investment in both the public and private sectors. Investment activity in the public sector gets more pronounced in modern underdeveloped countries where the responsibility for initiating the process of growth is taken up by governments. If government investment is to increase, real resources normally used for consumption or investment in the private sector are to be transferred to the public sector. If the demand for these resources in the private sector remains the same, then government's increased investment represents an addition to total demand. In other words, increased investment by the government causes an excess of aggregate demand over the normal supply of resources. Now, if government by means of physical controls or other direct measures restricts consumption and investment demand in the private sector, the transfer of real resources to the public sector can be effected without any rise in prices. On the other hand, if this transfer is to be brought about through the normal market mechanism, then government would have to find the means of buying these resources; that is to say, government will have to use its past savings or issue currency or borrow from the central and commercial banks. This can lead to an inflationary trend in prices. In fact, it is this rise in prices which helps in raising up the actual level of savings to equality with the higher rate of investment. A moderate dose of inflation by increasing the money incomes of the profit earners as against wage earners, transfers real resources from the wage earners and the fixed income earners whose propensity to consume is high, to the businessmen or the profit earners whose propensity to save is high and thus facilitates larger investment. Thus investment is not made equal to savings which are already available but the level of investment is raised first, in the interests of rapid economic development in anticipation of increased savings which under the present technique are brought about through indirect, forced means. In the years after the Second World War, genuine savings depending on the propensity of the people to save have greatly lost in relative importance as a determinant of the level of investment. The relatively low level of savings ceased to operate as a hindering factor in the process of growth; on the other hand, the structure of savings has got altered in view of the need for a constant or often rising level of total investment.[13]

It is immaterial in which sector of the economy excess demand starts. The point to remember is that as long as excess demand in any quarter is not offset by restriction of demand in other quarters, there is the possibility of inflation. In an advanced free enterprise economy where the private sector is well organized and has considerable scope for expansion, the rise in the level of investment activity in the public sector, even when it diverts resources away from private business would at the same time, by increasing the purchasing power available with the public as a result of increased public spending, provide an incentive for expansion of private business. To the drain of resources away from the private sector, private business would react by resorting to bank credit. This would obviously augment the aggregate excess demand in the economy. Also, if labourers want higher real incomes, their money wages are to be raised, and if reduction in employment is not possible because of Trade Unions, employers will have to borrow from banks in order to pay higher wages. However, in a developing economy where the government plays an important role in economic expansion, excess demand comes mostly from the public sector. And government's economic activity involving excess of outlays over normal receipts, causes prices to rise.

The Role of Money and Banking Institutions in Inflation

Although the root cause of inflation is excess demand, it is by and large a monetary phenomenon. A general rise in the level of prices can be said to have reached the stage of inflation only when the rise is continuous and self-propelled. It is obvious that a continuous rise in prices cannot be maintained unless it is possible to finance the prevailing scale of production at the higher level of prices. The stock of money available with the public at any point of time in the form of currency and deposits is used to finance production, consumption and investment. A rise in prices initiated by a rise in the demand for

[13]Bombach, Gottfried, ' Price Stability, Economic Growth and Income Distribution,' *International Economic Papers*, No. 10, p. 29.

resources for investment reduces the liquidity of the public and thus should normally help in bringing the inflationary process to a halt. In other words, unless the supply of money is increased in response to the need for more money arising out of an initial excess demand, the inflationary spiral cannot become operative.

The main sources of supply of money in a modern economy are the central and commercial banks. The central bank can facilitate expansion of money supply through its lending to the government as well as through its preparedness to come to the help of the commercial banks when they expand credit. Thus when the central bank lends to the government and when the government makes use of the credit made available by issuing cheques to its employees, creditors, contractors, etc., against the credit newly created, and when the latter deposit the money with the commercial banks, the reserves of the commercial banks are augmented. Also, if there is pressure on the commercial banks.for funds because of increased needs of the business sector, the central bank's action to relieve this pressure by lending to the banks through rediscounts or purchase of securities or advances would strengthen the free reserves of the commercial banks. It is thus clear that in any inflationary process the central bank should bear part of the responsibility. The role of commercial banks in this process is equally important. In a period of economic expansion when the demand for bank accommodation is high, it would be difficult for the banking system to resist the temptation to expand credit with a view to make profits for themselves. The necessary financial resources to meet the increasing demand would be found by the commercial banks by borrowing from the central bank directly or by rediscounting commercial, industrial or agricultural paper with the central bank. In this the role of the commercial banks may be said to be active in so far as their lending activity directly leads to an increase in money supply and thus helps to raise the level of effective demand. The role of the commercial banks in an inflationary process however may be passive, if they do not expand credit in spite of pressure from business but are compelled to expand credit in order to help the government or to avoid the social consequences of strikes or unemployment. All these would show that in the ultimate analysis, monetary authorities are the ones that bear the responsibility for a continuous inflation.[14]

Inflation and Economic Development

To the extent a rise in prices brings about a redistribution of incomes in favour of investors like private business and the government and reduces consumption, it does facilitate larger investment and makes possible a higher rate of growth. A mild dose of inflation has been recommended not only in situations that arise frequently in underdeveloped countries where the existing level of volun-

[14]Bernstein, E. M. and I. G. Patel, 'Inflation in Relation to Economic Development,' *I.M.F. Staff Papers*, Vol. II, No. 3, November, 1952, pp. 363-98.

tary savings is inadequate to bring about a continuous higher rate of real output, but also in advanced countries where the rate of growth of output is much higher than in the low income countries. Thus Professor Hansen makes a strong plea for creeping inflation on the ground that by keeping up the level of effective demand and by bringing about changes in the distribution of incomes, it helps in accelerating national income growth. The Staff Report on Employment, Growth and Price Levels prepared for consideration by the Joint Economic Committee of the U.S.A. in 1959 points out that the rate of growth of Gross National Product in the U.S.A. tapered off after 1953 and was substantially lower than the rate of 4·6 per cent achieved during the earlier part of the post-war period. According to this Report the " single most important requirement for expansion of the economy is the growth of demand at a rate equal to the expansion of productive capacity ".[15] A rise in price level is indicative of rise in effective demand which means that measures at price stabilization, to the extent they are effective, would scotch the growth process. Professor Kaldor stresses the effect of inflation on real rates of interest as an incentive for larger investment. In making long-term investments the businessman compares the costs represented by the risk factor and interest charges with the gross returns. Given the risk factor, a lower rate of interest would encourage greater flow of resources into investment or looking at it in another way, ensure the flow of the same amount of resources into investments even when gross returns are lower. When prices rise, money rates of interest also go up. But if prices rise faster than real output, then real rates of interest fall below the money rate of interest. Real rate of interest is calculated by the formula

$$r = \left(\frac{100+i}{100+ \Delta p} - 1 \right) 100$$

where r is the real rate of interest, i is the actual average rate of interest charged on bank loans and Δp is yearly increase in cost of living in percentage terms. Thus if actual rate of interest is 6 per cent and annual increase in cost of living is 10 per cent, then real interest is 3·7 per cent. Hence when prices are rising as in a period of inflation, real rate of interest would tend to fall and there would be greater incentive for investment. A policy of stable incomes and falling prices is accordingly not consistent with economic growth at all. And Kaldor proceeds to argue that by maintaining prices sufficiently high, booms can be perpetuated. And a slow and steady rate of inflation provides a most powerful aid to the attainment of a steady rate of economic progress.[16]

Opinion however is sharply divided on this issue. In recent years a formidable array of empirical data has been brought forth which shows that the advantages of inflation from the point of view of economic growth are very much exagge-

[15]Staff Report on Employment, Growth and Price Levels Prepared for Consideration by the Joint Economic Committee—Congress of the U.S.A., December 24, 1959. A review by Calvin B. Hoover. *Quarterly Journal of Economics*, August, 1960, pp. 374–92.

[16]Kaldor, Nicholas, ' Economic Growth and the Problem of Inflation,' Part II, *Economica*, November, 1959, pp. 287–98.

rated. On the other hand, many distinguished economists have drawn attention
to the dangers of inflation which far outweigh the few benefits which at best
are questionable.

From the theoretical point of view inflation can help economic growth in
so far as it brings about a redistribution of incomes in favour of the investing
classes. A larger volume of savings is thus made possible and the rise in the
level of investment that is assumed to result from the availability of resources
ensures increase in national product. It is thus clear that the effectiveness
of inflation in raising the rate of economic growth depends on two
basic conditions : (a) that levels of consumption in the aggregate are
brought down, savings are increased and the resources thus released are
transferred to the investing classes which of course would include both
the public and private sectors, and (b) that these resources are not dissipated but profitably invested in enterprises which would really help
economic growth.

But the claim that inflation helps in the transfer of resources to the investing
classes has not been fully borne out by facts. A study of inflation in the U.S.A. in
1939–52 shows that during these years labour's share of total personal income
rose by 6 per cent (from 64 to 70 per cent) contrary to the general notion that
wages and salaries lag behind other incomes during inflation. Unincorporated
businesses excluding farming retained a stable share of total personal income,
again contrary to the general notion that the business share increases during
inflation. Against the usual prediction, the farm share declined by one per cent
of the total overall, the picture is one of a substantial gain in the labour
share mainly at the expense of the interest share:[17] Criticizing Professor
Hamilton's thesis that profit inflation promotes capital formation because of
the lag of wages behind prices,[18] David Felix points out that " Spain under-
going the greatest price inflation during the 150 to 200 years of the price
revolution had the least profit inflation—limited to a few decades in the 16th
Century. France with the least price inflation had the greatest profit inflation.
England with less profit inflation than France had a greater rate of industrial
growth . . . . Clearly price inflation was not synonymous with profit inflation
and a widening spread between wage and price indices did not necessarily
mean a more rapid rate of growth."[19]

On the other hand, it has been argued that a better and more equitable
distribution of income and wealth is conducive to economic growth. This
view is based on the premise that economic expansion is possible only if the
increased output resulting from economic growth is readily absorbed by the

[17]Bach, G. L. and Abert Ando, ' The Redistributional Effects of Inflation,' *Review of
Economics and Statistics*, February, 1957, pp. 3 & 4.

[18]Hamilton, E. J., ' American Treasure and the Rise of Capitalism,' *Economica*, IX, 1929,
pp. 338–357; also ' Prices and Progress,' *Journal of Economic History*, XII Fall, 1952, pp. 325–49.

[19]Felix, David, ' Price Inflation and Industrial Growth,' The Historic Record and
Contemporary Analogies. *The Quarterly Journal of Economics*, August, 1956, p. 444.

community. Thus more industrial goods will be manufactured and put on the market if the demand for such goods is increasing. A shift in the national income in favour of the wage earning classes who constitute the bulk of society encourages mass production of goods as well as fosters technological progress; and a large-scale consumers goods industry makes a large-scale producers industry possible. In substantiation of this thesis the experience of the U.S.A. in some years of the 19th century and the early years of the 20th century has been cited. In the years 1884–1898, capital formation reached the high level of 16 per cent of national income per annum; and it was in this period that owing to a lag in the secular decline of wages behind prices, national income was better distributed than at other times between 1869 and 1914. Between 1920 and 1929 capital formation declined to 10·2 per cent of income per year; in the same decade the incomes of the top 5 per cent of spending units increased by 29 per cent, while the lower 95 per cent lost 4 per cent. In fact the disparity in the distribution of income and wealth as between different classes of the community is relatively less in richer countries like the U.S.A. and U.K. than in poor countries like Ceylon, India and some Latin American countries. Australia and Argentina differ much in standards of development—the former being much richer and more economically advanced than the latter, although in natural endowment they are very similar; and in the distribution of income and wealth, inequality is much less in the former than in the latter.[20] It is also worth noting that in periods of inflation or boom in the underdeveloped countries which are predominantly agricultural, there is a considerable augmentation of agricultural incomes in the form of windfall gains, but these incomes do not flow into industrial investment, nor are they productively employed even within the agricultural sector.[21]

Even assuming that inflation results in the transfer of real income from the wage earning to the profit earning class in a substantial measure, it does not necessarily follow that these resources will get profitably invested. Taxes on profits are generally lower in underdeveloped countries than in the high income countries. Hence the disposable income of business classes available out of the incomes transferred through inflation is proportionately greater. As such, the businessmen find it possible to spend a good part of their income in any manner they like. A part of their total spendings may confer greater ownership or private benefits. Among such spendings may be mentioned investments in holding foreign assets or in other lines of speculation which yield large profits and possibly capital gains. A part of additional income may be invested in the development of industry or agriculture which increases national production and thus confers large use or social benefits.[22] But left to themselves,

[20]Strassman, Paul W., ' Economic Growth and Income Distribution,' *The Quarterly Journal of Economics*, August, 1956, pp. 427–37.

[21]Felix, David, *ibid.*, p. 460.

[22]Bernstein, E. N. and I. G. Patel, ' Inflation in Relation to Economic Development,' *International Monetary Fund Staff Papers*, Vol. II, No. 3, November, 1952, pp. 363–98.

the businessmen in low income countries are likely to prefer investments whose ownership benefits are high such as foreign assets and gold holding, accumulation of inventories, real estate investments, investments in palatial buildings, acquisition of luxury goods, etc., rather than investments whose social benefits are high. Thus in the absence of strict regulation and control of private investments, it is likely that a large part of the forced savings arising out of inflationary price rise will be dissipated and fail to add to capital formation in the country.

These limitations of inflation as a means to promote economic development raise serious doubts about the view that a mild rise in prices is not only not harmful but is actually helpful to and indicative of economic growth. Recent statistical findings relating to the subject present a serious challenge to this notion which is usually taken for granted. These statistical data show that there is no correlation between inflation and economic growth. The years since the close of the Second World War have witnessed sharp inflationary trends in most of the developed as well as underdeveloped countries. But the countries in which rise in prices was very marked did not experience any corresponding increase in real output, nor was growth of income low in other countries where price rise was moderate or small. Between 1947–48 and 1956–57 general prices rose at an average annual rate of 8·5 per cent in Australia, 5·2 per cent in New Zealand and 5 per cent in U.K. but real income per head of the occupied population increased at 1·1 per cent, 1·8 per cent and 1·5 per cent respectively. And in the U.S.A. price rise was 2·3 per cent and the annual increase in output was 2·2 per cent; in Germany increase in prices was moderate at 2·1 per cent but real output rose by 4·6 per cent per year. In France the rise in price more or less corresponded with rise in output at 5·6 per cent and 5·5 per cent respectively. These figures show that economic growth and inflation are not invariably connected with one another in the short run. In reality, within the statistical material available at present, it is instances of a lower rate of inflation being associated with a higher rate of growth of real income that predominate.[23] On the basis of a statistical study of growth and price level in five developed countries of the 19th and 20th centuries covering mostly the 'take off' periods, Rattan J. Bhatia of the International Monetary Fund draws the conclusion that there is no correlation between growth in real income and price level.[24] In surveying the record of eight advanced countries over the last fifty to ninety years and of twelve since 1949, the Staff of the Joint Economic Committee of the U.S.A. Congress found that " there is no simple relationship between changes in output and changes in prices. Rapid economic growth has at different times been associated with rising, constant and falling price levels just as periods of slow growth or

[23]Phelps Brown, E. H. and M. H. Browne, ' Distribution and Productivity under Inflation, 1947–57,' *The Economic Journal*, December, 1960, p. 745.

[24]Bhatia, Rattan J., ' Inflation, Deflation and Economic Development,' *International Monetary Fund Staff Papers*, Vol. VIII, No. 1, November, 1960, pp. 101–14.

indeed of no growth have been marked by every manner of price behaviour."[25] Data relating to the less developed countries present the same story. Between 1946 and 1955 inflation in most of the Latin American countries was severe with of course considerable disparity in the rate of increase in prices between individual countries. But countries which experienced the highest degree of inflation were the ones which registered very negligible rates of growth. Rise in cost of living per annum was 120 per cent in Chile and in Paraguay but the increase in real product per capita in these two countries was 0·5 per cent and 1·5 per cent respectively. In Brazil, cost of living rose by 28 per cent and real income went up by 4 per cent. In the Dominican Republic, Ecuador and Guatemala, cost of living increased annually by 1 per cent, 3 per cent and 4 per cent respectively and their real product per capita rose by 3·5 per cent, 2·8 per cent and 2·3 per cent. In Venezuela rise in cost of living was 3 per cent and increase in output 4 per cent, while in Cuba prices fell and real product rose by 2·8 per cent.[26] It thus appears that the assumption that inflation ensures economic growth is only a theoretical notion not borne out by statistical evidence. Undoubtedly, deflation serves as a drag on economic expansion but there is little evidence to show that inflation accelerates long run growth.

That inflation does not always facilitate the transfer of real resources to profit earners, that even when such transfer is made there is no guarantee of these resources being invested in worthwhile undertakings and that on the whole the assumption that inflation promotes economic growth stands on very flimsy grounds are certainly matters of importance to be seriously considered before any glib advocacy of inflation or its continuance is made in underdeveloped countries. Apart from these, there are certain obvious evils of inflation of a socio-economic nature which deserve attention, and which should not be passed over lightly because of their very obviousness. Inflation aggravates the disparity in the distribution of income and wealth. Much of the increased earnings of the business classes and the profit earners are in the nature of windfalls and constitute an eyesore to the wage earners and fixed income earners who are left with a sense of deprivation and a feeling of social injustice. This state of affairs is conducive to much social ill will and conflict. The economic gain which is supposed to result from inflation in the form of higher investments is to some extent offset by other developments. Thus in the absence of controls it is likely that savings will be exported by those who have lost confidence in the domestic currency which rapidly declines in value. While forced savings may arise because of inflation, there is a loss to the nation's economy in so far as inflation discourages voluntary savings. A constant level of interest rates ensures stability, creates confidence among the

[25]*Report on Employment, Growth and Price Levels*, Staff of the Joint Economic Committee of the U.S.A. Congress, December 24, 1959, pp. 11–13, quoted in Phelps Brown, E. H. and M. H. Browne, *ibid.*, p. 745.

[26]Maynard, G., ' Inflation and Growth: Some Lessons to be drawn from Latin American Experience,' *Oxford Economic Papers*, June, 1961, p. 184.

business classes and imparts an element of certainty in their estimates of business costs. But inflation, while it reduces real rates of interest affects the stability of the money rates and adds to the uncertainties of calculations of the costs of any long-term investment projects. Lastly, inflation creates an external imbalance also in the form of external payments deficits resulting from increased imports and fall in exports. External imbalance of this nature would in turn necessitate exchange and other controls which have a restrictive effect on spontaneous productive efforts that promote economic growth in the country. There is besides the possibility, especially in underdeveloped countries, of a mild or creeping inflation gathering momentum rapidly and developing into inflation of the run away type. The social and economic evils indicated above, would then get considerably magnified. This danger is to be particularly guarded against in underdeveloped countries which do not have the necessary experience in monetary management, or an administrative machinery sound enough to take care of such a situation.

All these would point to the need for a great deal of caution in the matter of inflationary methods of financing economic development. Undoubtedly the safer method and the one which would be beneficial to the economy in the long run is to devise and adopt such techniques of financing and implementation of the schemes of development that would bring about economic development with price stability. This however, is difficult of attainment in underdeveloped countries and a certain amount of increase in prices seems inevitable. In countries which have stagnated for long, with very low levels of income and savings, economic development cannot be accelerated unless there is a stepping up in the rate of investment. Such acceleration involves an excess of investment over savings. Rigidities in factor supply and other production bottlenecks common in the low income countries create inflationary pressures only too quickly when any effort is made to step up the rate of investment. Besides, the inflationary potential of the type of investments that are required in order to promote economic growth is usually great. The emphasis on industrialization necessitates large investments by government for the development of key industries and transport and other public utilities. But the starting and expanding of major industries and the building up of factories require a large amount of real resources in the form of raw materials and labour power. The supply of raw materials depends on the growth and productivity of the agricultural sector. Also, the employment of more labour raises the demand for food. But from the point of view of the effect of investment on output, there is a difference between the industrial and agricultural sectors. By and large, while investment in the industrial sector takes time to fructify in the form of real consumption goods, a good part of the total investment in the agricultural sector results in an immediate increase in the supply. In other words, in the short period, investment in the industrial sector leads to the creation of additional money incomes to a greater extent than investment in the raw materials sector. Thus, while the demand for raw materials increases as the industrial sector expands, the amount of money that can be offered is also increasing. Obviously then, if this excess demand should not exert a pressure on the price front, there must be a proportionate increase in the supply of raw materials. Otherwise, when there is a relative shortage of primary products, the economy experiences a rise in wholesale prices. Manufacturers of final products raise the price of their goods in response to rise in costs. The cost of living goes up, and wage earners press for higher wages. This further raises costs of production, drives up other money incomes as well, and brings about a full-fledged inflationary trend. This sequence is observable in the recent experience of India. While the emphasis was on primary production and agriculture in the First Five-Year Plan, it shifted to large industries and economic overheads in the Second. In the Second Plan period the rate of industrial investment significantly increased but agricultural production slackened. The fact that the rise in the general wholesale prices has been greater than the rise under manufactures, but less than the increase in the prices of food articles and industrial raw materials, shows clearly that the last mentioned group of articles has exerted a preponderant influence on the general price structure. The important point to note is that simultaneously with a decline in agricultural output, an upward pull on the prices of these articles has been caused by higher investment in the industrial sector.

The foregoing brief analysis of the nature of inflation in underdeveloped countries indicates two types of imbalances which account for price rise. In the first place, there is imbalance between savings and investment, the latter outrunning the former; secondly, there is imbalance between the manufacturing or industrial and the primary or agricultural sector. Logically therefore, inflation can be prevented if investment is adjusted to the level of savings available in the economy and a balance is maintained between the industrial and agricultural sectors. This corrective measure would call for a reversal of the programmes of development drawn up and already being implemented in many of the low income countries; it also requires the bringing into operation of both monetary and fiscal measures of a comprehensive nature.

Monetary Policy and the Control of Inflation

Rise in prices resulting from over-investment or an unbalanced development between agriculture and industry represents the primary stage of inflation. It develops into the secondary stage when the uptrend in prices becomes continuous and more pronounced, fed by expansion in the supply of currency and credit. It is clear that inflation cannot continue for long unless the purchasing power available with the public is steadily augmented. It is at this stage that the central bank and the commercial banks bear the responsibility for the continuance and worsening of inflation. The measures that can be adopted at this stage as against the primary stage are mostly monetary, involving regulation of credit as well as physical controls of various types. Monetary policy to control inflation is thus essentially of a remedial kind. It attempts to slow down or control the rise in prices and introduce an element of stability by restricting the powers of the banking system to expand credit. Obviously, such a policy has to become operative through the agency of the central bank, the chief monetary authority of the state.

The fact that inflation is essentially a monetary phenomenon makes it amenable to monetary measures of control. If secondary inflation stems from the ease with which credit is expanded by the banking system, it follows that the uptrend in prices can be checked by restrictive monetary policy. In addition, there is a special reason why control of credit is of significance to underdeveloped countries in their attempts to check the uptrend in prices. In underdeveloped countries the relationship between money supply and prices is much closer than in the economically advanced countries having well organized monetary and financial institutions. Thus in Chile between 1937 and 1950 money supply increased over 800 per cent and cost of living went up by 549 per cent. The fact that in this country the ratio of Gross National Product to money supply remained constant in the years 1943 to 1950 when there was sharp inflation also illustrates the close relationship between the volume of money and price level.[27] A similar phenomenon has been observed in the case of Mexico and Cuba about the same period.[28] In India in the ten years covered by the first two Five-Year Plans 1950–1960, money supply increased by 40 per cent and the wholesale price level rose by about 25 per cent. In the same years the ratio of money supply to national income averaged 20 per cent with only very slight variations in either direction. This would mean that in these countries changes in the volume of money quickly react on the price front. When the country has experienced inflation for some time, people lose confidence in money and are unwilling to hold as savings any appreciable proportion of the new additions to money. As a result, variations in money supply have a pronounced effect on price level. It is observed that by 1939 inflation had continued for a number of years in Chile and money was no longer regarded as a convenient store of value.[29]

It would thus appear that the classical quantity theory of money has much relevance to contemporary underdeveloped countries. Fisher's equation relating to the value of money assumes full employment. Under such conditions lack of response of the supply side to increased demand causes prices to rise. The greater this rigidity of supply and the more constant the velocity of circulation of money, the closer will be the relationship between the quantity of money and price level. But if there is underemployment, any increase in demand facilitated by expansion of money supply would encourage increased

[27]Grove, David L., 'The Role of the Banking System in Chilean Inflation,' *I.M.F. Staff Papers*, Vol. II, No. 1, September, 1951, p. 37.

[28]Wallich, H. C., *Monetary Problems of an Export Economy, the Cuban Experience*, 1944–47, Harvard, 1950, p. 208.

[29]Grove, David L., *ibid.*, p. 37.

production, and to the extent supply increases, price rise will be restrained. In underdeveloped countries with low standards of life and low levels of consumption, increased money supply will tend to get absorbed fully in the transactions sphere. On the other hand, supply is not perfectly elastic in such countries. In many of these countries manufactured consumption goods are imported and it takes time before supply can be augmented in response to increased demand. Also factor rigidities, the lack of capital equipment and deficiency in technical and organizational skill present serious difficulties in the way of increased production. Thus from the point of view of the reaction of money supply on prices, the low income countries are in a situation corresponding to full employment. Moreover, lack of confidence in domestic currency increases velocity of circulation so that the initial increase in money supply creates a multiplier effect in respect of price changes.[30] This indicates that in underdeveloped countries it would be possible to manipulate prices by regulating money supply with a greater degree of certainty than in the case of developed countries.

While the close relationship between money supply and price level in underdeveloped countries adds to the effectiveness of monetary policy, the fact that the multiplier effect of an initial increase in money supply on prices is much pronounced makes it necessary to adopt a really restrictive monetary policy in order to control prices. Government's borrowing from the central bank in order to finance its increased investment outlays will have a twofold effect on credit and price situation. Firstly, there is credit creation by the central bank in favour of the government and a rise in prices resulting from increased spendings by government. Secondly, to the extent the private sector also is keen on securing an adequate supply of real resources for investment and consumption, it would react by bidding up prices in a competitive manner and get the necessary financial resources through borrowing from the commercial banks. And credit expansion by the banking system is facilitated by the acquisition of larger deposits through the initial increase in government spending. This defensive reaction of the private sector would bring about further rise in prices as long as credit is available. Hence when excess demand arises in the public sector its inflationary impact can be contained only by restraining investment activity in the private sector. In other words, in any scheme of financing development projects, if inflation is to be avoided, credit expansion in any one sector has to be matched by countervailing contraction in the other sector. The need of the private sector for bank credit is met by the commercial banks borrowing from the central bank and on the basis of this, by expanding credit to private business. The usual methods adopted by central banks to control credit operate on these two stages namely, primary expansion of credit by the central bank to the government, and secondary expansion of credit by commercial banks to the private sector. If the increase in money supply

[30]Van Philips, Paul A. M., *Public Finance and Less Developed Economy*, Martinus Nijhoff, 1957, pp. 72–73.

resulting from the primary expansion of credit is more than what is warranted by the conditions of the economy, the inflationary effect of such monetary expansion can be controlled by a matching restriction of the secondary expansion of credit, namely, increase in commercial banks' credit to private business. In brief, if monetary policy aims at keeping price level within limits in the context of economic development, and if rise in prices is facilitated by the expansion of credit by both the central and commercial banks, and if expansion of credit by the central bank to the government is absolutely necessary and cannot be reduced, the only way open to the monetary authorities is to restrict credit to private business to the extent credit to the public sector has expanded. The greater is the expansion of credit by the central bank in favour of government, the greater should be the restriction on credit creation by the commercial banks.

In practice however, such a severely restrictive monetary policy is not possible in an economy where free scope is provided for the private sector in business, and where activity in that sector is considered as much necessary and important for the nation's economic progress as activity in the government sector. Nevertheless, anti-inflationary monetary measures have to run along these lines even if it is not possible to carry them to the extent required in theory. Recent measures taken in India to counteract inflationary price trends are illustrative of the scope of monetary policy in underdeveloped countries and of the extent to which such measures are capable of achieving their objectives.

Anti-inflationary Measures in India

As in many other countries prices started moving up rapidly in India with the outbreak of the Second World War in 1939. The upthrust in prices very soon gathered an inflationary momentum. The general wholesale price index shot up from 100·0 in August 1939 to 244·1 at the close of the War.[31] After the end of hostilities, political disturbances in the country and the Korean boom gave a further boost to price rise. In June, 1950, the index of prices reached 395·6. Correspondingly money supply had increased from Rs. 5,320 million in 1939–40 to Rs. 21,210 million in 1945–46. Since 1950, the major factor responsible for price rise in India has been the large spendings by the government for investment purposes under the Five-Year Plans. Deficit financing was quite modest in the initial stages of planned development. This combined with increased agricultural production kept prices fairly steady till towards the close of the First Five-Year Plan. The sharp step up in investment expenditure in the last two years of the First Plan, further acceleration of investment in the Second Plan, increased deficit financing and the greater emphasis on heavy industries and on economic and social overheads helped in a sharp upthrust in prices in the Second Plan period.

. [31] Base: Week ending 19th August, 1939 = 100.

In their attempt to control prices the Government of India and the Reserve Bank have relied mostly on monetary measures. Most of the direct physical controls which were invoked during the war years were given up after the close of the war. Instead, attention came to be focussed on the credit policy of the banking system, and steps were taken to restrict primary expansion of credit by the central bank as well as secondary expansion by the commercial banks. About the middle of May, 1951, the volume of commercial bank credit, i.e. advances and discounts, rose to Rs. 5,860 million, the highest point to be reached till then. The currency notes in circulation amounted to more than Rs. 12,000 million exceeding the peak level attained during the war period. It was to meet this threat of an undue expansion of currency and credit that the Bank Rate was raised from 3 per cent to $3\frac{1}{2}$ per cent on November 14, 1951. As a further means to tighten the grip, the Reserve Bank announced its decision not to buy government securities directly from the banks in the busy season and its willingness to grant loans and advances at the new Bank Rate against government securities. Although as a result of this step the rate of increase in money supply and scheduled bank credit tended to decline, the restrictive effect of the higher Bank Rate was quite negligible. The level at which bank advances stood in the busy season of 1951–52 (Rs. 5,970 million) was higher than the maximum reached in the previous busy period. The advances-deposit ratio, which is a dependable index of the degree of expansion of bank credit, reached 70 per cent in March, 1952 against 65 per cent, the previous highest.

The second phase in the expansion of bank credit since the commencement of planning, started in 1954 and gained considerable momentum in the next year. Over the three busy seasons in the years 1954 to 1957 bank credit expanded by Rs. 950 million, Rs. 1,600 million, and Rs. 1,700 million respectively. This rise in bank credit and increase in money supply from Rs. 19,210 million at the end of 1954–55 to Rs. 23,890 million at the end of 1957–58 was necessitated by the rapid rise in investment and business activity in both the public and private sectors, but it was feared that the rate of increase in credit was much greater than what circumstances would justify. On March 1, 1956, therefore, the Bank raised its lending rate under the Bill Market Scheme from 3 per cent to $3\frac{1}{4}$ per cent (i.e. $\frac{1}{4}$ per cent below the Bank Rate) and later to $3\frac{1}{2}$ per cent effective November 21, 1956. But at the same time, some relaxation was made in the Bank's policy of open market operations. From the beginning of November, 1956, the Reserve Bank started making discriminating purchases of government securities and also liberalized to some extent the facilities under the Bill Market Scheme. In the next year, further measures to tighten credit were adopted. As a result of the government's raising of the Stamp Duty on usance bills, the effective borrowing rate of scheduled banks against usance bills further increased by $\frac{1}{2}$ per cent. Simultaneously, the Bank's lending rate on advances against government securities was increased from $3\frac{1}{2}$ per cent to 4 per cent. With effect from May 16, 1957, the Bank Rate itself was raised to

4 per cent, but the Stamp Duty on usance bills was reduced to one-fifth of one per cent so that the effective borrowing rate of scheduled banks against usance bills was lowered to 4½ per cent.

Other restrictive measures somewhat of an unorthodox kind have been adopted more recently. On March 11, 1960, the Reserve Bank invoked for the first time its powers to vary the reserve ratios of scheduled banks by requiring them to maintain with it additional balances equivalent to 25 per cent of the increase in their total deposit liabilities since that date. Later, these reserve requirements were raised to 50 per cent of the increase in demand and time liabilities. On September 21, 1960, an important step was taken by the introduction of a three-tier system of credit control. This involved, the charging of penal rates of interest for borrowing from the Reserve Bank by banks in excess of the quota fixed for each; an increase in the average lending rate by banks to their customers by half a per cent; and the fixation of a limit on the interest rate paid by banks on short term deposits. Also, selective credit control measures have been increasingly adopted. These include imposition of minimum margin requirements in respect of advances by scheduled banks against commodities and equity shares and also periodical appeals and directives from the Governor of the Reserve Bank to the commercial banks reiterating the need for refraining from excessive expansion of credit.

Despite the fairly wide sweep of these measures, their effectiveness in controlling price level or inflation has been quite insignificant. Prices have continued to be on the uptrend. Over the years 1956–61 covered by the Second Five-Year Plan, the general wholesale price level in the country went up by 12 per cent. The annual rate of increase in prices in the three years, 1958–59 to 1960–61, was nearly 4 per cent as against a little more than one per cent in the corresponding years of the First Plan. Money supply increased from Rs. 22,200 million at the beginning of the Second Plan to Rs. 28,740 million at its end. Between 1957–58 and 1960–61, the working class consumer price index compiled by the Labour Bureau of the Government of India registered a rise of 13 points. There are unmistakable symptoms of inflation in the Indian economy today. Among these may be mentioned the increase in the velocity of circulation of money, fall in the liquidity preference of the people, or the greater urge to spend money quickly so as to escape the loss arising from decline in its value, speculative rise in the values of fixed assets such as landed property, the tendency for wages to rise because of higher prices and higher cost of living and prices to go up because of wage rise and increased costs of production, speculative cornering and hoarding of goods, etc. The main factor responsible for this situation is the increasing outlay of the government on investment and deficit financing on a large scale. Against these forces tending to push up prices steadily, the monetary measures adopted to keep the price line seem to be of little avail.

And the reasons for this ineffectiveness of monetary policy are not far to seek. A restrictive monetary policy stringent enough to control an inflationary trend in prices is likely to have a dampening effect on private investment and would therefore slow down the pace of economic growth. Rapid economic development is the dominating concern and if it is a question of choice between a mild dose of inflation and economic growth on the one hand, and relative price stability and economic stagnation on the other, the preference lies definitely in favour of the former. At each stage in the adoption of anti-inflationary measures, the government and the central banking authority have kept an eye on the possible repercussions of such a policy on the production front. And they have been only too quick to reverse the policy or tone it down considerably, the moment they felt that it would hinder or threaten economic growth. In other words, the monetary authorities have been greatly handicapped in the implementation or continuance of their well-intentioned policies by the constant fear of a slowing down of the tempo of economic advance. This half-hearted attitude of the monetary authorities in the formulation as well as execution of anti-inflationary measures is certainly one of the main reasons for their limited effectiveness.

Limitation of Monetary Policy in Underdeveloped Countries

But the basic reason why monetary policy cannot hope to attain that measure of success in underdeveloped countries as is possible in developed countries is the fact that economic underdevelopment is reflected in the underdeveloped state of the capital and money markets. In these countries currency is more important than bank deposits so that even when the central bank is able to control the volume of commercial bank credit, it leaves mostly out of control the more important section of money supply. To the extent a restrictive monetary policy has to operate on the credit portion of money supply, the limited scope for such a policy in backward countries is obvious. Also, since many of the underdeveloped countries earn a good proportion of their income through a few primary export commodities like rice, cotton, jute, rubber, tin, etc. their domestic price level is easily influenced by world demand for their export goods and their prices in the external markets. Imported instability of this kind is not easily amenable to domestic price control measures.

The traditional means of control exercised by the central banks are the Discount Rate, Open Market Operations and the variation of commercial bank reserves. The effectiveness of these techniques is considerably limited in underdeveloped countries because of the fact that their money and capital markets are unorganized and not well integrated with the central banking system. Bank Rate can be effective only if the contact between the central bank and the commercial banks is close and the demand for credit is sensitive to cost. In underdeveloped countries it is quite common for commercial banks to keep cash reserves in excess of legal reserve requirements. The margin of difference between legal reserves and actual reserves provides considerable leeway for the commercial banks to depend on their own resources for expanding credit when there is need for it. In other words, a higher bank rate is ineffective in so far as the commercial banks arc not compelled to go into the Bank at a time when the latter expects them to go; nor can the central bank be certain at what stage or at what level the higher discount rate can be made effective. Another reason why discount rate quite often fails to be effective, is the lack of suitable bills for discounting. This prevents the wide use of rediscount facilities offered by central banks. Thirdly, the existence of quite a good number of foreign banks in the underdeveloped countries makes it difficult for the central bank to have a close control over the banking system. The branches of the big foreign banks are able to get resources from their parent institutions abroad in times of need, and can therefore to a large extent ignore the policy of the central banks in the countries in which they are operating. Lastly—and this is not special to low income countries—a change in discount rate has limited effect when there is a strong expectation of falling or rising prices. Thus when inflation has continued for sometime, and the business community expect the rise in prices to continue, they would not hesitate much to borrow from the central bank even when the rate of discount is quite high with the result that the volume of bank credit cannot be influenced to any appreciable extent. That the foregoing explanation is not an exaggeration is borne out by experience in the Philippines where when the central bank in order to stimulate economic activity reduced its discount rate from 2 to $1\frac{1}{2}$ per cent early in 1954, the rates of commercial banks instead of going down as expected, actually went up.[32] The possibility of raising the bank rate to any significant extent is also limited by the fact that it would raise governments' cost in connection with economic development. This is of particular importance since in most of these countries the public sector is playing an important role in economic development and government is depending to an increasing extent on borrowing against its securities for purposes of financing economic development.

Open market operations also fail because of the above reasons. The principle behind such operations is that by selling or buying eligible securities the central bank can reduce or increase the liquidity of commercial banks and thereby affect the volume of bank credit. Obviously, the success of this policy depends on the existence of a large amount of government securities and their marketability. The supply of government securities in the underdeveloped countries has increased in recent years but their marketability has not improved because of their low interest rates and earnings. While government securities are attractive to the commercial banks from the point of view of safety, the interest rate of 4 per cent or 5 per cent on them compares unfavourably with the yield of corporate securities of sound credit risk ranging from 8 to 12 per cent per annum. Hence the commercial banks prefer the latter or as it happens in many cases, they attach greater importance to liquidity position and hold their excess reserves in liquid assets such as cash, gold, foreign exchange, etc. The

[32] *Economic Bulletin for Asia and the Far East*, U.N., Vol. VII, No. 3, November, 1956, p. 41.

relative illiquidity of government securities is in some measure due to the absence or inadequacy of capital markets. However, any attempt to develop the marketability of government securities will have to face the problem of raising the government bond rates sufficiently high. In view of the prevailing high market rates of interest, the establishment of a bond market would only depress the value of the government securities and wipe out a large part of the capital value of such securities. On the other hand, raising of the interest rate on government bonds in order to increase their marketability would directly raise the government's cost of borrowing.[33]

A third method of controlling credit creation by commercial banks which has been resorted to in some of the underdeveloped countries, is for the central bank to raise the minimum reserve requirements of the banks. By raising the reserves which the banks are to keep against their deposits, a part of the commercial banks' assets can be immobilized and their powers to expand credit correspondingly restricted. But the scope of this measure is also limited in view of the excess reserves kept by the banks and also because of the existence of branches of foreign banks which can rely on resources from abroad. Also, to the extent that commercial banks keep government securities, they can replenish their resources by selling such securities in times of pressure. One method suggested to control the practice of commercial banks maintaining excess reserves is to require them to keep government securities as additional reserves. Such a measure it is hoped, would reduce the switching operations above mentioned, minimize fluctuations in the government bond market and also reduce the need for central bank support to the government bond market. Some countries in Europe like Belgium, Italy, France and the Netherlands have introduced this method and among underdeveloped countries Pakistan and the Philippines have taken a somewhat related step.

It is clear from the foregoing brief account of the nature of monetary institutions and practice in underdeveloped countries, that monetary measures to control inflation cannot be very much successful. While in developed countries the springing up of a large number of financial intermediaries affecting the liquidity position of commercial banks has reduced the scope of the traditional monetary measures of control, in underdeveloped countries the backward and ill-developed nature of the monetary institutions limits the effectiveness of monetary policy considerably. Even those monetary institutions which exist in an underdeveloped form in the low income countries are of an exotic variety introduced from abroad with little reference to the peculiar conditions and organization of the economy in these countries. The banking and financial systems in the Western countries have evolved over centuries through private enterprise and government co-operation. They have developed alongside of spontaneous economic progress and as such they are capable of dealing with the problems and meeting the requirements of a growing economy. But in underdeveloped countries like India, we find the existence side by side, of

[33] *Economic Bulletin for Asia and the Far East*, U.N., Vol. VII, No. 3, November, 1956, p. 42.

financial and banking institutions of the modern type as well as indigenous and antiquated organizations. We thus have the evils of both. Techniques which have been successful in a country with an advanced and wellknit monetary system fail, or function unsatisfactorily, in a different organizational and institutional set up. In India roughly about 35 per cent of the total national income is outside the purview of monetary transactions. And even in the monetized sector, only about 50 per cent of the financing of industry and trade is done by the organized part of the money market and the remaining 50 per cent of the financing is done by non-bank agencies. It is therefore clear that the traditional central bank techniques of credit control would not be of much use. In addition, the emergence of various new financial institutions like credit corporations and other organized credit agencies has created the need for new methods of control. The situation thus calls for a close study of the monetary institutions functioning in the organized sector of our economy, as well as outside it, their role in financing development and the extent to which they are amenable to control, so that more satisfactory techniques of management and control suited to the requirements of the economy can be evolved.

MONETARY POLICY FOR PROMOTING ECONOMIC DEVELOPMENT

Unless inflation tends to be chronic in underdeveloped countries, the objective of monetary policy to control rise in prices is a short term one. It represents the negative aspect of monetary management. But far more important than maintaining stability in price level is the long term objective of promoting economic growth. This represents the positive aspect of monetary policy in low income countries. From the point of view of long term growth, monetary policy should aim at providing means to better mobilize and canalize financial resources for investment. It should also have the objective of promoting the development of banking and financial institutions and fostering the banking habit in the community.

Development of Banking and Mobilization of Savings

The justification for inflationary methods of financing economic development is that the potential savings in underdeveloped countries are greater than actual savings and that inflation is a more effective way of raising the level of savings than taxation or internal borrowing. It thus follows that if steps can be taken to increase and mobilize voluntary savings, the necessity for deficit financing or inflationary methods of financing becomes correspondingly less. This points to the need for starting more and more banking and other savings institutions in the country and for promoting the banking habit among the people. In the underdeveloped countries, the area of the non-monetized sector is quite large. This covers mostly the rural areas where savings are made rather in kind than in cash. Where agriculture has become commercialized and the villages are brought into the system of exchange economy, a large part of the monetary savings is drawn away into the unorganized money market attracted by high rates of interest, and is for all practical purposes lost for profitable investment. It is possible to tap these resources only if banking spreads to the rural areas also. But the development of banking and economic growth are interdependent. In a free enterprise economy capital will be ventured into banking and finance only if such investment is attractive from the commercial point of view. In the process of industrialization and economic growth, the need for financial facilities also increases so that banks will get started in response to the need. The development of banking in turn would foster the growth of industries, trade and commerce. This happy synchronization is, however, not possible in underdeveloped countries which have economically stagnated for long. The scarcity of capital combined with the unpreparedness of private business to venture into the field of banking in rural areas, points to the need for public encouragement or enterprise in this direction. This is the only way of breaking the deadlock in which banking and industrialization in underdeveloped countries are involved. Such a development would not only help in the mobilization of domestic savings but also promote the growth of a money market and the integration of the banking and financial system of the country. Then monetary policy would assume new meaning and significance in so far as banking will become broad-based and better organized, and the contact between the monetary authorities and the financial agencies would become closer. The improvement in organization and better integration of the monetary institutions would increase the effectiveness of monetary policy.

Recent years have witnessed development along these lines in India. In the first place, certain measures have been taken by the Reserve Bank of India in order to exercise greater control over the banking system. The decision of the Reserve Bank, late in 1951, not to buy government securities for meeting the seasonal requirements of commercial banks, but to make only advances against government and other approved securities at the Bank Rate and the introduction of the Bill Market Scheme[34] not only forced the banks to approach the Reserve Bank for funds but also facilitated their getting accommodation from the central bank. The Reserve Bank thus acquired greater control over the commercial banks, and the opportunity to scrutinize the loan applications of commercial banks helped it to control or prevent non-essential borrowing. Subsequent extension of the Bill Market facilities and the declaring of certain

[34] Under the Bill Market Scheme introduced in January, 1952, the Reserve Bank of India undertook to provide accommodation to Scheduled banks by granting demand loans against the promissory notes of scheduled banks supported by usance bills or promissory notes of their constituents. In order to popularize the bill and make it a regular instrument of credit, advances against such bills were to be made by the Reserve Bank at $\frac{1}{2}$ per cent below the Bank Rate; also the Bank undertook to bear half the cost of the Stamp Duty on the conversion of the demand bills into time bills. The minimum limit for a single advance at any time was fixed at Rs. 2·5 million and the minimum value of individual bills tendered to the Bank was fixed at Rs. 1,00,000 each.

types of export bills to be eligible for rediscounting, largely extended the scope of the Reserve Bank's control over commercial banks. The tendency on the part of the commercial banks to rely increasingly on the Reserve Bank for funds is seen in the steady rise in the Reserve Bank's advances to scheduled banks under Section 17 (4) *A* and *C*. Simultaneously, the ratio of the scheduled banks' cash in hand and balances with the Reserve Bank to aggregate liabilities declined from about 11 per cent before the commencement of the First Plan period to about 8 per cent in 1956–57 and to 6·5 per cent in 1961–62. Also the excess of their balances over the statutory minimum steadily came down from Rs. 220 million in 1950–51 to an average of about Rs. 100 million over the years 1955–56 to 1961–62. These changes indicate the pressure on bank funds as well as the effectiveness of the measures to provide greater borrowing facilities by the Reserve Bank which made it unnecessary for the commercial banks to maintain a very high cash ratio.

An important step has been taken by the government in the direction of expanding banking facilities in the rural areas. There has of late been substantial increase in the income of the people in the agricultural sector of our economy. Recent price trends indicate that the terms of trade have on the whole been favourable to agriculture. It is therefore fair to assume that there is much scope for the expansion of banking in the rural areas of the country. However, the progress made in the development of banking has been not encouraging. Between January 1951 and the end of 1959 the number of offices of scheduled and non-scheduled banks in India increased from 4,119 to 4,851. What is required is greater diversification and decentralization in banking. In actual fact, there has been a great deal of concentration in particular areas of the country. Of the 347 reporting banks in 1959, only 29 or 8·4 per cent had paid up capital and reserves of over Rs. 5 million. These 29 banks accounted for Rs. 15,000 million out of the total deposits of Rs. 16,640 million that is, for 90 per cent. There is thus little difference now from the position in 1952 when 6 per cent of the total reporting banks had capital and reserves of over Rs. 5 million and accounted for 86 per cent of the total deposits. Apart from this concentration, there is considerable disparity in the development of banking in different areas of the country which cannot be explained by the mere difference in standards of economic advancement. It was to set aright this imbalance in the development of banking that the government launched in 1955 a programme for the opening of branches of the State Bank in the rural areas of the country.

Thirdly, some modifications have been effected by the Reserve Bank on the administrative side to ensure greater integration of the banking system and to enhance its control over the commercial banks. Since 1949 when the Banking Companies Act came into operation, the Reserve Bank has been maintaining a close supervision of the commercial banks with a view to improving the efficiency and the tone of the banking system as a whole. Under Section 11 (1) and Section 11 (3) of this Act, banks with paid up capital and reserves of less

19

than Rs. 50,000 are required to cease transacting business. At the same time, steps are taken to promote amalgamation of small banks in the interests of depositors and greater stability and in order to prevent the springing up of mushroom growths which cannot be operated efficiently. Furthermore, the system of inspection of commercial banks by the Reserve Bank started in March, 1950, provides an opportunity for the Reserve Bank to acquire an intimate knowledge of the conduct of business by these banks. These regular inspections have resulted in the exposure of some of the common defects of small sized banks and in the general toning up of the banking system. The recent introduction of the Deposit Insurance Scheme in Indian banking is an additional welcome measure which would go a long way towards creating confidence among the public in banking and in promoting the banking habit.

All these would mean that in India in recent years greater and greater control has come to be exercised by the government in the development as well as organization of banking. It is neither possible nor desirable to lay down any fixed pattern of development of banking institutions as an ideal one in a growing economy. Much depends on the nature of the economy, the habits of the people and their tradition, and the ideology of the government. Obviously, the type of financial and banking institutions which fit in well in the economy of a country where there is considerable scope for free enterprise and where the activity of the public sector is narrowly restricted, will not be so in another country where the organizational set up of the economy is different. Since it has become more or less obligatory on the part of the governments in underdeveloped countries to take the lead in economic development through government enterprise and investment, the responsibility of determining the shape and form of the financial system that would adequately meet the special needs of such economies has to an equal extent devolved on them. Recent developments in banking in India—the nationalization of the Imperial Bank, the establishment of special credit institutions and the forging of closer links of control between the central bank and the commercial banks—are in line with the scheme of economic development envisaged by the government. Given the pattern of economic development it is meaningless to expect the banking and financial institutions to shape in a different mould.

Canalization of Savings

Monetary policy can contribute to economic development not only by providing the means to mobilize the savings available in the country but also by canalizing them into proper lines of investment. In an indirect sense anti-inflationary measures help growth to the extent they succeed in preventing the wastage of resources in the form of conspicuous spending on consumption as well as on uneconomic investment. But the chief defect of quantitative measures such as discount rate and open market operations is that they are indiscriminatory in their effects. If inflation results from over-expansion in one or more

sectors of the economy, it would not be possible through the traditional techniques of control to restrain these sectors and at the same time encourage the
depressed sectors. If the monetary measures adopted are of a half hearted
nature and are for that reason ineffective, disequilibrating expansion would be
allowed to continue; on the other hand, if stringent steps are taken, they would
affect all sectors of the economy indiscriminately.[35] High interest rates will hit
the weaker industries and the smaller firms the hardest. And firms which
are most vulnerable to a credit squeeze are not necessarily always those which
it is economically most desirable to cut off. Monetary policy in the context of
economic development should therefore have two aspects. It should on the
one hand restrict inflation, but it should achieve this by curtailing expansion
of those industries or sectors whose expansion is not conducive to growth; on
the other hand, it should be able to divert savings away from such wasteful
lines of investment and direct them into really beneficial undertakings. In
other words, monetary policy should be of a qualitative nature and capable of
discriminating between economic and uneconomic outlays; it should strike
at the latter and favour the former.

Qualitative credit control measures may be general or specific. Voluntary
credit restriction or restrictions by exhortations and moral suasion are of the
general type, while controls of particular credit institutions or of credit facilities
granted to particular purposes belong to the specific category. Individual
credit institutions are controlled by varying their reserve requirements or
by influencing their assets structure. Restrictions with regard to the purpose
for which investment is made are imposed by fixing ceilings for investments,
by direct stipulation of the purpose for which loans can be used, by the adoption
of selective rediscount policy by the central bank, by prior deposit requirements
as in the matter of imports, by margin requirements as collateral for specific
loans, etc.

Credit control measures of the above type can help economic growth in
three ways. Firstly, selective or qualitative credit control can restrain inflation
with minimum of harmful effects on the economy as a whole. In a time of
inflation, bank advances to business tend to rise rapidly. Advances to enterprises or businesses which are not desirable from the point of view of the
national economy can be restricted by the monetary authorities demanding
higher margin requirements for certain types of collateral. These may be
advances for speculative building up of inventories, purchase of real estate,
gold or foreign exchange. The monetary authorities may declare that loans
advanced should not exceed a certain percentage of the value of the collateral,
say, 60 per cent or 80 per cent. There are, however, two difficulties in this
line of action. Valuation of the collateral presents a problem. Again this
policy will be successful only on the assumption that particular types of collateral are offered for particular investment purposes. To the extent this assump-

[35]Rousseas, Stephen W., ' Velocity Changes and the Effectiveness of Monetary Policy,'
1951–57, *Review of Economics and Statistics*, February, 1960, p. 27.

tion is incorrect, such a measure would not have much of a selective nature, but would have only a general restrictive effect.

Secondly, selective credit control measures can be made use of to prevent dissipation of savings into unproductive channels. In the Western countries, selective credit control has aimed particularly at bank advances against credit sales and purchases. In so far as credit purchases mean using future earnings for current consumption, they would add to inflationary pressure in boom periods and would result in dissipation of savings. Thus in Britain in 1947, the Bank of England made an appeal to banks to discourage loans for the purchase of real property and not to expand credit for financing instalment buying. A similar appeal was made when the Bank rate was raised to 7 per cent in 1957. Banks were required to see to it that loans to the private sector did not exceed the average of the previous twelve months. In the U.S.A. such measures have been adopted in respect of three fields of credit—credit for the purpose of acquiring or holding of marketable securities, credit for the purchase of new housing and also instalment credit for buying specified types of consumer goods. It is however, not possible to implement this policy really effectively, in so far as it is not easy for the banks to ascertain the extent to which loans granted to traders, businessmen or manufacturers are used for financing instalment buying. It is also possible that loans granted and taken for other approved purposes may be used for instalment buying. Credit can also be denied or discouraged to particular forms of investment which are undesirable from the national economy's point of view. Thus in Switzerland in 1951, the National Bank asked for the co-operation of the banking system in curtailing credits to the building trade with a view to restrain a housing boom. To the extent prevention of credit flow to particular channels makes available resources for investment in desired enterprises, these measures can be considered as an indirect means of promoting profitable investment and thus helping economic growth.

Thirdly, qualitative credit control measures can be employed to positively assist in the flow of savings into desired channels. In general, resources can be canalized into particular lines of investment through the lowering of margins or lengthening of the period of repayment or by giving other types of inducement. Thus inducement can be given to commercial banks for making available their resources for particular purposes by the central bank offering rediscounting facilities at rates lower than the Bank Rate, or by the central bank placing at the disposal of the commercial banks, loans, provided they are granted for certain specific purposes, or again by requiring the commercial banks to ensure that loans to agriculture or industry do not fall below a minimum level, etc. By setting up special credit agencies like Investment or Finance Corporations, the government can make available through such intermediaries funds collected from banks and the public for desired investments. Of late, such measures have been taken in some of the Latin American countries. It has however been reported that they have not been much successful " because the borrower can construe a productive purpose for a programme which really aims at maximizing his profits ".[36]

To the same category of selective control would belong discrimination in credit policy with a view to encourage exports. In Britain and Sweden, export trade and some industries are specified for encouragement and comprehensive measures are taken to discourage the flow of credit to investments other than those specified. Pressure on Sterling necessitated credit restriction in Britain in 1949 but exceptions were granted in favour of those industries or businesses producing goods for export to hard currency markets or goods which would substitute imports from hard currency areas. Belgium has adopted a selective rediscount policy in respect of financing foreign trade by raising the discount rates for bills financing imports in periods of adverse balance of payments and by lowering it in periods of export surplus. The novel method of requiring importers to deposit with the authorities in advance of their purchase of foreign exchange, a part of the local currency equivalent of their imports, prevails in Peru, Ecuador, Colombia, Finland, Israel and Indonesia.

Qualitative credit control measures have become popular in both developed and underdeveloped countries in recent years. Since 1951–52, variation in reserve requirements as a means of credit control has been largely used in New Zealand, Germany, Colombia, Brazil, Peru, France and Australia. The Voluntary Credit Restraint Programme was initiated in the U.S.A. in March, 1951. Sweden also relies considerably on this method. Advances by banks to particular trades which are a potential source of inflation have been restricted in Norway, Greece, Chile and Paraguay. In September, 1953, the National Federation of Bankers' Association in Japan decided to adopt voluntary measures to control bank lending for speculative and non-essential purposes. Similarly, the Commonwealth Bank of Australia recently urged the trading banks to be less generous in respect of new credit to capital expenditure schemes. The method of moral suasion involving the issue of directives and requests by the currency authorities to commercial banks is now recognized as an essential part of the monetary policy in U.K., Australia, Canada, New Zealand, the Netherlands, Norway and Sweden.

In India the Reserve Bank had recourse to the directive method for regulating the expansion of bank credit on two occasions during the war and later in 1946. It was however, only in 1949 that the necessary powers to exercise this sort of control were conferred on the Reserve Bank by the Banking Companies Act. Later by the Reserve Bank Amendment Act of 1956 the Bank acquired powers to exercise credit control by varying the reserve requirements of scheduled banks. Armed with these powers the Reserve Bank started to put into operation the methods of selective credit control. On May 17, 1956 a directive was issued to banks to refrain from excessive lending against paddy and rice. This restriction was removed at the end of 1956 but renewed on February 9, 1957.

[36] Adler, John H., ' Fiscal and Monetary Implications of Development Programmes,' *The American Economic Review, Papers and Proceedings*, May, 1952, pp. 584–600.

Since then, selective credit control measures have been increasingly made use of to control bank advances against various commodities like paddy, rice, wheat, other coarse grains, gram and pulses, and cotton textiles including yarn. To control advances to finance speculative purposes, the restriction was later extended to bank advances against certain securities. These measures however, have not in all cases achieved their purposes.

At any rate, it would appear that qualitative credit control measures have come to stay in most countries. But the record of selective control measures has not been very encouraging. Credit control in respect of stock market credit in the U.S.A. has been reported to be successful but in the same country restriction of consumer instalment credit has been attended with only limited success. In France selective control measures are not found to be much effective. The success of selective control measures in U.K. has been attributed to the high degree of concentration of banking in that country and the high sense of public duty among the British banks. In contrast to this, the criticism against qualitative measures of credit control is raised in Australia on the grounds that they involve undue interference by the central bank with the functioning of commercial banks and vexatious regulation. Besides it is stated that selective control tends to divert business to other financial institutions.[37] There is much substance in the contention that selective credit control techniques involve the central bank more deeply in the operations of the commercial banks and that banking mechanism will become more expensive and complex. It is difficult for the monetary authorities to discriminate correctly between speculative and non-speculative loans or between normal and abnormal uses of bank credit.[38] Complaints are sometimes made that small private companies find it difficult to raise additional finance. The point has also been raised that the central bank or monetary authority can make its influence felt only in respect of lending but the actual investment decision rests with the borrower which cannot be reached by the banking system. Furthermore, the claim in favour of selective control that it would help economic growth is questioned on the ground that preferential treatment by itself is not enough; there are various bottlenecks to increased production in underdeveloped countries the removal of which alone can ensure economic progress. Adoption of these monetary measures is likely to bring in a political element in matters of finance and business which would not be liked normally; nor would the controls and regulation which it involves be accepted without any misgivings or objection.

Despite these shortcomings, selective credit control measures may be expected to gain greater popularity in the present day underdeveloped countries. What a developing economy requires when it is faced with the threat of inflation is

[37]Navani, U. S., ' Selective Credit Controls Abroad, ' *Journal of the Indian Institute of Bankers*, January, 1959, pp. 31–47 and April 1959, pp. 107–18.

[38]Sen, S. N., ' Selective Control of Bank Lending, ' *Journal of the Indian Institute of Bankers*. January, 1960, p. 13.

some means to curb it with the least harm to growth and stability. To the extent that selective controls can aim at specific sources of inflation, they may be expected to produce better results with lesser chances of adverse consequences than the Bank Rate technique. The argument that the implementation of a qualitative credit control policy would endanger political freedom cannot carry much conviction in countries where governments play an important role in schemes of economic development and expansion. Planned development involves and necessitates the use of controls and restrictions. There is besides, great scope for the use of qualitative credit control measures to promote development along desired lines. With the growth of industrialization and the development of credit institutions and with improvement in administrative standards, it is likely that qualitative measures of credit control will be more widely used by the less developed countries not only for purposes of controlling inflation but also as a positive means to guide economic development.

Chapter IX

TAX POLICY

SINCE THE time of the early classical economists when the doctrine of laissez faire held complete sway, the attitude of economists to the role of the state in a nation's economic life has undergone considerable changes. Adam Smith argued that the state's activity should be confined to the maintenance of law and order and to the ensuring of political security and the development of means of transport. Taxation and public expenditure would therefore be kept at a minimum level. In the nineteenth century, this principle of innocuity in financial policy gave place to the ideal of distributive justice. Thus Bentham and the Utilitarians pointed out the need for shaping public expenditure and tax policy in a manner that would ensure an equitable distribution of wealth and income and maximize total satisfaction of the people. The onset of the Great Depression of the 1930s and the Keynesian diagnosis of the ills of a free enterprise economy directed attention to the importance of maintaining higher levels of investment in step with the rise in savings. With the realization of the fact that the state's expenditure and tax policy results in the mobilization of resources as well as in a change in the pattern of distribution and utilization of these resources, emphasis shifted to the functional aspect of public finance. According to the principle of functional finance fiscal policy would influence both savings and investment—the two crucial factors determining economic stability or instability. In so far as increase in public investment would offset the effects of a fall in private expenditure in depression, and a suitable tax policy helps in enlarging public savings, it would be possible for the state to match not only savings and investment, but also promote further expansion of the economy.[1]

As in the case of monetary policy, fiscal policy also has to aim at attaining in underdeveloped countries an objective different from that in advanced economies. In the latter, the private sector is responsible for making a large proportion of total investment and is capable of generating savings necessary to finance this investment. But in most of the poorer countries the private sector is not well developed and the interdependence between growth rate and the level of consumption is not close. The role of public finance has therefore to be a more positive one than in the developed countries and the additional expenditure of the government has to be of the ' real ' type than

[1]Gurley, John G., ' Fiscal Policy in a Growing Economy,' *Journal of Political Economy*, 1953, p 523.

of the ' transfer ' type.[2] Apart from this, is the fact that in many low income countries a good part of the available supply of goods is from imports and a raising of the level of spendings invariably leads to larger imports. As a result, a policy of stimulating effective demand which may be successful in a developed country benefits only the foreign producer if adopted in a backward economy. Hence the objective of fiscal policy is not to raise the level of consumption but to increase the nation's savings and to transform these savings into productive investment. Given the availability of large savings, a rich country can afford to adjust the level of taxation and the scale of borrowing with reference to financial needs. But in a poorer country the position is reversed. The sequence here is from higher taxation to increased state expenditure rather than in the opposite direction.[3]

As a means to regulate economic activity as well as to stimulate or generate it, fiscal policy is superior to monetary policy. The effect of monetary policy is indirect in so far as it attempts to influence the spending and saving decisions of individuals and business through regulating the flow of credit and money supply. But fiscal policy affects economic activity directly. By transferring resources to the government in the form of taxes and loans, the scope for spending by the parties who pay the taxes and contribute to the loans is reduced, while through public expenditure the level of spendings in the economy can be regulated. Fiscal policy as compared with monetary policy is of greater significance to underdeveloped countries since in these countries the monetary mechanism is not well developed and the tools of monetary policy operate haltingly, whereas the fiscal system even when it is not so refined as in advanced countries can yet be made to function on the whole satisfactorily.

The increasing functions of modern governments have naturally resulted in a sharp rise in the level of public expenditure in both developed and underdeveloped countries. However, the disparity between the per capita public expenditure in these countries continues to be wide. In the countries of Asia and the Far East, it varies between $ 10 and $ 70 per head while in Sweden, the U.K. and the U.S.A. it ranges from $ 300 to $ 400. This difference is mostly due to the corresponding variation in the per capita incomes of these two groups of countries. Thus as a percentage of the national product, per capita public expenditure varies between 10 per cent and 30 per cent in all countries irrespective of their standards of economic achievement. The close correlation between per capita public outlays and the size of the national product even among the less developed countries is illustrated by figures relating to some countries of the ECAFE region. Expenditure per head is the highest in Japan ($ 70) which in point of economic development is closer to some of the advanced economies of today than to the backward ones, while in Burma it is as low as $ 14 per head.

[2]Van Philips, Paul A. M., *Public Finance and Less Developed Economy with Special Reference to Latin America*, Martinus Nijhoff, 1957, p. 84.
[3]*Taxes and Fiscal Policy in Underdeveloped Countries*, U.N., 1954, p. 7.

However, the rate of increase in public expenditure in recent years in the low income countries is as marked as in the advanced economies. The disparity in the extent to which public expenditure has increased as between various countries reflects broadly the difference in the powers and responsibilities which governments have assumed. In the Philippines public expenditure increased by 50 per cent between 1950 and 1958 but it went up by six times in China. The remarkable increase in China as compared with the slow and moderate growth of public expenditure in the Philippines was due to nationali-zation in the former which not only swelled up public expenditure abnormally, but also accounted for a large increase in the states' revenue collections which went up by six and a half times. In the same period, government expenditure in Burma as a percentage of the Gross National Product increased from 15 per cent to 28 per cent; in Ceylon from 19 per cent to 26 per cent; in Mainland China from 16 per cent to 33 per cent. Corresponding figures for India are 9 per cent and 16 per cent, Pakistan 10 per cent and 15 per cent, and Thailand 11 per cent and 14 per cent. In Japan, the rise was small—from 24 per cent to 26 per cent—while in the Philippines the percentage has alternated between 11 per cent and 12 per cent over these years.

To some extent this rise in public outlays was due to the rise in prices and cost of living. But that these factors played only an insignificant part is indicated in the figures in Table 29. In fact among the East Asian countries only in one, namely, Indonesia, did the rise in prices come anywhere near the rise in public expenditure. In most others, prices and cost of living increased by about 20 per cent or less while expenditure of the government more than doubled.

Table 30

INDICES OF GROWTH OF GOVERNMENT EXPENDITURE, GOVERNMENT
REVENUE AND PRICES 1958 (1950=100)

Country	Government Expenditure at Current Prices	Government Revenue at Current Prices	Wholesale Prices	Cost of Living
Burma	278	189	108	104
Ceylon	162	141	...	104
China (Mainland)	602	642	118	...
India	237	168	106	115
Indonesia	332	225	250	290
Japan	287	253	140	140
Philippines	150	167	94	95
Pakistan	233	147	...	129
Thailand	261	261	136	170

SOURCE : *Economic Survey of Asia and The Far East*, 1960, U.N., p. 67.

The major factors responsible for the phenomenal rise in public outlays in underdeveloped countries in the last few years are, increase in public investment expenditure, mounting defence expenditure and rise in the cost of public administration. The forces at work in pushing up the investment expenditure of the governments have been explained at some length in a later chapter.[4] Defence outlay went up sharply as a result of the acquisition of political freedom and the taking over of the full defence responsibility by the national governments from the metropolitan countries. Independent political status also involved growing outlays on representations abroad—embassies, legations and consulates—and on international conferences. From the point of view of economic development, much of this expenditure is of little value. But the national governments feel it necessary to bear this as a mark of free status and as a means to improve their position in the international comity of nations. In many of the East Asian countries defence expenditure has been mounting up fast due to political uncertainties and the general feeling of insecurity. As a proportion of Gross National Product, defence expenditure in Burma increased from 3·8 per cent in 1950 to 7·7 per cent in 1958, in Ceylon from 0·2 per cent to 1·1 per cent, in India from 1·9 per cent to 2·1 per cent and in Thailand from 1·4 per cent to 2·9 per cent. On the other hand, in Mainland China and Japan, there is a decline in this proportion. As for spendings on representations abroad, the increase between 1950 and 1958 was by about 150 per cent in Burma, Indonesia and Pakistan, and 234 per cent in Ceylon, while in India it doubled.

The expanding role of the governments in national economic development and the increase in their functions explain the rapid growth of expenditure on public administration. Among the ECAFE countries, expenditure on general services of the government excluding national defence, ranges from 5 per cent of the total public expenditure in Japan (1957) to 28 per cent in the case of the Federation of Malaya. In Ceylon it is 12 per cent; in India 14 per cent and in Pakistan 17 per cent. There is no denying the fact that the expansion of outlay under this head is inevitable in a growing economy as the trend in public expenditure in India would illustrate. Of the four heads of revenue expenditure—civil administration, defence services, direct demands on revenue and miscellaneous—the rise under the first two items is particularly significant. Under civil administration, the increase has been due mostly to scientific, educational and medical departments. Entry of government in the industrial field accounts for the significant enlargement of public allocations to Industry and Supply. Under civil administration, the sharp shooting up of expenditure has been caused by increase in work and the creation of new departments like statistics, information, social welfare projects, etc. Along with increase and expansion of departments, the number of people in administrative services has also increased in accordance with Parkinson's law and the size of the wage bill in public services has gone up considerably. Yet there are reasons to feel

[4]Chapter XVI.

that the quality and standard of efficiency of public service have failed to improve in proportion to the cost of such service. There is much truth in the view " that the unwieldy government apparatus in underdeveloped economies covers a large measure of disguised unemployment and functions inefficiently and sluggishly ".[5] In view of inadequate financial resources in low income countries it is imperative that administrative efficiency is toned up so that more resources can be made available for development expenditure.

In order to meet this increasing demand on the government, the financial resources at the disposal of the state have to be considerably augmented. The ultimate source of government expenditure is national savings, that is,. the difference between aggregate production and aggregate consumption. But given the value of potential savings in an economy, the actual amount which becomes available to the state depends on the efficiency with which the resources are mobilized. The very fact that savings in underdeveloped countries are inadequate in relation to the needs, makes the task of mobilization and proper utilization particularly important. The normal means adopted by modern governments in this respect are three: taxation, internal borrowing and deficit financing. The former two draw upon current and past savings while inflationary methods of financing make use of anticipated savings. Internal borrowing and deficit financing have only limited scope in most of the low income countries. In developed countries the size of national debt is about 100 to 200 per cent of national income, while in the poorer countries it is only 20 to 30 per cent. The experience of the Government of India in recent years in the matter of mobilizing voluntary savings of the community through small savings schemes and the flotation of loans has not been very encouraging. It may be said that the contribution of voluntary savings to the national investment effort can at best have only a marginal effect. Deficit financing is even less reliable than internal borrowing as a means to augment the state's resources. Although this method of financing economic development has been made use of in recent years in many underdeveloped countries, the dangers and uncertainties involved in this method are increasingly becoming obvious, and countries like India which once enthusiastically welcomed it have now adopted a more cautious attitude towards it.

Taxation thus remains the most important means available to the state for collecting the nation's resources. Not only does it contribute to by far the major part of the government's financial resources but it has also one decided advantage in so far as, its yield can be more accurately estimated and its economic effects are better known and can be better foreseen than in the case of voluntary or forced savings. In fact the extent to which underdeveloped economies can finance their schemes of investment with minimum danger to economic stability depends upon the manner in which they make use of the tax machinery for mobilizing domestic savings.

[5] Van Philips, Paul A. M., *Public Finance and Less Developed Economy with Special Reference to Latin America,* Martinus Nijhoff, 1957, p. 95.

THE OBJECTIVES OF TAXATION IN UNDERDEVELOPED COUNTRIES

In view of the great importance of taxation as a means to mobilize domestic savings in underdeveloped countries, the primary objective of taxation should be to transfer as large a volume of resources as possible from the community to the state with minimum adverse effect on private incentives for investment and production. It is a generally accepted view among experts who have studied the problem of financing of economic development in the less developed countries, that the tax effort in these countries has not been adequate enough to mobilize fully the available resources. There is considerable scope for increasing tax revenue by deepening and broadening the tax system, by reorganizing the structure and composition of taxation and also by toning up the tax machinery. Apart from this major objective, there are other purposes for which taxation can be employed in developing economies. Firstly, taxation can be made to help private capital formation both directly and indirectly. The tax policy of the state should not merely have a neutral aspect in not hampering private productive effort but should also be assigned a positive role in providing incentives for private enterprise. Secondly, taxation can be made use of as a means to control fluctuations which in underdeveloped countries normally develop from the export sectors of the economy, and also as an agency to ensure stability in economic growth. It may also be added that although the principle of equity or social justice cannot be given as much importance in underdeveloped countries as in economically advanced countries, yet to the extent equity in the distribution of the burden among the different classes of income earners helps in calling forth greater productive effort, it should be accepted as an objective of tax policy if circumstances permit its adoption.

We may now examine how far these objectives of taxation have been attained in contemporary underdeveloped countries. A brief review of the tax system in these countries would bring to light the problems and difficulties which they face in this connection and suggest scope for improvements so that taxation can be made to play a significant role in economic development.

Taxation as a Means to Mobilize Domestic Resources to the Fullest Extent Possible

Recent economic history provides examples of some countries which have successfully relied upon taxation as the major means of financing economic development. Heavy taxation of land in the 1870s brought in about $\frac{4}{5}$ of the total government revenue in Japan. These resources were utilized for the building up of the economy, while industry was lightly assessed. Taxation in Latvia in the 1920s resulted in large accumulation of state funds in the central bank from which these were made available for private industrial expansion. Also in Poland and Turkey in the period between the First and

Second World Wars, taxation was successfully made use of as a means to finance economic development. But the most notable example of a country making use of taxation for economic development is Soviet Russia since 1918 under the Five-Year Plans.

But the experience of most of the underdeveloped countries of today in this respect is different. A reference to Table 30 would show that in most of the low income countries of East Asia the growth of public outlay has outpaced the increase in public revenue. This has been due as much to the spectacular increase in the developmental and non-developmental expenditure of the governments as to the failure of the tax system to absorb a good proportion of the increase in incomes of the community. Of the nine countries listed in the table, only in three, China, the Philippines and Thailand has increase in public revenues exceeded or equalled the increase in public expenditure. In all the others there is considerable disparity between the growth of outlays and receipts; in India and Pakistan, increase in government revenues between 1950 and 1958 has been only 70 per cent and 60 per cent respectively of the increase in government expenditure.

Normally as economic growth takes place, tax revenue tends to become a growing proportion of the national income. The disparity in the ratio of tax revenue to national income as between advanced and underdeveloped economies corresponds to the difference in their incomes and wealth. In many of the ECAFE countries the ratio of the central governments' tax revenue to Gross National Product is below 10 per cent while in countries like France, Germany, the U.K., the Netherlands, Norway and Australia it ranges from 25 per cent to 40 per cent. Even among the less developed countries of Asia, there is much variation in the proportion of national product collected by means of taxation. Mainland China raises about one-third and Japan about one-fifth, Burma and Ceylon about one-sixth to one-fourth, while the other countries are able to collect about one-tenth to one-eighth of the national product. It is also worth observing that over the last few years, this ratio has not shown any improvement except in the case of China, Malaya and Ceylon. In India the proportion of total government tax revenue to national income increased from about 7·5 per cent at the beginning of the Second Five-Year Plan to about 8·9 per cent at its end. The Indian Taxation Enquiry Commission (1953–54) points out that in the Second World War and post-war years, national income in money terms increased by about four-fold and the per capita tax contribution also went up just in proportion. In other words there has been very little addition to the national tax effort in average terms over the last two to three decades.[6] While in recent years India has made some good progress in industrialization, her fiscal system still remains quite underdeveloped to the extent that the country ranks among the lowest in terms of the percentage of revenue collected to its national income.[7]

[6]*Report of the Indian Taxation Enquiry Commission*, 1953–54, Government of India, Vol. 1, p. 21.
[7]*Economic Survey of Asia and the Far East*, U.N., 1960, p. 85.

The failure of most of the underdeveloped economies to mobilize properly their resources through taxation is largely due to the defects in the tax system and the inefficient manner in which the taxes are administered and collected. This becomes clear on a closer view of the operation of particular taxes in these countries.

Direct Taxes in Underdeveloped Countries

Developed countries derive the major part of their tax revenue from direct taxes, particularly the income tax. Such taxes have the advantage of flexibility ; their yield rises and falls automatically with national income. In addition, they have the merit of greater certainty in respect of their yield as well as their economic effects. Underdeveloped countries rely more on indirect taxes, especially customs duties and excise. In some of the British dependent territories which have now attained political freedom, the income tax has been in existence for quite a long time, while many others have adopted it in recent years.[8] But the administration of these direct taxes—income tax and land tax—in the underdeveloped countries has not been satisfactory and the revenue from these sources forms a much smaller proportion of the total public revenue and the total national product than in the developed economies. In the U.S.A. direct taxes account for about 78 per cent of the federal government revenue; in the U.K. it is 57 per cent and in Japan 50 per cent. In India, the two direct taxes, land tax and income tax together contributed to about 28 per cent of total government revenue in 1950 and 25 per cent in 1958. The proportion in the other less developed countries ranges between one-fifth and one-fourth of total revenue.

The fundamental reason for the very low yield of income tax in the less developed economies is the low level of national incomes. Apart from this, economic and social backwardness presents many difficulties in the way of proper assessment and collection of taxes. Among these may be mentioned the low standard of literacy, the absence of the habit of keeping accounts of personal incomes and expenditures, the existence of a large non-monetized sector and the lack of a civic sense on the part of the people. The average income per head in underdeveloped countries is so low that the income tax covers only a very small proportion of the population, whereas in countries which are economically better off like Japan, the coverage is much wider so that in the latter countries the income tax may be considered as a mass taxation. Thus in India the income tax covers only less than 600,000 individuals, 55,000 Hindu undivided families and about 50,000 business partnerships and companies. Assuming that on an average, five persons are effectively covered per

[8]Among countries of Asia and the Far East, the income tax exists in a well-developed form in Pakistan, India, Ceylon and Burma. The income tax was introduced in India in 1860 when it comprised the present territories of Burma and Pakistan. The Philippines came to have an Income Tax in 1913. Malaya, Brunei and Hongkong, Southern Korea, North Borneo, Sarawak, Singapore and Thailand adopted it after the Second World War. Nepal introduced it only in 1959-60.

assessee, the tax is effective in relation to less than one per cent of the total population. Taxable potential incomes of the country (i.e. national income plus taxable transfer incomes which are not included in national income) would amount to Rs. 130–140 billion. The income assessed to income tax, including those of partnerships and companies comes to only about Rs. 10 billion and tax collected to only Rs. 2·2 billion. This would mean that 99 per cent of the population and about 93 per cent of the potentially taxable income in the country remain outside the purview of the income tax system[9].

One important reason for this low coverage is the fact that the minimum exemption limit is high in relation to the average per capita income. In several of the underdeveloped countries the minimum exemption limits are higher than in countries which are much richer. A man with wife and three children has to earn over 19 times the national per capita income before he pays any tax on income in Burma, 15·6 times in the Philippines, 12·5 times in Ceylon, 11·5 times in India and nearly 10 times in the Federation of Malaya. Among Asian countries only in Japan is the multiple low enough (3·4 times) comparable with 1·3 in U.S.A., 1·9 in U.K. and Canada, 2·1 in France and 0·7 in Australia.[10] The basic exemption limit for a single person without dependants in Burma, Ceylon, India, Pakistan and the Philippines in 1954 was substantially higher than that of $ 336 in the U.K. and even that of $ 600 in the U.S.A.[11] Not only is the exemption limit high in many underdeveloped countries, but the income tax rates over a wide range of lower and middle brackets of the relatively high incomes are very low. Thus while a family of five with an income twenty times the per capita national income pays 35 per cent of the income by way of income taxes in the U.S.A., 43 per cent in Australia and 44 per cent in the U.K., its counterpart in Ceylon and India pays only 2 per cent and in Philippines only 1 per cent. This disparity is maintained at higher levels of income also. Thus if the family's income is hundred times the per capita national income, the proportion paid by way of income tax is as high as 78 per cent and 69 per cent of the income in U.K. and U.S.A., 59 per cent in Australia and 55 per cent in Canada compared with 23 per cent in Ceylon, 21 per cent in India and 11 per cent in Burma. In justification of the high exemption limit and relatively low rates in underdeveloped countries it is mentioned that the lowering of the exemption limit would add considerably to the difficulty and cost of administration and that it would be inequitable in so far as the lower income groups are subjected to high indirect taxation. But in view of the decided advantages of an income tax in a growing economy and its usefulness as a reliable means to mop up a portion of the increasing incomes of the community resulting from economic advancement, it is necessary to consider the feasibility of making the income tax more broad-based and comprehensive.

[9]*Economic Survey of Asia and the Far East*, U.N., 1960, p. 94.
[10]*ibid.*, p. 94, Table 36.
[11]*Economic Bulletin for Asia and the Far East*, U.N., November, 1956, p. 48, f.n.

Laxity of administration is another factor responsible for low yield. While the tax payers complain about defects in the assessment procedure such as delay in the grant of refunds and in completing assessments and about allowance of insufficient time for compliance with notices, the tax administration is worried over large-scale tax evasion and consequent loss to the treasury. This is as much true of less developed countries as of advanced ones. In making a strong plea for reform of income taxation and the reduction of tax rates, the Research and Policy Committee of the Committee for Economic Development in the U.S.A. point out that the tax " returns have become so complicated that the differences between natural errors and calculated errors become increasingly difficult to distinguish. If enough tax payers feel that errors are rarely detected, or that misrepresentation can be passed off as error, cheating could become the rule rather than the exception. "[12] From the economic point of view there is a waste involved in the effort and time devoted by tax payers and their counsellors to minimize taxes. Tax morality thus gets impaired and there is a real risk that the income tax will be discredited.[13] In his recent report on Indian Tax Reform Professor Kaldor draws attention to the widespread tax avoidance, and tax evasion in India particularly since the last war, due to fraudulent concealment of income by means of false entries in the account books. No correct estimate of the extent of such concealment is possible, but according to Kaldor " Conversations with individual businessmen, accountants and revenue officials, reveal guesses which range from 10–20 per cent of assessed income at the minimum to 200–300 per cent at the maximum ".[14] The magnitude of the problem of concealment of income and tax evasion is indicated in the findings relating to another underdeveloped

[12]*Taxation for Growth*, Committee for Economic Development, U.S.A., 1957, p. 11.

[13]*Tax Reduction and Tax Reform—When and How?* Committee for Economic Development, U.S.A., 1957, p. 9.

[14]Kaldor, Nicholas, *Indian Tax Reform—Report of a Survey*, Government of India, 1956, p. 103. The loss to the state arises out of tax avoidance through legal loopholes and tax evasion through administrative deficiencies. The latter takes the form of hiding or understatement of assessable income. The legal loopholes lie in the definition of tax base, namely, ' taxable income '. Other loopholes include the escape from personal income tax liability through undistributed profits in closely held companies or trusts. A third loophole is the system of perquisites such as office provided cars, living accommodation, travel or expense accounts in general which are charged off to business expenses. As regards the magnitude of tax evasion in India, according to Kaldor (*Indian Tax Reform*, pp. 103–06) the tax annually evaded was on income totalling Rs. 5·8 billion or about three quarters of the income assessed to tax in 1955–56 and the magnitude of the revenue lost through evasion was of the order of Rs. 2·3 billion as compared with Rs. 1·8 billion collected from all classes of assessees in that year. The Central Board of Revenue of India estimated the income evading tax assessment at about 40 per cent of the first estimate. Even the lower estimate suggests that income evading income tax was about 30 per cent of the income assessed to tax and that revenue lost might be well over one half. In Pakistan also, the voluntary disclosures in response to the two-month amnesty granted in November 1959 indicated that the tax evaded each year exceeded half of the income tax collected. *Economic Survey of Asia and the Far East*, U.N., 1960, p. 96 and f.n.

20

country—the Philippines. According to the Bell Report of October 1950, 9,350 individuals with taxable incomes filed their returns but the central bank estimated the number of individuals within that income range at 88,000. The amount of taxable income according to official records was p29·2 million but the central bank's estimates of assessable income was p232·3 million. If the central bank estimates are correct, only 11 per cent of the people with taxable income filed their returns and only 13 per cent of the income was reported.[15]

Measures to increase the yield of income tax have taken the form of adjustment in the structure of tax rates and supplementing income taxation by allied direct taxes. In India the slab system of graduation was introduced in 1939 in the place of the step system. The present minimum exemption limit is Rs. 4,000;[15a] and the basic income tax rates range from 3 to 18 per cent. In addition, a super tax is levied on incomes above Rs. 20,000 the rates of which rise from 5 per cent to 45 per cent. Over and above these, a surcharge for purposes of the Union Government is added to both income tax and super tax. Also businesses are subjected to corporation tax. As a result, the burden on the higher income ranges is made quite heavy. The rates in India on the middle income brackets among incomes assessable to income tax are lower than in most of the developed economies, but the rates on the top brackets are quite so high as in the advanced countries. The maximum rate practically comes to 92 per cent and this, it has been represented by business classes, is ruinous to private incentive and hampers investment. The plea is therefore made for fixing a maximum limit to the rates at 80 per cent or less as it has been done in some Western countries like West Germany, Netherlands, Sweden and Norway.[16] Besides in recent years, some new direct taxes such as the estate duty have been introduced supplementing the income tax. In 1956 Prof. Kaldor recommended the reform of income taxation in India by fixing a maximum limit to income tax rates at 45 per cent and by broadening the tax base through the introduction of an annual tax on capital; the taxation of capital gains; a general gift tax and a personal expenditure tax (the latter in partial substitution of the super tax on income). Part of these recommendations was adopted by the Government of India. In the budget of 1957–58 a wealth tax and expenditure tax were introduced and subsequently, the gift-tax also was adopted. However, the existing rates of income tax were left untouched. The introduction of these new taxes has not helped in any real broad-basing of the Indian tax system except that the scope and burden of administration have been increased. The revenue from these additional levies has also been quite meagre. The taxes on wealth yield about Rs. 100 million while their cost of collection comes to about 2·5 per cent of the revenue. The

[15] 'The University of the East,' *Economic Research Journal*, March, 1956, p. 186, quoted in *Economic Bulletin for Asia and the Far East*, U.N., November, 1956, p. 48, f.n.
[15a] i.e., in respect of a married individual and two children.
[16] *The Indian Finance*, Annual Number and Year Book, Calcutta, 1959, p. 84

expenditure tax and gift tax yield about Rs. 9 million each. Together the revenue from these three taxes accounts for only 2 per cent of the tax revenue of the Union Government. The revenue from income tax other than corporation tax increased from Rs. 1,330 million in 1950–51 to Rs. 1,720 million in 1958–59, but has declined since then to about Rs. 1,674 million in 1960–61. The corporation tax however, shows a steady rise in yield from Rs. 405 million in 1950–51 to about Rs. 1,110 million in 1960–61.

The major direct tax in many underdeveloped countries is the traditional land tax. But the method of taxing farm income shows considerable variation among these countries. In China (Mainland) and in the Republic of Korea, land tax is a taxation in kind on gross produce and was responsible for about 24 per cent of the total tax receipts of the government in 1953–54. In Iraq and Syria, the land tax takes the form of a tax on marketed produce. It yielded about 20 and 15 per cent respectively of the tax revenue in 1951–52. In some countries of the Middle East and Far East it is a tax on annual rental value (Egypt, India, Burma, Pakistan, Cuba, Iran). In the Latin American countries, it is mostly a charge on capital value (Paraguay, Panama, Costa Rica, Mexico, Chile, Nicaragua, El Salvador, Guatemala, Bolivia, Brazil). In the East Asian countries, in spite of the fact that land tax has existed for centuries, its contribution to total revenue has been not only meagre, but has shown a tendency to decline in recent years. In Nepal, South Korea and Afghanistan, the contribution of land tax is quite substantial but there is a pronounced fall in their yield in the last ten years or so. Thus in Afghanistan, land tax collections formed 12 per cent of total tax revenue in 1951 but came down to 3 per cent in 1956. In South Korea it declined from 28 per cent to 10 per cent between 1949 and 1958 while in Nepal the fall was from 42 per cent in 1952 to 24 per cent in 1958. In India, land revenue formed about 20 per cent of total tax revenue in 1939; it is now about 7 per cent. Revenue from land tax depends to a large extent on the proportion of national income originating in the agricultural sector. In some of the Latin American countries, this proportion is relatively low, lower than in the South-East Asian countries. In Chile it is 18 per cent of the total income and in Mexico 19 per cent, and the proportion of land revenue to total tax revenue forms less than 5 per cent in these countries, while in most of the South-East Asian countries it ranges from 5 per cent to 10 per cent.

As an economy develops, national income and per capita income increase and the tax-paying capacity of the people rises. The very fact that the agricultural sector is very extensive and contributes to the major part of national income is justification for increasing the scope of land taxation in underdeveloped countries. Agricultural development is one of the main planks in the programmes of planned economic progress and a good share of the state's investment expenditure is devoted to the agricultural sector. Apart from this, there are certain special reasons why resources of this sector are to be fully exploited in a growing economy. The existence of a large non-monetized sector and low standard of literacy of the people make it difficult for the state to collect an adequate share of the income from the agricultural sector by means of a personal income tax or through large-scale use of indirect taxes. Since the close of the Second World War, inflationary tendencies in many countries, increase in civil administration charges and investment outlays of the state, combined with the revenue inflexibility of land taxes, have focussed attention on the need for making land tax more flexible and a more fertile source of income for the state. Also, the measures at land reform, and tenancy legislation have facilitated and suggested measures to improve the land tax system.

However, land tax as such, cannot be made to yield larger revenue to the state to the extent that other taxes such as the income tax or sales tax can be made to yield. The inelasticity of the land tax is of an organic nature in the sense that " it comes from within the tax as a result of the application of a stable tax rate to a tax base that is not kept current ".[17] Apart from its non-progressive nature, the land tax in its traditional form has other defects especially from the point of view of equity. It fails to take account of the real tax-paying capacity of the people, does not provide for minimum exemptions and family allowances and makes no discrimination between earned incomes and unearned incomes. Any measures at reforming the land tax with a view to introduce an element of real flexibility into it should realize its structural deficiencies. In other words, no attempt at increasing the yield from land tax would be successful so long as it is maintained in its present form. What is required is a thorough overhauling of the system of land taxation so as to bring it into conformity with a progressive form of direct taxation such as the personal income tax.

It is here relevant to point out the disparity in the method of land taxation in a developed and an underdeveloped country. In the majority of advanced economies, taxation of agriculture has taken a definite form; it comprises a general income tax covering income derived from agriculture and a property tax on farm real estate. The latter is based either on the capital value of the property or on the annual value or rent. This form of land taxation makes it a flexible source of revenue. Thus in the states of the U.S.A., the rates on capital value are adjusted with reference to budget requirements. Obviously it requires an efficient administrative machinery which the less developed economies lack. Even among the low income countries where unconventional methods of taxing agricultural income have been adopted, the yield has been more satisfactory than where the traditional methods are in force. In countries like India and Pakistan the tax is on annual rental value and based on a cadastral survey made once in fifteen or twenty years. Such surveys involve considerable expense to the Treasury and in the period which intervenes between assessments, the yield of the land tax ceases to have any relation

[17]Wald, Haskell P., *Taxation of Agricultural Land in Underdeveloped Economies*, Harvard, 1959, p. 203.

to the actual returns from land. Not only is the system rigid but it is presumptive and notional and fails to take into account the paying capacity of the assessee. The system thus becomes both inflexible and inequitable. The introduction of the Agricultural Income Tax in the Indian States and the imposition of surcharges on land tax and the betterment levy have to some extent introduced an element of flexibility and progressiveness, but the existing arrangement still leaves much to be desired. The cost of administration of the tax is high while the yield per unit of cost is small.

Unconventional methods of taxing land and farm output have been adopted by some of the underdeveloped countries. Ceylon, Malaya and Thailand, instead of levying land taxes, levy export duties on their principal export crops. The Philippines has a general tax on real property. In China and in the Republic of Korea, collection is made in kind which makes the tax yield vary with returns from land. In Burma, the profits of the State Agricultural Marketing Board constitute a source of revenue, yielding about $\frac{2}{3}$ of the government revenue from all sources. In India the Taxation Enquiry Commission suggested a revision of land revenue assessment after standardization once every ten years with reference to changes in the price level. Also new taxes such as a property tax, net worth tax, capital gains tax and a tax on the value of land at sale have been suggested. While most of these new impositions may help in transferring a larger amount of agricultural incomes to the state, their feasibility in the economically backward countries is limited, because of administrative difficulties. Reform in this direction in some countries has not been successful. The net worth tax was adopted in Japan following the recommendations of the Shoup Mission in 1950 but was found to work unsatisfactorily and given up subsequently in 1953. Iran adopted in 1933, a 3 per cent tax on the value of agricultural commodities entering the market for sale in the place of the earlier land tax of the central government. This however, was abolished ten years later, and agriculture income was included in the general income tax; in 1946, the government experiencing difficulty in the operation of this form of agricultural taxation, re-established the old land tax system.

By retaining the traditional structure of land taxation and by adding to it supplementary levies, the tax system is only made more complicated and costly without any commensurate benefit in the form of additional revenue. Nor do such *ad hoc* measures at improvement have any great effect in making the tax less regressive or more equitable. Land tax if it is to meet the requirements of a growing economy and help in promoting economic development, should be a means of mass taxation; it should be productive from the revenue point of view and be sufficiently progressive so as to mobilize a higher share from the wealthier recipients of agricultural income; it should cover unearned increments or windfall incomes arising from rise in prices and in land values and should also provide scope for special assessments for regulatory purposes. Reform must therefore lie in the direction of integrating the various present levies bearing on land and agricultural income into one comprehensive but simpler system. When thus improved, land tax would become more personalized and therefore more equitable and progressive. This can be done if the scope of the general income tax is extended to comprise income from land also. But it may not be practicable in most of the underdeveloped countries where income tax itself is a recent innovation, and is not functioning quite satisfactorily. Short of this ideal arrangement, some device should have to be found out in which the principles of income taxation could be extended to the taxation of land and agricultural income as well.

Indirect Taxes

Indirect taxation continues to be the mainstay of public revenue in a large number of underdeveloped countries. While in the developed countries indirect taxes are designed as a means to bring the general population within the tax net, and to serve as a balancing factor against the direct taxation of the upper income groups, they are meant in the underdeveloped countries primarily to be for revenue or protective purposes or for helping to preserve foreign exchange. Such taxes are also made progressive by varying the rates according to the nature and value of the commodities taxed, and by differentiating between articles of popular consumption and luxuries. They are best suited to underdeveloped countries because their collection is easy, and their cost of administration is comparatively low; they reduce consumption and promote savings, their disincentive effect on private investment is limited and they bring in large revenue to the Treasury. Egypt in the early 1950s derived about 50 per cent of its public revenue from customs duties particularly import duties of a selective type on luxuries. In India, direct taxation reached high levels by 1948 when income taxes formed about 60 per cent of the total revenue but since then, there has been a shift towards indirect taxation. Figures in Table 31 illustrate the relative position of indirect taxation in the budgets of some of the underdeveloped countries of Asia.

Indirect taxes can be classified into two—taxes on foreign trade and taxes on internal transactions. Of the former, import duties are of greater importance in most of the underdeveloped countries except in those which are large exporters of primary products and industrial materials. In several countries import duties were at one time primarily intended for protecting domestic industries, but in recent years these duties have been increasingly made use of to reduce conspicuous consumption, to save foreign exchange and to encourage domestic industrialization by adopting a discriminatory rates policy according to which higher rates are charged on articles of consumption especially of the luxury variety, and machines and capital goods are either allowed tax free or lightly taxed. In the taxation of imports *ad valorem* duties are preferable to specific duties because the former are more flexible and productive of larger revenue. Besides, discrimination between different types of imports is easier under *ad valorem* than under specific rates. Taxes on manufactured imports help

Table 31

GOVERNMENT REVENUE FROM INDIRECT TAXES IN SOME ECAFE COUNTRIES

Country	Year	Per cent of Total Revenue		
		Import Taxes	Export Taxes	Excise and Sales Tax
Burma	1950	22	3	11
	1958	28	3	18
Ceylon	1950	31	27	7
	1958	25	28	8
Federation of Malaya	1950	33	34	3
	1958	36	17	3
India	1950	16	10	27
	1958	8	2	40
Indonesia	1950	14	13	12
	1958	8	1	23
Philippines	1950	16	...	51
	1958	26	...	33
Thailand	1950	27	8	13
	1958	29	5	21

SOURCE : *Economic Survey of Asia and the Far East*, 1960, U.N., p. 87.

domestic industrialization in a direct as well as indirect manner. If high taxes are levied on import goods which can be substituted by domestic production, it would directly promote industrialization. If domestic substitutes cannot be produced, demand for other commodities may rise in the place of import goods which are stopped; and if demand for domestic production does not rise, larger savings become available in the economy.[18]

Among the underdeveloped countries, those which are exporters of primary goods derive a substantial portion of their revenue by taxation of export goods, for example Ceylon, Malaya, Thailand. The extent to which a large revenue can be obtained by taxing exports depends on the conditions of production in the home country and the nature of demand in the foreign markets. Export taxes are not only easy of administration but they can be used as means to promote greater economic stability. This is done by raising or lowering the rates with reference to price and demand conditions and by building up cash reserves from the buoyant government revenues in times of boom. Such a policy was adopted recently in respect of rubber and tea in Ceylon. Similar adjustments have been made by India in the export of jute and by Thailand in the case of rice. Apart from regular export duties, some countries are deriving revenue from export goods in an indirect way. Thus in Burma, the

[18]Van Philips, Paul A. M., *Public Finance and Less Developed Economy with Special Reference to Latin America*, Martinus Nijhoff, 1957, p. 134.

State Agricultural Marketing Board fixes the domestic price of rice at a low and stable level but sells it abroad at a higher world price and makes profits. Thailand in 1947–55 earned a large revenue by selling to importers foreign exchange at rates higher than the unfavourable exchange rates applied to exports of rubber and tin and out of the profits acquired in this manner built up a Stabilization Fund. It has however, to be added that taxation of foreign trade, while productive of large revenue normally, has one serious defect, namely, its uncertainty. From the point of view of economic development this is an important matter because lack of stability in the yield from an important source of revenue affects decisions relating to public investment expenditure.

Table 31 shows that in most of the countries listed in it, the proportion of revenue from export duties has significantly fallen in the last decade. In Burma and Ceylon it has remained constant but in Malaya, India, Indonesia and Thailand the decline is marked. In India between 1950 and 1958 both import revenue and export revenue declined—the first from 16 per cent to 8 per cent of total revenue and the second from 10 per cent to 2 per cent. The decline in export revenue is due primarily to the change in external demand conditions. Since the Korean boom, a buyer's market has developed for the Indian export commodities, and against this trend it has been found necessary to reduce export duties steadily or abolish them altogether with a view to push up or even maintain the level of exports. As may be expected, import duties have declined with the progress of industrialization in so far as in the interests of economic development the importing of most of the consumption goods has been considerably restricted or stopped, while in the case of imports of capital goods, plants and machinery, duties have been negligible or nil. It is therefore not possible to rely much on taxation of foreign trade as a means to secure a large volume of revenue for the state. Taxes on foreign trade would thus serve mostly as a means to restore the balance of payments position of the country.

Of taxes on internal transactions, excise duties and sales taxes are the most productive of revenue. These taxes are a means of reaching the masses of consumers who are exempted from payment of income tax. They reduce consumers' spending and widen the margin of savings in the economy. A sales tax falls only on spending and not on income which may well include savings. The cost of collection is comparatively low, it can be graduated by differentiating the rates according to the nature and value of the commodities, and the yield can be varied with reference to budgetary needs and income and price changes in the economy by means of rate adjustments as well as by subjecting additional articles of consumption to taxation. The ease with which large revenue from this source can be collected depends on the elasticity of demand of the goods. The revenue will be larger and more easily collected if price elasticity of demand is small and income elasticity is high. They are particularly suited to underdeveloped countries which have started growing, inasmuch as it would be possible to take advantage of industrial expansion and rise in the community's level of spending to add to the states' revenue collection.

In India the decline in the yield of taxes on foreign trade has been offset by a substantial increase in the collection of revenue from internal transactions. Between 1950–51 and 1960–61, while total gross revenue of the Union government increased more than two-fold from Rs. 3,570 million to Rs. 7,301 million, Union excise revenue increased more than five-fold from Rs. 675 million to Rs. 3,413 million. As a percentage of total gross tax revenue, Union excise increased from about 19 per cent in 1950–51 to about 47 per cent in 1960–61. On the other hand. between these points of time customs revenue increased slightly from Rs. 1,572 million to Rs. 1,700 million but as a proportion of total revenue it declined appreciably. The steady rise in excise revenue is due to increased industrial production, rise in the purchasing power of the people and levels of consumption, increase in the rates of duties and the imposition of levies on a widening list of articles. Until the beginning of the First Five-Year Plan, the number of commodities subject to excise was only about twelve. Since then the excise duty has been levied on an increasing number of articles, so that at present excise duties have been collected from as many as sixty articles. In fact excepting salt and cereals practically all necessities have been brought within the scope of the excise levy. In extending the coverage of indirect taxation particularly of excise, the government has taken up the position that tax policy in the present context of economic development should aim at discouraging imports and consumption and encouraging exports and investment. In defence of additional excise duties, it is argued that " with the industrial expansion in the country it is now possible to spread the excise net wider ".[19] It may also be noted that while at one time excise duties were imposed as a countervailing measure against import duties, the position is now reversed. The shift in recent years is towards levying import duties as a countervailing charge on the foreign producer against heavier excise taxation, so that the indigenous producer is not placed at a disadvantage. While the need for increasing tax revenue is understandable, and the objective of discouraging imports and encouraging exports may be considered as both reasonable and necessary in the context of industrial growth in the country, it has, however, to be examined whether the present measures are really well conceived and conform to the basic principles of a scientific tax system. That the levy of such a large number of duties on articles of consumption has added to the cost of living and to the inflationary pressures in the economy cannot be disputed. Moreover, it may be questioned whether the imposition of duties on numerous articles which enter into production would not hamper exports of the country and would not thus go against one of the main considerations in our fiscal policy. The criticism is often made that the contribution of these impositions to the revenue resources of the state is less than in proportion to

[19]Finance Minister's Budget Speech, 1961–62.

their cost of collection and the disturbance and dislocation they cause in production. The United Nations experts have observed that " the tendency of many underdeveloped countries to add to new taxes and supplementary rates on top of old ones and to complicate the tax system, thereby lessening its efficiency, is particularly noticeable in the field of indirect taxation ".[20] It would therefore be in the interests of a sound tax policy if some of the petty vexatious duties whose nuisance effect is greater than their revenue effect are scrapped, and the rates on some other specific articles are raised and the administrative machinery is also geared up to higher levels of efficiency.

Taxation and Incentives

The need for enlarging public savings—meaning an excess of government tax and other revenues (borrowing excluded) over government non-developmental current expenditure—especially in an economy in which government takes the lead in economic development is obvious. The ultimate source of resources for investment in the public as well as private sector is the same namely the aggregate savings of the economy. It therefore follows that so long as the savings margin is not widened, any increased mobilization of savings by the public sector through taxation or internal borrowing or deficit financing would impinge on the resources available for the private sector. However, it is possible for the government to adopt its tax or borrowing policy in such manner as would help mobilization of savings without impairing private incentives for investment. Apart from this, tax policy can be designed to play a positive role in encouraging or stimulating private productive effort. The offering of such incentives to the private sector is essential in an economy where the private sector is expected to contribute as much to economic development as the government. In any scheme of taxation, the advantage arising to the economy as a result of diverting resources to the public sector should be balanced against its adverse reaction on private investment. Thus a tax system should be considered as ill conceived if it does not raise enough revenue and ensure its proper application which would offset losses caused on enterprises outside the government sector. It is possible that taxation in underdeveloped economies when not well planned, would fall too heavily on well organized industries which are the spearhead of economic development. It has been mentioned that the decline of mining in the Mexican economy in the late 1940s might have been caused by high taxation.[21] The need for adjusting the tax structure so as to provide a real incentive for the ploughing back of profits into fresh business, or aiding the accumulation of savings likely to flow into investment has been recognized by the Government of India since 1947.

Incentives for private capital formation can be offered not only directly through tax measures but also indirectly by enlarging government savings

[20]*Taxes and Fiscal Policy in Underdeveloped Countries*, U.N., 1954, p. 39.
[21]*Domestic Financing of Economic Development*, U.N., 1950, p. 37.

and investment. The building up of an infrastructure through public investment in economic overheads such as power, transport and communications
and social overheads like education, public health and technical training will
benefit the private enterprises affected by taxation, widen the range of profitable
new investment opportunities for private business, and help in promoting
private capital formation and production. Furthermore, in the absence of
properly developed money and capital markets, many governments of underdeveloped countries help financing of private enterprise by releasing public
resources collected by means of taxation through special financial institutions.
Another way of providing financial facilities to private industry is by placing
the tax-generated savings at the disposal of private entrepreneurs through
the private banking system. Thus when tax proceeds are used for the retiring
of bank held public debt the banking system is enabled to extend credit for
the financing of private investment projects.[22]

The basic objective of tax incentives has a negative aspect of regulating or
restricting the flow of private investible resources into unproductive channels
and also a positive aspect of encouraging such flow into those enterprises and
lines of investment that would promote domestic capital formation and the
production of goods and services essential for economic growth. In a free
enterprise economy where the price mechanism regulates the flow of investment
expenditure, it is possible to encourage private investment by widening the
scope for profit making. This can be achieved by reducing costs of production,
increasing productivity, minimizing risks, restricting possible losses by guaran-
teeing a certain measure of security and also by ensuring some amount of
freedom to utilize the profits in the manner deemed suitable by the enterprises
making such profits. Most of the tax concessional measures relate to the taxation of incomes. Thus as regards personal incomes subjected to income tax,
the system of progression helps not only in reducing lavish consumption but
also in raising revenue for the government. Besides, in order to strengthen the
private individual's incentive to save, exemptions are granted in respect of
that part of the income which the tax payer saves. Interest received from postal
savings banks and some government securities is exempt from income
tax in Ceylon, India, Pakistan and Thailand; also, life insurance premia
are excluded partly or wholly from taxable income in India, Japan and
Pakistan.

However, it is taxation of business incomes that gives ample scope for incentive measures; but it is also here that the conflict between the needs of high
taxation and the disincentive effects of such taxation appears sharp. Tax
incentives to private businesses take different forms. One method of helping
private businesses to enlarge their scale of operations is to encourage the
ploughing back of profits into investment. This is attained by means of tax
concessions on reinvested profits in the form of either an exemption from
income tax on the amount of ploughed back profits or a reduction in the tax

[22]*Taxes and Fiscal Policy in Underdeveloped Countries*, U.N., 1954, p. 7.

rate or the tax base.[23] This would be a necessary inducement if investments out of retained profits are a residual element in business earnings as when greater importance is attached by business to stability in dividend rates than in reinvestment of profits. Thus a study of business investments in India in the years 1947–52 made by the Indian Taxation Enquiry Commission (1953–54) indicates that " there is a clear tendency to keep distributed profits steady or rising in absolute terms so that the impact of any adverse turn in business conditions as in 1949 and 1952 (and partly even in 1947) falls with disproportionate weight on retained profits ".[24] An indirect method of encouraging reinvestment of profits is to subject dividend payments to high rates of taxation. This, however, is objected to on the ground that such taxation will discourage the flow of private savings into business. But the study above referred to points out that this possibility is not borne out by facts. The Commission in fact make the conclusion that " the amount of retained profits and its proportion to profits are influenced more by the volume and rate of profit than by the volume and rate of taxation " [25]

Private business investment is sought to be encouraged also by permitting higher rates of depreciation to new enterprises as is done in Ceylon, Pakistan and India. Such accelerated depreciation allowances provide for the more rapid recapture of productive investment. If investment is continuous in a business, it retains this benefit indefinitely so long as a fresh investment is made each year. Otherwise, the benefit amounts to a postponement of tax liability. Also extensive carry-overs of business losses in one year may be allowed to offset business gains in other years. The net tax liability of a company over good and bad years is thus reduced and the deterrent effect of possible losses in the initial stages is minimized. Besides, the starting of new enterprises is encouraged by giving tax exemptions for a given initial period of time which enable the business to establish itself on a sound footing. For the same purpose a system of development rebates has been created in Ceylon and India. In Ceylon, the normal development rebate amounts to 20 per cent of the cost of new machinery and plant installed in any year. But if the enterprise is one which is considered to be essential for the economic progress of the country, the rate of concession is increased to 40 per cent. The rate is 25 per cent in India and 50 per cent in Japan. Such development rebates are granted over and above the usual depreciation allowances and amount to a direct tax relief to the enterprise. The provision of a tax holiday for new enterprises is also an incentive for inducing investment to be made along desired channels. Such concessions are confined to approved industrial undertakings in Ceylon, India, Pakistan and Philippines. The holiday period varies from three years

[23]Thus in Burma, profits reinvested within one year are exempt from income tax and in Pakistan tax exemption is granted if reinvestment is done within one year of their accrual and if not more than 40 per cent of the profits is distributed. *Economic Survey of Asia and the Far East*, U.N. 1960, p. 90.

[24]*Report of the Indian Taxation Enquiry Commission*, 1953–54, Government of India, Vol. I, p. 124.
[25]*ibid.*, p. 127.

in Afghanistan, Japan and Burma to five years in India and Ceylon. In the Philippines according to the provisions made in 1953, the complete tax holiday was to extend up to the end of 1958, with subsequent progressive increases in tax liability rising from 10 per cent to 100 per cent in 1963. The eligibility of an enterprise to earn such concessions in that country depends on whether the industry in question would contribute to the establishment of a stable economy, on the proportion of imports required in the productive operation, and whether the industry could be set on a sufficiently large scale with up-to-date practices and techniques.

With a view to promote large-scale businesses on the assumption that they are the source of important external economies, tax concessions are granted to big joint stock organizations in some countries. Thus in Egypt only corporations and share partnership companies could avail themselves of the tax benefits granted in 1953. And in India exemption from income tax is given only to new industrial undertakings which employ at least twenty workers or are run with the aid of power and employ ten or more persons. In Ceylon, the tax privileges are accorded only to new undertakings that use electric energy and employ more than twenty-five persons.[26] Egypt and Israel have adopted special tax devices to encourage the development of a capital market.

Taxation of land has been made use of to encourage economic utilization of land and to increase agricultural productivity; and also in a negative way, to discourage neglecting of agricultural land. Levying of a tax on the potential yield of land rather than on its actual yield as was recommended by a mission of the International Bank to Colombia in 1950 is a means of raising land productivity.[27] Exemptions from land tax, for a certain period of time, of newly reclaimed land or land brought back into cultivation after it has lain fallow for a number of years, and also exemption in respect of investment in irrigation or the application of better methods of cultivation also fall into the same category. In Viet Nam, tax incentives are offered in the form of reduced rates to land owners accepting the new type of tenancy. In China (Mainland) tax concessions are granted to co-operative farms. Suitable tax policy can also be devised to bring about shifts in agricultural production as for example from production of food crops to cash crops or the other way, by exempting or taxing at a lower rate, lands which will be utilized for the growing of the desired crop. On the other hand, penalty taxes can be imposed on land which is neglected. Thus speculative holding of land with a view to reap windfall profits may be subjected to a penalty tax. In Australia and New Zealand, taxes are designed to discourage large holdings especially by absentee landlords. Absentee owners are subject to additional taxation in Argentine, and in Chile there is a surcharge on non-cultivated land.[28] The United Nations experts on

[26]*Processes and Problems of Industrialization in Underdeveloped Countries*, U.N., 1955, p. 53.
[27]*Economic Bulletin for Asia and the Far East*, U.N., November, 1956, p. 50, f.n.
[28]Wald, Haskell P., *Taxation of Agricultural Land in Underdeveloped Countries*, Harvard, 1959, pp. 220–21.

taxation in underdeveloped countries have suggested the extension of capital gains tax to land as a means to combat excessive speculation. Or in its place, a transfer tax is recommended with high rates applicable to those cases where the interval between two sales is short, and lower rates in those cases where the interval is long.[29] In Venezuela unexplored oil fields are taxed very heavily because speculative investments are made in such lands. Prevention of such speculative activity · is obviously necessary in the interests of productive exploitation of natural resources.

Although indirect taxes are designed primarily to bring in a large revenue to the state, it is possible to make use of such taxes to some extent, for non-fiscal purposes also. Exports can be promoted by manipulation of taxes on export articles. Indonesia has thus provided favourable tax treatment to small holders in rubber production. In Japan amounts transferred to reserves to provide for export losses are deductible as business expenses in computing the taxable income of companies.[30] Tax concessions are granted in respect of export commodities like tea and jute in India.

An Assessment of Tax Incentives

While tax measures can be used successfully as a means to finance and induce economic development, the practising of such a policy requires as a precondition, a sound system of tax administration which many underdeveloped countries do not have. In view of this difficulty, the advantage of tax incentives is sometimes questioned by critics. There is, in the first place, the danger of tax concessions being converted into tax loopholes. Tax payers, especially businesses would be quick to avail themselves of exemptions and concessions by meeting the formal requirements of the concession provisions without taking the trouble to carry out the underlying intent of the concessions. There is also the tendency for getting extended the period of concessional treatment as long as possible. This only perpetuates inefficiency. Besides, more and more industries would come forward claiming preferential treatment. This has been the experience of the Philippines and Mexican governments.[31] Concessions in respect of foreign-owned companies also present a problem.

Economists who set great store by private enterprise as the means to economic development doubt the usefulness of adopting taxation for incentive purposes. This at best, according to them, is a negative way. Limitation of taxation is a better method. High level of profits, luxury living and disparities in income and wealth are the real stimulants for private investment and human effort. The tolerating of such conditions goes against the sense of distributive justice, but it is a price necessary to be paid for ensuring spontaneous economic growth. This argument loses much of its force when once the role of the government in

[29]*Taxes and Fiscal Policy in Underdeveloped Countries*, U.N., 1954, p. 36.

[30]*Economic Survey of Asia and the Far East*, U.N., 1960, p. 99.

[31]*Economic Bulletin for Asia and the Far East*, U.N., November, 1956, p. 49.

economic development in underdeveloped countries is realized. For it cannot be denied that if the government has to undertake large investment outlays, the major question is how the necessary resources can be mobilized with the minimum danger to the private investment-incentive factor. There is however, general agreement regarding the view that sound taxation whether in developed or underdeveloped countries should involve the transfer of real resources from the community to the public sector which would otherwise be utilized for conspicuous consumption or speculative investments. If the tax system is well conceived and broad-based with adequate provision for progression in respect of higher incomes and windfall earnings, and includes other suitable fiscal measures to foster private initiative, it will not retard private investment but would, on the other hand, only modify the pattern of national investment in the direction of fuller and better utilization of resources. But tax concessions and exemptions involve a cost to the government in the form of lower tax revenues and it is therefore proper that such sacrifices are made only if there is an assurance of satisfactory returns for the economy as a whole. Hence, unless the tax concessions provide a real stimulus to private investment, and unless the private sector makes good use of the incentives for increasing production so that the initial losses of the government can be offset by the increased taxable capacity of the community at a later stage, such concessions are not economically justifiable.

It is not the high rates of taxation as such but the laxity in the application of the rates and enforcement of tax rules as well as the absence of tax discrimination between those who play the rules of the game and those who do not, that make taxation burdensome and inimical to economic growth. In the matter of incentive taxation the importance of bestowing great care on the choice of the devices for stimulating private investment as well as on their application cannot be exaggerated. There is a real dilemma in the matter of taxation in underdeveloped countries. While on the one hand, increased taxation is necessary to finance government investment outlay, there is on the other hand, the danger that additional and heavier taxation in the absence of proper safeguards would dampen private incentives. In fact, those measures of taxation which are effective in capturing a large share from the gains of economic development are the very ones that affect the returns from private investment. The sound principle which can be here observed is to " combine high rates of taxation in general, with preferential treatment for categories of desired developmental activity ".[32] But apart from such preferential treatment in respect of taxation, the real factor which should stimulate economic activity is economic development itself. Tax liability is only one of the factors affecting investment decisions. The major factor is the attitude of private business to economic prospects in general. Thus a proper scheme of economic development, if well planned and well executed would provide the necessary congenial climate for economic growth in the private sector to take place. There is no

[32]*Taxes and Fiscal Policy in Underdeveloped Countries*, U.N., 1954, p. 11.

denying the fact that political security and the provision of the economic infra-structure by the government and the rise in the level of effective demand resulting from public spendings and investment outlays, furnish the real stimulus for private investment much more than tax exemptions and conces-sions.

Taxation and Economic Stability

Undoubtedly, fluctuations in the levels of economic activity and investment are a serious dampening factor in economic expansion in the richer as well as in the low income countries. But the nature and pattern of cyclical fluctua-tions are different in these two groups of countries; and the measures to counteract such fluctuations which are successful in developed countries need not be so in underdeveloped countries unless such measures are adapted suitably to meet the special requirements of the latter. This is particularly so in the matter of taxation. Business cycles in underdeveloped countries are of an imported variety stemming primarily from the fluctuations in foreign trade. This naturally suggests that an important means to regulate such fluctuations is to be found in the taxes levied on foreign trade.

Since slackness in private investment activity causes unemployment and brings about a fall in effective demand, deflationary trends in advanced free enterprise economies are sought to be rectified by a compensatory fiscal policy involving shifts in the level of taxation, governmental borrowing and public expenditure. The economic mechanism in underdeveloped countries is such that it is incapable of generating economic fluctuations independently. But in many of these countries exports constitute an important source of national income so much that fluctuations in the levels of exports create boom or depres-sion conditions in the economy. In the late 1940s and early 1950s exports of mineral products in Bolivia, copper and nitrates in Chile, sugar and sugar products in Cuba, coffee in El Salvador, coffee and bananas in Guatemala, oil exports in Iran and Venezuela and tea and rubber in Ceylon constituted between 80 per cent and 90 per cent of the total value of exports. In 1951, rubber and oil accounted for 62 per cent of the total exports of Indonesia and rice formed 63 per cent of the total exports of Thailand in 1949. As a proportion of the total national product the sugar sector contributed about 30 per cent in Cuba in 1945-47 and coffee about 12 per cent in El Salvador (1946). It is thus obvious that a fall in the quantum of exports or in their value because of fall in prices in the export markets would have a serious repercussion on the economy of these countries. These are exposed economies in the sense that the rise and fall in the national incomes of advanced economies to which their exports are directed will be reflected in a similar fluctuation in their national incomes and levels activity. Exports are a destabilizing factor in under-developed economies even as private investment is a destabilizing factor in advanced economies. Developed economies thus constitute the cyclical centre while the underdeveloped countries are the cyclical peripheri.[33]

When once an underdeveloped economy is thus exposed, the pattern of income fluctuations is similar to that happening in the industrial countries of the world. In an export boom earnings are large, domestic investment activity is accelerated and the multiplier effect is seen in increased money incomes, rise in levels of employment and in effective demand, while when export demand slackens, the multiplier operates in the reverse way producing depression conditions. But since the major causes of fluctuations are different from that of developed countries, it will not be surprising if the usual techniques of cyclical control practised in advanced economies—restriction of private investment in boom period and stepping up of government investment in a depression to counteract the set back in private investment—do not have any appreciable effect in underdeveloped countries. Thus the manipulation of monetary demand will not influence investment or the volume of exports of the economy for the simple reason that the effective demand relevant to the export sector is the one operating in a foreign country. It is clear that what really helps in maintaining stability in underdeveloped countries is conditions of economic stability in developed countries; and the measures which the former can take have necessarily to be of a defensive nature.

Apart from the basic difference in the nature of fluctuations which call for different techniques of control, the fact that the economic system is not well developed and integrated in underdeveloped countries makes it impossible for the usual techniques of monetary and fiscal controls to function satisfactorily. Since the economies of the richer countries are diversified, industrialized and elastic, and their monetary and financial systems are integrated and closely knit, any reduction in transfer payments or increase in public works outlay would have a quick and ready effect in higher levels of employment and income. On the other hand, in underdeveloped economies where conditions are different, any injection of purchasing power through compensatory fiscal policy would run off into higher prices because of inelastic domestic supplies or into larger imports. Much of the multiplier effect is thus thwarted or transmitted abroad. Among Asian countries, in Japan alone, where the pattern of the economy conforms more nearly to the characteristics of an advanced capitalist economy, have recent attempts at controlling business fluctuations by the use of the usual fiscal and monetary policies been found to work satisfactorily.[34]

Compensatory fiscal policy in underdeveloped countries should therefore aim at insulating the domestic economy against the expansionary effects of an export boom and at offsetting the decline in the private investment activity in depression by increased public investment expenditure. The absorption of excess purchasing power generated by larger export incomes is relatively easy in a pre-industrial country through the use of tax measures. By levying

[33]Van Philips, Paul A. M., *Public Finance and Underdeveloped Economy with Special Reference to Latin America*, Martinus Nijhoff, 1957, p. 150.
[34]*Economic Survey of Asia and the Far East*, U.N., 1960, p. 117.

21

additional taxes or by raising the rates of export duties and income taxes a good share of the excess earnings could be mopped up. This serves the purpose of not only controlling inflationary pressures and preventing dissipation of incomes on unproductive expenditure but also of making available to the public treasury, financial resources for investment at a time when the tempo of activity in the private sector slackens. Obviously, the effectiveness of tax policy in this line depends on the nature of the tax system and the type of taxes which are incorporated in it. Thus according to the Indian Taxation Enquiry Commission, the Indian tax system was resilient enough to mitigate to some extent the inflationary pressures during the period of war, 1939–45, as well as in the post-war years; and this was due partly to the elasticity of the central tax system and partly to the imposition of the Excess Profits Tax and of new excise duties such as those on tobacco. When prices rose during war time, the yield of direct taxes reached as high as 68 per cent of the central tax revenue. This combined with higher export duties and other indirect taxes helped in impounding a substantial fraction of the additions to money incomes.[35]

Tax policy however has little chance of success in counteracting depression conditions. Elimination of export duties and reduction in internal commodity taxation may help to some extent to offset the influence of fall in external demand and to sustain domestic demand. The effect however cannot be appreciable in view of the obvious fact that recessionary trends are due not so much to fall in effective demand at home as to decline in the external demand for the country's export goods. A more effective way of meeting the situation would be for government to step up its expenditure. This would necessitate the withholding of investment outlay during a boom when the revenue resources of the government are buoyant and the level of private investment expenditure is also high, and conserve a part of the resources for utilization in depression period. The excess revenues mobilized during the period when export earnings are high, should be utilized for the building up of a budget stabilization fund. It is important that these resources are not invested in banks (lest they would only aggravate inflation) but should be preferably accumulated in the form of foreign exchange. When exports decline, this fund can be drawn upon to finance import of capital goods as well as to start investment projects like public works. Such an arrangement would ensure monetary stability as well as promote economic growth. The building up of a foreign exchange stabilization fund distinct from the budget equalization fund would help in cushioning the effects of a worsening of terms of trade when exports fall by making it possible to reduce the export duties and draw on exchange reserves. The experiment in this direction carried out in Ceylon in recent years illustrates the scope of such a policy in an underdeveloped export-oriented economy. In that country in 1954–56 when the tea boom resulted in an accumulation of foreign assets and increase in public revenues, public expenditure was trimmed

[35]*Report of the Indian Taxation Enquiry Commission* 1953–54, Government of India, Vol. I, p. 161.

and the inflationary impact of export surpluses was controlled by budget surpluses. As a result, price level remained stable; however, in subsequent years when the budget deficit widened because of rise in current and capital outlays, the balance of payments deficit was not sufficient to offset the inflationary effect of the former. On the whole, the counter cyclical fiscal policy tried in Ceylon in the two periods of export cycles between 1950 and 1957 was successful on the revenue side. Since a large part of national revenue is obtained from exports, it was possible to build up surpluses during the boom period but government expenditure failed to move in a compensatory way; it tended to increase in the boom periods and to contract in the downward phase of the cycle.[36] This again points to the limitations of the administrative mechanism. Obviously as Wallich has stated " it is difficult to convince government and the public that the time to spend is not when the money is available ".[37]

In the ultimate analysis, the real safeguard against the transmission of business cycles from developed countries to underdeveloped countries through foreign trade is for the latter to change the form and pattern of their economies. So long as foreign trade plays a large part in the determination of the size of their national incomes, the real solution against cyclical fluctuations is not a negative one of insulating the economy against the influence of foreign trade but a positive one of developing and diversifying the domestic economy so as to make it less ' exposed '. This involves fundamentally the building up of the industries of the country which would help in domestic utilization of the export products and absorb the abundant labour engaged in agricultural pursuits, and the improving of the financial and administrative mechanism with a view to promote the evolution of better and more reliable financial and monetary means of control. Diversification of the economy will reduce the dangers of inflation and deflation arising out of foreign trade, while the reform of the fiscal and monetary mechanism would strengthen the means at the disposal of these countries to control such instability.

TAX REFORM IN UNDERDEVELOPED COUNTRIES—THE NEED FOR IT

There are two valid reasons for increasing the tax effort in underdeveloped countries. Firstly, since savings are meagre and the rate of capital formation is low, any further increment in savings would form a substantial addition to the existing rate. Also, for the reason that capital requirements are large in relation to its availability, it may be assumed that any addition to the existing stock of capital will have a relatively high yield. Some government expenditures for development purposes such as transport or hydro-electric projects,

---

[36] *Economic Survey of Asia and the Far East*, U.N., 1960, pp. 111–12. See also Kanesathasan, S., ' Export Instability and Contracyclical Fiscal Policy in Underdeveloped Export Economies: A Case Study of Ceylon since 1948,' *I.M.F. Staff Papers*, April, 1959, pp. 46–74.

[37] Wallich, H. C., *Monetary Problems of an Export Economy*, Cambridge, Mass., 1950, p. 308.

show a high marginal value while certain private economic activities have a low or even negative social value such as the stocking of luxury goods in private trade. Given the productivity of public investments, the transfer of resources to public investment by means of higher taxation is justifiable. The marginal significance of any addition to total tax revenue when it is very low to begin with, can be illustrated by a simple arithmetical example. If tax revenue is 12 per cent of national income and one third is devoted to development expenditure, the collection of an additional 2 per cent of income would represent 16 per cent increase in tax revenue. If the extra revenue of 2 per cent of national income is used exclusively for development, government's development expenditure would go up by 50 per cent, i.e. from 4 per cent of national income to 6 per cent.

Secondly, the type of taxes that have been levied in underdeveloped countries and the way in which they are administered are such that they leave room for the supposition that taxation has not been carried to the limits of taxable capacity in these countries. The concept of taxable capacity is relative in the sense that it depends upon the purposes for which tax proceeds are utilized, the nature of the economy, the attitude of the people and the manner in which taxes are administered and collected. Looked at from the point of view of the tax payers, the limits of taxable capacity may be said to be reached when taxation impinges on consumption levels. Such restriction of consumption would hinder economic growth by affecting productivity of labour. From the overall economic point of view, the upper limit of taxation is reached when the increased productivity of the public sector resulting from additional tax resources is more than offset by a decrease in the productivity of the private sector. Broadly speaking therefore, the limit of taxable capacity in a country is the extent to which taxes can be imposed without affecting the incentives for saving and investment. Thus under an efficient tax system, a larger volume of public resources can be mobilized by taxation without impairing incentives or the productivity of the private sector than if taxes were imposed and administered in a lax manner. A sound tax system in which the tax burden is equitably distributed, that is the burden is made to be borne by different classes in proportion to their capacity to bear the burden, will elicit greater public cooperation and encourage people to put forth greater effort in productive enterprise. On the other hand, inequitable distribution of the burden is an obvious disincentive factor. In other words, the mere existence of a large number of taxes and their high rates need not imply that taxation is carried to the limits of taxable capacity; it depends more on the enforcement of tax obligations and the extent to which transfers are actually made. It also depends on the purpose for which the tax proceeds are utilized. If purchasing power is diverted to the government from private hands with economic advantage, taxable capacity is enlarged. And, it is reduced if tax revenue is used for financing government expenditure of low productivity. Prof. Colin Clark feels it plausible to assume that the safe top level of taxation is 25 per cent of the national product.[38] While it is unsafe to fix any such definite limit without reference to the nature of the economy and the functions and services of the government, this proportion may nevertheless be taken as an indication of the extent to which taxation can be relied upon as a means to find resources for the public sector. Very few, if any, underdeveloped countries collect about one-fourth of the national product by taxation. As against this, the fact that there has been substantial improvement in the economies of these countries and their national and per capita incomes have risen, while the proportion of tax revenue remains a constant ratio of the national income, provides good economic reasons to suppose that taxation has not been made use of to the necessary and justifiable extent.

It is therefore clear that the prime consideration in tax reform in under-developed countries should be to increase the yield of taxation without impairing national economic efficiency. The principle of equity or fairness in the distribution of tax burden has to be assigned only a subordinate role. In the present institutional set up and structure of taxation in underdeveloped economies, the scope for increasing public revenue lies in three directions: (a) Securing larger revenue from public undertakings; (b) Simplification of the tax system and (c) Improvement of tax administration.

(a) Revenue from Public Undertakings

Public undertakings contribute a good proportion of the non-tax revenues of modern states. In Soviet Russia, about 90 per cent of public revenue is derived from the national enterprises and through the turnover tax on the products of public enterprises. Even in free enterprise economies like the U.K. and France, the nationalization of some basic industries in the post-war years has considerably expanded the scope of the public sector but the industries which have been nationalized have not been an important source of revenue to the state. In France, the operation of public enterprises has resulted mostly in recurrent deficits. But in some of the countries of Southern Asia and the Far East, State ownership of certain basic industries and also state trading in a few articles of export have yielded large profits. Thus in Burma, export of rice through the State Agricultural Marketing Board, and in Thailand the ownership by the state of industries like cement, cotton textiles, paper, sugar, etc. and the export of rice through the Government Rice Bureau, contribute substantially to government revenues. In Ceylon and Indonesia, several public enterprises have been established in recent years.

Apart from being a source of income to the state, such undertakings by the government are useful in other ways. Public-owned profit-making enterprises serve as a yard stick to measure the efficiency and tax paying capacity of

[38]Clark, Colin, *Welfare and Taxation*, Oxford, Catholic Social Guild, 1954, quoted in Van Philips, Paul A. M., *Public Finance and Less Developed Economy with Special Reference to Latin America*, Martinus Nijhoff, 1957, p. 113.

private enterprises and the fairness or otherwise of the prices charged by them. Also, the assumption of direct responsibility by the state in the running of these undertakings brings the public authorities into closer touch with economic realities and enables them to better understand the problems of private business and thus enhances their competence to formulate development programmes, lay down economic policies in general and control the process of development.[39]

The objectives of government entry into business in India have generally been non-fiscal. These are, firstly, the undertaking of basic public utilities like railways and projects of outstanding public benefit like power projects and irrigation; secondly, the setting up of basic industries of national importance; thirdly, the establishment of certain capital goods industries which are not very attractive to private enterprise and lastly, the initiation of pioneering enterprises with a view to induce private entrepreneurs to enter new fields of industry. The operation of some of these enterprises has been a source of increasing income to the state but the main factor behind the extension of state enterprise has been the promotion of some broad public purpose rather than revenue or profit. The total investments in the various industrial and commercial undertakings of the Union government as at the end of 1953–54 amounted to about Rs. 600 million. The Third Plan envisages an investment of Rs. 12,160 million in industrial projects in addition to Rs. 4,660 million in mineral projects while the State governments are expected to make an investment of Rs. 640 million in industrial and Rs. 110 million in mineral projects. In view of these large outlays and the contribution which these public undertakings are making to national development, it is but fair that they are expected to add to the budgetary resources of the state. The need for securing an increasing amount of revenue from public undertakings is stressed in the Five-Year Plans. In presenting the Budget for 1961–62, the Finance Minister remarked that Government " have in the last decade invested large sums in various industrial undertakings in the public sector. It is of basic importance that these enterprises should function on sound commercial principles and should make adequate profits which can be ploughed back into further investments."

There is, however, a large body of opinion which views public undertakings as primarily a means to provide a national service. These are not commercial ventures and as such, should not aim at making a profit. This may be a sound principle so far as developed countries are concerned, in which the private sector is well organized. Even in an underdeveloped economy, there are certain types of investments like those in public utilities, railways or development of ports and harbours where the objective is to encourage demand and widen the domestic market. But if the state has made heavy investments in commercial and industrial ventures, so long as they are run along sound commercial lines, they should be considered as supplementary to private investment, and on this ground such undertakings are justified in adjusting their price policy with a view to ensure a fair rate of earnings. Profit making

[39]*Domestic Financing of Economic Development*, U.N., 1950, p. 50.

by enterprises of this nature in India is defended on several grounds. In the first place, many of these undertakings involve huge initial investment and they run at a loss for some years and start yielding only after an interval of ten or twenty years, e.g. power and electricity projects. Thus at any point of time, new undertakings may be running at a loss while older investments on similar enterprises may be yielding substantial net receipts. Such receipts are necessary to offset the losses of new projects and to finance the development of additional projects. This has been the experience in respect of electricity undertakings and irrigation projects in Punjab and Uttar Pradesh. An element of taxation in the pricing of such services is therefore permissible and necessary. Secondly, state enterprise in India has a dynamic role to play in the process of economic development and public undertakings in several instances are of the pioneering type which break new ground and which show the way to private enterprise to follow. State enterprise is no longer confined to the function of providing the basic frame work for economic development but takes a hand in capital and producer goods industries as well. To the extent that some of the undertakings are of an industrial and commercial nature, the pricing policy based on profit motive that is natural in free enterprise should be equally applicable to government enterprises. Thirdly, many of these undertakings benefit particular classes of consumers. While public utilities like railways are of service to the common tax payers in general, electricity undertakings or irrigation projects benefit particular groups of people or localities, and when the earnings of the beneficiaries are increased nothing can be said against the adoption of a suitable price policy which would facilitate the collecting of a proportion of the additional earnings. Viewed in this manner, profits from public undertakings may have less to commend than direct taxation, but not less suitable than indirect taxation as a means of raising revenue.[40]

(b) Simplification of the Tax System

One sure way of increasing the net revenue yield of taxes is to reduce the cost of collection by simplification of the tax machinery. Many specialists who have studied the problem of taxation in underdeveloped countries are of the opinion that the tax system in these countries is too complicated and that there is considerable scope for economizing in collection. Several of the taxes are of an *ad hoc* type super-imposed on some of the basic taxes without proper consideration of their net yield over and above the cost of collection. One of the fundamental canons of sound taxation namely, the principle of economy is thus violated. There is much truth in the maxim that an old tax is no tax. Any new tax, whether direct or indirect, causes an adverse reaction among particular classes of tax payers but the resistance dies out after some time and

[40]*Report of the Indian Taxation Enquiry Commission* 1953–54, Government of India, Vol. I, pp. 200–03.

the tax authorities are tempted to add more and more fresh taxes. But since the ultimate source of all taxes is the income of the community, diminishing returns set in in the yield of taxes while the cost of collection steadily rises. Thus in India the wealth tax, the capital gains tax, the gift tax and the expenditure tax have been added to the list of direct taxes, partly with a view to close the loopholes in the income tax system and partly with a view to add to the tax resources of the state. Similar additions have been made to the taxation of land, in the form of agricultural income tax, inheritance tax, betterment levy, etc. The excise taxes in India are too numerous and their cost of collection has increased more than in proportion to their yield. Between 1955–56 and 1960–61, the total tax revenue of the government of India increased from Rs. 4,110 million to Rs. 7,300 million while the cost of collection of taxes rose from Rs. 120 million to Rs. 220 million i.e. while the yield increased by 77 per cent, the cost of collection increased by 83 per cent. Basic excise duties levied by the Union government on eleven articles yielded Rs. 690 million in 1950–51 and the revenue from these items increased to Rs. 2,520 million in 1960–61, while about a score of items added on since the beginning of the First Plan accounted for only less than Rs. 1,250 million in 1960–61. Of the articles added to the list since 1950–51, the yield from only five— cement, paper, vegetable non-essential oils, refined diesel oils, and industrial fuel oils—shows any substantial increase while in the others the revenue in some cases has declined or has improved only to a very negligible extent. In the Budget for 1961–62, excise duty on fourteen commodities was raised while eighteen new commodities were brought under taxation, but the additional yield expected was only Rs. 310 million or an increase of less than 9 per cent of total excise revenue or 4·5 per cent of total tax revenue of the Union government. As regards direct taxes, the revenue from expenditure tax and gift tax has been negligible and has not increased since their first imposition.

It is therefore important that the tendency to seek increased revenues through the imposition of new commodity taxes should stop, and greater reliance should be placed on those duties which cover a large section of the population and the yield of which has been high and increasing in relation to their cost of collection. A good number of the many vexatious duties which rank the lowest in point of productivity deserve only to be scrapped. If the loss of revenue resulting from their abolition can be made good by adding to the rates of existing major items and if greater attention is devoted to the proper administration of the basic taxes, the net yield of taxation can be increased and at the same time the tax system can be considerably simplified. This applies to the direct taxes as well. It was pointed out earlier that in a growing economy which is predominantly agricultural, the primary sector in the economy should be made to contribute a good share to the tax revenue of the government. The land tax administration in India has grown complex and top-heavy while the contribution of land tax to total revenue has steadily declined in recent years. In the present context, the proposal to abolish land tax and merge the income from land with the general income for purposes of income tax assessment appears premature. But short of this step, it would be possible to improve the system of both income and land taxation by the adoption of a modified form of Schedular Income Tax system popular in the Latin American countries in the place of the global system which obtains now. By combining some of the basic features of the Schedular and the Unitary systems of income taxation, it would be possible to assess the income arising from different sources correctly and arrive at the best coverage of all income earners. General income that is now assessed to income tax can be classified into different categories, like professional income, business income, capital gains, etc. and different rates on these categories may be applied with varying degrees of progression according to the tax-paying capacity of the different classes of income tax payers.[41] A similar classification is possible in respect of income from land. The present system of land tax assessment can be adapted to meet the needs of taxation of income from agriculture and as a counterpart to the schedules of general income, a classification of income from agriculture can be made with reference to the nature of the crops grown, the fertility of the soil and the system of land holding. This would make the system of income taxation and land taxation more uniform, impart a greater degree of flexibility to the direct tax structure, and reduce the complexity, of the existing arrangement. Improvement along these lines would meet the requirements of a developing economy in which income from agriculture is a more significant component of total income than that from industries, businesses and professions and in which as much importance is attached to the development of agriculture as to the promotion of industries.

(c) Reform of Tax Administration

Since economic growth in several of the underdeveloped countries involves increasing investment outlays by the state, it is necessary that the financial resources at the disposal of the government should expand at least in step with the rise in national incomes. This is possible only if the tax system is such and the taxes so graded that something like 40 to 50 per cent of the increase in income is automatically sucked up by taxation. Such a fairly high rate of marginal taxation not only checks inflation and functions as a stabilizing factor but also enables government to accelerate its rate of investment. Marginal tax rates can be maintained high if the income tax is progressive enough, and the rates of commodity taxes are much higher in respect of luxury articles

[41]Despite differences in rates according to the size of income earned, the present income-tax system impinges heavily on the salaried classes, who pay 100 per cent of the assessment while earners of business incomes and some professional incomes escape full payment by making effective use of the many loopholes. The adverse effect of this on the morale of the tax-payers and on standards of efficiency in public services is specially stressed by Kaldor. See his *An Expenditure Tax*, Allen & Unwin, London, 1955 and *Indian Tax Reform*, Government of India, New Delhi, 1956, p. 8. A necessary improvement is the reduction of the rates on such incomes.

than of necessaries. Even with such a system of taxation, the extent to which resources can be mobilized depends on effective enforcement of the taxes. It is also important that evasion is kept at the minimum and the charges of collection do not rise disproportionately to the revenue from taxation.

In actual fact however, the tax machinery is defective in underdeveloped countries and there is considerable laxity in administration, with the result that the marginal rate of taxation is even less than the average rate. The institutional set up and conditions of administration are such that the finer arts of taxation cannot be practised in these countries. Administrative backwardness invariably co-exists with economic backwardness. In these countries, the system of tax administration as well as general administration is transplanted from advanced countries abroad without proper adaptation to the different social structure and economic environment obtaining in the former. Thus the tax system in the Latin American countries is based on the Franco-Spanish model while the system prevalent in some of the backward countries of the British Commonwealth are of the British pattern. In some of the low income countries, the social structure is still of a feudalistic type. Richard Goode, a member of the United Nations Technical Assistance Mission to Bolivia has set forth six important conditions for the successful operation of the income-tax. These are, the existence of a predominantly money economy; the existence of a high standard of literacy among tax payers; prevalence of accounting records honestly and reliably maintained; a large degree of voluntary compliance on the part of tax-payers; favourable political conditions in the form of a free democratic government, and lastly, honest and efficient administration.[42] Nearly all of these conditions are absent in the majority of the underdeveloped countries. While the form of government in most cases is largely democratic, the monetized sector of the economy is narrow, standard of literacy is less than fifty per cent, accounting records are not common or are ill maintained, tax compliance is very much limited and administrative system is far from efficient. As a result, not only is tax revenue a much smaller proportion of aggregate national income than in advanced countries, but the scope for mopping up an increasing portion of additional incomes is also narrowly restricted.

To be effective, the tax system of a country should be adapted to its social and economic environment. What has been found to work efficiently in an advanced free enterprise economy fails in a poorer country with a different cultural and social pattern. The limited success of financial programmes suggested by Western experts in underdeveloped countries such as the Shoup Mission proposals for Japan in 1950 and those made by Kaldor for the same country later, is illustrative of this point. But adaptation of the foreign techniques in a less developed country to suit its social institutions is as difficult as it is necessary. It has been remarked that if a developed economy has a

[42]Proceedings of the Forty-fourth Annual Conference of the National Tax Association, 1951, quoted in *Taxes and Fiscal Policy in Underdeveloped Countries*, U.N., 1954, pp. 20–21.

backward fiscal system it would be easier for that country to adjust the tax system to its requirements, than for an economically backward country to adjust an advanced system of fiscal administration to its underdeveloped economic structure.[43]

However, the difficulty of transferring the techniques of administration to the underdeveloped countries in respect of certain taxes is less than in the case of others. Thus to the extent that taxation of land is closely linked to the systems of land tenure and the agrarian structure of an economy, the method of taxation which functions efficiently in one country may not be successful in another. On the other hand, the techniques applicable to a tax like the corporation tax can be transferred from one country to another in so far as the organization of the corporation and the corporate method of doing business will be in much the same form in the two countries. And even when the under-developed country is a predominantly agricultural one, if agricultural opera-tions are done along corporate lines as in large-scale sugar or rubber planta-tions, the system of corporate taxation applicable to manufacturing establish-ments in developed countries can be transferred to the less advanced countries.

Apart from the adaptation of Western techniques of taxation to suit their requirements and institutional set up, the underdeveloped countries can considerably enlarge their revenue resources by improving their existing tax machinery. Expert advice in this direction is becoming increasingly available to the poorer countries through the United Nations Expanded Programme of Technical Assistance. Countries which have sought the advice of such tax experts have been amply rewarded by increase in their tax revenues of the order of twenty to hundred times the cost of operation.[44] It is also within the power of low income countries to develop their financial institutions, to improve accounting practices, to standardize book-keeping methods, to provide proper training for tax officials and to bring up the levels of general administrative efficiency. Also, better economic conditions and rise in the standards of literacy would promote a greater degree of tax compliance on the part of the community. Improvements along these directions would be of a cumulative nature in the sense that while they enable the state to acquire an increasing share of the national income through taxation and facilitate larger public investments, economic development resulting from such activity would in turn foster the necessary social and institutional changes.

[43]Bloch, H. S., ' Economic Development and Public Finance,' *The Progress of Underdeveloped Areas*, Ed. Hoselitz, Bert F., Chicago, 1952, p. 253.

[44]*Economic Bulletin for Asia and the Far East*, U.N., November, 1952, pp. 3–5.

Chapter X

DEFICIT FINANCING

WHEN THE current resources of any spending unit or administrative body fall short of its outlays there is a deficit in its budget. The term deficit financing denotes the measures adopted to cover this deficit and balance the expenditure against the receipts. Normally, deficit financing relates to the financial activities of the state. Even in economically advanced countries under the capitalist system, the state's investment activities have considerably expanded in recent years. And such expansion has been justified and recommended by economists on the ground that ownership and operation of utility services by governments is necessary in the public interest, that large investment schemes like highways and hydro-electric projects have necessarily to be undertaken by governments and that in order to promote social welfare, more is to be spent by the state on public health and education and other welfare schemes. Furthermore, it is commonly accepted that in order to ensure and promote economic stability public investment on a large and increasing scale is necessary.[1] Most of these arguments are as much relevant to underdeveloped as to developed countries. The fact that the former are economically backward and cannot rise out of the rut of economic stagnation unless a large initial effort to raise the level of investment is made, is a special argument of considerable force in justification of large public investments. In reality the preponderant role that the state has to play in initiating the process of growth constitutes one of the major factors which necessitate deficit financing in underdeveloped countries.

The need for large investments by the state has increasingly been realized in the underdeveloped economies of today. But against the mounting investment expenditures, the normal financial resources of the states—receipts from government undertakings and taxation—have failed to respond satisfactorily and as a consequence, economic development through the agency of the state, has strained the public budgets and caused budgetary deficits. We have seen in the previous chapter that the tax revenues of most of the states of this category have remained below 10 per cent of the national product as against 25 to 40 per cent in economically advanced countries. Tax revenues form what are called compulsory savings. As an economy grows, and the scale of expenditure of the state rises, the tax system should be resilient enough

[1]Copland, D. B., *Public Policy—The Doctrine of Full Employment*; Harris, S. E., *The New Economics—Keynes' Influence on Theory and on Public Policy*, Alfred Knopf Inc., New York, 1948, p. 216.

to provide adequate financial means to the government; but this responsiveness of the financial mechanism obviously depends upon the nature of the taxes levied, the efficiency with which they are administered and collected, and the scope for introducing new taxes as the economy gets more and more broad-based and the per capita income of the community rises. That tax administration is lax and inefficient in the poorer countries of the world is too well known a fact to require any elaboration. As a consequence, the government is forced to resort to borrowing internally and to deficit financing. The first is made possible by the voluntary savings of the community and the second results in forced savings.

It is necessary at this stage to be clear in our minds about the distinction between the practice of deliberately unbalancing the budgets in advanced countries with a view to maintaining the level of effective demand and thereby ensuring economic stability, and deficit financing in underdeveloped countries in order to promote economic development. It has been pointed out that in the advanced free enterprise economies such as the U.S.A., the replacement of monetary policy—Bank Rate and open market operations—by deficit financing as a technique for raising consumers' incomes through increased government expenditure and for stimulating productive activity, private employment and private investment, was not a deliberate innovation or a fully evolved new technique, but a practical rationalization of the experience of the government and the administration in the matter of economic and financial policy.[2] The recurring deficits in the U.S.A. budgets in the mid 1930s synchronizing with economic recovery, led to a disposition to regard budgetary deficits as themselves responsible for recovery and as a result deficit spending soon came to be regarded as a recovery measure. In the next few years, the purpose of deficit financing was considered as not merely pump priming or a means to give a temporary stimulus to the slackening private investment activity, but as compensatory financing or a more or less permanent feature of government's financial policy in which spending beyond the budgetary resources of the state was recommended as a measure to offset or compensate for the secular tendency for private investment to fall.

The theoretical justification for deficit financing in advanced economies is based on the assumption that the major cause of depression is the fall in effective demand in the Keynesian sense of the term. Deficit financing in such a context would increase money supply and the purchasing power of the people. As a result of the borrowing operation of the government the assets and deposits of the banking system are augmented which result in the expansion of credit and money supply and increase in the volume of spendable money income of the community. So long as deficiency in demand is the cause of economic depression or stagnation, the expansion in money supply and increased outlays by the state would encourage larger aggregate spendings, and with the rise

[2] Williams, John H., ' Deficit Spending,' *The American Economic Review*, February, 1941, pp. 52–66.

in the level of effective demand, there will be fuller utilization of the capital and labour resources and a revival of the tempo of economic activity.

But the efficacy of deficit financing as a means to promote recovery or maintain economic stability in advanced countries has been questioned and the technique itself has come in for a great deal of searching criticism. It has been argued for instance, that the recovery of the U.S.A. in the latter years of the world depression of the present century has to be attributed partly at least to the revival of private business activity which itself was due not so much to the rise in the investment of government but to other circumstances, and that government investment activity was not able to create the necessary confidence among the business classes, in view of changing international political conditions, uncertainties regarding labour relations and the prospects of private operators in public utility industries, etc. It has also been mentioned that large deficit spending encouraged wasteful expenditure in the public sector, and the consequent rise in cost and wages adversely affected the enthusiasm of private businessmen.[3] Moreover, the loading of the banking system with government bonds and securities because of deficit financing impaired the effectiveness of monetary and credit measures in the country. The exercise of the usual instruments of credit control proved to be therefore ineffective.

Before we examine the scope of deficit spending as a means to promote economic development in underdeveloped countries, it is necessary to bear in mind the fact that there is considerable difference in the connotation of the term ' deficit financing ' as between different countries.[4] Thus in the U.S.A., the term denotes the gap between the revenue receipts of the state and aggregate budget expenditure including capital outlay and covers all the means of closing the gap namely, use of cash balances, borrowing from the central bank and loans from the public. In India the term ' deficit financing ' has been defined in such manner as to focus attention on the inflationary potential of it. Thus while the term deficit refers to the short fall in both wings of the budget—revenue and capital—the financing part of it refers to the use of cash balances, and the short term borrowing of the government from the central bank and commercial banks. So long as total expenditure exceeds the normal revenue and other current receipts of the state, including the proceeds of loans, small savings, superannuation contributions and other funds available for the government, there is a budgetary deficit. And this deficit is financed by the use of the central and state governments' cash balances and short term borrowing from the central and commercial banks. Thus while internal loans are considered as one of the means of covering the budgetary gap in the U.S.A. the proceeds of such loans are taken as part of the current receipts of the government in India so that the budgetary gap is made to appear narrower.

[3]Haley, B. F., ' The Federal Budget: Economic Consequences of Deficit Financing,' *American Economic Review*, February, 1941, pp. 67–87.

[4]For various distinctions see Raj, K. N., ' Definition and Measurement of Deficit Financing,' *Indian Economic Review*, August, 1954, pp. 34–57.

The justification for this method of defining deficit financing in India is that the size of the deficit defined in this way points more pertinently to the excess spendings of the government over current production, and thus gives a clearer indication of the extent to which the financial activities of the state have inflationary potentialities. The drawing down of cash balances and government's resort to central bank credit have a direct effect on the currency in circulation. It is however, misleading to treat government's long term borrowings from the banking system as outside the category of financial transactions that have a bearing on money supply and inflationary situation in the country. In defence of this method of estimation it has been pointed out " that the monetary impact of governments' borrowings differs according to the subscribers " and that the " ownership of public debt does not remain with the same persons or institutions that bought it to begin with ". Hence " a deficit measured in terms of withdrawals of cash balances and net increases in floating debt gives on the whole, a reasonably reliable indication of the impact of the budget on money supply ".[5] But as Prof. B. R. Shenoy correctly points out, this criterion of the magnitude of deficit financing may apply to the first three years of the First Five-Year Plan period (1951–56) when on balance the Reserve Bank and the commercial banks were unloading on the market their holdings of permanent debt but not true of subsequent years when the permanent debt holdings of the banking system rose substantially.[6] In other words the exclusion of subscriptions to government loans by commercial banks as well as by the Reserve Bank from any computation of the size of deficit financing would result in an underestimate. Strictly speaking, the overall size of deficit financing at any point of time should comprise, reduction in cash balances, plus increase in the floating debt of the government plus increase in permanent debt held by the central bank and the commercial banks.

DEFICIT FINANCING FOR ECONOMIC DEVELOPMENT

While the theoretical justification for deficit financing in advanced free enterprise economies is that government's investment spending would raise money incomes and the level of employment and thereby compensate for the deficiency in private investment activity in a time of depression, budgetary deficits are recommended for a different purpose in underdeveloped countries. Deficit financing in these countries is designed not to raise the level of effective demand but to help in the increased mobilization of savings and in the building up of real capital. There are statistical evidences to show that there is much idle capacity in underdeveloped countries like India. But the existence of idle capital or idle labour is due to certain fundamental structural factors— such as the non-availability of technically skilled labour, lack of mobility of

---

[5]*The Second Five-Year Plan*, Government of India, 1956, p. 84.

[6]*Problems of Indian Economic Development*, Sir William Meyer Lectures 1955–56, University of Madras, 1958, pp. 58–59.

labour and also, in respect of fixed capital, due to the adoption of imported techniques of production which are often found to be unsuited to the factor supply situation in these countries. The real need for deficit financing in low income countries which are in the early stages of industrialization, arises from the fact that there is substantial difference between actual savings and potential savings. In view of the large investment undertakings of the government in these countries the need for much larger internal savings is obvious. But the means at the disposal of the government to mobilize all the potential savings of the community are inadequate and unsatisfactory.

Deficit spending by the government clearly indicates that investment demand is in excess of savings. So long as the structural rigidities mentioned above do not exist in an economy, and to the extent that resources remain unemployed because of lack of effective demand, investment spending by government through budgetary deficits would draw into service idle labour and capital and their mobilization and employment for productive purpose would add to output without creating any inflationary pressures. But if structural factors account for the unemployment of factors, the release of additional purchasing power would not help so much in an increase in output as in an increase in prices, and the extent to which prices would rise and assume inflationary dimensions depends directly on the degree of rigidity of factor supply and the failure of output to respond to any increase in demand. Furthermore, if deficit financing aims at the building up of costly capital equipment and economic overheads like hydro-electric projects, roads and railways, the inflationary impact will be all the greater. This is obviously because of the fact that unlike in the production of consumption goods, the larger investments in such capital schemes would increase the money incomes of large sections of the population while at the same time there is no likelihood of any immediate increase in the supply of consumption goods to offset the effect of larger purchasing power.

However, it is argued that such a rise in prices is helpful in underdeveloped countries where the state cannot hope to do much in mobilizing the available savings through the normal means of taxation and internal borrowing. Increase in taxation through higher rates or additional impositions restrict the consumption of the people and does increase the volume of savings. But in a democratic welfare state there are obvious limits to which taxation can go. At any rate in an underdeveloped country where the civic consciousness of the people is not well developed, where standard of literacy is low, and where tax administration is neither very strict nor efficient, the only other way of increasing savings is by bringing about forced savings through deficit financing. This also involves restriction of consumption and brings about a widening of the savings margin; but while in the case of taxation this restriction of consumption is direct and obvious, the restriction of consumption brought about by deficit financing is indirect and not always apparent. This then is an ideal way of stepping up the level of much needed savings without raising at least in the initial stages—when price rise is moderate—any great protest or social opposition. And the state is justified in resorting to this method for the further reason that the resources so collected will be employed for the building up of capital and thereby facilitate further increase in national product in later years. It is thus argued that to the extent deficit financing succeeds in increasing output and the level of incomes in the country in future, the inflicting of a sacrifice on the present generation in the form of higher prices and restriction of consumption or forced savings is justified. Deficit financing viewed in this manner would represent a technique of making present use of future anticipated savings.

The efficacy of deficit financing as a means to foster economic growth in an underdeveloped economy depends on the following factors: (a) The volume of savings mobilized is large in relation to the strain involved in implementing and operating this technique; (b) that the resources collected in this manner are productively employed so as to secure the maximum advantage out of it; in other words, these resources are employed in the building up of much needed capital which alone can promote growth in the country and not frittered away in meeting the consumption needs of the community; and (c) that while a moderate dose of inflation arising on the wake of deficit financing is permissible, the practice should not lead to runaway inflation, in which case, the remedy will become worse than the disease. That is to say, deficit financing should be moderate, should be regulated or adjusted according to the absorptive capacity of the economy and should not be allowed to exceed the optimum limit which is determined by the various social and economic circumstances in the country.

These three factors may now be examined in some detail. The volume of savings resulting from deficit financing depends upon the existing pattern of distribution of income and wealth, the size of the different income groups and the attitudes and consumption habits of the people. Since a moderate rise in prices attending or resulting from inflation may be necessary or at least harmless but runaway inflation is dangerous, the point at which rise in prices takes an inflationary turn should be considered as the upper limit beyond which deficit financing should not be permitted to go. This would mean that maximum use is made of deficit financing within these limits. Deficit financing helps in the mobilization of resources through rise in prices and the consequent transfer of incomes between different classes of income earners in the community. In a period of rising prices the real income of fixed income earners, and creditors declines while that of the debtors and of people whose incomes are unstable increases. To the first category would belong a good part of the middle class, salaried people and those who have invested in small savings, while business classes who are, by and large, among the richer members of the community, experience a swelling in their money incomes. To the extent rise in money incomes is greater than the rise in prices, their real income increases faster. But since there is no immediate upward or downward adjust-

22

ment of the earnings of labourers when there is a rise or fall in prices, the real income of this class of income earners falls in a period of rising prices. Thus when prices rise, there is a transfer of income and wealth from fixed income earners and wage earners to the richer classes and the business community. And since the propensity to consume of the latter class is less than that of the former, such a transfer of incomes results in larger savings of the community and a possible rise in the level of investment. It is clear that the more rigid the money incomes of the wage earners and the middle class, the greater is the scope for larger mobilization of resources through deficit financing. Also, the larger is the size of this category of income earners, the greater will be the yield of deficit financing. In most of the underdeveloped countries, however, the size of this class of people in relation to the other groups is smaller. The ratio of wages to profits is 2·1 : 1 in the U.S.A. and 2·3 : 1 in U.K., 1·6 : 1 in Puerto Rico, 1·5 : 1 in Colombia and South Rhodesia while in Ireland and Chile it is 1 : 1 and in Kenya it is 0·6 : 1.[7] This would mean that the scope for the diversion of incomes into savings through price rise is less in the underdeveloped than in the economically advanced countries, or putting it in another form, in order to realize a given amount of forced savings through deficit financing, a larger dose of inflation is needed in underdeveloped countries than in developed countries.

Transfer of resources to government can be brought about easily and in a larger measure through deficit financing if the price elasticity of demand is large and the income elasticity of demand is small.[8] This practically means that the extent to which real resources can be released for investment depends upon the effect of a rise in prices on consumption levels. Obviously, if production increases faster than consumption, the savings margin becomes wider. The level of consumption at any point of time depends upon the supply of goods, the extent to which money income increases and the consumption habits of particular classes of people. Since price elasticity of demand refers to the degree in which demand varies in response to price variation, it is clear that when price elasticity is large, a given increase in prices brought about by deficit financing would reduce consumption to a proportionately larger extent. And since income elasticity of demand relates to the extent to which consumption rises or falls with a given increase or decrease in money incomes, a low income elasticity of demand would mean that when money incomes rise, the level of consumption rises to a proportionately lesser extent. It is not possible to say anything definite about the degree of price elasticity and income elasticity of demand in the less developed countries of the world. It is, however, plausible to argue that since the level of consumption is already very low in most of these countries, any improvement in money incomes

[7]Axilrod, Stephen H., ' Inflation and the Development of Underdeveloped Areas,' *Review of Economics and Statistics*, August, 1954, p. 336.

[8]' Deficit Financing for Economic Development with special reference to ECAFE Countries,' *Economic Bulletin for Asia and the Far East*, November, 1954.

would result in an immediate rise in the levels of consumption. This is particularly true of the small income earners and the middle classes in the urban
areas of the country. On the other hand, it may be observed that the supply
curve becomes inelastic in the rural areas, and after a point a rise in money
incomes brings about a turn back in the supply curve, the rural folk taking
greater leisure and spare hours when they find that their money incomes can
be maintained stable even with lesser output. Even more difficult it is to
make any guess regarding the effect of rise in prices on consumption habits.
In a poor country about 70 per cent of the average annual expenditure of
the people is on food and necessaries. And any moderate rise in prices of these
articles will not depress consumption to any appreciable extent. In the case of
the higher income groups a rise in prices and incomes occurring simultaneously
will have hardly any effect on consumption levels. It is also a well-known
fact that a rise in incomes among these classes leads invariably to increased
demand for luxury and costly goods. Hence while the concepts of income
elasticity and price elasticity of demand have a theoretical significance in
respect of any analysis of the effects of price and income change on consumption and savings, they are of little practical value in measuring the effects of
deficit financing on the diversion of resources in a poor country.

DEFICIT FINANCING AND INFLATION

Apart from the fact that budgetary deficits imply excess of investment over
savings, there are certain other factors which help development of inflationary
conditions in underdeveloped countries when they resort to deficit financing
for economic development. These may be grouped under two heads: (a) monetary factors and (b) economic behaviour and attitude of the people.

(a) Monetary Factors

Although strictly speaking any rise in prices has to be explained in terms of
the operation of the supply and demand forces, the fact remains that the
inflationary effect of any excess demand in the economy is facilitated and foste-
tered by a rise in money supply. The relation between the size and technique
of deficit financing on the one hand and money supply on the other, has thus a
close bearing on inflationary trends resulting from deficit financing. In general,
it may be observed that if in a country which resorts to deficit financing for
economic development the money-income ratio is high, the chances of an
inflationary rise in prices are less than if the money-income ratio were low.
This observation is based on the simple fact that when money-income ratio
is high, any marginal increase in money supply resulting from deficit financing
would constitute a smaller proportion of the total, and for that reason its
effect will be relatively less. In underdeveloped countries where production for
domestic consumption and barter exchange are extensive and cash balances

in the hands of individuals are small, the money-income ratio is usually smaller than in the more developed countries. In the former, the money in circulation constitutes 16 to 30 per cent of the national income while in the latter the ratio is 30 to 60 per cent. In India it is about 20 per cent. This may therefore be considered as one of the factors that make underdeveloped countries easily susceptible to inflation from budget deficits.

On the other hand, expansion of money supply because of deficit financing is limited in underdeveloped countries in so far as the use of credit is less popular in such countries than in the economically advanced countries. The proportion of demand deposits to the total quantity of money is between 30 and 40 per cent in India, Burma, Malaya and Pakistan, while in countries like U.K. and the U.S.A. it exceeds 70 per cent. Among the Asiatic and Far East countries, Japan and Ceylon are exceptions in this respect with demand deposits forming more than 60 per cent of their money supply. The lower is the ratio of deposit money to currency. the lesser will be the pyramidding effect on credit of a given volume of deficit financing. This would in other words, have a restraining effect on the tendency of new money injected into the system to multiply itself.

(b) Economic Behaviour and Attitude of the People

In this connection we have to stress particularly the propensity to consume of the people, their rate of spending of money incomes and their psychological reaction to any given rise in prices. The higher the rate of spendings the greater is the velocity of circulation of money and the higher would prices rise. If the marginal propensity to consume is high as it is in the underdeveloped countries, when the money income especially of the middle and lower income groups rises, more will be spent on the purchase of goods and services for consumption. As such, there will not only be an upward pressure on prices, but the extent to which real resources can be diverted for investment in the public sector would also be limited. Given an increase in the stock of purchasing power available for each individual, effective demand is greater, the higher is the marginal propensity to consume. Marginal propensity to consume is determined by the level of income and the pattern of its distribution and the keenness of the desire of the people to improve their immediate living conditions. In underdeveloped countries the marginal propensity to consume is generally high, about 0·9, with the exception of Burma where crude statistics show that the propensity to consume based on private disposable income after tax is as low as 0·6. This means two things—firstly, the multiplier effect of the initial spending of the government is greater and therefore the inflationary effect will be larger; secondly, the spending of a large part of additional income on consumption leaves comparatively a smaller amount of real resources which can be diverted from the private consumers to the government for investment.

Equally important in this context as the demand for goods is the demand for services. A rise in the investment demands of the government would have a tendency to raise prices. And since demand rises not only for materials and capital goods but also for the services of labour, the price of the latter would also go up. In so far as wages of labour are an important item of the costs of production, any rise in the wage level would swell up costs and prices which in turn will lead to the demand for higher wages and thus set in motion the inflationary spiral. The fact that the wage earning class forms relatively a smaller proportion of the total population in the less developed countries as against the advanced ones and that labourers in underdeveloped countries are not so well organized in unions and their buying power is not very great, reduces the possibilities and magnitude of the wage cost spiral. But against this has to be mentioned the fact that the bargaining power of the wage earners is greater under inflationary conditions and since profits would also go up, the entrepreneurs themselves would be prepared to pay higher and higher wages. These two factors have to be taken into account in any consideration of the possibility of rise in prices via higher cost of living and higher wages.

The attitude of the people to change in money incomes and their reaction to a given rise in prices also play an important part in influencing the general trend in prices. In general, the private sector favours deficit financing for the simple reason that if in order to raise resources for investment the government relies on taxation and internal borrowing rather than on deficit financing, there would be a shrinkage of capital funds available for the private sector. On the other hand, deficit financing eases money conditions, and confers greater liquidity on the banking system. Besides, a rise in prices benefits the business classes who are the more important debtor class of the community and makes them more optimistic and venturesome in the matter of making new investments and launching upon new schemes of enterprise. If however, the private sector takes advantage of a tendency for prices to rise to make investments in consumption goods industries, the inflationary effect would be less than if in competition with the public sector they also concentrated on capital goods industries in which the scale of investment required is relatively large and the possibility of an immediate increase in the supply of goods to meet the rise in money incomes is very much limited.

A rise in money incomes however, need not necessarily cause a rise in the level of spendings of the community. If a large part of the additional money income is hoarded, it would mean that real resources are transferred without producing any inflationary effect. The hoarding habit in underdeveloped countries and the tendency to invest money income in jewels and other valuables neutralizes the effect of an increase in money supply. Also, the tendency to build up local stocks of food in a time of rising prices serves as a shock absorber in this respect. In addition, the fact that communications are not well developed in low income countries helps in containing inflation in particular regions and prevents mild inflation in one locality from being easily transferred to another.[9]

In a large measure, the extent to which a given dose of deficit financing would lead to inflationary conditions depends on the reaction of not only the business classes but of the consumers as well. The state of expectations of the people has a considerable influence on the inflationary impact of budgetary deficits. If prices have been maintained stable for a long time, the people would not expect any sudden rise in prices consequent upon deficit financing. On the other hand, if they have had recent experience of an inflationary trend in prices, even a mild dose of inflation would induce people to spend more for fear of a steady and continued decline in the value of money. This desire to exchange money quickly for goods would in turn aggravate the tendency of prices to rise. Consequently, the timing of deficit financing is of the greatest importance in determining its effect on the price level. The lesson here is that any increase in the scale of deficit financing at a time of rising prices has to be avoided in the interests of price stability. Besides, when such inflationary forces are set in motion, it becomes more and more difficult to achieve the purpose of deficit financing. The situation would be one in which since prices are rising, the state would have to resort to larger and larger amounts of deficit financing in order to transfer the same amount of real resources for investment in the public sector. The result will be runaway inflation. Speculative habits of the people have also much to do with the aggravation of inflationary conditions. The limits of deficit financing would be reached quicker and earlier in countries with a large speculative business community which is very conscious of price fluctuations. Speculation tends to exaggerate the disturbing factors affecting demand and supply. As an illustration it is mentioned that the impact of any given government deficit in Indonesia is likely to multiply itself rapidly because business people in that country are in the habit of speculating. This is in contrast to Burma " where business activities do not seem very sensitive to price fluctuations ".[10]

There is yet another reason why the inflationary consequences of deficit financing are likely to be more serious in underdeveloped countries. A sound and efficient administrative mechanism is a prerequisite for effectively controlling inflation which may result from government's excess spending over receipts. We have seen that mobilization of resources in a free enterprise economy is effected through the agency of price rise and the resulting transfer of incomes from the middle class and the labouring classes to the richer classes who are the primary savers of the community. The restriction of consumption as a consequence of price rise which is forced upon the fixed income earners is the means through which the savings are effected. It should be borne in mind that deficit financing tends to inflation when the spendings of the govern-

[9]Benham, F., ' Deficit Finance in Asia, ' *Lloyds Bank Review,* January, 1955, p. 22.

[10] 'Deficit Financing for Economic Development with Special Reference to ECAFE Countries,' *Economic Bulletin for Asia and the Far East,* November, 1954.

ment are much in excess of what the economy can absorb, that is to say, when the increase in the supply of real output does not respond adequately to increased spendings. To a large extent this lag is inevitable in so far as the expenditure is incurred on the formation of capital which does not immediately increase the yield of final output. It therefore follows that whether the spendings of the government are for building up of capital or for the production of consumption goods, so long as there is a time lag or there is inability to increase output immediately, spendings will exceed supply. Thus even when the government is utilizing the financial resources made available through deficit financing for augmenting the supply of final goods, as for example when government spends on minor irrigation, extension of agriculture, on cottage industries or community development projects, what we have to consider is the question whether these spendings do really help in increasing output quickly. The efficiency of the administrative mechanism here becomes obvious as a crucial factor. If the administrative system is weak and inefficient, if there is corruption, if works are not finished efficiently and on time, if what is spent by the government does not result in a tangible commodity or service according to schedule, but a large part of the spendings is absorbed by intermediaries, in short, if there is careless spending and wastage of financial resources, there is bound to be inflation. There is in this respect a close parallelism between deficit financing for war and deficit financing which is wasteful because of administrative shortcomings, inefficiency of workers and corruption. It is well known that inflationary threat of budgetary deficits in war is great, because resources are used for destructive purposes and their employment does not result in any increase in output. Even so, in peace time, if a large part of the spending of the government runs to waste, the same danger of excess spendings and inflation will arise. This is a fact the importance of which in the context of underdeveloped countries cannot be exaggerated. There is no denying the fact that the standard of administrative efficiency in underdeveloped countries leaves much to be desired, and consequently there is a considerable wastage of resources. It is worth examining whether a given amount of spendings in the government sector is more efficiently and economically handled than in the private sector. At any rate, the generalization can be made that to the extent spendings are not managed with efficiency and care and no sincere attempt is made to make a unit of expenditure go as far as possible in providing tangible output, there is an inherent danger of inflation.

MEASURES TO CONTROL INFLATION RESULTING FROM DEFICIT FINANCING

Measures to offset the inflationary effect of deficit budgets can be considered under two heads: (a) remedial measures and (b) preventive measures.

Remedial measures relate to the steps taken by government when once the symptoms of inflation have appeared. In so far as an inflationary upthrust in prices is due to excess demand in relation to supply, these measures would aim at controlling demand and regulating the flow of the limited supply of goods available. A well thoughtout tax policy can be successful in reducing the pressure of demand as well as in augmenting supply. Incentive taxation in the form of tax differentiation in respect of particular industries or tax exemptions with a view to promote savings or encourage investment in particular lines of enterprise, would help in containing inflationary pressures in the economy through their influence on the supply side. Since increase in the purchasing power available to the community plays an important part in making excess demand effective, it would be possible to reduce substantially the pressure of excess demand by absorbing by means of taxation and internal borrowing the marginal increments in money incomes. An additional point in favour of such a fiscal measure is the fact that the state's investments on development schemes confer benefits on the community at large and increase the money incomes of particular classes of people, and as such, government is justified in mopping up a part at least of the additional money incomes. Such a policy would have two benefits—firstly, the resources available to the state for investment is increased; secondly, the additional purchasing power which would have augmented the pressure of demand is transferred and made innocuous. In view of the large spendings by governments in underdeveloped countries on improvements in rural areas and for the development of agriculture in particular, an upward revision of the land tax or the levy of additional imposts on agricultural incomes may be strongly recommended.

When in the context of deficit financing the purchasing power with the community is increased, and there is a shortage in the supply of final goods and other resources in relation to demand, it is necessary that steps are taken to regulate the distribution of the available supply by means of controls so that inflationary pressures can be suppressed or kept within limits. This would include physical controls such as rationing, price controls and control of distribution. It should however, be added that it is difficult to have an efficient system of controls in underdeveloped countries which lack a good administrative machinery and in which the civic consciousness of the people is not of a high order.

Some control measures have a positive effect in so far as they can be operated with a view to distribute investible resources in such manner as would ensure improvement in the production of those goods the prices of which have a strategic significance in any inflationary process. Through control of capital issues and investment, financial resources can be made to flow into desirable channels or at least prevented from getting dissipated in unprofitable lines of investments. Apart from this, a suitable monetary policy involving control of credit and money supply—particularly of the selective credit control type—can succeed in directing investment into worthwhile undertakings and can prevent the scarce investible resources from flowing into unnecessary and costly schemes, like the construction of impressive and palatial buildings or luxury restaurants. Similarly, to the extent additional money incomes are utilized for the importing of luxury goods from outside and in so far as domestic inflation invariably leads to a balance of payments deficit, exchange control also becomes necessary in a growing economy. Most of the underdeveloped countries of today have adopted a strict system of exchange control. The objectives of such measures are firstly, to prevent the wastage of foreign exchange resources on unnecessary articles of consumption and secondly, to conserve foreign exchange and limit its availability for financing imports of essential capital goods and also those types of consumption goods which would help in keeping under control inflationary pressures in the economy.

In the matter of inflation as in the case of other economic ailments, prevention is better than cure. But the usual preventive measures which have been recommended and tried in many of the underdeveloped countries have not yielded very satisfactory results. One is the principle of limiting deficit financing to the size of foreign exchange available and the other is devoting the real resources released by deficit financing to the production of wage goods as far as possible. Emphasis on the need for making use of deficit financing for increasing the supply of consumption goods is based on the premise that so long as the supply of consumption goods increases in a country in step with the increase in the volume of purchasing power, there cannot be any inflationary rise in prices. It is the time lag between investment outlays and the emergence of an increased supply of final goods that constitutes an important source of inflation in a developing economy. Hence, it is argued that if the real resources diverted through deficit financing are utilized in those schemes of investment which yield quick returns and which facilitate production of wage goods or consumption goods, the threat of inflation can be considerably reduced. Thus development of cottage industries, improvement of agriculture through minor irrigation works, and increased production of food are all means which would conform to the aforesaid principle. The suggestion is therefore made that the development budgets of the underdeveloped countries are to be divided on the financial side into two categories; taxation and internal borrowing are to be used for collecting resources for investment in capital construction schemes while deficit financing is to be set apart for the production of consumption goods.[11] But it may be pointed out that even in investment schemes which are ostensibly designed to yield quick returns, a considerable amount of initial expenditure on capital formation is necessary and a time lag between investment and production, although a relatively short one, is inevitable. To that extent, there is the possibility of inflation. Furthermore, it may be questioned whether this is a wise policy. Deficit financing is resorted to in underdeveloped countries not so much to draw into use idle capital equipment or labour or to finance government investment as a balancing factor against decline in private investment, as to build up physical capital. If the primary objective is capital formation, a policy which aims at using the resources in

[11]Marathe, Sharad S., Deficit Financing and Economic Development, Sri Alladi Krishnaswami Aiyyer Shashtiabdipoorthi Endowment Lectures, University of Madras, 1953–54.

whatever manner collected, for the production of consumption goods and for increasing the stock and supply of these goods misses the main purpose for which resources are strained out of an underdeveloped economy. Certainly the need for increasing the production and supply of final goods quickly as a means to keep inflation under control cannot be disputed. But to devote undue attention to such investments and to confine deficit financing to the execution of such projects would be indicative of a mistaken notion of the whole *raison d'etre* of deficit financing.

The thesis that there will not be inflation so long as the size of budgetary deficits for financing economic development does not exceed the available external balance of the country is based on the fact that external balances represent past savings so that any excess of investment over current domestic savings reflected in budgetary deficit could be offset by making use of foreign balances. Hence if the decline in foreign balances is equal to the excess of investment over domestic savings, it would only mean that external past savings are drawn into use and added to domestic savings thus wiping out any excess investment. In such a case, deficit financing would be non-inflationary. It was on this principle that the Bernstein Mission in India (1953) suggested that in fixing the scale of deficit financing the amount of sterling reserves available to the country should be taken as a limiting factor. Deficit financing involves the creation of credit by the banking system for the benefit of the public sector or private sector or both but " creation of credit equivalent to the reduction of reserves attributable to a balance of payments deficit on either current or capital account is not inflationary and indeed, is necessary to restore the money supply and thereby prevent deflation in a country in which the money supply is properly related to economic policy and the balance of payments deficit is an appropriate deficit that can be financed ".[12] And the Mission further elaborates the argument that when credit is created or money supply is increased on behalf of the government, real resources are made available to both the public and private sectors. The benefit to the former is obvious, but to the extent money supply increases because of borrowing of business from the commercial banks, real resources are made available to the private sector also. Besides, it is pointed out that any increase in money supply resulting from deficit financing would not lead to inflation so long as the volume of money supply is within the limits set by the fall in foreign reserves and does not exceed the additional requirement of money resulting from economic development and increased production and the increasing monetization of the economy.

This assumption however has to be interpreted with care. Whether deficit financing when it is confined within the limits set by external deficit would lead to inflation or not depends on the purpose for which and the party on whose behalf the balance of payments deficit is incurred. Balance of payments

[12]*Economic Development with Stability*, A Report to the Government of India by a Mission of the International Monetary Fund, New Delhi, 1954, p. 46 f.n.

deficit is caused by the excess of imports over exports and this excess of imports may be for meeting the requirements of government or private business. Thus in the case of India when government imports goods from foreign countries in excess of the exports of the country, the necessary foreign exchange may be acquired from the Reserve Bank through borrowing which is deficit financing. This would not lead to any increase in money supply because the assets and liabilities of the Reserve Bank would remain the same. The decline in the foreign exchange assets of the Bank would be replaced by other assets in the form of government debt. The transaction would not therefore cause any inflationary pressure. On the other hand, if external deficit is caused by increased imports of private business and if on the ground of external deficit government also resorts to deficit financing there will be excess credit creation. This is because of the fact that when private business acquires the foreign exchange to finance the excess imports, credit is expanded by the banking system on account of this financial operation. The expansion of credit on behalf of the private sector would be matched by the balance of payments deficit. If on top of this, government resorts to deficit financing on the assumption that the decline in foreign reserves would have an offsetting effect on domestic creation of credit, it is in effect counting balance of payments deficit as a safeguard against the inflationary effect of budgetary deficits twice over, and piling up one deficit over another.[13] This would lead to excessive increase in the supply of money or over-expansion of credit and would bring about inflation.

The purpose for which balance of payments deficit is incurred also determines directly the inflationary potentialities of deficit financing even when it is within the limits of or equal to the size of external deficit. As the economy expands, and the increasing purchasing power released through deficit financing presses on the available supply of wage or consumption goods, there is bound to be a rise in prices if no immediate increase in the domestic production and supply of these goods is possible. In such a situation foreign reserves can be drawn upon or external borrowing may be resorted to, in order to finance the import of consumption goods. This would have an obvious restraining effect on the price trends in the country. However the situation becomes different if external deficit is due to the importing of capital goods for investment purposes. The investment goods do increase the supply of real resources. But their installation and the starting of their operation necessitate additional domestic savings if inflation is to be avoided. These additional costs involved in the installation of the equipment and in the procurement of materials, etc. involve further spendings which if financed through budgetary deficits cannot fail to have an inflationary impact on domestic price level, unless these additional investment costs are matched by increased domestic savings. It is thus clear that the popular assumption that deficit financing or domestic

[13]Shenoy, B. R., *Problems of Indian Economic Development*, Sir William Meyer Lectures, 1955–56, University of Madras, 1958, pp. 64–65.

expansion of credit would have a neutral effect on money supply and prices, provided the scale of such financing does not exceed the extent of external payments deficit, is incorrect. In reality it is hard to fix any upper limit to the size of deficit financing in any definite manner, in an underdeveloped country. The purpose for which such method of financing is resorted to, the type of goods to be imported, supply and credit conditions in the country, domestic savings available, all these are relevant to drawing the safe upper limit.

The conclusion therefore emerges that while in an underdeveloped country certain factors like, limited use of credit, hoarding habits of the people and the need for more money to meet the requirements of a growing economy serve as useful cushioning agents against any inflationary threat of deficit financing, yet the factors which operate in the opposite direction far outweigh the former. Shortage of capital equipment, need for long term investments, a high marginal propensity to consume, low money income ratio and the very small size of the middle class—which are characteristic features of an under-developed economy—considerably limit the scope of deficit financing. Further-more, these countries do not have an adequate tax system to absorb effectively the marginal increase in money incomes. In the absence of a good administra-tive machinery, price control measures cannot function satisfactorily. On the other hand, the general shortage of foreign exchanges and the great dependence on foreign export markets serve as real obstacles to deficit financing on a large scale.

A NOTE ON DEFICIT FINANCING IN INDIA

Deficit financing for purposes of economic development in India was first recommended in the Bombay Plan (1943). A good part of the outlay under the First Five-Year Plan was deficit financed; however, the approach of the government to this method of financing was hesitant and rather apologetic. In the Second Five-Year Plan the role of deficit financing as a means for econo-mic development was explicitly recognized.

The First Five-Year Plan originally envisaged a total outlay by the Centre and the states of Rs. 20,690 million. (This was later raised to Rs. 23,777 million of which the Centre was to spend Rs. 13,895 million and the states Rs. 9,882 million.) The resources for incurring an outlay of Rs. 20,690 million over the five years 1951–56, were to be found to the extent of Rs. 12,580 million by way of taxes, loans, small savings, etc. and the balance of Rs. 8,110 million was to be covered partly by external assistance (Rs. 5,210 million) and partly by deficit financing (Rs. 2,900 million). Actual outlay on the First Plan in the five years turned out to be Rs. 20,124 million of which the Centre accounted for Rs. 11,149 million and the states Rs. 8,975 million. Resources collected by the Central Government by means of taxation and from railways, and private savings through loans and small savings, deposits funds, etc. amounted to Rs. 7,776 million. Deducting from this a sum of Rs. 3,497 million transferred to the states, the amount actually available for utilization by the Centre was Rs. 4,279 million. Since external assistance was available to the extent of Rs. 2,032 million, the total resources available for the Centre amounted to Rs. 6,311 million leaving a budgetary gap of Rs. 11,149 million minus Rs. 6,311 million or Rs. 4,838 million. The states' resources including the assistance of Rs. 3,497 million from the Centre aggregated to Rs. 8,494 million, causing thus a deficit of Rs. 481 million at the state level. Thus the overall deficit of the Centre and the states was Rs. 5,319 million which formed about 26 per cent of the aggregate developmental outlay.[14]

When the First Five-Year Plan was formulated, it was hoped that deficit financing would be of the order of Rs. 2,900 million which corresponded to the drawal of sterling balances. Although external assistance was available to the extent of Rs. 2,960 million, only about Rs. 1,880 million was actually utilized in the First Plan period. In the first three years of the Plan, the Union Government's deficit was covered mostly by drawing on its cash balance and in the last two years by borrowing from the Reserve Bank. Thus at the end of the First Plan period, floating debt of the Central Government increased by Rs. 3,469 million, sale of securities held in reserve amounted to Rs. 252 million and withdrawal from cash balances was of the order of Rs. 1,117 million, the three items adding up to Rs. 4,838 million. As regards the states, their deficit of Rs. 481 million was covered to the extent of Rs. 211 million by increase in floating debt, Rs. 102 million by sale of securities held in reserve and Rs. 168 million by withdrawal from cash balances.

On the whole deficit financing did not have any noticeable effect on money supply and prices at least until the close of the First Plan period. In the five years 1951–56 money supply increased by Rs. 2,050 million or 14 per cent. The Central Government's budget for the first year of the plan showed a small surplus and the deficit in the next year 1952–53 did not have any expansionary effect because of certain offsetting factors such as the availability of external finance in the form of loans and grants, decline in private investment which itself was due to the tighter monetary policy and severe controls on private investment, and the sharp decline in scheduled bank credit. However, the significant step up in development expenditure in the last two years of the Plan, budgetary deficits and balance of payments surplus combined to expand money supply substantially. Thus while in the first three years of the Plan money supply declined by Rs. 1,850 million, it increased by Rs. 3,900 million in the last two years. Despite this monetary expansion the general price level

---

[14]These aggregate figures are based on actuals for the first four years of the plan and revised estimates for the final year. The actual budgetary deficit and the outlay on the plan in 1955–56 turned out to be less than the revised estimates. Thus the outlay on the First Plan in the five years was Rs. 19,600 million and deficit financing was of the order of Rs. 4,200 million or 21 per cent of total outlay. (*Review of the First Five-Year Plan*, Government of India, New Delhi, May, 1957, p. 34 and tables on pp. 39–47.)

was not affected. This was due largely to the considerable increase in agricultural output in 1953–55 and the fact that deficit financing in these years served only to neutralize the post-Korean deflationary forces. While money supply increased by nearly 7 per cent in 1954–55, the level of wholesale prices actually fell by some 5 per cent. In the last year of the Plan (1955–56) however with larger investment outlays and budgetary deficits and further increase in money supply and a decline in agricultural production, the price level showed a marked uptrend, indicating that the limits of the economy's capacity to absorb deficit financing were being rapidly reached.

Deficit financing in the Second Five-Year Plan period was not only of much larger dimensions than in the First Plan, but it came on top of a rising trend in price level. The Second Plan envisaged a total outlay of Rs. 48,000 million which was to be met to the extent of Rs. 8,000 million from current revenues, Rs. 12,000 million from borrowings from the public, Rs. 4,000 million from Railways, Provident Funds and other deposits, Rs. 8,000 million external finance, and Rs. 12,000 million deficit financing, leaving a gap of Rs. 4,000 million to be covered by additional taxation and further deficit financing. It may be pointed out that deficit financing which the planning authorities considered as possible in the Second Plan period was much in excess of the estimates made by some economists and other specialists. Thus the Commission of the International Monetary Fund in 1953 suggested that the scale of deficit financing should be related to the availability of sterling balances and regarded Rs. 333 million per annum or about Rs. 1,650 million over the five years as a feasible maximum. Dr. B. R. Shenoy pointed out the need for fixing the scale of deficit financing with reference to the requirement of cash balances with the public which itself could be assumed to vary with the increase in the national product. He recommended Rs. 1,800–2,200 million for the five-year period.[15] In his Report on Tax Reform in India, Professor Kaldor stated that the amount of deficit financing which the economy could bear was not likely to exceed Rs. 1,500 million a year or say Rs. 8,000 million over the five-year period.[16] The Economic Commission for Asia and the Far East considered Rs. 12,000 million as the upper limit for deficit financing in the Second Plan years and stressed the fact that to raise the sum further might leave a large quantity of excess purchasing power without any corresponding cover.[17]

A review of the progress of the Second Plan shows that on the resources side, the performance was disappointing. Against the anticipated receipts of Rs. 12,000 million from current revenues over the five years, the actual amount available in the first three years totalled only Rs. 4,275 million or less than

[15]Shenoy, B. R., *A Note of Dissent—Second Five-Year Plan, the Frame Work*, Government of India, New Delhi, 1955, p. 167.

[16]Kaldor, Nicholas, *Indian Tax Reform, Report of a Survey*, Government of India, New Delhi, 1956, p. 1.

[17]*Economic Survey of Asia and the Far East*, United Nations, 1955, p. 112.

36 per cent, and this in spite of strenuous efforts on the part of both the central and state governments to collect the maximum amount possible from additional taxation. The yield from public loans at the centre and the states and from small savings was also not quite satisfactory. It was assumed that income would increase in the five-year period by 25 per cent, and consumption by 21 per cent so that the savings margin would be widened from 7 per cent of the national income at the beginning of the Plan to 10 per cent at the end of it. In actual fact, in the first three years, national income increased by only 10 per cent and the collections through taxation as a proportion of national income increased from 7·6 per cent in 1955–56 to 9·2 per cent in 1957–58. This deficiency on the normal resources side necessitated resort to deficit financing to the extent of Rs. 9,000 million even in the first three years. In these years the total outlay on the plan was about Rs. 25,000 million financed to the tune of 46 per cent by domestic resources, 19 per cent by external assistance and 35 per cent deficit finance. Of the total deficit of Rs. 9,000 million incurred by the centre and the states, the major part (Rs. 8,300 million) was covered by increase in the floating debt of the government with the Reserve Bank and a small part of about Rs. 700 million was covered by withdrawal of cash balances. Thus while in the First Plan, about one-fifth of the total outlay was deficit financed, the proportion of this method of financing exceeded one-third of the total even at the end of the first three years of the Second Plan. However, in the last two years of the Second Plan, budgetary deficits were considerably reduced. It is estimated that over the five years 1955–56 to 1960–61 the total Plan outlay aggregated to Rs. 46,000 million; and this was financed to the extent of Rs. 11,520 million through taxation and surpluses of public enterprises, Rs. 14,100 million by mobilization of private savings through loans, small savings, etc., Rs. 10,900 million through external assistance and the rest Rs. 9,480 million through deficit financing.[18] Thus against the original estimate of deficit financing of Rs. 12,000 million, the actual turned out to be less by Rs. 2,520 million. And the proportion of deficit financing to total outlay on the Second Plan was 26 per cent while it was 21 per cent in the First Plan.

Inflationary pressures in the Indian economy which have become noticeable of late, have been due not only to the large size of deficit financing but also to the pattern of investment in the Second Plan. As against the First Plan, there was a shift in emphasis from agriculture to major industries and capital intensive schemes in the Second Plan. About 60 per cent of the entire investment outlay in the Second Plan was on large and medium industries, mining, transport and communications and electric power projects. Investments like these while essential for the construction of a strong base for the economy to grow, have undoubtedly a large inflationary potential. On the other hand, projects in which the lag between capital formation and the generation of additional real income is much shorter, like agriculture, National Extension

[18]*Report on Currency and Finance*, 1960–61, Reserve Bank of India, Bombay, p. 79.

and Community Development together with some schemes under Irrigation and Flood Control accounted for Rs. 11,600 million or 30 per cent. It is worth observing that the items in the first category absorbed 44 per cent of the total plan expenditure in the First Five-Year Plan, while the items in the second category totalled Rs. 11,330 million or 56 per cent. It is relevant to note also that apart from the outlays, the actual progress made in the first three years of the Second Plan in respect of investments in the larger slow yielding schemes was much more marked than in the case of the quick-yielding investments.

The effect of the increasing reliance placed on deficit financing for economic development is seen in the trends in money supply and prices. The volume of money with the public increased from about Rs. 22,000 million in 1955-56 to about Rs. 27,000 million by the middle of 1960. This was the net result of the expansionary force of government's budgetary deficits and credit creation for the private sector and the contractionary effect of the decline in foreign reserves.[19] On the other hand, industrial and agricultural production improved only slightly, with the result the general level of prices registered a sharp up-trend—the index number of wholesale prices (1952-53=100) rose by 23 points (from 100·0 to 122·9) between April, 1956 and June, 1960. The trends in relative prices in the five years highlight the crucial role played by food prices in the general inflationary situation in the country. Although the trend of prices has been upward since 1955, there is a distinct and sharp upturn in 1958-59. Against an average annual rise of 3·5 points in 1955-56 to 1957-58, the rise was by 6 points in 1958-59 and this higher rate of increase has continued since then. A significant fact to be noted in this connection is that in 1957-58 the very year when the output of industrial materials declined moderately, and food production fell substantially by as many as 7·5 points, deficit financing touched the peak level of nearly Rs. 5,000 million. This draws pointed attention to the importance of proper timing of deficit financing, and underlines the need for regulating financing of economic development by means of budgetary deficits with reference to the production and supply conditions in the country.

Against this background, the cautious approach of the planning authorities to deficit financing in the Third Five-Year Plan is understandable. With a marked rise in prices in recent years and with the rapid decline in foreign reserves, the need has been felt to reduce deficit financing drastically. Not only was the size of budgetary deficits brought down substantially in the last two years of the Second Plan, but deficit financing has been assigned a much smaller role in the Third Five-Year Plan compared with the Second Plan. The total investment outlay envisaged in the Third Plan is Rs. 104,000 million. It is assumed that a 33 per cent increase in money supply over the Third Plan would be warranted by the expansion of the economy and increasing monetiza-

[19]Thus between 1955-56 and 1959-60 bank credit increased from Rs. 7,610 million to Rs. 11,280 million while Foreign Exchange Reserves declined from Rs. 8,250 million to Rs. 3,630 million.

tion. This would allow for the creation of additional money to the extent of Rs. 9,500 million. Since part of the money supply comes through the banking system, the amount of budgetary deficits that could be considered permissible for the Third Plan period is fixed at Rs. 5,500 million. This constitutes a bare 7·3 per cent of the total outlay in the public sector.

Chapter XI

FOREIGN TRADE

THERE IS a close relationship between the economic growth of a country and its foreign trade. Economic development and rise in the level of national income influence the pattern and volume of foreign trade while changes in the conditions of foreign trade directly affect the composition and level of national income. Given the size of national income and volume of foreign trade, any change in either of these would set in motion certain forces which tend to bring about a sort of balance between the two. According to traditional theory, if two countries are on the gold standard, increased exports of one country would result in the inflow of gold which affects price level and the rise in prices would slow down exports and increase imports as a result of which an adjustment is brought about in the trade relation between the two countries. A later refinement of this theory consists in explaining the adjustment in terms of the income effect or changes in the income levels of the two countries which affect their level of exports and imports. According to this view, the prime mover in the restoration of balance is not the quantity of money and the price level, but the level of income and spendings of the community which react on the volume of exports and imports.

The impact of foreign trade on the economic development of a country can be explained by starting from the assumption that there is a normal balance between these two in the form of a given ratio of the value of foreign trade to national income and that this initial balance is disturbed by a substantial rise in exports due to exogenous factors. Any increase in the exports of a country while imports remain constant, means that there is an excess of external demand which would influence investment and thereby the level of economic activity and the national income of the country having an export surplus in the same manner as an increase in effective demand at home will have on national income. Normally exports are balanced by imports. Since payments have to be made for the imports, the net additional income earned through foreign trade is the difference between the value of exports and imports. Imports constitute a part of current income; hence if exports exceed the imports of a country and the country has a surplus balance of payments, this excess is treated as investment for national accounting purposes. The total investment of a country in a period of time, say a year, is therefore, the sum of domestic investment and foreign investment in the form of a surplus earned in international trade. Realized savings are necessarily equal to domestic invest-

354

ment plus foreign investment. Therefore when balance of payments is in equilibrium, it means that there is neither excess investment nor excess savings arising out of foreign trade. But if there is a balance of payments surplus it means that there is excess investment which will have an inflationary or expansionary effect; and a balance of payments deficit is of the nature of excess savings and will have the opposite contractionary effect.

A rise in the level of aggregate investment represented by an export surplus would however work itself out normally through international trade in a manner that would restore the balance in external trade. Increase in investment whether it is domestic or foreign, will raise the level of spendings and income. But this rise in domestic income in turn will attract more imports with the result that the total expansionary effect of an export surplus is reduced to the extent of the leakage involved in increased imports. This is so because increase in imports will raise the level of activity in the countries whose goods are imported, and therefore from the point of view of the importing country, should be regarded as equivalent to savings in respect of their non-expansionary or even deflationary effect on income. This would also mean that if starting from a position of equilibrium in its external payments relations, a country experiences an increase in imports with exports remaining constant, this would have a dampening effect on the level of activity and domestic income, the overall effect however, being modified to the extent of this country's exports increasing in consequence of the rise in income in the foreign country.

Obviously, the effect of an export surplus on investment and demand is of particular significance to advanced capitalist economies where the problem of maintaining a steady rate of growth is linked up with the problem of ensuring a high level of aggregate demand. On the contrary, in underdeveloped countries, the basic economic problem is altogether different and the advantage of foreign trade to these countries has to be judged with reference to its effect on the building up of capital, in generating economic activity in new lines of enterprises, in making available external resources for the importing of capital equipment and technical personnel, in short, in making economic growth possible.

Turning to the effect of growth of national output on foreign trade, it may be observed, that economic growth is made possible by stepping up the rate of investment which increases the productive capacity of the economy. But additional investment involves also an increase in income which would lead to increased imports. It thus follows that additional investment will have an adverse or beneficial effect on the balance of trade of a country according as its marginal propensity to import is high or low. If the savings are large and the capital productivity co-efficient is high and there is a positive foreign trade balance to begin with, the rate of growth of productive capacity will be high. Hence in underdeveloped countries whose savings margin is very narrow and who often have a negative foreign balance ratio, the extent to which productive capacity will rise through foreign trade is limited. It also follows that if in an underdeveloped country the level of domestic investment is stepped up, and the rate of expansion is accelerated, so that the demand effects exceed the supply effects, the country will have an adverse balance of trade which will necessitate inflow of capital in order to sustain the rate of investment. When once the rate of growth of the economy is accelerated by stepping up the rate of investment, it can be maintained only if the higher rate of investment is kept up. Output capacity which reflects growth of income, in any particular period of time depends on the investment in the preceding period and the ratio of the increment in output to the increment in capital. Part of this increased output is domestically consumed and part is exported. The amount of output available for domestic investment is the difference between total output on the one hand and domestic consumption and exports on the other. Thus if marginal propensity to consume and marginal propensity to import are given, exports and domestic capital formation compete for the excess of new supply over domestic consumption. If increase in exports resulting from new investment is equal to increase in imports and the increase in domestic investment is such that the money income-generated is in equilibrium with increase in productive capacity, then this rate of growth should be considered as the one which will have no adverse effect on the balance of trade of the country. If investment exceeds this limit, trade balance will turn passive, i.e. exports would not increase in proportion to rise in imports. Thus the extent to which a given rise in the level of investment would affect the balance of trade of a country depends on whether investment exceeds or falls short of the optimum level and also on the ratio of the marginal propensity to import.[1]

THE GAINS OF UNDERDEVELOPED COUNTRIES FROM INTERNATIONAL TRADE

Normally, the volume of external trade of a country increases with economic growth. The expansion of foreign trade is in fact an indicator of economic development. The economic history of nearly all advanced countries of the world, U.K., Germany, France and Japan shows that the growth of national product has been attended with a simultaneous increase in the volume of foreign trade. The one great exception to this general rule is the Soviet Union. The peculiarity in this country is to be explained partly by the economic policy of the government and partly by the vastness of the country and the abundance and variety of its resources which have helped to bring about what is called self-contained development. The normal trend however, is for both foreign trade and national income increasing together. Economic development means production of more and better goods. Export capacity is thus increased. It also implies rise in the level of investment, greater employment, increase in aggregate and *per capita* incomes and hence larger consumption demands also. Changes in consumption and investment would not only promote domestic

[1] Ingram, J. C., ' Growth in Capacity and Canada's Balance of Payments, ' *The American Economic Review*, March, 1957, pp. 95–97.

economic activity but also lead to increased imports and exports. It thus
follows that changes in the balance of payments position of particular countries
are caused by differences in their rates of growth. In general, the richer and
more developed countries of the world have higher rates of growth than the
less developed ones. Apart from this difference in the rates of income expansion,
structural and institutional factors also account for differences in the balance
of payments experience. In other words, although basically the factors responsible for balance of payments difficulties of developed and underdeveloped
countries are the same, yet the fact that the richer industrial countries are
well developed and have large resources which are easily shiftable, not only
reduces the severity of their external payments problems, but also explains
why they are able to tide over a crisis with greater ease than poorer countries.

The effect of variations in a country's balance of payments or income on
the economy and foreign trade of another or other countries, depends to a
large extent on the size of the countries concerned, the standards of economic
life attained by them, their relative position in international trade, i.e. their
share in the total volume of international trade, and the elasticity of demand
and supply of their imports and exports. Even among the poorer countries,
those which are small in area and in population are in a more unenviable
position. Their dependence on external trade is greater than that of bigger
countries. While they have little effect on the pattern and terms of trade of
other countries, they are themselves influenced to a greater extent by the course
and behaviour of national income of richer countries. The smaller among the
underdeveloped countries cannot have a diversified economy because of the
scarcity of natural resources. Their exports trend to be confined to one or a
few articles, but their consumption pattern is more diversified so that they
depend to a large extent on foreign imports to meet their consumption requirements. Arranging the different countries of the world into six categories
according to the size of their population, it is found that in countries of the
first category (i.e. countries with large population) the average foreign trade
ratio in the years 1950–54 was 0·21 while in the smaller countries the ratio
was 0·41.[2]

Under conditions of free trade, an underdeveloped country benefits from
its external trade in so far as it helps in augmenting capital formation. Since
the level of production and per capita incomes are very low, it would not be
possible in many of these countries to further depress the already low levels of
consumption. It is obvious then that the vicious circle of low production and
low savings can be broken only if external resources are made available. In
the absence of a free flow of foreign capital or external aid, the only way open
for the underdeveloped countries is to increase their export earnings. From
the point of view of growth these export earnings are significant in so far as

---

[2]The foreign trade ratio for each country is calculated by dividing the sum of commodity
exports and imports by the sum of national income and imports (all in current prices)—Kuznets,
Simon, *Six Lectures on Economic Growth*, Free Press, Glencoe, Illinois, 1959, pp. 93–94,

they represent a marginal increment to national income and as such, may play a crucial role in accelerating domestic capital formation. Export earnings help in importing much needed capital goods from advanced countries of the world which the underdeveloped countries left to their resources and technical backwardness, cannot produce. Furthermore, expansion of external trade means an increase in effective demand and extension of the markets available for the products of the underdeveloped countries. Normally, in the absence of any innovation by means of which a ' new ' commodity is produced, expansion of one industry has to be at the expense of another industry. And innovation is difficult and rare in an underdeveloped country. This problem can be solved if increased output resulting from the expansion of one or more industries is exported and disposed of in external markets. Since the export sector can be readily controlled, the larger earnings arising out of increased exports can be profitably diverted for investment purposes.

The development and expansion of export–oriented industries help growth not only through the earnings of foreign exchange but also by indirectly assisting other industries in the country. The development of an export–oriented major industry facilitates and encourages the development of other industries which help in general economic growth. Quite often, the emergence and expansion of particular industries provide the necessary impetus and the means to ensure rapid growth of the economy as a whole. The yield of one or a few industries in a country may increase more than in proportion to the yield of the other industries. The expansion of the domestic market and higher levels of consumption offer an incentive for increased investment and production. Prof. Haberler lays much emphasis on this galvanizing influence of competition as one of the important benefits of foreign trade and an agent providing a strong motive force for the starting and developing of new industries. Also, the overhead facilities which have to be provided for the export industries constitute an important source of large external economies to other enterprises which may or may not be directly connected with the former.

The economic history of Great Britain affords an excellent illustration of the manner in which a country is benefited by foreign trade in developing her industries and also the extent to which an industrialized nation by means of its trade relations with primary producing countries can help in the industrialization and economic growth of the latter. While in the 18th century, Britain's export of cotton textiles played an important part in the building up of her industrial structure, in the 19th century as the country advanced rapidly in industrialization, her foreign trade came more and more to be in the nature of export of a variety of manufactured goods and import of raw materials and food stuffs which contributed to some extent to the building up of the economies of many primary producing countries. British imports rose from about 12 per cent of the national income at the beginning of the 19th century to about 30 per cent at the end of the century. Britain was the centre of international trade and Prof. Nurkse points out that the " Centre's increasing demand for raw materials and food stuffs created incentives for capital and labour to move from the Centre to the outlying areas accelerating the process of growth transmission from the former to the latter ".[3] The countries which benefited by this pattern of international trade were the new countries in the world's temperate latitudes—Canada, Argentina, Uruguay, South Africa, Australia and New Zealand. From the point of view of these countries therefore, external trade was undoubtedly an engine of growth. Between the middle of the 19th century and the early years of the 20th century, the proportion of British imports from the new countries—Canada, Argentina, South Africa, Australia and New Zealand—increased from 8 per cent to 18 per cent while that from the U.S.A. and industrial Europe remained more or less constant at about 40 per cent. Parallel with this trend in British imports, was the outflow of capital from Britain to the new countries which increased from 10 per cent of the total British exports of capital in 1870 to 45 per cent in 1913. As the external trade of these countries with Britain increased, their export earnings also swelled up, while at the same time the inflow of foreign investment helped in domestic capital formation and in the rapid growth of their economies, thus setting in motion a cumulative process of economic expansion.

Nevertheless, the importance of foreign trade in economic growth must not be exaggerated. It should be remembered that in only some of the under-developed countries in the 19th century did external trade contribute substantially to economic advancement. What is true of Canada, South Africa, Australia and New Zealand is not true of China, India, tropical Africa and Central America. As against the former, the latter were relatively neglected by the expansion of export demand as well as of the flow of capital.[4] These countries had something of a dual economy with a well developed export sector and a primitive domestic sector. Foreign trade fostered the growth of the former sector without in any way affecting the latter. In other words, circumstances that favoured the proper utilization of the opportunities presented by increased external trade in countries like Canada, Australia and New Zealand were not available in the other countries, and the opportunities were not seized upon and made proper use of in these countries. The major factor responsible for this difference is to be found in the fact that international trade patterns are determined primarily by economic considerations. Britain's imports from the primary producers increased considerably in the 19th century and the outflow of capital to these countries was substantial because it fitted in with the pattern of economic development of Britain at that time. The external trade of Britain was not designed with a view to develop the economies of the countries with whom she had trade relations. The overhead facilities and the external economies that became available in the primary producing countries were the indirect benefits of foreign trade and the extent to which

[3]Nurkse, Ragnar, *Patterns of Trade and Development*, Wicksell Lectures, 1959, Stockholm, 1959, p. 15.

[4]Nurkse, Ragnar, *ibid.*, p. 18,

such facilities were utilized for the overall economic development of the country, depended on political, social and economic factors—the attitude of the people, their spirit of enterprise and the facilities offered by the governments concerned. In the absence of these helpful factors, foreign trade would result more in exploitation than in economic growth.

The existence of self-contained and non-competing groups in the form of foreign and domestic sectors in underdeveloped economies is only one of the factors limiting the scope for expansion in such economies. As between manufactures and agricultural production, the spread between cost of materials and value of the final product is much greater in the former than in the latter. The multiplier effect of an initial investment is therefore larger in manufacturing industry. While expansion of foreign trade of some of the primary producing countries in the 19th century undoubtedly led to the acquisition of foreign exchange and increased capital formation, the fact still remains that had comparable investments been made in secondary industries national income in these countries would have increased faster and economic progress would have been more rapid and spectacular. The economic history of countries like China, India and Malaya shows that the main reason why they did not benefit much from external trade was that foreign investments for developing export industries failed to get properly integrated in their economic structure. Investments were made by foreign enterprisers and businesses in the production of food and industrial raw materials with a view to get as large returns as possible. These countries at best remained merely as outposts of the economies of the more developed countries and the foreign capital that was employed aimed at benefiting the investing country and not the countries where the investments were made. Quite often, the foreign enterprises were in monopolistic and monopsonistic position; and specialization in food and extractive industries removed most of the secondary and cumulative benefits of the investments from the point of view of the primary producing countries which attracted capital from outside. The pattern of the economy of these countries was oriented to the needs of the developed countries and offered little scope for any technical progress or internal and external economies.[5] Besides, to the extent productive facilities were foreign owned, even when productivity in particular concerns was large, the benefits in the form of large returns accrued primarily to the foreigner.

Much stress is laid by some economists on the benefits from external trade and investments in the form of improvement in the standards of life of the people in the primary producing countries and also better organization and rise in standards of literacy and education. In this respect also, India, China and some other South-East Asian countries did not gain. The contribution of external trade to the formation of social and human capital is certainly of equal importance as increased national product. But the formation of this

[5]Singer, H. W., 'The Distribution of Gains between Investing and Borrowing Countries,' *The American Economic Review—Papers and Proceedings*, May, 1950, pp. 473–85.

type of capital as much as the expansion of markets and increase in demand which are assumed to follow from foreign trade, depends to a large extent 'on the manner in which the initial gain is distributed, whether it goes into the hands of the foreign investor or to the large number of wage earners who are employed in the export-oriented industries. The existence of under-employment and disguised unemployment and the tendency for labourers to follow traditional occupations, combined with the limited regional mobility of labour and its large turnover, helped to keep down the wage level in underdeveloped countries at a time when large foreign investments were made in some extractive industries. The employer took low wage level for granted with the result that the low wage rate tended to become fixed and permanent. It was this belief that led to compulsive methods of obtaining labour through taxation and administrative pressure when the necessary labour was not forthcoming at the prevailing wage rate. The importation of cheap Indian and Chinese labour for employment in the plantations of Malaya, and the adoption of similar tactics in Australia and North America are an illustration of this point. It is therefore not surprising that the economies of these countries did not benefit by foreign trade or investment. Their income level remained stagnant, effective demand did not rise and markets did not expand.[6]

Another factor which has been sometimes mentioned in explanation of the failure of some underdeveloped countries to gain from external trade is their failure to make use of export earnings when available, for increasing domestic capital formation. When the demand for export products increased and export earnings rose correspondingly, these countries found it irresistible to use the incomes for further expanding the primary goods industries rather than to divert the earnings for importing capital goods or for investing in major industries. On the other hand, the tendency was to devote greater attention to manufacturing industries when the earnings from primary production decreased. Thus they failed to industrialize in a boom because things were as good as they were and failed to industrialize in a slump because things were as bad as they were.[7] This failure however was due as much to the unstability of external earnings as to the lethargy and lack of enterprise on the part of the people.

THE FOREIGN TRADE PROBLEM OF UNDERDEVELOPED COUNTRIES

A rough measure of the extent to which an economy benefits by its external trade is the size of its net earnings from exports. This in turn is determined by the supply of export goods and the nature of their demand in foreign markets, the import requirements of the country and also the unit value of export goods

[6]Myint, H., ' The Gains from International Trade and the Backward Countries, ' *Review of Economic Studies*, Vol. XXII, 1954–55, pp. 129–42.

[7]Singer, H. W., ' The Distribution of Gains between Investing and Borrowing Countries, ' *The American Economic Review—Papers and Proceedings*, May, 1950, p. 482.

compared with that of imports. The significance of these three factors exports, imports and the terms of trade—in determining the size of foreign trade earnings of underdeveloped countries may now be examined against the background of world trade.

(a) Exports

Considerable emphasis has been laid on export promotion in underdeveloped countries like India in view of the close correlation between export earnings and domestic investment. Of the aggregate annual export earnings only a small portion is available for adding to the capital stock of the country. This is so because the bulk of current export earnings is needed for financing the regular imports defined as maintenance imports. If the country is indebted to foreign countries and has to make annual external payments in order to meet its foreign debt obligations, only the balance available over and above mainte-nance imports and service charges of foreign loans can be used for domestic capital formation.[8] Hence the larger the propensity to import and the heavier the debt service charges, the smaller would be the contribution of exports to domestic investment. This means that in the absence of fresh foreign loans, a considerable stepping up of exports is an imperative need for promoting capital formation. The extra exports needed to finance one rupee of extra foreign debt service are considered to be the reciprocal of one minus the propensity to import. Thus if propensity to import is $\frac{6}{10}$ and debt service is one rupee then exports are to increase by Rs. $2\frac{1}{2}$. Of this Re. 1 will go for debt service and Rs. $1\frac{1}{2}$ would be available for importing goods to meet the consumption requirements resulting from economic growth. This leaves nothing for making additional investments; hence, to meet this need, exports are to increase to a greater extent. In a small country like Rhodesia where the burden of external debt is heavy, propensity to import capital and consumption goods has been estimated at 0·73 so that an extra export of £ 100 would improve merchandise trade balance by only £ 27.[9] In other words, if debt service obligations amount to £ 27, given the propensity to import, exports needed are £ 100, and if additional imports are required to augment domestic capital stocks, exports are to increase correspondingly. This analysis is of particular signifi-cance to India in the present context. An exact estimate of our foreign exchange requirements is necessary in our programme of planned investment. The non-resilience of our exports, the considerable increase in our import requirements for investment purposes and the fact that our foreign debt service obligations are expected to rise significantly in the Third Plan period call for sustained effort to increase our exports. It is also important to distinguish between the

[8]Mandelbaum, K., *The Industrialization of Underdeveloped Areas*, Basil Blackwell, Oxford, 1945, p. 89.

[9]Enke, Stephen, ' Western Development of a Sparsely Populated Country—the Rhodesias,' *The American Economic Review*, June, 1960, pp. 387–400.

propensity to import capital goods and the propensity to import consumption goods. For, obviously, given the propensity to import the former category of goods, the higher the rate of investment expected, the higher should exports have to be increased in order to finance the import requirements.

While in underdeveloped countries the need for stepping up exports is great, most of them are experiencing in recent years increasing difficulty in this direction. Normally, the income elasticity of demand for the articles imported by advanced countries is less than that of the imports of the primary goods producing countries. As the income of the latter group of countries increases, they require more and more of machines, plants and other capital goods for investment and a larger supply of luxury articles and other manufactured products for consumption. But food materials and other raw produce constitute the bulk of the imports of industrial economies, and the demand for these goods does not rise in proportion to income expansion. Thus between 1938 and 1954 total production of industrial countries increased by 77 per cent, but the quantities of food stuffs taken increased by only 35 per cent.[10] According to an estimate made by Prebisch, the former Executive Director of the Economic Commission for Latin America, the income elasticity of the United States demand for primary goods is 0·66 and that of Latin America for industrial products is 1·58.[11] Nor is the demand for raw materials likely to go up to any significant extent in so far as most of the advanced countries of the world are taking steps to make themselves less dependent on other countries in the matter of raw materials by economizing in the use of such goods and by developing synthetic substitutes.[12] Since by and large, the imports of industrial countries are the exports of primary producing countries, it follows that given a certain rate of increase in incomes in developed and underdeveloped countries, the imports of the latter increase to a much greater extent than the imports of the former and consequently their balance of payments position deteriorates. This is only aggravated by the fact that there has been a secular trend for income in industrial countries to go up at a much faster rate than incomes in primary goods producing countries so that the exports of the latter form a smaller and smaller proportion of the national incomes of the former. Apart from this, differences in the elasticity of demand account for sharper trends in imports in the different phases of the cycle in underdeveloped coun-

[10] *Trends in International Trade*, GATT, Geneva, 1958, p. 43.

[11] Quoted in *Economic Development* by Charles P. Kindleberger, McGraw-Hill, New York, 1958, pp. 246–47.

[12] This point however tends to be exaggerated. In an interesting article B. C. Swerling mentions that while production of such synthetic substitutes is increasing, the manufacture of such substitutes itself requires other raw materials. Thus synthetic production of rubber in the U.S.A. provides an expanded outlet for black strap molasses or invert sugarcane syrup from abroad. There is also increasing need for new raw materials—metallic minerals, petroleum, etc. Atomic fission promises larger exports of uranium from some underdeveloped countries— Swerling, Boris C., 'U.S. Commodity Imports in the Longer Run,' *Economic Journal*, March, 1952, pp. 37–39.

tries as compared with the richer industrial countries. In times of boom when world income is rising, the total imports into agricultural countries will be rising faster than those into the industrial countries; and in times of depression imports into agricultural countries will shrink to a greater extent than the imports into developed countries.[13]

Foreign trade of underdeveloped countries is very much susceptible to cyclical changes in the incomes of industrial economies mainly because of the fact that the degree of concentration of exports is greater in the less developed countries of the world than in the economically advanced ones. A recent study based on 150 groups of export and import articles of both developed and underdeveloped countries shows an inverse correlation between the concentration of exports and degree of economic development. The more developed and the more industrialized an economy, the more diversified are its exports.[14] Roughly 90 per cent of the foreign exchange earnings of the low income countries are derived from the export of primary products. Since the ratio of their export earnings to national incomes is also large, any variation in the demand for their exports will have a serious repercussion on their incomes. This explains why cyclical fluctuations in a large industrial country like the U.S.A. produce similar income changes in countries which are exporting primary commodities to the U.S.A. There is in fact a very distinct and close correlation between the highs and lows of national income in the U.S.A. on the one hand, and those of exports, exchange reserves and national incomes in the underdeveloped countries on the other. It is true that balance of payments disequilibrium is normally set aright through changes in income; but this is not applicable to the primary producing countries because the scope for such adjustments in these countries as against the high income countries is very limited. If the country is large, the increase in imports would itself encourage exports. But this automatic adjustment is not possible in the matter of trade between a large industrial country on the one hand, and a small underdeveloped one on the other.

Not only are fluctuations in export earnings considerable, but their effect on national income is also greater in underdeveloped than in developed countries. Generally, the relation between foreign reserves and domestic money supply is close in the low income countries. A favourable balance of trade therefore results in greater liquidity of money, and this increased liquidity intensifies the upswing. Liquidity of money also facilitates speculation which adds to the inflationary pressures in the economy. When there is a decline in exports, fall in exchange reserves and decrease in money supply and bank reserves accelerate the down trend.[15]

[13]Chang, Tse Chun, *Cyclical Movements in the Balance of Payments*, Cambridge, 1951, p. 51.
[14]Michaely, Michael, ' Concentration of Exports and Imports: an International Comparison,' *Economic Journal*, December, 1958, pp. 725–28.
[15]Wallich, C. Henry, 'Underdeveloped Countries and the International Monetary Mechanism,' in *Money Trade and Economic Growth* in honour of J. H. Williams, Macmillan, New York, 1951, pp. 24–45.

It is however wrong to explain the failure of exports of underdeveloped countries to rise in consonance with their needs solely in terms of the inelastic demand for such export goods in advanced countries and their import policy. The tendency for a shift in industrial production in the richer countries from light to heavy industries such as engineering and chemicals, and the rising share of services in the total output of these countries have undoubtedly prevented the importing of raw materials to the extent proportionate to their rate of growth.[16] But certain aspects of the economic policy of poorer countries have also not been conducive to any expansion of their exports. One of these is the increasing emphasis laid on industrialization in these countries. It is inevitable that as the underdeveloped countries launch on ambitious schemes of industrialization, their export of primary produce should decline relatively to the increase in their national incomes. Growth of secondary industries has stimulated a competitive drawing away of factors of production which otherwise might have been employed in export activities. This however, is inevitable if industrialization is accepted to be synonymous with economic advancement. But a real harm to export earnings arises when the assignment of high priority to industrialization programmes results in a tendency to neglect or discriminate against export activities. For then, the capacity to import will be curtailed at a time when the demand for imports is rising.[17] Also, to some extent, taxation of export goods has adversely affected the flow of exports. While such taxation would have facilitated capital formation in a boom period as in the Korean flare-up in 1950–51, in normal times especially when external demand is price elastic, it hampers exports.

Another depressing feature about the foreign trade of underdeveloped countries is the difficulty which they experience in converting their export earnings, inadequate as they are, into domestic investment. Prof. Dudley Seers points out that in the matter of investment possibilities of export earnings in underdeveloped countries, not only the size of such income but the distribution of it also has to be taken into account. Thus in Malaya, export income from rubber flows into the hands of individual entrepreneurs while that from tin, another important export commodity of this country, accrues to government and to big companies.[18] Also to the extent there are controls, export income does not easily get invested in the private sector, and its utilization for investment is determined by government's economic and import policy. Even when foreign exchange becomes available through exports, the entrepreneur in the poorer countries has to face the task of acquiring the most appropriate capital equipment from sources with which he is not familiar and, as quite often

[16]Nurkse, Ragnar, *Patterns of Trade and Development*, Wicksell Lectures, 1959, Stockholm, 1959, p. 23.

[17]*Processes and Problems of Industrialisation in Underdeveloped Countries*, U.N., 1955, p. 108.

[18]Seers, Dudley, ' An Approach to the Short Period Analysis of Primary Producing Economies,' *Oxford Economic Papers*, February, 1959, p. 8.

happens, has to get it from different firms in different countries and have it assembled with whatever technical help he can secure. The difficulty in this matter has however been eased of late, by the emergence of designers and manufacturers of complete plants for specific purposes and of various sizes. Thus Japanese firms have offered to sell to India and some other South-East Asian countries ready to assemble factories, each designed to produce one of a variety of common consumer goods.

(b) Imports

Economic growth normally necessitates larger imports. This obviously is because of increased investment needs and consumption needs arising out of larger money incomes. The composition of imports, however, depends upon the size of the country, the availability of domestic resources and also the pattern of income distribution. Thus rise in total wage bill and increase in population necessitate import of food, if food supply in the country cannot be adequately increased. Rise in the money incomes of the upper income strata of society necessitates import of the better variety of consumption goods or shifts domestic resources to the production of this category of goods. Lastly, rise in the profits of the private entrepreneurs and increased entrepreneurial activity of the state necessitate the importing of industrial raw materials and capital goods.

A study of the long term trends in the foreign trade ratio of the developed countries of the world by Simon Kuznets nevertheless shows that this ratio has remained more or less constant over a period of hundred years or so, although minor fluctuations over relatively shorter periods of time are observable. The relative constancy in the foreign trade ratio has been attributed by Kuznets to the complex and varied forces that determine the trends in foreign trade. Among these forces are mentioned technological changes and improvement in means of communication and transportation, changes in industrial structure, and also political and social factors. What is relevant in the present context is the fact that in most of the present day advanced economies the import ratio shows a steady upward trend from about the middle of the 19th century up to about the first quarter of the 20th century. This is particularly marked in the case of U.K., France and Canada. In Japan, the rise is significant since the early years of the present century up to about the outbreak of the Second World War. On the other hand, in the United States where the import and export ratios and the foreign trade ratio have been quite low, there is a further steady decline in the import ratio.[19] Since about 1925 the import

[19]Export   ratio   is $\dfrac{\text{Commodity   exports}}{\text{National   Income   }plus\text{   Imports}}$ and   Import   ratio   is $\dfrac{\text{Commodity imports}}{\text{National Income }plus\text{ Imports}}$ Simon Kuznets, *Six Lectures on Economic Growth*, Free Press, Glencoe, Illinois, 1959, p. 96.

ratios in U.K., France and Canada also show a downward trend. This is in conformity with the commonsense notion that smaller countries with relatively limited primary resources for industrial production would have to depend more and more on imports as industrialization progresses, unlike countries which are large and which have extensive natural resources like the U.S.A. and U.S.S.R. The decline in the import ratio of countries like U.K., France and Canada and to some extent Japan in recent years, reflects the shifts in industrial production from consumer goods to capital goods which require proportionately a lesser volume of imported materials.

From a review of the foreign trade of five underdeveloped countries—Argentina, Brazil and Mexico in Latin America and Australia and the Union of South Africa—in the British Commonwealth in the years 1910–1950, the Economic Development Branch of the Bureau of Economic Affairs of the United Nations makes the observation that in general, the process of industrialization in these countries in the first half of the twentieth century has been accompanied by an increase in total imports. According to this study, characteristic changes in the composition of imports have been a rise in relative expenditure on capital goods, raw and semi-finished materials and fuels (especially petroleum), and a decline in relative expenditure on consumer goods (especially foodstuffs and ordinary types of textiles). On the other hand, increasing industrialization of these countries has not perceptibly affected the structure of their exports the bulk of which continues to remain raw and semi-manufactured materials and foodstuffs.[20]

While increased imports of capital goods and industrial materials are a direct result of industrialization programmes, a large volume of imports is also necessitated by increasing incomes, rise in the standards of living and consumption habits of the people. Import requirements in connection with an investment programme can be cut up into two parts—direct requirements of imports needed in connection with the investment project itself and indirect requirements resulting from the higher money incomes of the community. The latter part is determined by the actual disposable money income of the people which is the difference between the total money income received and the payments of taxes and contributions to loans and other savings. In any planning of imports needed in a programme of development, the size of the imports required is calculated with reference to the marginal propensity to import of the community. Data relating to the marginal propensity to import in the underdeveloped countries are meagre and unreliable; and the average propensity to import figures show considerable variation; for China it has been estimated at 0·03, India 0·09, Pakistan 0·11, Japan 0·11, Union of Burma 0·17; South Korea 0·20, Thailand 0·23, Philippines 0·25, Indonesia 0·27, Ceylon 0·41, and the Federation of Malaya and Singapore 0·62. On the whole, propensity to import is lowest in countries which are nearly self-sufficient in food and clothing, and highest in those countries whose economies are engaged

[20]*Process and Problems of Industrialization of Underdeveloped Countries,* U.N., 1955, pp. 113–16.

largely in producing for export markets.[21] Apart from the size of the country and the domestic resources available, the rate at which income is increasing has also a bearing on import requirements. If income is increasing at a moderate rate, it is possible that domestic supply can be adjusted to the rising requirements, so that the marginal propensity to import may not deviate much from the average propensity, but if money income rises rapidly as in inflation, this adjustment becomes difficult and a large part of the additional income will spill over into imports.

A more careful analysis of the import requirements resulting from economic expansion should take into account the accelerator effect of investments on external trade. The assumption of a constant income elasticity of demand for imports when the rate of growth of income is constant, fails to take cognizance of the immediate and delayed effect of investment expenditure on imports. Aggregate investment takes the form of inventory accumulation and also building up of capital capacity. The accelerator is the ratio of this investment to income. Its value depends upon the scarcity or otherwise of the other resources in relation to capital, say for instance, labour. Thus if surplus labour is available as when there is under-employment, the value of the accelerator will be small and it reaches its maximum when output capacity is fully utilized. That is to say, so long as resources other than capital are unemployed, additions to capital stock would bring in relatively larger returns per unit of capital. As these resources get employed, more and more capital will be required in order to attain a constant rate of growth of income. Since in an underdeveloped country investment goods are mostly imported, it means that as the value of the accelerator rises there will be increased demand for investment goods, but after it reaches its maximum, the rate of increase in demand for imports brought about by the accelerator effect declines. To what extent the accelerator would work itself out in the form of enlarged imports depends on the elasticity of supply of imports and the elasticity of demand for them. In general, the greater is the elasticity of supply of foreign exports in relation to the elasticity of home supplies, the greater will be the effect on imports; also, the effect will be greater when the accelerated demand for imports is more inelastic.[22] To the extent the yield of capital tends to be proportionately high in underdeveloped countries in view of the relative shortage of capital and the abundance of labour, the value of the accelerator is likely to be low; and the proportion of demand for investment goods in relation to increase in income will be low But against this has to be set the fact that the demand for imported investment goods is both income and price inelastic while their supply in the advanced countries from where these are imported is more elastic.

There are two other factors which account for larger imports in under-

[21] 'Mobilization of Domestic Capital,' *Report and Documents of the Second Working Party of Experts.* U.N., 1953, p. 286.

[22] Giersch, Herbert, 'The Acceleration Principle and the Propensity to Import,' *International Economic Papers*, No. 4, pp. 198–214.

developed countries in their early stages of economic growth. The greater
interest taken by the State in these countries in initiating and engineering
economic growth has frequently involved resorting to methods of financing
which are of an inflationary nature. The result is a rise in real income and a
greater rise in money incomes. Inflationary pressures generated in this manner
have an adverse effect on the balance of payments position of these countries.
A rise in real income raises the standard of life of the people, increases their
capacity to consume, facilitates larger investment and thereby causes a greater
demand for both consumption and investment goods; but if money income
rises faster than real income—and this is the characteristic of inflation—excess
demand creates á strain on domestic resources as well as on foreign balance.
If exchange rate is unchanged, there is in the first place, a tendency for imports
to increase attracted by the price factor. Also, inflation involves a shift in
incomes towards the richer classes which may lead to an increase in the demand
for luxury goods. If restrictions are placed on the importation of such goods,
it is likely that excess demand will make itself felt on domestic substitutes of
imported luxuries with the result that a lesser volume of resources would be
available for the production of export goods. Or, if it results in a decline in
the resources necessary for the production of essential domestic consumption
goods, the shortage in this would aggravate inflationary pressures along the
usual wage cost line. In short, the pressure on foreign balances only reflects
the domestic imbalance inherent in inflation. Given the amount of domestic
supply, excess demand manifests itself either in inflation at home or in pressure
on demand for goods from outside or in both. The effect of the latter is balance
of payments difficulties and deterioration in foreign balances.[23]

Secondly, apart from inflationary methods of financing development, pressure
on external balance is exerted through increased demand arising from growth
of population. In most of the underdeveloped countries the rate of growth of
population is high. Since capital is scarce, growth in numbers increases
unemployment, reduces productivity, keeps down per capita incomes and
prevents a widening of the savings margin which is essential for raising the
level of income. On the other hand, there is need for additional food supplies
and if conditions of domestic supply are inelastic more and more imports
become necessary with obvious effect on foreign balances. This has been well
illustrated by recent trends in India.

(c) Terms of Trade

The size of export earnings of a country is determined not only by the volume
of exports as against imports but also by the value which exports command
in foreign markets compared with the price of imports. Thus terms of trade

---

[23] The effect of excess demand caused by inflation on external trade may be made clear by
the following identity: $Y=C+I+(X-M)$; $Y=S+C$; $S=I+(X-M)$; $S-I=X-M$. If $I>S$
then $M>X$: Y is national income, C consumption, I investment, X exports and M imports.

play an important part in the determination of the gains which a country gets out of its foreign trade. It is conceivable that gains would be negligible or negative even when exports are increasing faster than imports if the terms of trade are unfavourable. On the other hand, it is possible that substantial gains would arise even when exports are falling if the decrease in volume is more than offset by rise in the prices of exports in external markets. Since underdeveloped countries are mostly importers of manufactured goods and exporters of raw materials, their gain from this source is determined by the relative movements in the world prices of manufactures compared with industrial raw materials and foodstuffs. There is however, no unanimity of opinion regarding the trend in terms of trade, whether it is favourable to primary producing or industrial countries. One view is that with economic development, terms of trade of underdeveloped countries improve while that of advanced industrial economies turn adverse. In explanation of this hypothesis it is mentioned that while the output of manufactured goods can be expanded and their costs can be lowered easily, the supply of primary products is less flexible and their costs go up when any attempt is made to increase their output. The tendency for prices of primary goods to rise in relation to manufactured goods is also due to the fact that as development takes place, the divergences in the matter of factor proportions between developed countries and underdeveloped countries tend to decrease. Capital formation in underdeveloped countries increases the capital components of its products and facilitates the production of certain manufactured products which substitute imports. This would mean that such goods would no longer be imported unless their prices declined to the extent warranted by increased domestic supply. Secondly, as industrialization proceeds, underemployment in the backward sectors of the economy would be reduced and consequently the cost of labour employed in the different industries including export industries would go up, thereby pushing up the prices of these goods. In other words, with the decline in the magnitude of underemployment, exports become less elastic with respect to price increases than before development got underway.[24] In support of this thesis statistical evidence relating to some advanced economies is brought forward. Thus U.S.A. export prices rose to about double the pre-war level by 1953 while import prices went up by nearly three times.[25]

This view however, is questioned. Terms of trade were unfavourable in the early nineteen-fifties to countries importing raw materials because of international political developments particularly the war in Korea which set in motion a feverish stock-piling programme among some of the developed countries of the world. The result was a shooting up of the prices of industrial raw materials. As against developed countries, some of the primary producing countries benefited by this situation. In nine out of eleven South-East Asian countries the terms of trade were more favourable in 1951 as compared with the year

[24]Wolf, Charles (Jr.), *Foreign Aid: Theory and Practice in Southern Asia*, Princeton, 1960, p. 273.
[25]Thorp, W. L., *Trade Aid or What?* Johns Hopkins, Massachusetts, 1954, p. 65.

before the Korean War. This however, was very shortlived. There was a setback in 1952 and the recovery in the next year was quite moderate.[26]

On the other hand, statistical data relating to a longer and more normal period of time show that the long term trends in the terms of trade have on the whole been favourable to industrial countries and adverse to primary producing countries. On the basis of a detailed analysis of the terms of trade of some European countries and North America in post-war years, Kindleberger comes to the conclusion that " few generalisations on the terms of trade between world manufactures and world primary products are valid but that they tend to turn against underdeveloped and in favour of developed countries ".[27]

It is in fact difficult to specify the factors which account for the movement of terms of trade against or in favour of one country or another at any particular period of time. Quite often terms of trade are affected by the fall or rise in the prices of a few key commodities. And if these commodities enter largely into international trade, their influence on terms of trade would be significant. But the rise in their prices would be due to a host of factors the relative significance of each of which cannot properly be ascertained. Thus fluctuations in income, short period elasticities of supply and demand for import and export commodities, harvest fluctuations, major labour disturbances, and other more or less random influences, all are important factors to be considered in this context.[28] It is however, possible to make some generalization about the determinants of terms of trade from the point of view of primary producing countries.

The major factor covering in a way all other minor factors is the nature of demand for imports and the supply of exports. The greater is the elasticity of demand for imports of a country and the lower the elasticity of demand for its exports, the greater are the chances of terms of trade turning in its favour. If the supply of exports is relatively inelastic, world prices would go up when there is increased external demand. But if external demand is stagnant or falling, difficulty in reducing supply would depress the prices. Since industrial expansion necessitates import of raw materials, it is likely that prices would shift in favour of the exports of agricultural countries. But the rise in income of the latter countries would in turn increase imports from other countries so that in the end the effect on terms of trade would depend on the relative elasticities of demand and supply in both classes of countries.[29] As has been observed earlier, the demand for the exports of underdeveloped countries in developed countries is more elastic than the demand for the exports of developed countries in underdeveloped countries. For this reason, the bargaining power of under-

[26]*Economic Bulletin for Asia and the Far East*, U.N., May, 1954, p. 24.

[27]Kindleberger, C. P., ' The Terms of Trade and Economic Development,' *Review of Economics and Statistics*, February, 1958, p. 72.

[28]Rostow, W. W., *Process of Economic Growth*, Oxford, London 1953, pp. 202–08.

[29]See for a detailed analysis of this point, Johnson, Harry, *International Trade and Economic Growth*, Allen and Unwin, London, 1958, pp. 65–93.

developed countries in the matter of foreign trade tends to weaken. Over the years there has been a tendency for the prices of agricultural commodities to decline in terms of manufactured goods. This is illustrated in a United Nations study which shows that at the late stages of the depression of the 1930s, a given quantity of the exports of the underdeveloped countries could pay for only 60 per cent of the quantity of imported manufactured goods that they could buy at about the close of the 19th century.[30] As regards capital goods which are in great demand in the semi-industrialized and developing economies, supply is relatively inelastic in the economically advanced countries which export these goods, because of high levels of employment and full utilization of capacity in them. This explains why prohibitive prices are paid for them by countries where they are required for investment.

In a large measure, the relative movements of the terms of trade of different countries are to be explained in terms of the ease or difficulty with which resources can be shifted from one enterprise to another with a view to secure attractive prices. The facility with which resources can be shifted depends on the nature of the resources, the skill, foresight and enterprise of the entrepreneurs and the mobility of labour. If resources are shifted easily so as to bring about a relative shortage in the supply of some commodities and increase in others, potential competition can be eliminated and prices both internal and external can be prevented from falling. Normally, the shiftability of resources in developed economies is greater than in the underdeveloped countries, chiefly because the proportion of capital employed in production in the former is very much greater than in the latter. Among the factors of production capital is the most mobile. Even in agricultural operations the input of capital in countries like the U.S.A. or Canada is several times greater than in countries like India or China. In the latter countries, since much labour is combined with a small amount of capital, and since labour is tradition-bound and by nature relatively immobile, the scope for regulating output of different types of goods by shifting of resources is considerably limited. It is this difficulty to vary supply that affects prices and terms of trade more than any monopolistic restriction.[31]

Whatever be the forces operating on terms of trade at any particular period of time, the effect of such changes on the economy and balance of payments position of the countries concerned is of great significance. This is particularly so in the case of primary goods producing countries because of the high foreign trade ratio to national output in such countries. A small change in terms of trade would therefore have a disproportionately large effect on the domestic economy. It has been calculated that a 10 per cent change in the terms of trade of underdeveloped countries would modify their capacity to import by as much as 1,500 million dollars a year. The Secretariat of the Economic

[30]*Relative Prices of Exports and Imports of the Underdeveloped Countries*, U.N., 1949, p. 7.

[31]Kindleberger, C. P., *The Terms of Trade—A European Case Study*, John Wiley, New York, 1956, pp. 253–54.

Commission for Latin America has estimated that the improvement in the terms of trade for Latin America from 1946 to 1952 made available to that continent more than 11,000 million dollars, i.e. about 4·3 per cent of the aggregate product of the area for the whole seven-year period.[32]

RECENT TRENDS IN EXTERNAL TRADE OF UNDERDEVELOPED COUNTRIES

Recent trends in the exports and imports and terms of trade of the underdeveloped countries bring to light the significance of these factors in the economic position and the prospects for growth in these countries. Broadly speaking, four important features in the external trade of underdeveloped countries can be distinguished. Their imports from industrial countries have increased substantially, but their exports to these countries show a relative decline; and they have suffered from instability in their export markets; also, their balance of payments problem has been aggravated by adverse price trends.

(a) Increase in Imports from Developed Countries

Economic growth in underdeveloped countries has necessitated larger and larger imports from advanced countries. Between 1938 and 1957 world trade increased from 21,400 million dollars to 97,500 million dollars. In the same period imports into non-industrial areas increased from 6,600 million dollars to 34,300 million dollars. Thus between these two points of time, while world trade increased by 4½ times, imports into non-industrial countries increased by more than 5 times. This increase in imports is accounted for mostly by capital goods. The share of capital goods in total imports increased from 19·7 per cent in the pre-war years to 27·8 per cent in 1954–55 against 29·0 per cent and 32·7 per cent in the case of raw materials; the proportion of semi-manufactured goods remained more or less constant at 26·4 per cent and 26·1 per cent while consumer goods declined substantially from 24·9 per cent to 13·4 per cent. The rise in capital goods imports occurred in countries where total imports fell as well as in those where they increased. This shift in the composition of imports has been closely linked to the widespread intensification of investment activity in the primary producing countries since the close of the Second World War. In many countries governments gave priority to the importation of capital goods.

Another noteworthy change in the pattern of imports has been the decline in the relative share of food imports in the net food importing countries. Thus in Malaya and Ceylon in the early post-war years food imports constituted 47 per cent and 57 per cent respectively of total imports. Between 1948–49 and 1954–55, of the total increase in imports in these two countries food imports accounted for only 5 per cent in Malaya and 30 per cent in Ceylon.

[32]Quoted in Myrdal, G., *An International Economy*, Routledge and Kegan Paul, London, 1956, p. 234.

Food imports in Egypt, Pakistan and Philippines decreased in absolute terms. In those countries which have made some progress in industrialization, there has been a sharp decline in the imports of manufactured goods. This trend is particularly noticeable in the Latin American countries. But expansion in manufacturing production has caused in its turn an increase in the demand for imported industrial materials.

By and large then, economic growth in the underdeveloped countries of the world in the post-war years has been attended with an increase in the imports of capital or investment goods and industrial raw materials. Food imports in some of these countries have increased, while in others they have fallen. However, the rate of increase in food imports has been less than that under capital goods. The decline in imports of consumer goods has been brought about not only by increased domestic production, but also by government policy which has aimed at restricting unnecessary imports so as to save foreign resources for the procuring of much needed capital equipment.

(b) Decrease in Exports to Developed Countries

While the demand for the export goods of developed countries has increased with economic development in the non-industrial countries, the demand for primary products (the export products of underdeveloped countries) has not increased in proportion to the rise in the national income of the advanced countries. In the three years 1955–57 exports from non-industrial countries (excluding the U.S.S.R., Eastern Europe and China) increased from 28,220 million dollars to 30,880 million dollars, i.e. by 9 per cent while in the same period, exports of industrial countries rose from 53,440 million dollars to 66,690 million dollars or by 25 per cent.[33] The demand for most of the industrial raw materials in world's markets has either stagnated or has been increasing haltingly except in the case of fuels, particularly petroleum. From 5 per cent of total export value in 1928 the relative importance of petroleum and petroleum products rose to 10 per cent in 1937–38 and 20 per cent in 1955. On the other hand, demand has been the weakest in respect of certain agricultural raw materials such as natural fibres. This has been largely due to technological developments in industrial countries which have made industries less dependent on imported raw materials. Also some of these advanced countries have been making successful attempts to become as far as possible self-sufficient in the matter of agricultural products.

Relative decline in the export of traditional articles has been due not only to fall in external demand but also to supply conditions. Some underdeveloped countries have been quick enough to adjust their export pattern to changing needs, by diversifying their exports and by increasing the output of commodities for which foreign markets are expanding. Thus while between 1950 and 1955, the proportion of tea exports of India in world markets declined from 46 to

[33] *Trends in International Trade*, GATT, Geneva, 1958, p. 20.

40 per cent, Ceylon maintained her tea exports more or less at a stable level. In the same period the share of cotton exports of Egypt declined from 15 to 12 per cent, but Mexico and Brazil increased their share of cotton exports from 5 to 10 per cent and 7 to 10 per cent respectively. Apart from this, in several other countries fall in exports was due to increased domestic consumption of export commodities. Inflationary conditions, higher cost of production, governments' regulatory measures, currency inconvertibility and other similar factors have also stood in the way of expansion of exports.

Disparity in the movement in exports of the underdeveloped countries to some extent accounts for differences in their rates of growth. On the whole, high rates of domestic economic growth have taken place in countries whose exports have shown the greatest buoyancy, while countries whose exports have been sluggish, have registered only moderate rates of growth. Also, it is observed that countries which have increased their exports in step with domestic expansion have experienced less strain on the balance of payments front. As against this, countries like Argentina, Egypt, India and Pakistan, whose exports have not risen substantially, and as a result import capacity has not much improved, have experienced continuing or increasing pressure on their external balances. To a large extent high rates of income growth in Brazil, Colombia, Mexico, Peru and Venezuela (5 to 7 per cent per year) were due to favourable trend in exports while in countries like Cuba relatively slow increase in real product (about or less than 2·5 per cent per year) can be attributed to stagnation or even decline in exports.

It should however be added that the trend in exports affects the rate of domestic growth as much as the latter affects the former. The volume of exports of a country in any period of time is determined by external as well as internal factors. The decline in export earnings may be due to fall in external demand as well as to increased domestic absorption in which case a fall in exports may synchronize with domestic economic expansion. Furthermore, rapid economic development if it is attended with rising prices, attracts increased imports and adversely affects the volume of exports. Much therefore depends on the pattern of domestic growth and the extent to which growth depends on imported goods and affects the supply of export commodities.

(c) Instability in Export Markets

The problem of adverse balance of trade has been aggravated by instability in the export markets of underdeveloped countries. Both the prices of exports and their volume have varied widely with the result that total export proceeds have been quite unstable and as such, could not have been of any great use in domestic capital formation. In the first half of the present century, year to year price fluctuations of the export commodities of underdeveloped countries have averaged about 14 per cent, while fluctuations in the volume of exports of primary commodities were between 18 and 19 per cent a year. Cyclical fluctuations—each full cycle covering 4½ years—averaged about 27 per cent in respect of prices and 10 per cent to over 50 per cent in respect of volume. Long term price changes amounted to between 4 and 5 per cent a year in either direction. Changes in export volume due to long term factors were similar in magnitude to long term price trends—about 4 per cent a year. The combined effect of price and volume variations is seen in the size of export proceeds which shows an year to year fluctuation of 23 per cent between 1901 and 1950, and a cyclical fluctuation, over each period of a little over four years, of 37 per cent. Changes in export proceeds due to long term factors were at the rate of about 6 per cent a year. The fact that export proceeds varied more widely than price or volume fluctuations taken separately, indicates that changes in price and in quantity had a destabilizing effect on each other. It is relevant to add that inflow of foreign capital in this period did not have any compensatory effect on the instability in export proceeds. The inflow of long term and short term capital combined, aggregated to only about 10 per cent of foreign exchange earnings from exports and until recently showed a declining trend. What is worse, capital inflow fluctuated even more than earnings from export proceeds, particularly before 1939. Year to year fluctuations of capital inflow were on the average more than three times as wide as fluctuations in export proceeds. The tendency for capital inflow to fluctuate in the same direction as export proceeds further aggravated the problem.[34]

(d) *Adverse Price Trends*

In the six years since 1949 covering the Korean war and its aftermath, some of the primary producing countries in South-East Asia like Burma, Ceylon, Malaya and Thailand benefited by a favourable movement in the terms of trade which may be presumed to have assisted substantially in domestic capital formation. Given the prices of export and import commodities, the gain from terms of trade refers to the extra earnings derived from a favourable shift in the terms of trade. These extra earnings are in the nature of windfall income and can be utilized for investment by the government or private entrepreneurs. However, in the same period because of the setback in textile prices, the gain from exports declined in the case of Japan and India. The main sources of terms of trade gain were rubber and certain mineral products on the export side and textiles on the import side. However, in these years the gains from trade of the East Asian countries fluctuated widely. The trade gains for the region since 1949 rose to a peak in 1951, fell to one-fourth in 1953 and again more than doubled in 1955.[35] Subsequent to 1955, terms of trade have turned on the whole adverse to underdeveloped countries. Thus between the last quarter of 1954 and the first quarter of 1958, the index number of prices of primary products (1953=100) declined from 103 to 96 while manufactured

[34]*Instability in Export Markets of Underdeveloped Countries*, U.N., 1952, pp. 3–7.
[35]*Economic Bulletin for Asia and the Far East*, U.N., May, 1957, pp. 18–39.

goods registered a rise from 98 to 107. Among the primary products, however, minerals including fuels moved up from 99 in 1954 to 119 in the first quarter of 1957 and then receded to 109 in the first quarter of 1958. As a result of the shift in the prices of manufactured goods and primary products, the terms of trade of the latter against the former declined from 105 to 90.[36] From another point of view, while the index number of volume of exports (1928=100) from non-industrial countries (excluding the U.S.S.R., Eastern Europe and China) of the world increased from 138 in 1955 to 151 in 1957, the unit value remained constant (197). On the other hand, in the same period, while the index number of volume of exports from industrial countries moved up from 139 to 162, the index number of the unit value of their exports rose from 83 to 193 i.e. an increase by about 133 per cent. Even among the less developed countries, there is evidence to show that semi-industrialized countries like India have been the worst hit.

INDIA's POSITION IN WORLD TRADE

India's share in world trade is about 3·5 per cent. As a share of total national product, exports in recent years constitute about 6 per cent and imports 7 per cent. The trends in the foreign trade ratio of the country in recent years are shown in Table 32. Foreign trade ratio is calculated as the proportion of the value of exports and imports at current prices to the total availability of output, i.e. national product plus imports.[37]

Table 32

FOREIGN TRADE RATIO OF INDIA 1951—1960

Year	Foreign Trade Ratio	Import Ratio	Export Ratio
1951–52 —	0·16	0·09	0·07
1952–53 —	0·12	0·06	0·06
1953–54 —	0·09	0·05	0·04
1954–55 —	0·12	0·06	0·06
1955–56 —	0·13	0·07	0·06
1956–57 —	0·13	0·07	0·06
1957–58 —	0·14	0·08	0·06
1958–59 —	0·11	0·07	0·04
1959–60 —	0·11	0·07	0·04
1960–61 —	0·11	0·07	0·04

From a relatively high level of 0·16 in the first year of the First Plan period foreign trade ratio receded to 0·09 in 1953–54; since then it revived and reached

[36] *Monthly Bulletin of Statistics*, U.N., June, 1958.
[37] See *ante*, p. 366 f.n.

the high of 0·14 in 1957–58. In the next year, it declined to 0·11 and has remained constant in the subsequent years. It may also be observed that since the commencement of the Second Five-Year Plan, export ratio has decreased appreciably, while import ratio has remained more or less unchanged.

The trends in the foreign trade of the country may be explained in terms of: (a) external factors affecting exports; (b) domestic factors affecting demand for imports and (c) import and export policy of the government.

Both imports and exports were high in 1951–52. This was due mostly to external factors, particularly the outbreak of hostilities in Korea. The large inflationary potential inherited by the Western countries from the Second World War was further augmented by increasing government budget deficits and the marked step up in domestic investment activity, especially in stock building following the Korean War. This accounts for increase in the exports of India as well as a rise in the cost of imports. Acute shortages in the industrial raw materials like raw cotton and raw jute as a result of partition swelled up the imports of that year considerably, while the fall in the production of food because of failure of the monsoons aggravated the situation. In the next two years imports as well as exports declined. The major cause for this down trend in the volume of trade of the country was the appearance of recessionary conditions both in India and abroad. With the ending of the Korean War boom and the slackening of the investment and stock piling activity in the industrial countries, and the emergence of mild recessionary conditions in America in 1953, there was a decline in both the volume and the prices of Indian exports. The decline in imports which was sharper than the decline in exports was due partly to the slackening of economic activity at home and partly to the tighter import policy of the government at this period.

Since about the close of the First Plan period, there has been a significant and steady rise in imports with exports stagnating or declining. This has been due largely to the rising investment activity at home. The outlay on planned development in India (Government investment) rose from about Rs. 2,000 million at the commencement of the First Plan to Rs. 5,000 million in the first year of the Second Plan (1956–57) and to about Rs. 8,000 million in the final year (1960–61). Imports rose from less than Rs. 6,000 million in 1953–54 to Rs. 7,500 million in the first year of the Second Plan and exceeded Rs. 10,000 million at the end of the Second Plan, while exports have averaged about Rs. 6,500 million over this period. The balance of payments position of the country in the First Plan period was far more satisfactory than was originally expected. Against an estimated annual deficit of Rs. 1,800–2,000 million, the actual deficit turned out to be much less—the deficit of Rs. 1,630 million in 1951–52 being followed by surpluses of Rs. 600 million, Rs. 470 million, Rs. 60 million and Rs. 150 million in the next four years. For the entire five-year period the deficit totalled only Rs. 300 million. On the other hand, the deficit on current account excluding official donations in the Second Plan period aggregated to Rs. 19,200 million or an annual average of Rs. 3,840 million against the anticipated amount of Rs. 2,240 million. The total deficit for the quinquennium exceeded the estimates by Rs. 8,000 million. The average annual export earnings in this period (Second Plan) of Rs. 6,120 million exceeded the estimates slightly by Rs. 190 million but were short of the average attained in the First Plan period by Rs. 100 million. As against this, payments for imports per year averaged Rs. 10,740 million, exceeding by nearly 24 per cent the plan estimates, and by 50 per cent the First Plan actuals.[38]

Increase in investment activity particularly in the government sector mostly accounts for the marked increase in imports. While the annual average of total imports in the Second Plan period exceeded by about 50 per cent the average of the preceding five years, imports on government account increased by 140 per cent and private imports by less than 25 per cent. Taking the Second Plan years as a whole, in absolute terms imports on government account have considerably increased, while imports for the private sector have decreased. It should be added that the bulk of government imports has been capital goods. Of the total government imports in the years 1956–57—1958–59, food materials accounted for about Rs. 3,900 million while much of the balance of about Rs. 9,300 million constituted machinery and other capital equipment. The influence of higher investment activity at home is seen also in the fact that aggregate imports on both government and private account, of machinery and vehicles averaged Rs. 3,250 million per annum as against the First Plan actuals of Rs. 1,500 million only. Similarly iron and steel imports averaged Rs. 950 million annually; in the First Plan they averaged Rs. 320 million only.[39]

As against imports, export earnings fell in most of the years of the Second Plan. A number of traditional commodities such as jute and cotton manufactures, raw cotton and vegetable oils brought in lower earnings over the Second Plan period than in the First. While the volume index of India's imports (1953=100) increased from the average for 1951–55 of 118 to 168 in 1957, that of exports increased from 102 to 115 in 1955 and 119 in 1957 with a setback to 110 in 1956. The production of export goods did not show any appreciable increase. Much of this non-resilience has to be attributed to the fact that India was exporting to trade partners whose imports were stationary or declined, and failed to take advantage of the opportunities available in some newly developing countries. Use of substitutes, the manufacturing of synthetic products, conservation and better utilization and economizing in the use of domestic materials and attempts to make themselves self-sufficient in some of the imported raw materials—all these should have contributed to prevent any rise in the demand for such materials in advanced industrial countries even when their national incomes were rising rapidly. Apart from these, fluctuations in economic activity in industrial centres continue to exert an

[38]*Report on Currency and Finance, 1960–61*, Reserve Bank of India, Bombay, pp. 110–11.
[39]*ibid.*, p. 112.

adverse effect on the foreign trade of primary producers and semi-industrialized countries like India. As a result of the recession in the U.S.A. and the West European countries in 1957–58, exports of staple commodities like tea, jute manufactures, cotton manufactures, raw cotton and vegetable oils from India showed substantial declines.

The price factor also has played a part in the stagnation of exports. In the matter of exports of cotton textiles and tea in 1960, it has been reported that Indian goods are at a disadvantage in so far as other competitors are able to dump their goods in overseas markets at a much cheaper price. As regards tea, there is increasing competition from East Africa and Indonesia. In both these countries it is found possible to keep down prices because of government policy. The East African tea is exempt from export duty and the industry in Indonesia is subsidized by the government. On the other hand, the Indian product is subjected to several taxes like export duty, excise duty and sales tax which inflate the prices and make it all the more uncompetitive.[40] Besides the burden of taxes, inflationary conditions at home, increasing domestic demand, rising costs of production, all these have made it difficult to maintain competitive prices of our export products abroad. The decline in the sales of cotton manufactures in the South-East Asian markets has been ascribed to growing competition from countries like Japan and China. Restrictive import policy adopted by some countries in recent years has also had an adverse effect on Indian exports.

Mention may also be made of increasing domestic absorption of articles of export because of industrialization in the country. With rising levels of personal incomes, demand for exportable consumer goods should also have substantially risen. To the extent capital formation produces a large expansion in money incomes, the result would be increased demand for consumption goods. And in the absence of an elastic supply of goods of this category, there is bound to be a spill-over of expenditure into imported consumption goods. Any further restriction of the import of consumer goods and the maintenance of the imports of capital goods would only aggravate the trend of effective demand outrunning the resources available for consumption. If import is blocked excess demand would impinge on the exports.

While export figures seem quite discouraging, the need for increasing our export earnings has been keenly felt. The foreign exchange requirements of the Third Plan are much higher than of the Second Plan. This is because of three reasons. In the first place, since great emphasis is laid on capital goods and heavy industries, there is bound to be greater need for the importing of capital equipment and machinery on a large scale. Secondly, domestic savings have not shown any great expansion in the last few years. At any rate it is doubtful whether increase in internal resources that can be mobilized will be in proportion to the increase in the size of the Third Plan. Thirdly,

[40] *Indian Finance*, Calcutta, September 16, 1961, p. 526.

the problem of repayment of loans already taken and the need for interest payments on a large scale will arise in the next plan period which would also necessitate substantial foreign exchange earnings.

Of the total investment outlay of Rs. 104 billion envisaged in the Third Plan, the allocation to industry, minerals, transport and communications is Rs. 43 billion. The need for the building up of capital goods industries for generating self-supporting forces of growth cannot be disputed. It is by this means that the rate of increase in national income can be stepped up to any appreciable extent, so that savings would increase even when a good proportion of the annual addition to income is used up for consumption by a rapidly growing population. On certain assumptions it is possible to make a rough estimate of the imports of capital equipment necessary in a semi-industrialized country like India. If net investment is 7 per cent of national income and depreciation allowances amount to 5 per cent, gross investment is 12 per cent of national income. Capital-output ratio in India is estimated to be about 2·5 : 1. If so, net investment of 7 per cent of national income would yield an addition to income of 2·8 per çent. If population is increasing at 2 per cent annually, increase in per capita income amounts to only 0·8 per cent per year. If it is desired to increase income by an additional 2 per cent, then net investment has to be increased by 5 per cent that is the rate of net investment will have to rise from 7 per cent to 12 per cent. Gross investment would then rise to 12+5=17 per cent, i.e. gross investment has to increase by 42 per cent (from 12 to 17 per cent). Imports of capital goods may be assumed to rise in the same ratio as the rise in gross capital investment i.e. by 42 per cent. It is estimated that in semi-industrialized countries imports of capital goods form about 28 per cent of total imports.[41] If capital investment is to go up by 42 per cent, then imports of capital goods will have to increase by 0·28 × 42 = about 11·75 per cent. At 28 per cent of the total imports, the value of capital goods imported in India will be roughly Rs. 3,000 million. According to the above calculation this amount will have to rise to about Rs. 3,350 million. Thus over the five years, the aggregate value of capital goods imports will be of the order of Rs. 16,750 million. This is only a rough calculation but it indicates the extent to which foreign exchange requirements would have to increase if a certain rate of growth of national income is to be achieved. Recently an Indian economist has calculated that over the next fifteen years or so, the volume of Indian exports, and the country's import capacity, will not rise by more than 33–50 per cent. According to the Planning Commission, if national income is to be raised by about 150 per cent by 1975–76 over the level in 1955–56, investment will have to be increased by 500 per cent. Since export earnings would increase at a much slower rate, these would form only 3 to 4 per cent of national income in 1975–76 as against 6 per cent in 1955–56. But in the same period, investment will rise from 7 per cent to 17 per cent of

[41] *Trends in International Trade*, GATT, Geneva, October, 1958, p. 50.

a much larger national income. This would mean that slow development of the exports will act as a built-in depressor upon economic growth.[42]

In view of this need, the sense of urgency with which the government of India have adopted a series of measures in the interest of export promotion is understandable. Measures that have been taken so far in this direction include bilateral trade agreements, institution of Export Promotion Councils, and the State Trading Corporation, provision of adequate financial facilities for exporters, better dissemination of commercial intelligence, propaganda abroad through embassies and delegations, exhibitions and fairs, foreign market surveys, etc. The Export Promotion Committee which submitted its report in 1957 envisages an increase of our annual exports from Rs. 7 billion to Rs. 7·5 billion and has recommended, among other things, diversification of exports and export markets, creation of an export consciousness among Indian traders and industrialists, adoption of better methods of production, competitive prices, better advertising and salesmanship, increase in productivity, reduction of costs through tax concessions and refunds of certain duties, facilitation of easier transport, extension of Export Promotion Councils—in all 85 recommendations—but most of these recommendations are in the nature of an expansion of the scope of existing arrangements. Such measures can at best touch only the fringe of the export problem of the country. What is required is a thorough reorientation of our traditional approach to exports and the devising of a new commercial and export policy which would fit in with the change in the structure of our economy and meet the requirements of domestic economic expansion.[43]

COMMERCIAL POLICY FOR ECONOMIC DEVELOPMENT

Any measures taken towards strengthening the export front should be based on the recognition of the fact that foreign trade which was an engine of growth from the point of view of the less developed countries of the 19th century is no longer true in the 20th century. We have seen that in the 18th and 19th centuries the progress of industrialization in Britain was attended with a steady increase in the demand for raw materials and an outflow of British capital to the countries which supplied the raw materials. Economic expansion in Britain thus induced development in some primary producing countries also in so far as investments were made in the construction of roads and railways and in the development of some of the primary industries especially plantation industry. To the extent the latter group of countries succeeded in utilizing their foreign exchange earnings in broadening their economic base as was done in Canada and Australia, they reaped external economies which helped

[42]Patel, S. J., ' Export Prospects and Economic Growth in India,' *Economic Journal*, September, 1959, pp. 504–05.

[43]*Report of the Export Promotion Committee*, 1957, Ministry of Commerce and Industry, Government of India.

the process of growth. But the pattern of international trade has changed considerably since then. In the latter half of the 19th century and in the 20th century, North America and Western Europe registered as rapid an economic advancement as Britain experienced in earlier years. But progress of industrialization in these countries has not benefited primary producing countries. While on the one hand the demand for raw materials has not kept pace with the rate of increase in incomes of the advanced countries, foreign capital has tended to flow into other industrial countries or some of the oil countries and away from the traditional primary producing countries. The movement of terms of trade against the agricultural countries, the inelastic demand for their export products and their failure to shift their resources to the production of goods other than the customary export items have placed them in an unenviable position, in which they can no longer look upon external trade as a means of lifting themselves up from economic stagnation.

It thus follows that the traditional theory of international trade which was once applicable to both developed and underdeveloped countries of the world is no longer applicable equally to the highly advanced and backward economies. The main reason is that the discrepancy between their standards of economic development has considerably widened and their economic structure has undergone significant changes. The major limitations of the classical comparative costs theory spring from its assumptions. Specialization in production between industrial countries of a more or less equal standard in economic development may be based on comparative advantage in the production of one or another article under free trade conditions. But in the 19th century, specialization between developed and underdeveloped countries arose not out of comparative differences in resources or ability to produce particular goods, but out of distinct differences in resources, climate and other conditions.[44] In the case of underdeveloped countries there was specialization in primary goods because circumstances were such that they could not choose other production. There was no possibility of making a choice by comparing one line of production or investment with another. Secondly, the comparative cost principle is relevant to developed countries because in such countries capital and labour resources are very mobile, so that they can be shifted between different enterprises and allowed to concentrate on those in which they have a relative advantage. This obviously is not possible in the case of pre-industrial countries where factor resources are immobile and adjustment in the output of particular industries or shifting of resources between industries is not possible, with the result that when once a particular scheme of production is attuned to a particular commodity or to a particular market, it gets fixed and is not likely to change in response to any variation in profits or earnings. This rigidity partly explains why specialization and international division of labour have not brought about equality of incomes. Specialization of poorer countries in primary production

[44]Myint, H., ' The Classical Theory of International Trade and the Underdeveloped Countries,' *Economic Journal*, June, 1958, p. 325.

did not result in any increase in productivity but only led to the using up of more resources. Thus expansion of plantation industries drew into employment labour resources but it did not result in any great technological improvement or increase in the productivity of labour. Certainly, specialization of one group of countries on primary production in which the income generating effect of investment is limited, and another group on industries in which the scope for external economies is much larger and the cost price differential is much wider, cannot help in narrowing the difference in incomes of the two groups of countries, but would only widen it further. Free trade would facilitate the international absorption of the surplus produce of some countries, but in the context of competition among countries of different standards of development, it would not benefit the poorer among them so much as it would the richer ones. The comparative cost theory not merely fails to explain the growing inequality in income of different countries; it is in fact not related to the special problems of development which the backward countries face. At any rate, the specialization which would follow from the doctrine of comparative costs would cause, and has in reality caused, more harm than good to the primary producing countries. As Professor Myrdal points out, initial differences get enlarged by free trade.[45] There is a circular causation involved in this. Specialization in primary production accounts for low income and low capital formation, while specialization in industrial production facilitates further expansion. Lastly, the comparative cost theory is based on static premises such as the assumption of fixed factor endowments.[46] But modern technology offsets the initial disadvantage or advantage of particular factor endowments, and easy international movement of capital and labour makes it possible to shift to production of goods or services which would not have been possible with the initial endowment of factors.

These limitations of the classical theory of international trade point to the irrelevance of the free trade principle in the present context of developed and underdeveloped economies. Free competition may be fair competition between countries of more or less the same economic status, but not between highly industrialized and rich nations on the one hand, and poor underdeveloped primary producing countries on the other. If the comparative cost doctrine and the concomitant principle of free trade are accepted in good faith, it would only leave the poorer countries of the world where they are. Since in the matter of external trade between developed and underdeveloped countries what is good for one is not good for the other, Prof. Myrdal advocates a double standard morality in international trade relationship. According to him the underdeveloped countries " need to be staunch free traders, and even

[45]Myrdal, G., *Economic Theory and Underdeveloped Regions*, Indian edn., Vora, Bombay, 1958, p. 164.
[46]Myint, H., ' The Gains from International Trade and the Backward Countries,' *Review of Economic Studies*, Vol. XXII, 1954–55, p. 130; also Kindleberger, C. P., *Economic Development*, McGraw-Hill, 1958, pp. 242–46.

preserve for themselves the right to give export subsidies, so far as the advanced countries' imports from them are concerned, but restrictionists in respect of their own imports ".[47]

The plea for a protective tariff in order to foster industrialization in low income countries is not however without its critics. Prof. Nurkse argues that infant creation should precede infant protection, that without adequate domestic savings no investment in any scheme of enterprise is possible and that protection by itself cannot generate the savings necessary for the purpose of building up an industry.[48] It has also been argued that protection quite often does more harm than good and that many of the advantages claimed to result from a protective external trade policy may be secured by the safer and more reliable monetary and other economic measures.[49] However many economists are agreed on the point that in the circumstances of present underdeveloped countries, industrialization is essential for economic progress and that in the initial stages, a protective trade policy has to be adopted. Several reasons in support of this policy are brought forward. Firstly, the building up of certain key industries which yield large external economies is necessary to generate forces of economic growth but, in the face of keen competition from advanced economies, it is difficult or impossible to start such industries unless a large measure of protection is granted, at least in the initial stages. The advantages of such external economies cannot be measured in terms of cost and gains on the purely commercial principle, yet they are of the greatest importance in the less developed countries. Secondly, protection helps diversification of industries and thus provides an insurance against instability arising from foreign trade. Thirdly, to the extent protective shelter fosters industrialization, it helps in reducing unemployment and underemployment which are a common evil in most of the underdeveloped countries. Fourthly, it is claimed that protective tariffs contribute to maintain better balance between agriculture and industries in respect of relative costs of production in the two sectors. In the absence of easy mobility of labour, wages tend to be much higher in industries than in agriculture in pre-industrial countries. This weakens the competitive strength of the former. Industries therefore need protection so that they can be placed in an equitable position with agriculture.

However, in a planned economy where growth is sponsored and regulated, it is important to see that protection granted to some industries is conducive to the general growth of the economy and that it does not endanger the prospects of other non-protected industries. In other words, protection should fit in with the overall scheme of economic progress. Protection has its costs; hence it is appropriate to examine whether the activity of the industry asking

[47]Myrdal, G., *ibid.*, p. 109; also, *An International Economy*, Routledge and Kegan Paul, London, 1956, p. 292.

[48]Nurkse, Ragnar, *Problems of Capital Formation in Underdeveloped Countries*, Basil Blackwell, Oxford, 1955, pp. 104–10.

[49]Black, J., ' Arguments for Tariffs,' *Oxford Economic Papers*, June, 1959, pp. 191–208.

25

for protection would result in a net saving of foreign exchange, which is a scarce factor, in low income countries. Against the foreign exchange earnings which the industry when developed will bring in, has to be set the possible loss in foreign exchange, if the industry is started with external capital which necessitates the payment of foreign exchange to service the external aid, and also the loss in foreign exchange that may arise if the industry in question absorbs domestic raw materials which would otherwise have been exported. The possibility of protection generating inflationary pressures should also not be ignored. Restriction of imports reduces domestic availability of goods required for consumption or production. It may then push up the cost of living or raise the cost of materials needed in other industries and thus swell up the prices of end products.[50]

Since external trade is of vital importance to underdeveloped countries, protective commercial policy may be deemed to be successful if it helps in the development of such industries whose product commands a ready market in foreign countries. In other words, protection should result in large export earnings. Although in recent years there has been a freer flow of foreign capital into low income countries from government and international agencies, the receiving countries would be wise if they do not regard borrowing of foreign exchange as a substitute for earning of foreign exchange. Even when foreign capital becomes available to close a temporary gap in the trade balance, the servicing charges of such external obligations necessitate the building up of an export surplus. In the circumstances obtaining in contemporary underdeveloped countries, export promotion is possible along three lines: (a) diversifying exports i.e. finding out new commodities for export; (b) diversifying export markets i.e. finding out new external markets where domestic products can be disposed of and (c) restraining domestic consumption of exportable articles to the extent price conditions at home would permit.

(a) Diversifying Exports

It is now clear that the markets for the traditional articles of export of primary goods producing countries are rapidly shrinking. Excluding the Soviet area and the oil exporting countries, the value of exports of non-industrial countries in total world trade declined from 32·2 per cent in 1928 to 24·4 per cent in 1957, while the percentage share in imports increased from 26·9 per cent to 30·4 per cent in the same period.[51] Since the late 1920s exports from the primary producing countries to the U.S.A. and Western Europe have fallen from about 3·5 per cent to less than 3 per cent of the combined Gross National Product of this industrial area. If petroleum is excluded, the fall would be from 3·5 per

[50]*Economic Bulletin for Asia and the Far East*, U.N., May, 1957, p. 15.

[51]Nurkse, Ragnar, *Patterns of Trade and Development*, Wicksell Lectures, 1959, Stockholm, 1959, p. 21.

cent to less than 2·5 per cent.[52] The trade pattern of India illustrates the same trend. The major articles of export of India, jute, tea and cotton textiles, show negligible increase or even a decline in recent years in spite of strenuous efforts at export promotion. Between 1930–39 and 1950–54 world consumption of jute and jute manufactures increased from an annual average of 1·7 million tons to a little less than 1·8 million tons while output in India and Pakistan rose from 1·5 million tons to 1·7 million tons. The indices of supplies of Indian tea (1934–38=100) increased slightly from 156 in 1949–51 to 160 in 1952–54 but exports receded from 138 to 136. Output of cotton textiles in India was 3,660 million yards in 1950; this increased to 5,306 million yards in 1956. Exports in the same years decreased from 1,116 million yards to 744 million yards or from 30 per cent to 14 per cent of the total output. The main reason for the stagnation in exports is that " we are offering more of the same things to the same people who no longer want more of them ".[53] In spite of this poor showing, Indian economy is still relying heavily on these commodities in respect of its export trade. Tea, jute goods, cotton piece goods and metallic ores, minerals and metallic scraps, account for about 53 per cent of our earnings of foreign exchange.

It is therefore necessary to devote greater attention to articles other than the traditional ones. The export policy in the present context that would really serve the purpose is not straining ourselves unduly to expand the exports of the customary products, but trying to shift resources to new enterprises and lines of production which would bring out new goods. These commodities should be of such a nature as to meet the needs of different economies which are at different stages of economic development, and the markets for which would therefore be expanding and not shrinking. In short, a structural change in the composition of exports is what is required. This is the lesson that we learn from the balance of payments experience of industrial countries in the post-war years. This is no argument for slackening our efforts to promote the export of articles like tea, cotton, rubber, jute and cotton textiles, but a call for redrawing our exports pattern and for concentrating on those lines of enterprise which will really yield satisfactory returns. In view of the substantial earnings which the above-mentioned items bring in, they are not to be neglected, but it would be a sound policy if in making future investments for expanding such industries, the relative difference between their costs and earnings is compared with that of other industries for which there is scope for an expanding foreign market. Of late, the products of some of the consumer goods industries and the chemical and engineering industries in the country have made some impression on foreign markets. Exports of manufactured durable consumption goods like sewing machines, bicycles, radios, etc. have increased appreciably in recent years and the proportion of manufactured goods to raw materials

[52]*Economic Survey of Europe* 1957, U.N., p. 6.
[53]Patel, S. J., ' Export Prospects and Economic Growth: India.' *Economic Journal*, September, 1959, pp. 490-506.

in our total exports has gradually been rising. A few years ago India did not export any engineering goods. In 1960 the value of such exports reached Rs. 95 million. With increased production of steel in the Third Plan period and later, it would be possible to step up the exports of this category of goods considerably.[54] The success of export promotion would depend to a large extent on the way in which these dynamic goods industries are encouraged. It is in this connection that the plea for protection assumes considerable significance. Along with protection in the form of import restrictions, it would be a sensible policy if discriminating subsidization of some of these industries is resorted to. But any help in the form of protective tariff or subsidization should be based on a consideration of the prospects of export earnings of the industries concerned, whether such earnings would be progressively expanding and free from instability and of the effect of such a protective policy on other industries and on the economy in general. There is thus need for greater vision, alertness and enthusiasm, in fact true entrepreneurship, on the part of private businessmen as well as the government. For this reason, sufficient incentives are to be offered by government to the private sector, at least in a negative manner, by relaxing their fiscal, tax and foreign exchange policy, while the private sector on its part, should adopt a more dynamic attitude in opening up new lines of enterprise and investment. It is up to private enterprise to maintain quality of exports and promote larger trade through more prompt and efficient service.

(b) Diversifying Export Markets

Allied to the need for diversifying exports through encouragement of manufacturing industries is diversification of markets. Instead of banking too heavily on the traditional markets in highly industrialized countries it is necessary to look forward to the smaller industrial nations and the other less developed countries to secure markets for export goods. This is of great importance in view of the fact that our manufactured products have to compete with similar products of much stronger rivals. We have had large trade deficits with our major trade partners—the U.K., U.S.A. and the members of European Common Markets. Our imports from the latter group of countries of which West Germany is the most important, amounted to Rs. 1,910 million in 1959–60 and Rs. 1,950 million in 1960–61, while our exports to that region in the two years were of the order of Rs. 500 million and Rs. 520 million respectively, leaving a trade balance of Rs. 1,410 million in 1959–60 and over Rs. 1,430 million in 1960–61. The joining of Britain in the European Common Market would worsen the situation. This makes it all the more necessary to find out new markets for our exports. The possibility of considerably increasing the exports of our manufactured consumption goods and small machinery to countries which are even less developed than ours is to be fully investigated

[54]Kilnani, K. R. F., ' Changing Pattern of India's Foreign Trade,' *Industrial Times*, Bombay, August 15. 1961, pp. 47–49.

and exploited. The fact is that all those countries which are broadly categorized as underdeveloped countries, but which in actual fact are of different standards of development, have awakened to the need of building up their economies through industrialization. This provides an opportunity to sell the products of a semi-industrialized country in the markets of other countries which are at a lower stage of development. There is considerable scope for expanding our markets in some regions of Africa, like Libya, West Africa, Equatorial Africa, and Belgian Congo, the Middle East countries, and the South-East Asian countries, like Indo-China, Thailand, Indonesia and also Eastern Europe and Latin America. Some of these regions are in the midst of vigorous economic development and industrialization. The prospects of our exports would be brighter to the extent that standards of life in these countries improve. In so far as India is one of the foremost among these countries in point of industrial development, there is an opportunity to gain a headway in those foreign markets provided our exports are organized ahead for this expansion. For this purpose, it is important to acquire an adequate knowledge of the export prospects. It is also imperative that greater competitive strength is imparted to our export products by keeping down prices and maintaining high standards of quality. Equally important is greater co-operation among the underdeveloped countries. The considerable emphasis laid by the Government of India to maintain the quality of products high and prices low in recent years, and the efforts of the countries of South-East Asia to form an Asian Common Market with a view to promote regional trade and strengthen their position in the face of increased competition from industrial nations, are therefore to be considered as very welcome trends.

(c) Restraining Domestic Consumption

As stated earlier, imports of capital goods are bound to increase substantially in the next few years. Nor is there any great scope for further restricting (except to the extent that food imports can be stopped when the country becomes self-sufficient) the import of the few items of manufactured consumption goods. Since our consumption level is already low, it is unwise to think of further pressing it down. Domestic consumption can, however, be regulated in a manner which would help not so much in restricting imports as in promoting exports. Thus wastes arising out of the production of a wide variety of more or less similar consumption goods can be avoided if production of some of the manufactured goods can be standardized. In a country where per capita income is very low and where resources are very much limited, it is certainly uneconomic to produce and distribute a wide variety of more or less similar products particularly of the quasi-luxury category. Greater attention is to be devoted to utility than variety or superficial attractiveness. Of the consumer goods produced in the country for domestic use as well as for exports, it should be possible to discriminate between the two and standardize the first group as far as possible. In cases of consumption goods produced at home and which are competing with similar imported goods, it would be advantageous to increase domestic output by means of large-scale standardized methods of production and altogether stop imports. Such standardized products can then become virtual import substitutes. In so far as expansion of production in this manner would not involve a proportionate increase in the use of resources as it would if variety is required, there is real economizing and there would not be any adverse effect on the scale of output of other exportable commodities. Obviously measures to expand exports and to restrict imports would tell on the consumption habits of all classes of consumers, particularly, the well-to-do and richer classes. But this is a cost worth paying in order to build up the economy rapidly with minimum danger to internal or external stability.

Chapter XII

EXTERNAL CAPITAL : THE PROBLEMS OF UTILIZATION

THE IMPORTANCE OF FOREIGN CAPITAL IN ECONOMIC DEVELOPMENT

ECONOMIC DEVELOPMENT involves the increased utilization of resources for investment purposes; it also requires expanding the supply of consumption goods in order to meet the growing demand for such goods as national income rises. To a large extent the supply of both investment and consumption goods comes out of domestic resources. But normally as an economy develops, it has to import from foreign countries some investment goods like machines, plants and other capital equipment and also certain consumption goods which it cannot produce out of its own resources to the extent they are required at home. To pay for these imports, the country has to earn enough foreign exchange through its exports. If foreign exchange requirements are greater than the value of exports it means that there is a gap between foreign exchange needs and foreign exchange earnings and this gap is closed by the borrowing of foreign exchange. Thus external resources are earned or borrowed or obtained free in the form of grants or aid. When we talk of external capital used for domestic capital formation or for promoting economic growth, we have in mind primarily the foreign borrowed capital and also external aid and grants.

External capital is required to finance the procurement of real resources from foreign countries. It is clear that even if internal resources are adequate to cover the cost of both the domestic and external components of a programme of development, external assistance becomes necessary in so far as the mobilization of a given amount of financial resources in a country does not guarantee the releasing of an equivalent amount of foreign exchange that is required to carry through an investment programme. Collections through taxation borrowing and inflation do represent savings of the community which can and are used for investment. As a result of this activity, the community is deprived of a certain amount of real resources which it could have otherwise disposed of. The major part of the financial resources mobilized in this manner might have been utilized for the consumption of domestic goods and services and a smaller part for purchasing external goods and services. Thus of the total amount of financial resources collected by the state, that part alone which could have been used for the procuring of foreign goods represents the additional foreign exchange acquired by the state. It is thus obvious that if the foreign exchange requirements exceed this amount, other methods would have to be adopted, for example, external borrowing or utilization of past foreign savings in order to acquire the needed foreign exchange.

In reality, the domestic savings available in low income countries are meagre and what is collected by the state through taxation and internal borrowing are insufficient to meet the investment requirements. In such a situation, an under-developed country can be freed from the vicious circle of low income, low savings, and low productivity only with the help of resources from outside. These resources are transferred in the form of imports and constitute therefore a direct addition to the available real resources of the less developed country. The use of foreign capital in economic development therefore implies primarily the supplementing of domestic resources available for investment by external resources. In theory, such a movement of resources represents a transfer of capital from where its marginal efficiency is low, to where it is high and contri-butes in this manner to a decrease in the inequality of international living standards.[1]

In addition to providing foreign exchange directly for financing the import of capital equipment and also of consumption goods, external capital helps in accelerating the pace of economic progress in many ways. In an underdeve-loped country which is incapable of earning sufficient foreign exchange through its external trade, external assistance by making available foreign exchange enables the starting of projects which could not have been undertaken. It is likely that in the absence of such facilities an underdeveloped country would have given high priority to projects requiring little foreign exchange or which would be capable of earning large foreign exchange, but which may not be essential from the national economic point of view, or help in promoting domestic economic growth.[2] Foreign capital facilitates the mobilization of domestic resources and makes it possible to start highly capital-intensive programmes of development, as for instance the Aswan Dam in Egypt, which the low income countries left to their own resources would be incapable of achieving. It ensures the speeding up of capital formation which is often necessary because of political and economic reasons. In a democratic set-up, in which a political party may be in power for only a short period of time, say five years, if an investment project is to be taken up at all, it should be one which can be completed within a fixed period of time. Quite likely, the autho-rities may shy away from costly schemes if external capital is not available and if domestic resources alone are not sufficient to ensure the quick execution of the work. Moreover, from the economic point of view, some schemes have necessarily to be undertaken in a big way, involving large expenditure on a series of complementary investments which have to be taken up simultaneously. Or the presence of a rapid growth of population may necessitate a high initial

[1]Tinbergen, Jan, *International Economic Integration*, Amsterdam, 1954, p. 62.
[2]‘ Mobilization of Domestic Capital,’ *Report and Documents of the Second Working Party of Experts*, U.N., 1953, p. 274.

speed of development lest any slower tempo of development fail to make any impression in the matter of per capita incomes. It may also be added that through foreign financing it would be possible to give capital formation a longer time range. If the inflow of foreign capital is steady and assured, the economy can plan for a number of years ahead, and undertake schemes of development which would take a long period of time for completion.[3]

Secondly, the employment of external capital for economic development reduces the strain on the domestic economy which normally an acceleration of investment would cause. Primarily, the burden of economic development in the initial stages is in the form of reduced consumption; for obvious reasons in a low income country, any attempt to augment the resources for investment would impinge upon consumption levels. But the influx of foreign capital helps to maintain consumption at higher levels than would otherwise be possible. In a country where the standard of consumption is already very low, the fact that foreign resources would help in maintaining or even raising the levels of consumption in the early stages of growth, is of considerable significance. This may be necessary to ensure social goodwill, but higher levels of consumption may also add to the economic efficiency of the community and thereby facilitate increased production. In such a case, the expenditure on increasing the supply of consumption goods may be even considered as a form of investment. Moreover, utilization of foreign capital for augmenting the domestic supply of consumption goods through increased imports, contributes to maintaining a certain fairness in the distribution of the burden of development between different generations.[4] To the extent repayment of foreign obligations at a future point of time and the payment of interest charges would necessitate additional taxation, it would be possible to make future generations bear part of the strain of capital formation and economic development.

As regards the effect of foreign capital on internal stability in the borrowing country, there is some ambivalence. In a growing economy, domestic instability manifests itself in the form of inflation caused by excess of investment over savings. Normally, the availability of external resources should relieve the pressure on domestic savings. Foreign capital can be utilized in the form of import of capital goods as well as consumption goods. The former eases the strain on the demand for local investment goods and the latter adds to the supply of consumption goods and thus reduces the pressure on supply. Eitherway inflationary pressures are kept under control. There is, however, the possibility of an opposite effect resulting from the use of external capital. The availability of foreign resources may create or aggravate internal disequilibrium in so far as these represent a net addition to the resources available for investment and hence when there is no problem of scarcity of resources, there will be greater temptation to launch upon too ambitious programmes of investment.

[3] *Formulation and Economic Appraisal of Development Projects*, Vol. I, U.N., 1951, pp. 103–04.
[4] *ibid.*, pp. 104–05.

If so, there is always the likelihood of inflation when additional investment facilitated by foreign resources is not matched by domestic savings. An attempt to finance the domestic project out of domestic resources alone will be deflationary if it involves collecting from the community's purchasing power more than what is released through government expenditure. But, to the extent the resources collected by the state fall short of the amount released through investment spending, an inflationary potential is created. This is the theoretical basis of the view that financing an investment programme even with foreign capital will tend to inflation if domestic savings are not raised to a matching level. Furthermore, the additional foreign resources have a direct effect upon the volume of money supply in the country and thus stimulate increased spendings by the community. The inflow of foreign capital adds to the foreign exchange resources available for the economy. These may be acquired in the first instance by the government or business firms and may be exchanged for bank deposits. The improvement in the reserves position of the banks induces expansion of credit and brings about a fall in interest rate and easier money conditions.[5]

However, the beneficial effect of external capital in strengthening the external payments position of the borrowing country cannot be disputed. Generally, domestic instability in the form of inflation is reflected in the external balance of payments of the country. If investment is equal to savings there is internal stability. The exports of a country constitute a form of investment and imports represent a form of savings. Since internal stability has a close bearing on external stability, the over-all equilibrium conditions of an economy can be properly viewed only if the effect of external trade is also brought into the situation. There can be over-all equilibrium only if the value of exports plus domestic investment is equal to the value of imports plus domestic savings. It therefore follows that when domestic investment exceeds domestic savings, equilibrium can be maintained only if imports are made to exceed exports. Thus if domestic investment is 25 and exports 100, domestic savings 25 and imports 100, there is both internal and external equilibrium. If domestic investment rises to 50 and savings remain at 25, over-all equilibrium can be maintained only if either imports rise to 125 or exports fall to 75. It means that under these conditions if investment level has to be higher than savings level—and this is what happens in developing economies—and exports level is not to be allowed to fall, the excess of imports necessary to maintain or preserve stability, has to be financed by means of foreign borrowing. In reality, in a developing economy there will be a persistent tendency for imports to exceed exports with the result that the gap in external balance of the country can be closed only with the help of foreign loans or aid.

Apart from the direct effect of foreign capital in relieving balance of payments pressure, it has an indirect effect also in so far as it helps to improve the terms

[5]Polak, J. J., 'Balance of Payments Problems of Countries Reconstructing with the help of Foreign Loans,' *Quarterly Journal of Economics*, February, 1943, pp. 208–40.

of trade of the country which gets command over foreign resources This follows from the fact that the capital receiving country is not under any compulsion to match its imports by exports immediately, so that it can hold back its goods from external markets and wait for favourable opportunities to sell. In other words availability of foreign finance strengthens the bargaining position of the country in its dealings in international trade. This also enables the country to maintain the exchange rate of its currency at a higher level than would be possible if foreign capital were not available.

To what extent foreign capital can help economic development is illustrated by the economic history of most of the advanced countries of the world today. In the 17th and 18th centuries when Britain witnessed a remarkable industrial awakening, she drew heavily on the capital resources of Holland. In the last quarter of the 19th century the U.S.A. was a large borrower of external capital. Foreign borrowing by this country in the years 1874 to 1897 was so large that current trade surpluses were insufficient to service the debt; consequently, it became necessary to utilize some of the foreign exchange resulting from new loans for paying interest and dividends on old loans. Similarly in Canada in the first three decades of the present century, particularly in the years 1900–1913 and 1920–1929, the influx of large foreign capital synchronized with the rapid industrial growth of the country.[6] In both these countries the inflow of foreign capital was large and continuous, and helped substantially in the laying of a broad base for the industrial structure of the economy. The significant contribution of foreign capital to the economic growth of Canada is recognized in the Report of the Royal Commission on Canada's economic prospects which states " the growth of the country at any stage in its history would have been much slower without large supplies of capital from foreign countries principally from the United Kingdom and the United States. All our periods of great economic activity and expansion in peace time have been characterized by heavy inflows of capital from abroad."[7] Many of the younger among the industrial nations also lay great stress on the need for external resources in order to further strengthen their economies. In its review of the desirability of overseas borrowing, the Royal Commission on Monetary Banking and Credit Systems in New Zealand (1956) points out that the country having become accustomed to high standards of living and high levels of expenditure on consumption goods is confronted with the problem of inadequate savings to meet the minimum required rate of investment and as such would have to resort to external capital for financing additional development. The attitude of Australia is similar. The official view about foreign capital as expressed in the *Economic Survey* of 1957 is that in view of certain special reasons such as the great distances of the country, and the fact that expansion is taking place in an age of costly capitalizing techniques, the Australian need for capital is high; but since the

[6]*Processes and Problems of Industrialization of Underdeveloped Countries*, U.N., 1955, p. 81.

[7]Quoted in Conan, A. R., *Capital Imports into Sterling Countries*, Macmillan, London, 1960, pp. 88–93.

inflow of foreign capital taken with domestic savings is inadequate in relation to the need, much emphasis has to be laid on avoiding any policy which would hamper or restrict the inflow of capital on the scale desired.[8] Considerable importance is attached to foreign capital in the development plans of the East Asian countries also.

Of late, however, there has been a reaction against the extollation of foreign capital as an agency for accelerating economic development in poorer countries. Some writers take the line that the importance of external finance in economic growth has been very much exaggerated and that normally the contribution that foreign assistance makes to the building up of industries or to capital formation is much less than what the figures relating to the international transfer of capital would suggest. Singer puts forward the thesis that private foreign investment has not helped so much in the industrialization of under-developed countries as in the exploitation of their natural resources for the benefit of the foreign investing country. The inflow of such foreign capital only helps in maintaining the condition of the less developed countries as primary producers in the interests of further industrialization of richer countries which are already industrialized. As a result, the system of international division of labour gets strengthened and hardened to the benefit of the industrial countries and to the detriment of the low income countries.[9]

It is pointed out that although countries like, Sweden and Denmark did borrow from foreign countries, yet at certain important stages in their economic growth little reliance was placed on foreign capital or foreign enterprise. And this is mentioned as an instance to prove that dependence on external capital is not inevitable. There is some point in this argument but it has to be remembered that the conditions under which growth took place in these countries were very much different from that obtaining in contemporary underdeveloped countries. Youngson shows[10] that there was rapid economic growth in these countries in certain periods of their history when there was no great inflow of foreign capital because of the following reasons. In the first place, the quantity of capital required in these countries during their early stages of industrialization was much less than what the present day under-developed countries in corresponding stages of economic advancement require. The disparity between different countries in the matter of income and wealth was not so wide in the 18th century as in the 20th. It is this glaring disparity that impels the low income countries of the present day to desire a much higher rate of growth of income, and economic progress at a much faster pace than was possible two centuries ago. Secondly, the level of per capita income and consumption, the pattern of distribution of income, the rate of population

[8]Quoted in Conan, A. R., *Capital Imports into Sterling Countries*, Macmillan, London, 1960, pp. 88–93.

[9]Singer, H. W., 'The Distribution of Gains Between Investing and Borrowing Countries,' *American Economic Review — Papers and Proceedings*, May, 1950, p. 473.

[10]Youngson, A. J., *Possibilities of Economic Progress*, Cambridge, 1959, pp. 285–88.

growth and the nature of economic development were such in these earlier cases of economic progress as to make financing of investment out of current savings relatively easier. Thirdly, many industries in Sweden and Denmark in the early days of economic growth were built up or expanded by means of very heavy reinvestments of business profits. And in view of the absence of labour organizations pressing for higher wages and of any taxes on profits, the private entrepreneurs found it possible to convert a large part of their annual profits, which they earned by their hard labour and diligence and their unostentatious ways of living, into fixed capital. Lastly, these countries were able to acquire foreign exchange out of primary commodities. This was the case of Sweden before 1875 and Denmark before 1880. They had not to borrow from outside in order to acquire the foreign exchange needed for domestic capital formation.

An additional point mentioned in this connection is that even in the case of those countries where economic expansion was facilitated by a large inflow of foreign resources, the import of external capital was necessitated not by the inadequacy of domestic savings but by the fact that in the absence of a satisfactory system of financial institutions a large part of the savings which the economy was capable of generating could not be properly mobilized, and canalized into investment. Among the present day developed countries which have drawn heavily on foreign resources for financing domestic investment, the U.S.A. stands most prominent. Between 1843 and 1914 net foreign indebtedness of the U.S.A. rose from $200 million to $3,700 million. This large external borrowing was primarily due to the underdeveloped nature of the country's banking system and financial institutions. In Denmark about the middle of the last century, despite the boom of the 1840s which swelled the pockets of the farmers and provincial merchants, businessmen complained of lack of funds and began to depend on Hamburg for capital. The real cause of the trouble in Denmark then was the inadequacy of the banking system and the failure to mobilize domestic savings, rather than any absolute want of the ability of the country to save. It was only in the latter half of the 19th century, that the problem of scarcity of money for investment, while money lay idle where it was not required, was sought to be met by the development of banking and other financial institutions. When banks did develop, foreign indebtedness significantly declined, and programmes of railway construction and industrialization were undertaken largely without any foreign financial aid.[11]

Writers who are sceptical about the advantages of foreign capital in economic development seriously question the assumption that the total volume of external resources brought into a country in the form of loans, grants and aid is a measure of the extent to which domestic resources are augmented. They point out that there is considerable divergence between the aggregate amount which a country borrows from outside over a period of time, and the actual amount which it utilizes for development. It is argued that invariably when a

[11]Youngson, A. J., *Possibilities of Economic Progress*, Cambridge, 1959, p. 180.

country draws resources from foreign countries for domestic investment purposes, the import of goods and services is very much in excess of what the
importing country can absorb or satisfactorily utilize. While a certain minimum
amount may be necessary to supplement domestic resources, and does add to
capital formation, it happens that after sometime, the size of foreign capital
apparently employed in the country tends to increase rapidly because of the
compound interest factor. The payments on account of amortization and
interest charges due from the borrowing country would be mounting up which
would necessitate further borrowing to meet these payments. This leads to
excess borrowing which has no relevance to the extent to which the borrowing
country has actually depended on foreign capital for its development. Thus
while the net long-term borrowing of the U.S.A. between 1850 and 1914
amounted to three billion dollars, it was throughout either matched or exceeded
by net payments of interest and dividends amounting to $ 5·8 billion over
the period.[12] In the case of New Zealand, while the inflow of foreign capital
between 1840 and 1847 occurred in a crucial period of the country's economic
development, yet after 1887 it was not foreign capital that helped New Zealand's development, but her own internal savings. In that period, a large part
of the country's surplus resources was utilized for the amortization of foreign
loans and for meeting the huge interest charges. Economic development in
the latter period was possible only because internal resources which were
saved, exceeded the above payments. Without external technical assistance New
Zealand could not have developed herself, but the point that is stressed here
is that more than the amount borrowed from outside was paid out by way of
repayment of capital and interest out of domestic savings.

This explanation is unconvincing. New Zealand (and this applies to other
countries as well) was able to enlarge her domestic resources and transfer to
foreign countries a larger amount than what she was able to utilize, only
because foreign capital was available in the early stages of her economic
growth. What is really significant is that foreign resources became available
at a crucial stage in the development of the country. A debtor nation will
not continue to be debtor indefinitely; nor is it expected or desired to be so.
After all, foreign capital is needed only for promoting economic growth which
would become self-sustained, so that the country after a time would be able
to stand on her own legs and would no longer need external loans. It is true
that over the years, the payments on account of amortization and interest
charges exceeded the receipts which were actually absorbed into domestic
capital formation. Also for making such payments, the country was forced to

[12]Knapp, John, ' Capital Exports and Growth,' *Economic Journal*, September, 1957, p. 432.
Prof. Knapp cites the case of Germany in Hitler's time and of the U.S.A. during the First World
War, when the two countries were able to increase their output without recourse to external
borrowing. This however misses the point in so far as these two countries at the time under
reference had already built up their economies and were in a position to further expand with
the help of their own resources.

resort to fresh external borrowings. Hence it is correct to say that the aggregate receipts of resources and aid from outside were much in excess of the extent to which foreign capital helped in economic development.ᐧ But it is incorrect to conclude from this that since over a long period of time the payments made by the borrowing country to the creditors exceeded what she actually invested out of the external resources, she is not in a net debtor position and as such owed nothing in her economic development to foreign resources. This may be true in an accounting sense of the term, but not true in the economic sense.

What is true of New Zealand is equally true of many underdeveloped countries of today which are relying largely on foreign capital to supplement their own meagre resources. The real contribution of foreign capital to economic growth lies in the fact that it operates as a catalytic agent and makes development possible where it would have been otherwise impossible. So long as the per capita incomes of the pre-industrial countries are low, their savings margin will be low, their rate of investment will be low and they will continue in the vicious circle of poverty. If the proposition that the major problem of economic development in backward countries is to raise the rate of capital formation from about 5 or 7 per cent of their national incomes to 10 per cent or more, is accepted, the contribution of foreign capital to economic development becomes obvious. The marginal increment in the resources for investment has a considerable strategic significance for it can make all the difference between self-sustained growth and economic stagnation. Growth may start from the development of a particular industry or a particular region. Concentrating of investment on such an industry or a region may not be possible either for the public sector or private enterprise because of political reasons and also because of difficulty of co-operative effort on the part of independent entrepreneurs to choose a particular region or enterprise for development. In such a situation, the inflow of external capital into those particular sectors of the economy may help in the development of not only that region or industry but also in the expansion of the entire economy. ' Triggering off' economic growth in this manner involves an initial investment which in point of size and cost has no relation to the future prospects of expansion which it makes possible. As Professor Hirschman points out, even the importing of certain goods or raw materials with the aid of foreign capital would create a market for these goods and raise the general level of demand. Such imported goods could have been produced at home but are actually not produced because of the absence of a market for them. Hirschman's thesis is that instead of waiting for the market to develop in order to produce a commodity, it would be better and more beneficial to growth if the commodity is first brought in and a market is made to develop by the inducement of supply. When once new commodities are imported and an industry is developed that would absorb these goods, a local market for the import goods will spring up, and as a result domestic production of such goods would become an economic feasibility.[13] All this would mean that the value of foreign capital in promoting economic growth is not related so much to its size as to the timing of the inflow and the channels into which it flows—whether it is used up in consumption or invested in those strategic sectors of the economy that could assist in the development of supplementary and ancillary industries and thus foster overall economic growth.

The employment of foreign capital for purposes of economic development raises two important problems: firstly, its proper utilization, secondly, the problem of repayment.

UTILIZATION OF FOREIGN CAPITAL

Utilization of foreign capital involves an assessment of the actual requirements of the economy with reference to its absorptive capacity and also a careful choice of investment schemes in which the employment of external capital will be most productive from the point of view of development of the whole economy.

An estimate of the total foreign exchange requirements over a period of time has to be based on a calculation of the external capital components of different programmes of investment. To the extent foreign exchange earned through exports is insufficient for the purpose, recourse is to be had to external borrowing. The foreign exchange requirements of any scheme of economic development are made up of two components: (a) Foreign exchange needed for importing capital goods, plants, machinery, etc. to start the programme. This being a direct charge, it can be easily calculated and can therefore be accurately provided for in the budget. (b) Foreign exchange required indirectly in order to meet the recurring needs for imports resulting from the investment. Even in an investment project like increasing the output of raw materials such as rubber or jute, which clearly do not require any foreign exchange in the initial stages, foreign exchange budgeting is necessary in so far as the higher levels of employment and higher money incomes resulting from investment expenditure would increase the demand for better food, better clothing and finer kinds of consumption goods. In addition to the increased demand for consumption goods, the need for larger supplies of raw materials, spare parts of machinery, service of foreign technical personnel, etc. is also to be taken into account. These have mostly to be imported. As regards consumption goods, if it is not possible to increase their supply with domestic resources it would be necessary to acquire foreign exchange to finance their imports. Even if internal resources are diverted to the production of these goods, it is likely that export production or the investment schemes themselves would be affected, with the result that the foreign exchange problem far from being eased is very likely to be aggravated. It is therefore necessary to emphasize the fact that in any national scheme of economic development, the foreign exchange requirement has to be calculated in respect of nearly every particular

[13]Hirschman, A. O., *The Strategy of Economic Development*, Yale, New Haven, 1958, p. 205.

scheme of investment or development. Otherwise, there is always the possibility of under-estimation and unexpected shifts in the balance of payments position of the country. Obviously, a calculation of this kind covering the entire economy is relatively easier in a rigidly planned authoritarian economy than in a free enterprise economy. However, even in mixed economies where economic development is planned, it would be possible to make an estimate of the foreign exchange requirements of both the public and private sectors on the basis of information relating to individual projects of investment.

The magnitude of indirect demand for imports depends on several factors such as the size of the country and its natural resources, the pattern of distribution of wealth and income, whether the economy is diversified or not, whether it is resilient enough to produce the variety of goods needed to meet the demand of the people, etc. Generally speaking, the amount of indirect foreign exchange requirement will be relatively less in a vast and fairly industrialized economy like India and large in a country which is small in size and less developed and less endowed with natural resources like Ceylon or Malaya. This is another way of saying that the propensity to import is higher in the latter type of country than in the former. The fact that foreign exchange requirements to finance indirect imports resulting from large investment spending will be greater in a small country with an export-oriented economy than in a larger and fairly developed economy is illustrated by the data presented by some of the underdeveloped countries of South and South-East Asia at the commencement of the Colombo Plan, indicating their foreign exchange requirements. These estimates are shown in Table 33.

Table 33

IMPORT REQUIREMENTS UNDER THE COLOMBO PLAN   (1951–56)
IN SOME ASIAN COUNTRIES
(*Figures as per cent of total investment outlay*)

Country	Primary Import Incidence of Plan	General Secondary Incidence on Imports	Total Needs for Imports in Plan
India	18	10	26
Pakistan	40	10	46
Ceylon	38	34	59
Malaya and North Borneo	18	56	65

SOURCE: Vries, E. De., ' Financial Aspects of Economic Development ', *Formulation and Economic Appraisal of Development Projects*, Vol. I, U.N., 1951, p. 351.

The figures in Table 33 show that the secondary incidence of imports in the smaller and less industrialized countries—Ceylon and Malaya—is much greater than in the bigger countries like Pakistan and India. Primary imports constitute 18 per cent of total investment outlay in both India and Malaya but there is wide difference in the secondary imports required. The fact that the secondary incidence on imports is only 10 per cent of the investment outlay in India and Pakistan means that if these countries were able to secure 18 per cent and 40 per cent respectively of their investment expenditure by way of primary imports from foreign countries, they could carry through their investment programmes without their economies being subjected to any great strain or inflationary pressures. On the other hand, in the case of the small country of Malaya although the initial import requirements were estimated at 18 per cent as in India, it was felt that the income generated by this outlay would result in such a large order of increased demand for imported consumption goods that the economy would not be in a position to cope with it unless a large amount of foreign exchange (56 per cent of investment expenditure) became available to finance it.

The demand for imported consumer goods comes from private consumers and the size of this demand is determined by their money incomes as well as their propensity to import. Hence to the extent part of the additional money income generated by investment spending is appropriated by the state by way of taxes and internal loans, the actual demand for consumption goods will be reduced and the requirement of foreign exchange necessary to finance imports of consumption goods will be correspondingly less. At the same time, when the state taxes the people it acquires control over additional foreign exchange which otherwise would have been utilized by the community. Thus if investment involving foreign exchange is in the public sector, the state has to calculate the aggregate foreign exchange requirements as the sum of the initial foreign exchange directly required to finance capital imports and that part of the additional incomes net of taxes and loans which will be available to the income earners to spend on foreign goods and services. For illustration, let us assume that the domestic outlay on investment is 1,000. When this amount is spent on capital formation, the purchasing power available to the community increases to a corresponding extent. Of this income of 1,000, the state collects by way of taxes and loans 400 so that the disposable income of the community is reduced to 600. If the propensity to import is 0·20, the value of indirect imports needed is $\frac{1}{5}$ (1,000−400) =120. If the direct imports required for the above investment is 500, the aggregate imports direct and indirect will be 500+120=620. It should be added that when the state collects its revenue by way of taxation, it acquires foreign exchange which is equal to the amount that the tax payers would have utilized for imports if they had not parted with a portion of their incomes for payment of taxes. Since in the above illustration the propensity of the community to import is assumed to be 0·20, it means that when the state collects 400 by way of taxation the amount of foreign exchange which it acquires is 0·20 (400) =80. It is therefore incorrect to say that the foreign exchange needed for a development project is the difference between its total cost and the resources that can be collected through taxes and loans. This is obvious because as has been mentioned earlier,[14] even

14See p. 391.

if the domestic resources mobilized by the state are equal to the cost of the programme, the amount of foreign exchange that would become available for the state would be only a part of the resources, viz. that part which the community would have spent on imports in the absence of taxes and loans. It also means that a project can be financed exclusively out of domestic resources only if the resources collected by the state are much in excess of the cost of the scheme; and this excess depends on the propensity to import of the community; the higher is the propensity to import, the lower will be this excess and *vice versa*. On the same reasoning it can be shown that the statement that the foreign exchange requirement of an expenditure programme is equal to the sum of direct foreign exchange needed for investment and the foreign exchange required for financing the increase in imports caused by the higher spending power of the community is only roughly indicative of the actual magnitude involved. This can be right only if no tax is levied by the state on the additional income created. In the absence of taxes and loans, a part of the additional income will be spent on imports and the indirect requirement of foreign exchange will be equal to this expenditure; but if the community is deprived of part of this additional money income because of taxation and loans, the amount of expenditure on imports, assuming propensity to import to remain the same, will be less.

While the view that foreign exchange required in connection with a development programme should be equal to the value of direct and indirect imports arising out of the investment is correct, it is not proper to base the estimate of foreign capital requirements on these considerations alone. The capacity of the recipient country to absorb and properly utilize external resources is also an important factor to be taken into account in this connection. In other words, the extent to which an economy in the early stages of growth may resort to foreign borrowing with advantage, is not the sum of the foreign exchange requirements of each individual project but an aggregate depending upon the economic conditions of the capital importing country and the pattern of development which it envisages. It is quite possible that the estimated demand for foreign capital based on individual project requirement may fall below or exceed the absorptive capacity of the economy concerned.

Primarily, the capacity of an underdeveloped country to absorb external capital depends upon the availability of domestic resources. This is obvious in so far as capital has to be combined with the other complementary factors of production in any productive effort. We have seen that in most of the primary producing countries of the world today, domestic capital is not only scarce, but also shy, not tending to flow into venturesome new enterprises. The limited savings available are not properly mobilized and this because of the lack of investment habit and the undeveloped nature of financial and banking institutions.[15] Natural resources in many of these countries are limited,

[15]See Chapters V and VI.

and even when they are relatively abundant, the harnessing of them for productive enterprises requires huge initial investment. Labour may be plentiful and cheap in the sense that the services of labour can be acquired at a low rate of daily wage, but costly or expensive in so far as labour turnover is much quicker and the standard of efficiency is far lower than in the economically advanced countries. Equally significant is the fact that technically skilled labour which is necessary to build up and man modern industries is inadequate. Furthermore, scarcity of entrepreneurial skill limits considerably the scope for full utilization of foreign capital. In such a situation it becomes necessary to bring in not only external financial resources and capital equipment, but also import technically skilled labour as well as entrepreneurial skill. Lastly, it is possible to make proper use of external resources, especially in the form of capital goods only if the standards of education of the people, their capacity to co-operate, their social discipline, intelligence and technical knowledge are of a fairly high order.

These limitations affect not only the size of foreign capital inflow, but also determine largely the types and forms of external capital that would fit in with the mode of investment in the recipient countries. Thus if private enterprise is well developed in a country and entrepreneurial skill is available, foreign private capital would be encouraged to flow in. Availability of natural resources and insufficiency of local entrepreneurial talents attract direct investment. On the other hand, if the administrative system is efficient and the government is stable and takes a leading part in economic development, it is likely that foreign resources would become available through foreign governments or international agencies. Even when complementary resources are limited, the existence of a sound administrative system and a government which is capable of planning and operating developmental schemes efficiently, is an extenuating factor and raises the absorptive capacity of the economy for that reason.

On the ground that local capital and other resources are meagre, it is argued that foreign capital should be made to fit in with the economic set-up of the borrowing country and that it would be advantageous if external resources are utilized by governments for the building up of social and economic overheads which will not be attractive from the point of view of private entrepreneurship, and also if foreign capital is spread thin over the economy and not concentrated on big capital-intensive schemes. Investment of external capital in big industrial enterprises in such a situation is considered to be an act of improvidence.[16] This, however, may be true of only very backward economies where basic facilities for investment are lacking, but not applicable to countries which already have registered some progress in economic advancement. In countries of the latter type, concentration of investment on capital-intensive schemes may be necessary, for stepping up the rate of capital formation.

[16]Belshaw, Horace, *Population Growth and Levels of Consumption*, Allen and Unwin, London, 1956, p. 195.

Nevertheless, the fact cannot be ignored that some sort of preparation of the ground of the domestic economy is necessary in order to attract and properly absorb foreign capital. The history of Japan affords an illustration of this point. In the last quarter of the 19th century when the framework of a modern economy was created in Japan, the inflow of foreign capital was quite negligible. Full scale industrialization was deferred in this period, but the limited resources available were utilized in the best manner possible in developing and reorganizing agriculture, in building up small industries, in improving financial institutions and in bringing about changes in social attitudes. In the next stage in Japan's industrial expansion, covering roughly the first fifteen years of the present century, industrialization on a large-scale started, and the progress was steady and rapid, thanks largely to the sound basis which had been laid in the preceding period. With industrialization, foreign capital also flowed into the country mostly in the form of government borrowing from foreign private investors and the economy was in a position to take full advantage of this inflow of external capital.[17]

The utilization of foreign capital involves two considerations—the first a general one, relating to the extent to which application of external resources would help in domestic capital formation and strengthen the balance of payments position of the country; and the other relates to the somewhat technical issue as to whether foreign capital is to be used for the development of specific projects or for the overall development of the economy. Employment of foreign capital facilitates the better utilization of domestic capital resources, steps up the rate of investment and capital formation and accelerates income growth in the usual multiplier way. The increased income created by the initial investment of foreign capital is in the form of consumption and producers goods which are absorbed in the country or exported. To the extent additional supply of goods is exported, the country earns foreign exchange which increases the flow of foreign resources and promotes further investment. Producers goods internally absorbed directly add to domestic capital formation. It therefore follows that the expansionary effect of foreign loans is inversely related to the proportion of consumption goods imported or consumed out of the external resources in the capital receiving country. Thus if the flow of foreign capital is one per unit of time, and the marginal propensity to consume is equal to unity, all the money put into circulation through higher investment activity will be drained away as payments for consumption goods, and as such the rate of investment cannot exceed the rate of foreign lending. On the other hand, if propensity to consume is less than unity, the initial inflow of foreign capital will have an expansionary effect on the level of investment in the country. Prof. Polak points out that if the marginal propensity to consume is about $\frac{3}{4}$ and marginal propensity to import about $\frac{1}{4}$ a level of investment of about $1\frac{1}{2}$ to 2 times the level of capital inflow could be maintained. He calls

[17]Kuznets, Simon & Others, Eds., *Economic Growth: Brazil, India, Japan*, Durham, N. C., 1955; Reubens, Edwin P., *Foreign Capital and Domestic Development in Japan*, pp. 181-83.

the ratio of the actual rate of investment to the initial rate of capital inflow as " the expansion ratio ".[18]

Polak's classification of goods produced out of external resources into three categories according as their effect on external balance is favourable, neutral or adverse, has been referred to in an earlier chapter.[19] He argues that from the point of view of exchange earnings, a country making use of foreign capital for domestic investment would be well advised to concentrate on the first category of goods, avoid the third type goods and choose the second one only if other conditions weigh in its favour. However, choice between the three types of investments will be influenced also by the nature of external capital inflow—its magnitude, duration and rate—because the burden of service costs depends on it. This is illustrated and explained by Polak by taking two extreme cases. In the first two types of goods whose expansion ratio and capacity to yield export surplus is high, if we assume that foreign capital inflow is limited to a period of ten or five years, the foreign exchange earnings of the investment would be moderate or even negative in the initial period, but would show considerable expansion afterwards. But if the assumption is made that in the case of the third category of goods, external capital inflow is continuous, foreign exchange earnings of investment in this type of goods in the early period may be actually higher than in the former because of the continuity of the flow of resources from outside, but in the subsequent years there would be a decline and chronic foreign exchange shortage because of the interent nature of the goods produced, viz. their adverse effect on balance of payments. The conclusion is therefore drawn that a country's investment programme may lead to foreign exchange difficulties because the rate of investment is too high in relation to the magnitude of the initial capital inflow, or investment is wrongly distributed or because the rate of capital inflow declines too rapidly. Hence in order to avoid these difficulties governments of borrowing countries should keep total investment within the limits set by the initial inflow, divert a large part of the investment to large export yielding projects and be assured of the length of the period over which capital inflow would continue.[20]

It is however necessary to point out that Prof. Polak's analysis relates primarily to countries reconstructing their war-ravaged economies with foreign loans and not to underdeveloped economies which have to build up their economies practically from the very foundations. The economic problems confronting the two types of countries are dissimilar. Particularly in the case of advanced countries like Japan and Germany which lost heavily in the war, the after-war problem was mostly one of rebuilding and reviving their econo-

[18]Polak, J. J., ' Balance of Payments Problems of Countries Reconstructing with the help of Foreign Loans,' *Quarterly Journal of Economics*, February, 1943, pp. 208–40.

[19]Chapter VII, p. 249.

[20]Polak, J. J., ' Balance of Payments Problems of Countries Reconstructing with the help of Foreign Loans,' *Quarterly Journal of Economics*, February, 1943, pp. 208–40.

mies, and foreign capital was used for that purpose. So long as the enterprise, skill, intelligence and co-operative spirit of the people and the tradition and background of an advanced economy were left unimpaired, it was easier to reconstruct the economy than in the case of underdeveloped countries in which the problem is to build the basic structure itself. While therefore it is important for these countries to ensure a steady inflow of foreign capital, it would be unwise to concentrate investment on export oriented industries at the cost of basic social and economic overheads, public utilities, etc.

Nevertheless the attention which Prof. Polak has drawn to the need for keeping down the levels of consumption in countries making use of foreign capital is of value to economically backward countries. If marginal propensity to consume is near unity, the risk of foreign exchange shortage becomes great. As the poorer countries come into closer contact with the rich and highly industrialized countries of the world they are irresistibly tempted to keep up their standards of living and maintain their levels of spending above what the real resources at their disposal and their capacity to produce would warrant.[21] The result is, the development of inflationary pressures at home and a chronic tendency towards disequilibrium in the balance of payments. If against this danger, import of luxury articles is stopped or restricted, there is no guarantee that domestic capital formation will be augmented, because there is the likelihood of scarce capital locally available being diverted towards the production of similar luxury goods at home with very little beneficial effect on capital formation. It is therefore necessary to either take measures against demonstration effect affecting levels of consumption at home, or to keep down levels of consumption by means of physical controls or by means of a suitable tax and fiscal policy.[22]

The second aspect of the problem of utilization of foreign capital is the choice between investment in specific projects and investment in enterprises which would promote general economic growth. The advantage of investing foreign capital in specific projects which become productive in a short period of time is that it avoids any wastage or dissipation of foreign resources and at the same time ensures that the project in which investment is made, quickly reaches the stage when it can easily pay its way. If the project in addition to being a specific one, is also one that earns foreign exchange after a fairly brief gestation period, it would minimize the danger of foreign exchange difficulties and balance of payments disequilibrium. It is for this reason that the International Bank for Reconstruction and Development insists upon loans granted to underdeveloped countries being utilized for the setting up and development of projects which are economically feasible and productive, which will, when developed, earn sufficient amount of foreign exchange to meet the interest and amortization charges, and which in the absence of external aid could not

[21]Nurkse, Ragnar, ' Some International Aspects of the Problem of Economic Development,' *The American Economic Review—Papers and Proceedings*, May. 1952, pp. 571–83.

[22]Nurkse, Ragnar, *ibid*.

have been developed. This is also the principle behind the lending policy of the Export Import Bank of the U.S.A. Similarly the European Recovery Programme intended for the building up of the European economies which had been seriously dislocated by war, laid it down as a condition that external aid was not frittered away on consumption expenditure, but used to finance productive enterprises. Also, most of the grants made by advanced economies to the less developed countries are of a specific nature based on a direct relationship between the donor and the donee, in which the former understandably enough, wants to know what is done with the money. Besides, the fact that when grant is tied, the recipients feel no loss of prestige as they would otherwise, is a point in favour of such specific arrangements in the matter of external assistance.

However, from the point of view of economic development of low income countries, the system of tying up external aid to specific projects and the insistence on its being used to finance only productive enterprises seem to be based on an inadequate appreciation of their problems and hence not always advantageous. In the first place, there is no assurance that when external finance is made available in the form of loans or grants on a project-wise basis, it would be used exclusively for the purpose for which it is granted. There is the possibility of its being transferred from one project to another by a cunning twist of the terms of agreement as it happened in Austria under the European Recovery Programme.[23] Secondly, the basic principle requiring that external assistance, if it is to be of real benefit should be used for specific productive projects has come in for some criticism. There is no disputing the fact that many large capital-intensive undertakings such as railway construction, hydro-electric projects and public utilities may not be immediately productive from the strict accounting point of view, but they add to the basic capital structure of the economy and indirectly help in the development of many other industries and thereby promote the over-all growth of the economy. Thus development of ports and railways expands domestic market, helps in the better utilization of resources and the industrialization of the country. The T.V.A. is an illustration of this point. Such investments are important sources of external economies which bring about considerable profits to particular industries and enable debt charges to be covered on the whole, even if a few industries were run at a loss.[24] The point to remember here, is that economic growth is a general process affecting the entire economy and the failure or success of a particular undertaking is not to be judged with reference to the profit it yields, but in the context of its impact on the entire economy. Unlike in the nineteenth century, the present day borrowing by underdeveloped countries from foreign countries is usually for general economic development and not for specific

[23]Nurkse, Ragnar, *Problems of Capital Formation in Underdeveloped Countries*, Basil Blackwell, Oxford, 1955, pp. 95-96.
[24]Mandelbaum, K., *The Industrialization of Backward Areas*, Oxford, 1945, p. 11.

industries. Hence on the lender's side, the balancing between cost and returns in the private balance sheet sense is neither possible nor advisable.[25]

On the same grounds, the soundness of the principle requiring that external capital should be invested in only those undertakings that would be good earners of foreign exchange may be questioned. In so far as the servicing of foreign loans does involve a cost, and necessitates the earning of foreign exchange to meet the obligations, the importance of producing an export surplus should not be minimized. It has been observed that if at any period of time the service charges on foreign loans exceed the inflow of capital, it would require a greater reduction in a country's national income than the service charges themselves.[26] Nevertheless, the significance of this point should not be exaggerated to the extent of ignoring other important considerations. It has to be repeated that in the ultimate analysis, external balance of a country can be strengthened only by strengthening its economy. When the country develops economically and its resources are properly mobilized it would be found that not all the industries are foreign exchange earners. While in respect of some, foreign resources may be continually required, this would be offset by the development of other export oriented industries so that taken all in all, the country's balance of payments position would not cause any concern. The building up of economic overheads, the improvement in educational and public health facilities, development of technology and promotion of research, are perhaps more necessary for the formation of capital in a low income country than the organization and expansion of particular industries. Utilization of foreign capital in these lines of investment as well as in the building up of what is called human capital may create immediately balance of payments difficulties but all the same it is important and necessary. Whether foreign capital is well or ill utilized should not be judged merely in terms of its effect on foreign exchange earnings. The important criterion in the using of external capital is not the extent to which it reduces imports and increases exports, but its effect on the over-all productivity of the economy. It has therefore been pointed out that the principle which requires that foreign capital should be used in such manner as to bring about large foreign exchange earnings, is an administrative rather than a purely economic reason.[27]

PROBLEM OF AMORTIZATION AND INTEREST PAYMENTS

Equally important as the proper investment and utilization of external capital is the problem of finding out satisfactory means of meeting the charges arising from its utilization. These include amortization payments, interest charges and other service costs. The two major issues involved in the employment of

[25]Frankel, Herbert S., *The Economic Impact on Underdeveloped Societies*, Basil Blackwell, Oxford. 1953, pp. 56–81.

[26]Thorp, Willard L., *Trade, Aid or What?* Johns Hopkins, 1954, p. 176.

[27]*ibid.*, p. 173.

foreign capital for economic development, viz. its proper utilization and the meeting of servicing costs and repayment, are interdependent, because proper utilization of foreign capital means that the borrowing country brings itself up into a position when the burden of servicing the loans can be borne without any strain.

Servicing of foreign loans requires two things—firstly, internal financial resources are to be mobilized so as to meet the external obligations; secondly, there is the problem of securing foreign exchange to effect the transfer. Hence it may be seen that the capacity of the borrowing country to repay the loan and meet the interest charges depends on the following factors.

(a) First is the extent to which national income increases as a result of the investment of external finance. From the point of view of the individual project or industry in which the investment is made, it is not a matter of concern whether that particular industry could pay its way, that is, be productive enough and capable of yielding a sufficient amount of export products to meet the cost. But from the point of view of the entire economy it is obvious that unless national product rises sufficiently high it cannot meet its external obligations satisfactorily. It may be that investment of foreign capital gets concentrated into particular enterprises, basic and heavy industries, in agriculture and extractive industries or in public utilities and social overheads. But unless the capital so used up serves as a catalytic agent and helps in the generation of growth forces and raises the economy from its low standards, unless in short the borrowing country's economy is transformed, the country would find it hard or impossible to raise domestic resources to the extent needed for repayment of the amounts borrowed and payment of interest, etc. In fact, the capacity of the country to repay depends on the extent to which domestic savings exceed domestic investment.

The impact of foreign loan repayment on domestic income can be illustrated by a hypothetical example. Assuming that every year borrowings amount to Rs. 100, amortization extends over 10 years for each loan, i.e. every year Rs. 10 is repaid and interest charge on the loan taken every year is the same, it would be seen that at the end of the 10th year or beginning of the 11th year, the amount outstanding will be Rs. 550. Up to the 11th year the annual amortization payment will be increasing and reach a maximum at the beginning of the 11th year and thereafter remain constant.[28] The longer the amortization period, the longer time will it take for the outstanding payments to reach the maximum. At a certain point of time the amortization payment for a year will equal the capital borrowed in that year. Then the country may

---

[28] Let L be the loan taken every year, and let this loan L be amortized by an annual payment of m over a period of N years, the payments being made at the end of each year. $L=mN$. At the end of the rth year the annual amortization payment for all the outstanding loans will be mr, if $r \leqslant N$ and mn. if $r \geqslant N$. Also the total amortization amount on this date would be $m+2m+ \ldots +rm=mr(r+1)/2$ if $r \leqslant N$; and $m+2m+ \ldots Nm=mN(N+1)/2$ if $r \geqslant N$. Thus we see that the annual amortization amount goes on increasing during the first N years and then attains a constant level.

be said to have reached the saturation point in respect of foreign capital. But the interest on the outstanding capital will be over and above the capital inflow. Hence there is a maximum in foreign borrowing beyond which a country cannot go unless the size of capital inflow per year is increased. If the amount borrowed is Rs. 100 and amortization Rs. 10 for 10 years and interest rate 3 per cent, then at the end of 10 years amortization payment of Rs. 100 becomes equal to the inflow of capital. But interest payment above this will be Rs. $550+3/100=$Rs. $16\frac{1}{2}$. Hence from an accounting point of view, unless the increase in national product is sufficient enough to cover this cost, it is not worthwhile to import foreign capital.

(b) Proper mobilization of domestic resources for the purpose of meeting external loan obligations depends on the tax and fiscal policy of the state. In assessing the burden of repayment on the debtor country's economy we have to take into account not only the extent to which national income increases, but also the interest charge on the capital borrowed and the proportion of tax revenue to national income. Investment may be in the public or private sector. As for the former, resources can be collected through pricing by the state, and in the latter through taxation and borrowing. It is needless to mention here that taxation and borrowing would help also in restricting the levels of consumption and thus make available a larger margin of savings. Attention may however be drawn to the fact that the effectiveness of taxation for this purpose is determined by the way in which it can be used to mop up the additional income generated by the investment. In India, the proportion of tax revenue to national income is about 9 per cent. Since this would mean that about one eleventh of the new income created can be collected by way of taxation, it is possible to calculate the extent to which income should grow, given the rate of interest payable on borrowed capital. Thus if the rate of interest is one per cent, new income to be created is 11 per cent; and if the rate of interest is 5 per cent income should increase by 55 per cent. It is obvious then that if the rate of interest is lower or the tax collection is higher, the minimum economically feasible yield of the new investment can be lower. If as in the economically advanced countries, about 25 per cent of the national income can be collected by way of taxation, investment of foreign capital at 5 per cent interest will not be a burden even when the yield of the investment is 20 per cent. Conversely, it means that given the yield of the investment, such countries can afford to pay a much higher rate of interest on the capital borrowed than is possible in the case of poorer countries.[29]

(c) What is collected through taxation and borrowing is the savings of the community. These financial resources are to be transferred to the foreign creditor country through export surpluses. Exports earn foreign exchange and this foreign exchange is utilized for effecting the payment. Hence the capacity to repay of the borrowing country depends also on the growth of

[29]Vries, E. De, ' Financial Aspects of Economic Development,' *Formulation and Economic Appraisal of Development Projects*, Vol. I, U.N., 1951, pp. 345–49,

an exportable surplus resulting from the expansion of the economy. Assuming that the economy has developed satisfactorily with the help of foreign capital, the real burden of repayment has to be related to the aggregate export earnings of the country. Thus what is called the 'investment-service ratio' or the ratio of interest and amortization paid each year to foreign countries, which is a debit item on the balance of payments account, to the export earnings of the borrowing country, which constitute the credit item, indicates roughly the real burden of these charges on the debtor country.[30] These figures relating to some of the underdeveloped countries in South Asia show wide variation. It was 30 per cent in pre-war Indonesia, and for the post-war years it was 8 per cent for Ceylon, 5 per cent for India and Thailand, 4 per cent for Philippines and 1 per cent for China.[31]

The foregoing points bring to light the importance of continuity of inflow of foreign capital in underdeveloped countries. This is clearly necessary in order to offset the strain involved in the payment of interest charges and the low yield of many types of foreign investments in underdeveloped countries. It is in fact a relieving feature of the recent trends of foreign capital that much of the inflow is more or less of a steady nature. This is especially so in respect of public assistance and loans from international bodies like the World Bank in contrast to private capital. However as Prof. Conan points out, there are two limitations inherent in the international movement of capital in modern times. Writing about the sterling area countries he says that in these countries a large volume of foreign, private capital tends to get invested in manufacturing industries. The manufactured products have however to be sold mainly in the home market and add little to the volume of exports of the country. In a period of declining demand in foreign markets, the foreign exchange earnings of what little they can sell abroad fall appreciably. At the same time since the bulk of the manufactured products is sold in domestic markets, the profits of such industries will not be depressed so much as to deter further investment of the same type. Hence the foreign investments in industries would involve a continuing claim on the proceeds of exports at a time when these may be falling heavily.[32] Furthermore, to the extent foreign, private capital is invested in underdeveloped countries, their foreign liabilities will be increasing with every reinvestment of profits, quickly but imperceptibly. Under such

---

[30]Finch, David, ' Investment Service of Underdeveloped Countries,' *IMF Staff Papers*, September, 1951, pp. 60–85.

[31]' Mobilization of Domestic Capital,' *Report and Documents of the Second Working Party of Experts*, U.N., 1953, p. 296. In Australia this ratio fluctuated around 20 per cent in the early part of the present century but rose to 44 per cent in 1930–31. Since then, it steadily declined to 10 per cent in 1947–48. Between 1948–49 and 1951–52 it averaged 8 per cent. *ibid.*, pp. 327 and 331. Dr P. S. Lokanathan estimates that in India the annual principal and interest payment obligations on account of foreign loans will be Rs. 1,000 million in the Third Five-Year Plan period (1961–62—1965–66). Average annual value of exports expected in these years is Rs. 7,400 million. This gives an investment-service ratio of 13·5 per cent. ' Our Foreign Indebtedness,' Symposium in the *Kalki*, Madras, 1958, p. 6.

[32]Conan, A. R., *Capital Imports into Sterling Countries*, Macmillan, London, 1960, p. 59.

conditions unless foreign capital flows in an uninterrupted manner there will be balance of payments difficulties.

It is worthwhile to add that the strain on the balance of payments of under-developed countries using foreign capital to build up their economies has increasingly been realized by the creditor countries also, and international lending bodies have adopted certain measures to ease this pressure. Such measures include charging moderate or low interest rates, waiving of interest payments if there is any substantial decline in the debtor countries' exports (as was provided in the Anglo-American Loan Agreement of 1945) extension of the amortization period and deferment and acceleration of amortization pay-ments. Among methods to ameliorate the problem of currency transfers may be mentioned the provision in the Articles of Agreement of the World Bank for acceptance of domestic currency for a limited period when the borrowing member country suffers from an acute exchange stringency, and the granting of guarantee of convertibility by special agencies like the Investment Guarantee Programme under the United States Mutual Security Agency. Other measures which have been suggested in this connection are, deferment of the currency transfer of payments and the adoption of an index method under which the amount of currency transfer could be made to vary in accordance with trends in export prices, and world trade activity and the availability of dollars. The need for ensuring a continuous inflow of capital so that the gap between the current export receipts on the one hand, and the annual amounts to be paid by way of amortization, interest charges, etc. on the other, could be covered by fresh borrowing, has also been stressed. Apart from these, other measures like control of capital flight and inflow of hot money, lowering of tariffs and adoption of suitable commercial policies by the lending countries have been recommended. Most countries of the world realize that in the matter of tariff concessions, the U.S.A. should play the leading part. It has been urged over and over again that American tariff in particular should be reduced so as to make the U.S.A. a good creditor.

Repayment of external borrowings presents a problem to the creditor as well as to the debtor countries. This aspect of the problem of foreign lending from the point of view of a high income lending country such as the U.S.A. has been stressed recently by some American economists.[33] The granting of a loan necessarily involves increased exports of goods and services from the lending country. When a country advances loans or extends aid to another country it amounts to an act of investment and raises the over-all level of investment and employment and increases output in the lending country. Conversely, when the debtor is making a payment on account of principal and

[33]Buchanan, Norman S., *International Investment and Domestic Welfare*, New York, 1945, p. 179. Lary, Hal B., 'The Domestic Effects of Foreign Investment,' *The American Economic Review, Papers and Proceedings*, May, 1946, p. 678. Domar, Evsey D., 'The Effect of Foreign Investment on the Balance of Payments,' *The American Economic Review*, December, 1950, pp. 805–26, reprinted in *Essays in the Theory of Economic Growth*, Oxford, New York, 1957, pp. 129–53.

interest obligations, it has to increase its exports of goods. The creditor country can therefore accommodate these repayments only by increasing her import or decreasing her visible exports. Thus amortization and interest payments will have the opposite effect of lending. This reverse trend which would adversely affect investment and employment levels in the creditor country can be offset only by fresh increased investments abroad. The rate at which such foreign investments should increase depends upon the rate of inflow of amortization and interest payments. Domar has shown that the ratio of the inflow of funds in the form of interest and amortization to the outflow, i.e. new investment will gradually approach as a limit the expression,

$$\frac{\text{amortization rate} + \text{interest rate}}{\text{amortization rate} + \text{rate of growth}} \text{ (i.e. percentage rate of increase in new lending)}.$$

From this it follows that the faster the new investment grows, the smaller will be the ratio between the inflow and outflow of funds. It is in the interests of the lending country to keep this rate as low as possible, but it can achieve this only by lending at very low rates of interest or by increasing the rate of fresh lending or by both. If the rate of interest charged on external loans is higher than the rate of growth of foreign investment, the lending country cannot but face import balance and all its consequences. The total lending of a country is made up of private lending and government lending. If the rate of growth of national income per year is assumed to be 3 per cent and foreign lending by the government is a constant proportion of the national income, the rate of lending by government would be 3 per cent per year. The government cannot afford to charge a rate of interest of 3 per cent since the rate of interest on private loans will be much higher than this. To offset this, the rate of interest on government loans to foreign countries has to be kept well below 3 per cent. In view of this Domar concludes that the average rate of interest charged by the government of the U.S.A. on foreign loans of 3 or 4 per cent and by the Export Import Bank of $2\frac{3}{8}$ to 6 per cent is much higher than what is required to avoid the consequence of import balance arising out of foreign lending.[34]

But the magnitude of the problem involved in repayment of foreign capital from the point of view of the creditor nations appears to be exaggerated. If attention is confined solely to the trade movements connected with foreign lending, the consequences indicated above are real. But even if an import balance arises it is possible for the government concerned to meet this by other measures of a fiscal and monetary nature. Furthermore, it is incorrect to assume that the repayment of principal or amortization will necessitate export of goods from the debtor to the creditor country to the same extent as payment of interest charges would. The latter is a regular annual payment. From the point of view of the lending country, receipts on account of interest are in the nature of income, but receipts on account of amortization are in the nature of

[34]Domar, Evesey D., ' The Effect of Foreign Investment on the Balance of Payments,' *The American Economic Review*, December, 1950, p. 808.

capital payments. Prof. Nurkse points out that while an individual feels free in spending income receipts in any way he likes, this cannot be said of capital receipts. As regards the latter, they may be reinvested in a new loan in the same country or other countries. The payments on that account do not therefore necessitate an inflow of goods from the debtor countries. Such an inflow becomes possible only when the fundamental economic conditions of the creditor and debtor countries are reversed. That is to say, repayment of foreign loans would be necessary when the interest rate in the creditor country rises or savings fall short of investment. It takes a long period of time before such fundamental changes can take place so that, the above-mentioned problems involved in the repayment of capital would not arise, except in abnormal circumstances.[35]

[35]Nurkse, Ragnar, *Problems of Capital Formation in Underdeveloped Countries*, Basil Blackwell, Oxford, 1955. pp. 133–34.

Chapter XIII

EXTERNAL CAPITAL : TYPES AND TRENDS

FROM THE point of view of receiving countries, foreign capital may be divided into loan capital, direct investment and grants and aid. There is a difference between these categories of external capital in respect of their impact, the benefits which they confer and the strain which they cause on the economies of the receiving countries. Thus while loan capital involves regular servicing costs in the form of interest payments and amortization, grants and aid constitute a net gain to the country into which they flow. As regards direct investments, while no interest need be paid on these, they necessitate the transfer of resources from the beneficiary country in the form of periodic dividends and profits. Another way of classifying foreign capital is with reference to its source. On this basis, three main classes of external capital can be distinguished: (1) Private foreign capital, (2) Loans and Grants made by governments to foreign countries and (3) Loans and aid from International agencies. The relative significance of these three types of external capital and the recent trends in their movement may be briefly examined.

1. PRIVATE FOREIGN CAPITAL

Private capital or venture capital flows out in the form of loans, i.e. portfolio investment and also in the form of equity capital i.e. direct investment. In addition, private capital moves out through commercial banks for investment in foreign countries. Portfolio investment involves the transfer of capital from one country to another by means of holding of bonds and securities of a firm or company in the borrowing country by parties in the lending country; while direct investment relates to the investments made by entrepreneurs of a firm in one country in a subsidiary firm in another country. Apart from this, reinvestment of profits in a firm in a foreign country which results in its expansion and growth should also be considered as direct investment. The fundamental point of distinction in this case is that direct investment involves control by the investor of the enterprise in which investment is made.[1]

[1]I.M.F. *Balance of Payments Year Book.* Vol. V, 1947-53, p. 10. The distinction between portfolio investment and direct investment is, however, not clear cut. Portfolio investment normally means investment effected through the purchase of securities and bonds of companies and firms or of governments on the Stock Exchange; and direct investment or entrepreneurial investment refers to the investments made by foreign businessmen or companies which result

(a) Portfolio Investment

Private portfolio investment takes place through private parties in a country or its government selling bonds or securities in a foreign Stock Exchange Market. Thus capital is lent by private parties either to their counterparts or to the government of a foreign country. In the latter case, the foreign resources would be utilized by the borrowing governments concerned to finance government schemes or would be re-lent to private enterprise. In this kind of external borrowing, the initiative comes from the borrowing country and the risk is with the party which takes the initiative. Obviously, the price of such loans or the interest charges depends on the confidence which the borrower can create in the foreign capital market.

Among the advantages of portfolio investment may be mentioned the fact that a larger collection is possible at competitive rates of interest. Since the transaction is done on purely commercial lines, the borrowing country has greater freedom in the matter of utilization of the resources and can have greater control over the same. If the government is the borrower, it is always possible to make the inflow of foreign capital fit in with the programmes of investment in the borrowing country. The possibility of having greater control over the uses of such external finance minimizes or removes the chances of exploitation by the foreign investor.[2] Whatever be the nature of the obligation, it is always in the interests of the borrower country to relieve itself of the burden by reducing the debt. Here also, reducing of loans may be easier, while the

mostly in the expansion of the parent firm. Whether investment by means of purchasing securities should be treated as portfolio investment or direct investment is a disputed point in so far as when a foreign company is financed by the flotation of loans on the Stock Exchange of the investing country, it is possible for a big company in the latter country, to buy a great share of the securities in the company and thereby gain control over it. The first is then the parent company and to the extent there is control, this smacks of direct investment; but since financing is done through the Stock Exchange it is in the nature of portfolio investment. The attitude of the United Nations experts is to consider financing through purchase of securities, by and large, as portfolio investment. Thus in *Measures for the Economic Development of Under-developed Countries* (U.N., 1951), private direct investment is treated as investment in subsidiaries. And in *Processes and Problems of Industrialization of Underdeveloped Countries* (U.N., 1955), portfolio investment is defined as investment through purchase of bonds and securities. A. R. Conan clarifies the issue as follows, " In general practice, portfolio investment has in the past often been taken to refer to investment through the medium of securities traded on the Stock Exchange: as a result of such trading, several parties (perhaps a great many) would normally share the ownership of the undertaking in which the capital was invested and thus control would be dispersed. Direct investment on the other hand, implies the extension of a business through overseas branches or subsidiaries; the finance for these affiliates would normally come from the parent concern (not necessarily from a Stock Exchange flotation) and the investment would naturally involve effective control of the overseas undertaking by the parent."
—Conan, A. R., *Capital Imports into Sterling Countries*, Macmillan, London, 1960, p. 105.

[2]Nurkse, Ragnar, *Problems of Capital Formation in Underdeveloped Countries*, Basil Blackwell, Oxford, 1955, p. 89.

27

purchasing off of businesses built out of equity capital is not so.[3] Against these advantages have to be set certain drawbacks. The main disadvantage of external loan capital is the rigidity in the payment of interest charges. The burden becomes disproportionately high in depression when the capacity of the borrowing countries to make the payments is low. The United Nations Working Party of Experts on the Mobilization of Domestic Capital points out that portfolio foreign capital usually has an adverse effect on balance of payments for three reasons. Firstly although there is considerable scope for control over the utilization of such loans, the possibility of misapplication of the proceeds cannot be altogether ruled out. And to the extent there is uneconomic utilization, there is the possibility of strain on the external balances. Secondly, the inflow of capital of this type and the outflow of service charges on it represent a spontaneous movement of resources in and out of the country without reference to levels of national income, external trade position or inflationary or deflationary conditions in the debtor country. Thirdly, if a government issue of foreign bonds is not linked to any particular development project, there will not be any automatic improvement in the repaying capacity of the debtor country.[4] Moreover, while in theory, borrowing can be done at competitive rates in foreign Stock Exchanges, the fact is that underdeveloped countries are usually forced to borrow at very high rates of interest. Even at such cost it is quite often difficult to raise the loans because of the fear of the creditors regarding the balance of payments position of the debtor countries and the problem of the transferability of interest or amortization payments. One way of solving this problem is to match future export of raw materials or other goods resulting from investment with the amortization and interest charges anticipated. This may be advantageous from the point of view of the capital exporting country also, because it can export excess investment goods and in return get much needed raw materials.[5] But obviously this sort of arrangement is not possible in the case of all foreign loans.

(b) Direct Investment

As mentioned earlier, direct investment of foreign private capital takes place through the financing of subsidiaries of parent firms and also through the reinvestment of profits earned in the subsidiaries abroad. In recent years, the raising of tariff barriers against imports of certain commodities particularly of manufactured consumption goods in underdeveloped countries, has encouraged the setting up and expansion of subsidiaries by big foreign concerns.

[3]Rosenberg, W., 'Capital Imports and Growth—the Case of New Zealand,' *Economic Journal*, March, 1961, p. 106.

[4] 'Mobilization of Domestic Capital,' *Report and Documents of the Second Working Party of Experts*, U.N., 1953, p. 294.

[5]Kalecki, M., 'The Problem of Financing Economic Development,' *Indian Economic Review*, February, 1955, p. 161

Apart from direct transfers, provision of machinery and other equipment on credit by the parent company has contributed to total direct investment. Surveys of this sort of investment in Australia, New Zealand and India show that out of the total of such investments cash transfers account for about 23 per cent, credit 40 per cent and retained profits about 37 per cent.

Direct investment earns its income out of the profits it creates. There are no rigidly fixed service charges and the amount of income that is transferred to the investing countries directly varies with the earnings of such investment in the capital importing country. In other words, it does not impose a fixed burden of net payments on the borrowing country in times of declining economic activity and trade. Furthermore, to the extent that the private investors are keen on securing a reasonable amount of profit out of their investments, they bring with their capital the best of talents and skill to work. This combination of capital, technology and managerial skill contributes to the greater catalytic effect of this form of foreign capital. Since investment of this type is made purely on commercial considerations, chances of misuse are limited. The greater facility of expansion which foreign private capital affords through reinvestment and the chances it provides for varying degrees of participation with local capital are additional points in its favour. Since direct investments in most cases involve imports of commodities by the country receiving foreign investments, inflationary possibility of investments is reduced.

But direct foreign investment is not altogether advantageous from the point of view of the low income countries. Private capital of this type as compared with portfolio investment is less amenable to control by the borrowing country and the large profits that are transferred in a period of prosperity bring into glaring relief the fact that such capital is invested more to the advantage of the lending country than to the borrowing country. This is its major drawback. Though the rate of dividends is flexible, it will be higher than interest charges on the average. The obvious criteria for this type of investment is the availability of opportunities for making large profits. But in the absence of economic overhead facilities and an expanding domestic market which are a necessary condition if manufacturing concerns are to make any headway, foreign direct investments in underdeveloped countries gravitate towards extractive industries. Before the depression of the 1930s, of the total direct investment by the U.K. and the U.S.A. only 3 per cent was in manufacturing industries. To a large extent the aversion to foreign capital of this kind manifested in the less developed countries is due to the fact that such flow of capital takes place without any great co-ordination with the actual development needs of the recipient countries, but rather in response to the requirements of the investing countries, as in the case of petroleum investments in the immediate post-war years. At best, such investments contribute only indirectly to raising the standard of living in the low income countries. Besides, the flow of private foreign capital of this type tends to vary directly with the level of business activity and the chances of profit-making in the importing country and quite often inversely with the real needs of the latter. In periods of boom it flows unrestricted, while in periods of depression it tends to dry up, at the very time when its cessation does the greatest damage to the maintenance of world prosperity. While suspicion of the foreigner, employment of alien personnel, absentee ownership and the possibility of the affiliates or subsidiaries of the big foreign companies getting political influence in the country have been the causes of complaints by the capital importing countries, fear of nationalization, exchange controls, the tax policy and the political and economic views of the government in the countries where the direct investment is to flow have hampered the foreign investors.

(c) Trends in the Movement of Foreign Private Capital

In the four decades preceding the outbreak of the First World War, the out-flow of foreign capital in the form of portfolio and direct investment from some of the leading industrial countries of the world. especially the United Kingdom, Germany and France was of an unprecedented magnitude. This large outflow was facilitated by the legal and economic privileges enjoyed by the owners of capital in the advanced countries, the need for securing key raw materials to feed the rapidly expanding manufacturing industries in the metropolitan countries, and the prospects of attractive profits from pioneering industries. Of the total foreign investment of about £ 44,000 million nearly three-fourth was from the three countries mentioned above—the United Kingdom, Germany and France. About half of this investment was in Europe and North America and the Asian countries accounted for only about one-seventh. Although British capital which was flowing mostly to European countries in the 19th century turned towards the underdeveloped countries in the early years of the 20th century, the proportion of foreign capital absorbed by the latter group of countries remained small. During the interwar period, the size of this outflow declined considerably. Apart from the unsettled political and economic conditions brought on by the war of 1914–18 and the World Depression of the 1930s which created problems of balance of payments, exchange controls and restrictions on the international movement of capital, this decline can be attributed to a change in the attitude of both lenders and borrowers to the export of capital and the utilization of external resources for economic development.

The decline was particularly marked in the case of portfolio or loan capital. It was precipitated by the disintegration of the international capital market which began about the middle of 1928. Till then, portfolio investment had been the most common method of transferring capital from economically advanced countries which had enough investible funds to dispose of, to borrowers in the low income countries. During the depression years debt defaults, currency depreciations and trade restrictions all contributed to the rapid shrinking of this source of external finance. The rigidity of the service charges increased the real cost of loans in a period of declining prices and low business activity. Balance of payments difficulties magnified the risks of the lender while devaluation and currency inconvertibility raised the borrowers' service costs. Growing economic uncertainties increased the lenders' doubts about the repaying capacity of the borrower. The stringencies in the international capital market particularly affected the small borrowers and the poorer countries, for the obvious reason that operation in these markets even in normal times is economical only to larger and better known borrowers and not to underdeveloped countries.[6]

However, since the close of the Second World War, there has been a significant revival in the international flow of private capital. In the five years, 1924–28, a pre-depression period of high international investment activity, the total outflow of private capital approximated $ 5 billion or an annual average of $ 1 billion. In the seven years 1946–52, the net outflow of private long term capital from the industrial countries amounted to about $ 11 billion which works out to an average of $ 1·5 billion annually. The outflow of private capital from the main capital exporting countries (including retained profits of foreign branches and subsidiaries) in the four years 1955–58 exceeded $ 17 billion or $ 4·25 billion a year. Even allowing for rise in prices and also growth of population, the increase in the volume of private capital that has moved out has been substantial. As a proportion of the value of world trade, the size of private long term capital that has been transferred to foreign countries has remained more or less constant since the 1920s but the rate of increase in private international investment is higher than the rate of increase of world trade. The average annual outflow of $ 4 billion for the period 1955–58 is about twice the outflow in 1951–52. The more important among the high income countries which are large exporters of capital are the U.S.A., the U.K. and West European countries. The proportion of private capital to total capital exports (i.e. private capital and public assistance) of these countries shows much variation. Thus in 1957 export of private capital from the U.S.A. exceeded government loans and grants to foreign countries by about 50 per cent; in U.K. private capital exported was about three times as large as public capital, but in France public funds advanced to underdeveloped countries far exceeded private capital. But the governments of France as well as that of U.S.A. and U.K. have repeatedly emphasized the importance of private capital in financing economic development. Over the five years 1954–58, the gross outflow of private long term capital has averaged $ 2,700 million in the U.S.A. and $ 559 million in the U.K. while in continental Western Europe (Belgium-Luxembourg, France, West Germany, Netherlands and Switzerland) the average for the years 1954–57 was $ 1,000 million. The figures in Table 34 show the relative position of these countries in the matter of exports of private capital.

[6]*Processes and Problems of Industrialization of Underdeveloped Countries*, U.N., 1955, pp. 83–84.

Table 34

GROSS OUTFLOW OF PRIVATE LONG TERM CAPITAL FROM THE
MAIN CAPITAL SUPPLYING COUNTRIES 1954–58
(Millions of dollars)

Source of Supply	1954	1955	1956	1957	1958
United States	1,628	1,918	3,420	3,920	2,567
United Kingdom	585	364	557	755	533
Continental Western Europe	874	1,142	1,155	1,025	*N.A.*
	3,087	3,424	5,132	5,700	*N.A.*

SOURCE: *International Flow of Private Capital 1956–58*, U.N., 1959, p. 19.

The aforesaid trends in the movements of private foreign capital, namely, decline in the interwar years and marked revival since the close of the Second World War, are true of portfolio capital as well as of direct investment. However, in recent years the rise under the latter category has been more spectacular. In fact since 1945, the major part of the outflow of private capital from the high income countries has been entrepreneurial or direct investments. Between 1950 and 1957 the book value of outstanding direct investments of the U.S.A. in foreign countries more than doubled (from $ 11,788 million in 1950 to $ 25,252 million in 1957). In the period 1953–57 direct investment of the U.S.A. abroad was about ten times as great on the average as the net outflow of portfolio capital. The total value of the direct investments of the United Kingdom at the end of 1955 was estimated at £ 4,000 million. French private direct investments abroad increased at an annual average rate of $ 460 million between 1954 and 1957.

Two important features characterize the post-war revival in the flow of private portfolio capital. One is the emergence of West European countries— Switzerland, Federal Republic of Germany and the Netherlands—and Canada as lenders. In the early post-war years, domestic resources of these countries were fully utilized for reconstruction of their economies but in recent years growth and expansion of their economies has been accompanied by an expansion of their capital markets as well. Apart from lending to foreign private firms, the foreign investments of Switzerland, West Germany and the Netherlands have taken the form of private investment in IBRD bonds. An equally significant development has been the emergence of the U.S.A. as the leading nation in this form of foreign investment. While new flotations in the U.S.A. for foreign account exceeded $ 500 million every year in the decade 1920–1930, it did not reach $ 100 million in any year from 1931 to 1942. The revival after the Second World War was encouraged by the issues of the International Bank. The annual average new issues of foreign securities reached about $ 300 million in 1950–55 but since 1956, the increase in this line of investment has been considerably accelerated. New issues amounted to $ 457 million in 1956, nearly $ 600 million in 1957 and touched the peak of $ 956 million in 1958. Between 1946 and 1957 the private foreign portfolio of the U.S.A. increased from about $ 4 billion to nearly $ 6 billion. The outstanding value of U.S. foreign securities reached $ 6·5 billion in 1958, but this is still $ 1 billion below the level at the end of 1930. Further, it has to be noted that the purchasing power of dollar in 1958 was about half of what it was in 1930. Along with the rise in the magnitude of lending of this type, the number of foreign borrowers has also increased. While between 1946 and 1955 hardly more than half a dozen foreign borrowers other than Canada and IBRD issued dollar securities in the United States, the number increased to about twenty in 1958.

The general trend in the flotation of foreign issues in the capital market of the United Kingdom conforms to the pattern in the U.S.A. Foreign capital issues in the United Kingdom declined from an annual average of more than $ 500 million in 1920–1930 to $ 143 million a year in 1932–38. However, the revival since the close of the Second World War has not been very marked because the United Kingdom government has placed some restrictions in the post-war period on capital issues and further, the resources available for overseas investment have been practically reserved for Commonwealth private and public issues. In 1955 owing to the deterioration in the United Kingdom's external balances position, the Capital Issues Committee was asked to be more strict on the sanctioning of plans for new investments at home and abroad, and the Bank of England's discount rate was raised to 4½ per cent. The tight money policy adopted by the government and the raising of the interest rates were definitely a deterrent to borrowing or floating of new loans by many Commonwealth Countries. As a result of the stiffening of interest rates in the United Kingdom, the long term interest rates in the Commonwealth countries of New Zealand, the Union of South Africa and Australia tended to remain substantially lower than in the United Kindgom. Despite this factor, the pressure of applications for issues on the London Market for Commonwealth countries has been increasing and in early 1959, the government of the United Kingdom made an effort to stimulate private investment and undertook to loosen the restrictions on credit and spending. Capital issues on overseas account which declined to a very low level in the immediate post-war years rose to above £ 50 million in 1950. It reached an exceptionally high of about £ 80 million in 1954 and since then has averaged £ 60 million annually. Of the total new capital issues amounting to £ 74 million in 1958, Commonwealth countries accounted for £ 67·5 million or 91 per cent.

While British private venture capital has been concentrated on the Commonwealth countries, the U.S.A. portfolio investment has gravitated largely towards manufacturing establishments in advanced countries like Canada and to some extent to Latin America or to the petroleum industry in some of the underdeveloped countries. Thus in 1957, of the total private foreign portfolio of the U.S.A. of $ 5,919 million, as much as $ 3,894 million or 66 per cent was accounted for by Canada, $ 709 million by Western Europe and dependencies, $ 160 million by Latin America, $ 585 million by other countries and $ 571 million by International Institutions. Taking the foreign loan markets of the United Kingdom, the U.S.A. and other countries together, we find that although some of the Commonwealth countries which have secured loans from the British capital market are very much underdeveloped, yet the low income countries as a whole, account for only a small part of the foreign issues floated on the main capital markets since the end of the War. The obvious explanation for this situation is the increasing competition of the high income borrowers with long established credit standing which has resulted in the edging out of weaker and smaller countries. Thus Canada and Australia have had by far the largest share in both the United Kingdom and the U.S.A. portfolio investment. Among the Asian countries Japan alone has been successful in floating new issues in the United States Capital Market. It should however be added that the capacity to borrow of the underdeveloped countries has been increasing of late with the growth and expansion of their economies. They have increased their ability to market their securities in foreign countries through the organization of Industrial Finance Corporations, Development Banks or other similar public institutions. Organized capital markets are also emerging in some of the low income countries.

This trend in the outflow of private capital from the U.S.A. may be attributed to the following reasons: Firstly, in view of the problem of dollar shortage faced by many countries, American business finds it safer to invest in countries relatively free from this trouble so that there would be regular and reliable inflow of returns from foreign investment. Hence the tendency is to concentrate on dollar export or ' outward flow ' products. But such industries are usually not found in the underdeveloped countries. Secondly, it is an obvious fact that the ultimate determinant of the movement of capital out of the frontiers of a country is the chances of profits abroad compared with the prospects at home. All things considered, unless there is a net gain from investments in foreign countries, of a sufficient margin to offset the risks involved in such lending, capital will not move out. Because of the existence of untapped resources, the marginal product of capital in underdeveloped countries may be relatively high, but against this has to be set the fact that the non-availability of economic overheads and other sources of external economies would have a depressive effect on the productivity of capital in the pre-industrial countries. In actual fact, the margin of difference between the returns from capital invested in underdeveloped countries by Americans as compared with investments made in the U.S.A. itself is not sufficiently attractive so as to lead to any large movement of capital into the poorer countries. It has been estimated that in 1948 the returns on investment in the U.S.A. amounted to about 14 per cent on the capital as against 17 per cent abroad—a margin not wide enough to counterbalance the risk and other adverse factors involved in foreign investment.[7] This is also the reason which explains why foreign capital flows into manufacturing establishments in developed countries and primary or extractive industries in the backward countries.

On the other side, the political and economic conditions in most of the underdeveloped countries are not conducive to any large inflow of private capital. Most of these countries acquired political freedom only recently and the magnified spirit of nationalism manifesting itself in the form of unfriendliness if not hostility to any sort of foreign economic intervention is often mentioned as an important obstacle to the inflow of private foreign capital. Foreign investors are discouraged by various kinds of restrictions imposed by the governments in the underdeveloped countries. Among these are mentioned controls over the entry and conduct of foreign investments, threat of nationalization and expropriation, barriers against investments in certain types of industry, fixation of a maximum rate of earnings, steep progressive taxes on profits, stipulations regarding employment of a certain proportion of local personnel, heavy import duties on capital equipment, compulsory participation with domestic capital, restrictions on the transfer of profits, etc. Apart from political factors, economic conditions also do not appear favourable to the foreign investor. Instability in currency, lack of convertibility, scarcity of foreign exchange, exchange control and balance of payments disequilibrium add to the uncertainties and risks of foreign investment. This is an important reason why investment in oil industry is attractive to the American capital owner; countries purchasing oil even if they are soft currency areas are prepared to pay in U.S.A. dollars. The very fact that underdeveloped countries are poorly developed, and lack entrepreneurial ability, technically skilled labour and knowledge of technology is an obstacle to foreign investment. The size of domestic markets is limited with the result that the new products of industry cannot be absorbed in the country and have to be exported. It is also pointed out that investment opportunities in underdeveloped countries have declined. Prof. Nurkse shows that in the 19th century foreign capital moved out into new and unexploited countries like the U.S.A., Canada, Australia and Argentina along with people accustomed to the techniques and methods of capitalistic production. But in the 20th century, foreign capital is required by countries with a different social and economic background and where increasing pressure of population presents a serious obstacle to any programmes of industrialization.[8] Furthermore, the requirements of foreign capital in many of the underdeveloped countries have been restricted or controlled by government policy. The improvement in banking and financial institutions in these countries in recent years has helped in the better mobilization of domestic capital and to that extent has relieved the pressure on external

[7]Wolf, Charles, (Jr.) and C. Sufrin, *Capital Formation and Foreign Investment in Underdeveloped Areas*, Syracuse, 1958, pp. 53–63.

[8]Nurkse, Ragnar, ' International Investment Today in the Light of Nineteenth Century Experience,' *Economic Journal*, December, 1954, p. 744.

assistance. Besides, planned economic development has involved a restriction on the propensity to import as a means to ease the strain on foreign exchange resources and to ensure balance of payments equilibrium. At any rate, the requirements of foreign exchange in connection with economic development have been reduced to a minimum compatible with the economic growth of the country. This would mean that the decline in the inflow of foreign private capital into underdeveloped countries in recent years is due not merely to lack of profitable investment opportunities, but also to some extent to a slowing down of demand.[9]

(d) Private Capital Transferred through Commercial Banks

In addition to direct investments and portfolio capital, private financial resources of developed countries flow into foreign countries through the agency of commercial banks and other financial institutions. These credit flows are of a medium and short term nature. External assistance of this type may be classified into three: (i) participation of commercial banks in the loans of the International Bank and of the Export Import Bank of the U.S.A.; (ii) export credits granted to foreign buyers by commercial banks mostly under government guarantees and (iii) direct investment by commercial banks in foreign enterprises.

(i) Commercial banks in some of the advanced countries of the world make foreign loans through participations in the loans of the International Bank for Reconstruction and Development. Up to the middle of 1958, out of the 204 loans made by the International Bank, 132 involved private participation. Apart from this, the World Bank has in some instances extended loans in conjunction with commercial banks and issues on the market. Thus in 1957 an Indian government corporation obtained $ 5·6 million from the IBRD and at the same time raised a further loan of $ 11·2 million by selling bonds to five United States private banks. Similarly in 1959 Japan and Italy took loans in the U.S.A. partly from the commercial banks and partly from the World Bank. Private lending is also associated with the lending activities of the Export Import Bank of the U.S.A. In the latter half of 1958, out of the 117 new credits and allocations authorized by the Export Import Bank amounting $ 606·6 million, 73 totalling $ 162 million included private participation.

(ii) Export credits granted by manufacturers of capital goods in the industrial countries to importers in low income countries constitute another means for

[9]This assumption however is questionable. As may be shown in later pages, while the inflow of private capital has declined in underdeveloped countries, increasing reliance has been placed on loans and aid from foreign governments and international agencies. If really there is a decline in the demand for private capital, it is not because the underdeveloped countries have reached the point of saturation in respect of external resources, but because foreign private capital cannot be made to fit in with the requirements of planned development as easily as other types of foreign capital.

the outflow of private capital. Such export credits are insured in most cases by the governments of the capital exporting countries. Of late, this method of extending export credit has assumed some importance in countries like the United Kingdom, France, Germany and Italy. The slackening of world trade in 1957–58 and increasing competition among industrialized countries in maintaining or expanding their foreign markets have been mainly responsible for this new development. From the point of view of underdeveloped countries, export credits granted by the West European countries have been of considerable help in financing their schemes of development. However, this form of external assistance is not without certain defects. In most cases, the terms of such credits do not exceed a period of five years. Since the resources which the capital exporting countries can make available in this manner are dependent on their external payments position, it is likely that the expansion of short or medium term credit of this nature would bring about a reduction in the availability of long term credit. Easy credit terms may also have inflationary consequences in the capital exporting countries. They are essentially tied loans and have all the defects of loans of this type. The availability of export credit on easy terms conceals the urgency of tackling balance of payments disorders. They provide an illusion of external payments stability while it is really not. Moreover, as the export credits approach maturity, they impose a debt burden on the importing countries which do not realize the seriousness of it sufficiently in advance. The burden becomes more onerous, if the export proceeds of the underdeveloped countries are, as they normally happen to be, of a fluctuating nature. This has been the experience of some of the Latin American Republics, especially Argentina and Brazil.

(*iii*) Commercial banks have also separately, or in national or international syndicates, financed capital projects in developing countries. Thus since 1950, private French banks have financed a number of projects in Latin America, and British banks have extended similar credit facilities to Argentina, India and Turkey. Also private banks in the U.S.A., Belgium, the Federal Republic of Germany, the Netherlands and Switzerland have made loans to foreign enterprises or purchased foreign securities. In addition, commercial banks in the economically advanced countries have offered financial assistance to a number of low income countries enabling them to refinance outstanding credits, transform short term arrears into medium term debts and to work out amortization arrangements. As a result of their activity in participating directly in investments in low income countries and in supplementing official loans in some instances, private banks have to some extent at least, offset the inability of the poorer countries to raise loans in the international capital markets. They have undoubtedly added to the financial help which the underdeveloped countries badly need from high income countries for carrying out their development plans.

(e) Measures to Facilitate Increased Flow of Private Capital

From the foregoing brief review of the trends in the movement of foreign private capital in recent years it is clear that although the outflow of private capital from high income countries in the form of entrepreneurial investment, portfolio capital and credit granted by commercial banks has increased substantially since 1955, the benefit which the underdeveloped countries of the world have derived from it has not been in any way commensurate with the magnitude of the flow. The United Nations Study on the International Flow of Private Capital 1956–58, classifies the capital importing countries into four: (i) Advanced industrial countries which provide for each other large markets and investment opportunities; (ii) Rapidly expanding countries with a substantial industrial sector—Australia, Canada, Union of South Africa, Mexico, Brazil; (iii) Low income countries which possess natural resources mostly in the form of oil and non-ferrous metals ; and (iv) Low income countries which have neither important natural resources nor domestic markets for absorbing the output of large enterprises; most of the countries in Asia belong to this category. It is observed that a large part of entrepreneurial capital and the bulk of portfolio investments flow into the advanced industrial countries. Countries in the second group have attracted foreign capital largely in the form of establishment of branches and subsidiaries of big firms in the capital exporting countries; reinvestment of profits and portfolio investment have also contributed to the total volume of foreign private capital employed in these countries. In the third group of countries investment is made by large international companies for the development and exploitation of the natural resources. As for the last category of capital importing countries, the inflow of private capital has been quite meagre. Thus in Africa, Asia and the Far East where domestic capital formation hardly keeps pace with population growth and where capital needs are particularly great, the inflow of private long term capital is very small.[10] Yet the importance of this type of foreign capital in economic development has been increasingly recognized by the capital importing as well as the capital exporting countries. Accordingly, in recent years various measures have been taken by both these groups of countries for encouraging the outflow and inflow of private capital.

The enthusiasm with which underdeveloped countries welcome foreign capital depends mostly on the extent to which it would help in building up their economies without affecting their internal or external stability. In so far as most of these countries have adopted plans for economic development, it is understandable that they feel the need for channelling the resources, both foreign and domestic, into those lines of investment which conform to the pattern of development envisaged in the Plans. The policy of the Government of India in this matter is made quite explicit. It is the view of the government that in so far as " the investment of foreign capital necessitates the utilization of indigenous resources and also that the best use of foreign capital is as a

[10]*International Flow of Private Capital, 1956–58,* U.N., 1959, p. 11.

catalytic agent for drawing forth larger resources for domestic investment, it is desirable that such investment should be channelled into fields of high priority. The broad principle to be followed is that foreign investment should be permitted in spheres where new lines of production are to be developed, or where special types of experience and technical skill are required or where the volume of domestic production is small in relation to demand and there is no reasonable expectation that the indigenous industry can expand at a sufficiently rapid pace ".[11] In conformity with this basic principle, four important points are considered by the government before approval is given to foreign investment. Firstly, there must be a genuine programme of manufacture; secondly, the investment would be in a field where there is deficiency of indigenous capital and lack of technical knowledge; thirdly, the investment would result in a saving of foreign exchange; and fourthly, the project would lead to increased productivity. The emphasis is on the second and third points and in general, when proposals of foreign firms are made for investment in India, preference is given to those projects which cannot be developed in this country with domestic resources and which would bring into the country specialized knowledge and technical skill.

One of the main deterrents from the point of view of the foreign investor is the fear of nationalization of the industry in which investment is made. To allay this fear, some of the capital importing countries like Greece and Thailand have given assurances that they will not resort to nationalization of foreign enterprises, while in Cambodia, Indonesia and Ceylon, a declaration is made that they would not nationalize foreign enterprise for a fixed period of time. Besides, assurances are given to foreign investors about the payment of adequate compensation in the event of nationalization or expropriation and also that special provisions would be made for the repatriation of foreign capital and for the transfer of foreign investment income. Thus in India, in the case of the Standard Vacuum and other oil companies, guarantee is given by the government that they will not be taken over for a period of at least twenty-five years after operations are commenced, and after that period if they are taken over, adequate and reasonable compensation would be made and necessary facilities would be provided for transferring the amount invested in the business. Similarly, payment of fair and equitable compensation has been assured by the governments of Ceylon, Pakistan, Burma, the Republic of China and Indonesia. Another incentive offered by the underdeveloped countries to foreign private capital is in the matter of taxation. This includes in addition to removal of all discriminatory taxation against foreign enterprises, positive measures like exemptions from import duties on machinery and raw materials required for the industry. Some underdeveloped countries like Ceylon and Iraq have attempted to encourage the setting up of new industries through exemptions or reductions of income or profit taxes. Usually, these concessions are granted for limited periods from three to five years. Thirdly, steps have

[11] *The First Five-Year Plan*, Government of India, New Delhi, 1951, p. 438.

been taken to furnish adequate information to foreign investors regarding investment opportunities, as for example in Puerto Rico and Southern Rhodesia. In the former country, the Industrial Development Company established during the war, gives information and advice to foreign firms on legal matters, labour recruitment, site selection, capital raising and other problems. Ghana and Israel give positive help by providing basic facilities by improving sites, and also by providing such services as roads, water supply, power lines, etc. Besides, policies regarding nationalization, taxation, etc. have been clarified and published and the boundaries between public and private industry have been precisely defined and indicated. More important than these is the fact that there has been a significant change in the general attitude of many low income countries to foreign capital. Fear of exploitation and foreign economic domination has given place to greater self-confidence and friendliness. It is this change more than anything else, that would induce a free flow of foreign private capital into underdeveloped countries, for as the Sub-Committee on Economic Development of the United Nations Economic and Social Council has observed, " The most important requirement for promoting the flow of private capital is good faith and confidence, a sense of welcome, a sense of co-operation and a favourable response of investors. It is the fruit of favourable experience of private investors and tangible economic results in underdeveloped countries that must be relied upon as the final assurance required by the investor to promote an accelerated flow of foreign capital ".[12]

On the part of the capital exporting countries steps have been taken to encourage the outflow of private capital to newly developing countries by means of investment guarantees, tax concessions and by providing information regarding investment opportunities abroad. In the matter of offering guarantees to private investors against the risks of investing their capital in foreign countries, Japan and the U.S.A. have led the field. The Investment Guarantee system for Japanese investments abroad was introduced in April, 1956 by the amendment of Japan's Export Insurance Law, according to which the government offers protection to entrepreneurs against loss of capital and blocking of profits abroad in respect of overseas investments approved by the government. Since 1948, the U.S.A. government has had in operation an Investment Guarantee Programme which provides by means of inter-governmental agreements, insurance protection to United States foreign investors against the risks of inconvertibility of foreign currency receipts and loss through expropriation or confiscation. However, these measures have been attended with only limited success, the reasons being the high cost and delays and the practice of scrutinizing the records of the corporation which is not generally liked by the private firms. In addition, measures have been taken in recent years in the U.S.A. and the United Kingdom towards reducing the tax liability of earnings from investments abroad. By the Finance Act of 1957 the United

[12] Quoted in *Process and Problems of Industrialization of Underdeveloped Countries*, U.N., 1955, p. 89.

Kingdom set up Overseas Trade Corporations, the business profits of which are taxed only if and when they are distributed to shareholders in the United Kingdom. Proposals to form similar Corporations have also been made in the U.S.A. A third method adopted by developed countries in this line is the provision of adequate information regarding investment opportunities in foreign countries to owners of investible capital at home. In the U.S.A. the Office of the Economic Affairs in the Bureau of Foreign Commerce provides the country's businessmen with detailed information on foreign investment conditions and foreign laws and regulations and practices affecting investment. The supply of such information has been further facilitated by the setting up of the Office of Foreign Investment in April, 1955 which serves as a clearing house of information on investment opportunities overseas.

Apart from the action taken by developed and underdeveloped countries independently to encourage the flow of foreign capital, there have been mutual agreements entered into between the two parties for the same purpose. In the first place, bilateral treaty agreements provide for reciprocal 'national treatment' of foreign investments which minimizes the risks of discrimination against investments made by foreigners. The U.S.A. has entered into investment treaties with Colombia, Ethiopia, Haiti, Israel, Uruguay, the Republic of Korea, the Netherlands, Nicaragua and the Federal Republic of Germany. Since 1956 a large number of such bilateral treaties have been made which have facilitated easier transfer of capital from one country to another. Secondly, joint ventures have been formed by the co-operation of foreign investors, local investors and governments of the capital importing countries. This development has become common in Latin America, the Far East and India. In Mexico, the Nacional Financiera has participated with private American business in the establishment of important enterprises. Lastly, many developed countries have concluded agreements with low income countries to secure relief from double taxation. To this category would belong the Japan-U.S.A. Conventions of April, 1954, and the agreements of the United Kingdom with Burma, Ceylon, Federation of Malaya, Singapore, North Borneo and Pakistan. In India under the Finance Act of 1953, the government was empowered to negotiate double taxation relief agreements with foreign governments. Of late, the tax treaty agreements of developed countries like Canada, the United Kingdom and the U.S.A. with low income countries have been considerably extended. In 1956 the U.S.A. concluded an agreement with Honduras and in the next year with Pakistan. The agreement between the U.S.A. and the United Kingdom entered into in 1946 was extended in 1958 to a number of the latter's overseas territories.

These measures taken by the economically advanced countries in the matter of facilitating international transfer of capital are an indication of not only the extent to which underdeveloped countries have got over their suspicion of external capital and the recognition by them of the importance of foreign resources in accelerating domestic capital formation, but also of the growing sense of responsibility on the part of the advanced economies to help in the economic betterment of the poorer countries by making available their surplus funds for investment overseas. It may therefore be hoped that with improvement in international relations and better understanding of the needs and obligations of the different countries of the world, the prospects of the flow of international capital in the form of both entrepreneurial and portfolio investment would become brighter.

2. LOANS AND GRANTS FROM GOVERNMENTS

One significant feature of recent trends in the outflow of external capital to underdeveloped countries is the increasing extent to which the deficiency of private sources has been offset by the contributions from governments and international agencies. The international transfer of capital at government level is effected in the form of: (a) Loans and grants; (b) Technical Assistance and (c) Export of food surpluses.

(a) *Loans and Grants*

The ultimate source of government loans is of course the savings of the people and as such the risk involved in the payment of amortization and interest charges is shared by the nation as a whole through the government. The Export Import Bank of the U.S.A. set up in 1934 to help the foreign trade of the country is an agency through which public capital is transferred in order to facilitate the importing of American goods in foreign countries. The loans through this agency are usually made for short terms and supplement private capital resources. Since its primary objective is to promote domestic foreign trade it can be of benefit to the underdeveloped countries only to a negligible extent, and that of an indirect nature. Similarly, the United Kingdom made available public capital to many of her colonies and France to her dependencies in North Africa. Recently the Soviet Union has also entered this field by delivering capital goods at a low rate of interest—2 per cent—to be later repaid by the borrowing countries in the form of primary products. One advantage of government to government loans is that the borrowing government is in a better position than private individuals or businesses to understand the nature of the development required and the extent to which and the lines along which external capital can be utilized for the purpose. The successful employment of foreign capital by governments reduces the investment risks of private businesses. On the other hand, it is sometimes feared that increased availability of public loans at low interest rates would dampen the outflow of private capital.[13]

[13]Froomkin, Joseph N., · 'The Migration of Capital, People and Technology,' Williamson, Harold, F., and Buttrick, John, A., *Economic Development : Principles and Patterns*, Prentice-Hall, 1954, p. 295.

Grants and aids from the industrial countries for the economic development of the low income countries are a recent development in international finance. Soon after the close of the Second World War, there was a substantial outflow of American public capital to the war-devastated countries of Europe to help reconstruction. Also, the International Co-operation Administration under the Department of State of the U.S.A. has made available large funds mostly in the form of grants for building up the military defences in Korea, Taiwan and Viet Nam. However, only in the last few years have underdeveloped countries received foreign aid of this kind to facilitate their development schemes. Grants have an advantage over loans from the point of view of the grantor as well as the beneficiaries. They constitute a net addition to the real resources of the receiving countries which are relieved of the problem of servicing charges and repayments. They are therefore ideally suited for investments in economic and social overheads and help in building up the infrastructure necessary for industrial expansion. A large proportion of international grants has thus gone to provide better means of communication and to improve educational and public health facilities. A further point in favour of grants is that since they represent a net addition to the real resources available to the receiving country, their utilization is non-inflationary unlike in certain cases of loans. The developed countries which make the grants also benefit to the extent that capital exports in the form of grants unlike loans, do not create any balance of payments strain or affect their external trade by necessitating larger imports when amortization or interest payments are made by the receiving countries. It should however be added that there is a greater measure of control than in the case of loans by the donors in respect of the manner in which the grants are utilized. Normally, grants are assigned for financing specific projects and the receiving countries are in a way bound to utilize the grants in the manner indicated in the agreement. This combined with the fact that the countries which are assisted by such forms of foreign capital are not very happy over the donor-donee relationship has made international grants less popular than if economic considerations alone were taken into account.

(b) Technical Assistance

Experience has shown that lack of education and technical knowledge and skill constitutes one of the main obstacles to growth in many of the underdeveloped countries. Technical assistance from developed countries is designed to fill this gap. It takes the form of lending of the services of technicians, engineers and other expert personnel and providing training facilities for the people of the economically backward countries. Since assistance of this nature involves a financial obligation on the part of the countries granting such assistance, it should be regarded as a form of capital made available to the poorer countries. In the 18th and 19th centuries outflow of private capital from the industrial countries to the primary producing countries was frequently attended with a concomitant movement of technically skilled labour and entrepreneurship and hence the question of the proper utilization of foreign capital did not arise. In later years, however, this combined movement became rare and as a result, the non-availability of local co-operant factors came to be a deterrent to the free outflow of private capital. Hence technical aid and assistance have been organized on independent and separate lines with the specific purpose of filling this lacunae in underdeveloped countries. Such assistance which has assumed large dimensions in recent years, is offered by governments especially of the United Kingdom, the U.S.A. and the U.S.S.R. and also by non-governmental and International Agencies.

Since the primary objective of technical assistance is to develop the capacity of the people to make proper use of the resources, it plays only a subordinate part in industrializing an underdeveloped country directly. In the United Kingdom, technical assistance in some form to the backward colonies was provided as early as 1929 by the United Kingdom Colonial Development and Welfare Act, when an annual allotment of £ 1 million was made to aid and develop agriculture and industry in the colonies. The annual investment was raised to £ 5·5 million in 1940 and to £ 12 million in 1945. However, of the loans and grants made between 1946 and 1953 under this arrangement, only about 5 per cent was for industrial development proper. Assistance granted in the next few years covered quite a wide field of schemes such as cement works in Northern Rhodesia and Trinidad, ceramics and chemical industry in Kenya, textile mills and refinery for edible oil in Singapore, development of cattle ranching in Bechuanaland, sack factory and saw mills in Nigeria, timber milling in British Guiana, etc. From the purely commercial point of view, these ventures were not successful, but as a result of the introduction of new techniques, skill and capital equipment, such assistance undoubtedly helped in strengthening the base for industrial growth in some of the least developed regions of the world.

United States technical assistance on a notable scale commenced with the Technical Co-operation Administration in 1950. Although primarily intended to improve the standards of public health, agriculture and education in underdeveloped countries, American technical assistance has also fostered the development of some small industries in many parts of the world as well as some ancillary industries. Provisions have been made for lending the services of American technical personnel, and for the training of local hands in American Universities and Technical Institutes. Much American capital has flowed into underdeveloped countries in the form of technical assistance for organizing small scale and handicrafts industries in Mexico, India, Indonesia, Pakistan, Dominican Republic, Cuba and in several other Latin American countries. For improving the productivity of labour, training facilities in industrial work have been provided for in Iran, Egypt, Iraq, Israel, Jordan and the Lebanon. Compared with the assistance from the United Kingdom of a similar type, the

United States assistance seems to give relatively greater emphasis to industrial projects.

Technical assistance on a substantial scale has been given in recent years by the Union of Soviet Socialist Republics to Bulgaria, Rumania and Mainland China Technical assistance from the U.S.S.R. concentrates more on heavy industry and takes the form of capital equipment as well as expert advice. An instance of technical assistance on a multilateral basis is the institution of a Council of Mutual Economic Assistance in 1949 with Czechoslovakia, Eastern Germany, Hungary, Poland, Albania, Bulgaria, Rumania and the Soviet Union as members. Mutual assistance extended by the Council is in the form of exchange of plans for industrial projects, sharing of research results in the industrial field as well as the supply of Soviet experts for assistance in the planning, construction and operation of factories and provision for the training of workers and students from the less developed members of the Council in Soviet schools and factories.

Significant contributions in this line have been made by voluntary non-governmental agencies particularly of the U.S.A. and also by International Agencies like the United Nations and the Colombo Plan organization. The United Nations Technical Assistance started on an organized scale in December, 1948 with the provision of £ 288,000 in the budget for 1949. The annual allotment in subsequent years has been considerably increased. The programme was expanded in 1949 by enlisting the co-operation of all the specialized agencies of the United Nations in this field. Financing is made possible by the voluntary annual contributions of governments of member countries of the United Nations and of its specialized agencies. The objective as officially laid down is to strengthen the national income of underdeveloped countries through the development of their industries and agriculture. Assistance is granted on the basis of requests made by governments and is made to flow through official channels and the recipient countries are required and expected to perform as much of the preliminary work as possible in connection with the projects for which such assistance is made available. Technical assistance granted by the United Nations covers direct industrial activities especially small industries, provision of training facilities in the general field of industrial development, carrying out of manpower surveys, study of industrial relations, job analysis for statistical purposes and for raising the level of productivity and research projects in the industrial field. A good proportion of the total expenditure is incurred on social matters such as public health, education, etc. Industries alone absorb only about 5 per cent of the total outlay directly. This is due to the fact that most of the underdeveloped countries are not in a position to utilize this assistance in any large measure in industrialization and also because the assistance flows directly to governments and as such does not affect the large part of industries which are in the private sector.

The Colombo Plan is another internationally organized scheme for the exchange of technical aid. Most of the countries of South-East Asia are members, besides Australia, Canada, New Zealand. the United Kingdom and Japan. The U.S.A. has also taken much interest in it. As in the case of aid granted by the United Nations, the contribution of the Colombo Plan to major industries is limited. Since its organization in 1951, the contributions of the Colombo Plan have gone into small industries and have also taken the form of expert advice, exchange of trainees and experts, equipments for technical schools, etc.

The figures in Table 35 indicate the extent of United Nations technical assistance including the United Nations Children's Fund and other agencies to underdeveloped countries in 1958 and 1959 and also contributions to the assistance made by different member countries.

Table 35

U.N. TECHNICAL ASSISTANCE—RECEIPTS AND CONTRIBUTIONS BY DIFFERENT COUNTRIES 1958, 1959
(*Amount in million dollars*)

Countries	Receipts under Technical Assistance	Contributions to Technical Assistance
Africa	17·1	2·0
America: North and Central	21·1	121·6
America: South	20·2	6·1
Asia	54·8	9·5
Europe	...	51·8
U.S.S.R.	...	7·1
Other regions and undistributed	7·7	...

That technical assistance from governments and International Agencies has contributed substantially to the development of the economic potentialities of some of the poorer countries of the world is an obvious fact. It should however be added that the full benefit of this form of assistance can be reaped only if the recipient countries are well aware of the nature and magnitude of their needs and are prepared to co-operate whole-heartedly with the agencies which assist them and also are able to follow up the scheme after the period of assistance ceases. On the other hand, it may be said that technical assistance would not be of help if it merely aims at implanting Western techniques in the pre-industrial countries, without attempting to evolve a proper combination of Western know-how with local knowledge and tradition. A great deal of under-standing by the developed countries of the requirements and problems of the less developed regions and a proper appreciation of the help received in this form by the latter are an essential condition for the success of such measures of help. A suitable combination of capital assistance with technical aid is also necessary. Furthermore, in granting assistance of this nature, the over-all investment potentialities of the country and its economic possibilities and scope for general development are to be correctly estimated. Also, it is important that technical assistance is continued over a fairly long period of time, besides being steady and reliable. The real benefit of foreign assistance in any form depends on the extent to which and the speed with which the recipient country can be enabled to depend on its own resources and to develop its own skill and techniques for maintaining the growth of the economy.

(c) External Assistance in the Form of Export of Food Surpluses

The export of food surpluses by high income countries to backward economies constitutes another important source of external aid for the latter. A committee of experts of the F.A.O. who conducted a pilot survey in India in 1954-55 under the direction of Mordecai Ezekiel pointed out that surpluses of farm products in one country can be utilized for the employment of unemployed labour in underdeveloped countries in works like road-building, irrigation, construction of schools, warehouses, etc. which are labour-intensive and which would increase the countries' productive ability and speed up their development. But in so far as time has to lapse before these newly-created facilities result in increased production, additional employment by raising the levels of effective demand would cause inflation. This however can be prevented if food surpluses in other countries are transferred to the developing countries to help financing the projects as well as to meet the newly created demand until production in the recipient country sufficiently expanded.[14] From the point of view of underdeveloped countries, the economic significance of such food surpluses received from richer countries consists also in the fact that to the extent such consumption goods are available, domestic resources can be shifted from the production of consumption goods to the production of export goods which would earn foreign exchange for the importing of capital goods. Apart from stepping up capital formation in the low income countries, this would strengthen the balance of payments position of these countries. Besides, the import of food surplus sets aright any adverse trend in the terms of trade as between agricultural and manufactured products in the importing countries. The donor country also stands to gain in so far as such exports represent surplus production in the country and as such would mitigate the depressing effect of any excess production of agricultural commodities.

By far the most important source of this form of external assistance is the U.S.A. where the programme of sending food surpluses to needy countries was started in 1954 by the Agricultural Trade Development and Assistance Act of that year. The disposal of surplus agricultural commodities is effected in the U.S.A. under the provisions of Public Law 480. Under Title I of this Act

[14]Uses of Agricultural Surpluses to Finance Economic Development in Underdeveloped Countries, F.A.O., Rome, 1955.

such commodity transfers take the form of sales for local currency and under Titles II and III of the Act they take the form of donations and barter transactions. In the two years July 1, 1957 to June 30, 1959 commodity transfers authorized by the U.S.A. under Title II of Public Law 480, to the poor countries of Africa, America and Asia amounted to $ 101·3 million and the actual expenditure $ 80·0 million. In the same period, the donations of agricultural commodities by the U.S.A. to underdeveloped countries under Title III of Public Law 480, aggregated to $ 150·0 million of which Asia accounted for two thirds. Of the total donations amounting to $ 105·4 million to Asia in these two years, India and the Republic of Korea accounted for slightly over $ 27 million each.[15]

3. Loans by International Agencies

In the matter of making available external resources to underdeveloped countries, International Agencies serve as intermediaries between the lending and borrowing countries. The resources out of which loans are granted by International Agencies are the collections made in the capital markets of lending countries. The advances are in the first instance made to the agency so that the extent to which financial resources can be mobilized for this purpose depends on the confidence which such bodies can create among the ultimate lenders. But in so far as the initial borrowers are a body of specialists, there is an assurance of safety, and hence the price paid for such loans tends to be low. On their part, such agencies have to undertake the responsibility of seeing that the proceeds are properly utilized.

The most important International Agency doing this service is the International Bank for Reconstruction and Development which started operations on June 25, 1946. One of its major functions is to provide financial means to countries requiring funds to supplement their own, in their economic reconstruction and development schemes. In its lending policy the Bank is influenced by three objectives: first, to ensure that the loans granted are within the means of the borrower to repay; second, the projects financed are productive; and third, the loans are utilized in a manner agreed upon by the borrowing party and the Bank. Before a loan is granted, the International Bank makes a preliminary exploration through its specialists to make sure that the financing would come within the scope set by its policies and the requirements of its Articles of Agreement. Next, a critical examination of the particular projects is made for which financial help is required. In addition, a careful investigation is carried out about the economic condition of the country and its financial position, the scope for the development of the project, the domestic resources available, the possibilities of its successful execution, the extent to which it would help the general economy, etc. The Bank's experts also examine the technical feasibility of the project, conduct market surveys and scrutinize

[15]*International Economic Assistance in the Less Developed Countries*, U.N., 1960, pp. 35 & 36.

the plans and the financial arrangements. If these findings are satisfactory, the next step is taken which is concerned with the negotiations for the loan agreement. This relates to the processing of loans involving the drafting of the loan and guarantee agreements, disbursement of loan proceeds, fixing of rates of interest and other charges and repayment terms. The Bank's responsibility does not end with the actual granting of loans. The fourth stage is the administration of loans in which the Bank follows up the progress of the projects and makes effective contacts with the borrower during the life of the loans. It also makes an ' end use ' supervision of the loans in order to ascertain that goods purchased with the loan proceeds are properly installed, and necessary steps are taken to ensure the satisfactory progress of the project.

In the initial years of its operation, the International Bank favoured the financing of light consumer goods and processing industries which employ small amounts of capital per worker and can build upon traditional skills available in the low income countries. Later however, in consideration of the fact that light industries would be able to attract the required amount of investment finance from private entrepreneurs, the Bank began to give greater importance to investment in basic economic facilities—communications, water supply, power, etc. which in spite of their great importance in national economic development are not normally attractive from the point of view of private businessmen. Thus larger amounts came to be advanced for hydro-electric works, transport, communications, etc.

Of the loans made by the World Bank to underdeveloped countries up to the middle of 1954, 47·5 per cent was accounted for by electric power and 18·5 per cent by railways. Secondary industry absorbed only a little more than 5 per cent. The first loan of the Bank advanced directly to a private concern was for $ 31·5 million to the Iron and Steel Company in India about the end of 1952. Another industrial loan was of $ 20 million to Chile for the paper and pulp mills in 1954. Apart from these direct loans, the International Bank also provided industrial finance to underdeveloped countries through the agency of special banks in the borrowing countries. Thus in 1954 a loan of $ 9 million was made to the Industrial Development Bank of Turkey. Similar loans were granted through the Development Bank of Ethiopia and the Consortium of Commercial Banks of Mexico set up in 1950. In the two years ending June, 1959 total authorizations of the Bank's loans to underdeveloped countries amounted to $ 967·4 million of which disbursements aggregated to $ 686·7 million. This was distributed as follows: Africa $ 116·2 million; North and Central America $ 52·7 million; South America $ 82·6 million and Asia $ 435·2 million. Of the total amount of $ 435·2 million disbursed to Asian countries, $ 306·0 million or 70 per cent went to India. The Bank's practice in lending to underdeveloped countries in order to finance the foreign exchange components of their projects has helped in the execution of many investment schemes which otherwise could not have been undertaken and has thus contributed to the economic development of these countries.

In the course of its operation, some defects of the Bank's method of lending
have become manifest some of which have been rectified. The receiving underdeveloped countries have complained about procedural difficulties and about
the narrow interpretation being given to the articles of agreement which
restricted the Bank's lending operations to the provision of foreign exchange
needed for specific projects. The rate of interest charged by the Bank in
many cases is quite high, considering the economic status of the countries
which resort to it for loans, and in some instances balance of payments problems
have made it difficult for the poorer countries to pay even the minimum rates
of interest (5–6 per cent) which the Bank charges. The fact that the Bank is
prevented from equity financing which often is the most appropriate source
of capital for industrial enterprises is another limiting factor. Besides, the
provision that requires the guarantee of the government or the central bank
of the borrowing country in respect of the loans has discouraged private enterprises from resorting to it freely for fear of scrutiny of their records and accounts
by the government or the central bank.[16] On the other hand, from the point
of view of the Bank, the nature and magnitude of the risks involved in some
forms of manufacturing enterprises and the unpreparedness of some of the
borrowing countries to develop along sound lines and their inability to absorb
capital rapidly because of lack of skill, entrepreneurial ability or economic
and social overheads, are real obstacles to greater lending.

The Economic Significance of the Flow of Foreign Public Capital

A review of the inflow of foreign public capital into underdeveloped countries
in recent years reveals three important aspects which are of considerable economic significance. Firstly, the size of the inflow has increased very rapidly;
secondly, the increased inflow of public capital has offset to a large extent the
deficiency in the availability of private capital from abroad and has thereby
facilitated a better distribution of external resources among the receiving
countries; thirdly, external public capital has significantly contributed to
domestic capital formation in the low income countries.

The flow of public capital from governments and International Agencies
other than the centrally planned economies in the form of official loans and
bilateral grants to underdeveloped economies rose from an annual average of
$ 2 billion in 1954–56 to $ 3·3 billion in 1958–59 which represents an increase
of more than 60 per cent. The average annual rate of increase in this flow
has been about 15 per cent. This growth has not only been steady but also
faster than the rate of growth of the national income of capital exporting
countries and their export proceeds. This has been made possible by the rapid
growth of the national income of industrial countries as well as the greater
diffusion of economic strength among them. The marked increase in the

[16]The Institution of the International Finance Corporation is aimed at removing this
difficulty.

supply, of capital through official channels to the capital poor countries of the world could not however, have involved a corresponding strain on the economies of the developed countries. It has been estimated that such assistance formed only 3 to 4 per cent of the increase in the non-consumption expenditure in industrial countries. Had this part of the savings not been sent abroad, but used for capital formation at home in the advanced countries, they would have added to their domestic capital formation only by about 1 per cent in the year 1958–59. On the other hand, the benefit of this assistance to the underdeveloped countries was great. The trend in the outflow of public capital from the major capital exporting countries of the world in the years 1957–59 is shown in Table 36.

Table 36

INTERNATIONAL ECONOMIC ASSISTANCE PROVIDED BY SOME
HIGH INCOME COUNTRIES THROUGH THEIR GOVERNMENTS AND
INTERNATIONAL AGENCIES 1957–59

(Millions of dollars)

Contributing Country			1956–1957*		1957–1958*		1958–1959*	
			Grants	Loans	Grants	Loans	Grants	Loans
Australia	—	—	33·6	1·2	40·3	....	38·3	...
Canada	—	—	23·4	...	43·8	16·8	50·6	9·8
France	—	—	577·4	311·0	526·9	227·5	N.A.	N.A.
Italy	—	—	8·9	101·8	10·2	....	8·1	30·5
Japan	—	—	0·3	...	0·5	...	177·4	0·5
Netherlands	—	—	23·1	3·5	20·0	2·5	23·6	3·0
New Zealand		—	5·7	0·1	5·4	0·2	5·3	...
U.K.	—	--	113·5	42·4	141·7	34·2	135·8	94·6
U.S.A.	—	—⌐	1,169·9	275·5	1,180·0	582·2	1,132·2	865·1
Multilateral aid†		--	122·5	179·2	101·3	321·7	101·2	273·2

SOURCE: *International Economic Assistance to the Less Developed Countries*, U.N., 1961, p. 14, Table 2.

*Fiscal years.

†Granted by the International Bank, International Finance Corporation, Organization of American States, United Nations Children's Fund, United Nations Relief Works Agency for Palestine Refugees, United Nations Korean Reconstruction Agency and United Nations Technical Assistance. Loans made almost entirely by the International Bank; Grants made by the other agencies excepting the International Finance Corporation.

Over the three years, grants from developed countries were a little more than double the loans. In most of the capital exporting countries, loans have tended to decline while in the United Kingdom and the United States which with France are the major contributories, loans have increased at a faster rate than grants. Of the total assistance given by governments and International

Agencies, the contribution of the latter has increased more rapidly. In the years 1953–54 to 1958–59 assistance from International Agencies rose from $ 0·2 billion to $ 0·4 billion or from about 10 per cent to about 12 per cent of the total. Up to 1959, by far the most important International Agency offering aid to underdeveloped countries was the World Bank. In the beginning of the fiscal year 1960, new agencies like the European Economic Community Development Fund for Overseas Countries and Territories and the United Nations Special Fund started their operations.

This increased outflow of public capital has to some extent set aright the disparity in the distribution of external resources between the developed and underdeveloped countries on the one hand, and between the low income countries themselves on the other. We have seen that in recent years private capital from high income countries has tended to flow mostly to the other industrialized countries of the world or to oil countries in Latin America and the Middle East. This trend still continues but there is significantly a larger proportionate outflow of public capital to the other underdeveloped countries. In 1956–58, while of the total private foreign capital, 34·8 per cent moved into the exporters of petroleum, only 4·1 per cent of public capital went into these countries. On the other hand, the other countries absorbed about 96 per cent of the official capital. Even among poorer countries there is disparity in the inflow of private capital as between Latin America and the countries of Asia and the Far East. The inflow of U.S.A. private capital into Latin American countries has been quite substantial, while of the countries in Asia and the Far East, the Philippines appears to be the only underdeveloped country which has attracted significant amounts of private investment capital in recent years. This uneven flow of private capital between Latin America and the other underdeveloped countries has also been compensated appreciably by the increased inflow of official capital into the latter. Thus in 1957 the inflow of long term private capital in Latin America was about $ 1,500 million but the region's net receipts of long term official capital amounted to only some $ 130 million or less than one-tenth of private capital. In contrast to this, ten low income countries of Asia—Burma, Ceylon, the Republic of China, Indonesia, India, Iraq, Pakistan, the Philippines, Thailand and the Republic of Viet Nam—received less than $ 100 million of private long term capital but had a net inflow of more than $ 600 million in official long term capital and grants.[17]

Apart from disparity in the distribution of external resources as between different countries, there is considerable variation among underdeveloped countries in respect of receipts on a per capita basis. In relation to population, Africa continues to be the largest beneficiary of official international assistance while on a per capita basis, Asia received the smallest aid. Grouping the under-developed countries into three categories according to their per capita incomes (i.e. with per capita annual income of less than $ 100, $ 100–200, and above

[17] *The International Flow of Private Capital, 1956–58*, U.N., 1959, pp. 13 & 14.

$ 200) it is found that the per capita aid in the first category is $ 1·55, in group second $ 2·41 and in the third $ 3·65. In the years 1957–58 and 1958–59, the annual per capita aid varied from as much as $ 36·30 for Jordan to as little as $ 0·02 for Yemen. The aggregate average for all the three groups was $ 1·91 but Jordan and Libya received more than $ 30 per head and the Republic of Korea, Israel, Lebanon and Costa Rica got more than $ 10 per head while the per capita aid going to India, Ethiopia, Nepal, Yemen, Iraq, Ghana, U.A.R. and Venezuela was $ 1. It is however, significant that the disparity in the per capita distribution of external assistance is decreasing. Between 1953–54 and 1958–59 the number of countries receiving less than $ 1 per head declined by half. Also, as a group, per capita aid in this period increased to a greater extent in Group I (from $ 0·84 to $ 1·55) than that in Group II ($ 1·87 to $ 2·41). The rate of increase in Group III was however the highest (from $ 0·96 to $ 3·65) but this consists of mostly Latin American countries, several of which received large public loans in 1958–59 to meet their external payments deficits.

Another aspect of the increased inflow of public capital into underdeveloped countries is that it has involved a strain on their foreign exchange position because of amortization and interest payments. The rate of increase in the inflow of public capital as compared with the rate of increase in the export earnings of these countries is indicative of not only the extent to which external public assistance has added to domestic resources, but also of the increasing strain on their capacity to meet foreign debt charges. Between the years 1955–56 and 1958–59 export earnings of the underdeveloped countries increased by only 5 per cent while foreign public assistance increased by more than 60 per cent. As a result, the ratio of public external assistance to export earnings has increased from 9 per cent to 16 per cent. In India foreign public capital formed 8 per cent of her export proceeds in 1953–56 but rose to 23 per cent in 1957–59. The corresponding ratios for Burma were 3 per cent and 16 per cent and for Indonesia 1 per cent and 13 per cent. The strain on the external payments position has been particularly pronounced in the case of Asian countries which have tended to prefer loans to grants. Between the end of 1955 and the end of 1958 the volume of external public indebtedness increased in India from $ 308 million to $ 1,442 million, in Burma $ 17 million to $ 84 million, Philippines $ 91 million to $ 198 million, Thailand $ 73 million to $ 143 million and in Pakistan from $ 148 million to $ 200 million. Simultaneously, the external public debt service ratio (i.e. amortization and interest payments on external public loans as a proportion of current account receipts) increased from 0·5 per cent to 1·5 per cent in Burma, 0·7 to 1·7 per cent in India, 1·5 to 2·1 per cent in the Philippines, 1·3 to 5·5 per cent in Iran and from 2·3 per cent to 5·3 per cent in Pakistan. For the under-developed countries as a whole, the ratio has moved up from 4·9 per cent to 5·8 per cent. This underlines the need on the part of the low income countries to increase their supply of foreign exchange in order to ease the pressure of servicing of external debt. The severity of the problem can however be reduced if a steady flow of fresh assistance is assured from the richer foreign countries.

But this should not lead to any minimization of the great contribution which external public assistance has made to capital formation in the recipient countries. Since 1953–54 the ratio of public aid to domestic investment has risen substantially in underdeveloped countries and this rise has generally been accompanied by a corresponding increase in the rate of capital formation. Comparing the average of the years 1953–54 to 1955–56 with that for 1957–58 to 1958–59, it is found that in India external public assistance as a percentage of gross fixed investment increased from 5·6 to 10·6 while gross fixed domestic investment as a percentage of Gross National Product moved up from 8·0 to 11·5 in the same period. That is to say, as a proportion to domestic investment, external public assistance has increased at a faster rate than the rate of increase in domestic investment. This is true of other underdeveloped countries of Asia also as may be seen from the following statement. If we assume that all the external public assistance went into investment in the underdeveloped

Table 37

RELATIONSHIP BETWEEN PUBLIC ECONOMIC ASSISTANCE AND
CAPITAL FORMATION IN UNDERDEVELOPED COUNTRIES
1953–54—1955–56 to 1957–58—1958–59

Country	Public Assistance as Percentage of Gross Fixed Investment		Gross Fixed Investment as Percentage of Gross National Product	
	1953–54 to 1955–56	1957–58 to 1958–59	1953–55	1957–58
Thailand — —	10·4	16·2	8·7	10·2
Ceylon —	5·8	15·6	9·6	11·8
Burma —	3·7	14·3	17·0	20·3
India —	5·6	10·6	8·0	11·5
Philippines —	5·0	9·4	7·0	8·5
Iraq —	1·0	1·5	16·8	20·5

SOURCE : *International Economic Assistance to the Less Developed Countries*, U.N., 1961, p. 47 Table 30.

countries, it would mean that over one-fifth or possibly even one-third of the increase in domestic capital formation in these countries has been due to public foreign capital.[18] It is however possible that a good proportion of this form of assistance would have served to increase consumption. On the other hand, it should be pointed out that additional resources made available

[18]*International Economic Assistance to the Less Developed Countries*, U.N., 1961, p. 51.

in this manner would have been invested in basic industries or in social over-heads and public utilities, in which case they would have activated complementary domestic or foreign resources and helped substantially in generating forces of economic growth in the low income countries. If so, the contribution of external public capital to economic development would be greater than what it would indicate as a proportion of aggregate investment.

A NOTE ON EXTERNAL CAPITAL AND ECONOMIC DEVELOPMENT IN INDIA

About the middle of 1948 India's foreign liabilities aggregated to Rs. 5,042 million of which the official sector accounted for Rs. 1,781 million and the non-official sector for Rs. 3,261 million. The official sector comprises the central government, the state governments, port trusts, improvement trusts, local authorities and statutory corporations including the Reserve Bank of India. The major part of the liabilities of the official sector consists of loans and advances from governments of foreign countries and International Institutions. The foreign liabilities of the non-official sector are made up of direct investments, portfolio investments and miscellaneous obligations.[19] Direct investments are officially defined as those foreign investments " which are accompanied by the control and direction of the enterprise by foreign investors . . . . " Branches of foreign companies, the ownership and direction of which are wholly in the hands of foreign owners are an obvious instance of direct investment.[20] External capital received in the public sector is used mostly for building up the economic infra-structure—transport, communications, development of ports, hydro-electric projects, etc. while foreign resources flowing into the private or non-official sector get invested in manufacturing industries, plantations, trade, etc. For purposes of analysis it would be advantageous if the trends and utilization of external resources in the two sectors are considered separately.

External Capital in the Non-official Sector

In British India, foreign private investments played an important part in the development of railways and other public utilities, plantations, mines and some manufacturing industries such as jute. The value of foreign private investment in India just before the outbreak of the Second World War in 1939 was roughly estimated at Rs. 8,500 to 9,500 million.[21] But according to the Reserve Bank's

[19]Miscellaneous obligations (of Indian Joint Stock Companies) comprise loans and advances (including inter-company/inter-branch advances, etc.) and insurance liabilities representing actuarial reserve value (or cash surrender value) of life insurance policies payable abroad and unexpired risks in respect of non life policies—*Survey of India's Foreign Liabilities and Assets*, Reserve Bank of India, Bombay, 1957, p. 11.

[20]*Survey of India's Foreign Liabilities and Assets*, Reserve Bank of India, Bombay, 1957, p. 10.

[21]' Post-War Foreign Investment in India,' *Economic Bulletin for Asia and the Far East*, June, 1962, U.N., p. 1.

estimate the amount in mid-1948 was only about Rs. 2,560 million.[22] Although these two figures are not comparable because of differences in the methods of computation, in territorial coverage and in the concepts used, there can be no doubt about the fact that in the ten-year period 1939 to 1948, there was a substantial decline in foreign business investments in the country. Roughly this decrease might have been of the order of Rs. 5,000 to 6,000 million.

Of the countries which have contributed to private business investment in India, Britain is by far the most important. Thus out of the foreign liabilities of business enterprises in India at the end of 1955 aggregating to Rs. 5,220 million, Britain's share was no less than Rs. 4,020 million or 77 per cent; U.S.A. contributed Rs. 460 million, Switzerland Rs. 70 million, Germany Rs. 30 million and the other countries Rs. 640 million. However, the amount of private capital from the United Kingdom remained at about Rs. 4,000 million between 1956 and 1958 while there was a marked increase of the inflow from some other countries. The receipts from West Germany increased from Rs. 25 million in 1955 to Rs. 38 million in 1958 while that from Japan rose from Rs. 160 million to Rs. 620 million in the same period. Since 1955, the non-official sector has in addition to the usual receipts from private sources, been also benefited by loans from the International Bank for Reconstruction and Development. The first World Bank loan to the private sector was Rs. 150 million to the Indian Iron and Steel Company in December, 1952; the second was one of Rs. 77 million for the Trombay project in November, 1954; another loan of Rs. 48 million was made to the Industrial Credit and Investment Corporation of India in March, 1955. The total inflow of capital from this agency was Rs. 121 million in 1956 and Rs. 321 million and Rs. 253 million in 1957 and 1958 respectively. Over the years 1955-58 gross inflow of foreign capital into the private sector amounted to Rs. 1,737 million (or an annual average of Rs. 434 million) of which the International Bank accounted for Rs. 709 million. In 1957 foreign capital for the private sector from the Bank (Rs. 321 million) exceeded that from private sources by Rs. 62 million and in 1958 (Rs. 253 million) was very nearly equal to the inflow from private sources.

Total foreign business investments in the private sector in 1948 amounted to Rs. 2,558 million of which more than four-fifths were direct investments. A large part of the direct investments was accounted for by the assets of the branches of the foreign companies operating in India. The distribution of the foreign business investments among different enterprises in 1948 compared with that at the end of 1959 is shown in Table 38.

It may be seen from Table 38 that foreign business investments in India doubled in value over the twelve years 1948-59. Of the total increase of Rs. 2,554 million, plantations, petroleum and manufacturing industries accounted for no less than Rs. 2,339 million or 92 per cent. However, in the case of plantations, the rise in investments was due largely to the revaluation of assets and in the case of manufacturing establishments, not all the units experi-

[22]*Report on the Census of India's Foreign Liabilities and Assets*, 1948, Reserve Bank of India Bombay.

Table 38

COMPOSITION OF FOREIGN BUSINESS INVESTMENTS IN INDIA
IN MID-1948 AND END OF 1959

(In million rupees)

Industry	Mid-1948			End of 1959	
	Direct	Portfolio	Total	Total	Changes during 1948–59
Plantations	451	72	523	951	+428
Petroleum	220	3	223	1,193	+970
Mining	89	25	115	130	+15
Manufacturing	486	224	709	1,651	+941
Trading	406	26	431	284	−146
Transport	104	23	126 ⎱	422	+110
Utilities	156	31	186 ⎰		
Financial (excluding banks)	47	21	68	230	+161
Managing Agencies	129	14	144	230	+86
Miscellaneous	25	8	33	21	−12
Total	2,111	447	2,558	5,112	+2,554

SOURCE: *Economic Bulletin for Asia and the Far East,* June. 1962, U.N., pp. 2 & 3. Tables 1 & 2.

enced a rise in the value of external investments. In fact there was net decrease under cotton, jute and coir industries. A substantial decline in the investments in trading is also observable. The real contributors to increased foreign business investments in this period were, petroleum products and manufacturing industries excepting textiles.

Another aspect of the trend in foreign business investments in the period 1948–59 is that the major part of the increase took place in the earlier part, i.e. between 1948 and 1955. In these seven years, the increase was about 77 per cent while in 1956–59 foreign investments moved up by 23 per cent. But if an allowance is made for the revaluation of assets which accounts for about Rs. 470 million of the total increase of about Rs. 1,980 million between 1948 and 1955, the increase in foreign business investments in this period would constitute about three-fourths of the total increase over the years 1948–1959. This pattern in the trend was set mostly by the petroleum industry and also the cigarette and tobacco industry and the managing agency companies. In the first mentioned industry, there was an increase in investment of the order of Rs. 200 million in 1948–53 and a decline of about Rs. 20 million in the subsequent years. It would be seen that in the years 1948–59 taken as a whole, there was a slowing down of the inflow of foreign capital and in some cases even a decline in those industries which were in an earlier period very popular with the foreign investor (plantations, textiles, trading).

The gross accumulation of external private capital in the non-official sector in the period under reference can be found by adding to the increase of Rs. 2,554 million, the value of the outflow of capital from India. A rough estimate of this repatriation in the period 1948–53 by the Reserve Bank places it at Rs. 500 million. If to this is added the outflow of capital of the order of Rs. 870 million in the next six years we get the tota. of Rs. 1,370 million for the period 1948–59. Hence gross addition to foreign business investments in these years must have been around Rs. 3,920 million. Of this increase, revaluation of existing assets accounts for Rs. 490 million (Rs. 470 million in 1948–55 and Rs. 20 million in 1958). Reinvestment of profits has been estimated at Rs. 1,700 million. The balance Rs. 1,730 million was made up of inflow of fresh capital in the form of cash to the extent of Rs. 550 million and receipts in the form of investments in kind[23] to the extent of Rs. 1,180 million. This is summarized in Table 39.

Table 39

SOURCES OF THE INCREASE IN FOREIGN BUSINESS INVESTMENTS IN INDIA 1948–59

(In million rupees)

	1948–1953	1954–1955	1956	1957	1958	1959	1948–1959
Revaluation of assets	150	320	...	...	20	...	490
Retained profits out of current earnings	700	460	200	100	100	150	1,700
Fresh capital inflow from abroad	1,010	160	120	170	170	100	1,730
In cash	350	30	30	60	50	30	550
In kind	660	130	90	110	120	70	1,180
Gross additions to foreign business investments	1,860	940	320	270	290	250	3,920
Minus							
Repatriation of business investments by non-residents (capital outflow)	500	320	60	90	240	150	1,370
Net increase in foreign business investments	1,360	610	250	180	40	110	2,550

SOURCE: *Economic Bulletin for Asia and the Far East,* June, 1962, U.N., p. 6, Table 6.

Since fresh capital inflow from abroad amounted to Rs. 1,730 million in the years 1948–59 and capital outflow was Rs. 1,370 million, net inflow of foreign capital was only Rs. 360 million. Thus over this period increase in foreign business investments in the country was due mostly to retention of profits and to a small extent to revaluation of assets. The profits (after tax) earned by foreign controlled enterprises in plantations, petroleum, manufacturing and other industries totalled Rs. 1,554 million in the four-year period 1956–59.

[23]These are in the form of equipment and materials accounted for by companies which import goods on a consignment basis but do not fully remit the proceeds of the sale of these goods to the consignor companies.

Of this, a little less than two-thirds was distributed and a little more than one-third was reinvested. Profit retained in the plantation industry was actually negative, while in the case of petroleum Rs. 268 million out of a profit of Rs. 507 million was reinvested and the manufacturing concerns accounted for reinvestment of Rs. 216 million out of the profits amounting Rs. 521 million. However, in view of the fact that a good part of the earnings of the petroleum industry was used up to repay loans received earlier from the parent companies, the ratio of reinvestment to total profits was much less than what the above figures would indicate. If this factor is taken into account, the manufacturing concerns emerge as by far the most important sector in the matter of plough back of profits. This sector was responsible for reinvesting an increasing share of its rapidly growing volume of profits. As a proportion of the total reported profits of all foreign controlled enterprises, the profits of manufacturing enterprises increased from 20 per cent in 1953 to nearly 42 per cent in 1959 while the ratio of the profits retained in this sector to the total retained profits of all the foreign controlled enterprises increased from less than 29 per cent to 47 per cent in the same period. Apart from this method of financing expansion, the manufacturing sector benefited also by the inflow of fresh private capital. Of the net inflow of private capital into the economy in the two years 1958 and 1959, estimated at about Rs. 230 million, the major part went into manufacture. And within the manufacturing sector, expansion in medicines and pharmaceuticals, electrical goods and chemicals and allied products seems to be more pronounced.

Undoubtedly, the most important factor which has helped the increased inflow of foreign private capital into the manufacturing sector is the attitude of the government, which has of late become more favourable to this type of foreign investment. Not only has majority foreign participation been allowed in many private enterprises, but government has also given greater freedom to private enterprise for developing industries reserved for the public sector. As instances of this gesture may be mentioned, the permission granted to private steel companies to expand their operations although steel is reserved exclusively for the public sector, and similar concessions shown to fertilizer production, aluminium industry and the manufacture of synthetic rubber. The starting of joint ventures between the government and private firms especially in the oil industry in which government's equity participation is restricted to less than half is another variant of this encouraging attitude. Apart from this, government's double taxation avoidance agreements with the U.S.A., West Germany, Norway and Japan, and negotiations for similar agreements with the United Kingdom, Denmark and France, and India's decision to join the scheme for insurance cover against the risks of nationalization and expropriation, all these contributed to an improved outlook for foreign investments.

Nevertheless, the contribution of external private capital to total investment of the private sector in India appears to be quite meagre. Aggregate foreign

29

investments in the private sector over the four years 1956–59 have been estimated at Rs. 1,350 million of which the International Bank capital amounted
to Rs. 720 million. It is presumed that the total private sector investment in
the Second Plan period was of the order of Rs. 31,000 million.[24] This figure
does not include investments in the private sector financed out of resources
transferred from the public sector. Assuming that in the first four years of the
Second Plan period. investment in the private sector amounted to about four-
fifths of this total, external investments in the private sector would have contributed only a little more than five per cent.

But the real significance of the growth of foreign private investments in the
manufacturing sector consists in the fact that it is indicative of the evolving
pattern of the Indian economy. The type of foreign capital that flows into a
country and the nature and distribution of its investment reflect broadly the
standard of economic development and the political status of the country.
In a very backward economy with no political freedom, foreign capital flows
mostly into extractive export industries and also to some extent into public
utilities like transport and communications which facilitate proper exploitation
of such industries. India in the pre-independence era was in this position.
Next, when a country becomes politically free and is in a position to shape her
own economic policy, foreign capital would be invited and made to flow into
those channels which would ensure a stable rate of economic growth. Here
there is greater control of foreign capital the investment of which is made to
fit in with the over-all national requirements of the country. At this stage,
foreign resources from governments and international institutions have precedence over private capital in so far as the former are more amenable to control
and can be made to flow into those very lines of investment requisite for the
country's planned progress. This is broadly true of the investments in the
official sector in India in recent years financed out of external public assistance.
The third stage is reached when, as a result of the investment of foreign capital
made available through government and quasi-public institutions, the economy
is developed, industries are started, national income goes up and the domestic
market is expanded. When this stage is reached, the country provides opportunities for the investment of foreign capital in manufacturing industries. Private
capital from abroad is now attracted into manufacturing industries in the
borrowing country because of the expansion of the domestic market and the
availability of the requisite overhead facilities which ensure larger returns on
investment. The considerable industrial development that has taken place in
India in the last few years, the rise in national income and the tendency for the
proportion of the foreign investments in manufacturing concerns to increase
indicate that India is now in a transitional stage, and that with succeeding
Plans, there will be greater and greater need as well as scope for investment
of foreign private capital in manufacturing and consumer goods enterprises.

[24]*Third Five-Year Plan*—A Draft Outline, Planning Commission, Government of India,
New Delhi, June, 1960, p. 16.

External Capital in the Official Sector

While external capital in the form of direct and portfolio investments and that made available by the World Bank have been absorbed in the private sector in enterprises which are productive from the commercial and business points of view, foreign resources which the official or public sector has been able to acquire have flowed into public utilities, social overheads and also some industries and agricultural development, and have been distributed in accordance with the patterns of development set under the Five-Year Plans. Inflow of external capital since 1950 into the official sector has in fact been linked with planned development and has been used to meet the foreign exchange requirements of the programmes under the Plans. The foreign liabilities of the official sector increased from Rs. 2,008 million at the end of 1955 to Rs. 9,466 million at the end of 1959. The main sources from which this amount has been drawn are the U.S.A. and the World Bank, which together accounted for Rs. 6,538 million or 70 per cent of the total foreign liabilities of the official sector in 1959. The other contributing countries are the United Kingdom, the U.S.S.R., West Germany and Pakistan. The sources of external capital and its utilization in the First Plan years are shown in Table 40.

Table 40

**EXTERNAL ASSISTANCE : AUTHORIZED AND UTILIZED IN THE
PUBLIC SECTOR 1951–52 TO 1955–56**

(In million rupees)

	Total Authoriza-tions	Utilization					Total utiliza-tion
	1951–56	1951–52	1952–53	1953–54	1954–55	1955–56	1951–56
Loans:							
U.S. Govt. Wheat Loan	903	598	305	...	...	...	903
Indo-U.S. Aid Programme	393	...	...	...	...	45	45
International Bank	125	10	31	15	7	13	76
Total Loans	1,421	608	336	15	7	58	1,024
Grants:							
Indo-U.S. Aid Programme	1,025	...	41	144	127	270	582
Colombo Plan :							
Canada	323	...	71	20	20	86	197
Australia	111	37	2	2	8	2	51
New Zealand	17	3	...	...	...	...	3
U.K.	4	...	...	...	0·1	0·3	0·4
Ford Foundation	56	...	6	4	5	6	21
Indo-Norwegian Programme	7	...	...	1	1	1	3
Total Grants	1,543	40	120	171	161	365	857
Total Grants and Loans	2,964	648	456	186	168	423	1,881

SOURCE: *Review of the First Five-Year Plan*, Planning Commission, Government of India, New Delhi, May, 1957, p. 30.

The total authorizations in the First Plan period amounting to Rs. 2,964 million were made up of loans from the U.S.A. and the International Bank (Rs. 1,421 million) and grants under the Indo-U.S. Aid Programme which commenced in January, 1952, and also from the Colombo Plan countries, Ford Foundation and Indo-Norwegian Programme aggregating to Rs. 1,543 million. Excluding the United States Government Wheat Loan of Rs. 903 million which was fully utilized in the first two years, the annual absorption up to the last year of the Plan averaged only Rs. 140 million. The amount used up in the last year of the Plan was Rs. 420 million. Thus the total utilization over the five years was Rs. 1,880 million leaving a carry over of about Rs. 1,080 million.

Part of the external assistance was received by the official sector in the form of wheat from the U.S.A., Canada and Australia, which could not have directly helped in additional capital formation. The bulk of the external assistance however, was used for the procurement of industrial raw materials, steel, machinery, construction and equipment for irrigation and power projects, rolling stock for railways, etc. Thus the assistance under the Indo-U.S. Aid Programme was at first utilized on joint projects relating to community development, sinking of tubewells, river valley development and on the purchase of fertilizers and steel for agricultural purposes. Later it was drawn to finance schemes in the fields of transport and industrial development—purchase of locomotives and wagons for the railways, steel for industrial uses—and for the financing of major projects like the Rihand Power Project. The loans extended by the World Bank were for power projects and for the purchase of agricultural machinery. The Canadian loan was used for the purchase of transport equipment and materials for the wire and cable industry, locomotive boilers and electrical equipment and for financing some power projects—Mayurakshi Project, Kunda Hydro-electric Project and the Tungabhadra and Ramagundam Projects. In addition to these loans, substantial technical assistance was received from the United Nations and its specialized agencies. Thus foreign capital received by the public sector from foreign governments and International Agencies was used in the main on public utilities, power projects and on irrigation and thus helped in broadening the capital base of the economy.

Total external assistance available for the official sector (and to a small extent to the private sector also for utilization in industries) in the Second Plan period —1st April 1956 to 31st March 1961—amounted to Rs. 27,615 million. Of this, loans accounted for Rs. 13,918 million and grants and other assistance Rs. 13,697 million. The breakdown of this total amount according to source is given in Table 41.

The external assistance utilized in the Second Plan period represents an increase by about eight times over the utilization in the First Plan years. As a proportion of the total investment in the public sector it constituted 40 per cent in the Second Plan period as against 12 per cent in the First Plan. Loans form roughly about half the total external assistance available in both

Table 41

EXTERNAL ASSISTANCE: AUTHORIZED AND UTILIZED IN THE SECOND PLAN PERIOD APRIL 1956 TO MARCH 1961

(Million rupees)

Source	Aid Authorized during the Second Plan	Total Available for Utilization after 31st March 1956*	Estimated Utilization during the Second Plan	Aid Undisbursed as at the end of March 1961
(1) Loans:				
IBRD Loans	2,627	2,862	2,228	634
From the U.S.A.	1,085	1,085	368	717
Canada	157	157	157	...
U.K.	1,226	1,226	1,218	8
West Germany	1,339	1,339	1,197	142
Japan	276	276	160	116
U.S.S.R.	3,190	3,837	747	3,090
Switzerland	109	109	...	109
Poland	143	143	...	143
Yugoslavia	190	190	...	190
Czechoslovakia	231	231	...	231
Loan from the U.S.A. (repayable in rupees)	2,216	2,463	1,168	1,295
Total Loans	12,789	13,918	7,243	6,675
(2) Grants:				
From the U.S.A.	927	1,402	1,237	165
Colombo Plan countries	626	829	711	118
West Germany	21	21	6	15
Norway	19	19	19	...
Total Grants	1,593	2,271	1,973	298
(3) Other Assistance:				
P.L. 480 (Gross)	11,130	11,130	5,155	5,975
P.L. 665 (Gross)	150	268	268	...
Third Country Currency Assistance from the U.S.A.	28	28	25	3
Total other assistance	11,308	11,426	5,448	5,978
Grand Total 1+2+3	25,690	27,615	14,664	12,951

*Aid authorized in the Second Plan *plus* aid undisbursed at the end of the First Plan.

SOURCE: *Report on Currency and Finance*, 1961–62, Reserve Bank of India, Bombay, Statement 88.

the plans. Regarding the source of loans, an important feature is the considerable increase from the U.S.S.R. Of the total loans authorized in the

Second Plan period—Rs. 12,789 million—the U.S.A. accounted for Rs. 3,301 million (including Rs. 2,216 million repayable in rupees) and U.S.S.R. for Rs. 3,190 million. Loans authorized by West Germany were Rs. 1,339 million and by the United Kingdom Rs. 1,226 million. Together these four countries accounted for 70 per cent of the total loans authorized. The share of the U.S.A. in grants and other assistance is by far the largest. Of the total assistance authorized under these two heads—Rs. 12,901 million —the contribution of the U.S.A. was as much as Rs. 12,235 million or 95 per cent ; the balance was made available mostly by the Colombo Plan countries.

Out of the aggregate amounts of loans and grants available for utilization after March 31, 1956 (Rs. 27,615 million), about half (Rs. 14,664 million) was actually utilized in the Second Plan period. It should be noted that not all the total amount was designed to be absorbed before 1961. Thus three quarters of the Rs. 3,190 million loan authorized by the U.S.S.R. was earmarked for projects included in the Third Plan. Moreover, a good proportion of the external assistance received under various heads by the official sector is placed at the disposal of the private sector, particularly in steel projects and in various industries and also used jointly by the public and private sectors. Excluding the West Germany Credit of Rs. 112 million authorized for the purpose of repayment of liabilities arising out of the Rourkela credit, the total amount of external loans utilized in the Second Plan period was Rs. 7,132 million. Out of this, the public sector absorbed Rs. 4,124 million or 58 per cent while a sum of Rs. 886 million was made available to the private sector; and loans utilized jointly by the public and private sectors amounted to Rs. 2,122 million or about 30 per cent. Purpose-wise, the distribution of loans in the period 1951–52 to 1955–56 was as follows:

Table 42

PURPOSE-WISE DISTRIBUTION OF FOREIGN LOANS/CREDITS
ESTIMATED UTILIZATION DURING THE SECOND PLAN PERIOD

	Rupees (million)	Percentage of total
Railway Development	1,434	20
Power Projects	293	4
Steel and Steel Projects	2,540	36
Port Development	68	1
Transport	90	1
Industrial Development	2,550	36
Wheat Loans	157	2
Total	7,132	100

SOURCE: *Report on Currency and Finance*, 1961–62, Reserve Bank of India, Bombay, Statement 89.

Railway development absorbed about one-fifth of the total loans utilized in the period under reference, while steel and steel projects and industrial development together accounted for 72 per cent of the total. A rough idea of the contribution of external capital in the official sector to domestic capital formation can be had from the fact that in the decade April 1951 to March 1961 covered by the First and Second Five-Year plans, aggregate amount of external assistance in the form of loans and grants received in the official sector and utilized in the country was Rs. 16,545 million which formed about 32 per cent of public investment amounting to Rs. 52,100 million in this period. But as was observed earlier, it is not proper to measure the contribution of external capital, whether public or private, in terms of its magnitude or proportion to total investment outlay. Much depends on the manner in which it is invested and the nature of the real capital which it helps to build up. However, in so far as the major part of the external public capital in India has been utilized for the building up of the economic infrastructure, and to some extent for the formation of human capital also, it may be safe to infer that the use of public capital from abroad has significantly helped to generate the forces of economic growth and to bring the country nearer to the stage of self-sustained growth.

External Assistance for the Third Plan

The Planning Commission have laid considerable stress on the need for stepping up exports. It is estimated that exports over the Third Plan period could be raised to Rs. 37,000 million if strenuous efforts are made in this direction. Since no earnings are envisaged under invisible items (excluding official donations) the total export earnings of the economy in the period 1961–62 to 1965–66 will be only equal to the value of exports. Against this estimated earnings of foreign exchange of Rs. 37,000 million, have to be set the following payment items: (a) Imports of machinery and equipment for the Plan projects are estimated at Rs. 19,000 million; (b) Maintenance imports, i.e. imports required to meet the general needs of the economy in the form of raw materials, components, replacement machinery, etc. would involve payments of the order of Rs. 36,500 million; (c) Components, intermediate products, etc. for increasing the production of capital goods within the country are estimated at Rs. 2,000 million; (d) the repayment of foreign loans and credits falling due within the Third Plan period would amount to Rs. 4,500 million. Other capital transactions including payment of certain obligations to Pakistan and Kuwait would call for further foreign exchange resources amounting to Rs. 1,000 million. In all, net capital transactions would involve Rs. 5,500 million. All these four items on the payments side add up to Rs. 63,000 million. This means an excess of Rs. 26,000 million over the expected export earnings, and measures the extent to which external assistance would be required in order to carry through the projects in the Third Five-Year Plan. External assistance would thus form one-fourth of the total investment envisaged and about 43 per cent of the public sector investment.

The question arises whether this requirement would be met satisfactorily in the period 1965–66. Recent developments in the field of external assistance are however quite encouraging. Apart from the carry-over of total assistance available from the authorizations of the Second Plan, assistance from friendly countries is forthcoming in a liberal measure. The International Agencies as well as governments of developed countries in the West have come to recognize that foreign assistance for the economic development of low income countries, if it is to be really effective, is to flow on an assured basis over a number of years, that it should take into account not merely the requirements of particular projects but of the development of the economy as a whole, and that terms of repayment should be adjusted with reference to the paying capacity of the recipient country and the availability of an export surplus. Recently the International Monetary Fund provided a standby credit to the extent of $ 250 million (equivalent to Rs. 1,190 million) to help the country bridge a gap in the receipt of foreign aid funds pledged by the countries assisting India in its Third Five-Year development programme and overcome a drop in exports. Of greater significance in this matter is the commitment of aid to India made by the Aid India Consortium consisting of the U.S.A., West Germany, the U.K., Japan, Canada and France. In May 1961, these countries along with the International Bank and the International Development Association gave an assurance of assistance to the extent of Rs. 10,590 million ($ 2,225 million) in the first two years of the Third Plan. In the next year, Austria, the Netherlands, Belgium and Italy also joined the consortium, with the result that the assistance available from this source has increased to Rs. 11,260 million which falls short by only Rs. 380 million of the requirement of Rs. 11,640 million for the years 1961–62 and 1962–23. The U.S.A. aid which forms nearly half the total commitment of the consortium is to be released partly through the Development Loan Fund (for which the period of repayment is fixed at 50 years and the rate of interest at a nominal 1 per cent) and partly through the Export Import Bank on which the commercial lending rate will be charged. The United Kingdom loan is for 25 years and bears an interest of $5\frac{1}{2}$ to $5\frac{3}{4}$ per cent. The loans of West Germany extend over 12 to 20 years and the interest rates vary from 3 to $5\frac{1}{2}$ per cent. The French and Japanese loans are for 10 and 15 years. Out of the Canadian assistance, $ 36 million are grants and the balance of $ 20 million will be in the form of export credits. Half of the loan from Japan ($ 80 million) will be set apart to finance private sector projects. In addition to these loans, the U.S.S.R. has authorized two credits amounting to Rs. 2,380 million for use on the Third Plan projects. A number of other countries—Czechoslovakia, Yugoslavia, Poland and Switzerland—have also extended credits for projects in the Third Plan.

It thus appears that the external assistance promised by the friendly countries would adequately meet the requirements of India and help her to finance her development programmes without much strain on the external payments position. But it has to be remembered that much of this aid is in the form of loans requiring to be repaid after some years. The problem therefore that the country has to face, is the proper utilization of this assistance, utilization in such manner as would help in preparing the ground work for self-sustained growth as well as increasing agricultural and industrial output in the short run. It may be repeated that in the ultimate analysis, the ability of the country to meet the service and repayment obligations of foreign loans depends on the extent to which the economy is transformed.

Chapter XIV

THE ROLE OF AGRICULTURE

AGRICULTURAL DEVELOPMENT AND ECONOMIC EXPANSION

THE EXTENT to which the development of agriculture can help economic expansion has been well illustrated by the economic history of many of the developed countries of today. In Britain, the remarkable progress which agriculture made during the first quarter of the 18th century laid the ground firmly for industrial progress. In the second half of the 18th century, net wheat yield in England (after providing for seed) rose from 12½ bushels per acre to over 20 bushels. A century later, in Germany the start of the period of industrial revolution synchronized with rapid improvement in agricultural production; between 1850 and 1950 the yield per hectare of wheat rose from 1·2 to 2·7 tons and that of potatoes from 8 to 22 tons.[1] Increased productivity resulting in a marked rise in incomes in the agricultural sector, widened the savings margin and enabled the flow of resources into the non-agricultural sector either voluntarily or through forced savings, taxation or compulsory delivery of agricultural products. It is a fact well known in recent Japanese economic history that in the period of rapid economic growth in Japan from about 1885 to 1915 the productivity of the farm worker more than doubled as a result of better methods of cultivation, and the major part of this increased income of the agricultural community was drained away through heavy land taxation and made to flow into industry. The living levels of the rural population in spite of this improvement in incomes remained very low if not deteriorated. Of the Central Government's tax revenue 93·3 per cent was accounted for by land tax and even at the turn of the century it remained higher than 50 per cent. More recently, the U.S.S.R. and China have implemented a similar policy. Between the two World Wars, despite larger agricultural production and the drift of labour to the towns, the farm incomes per head were kept down in the former country; similarly in China during 1953–57, about 40 per cent or more of the tax yield from agriculture was utilized for development outside the agricultural sector.[2]

It would thus appear that agricultural development fosters economic growth through increasing the savings and enlarging the source out of which

[1]Clark, Colin, ' The Development of Agricultural Productivity,' *The Eastern Economist*, New Delhi, Blue Supplement, April 26, 1957.

[2]*Economic Bulletin for Asia and the Far East*, U.N., November. 1957, p. 63.

more and more investible funds could be canalized into the industrial sector of the economy. In reality, the impact of agricultural growth on economic progress has much wider scope. Specifically, apart from increasing the savings available for investment in the economy, progress in the primary sector helps overall economic growth by more adequately meeting the growing food requirements of the country, supplying the raw materials for industry, increasing the foreign exchange earnings through larger exports, expanding the market for industrial goods, promoting an exchange economy, facilitating the development of transport and means of communications, and by releasing labour for employment in the growing industrial sector.

A rapid increase in the food production of underdeveloped countries is urgently needed because of the high rate of growth of population and also the necessity to raise the consumption standards of the masses. Many of the economically backward countries are over-populated. Even in order to keep pace with the growth in numbers, food production in the low income countries of Asia and the Far East would have to go up at the rate of 1·5 per cent per year. In some of these countries like India, the annual rate of growth of population is above 2 per cent and hence food production has to be stepped up accordingly. An additional point to be considered in this connection is, that the present nutritional standards of the underdeveloped countries are deplorably low and there cannot be any meaning in economic development unless it helps in achieving improvement of nutritional levels. According to a United Nations inquiry, the average energy intakes in the underdeveloped countries of Asia and the Far East are amongst the lowest in the world and below those considered necessary to maintain normal levels of health. Actual food consumption falls short of minimum requirements by 12 to 18 per cent in Ceylon, India and the Philippines, and by 5 to 7 per cent in Japan and Pakistan.[3] It is thus clear that in these countries food production has to increase more than in proportion to the annual rate of increase in population. Furthermore, there is evidence to show that as national income and per capita incomes rise with economic progress, expenditure per person on food will rise although less rapidly than rise in income; that is to say, income elasticity of demand for food is positive, but less than unity. On the basis of data relating to urban household budgets in India and Japan, income elasticity co-efficients of about 0·7 and 0·6 have been estimated for the two countries respectively, for expenditure on all foods consumed in homes. In view of the fact that the present level of per capita consumption is very low in underdeveloped countries, the income elasticity of demand for food in these countries tends to be higher than in richer countries. Also, with rapid growth in urban population, the standard of consumption will rise. Improvement in social conditions and in transport and communications is also likely to raise the consumptive power of the peasantry. The rise in urban population underlines the need for increasing the marketable surplus of agricultural goods. However, there is likely to be a shift in the composition

[3] *Economic Bulletin for Asia and the Far East*, U.N., November, 1957, p. 24, f.n.

of demand for food articles as income rises. There will be a shift in demand in favour of more costly and nutritious items of food articles like vegetables and fruits, milk, eggs, livestock and fishery products. This shift in the pattern of demand is observable in the developed as well as economically backward countries. Thus in Japan, the elasticity of demand for all foods is 0·6 and that for staple foods, cereals, pulses, bread and other starchy foods is about 0·2 while for meat it is 1·1. Also in the same country, surveys made between 1951 and 1954 showed that even among cereals the elasticity of demand differs as between different categories. Income elasticities of expenditure for wheat and barley were found to be negative, while for rice it was positive, ranging from 0·09 to 0·25.[4] This trend in demand would therefore require a shift in the pattern of production of agricultural commodities as well. Where production is planned, and targets are to be fixed in respect of output, it would be necessary to take into account the elasticity estimates for individual commodities rather than for the aggregate of commodities.

Apart from increased food requirements, industrialization of an economy also necessitates the expansion of output of industrial raw materials. The development of consumer goods industries would require increased production of raw materials such as timber, pulp and paper or textile fibres. There is however, an important difference in the nature of demand for additional food production brought about by rise in the level of incomes, and the demand for industrial raw materials arising from the expansion of the industrial sector; while the income elasticity of demand for food is relatively limited, that for industrial raw materials is fairly high with respect to increases in income.

Any shortage in the production of food and raw materials in the context of a growing economy would upset not only its internal but its external balance as well. A developing economy in the initial stages of its growth has to import machinery and other capital goods from advanced countries. These imports have to be paid for by exporting agricultural goods and raw materials. Because of large investment expenditures and the inevitable lag between the increase in money incomes and the supply of necessary consumption goods, inflationary pressures tend to develop in the economy. Also when industrial production goes up, if there is shortage in the supply of food, the terms of trade will turn in favour of the latter and against the former, so that it is even likely that industrial expansion will be held up because of the price and cost factor. This sort of internal imbalance in turn is likely to lead to a deterioration in the balance of payments position of the country. To counteract inflationary trends and to maintain the growth of the industrial sector, it would therefore become necessary to import food. But this would deplete the foreign exchange earnings of the country. Furthermore, even when agricultural production increases, a

[4]The Food and Agriculture Organization of the U.N., *State of Food and Agriculture, 1956*, Rome, 1957, Ch. III and also ECAFE FAO ' Measurement of Price and Income Elasticities of the Demand for Rice and other Cereals in the ECAFE Region,' (1956) quoted in *Economic Bulletin for Asia and the Far East*, U.N., November, 1957, p. 38.

considerable part would be absorbed internally for domestic consumption consequent upon rise in incomes so that the volume of export surpluses and foreign exchange earnings would not improve in proportion to rise in domestic income. The only way of meeting this difficulty is therefore by increasing the production of exportable goods which in most of the underdeveloped countries happen to be primary goods. Undoubtedly, with industrial development of these countries, more and more of the articles which are now exported will be absorbed domestically. But until and unless industrial development has reached that stage at which these countries would be in a position to export manufactured goods, their foreign exchange position will be dependent mostly on the volume and value of exports of agricultural commodities. As such, priority has to be given to agricultural production as a source of foreign exchange earnings and also as a means to counteract inflationary pressures in the economy.

Besides supplying the necessary raw materials needed in the industrial sector, agriculture helps economic growth by providing a market for the finished goods of the industrial sector. Increase in agricultural production and the rise in the per capita incomes of the rural community together with industrialization and urbanization and the closer contact between villages and towns brought about by improvements in transport, lead to an increased demand for industrial products also. This is a significant factor in a large country like India where the vast majority of the population is agricultural. Rise in incomes brings about also a shift in the pattern of agricultural production. With the introduction of new crops and the opening up of the villages by modern methods of communication, agriculture becomes commercialized. Subsistence economy gives place to a market or exchange economy. Higher production and incomes in the agricultural sector will in due course swell the transactions in both the industrial and agricultural sectors and increase the volume of exchange between the two. As a result, an almost revolutionary transformation will take place in peasant agriculture, which will become increasingly integrated with the national and international economy.[5]

Lastly, agriculture helps industrial growth by ensuring the supply of labour to industry. Higher agricultural productivity reduces the number of persons required in agricultural operations to feed the total population of the country. Employment potential in the industrial sector is much greater than in the primary sector and if the rate of absorption of labour in the former is greater than the rate of population growth, industrial expansion can be maintained only by transferring labour from agriculture to industry. Thus with economic growth, the contribution of the industrial sector to national income will be increasing while that of the primary sector will be decreasing. Correspondingly, there will be an increase in the proportion of population engaged in industry and a decrease in the agricultural sector. Such migration of labour from the primary sector has obvious social advantages. It helps in a rise in the marginal

[5]*Economic Bulletin for Asia and the Far East*, U.N., November, 1957, p. 25.

value product of labour and also reduces the number of claimants to farm income. Since the marginal value product of labour in agriculture is lower than in industry, a transfer from the former to the latter would mean supply of labour at relatively low prices to the non-farm sector. This improves the efficiency in the distribution of labour resources in the economy, and is likely to bring about a better balance in growth between capital and labour.[6]

The foregoing points convey an idea of the contribution which agriculture can make to economic development by facilitating industrialization of the economy. The growth of industries in turn, has a beneficial effect on the agricultural sector. Obviously, there will be no incentive for producers of primary goods to increase output by extension of cultivation, introduction of new crops and the adoption of new methods of cultivation, unless they are sure of an expanding market for their products. Thus even as higher incomes in the agricultural sector help in the absorption of finished products of the non-farm sector, higher levels of activity and rise in income levels in the industrial sector raise the demand for farm products. Expansion of the urban market also promotes the development of means of communication and brings about commercialization of agriculture and the economic transformation of the agricultural sector. Increasing opportunities of industrial employment take away the surplus of the agricultural population, reduce the number of people dependent on agriculture and thus increase the output per head. Besides, industrial development is of direct benefit to agriculture by providing the latter with an adequate supply of the means of production—fertilizers, machinery and other equipment, power, etc. Finally, in so far as the agricultural sector constitutes the deficit sector in many underdeveloped countries incapable of generating sufficient savings to bring about any improvement, it requires financial resources from outside. Where however, agriculture is developing in step with industry, it is conceivable that the flow of savings will be in both directions.

Recognition of this close interdependence of the agricultural and industrial sectors of the economy has led to the suggestion that there should be a balance in the development of both these sectors in order to ensure stable overall economic growth. Balanced development in this sense is interpreted to mean the minimizing of the waste of productive resources which results from one sector of the economy operating as an effective limiting factor on the expansion of other sectors. One sector of the economy can hold back another in either of two ways—by failing to provide it with essential materials or services and also by failing to provide a market for its products or services. Thus if industrial production expands while the agricultural sector remains stagnant, the excess income of the industrial sector would exert a pressure on the limited supply of the primary sector with the result that inflationary pressures will be generated or external balance upset. On the other hand, if increase in agricul-

[6]Baker, C. B., ' Instrumental Goals and Economic Growth,' *Agricultural Adjustment Problems in a Growing Economy*, Ed. by E. O. Heady and others, Iowa State College Press, 1958, p. 259.

tural production takes place without corresponding expansion of the non-agricultural sector, the demand for agricultural products will fall short of supply, and this would lead to (assuming that export markets remain unchanged) depression in agricultural prices and fall in incomes and would thus hamper growth. It is however to be noted that the concept of balanced development does not mean equal growth of both sectors. Since as income grows, a relatively greater proportion of it is likely to be spent on manufactured goods and services than on agricultural commodities, there can be stable and balanced growth of the economy only if the rate of expansion of the industrial sector is faster than that of the primary sector. At any rate, it appears to be an unwise policy to concentrate too much of the investment on either of the sectors, neglecting the other. The Report of the World Population Conference in 1954 in Rome draws attention to the fact that too speedy indus-trialization in the sparsely populated countries of Latin America and Oceania in recent years. tended to divert much needed capital and resources from agriculture to industry, which not only seriously affected agricultural develop-ment but caused undesirable distortions in the general economy.[7]

Nevertheless, quite often extreme views are held in this matter by writers who emphasize that top priority is to be given to one or the other sector of the economy in any programme of planned development. In defence of the plea for large investments in the agricultural sector, the experience of developed countries like the United Kingdom is cited and it is urged that agricultural growth is a pre-condition for industrial expansion. It is particularly emphasized that in the case of underdeveloped countries which are predominantly agricul-tural, no economic progress can be possible unless development is initiated in the primary sector. Thus Professor Theodore Schultz remarks: " In a high food drain economy where most of the income of the community is represented by food, there is little room except in agriculture for new and better production possibilities, because the productive efforts required to produce food are so large a part of the whole ".[8] On the other hand, some writers hold the opposite view that in so far as productivity in agriculture in poorer economies is very low, and the pressure of population is so acute, it would be illogical and unwise to concentrate investment in the agricultural sector. The problem in such countries is to bring about a quick increase in incomes and transfer of popula-tion from the primary sector. The correct step therefore would be to emphasize development of the industrial rather than the agricultural sector. In opposing the views of the economists who stressed the need for agriculture-biased develop-ment in underdeveloped countries at the International Conference on Economic Growth held in Tokyo in April, 1957, Professor Kurihara pointed out that this would be an unwise policy because of three reasons: firstly, the marginal productivity of capital in agriculture is less than in industry. Hence it would

[7] *Proceedings of the World Population Conference*, Summary Report, U.N., 1954, p. 108.

[8] Schultz, T. W., *The Economic Organization of Agriculture*, McGraw-Hill, New York, 1953, p. 273.

be uneconomic to fritter away the meagre capital resources by investing in agriculture; secondly, propensity to save in the agricultural sector is less than in the industrial sector. Conspicuous consumption among the rich agriculturists and subsistence living among the vast majority of cultivators rule out the possibility of any good amount being saved; thirdly, in so far as there is a tendency for the terms of trade to move against agricultural goods, concentration on the development of agriculture would only have an adverse effect on the country's balance of payments. He therefore concludes that " a balanced increase in agricultural output and industrial output is a luxury which an advanced economy with abundant real capital can easily afford, but which a capital poor country can scarcely afford. With limited savings and capital using projects competing for those limited savings, an underdeveloped economy would do well to concentrate on the rapid development of its industrial sector and to let its agricultural sector develop by repercussion."[9]

This appears to be rather an extreme view. But the historical illustration which the protagonists of agriculture-biased development give in support of their thesis, viz. the historical precedence of agricultural development in relation to industrial expansion in countries like Britain, seems an unconvincing point in the context of the problems which contemporary underdeveloped countries have to face. England was the pioneer industrial country and although the European countries built up their industries in the course of the 18th and 19th centuries, they could not excel Britain and the healthy competition that prevailed was one of equals. But today there is a large gap in point of economic standards between the developed and underdeveloped countries and this gap is widening. Competition is not possible between these two groups and even where it is possible, it would be to the disadvantage of the latter. Low income countries have therefore to considerably accelerate the pace of their economic progress. Further, in the European countries of the 18th century, industrialization required more and more man-power and the drift of population from rural to urban areas was both welcome and necessary; and increased agricultural productivity helped industrialization by releasing labour for industrial employment. But in the overpopulated, underdeveloped countries of today, there is no problem of scarcity of labour in the industrial sector. In the urban as well as in the rural areas labour is superfluous. What industry requires is not additional man-power but additional financial and capital resources to fully utilize existing man-power. Hence increased productivity of agricultural workers and larger production in the agricultural sector are desired not because these would result in the releasing of labour for employment in industries, but because there would be larger supplies of food and raw materials and higher incomes for the majority of the population. In reality, however, the rapid increase in numbers combined with inadequate avenues for alternative employment has necessitated the increased dependence of

[9]Kurihara, Kenneth, K., ' Theoretical Objections to Agriculture Biased Economic Development,' *Indian Journal of Economics*, October, 1958, pp. 163-69.

population on agriculture and as a result the productivity per head decreases and the economy gets stagnated. This stagnation can be avoided only if savings are augmented with which excess labour can be drawn out of agriculture. The question at issue is therefore one of finding out the efficient means of generating savings in the economy. And in so far as industrial incomes have a tendency to rise faster than agricultural incomes, we have to depend more on industries as a source of savings than on agriculture. On the other hand, the major points in favour of development of agriculture in contemporary low income countries are, that increased agricultural production is necessary in order to support a growing population on higher levels of food consumption, and also to ensure increased supply of industrial materials and an expanding market for the manufactured products. Besides, the production of a larger and larger volume of food and other primary commodities would help in relieving inflationary pressures in the economy and in maintaining the external balance of payments position.

AGRICULTURE, THE DEPRESSED SECTOR

At one stage in the economic evolution of nations, natural resources and the utilization of land provided nearly the entire income. With increased agricultural output and the availability of savings, other means and methods of production, less directly dependent on the resources of land, are found and the proportion of national income contributed by cultivation of the soil declines. Clearly, the development of industries and tertiary services is made possible only because agriculture is able to contribute by way of production something more than what is required for consumption. But though agricultural expansion has contributed significantly to industrial development and to overall economic growth, the primary sector, as compared with the secondary sector continues to be a depressed one. This is true of developed as well as underdeveloped countries.

According to the Census of 1951, in India 70 per cent of the people are supported by agriculture, while the income generated in the agricultural sector is only about 50 per cent of the total national output. This would mean that per capita income in the primary sector is about $\frac{3}{7}$ of the per capita income in the non-agricultural sector. As industrialization progresses, there is a tendency for the share of agricultural income to decline until a certain level of disparity is reached at which point it becomes more or less stable. Thus Dr. Egbert de Vries feels that for every 10 per cent increase in per capita real income, the fraction of national income arising from agriculture drops by $1\frac{1}{2}$ percentage points.[10] And Colin Clark is of the view that the

[10]*The Balance between Agriculture and Industry in Economic Development*, a paper for the fourth meeting of Technicians of the Central Bank of the American Continent, May. 1954 (mimeographed) quoted in Coale, A. J., and E. M. Hoover. *Population Growth and Economic Development in Low Income Countries*, Oxford. India. 1959, p. 121.

" situation is fairly stable when the agricultural worker is receiving something between a third and a half of the average income of secondary and tertiary producers ".[11] Undoubtedly, such a trend in the relative incomes of the agricultural and industrial sectors of the economy is necessary as well as indicative of economic progress. But the question that arises is why as an economy progresses, the primary sector fails to absorb as much of the national resources, and to produce as much of the national income as the industrial sector does.

The reasons for this relatively depressed state of agriculture are manifold. But they all spring from the basic characteristics of agriculture. The fundamental factor is, that the quantity of input in the agricultural sector shows a tendency to decrease as compared with the secondary and tertiary sectors in all countries. While in industry practically all the factors are variable in quantity as well as quality, this is not true of agriculture. In a country which is very thinly populated and cultivable land is available in plenty, land cannot be a limiting factor in production. But with increasing population, when all available land is used up for cultivation or in other ways, the rigidity in factor supply makes itself felt. What extension is possible by way of reclamation of swampy or forest areas, or control of soil erosion has only a marginal effect. Thus unless the quality of the soil is improved to compensate for the fact that its extent cannot be increased, the income yielded by agriculture would rise only less than proportionately to the application of labour. At a time when the possibilities of scientific and technological progress in the use of land was not envisaged, it was this prospect of a steady increase in the application of labour to a given area of land that suggested the Law of Diminishing Returns. And this principle is essentially true even today. Thus in underdeveloped countries, scarcity of capital and lack of enterprise prevent the full use of technology and science in agricultural work, and also in combination with increasing population, tend to depress the marginal product to nearly the zero level.

Since land is fixed in supply while population is increasing, the share of land as a factor of production decreases. In actual fact, however, there has not only been this relative decline but in absolute terms also the extent of land used for cultivation purposes has tended to decrease. Prof. Schultz points out that in the U.S.A. the extent of land used for agricultural purposes declined from 1,618 million acres in 1910 to 1,570 million acres in 1945. But in the same period, the volume of agricultural production went up by 70 per cent. In France, between 1901 and 1947–48, the proportion of agricultural land rent to agricultural income receded from 25·2 per cent to 9·0 per cent, and in the United Kingdom between 1925 and 1946 net rent as a percentage of net agricultural income declined from 16·8 to 5·6. The explanation is to be found in the fact that while productivity of land is steadily improved by better methods of cultivation, use of fertilizers, etc. the actual area under cultivation tends to decline because of the use of land for farm buildings and

[11]*The Economics of 1960*, London, 1944, pp. 37–38.

other improvements. As a result, the economy of an advanced country like the U.S.A. or U.K. becomes less dependent on the original and indestructible properties of land.

As regards the other factors—capital and labour—although agricultural expansion has been made possible in developed -economies mainly by the increased use of capital in many ways, yet the flow of capital into the rural sector as compared with the urban sector is small. Particularly in the low income countries of Asia and Africa, the farmer is lagging far behind the industrialist because of the shortage of capital for investment. Improved methods of production which are technically feasible are not adopted, not so much because of lack of enterprise as because of the non-availability of funds. Being a depressed sector with per capita incomes barely sufficient to meet the primary consumption needs of the people, the agricultural sector is incapable of generating any large savings that will accelerate capital formation. Far from it being in a position to support industrialization through transfer of savings to the non-agricultural sector, the rural economy in the low income countries has come to depend on the savings of the rest of the economy even to maintain its existing position. Capital shortage which has necessitated capital rationing is due to the unattractiveness of investment in agricultural operations. Price uncertainty and income instability are characteristics of agriculture in all free enterprise economies. Such uncertainties result in capital rationing of a double type—the farmer is reluctant to invest his own money and the outsider is reluctant to lend to the farmer. Hence as may be expected, the rate of interest in the rural sector as compared with the non-rural sector is much higher in the poorer countries of Asia and Africa as well as in the richer and industrial countries.

So far as labour as an input is concerned, economic growth has involved the transfer of this factor from the primary to the secondary and tertiary sectors with a corresponding decline in the proportion of people employed in the cultivation of the soil. As observed earlier, the steady drift of population to the urban and industrial centres as industrialization progresses, is certainly an indication of economic advancement, because such a trend increases the productivity of labour in agriculture and thus makes further growth of industries and agriculture possible. But the point to remember in this connection is that as an economy grows, the non-industrial sector absorbs only a decreasing proportion of all the inputs. Obviously if more land, more capital and more labour are employed in the primary sector, total agricultural income and its proportion to aggregate national income will be rising. In a primitive economy, what the earning members of a family could produce was probably just sufficient to meet the consumption requirements of that family. As a result of economic progress one man is able to produce food for twenty or even a hundred families. In other words, the economy would require only five or one per cent of the population to be engaged in agricultural operations. However, the fact that only a relatively small number of people are supported in agriculture makes agriculture appear depressed.[12] Between 1900 and 1943 the proportion of working population in agriculture dropped from 37 to 15 per cent in the U.S.A. and from 40 to 22 per cent in Canada.[13]

Lack of entrepreneurial skill and the absence of enthusiasm and drive on the part of workers in the agricultural sector constitute another factor responsible for the low level of agricultural incomes. While the solid virtues of the character of the farmer cannot be disputed, the fact remains that in point of inventiveness, initiative and enterprise and the urge and enthusiasm for making money, the enterpriser in the rural sector makes a poor show when compared with his counterpart in industry. To a large extent, this is due to differences in circumstances, lack of opportunities and the difference in the accessibility to financial resources. However, where such enterprise has been forthcoming in the rural sector, progress has resulted, as the example of the pioneers in British agriculture during the era of agricultural revolution would amply testify. From a study of the rural economy of several countries in the 20th century, Bellerby draws the conclusion that before 1939 the worldwide average ratio of incentive income in agriculture to that outside was as low as 55 per cent.[14] Boulding remarks that entrepreneurial geniuses have no great scope in agriculture as in industry.[15] This is true of the labouring classes as well. Material welfare and the desire to acquire wealth are less keen motives in work in the case of agricultural workers as compared with industrial workers. Low standard of literacy, the dead weight of tradition and custom, lack of mobility, etc., which characterize the worker in rural areas have certainly stood in the way of his material advancement. The lethargy of the agricultural worker and his preference for leisure when his usual income is assured, explains the well known perverse supply curve of agriculture. The existence of a large number of small farmers in low income countries and their geographical dispersion make it difficult for these producers to organize themselves or combine in any productive effort. Also, the low

[12]Boulding, Kenneth E., ' Economic Analysis and Agricultural Policy,' *Canadian Journal of Economics and Political Science*, August, 1947, pp. 437–45. Reprinted in *Contemporary Readings in Agricultural Economics*, Ed. by Halcrow, Harold G., Prentice-Hall, New York, 1955, p. 197.

[13]Schultz, Theodore W., ' Two Conditions Necessary for Economic Progress in Agriculture,' *Canadian Journal of Economics and Political Science*, August, 1944, pp. 298–311. Reprinted in *Contemporary Readings in Agricultural Economics*, Ed. by Halcrow, Harold G., Prentice-Hall, New York, 1955, p. 207.

[14]Incentive income is used as an attempt to measure the return to human effort and enterprise in each sector of the economy and is defined in agriculture as the total income accruing to the agricultural sector divided by the number of farmers and their relatives after payments for rent, interest and the wages and salaries of employees have been subtracted. In other words, it is a rough measure of entrepreneurial income—Anne Martin, *Economics and Agriculture*, Routledge and Kegan Paul, London, 1958, p. 21.

[15]Boulding, Kenneth E., ' Economic Analysis and Agricultural Policy,' *Canadian Journal of Economics and Political Science*, August, 1947, pp. 437–445. Reprinted in *Contemporary Readings in Agricultural Economics*, Ed. by Halcrow, Harold G., Prentice-Hall, New York, 1955, p. 202.

standard of education in the agricultural sector, makes the task of disseminating technical information much harder.

But behind all these factors—lesser inputs and unfavourable social attitudes—lie the basic characteristics of agriculture which account for its relatively depressed state. Both on the demand and supply side, there is an element of inelasticity in agriculture. One of the major factors responsible for the low level of incomes in the rural sector is that the price as well as the income elasticity of demand for food—in several cases the major agricultural output—is low. As per capita income rises, the proportion of expenditure on food declines. On the other hand, the demand for manufactured goods increases, and there is a shift in demand towards varieties of goods which involve higher amounts of processing costs. This is based on the elementary fact which is observable in the family budgets of different income classes, in which as the income per family rises, the proportion of income spent on necessary goods steadily declines. In advanced economies where the application of scientific methods of cultivation and improved methods of technology has enabled farm output to increase enormously, the deficiency in demand for food articles has created quite a serious problem in the rural economy. From the data given below, it is observable that there is a close inverse correlation between the standard of economic development of a country and the income elasticity of demand for food.[16]

Country	Income elasticity of demand for food
U.S.A.	0·27
Sweden	0·32
U.K.	0·33
Germany	0·36
Ceylon	0·79

Prof. Schultz estimates income elasticity of demand for food at about 0·25 for all food products in the U.S.A. It may thus be easily seen that in so far as the proportion of national income spent on food declines with every increase in income, the agricultural sector will be receiving a lesser and lesser proportionate income. This obviously would reduce per capita income in the primary sector in relation to the industrial sector, unless there is a corresponding movement of agricultural workers out of agriculture. Thus if the income elasticity of food were to drop from 0·5 to 0·25 (in terms of the food purchased by consumers minus the cost of the services that have been added to farm products) as income rose 20 per cent, the consumption of farm products would increase 5 per cent instead of 10 per cent. Hence the problem which confronts

[16]Martin, Anne, *Economics and Agriculture*, Routledge and Kegan Paul, London, 1958, p. 21.

the primary sector in advanced economies like the U.S.A. is one of reconciling the low income elasticity of demand for food and the rapid progress in farm technology. According to Prof. Schultz, the elasticity of demand for farm products is not only low but it probably is declining.[17]

On the side of supply, it is a commonly observed fact that price changes bring about only a limited response in the form of output of primary commodities. One main reason for the farmers' relative insensibility to price changes is the cost structure of agriculture—the preponderance of what are called inescapable costs as against escapable costs. Escapable costs relate to those items of expenditure involved in production which can be reduced if demand for output falls, while inescapable costs are in the nature of fixed charges like minimum of income for the family, rent payments, interest charges, etc. In industry, in so far as escapable costs like wage payments constitute the major part of manufacturing costs, the size of output can be reduced by laying off of labour when there is an adverse movement in the price of the final output. Other factors which account for the relative inelasticity in the supply of agricultural produce are the comparatively small scale of farming business, lack of proper organization in the agricultural industry and the limited employment opportunities outside agriculture. These factors in addition to keeping down agricultural incomes, make the agricultural sector easily susceptible to economic instability. Such income fluctuations bear particularly heavily on the low income countries of the world because their resources, and therefore their staying power, are very limited. Since the normal level of their incomes is very low, a temporary fall even below that low level, brings much hardship.

The foregoing points make it clear that the basic factor responsible for the depressed state of agriculture as compared with industry in the industrial as well as the pre-industrial countries of the world is an economic one. The force of economic circumstances moves out resources into those sectors or enterprises where they would be used to the best advantage. So long as the demand for industrial goods rises to a greater extent than the demand for agricultural goods when there is an income increase, and the spread between costs and the value of the final product is higher, it is inevitable that in a free enterprise economy, resources would be drawn into that sector. But while such a movement of the factors and resources would help in national income growth, it does make the primary sector appear relatively backward in the overall set-up of the economy.

THE STATE OF AGRICULTURE IN UNDERDEVELOPED ECONOMIES

The underdeveloped countries are predominantly agricultural, but in point of contribution to national income and in the standards of development, the

[17]Schultz, Theodore W., ' Two Conditions Necessary for Economic Progress in Agriculture,' *Contemporary Readings in Agricultural Economics*, Ed. by Halcrow, Harold G., Prentice-Hall, New York, 1955, p. 205.

agricultural sector in these countries is far behind that of the advanced econo-mies. While in Africa and Asia more than 70 per cent of the population is rural, in Europe and North America the proportion ranges from one-fifth to one-third. In Asia, Africa and South America which contain most of the underdeveloped countries, per capita yields of agriculture are the lowest of the six continents. Production per head of the farm population in Oceania, North America and North-West Europe appears to be ten to twenty times greater than in the Far East, Near East and Latin America. According to Colin Clark's findings, the product per worker in agriculture in the under-developed countries averages about 250 International Units which is about $\frac{1}{18}$ of that of New Zealand and about $\frac{1}{2}$ to $\frac{1}{6}$ of the productivity in the advanced countries. India's place even among the underdeveloped coun-tries is very low. The productivity in India is about half that of countries like Ceylon, Java and Egypt and one-seventh that of Brazil. In point of output per unit area also, there is wide difference between the richer countries and the low income countries of the world. The output of wheat per hectare in India is about one-sixth of the yield in industrialized but densely populated countries like Belgium, West Germany, Switzerland and the United Kingdom. It compares unfavourably even with countries like Turkey, Egypt and Pakistan. Rice yield is 10·8 quintals per hectare in India as against 47·8 in Italy, 48·8 in Spain, 39·6 in Japan and 48·6 in Australia. Similar is the relative position of India in the yield of cotton.[18]

Not only is agricultural production low in underdeveloped countries, but it has remained low for long. While in the last few decades agricultural produc-tion increased remarkably in some of the advanced countries, it has remained disappointingly static in the poorer countries. Between the late 1930s and the middle of the present century, agricultural yield in the U.S.A. increased by about 45 per cent. In Japan, in the sixty years since the close of the 19th cen-tury, rice acreage increased by 25 per cent while yield of rice increased by 70 per cent and total agricultural production went up by 113 per cent. Between 1800 and 1940 in the U.S.A. the number of man-hours needed to produce 100 bushels of wheat declined from 373 to 47. While in 1820 in that country one farm worker supported 0·5 people, in 1946 one farm worker supported 14·5 people. On the other hand, considering the Asian and Far East Asian countries as a whole, the United Nations Commission feels that the growth of the region's food production since the Second World War has not, except in 1952–56, caught up with population growth, with the result that per capita food production in 1955–56 was 8 per cent less than before the War.[19]

Agricultural backwardness of contemporary underdeveloped countries is due primarily to three factors : (a) Low land labour-ratio ; (b) Low capital-

[18]Clark, Colin, *Conditions of Economic Progress*, 3rd edition, Macmillan, London, 1957, pp. 257-77. Data relate to the years around 1950. Agricultural output includes forest produce.

[19]*Economic Bulletin for Asia and the Far East*, U.N., November, 1957, pp. 23 & 24.

labour ratio and (c) Adverse social and institutional factors. Although the low income countries are not so densely populated as some of the industrial countries of Europe, yet most of them are over-populated in so far as the proportion of people subsisting on agriculture is much higher. Since the extent of the total land area is fixed, rapid growth of population and the failure of industries to absorb the growing population resulted in surplus of labour in rural areas. In India, the per capita availability of net area sown decreased from 1·11 acres in 1921 to 0·84 acre in 1951. If output per head is low because land-labour ratio is low, it is possible to increase per capita output only by increasing the capital per head, but in underdeveloped countries with very low per capita incomes, savings have been meagre and the capital available per worker is also very much limited as compared with the position in the developed countries. Since income is hardly sufficient to meet the basic consumption requirements, farmers cannot save much for investment, and governments cannot raise much revenue by means of taxation. Thus in India in 1951–52 it was estimated that rural investments in the form of shares, deposits and the like, amounted on the average to less than Rs. 4 per family and were mostly effected by the 10 per cent of cultivators with the biggest holdings.[20] An idea of the backwardness of low income countries in the matter of capital equipment per worker can be had from the great disparity in the use of fertilizers and tractors between different countries. Consumption of fertilizers per hectare of arable land in 1959 was 461 kilogrammes in the Netherlands, 278 in West Germany, 207 in Switzerland, and 180 in the United Kingdom, but only 31 in Greece, 29 in Spain and 1 in Turkey. In the same year, the number of tractors per thousand hectares of arable land was 29·2 in France, 80·9 in West Germany, 43·4 in the Netherlands, 83·1 in Switzerland and 59·1 in the United Kingdom, while in Greece it was 4·3, in Portugal 1·9, and in Turkey 1·7.[21]

The superfluity of labour and the scarcity of capital are reflected in rural unemployment and disguised unemployment. It has been estimated that in the countries of Asia, the number of men who can be fully occupied on one square kilometre of land for the production of rice works out at 42, for maize 25, and for rubber 35. For India, Tarlok Singh in 1945 estimated on the basis of the number of ploughs available in a given area, the number of men who can be fully employed in that area. His figures for one square kilometre of land are : Sind 12, Bombay 13, Punjab, Central Provinces and North-West Frontier Province 21, Madras 25, United Provinces, Bihar, Orissa and Assam 31

[20]*All-India Rural Credit Survey*, The General Report, Abridged edn. Reserve Bank of India, 1952, p. 264. At the end of 1953–54 after half a century's work, the co-operative agricultural credit societies in India had as capital, reserves and deposits, an aggregate amount of only Rs. 262 million, while the remainder of their working capital of Rs. 544 million came from outside sources mainly in the form of borrowing—Reserve Bank of India, *Statistical Statements Relating* to Co-operative Movement in India for 1953–54, Bombay, p. ii, quoted in *Economic Bulletin for Asia and the Far East*, U.N., November, 1957, p. 58 f.n.

[21]*The Eastern Economist*, Annual Number, 1962, New Delhi, pp. 80 & 83.

and Bengal 35.[22] The actual number of men available for work is much greater, and this excess of labour has resulted in low marginal productivity of labour or even zero marginal productivity. Since the transfer of the disguisedly unemployed part of labour from agriculture would not result in a fall in agricultural output, it is obvious that the contribution of labour at the margin is nothing. Professor Buck in his *Land Utilisation in China* has made a rough estimate of the marginal productivity of labour in the rice areas of that country by observing the contribution of a given area of land with varying labour inputs. In the rice area, the number of hectares per man ranged from an average of 0·53 to 1·25, that is to say, the labour input in the former is greater than in the latter. However, with this markedly differing levels of labour input per unit of land, output per unit of land remained practically constant at about 1,800 kilos of grain equivalent (converting all agricultural produce into grain equivalent with reference to their market prices in relation to a given quantity of grain) per hectare per year over the whole range. In other words, the marginal productivity of labour when the land is as crowded as this is zero. A similar calculation for wheat areas indicated a marginal productivity of only 80 kilos of grain equivalent per man-year, while the wage of the farm labour if it is employed is equivalent to 660 kilos of grain.[23] These figures may be taken as representative of the position in many other under-developed countries also. The point to be noted is that output per worker is very low or even nil, because there are too many labourers on a given area of land.

Such a situation in the low income countries calls for a transfer of population from the rural to the industrial sector. A shifting of resources in this manner helps and in turn is facilitated by industrialization. There is in this respect a significant difference between industrial countries and the pre-industrial and underdeveloped economies. Developed economies especially those in which land-labour ratio is high get over this difficulty easily because they have the advantage of already accumulated technical knowledge and capital and skill to cope with the problem. This is illustrated by the experience of the U.S.A. in the decade 1938–1948. In these years, increase in the demand for food pressed hard against available supply, and wholesale prices of farm products rose rapidly. But since technology was already advanced, it was possible to apply it to cultivation, and agricultural production expanded rapidly. In fact, rapid technological progress has facilitated a rather too fast movement of population out of agriculture. It has been estimated that in the U.S.A. between 1910 and 1950, because of technological improvements the output per unit of input in agriculture was made to increase at the rate of 1·35 per cent per year. Since over-all agricultural production increased at the

[22]*Poverty and Social Change*, 1945. Quoted in Colin, Clark, *Conditions of Economic Progress*, 3rd edition, 1957, Macmillan, London, p. 321.

[23]Quoted in 'The Development of Agricultural Productivity,' Colin. Clark, *The Eastern Economist*, Blue Supplement, New Delhi, April, 26, 1957.

annual rate of more than 2 per cent, it would appear that technological progress accounted for about 60 to 70 per cent of the agricultural improvement. The fact that per capita incomes in both the sectors of the economy in the high income countries are very much higher than in the underdeveloped countries, makes it appear that agriculture is not supporting as many of the population as would be possible. And the question is raised whether such transfer is not proceeding at a faster rate than would be in the interests of economic stability.

In contrast to this, in low income countries, which are over-populated, the pressure of population is so acutely felt in the primary sector that it seems that agricultural progress is possible only if such a transfer on a large scale is effected. Quite often, this is one of the main points raised in support of the thesis that rapid industrialization is of the utmost importance in these countries if only for the relief which it would give to the agricultural sector in the matter of population pressure. At any rate, it is obvious that out-migration of surplus labour from rural areas would, by reducing the number of claimants to aggregate farm incomes and by raising the marginal value product of labour, help capital formation in the primary sector of the economy.[24] But this transfer of population from the primary sector is as difficult as it is necessary in the pre-industrial countries. In poor countries even when productivity per head is low in the agricultural sector, there is only limited out-migration of labour because of limited knowledge, inertia and lethargy on the part of labour which is traditionally immobile and also because of the fact that in the absence of a rapidly expanding industrial sector, employment opportunities outside agriculture are very much limited. The pull of the narrow urban industrial sector is therefore very insignificant. It may also be mentioned that the very fact that surplus labour has continued long to subsist on the meagre resources of an impoverished agricultural sector makes it appear unsound from the immediate economic point of view to bring about any important transfer. Since physical productivity of labour is low, it becomes necessary to employ a large number of people in agriculture to satisfy minimum food requirements. All the same, this apparent dilemma can be solved only by first raising the physical product per head in agriculture. To the extent that this can be attained by reducing the number of people in agriculture as well as by increasing per capita output of existing labour, both the methods are to be adopted.

While in economically backward countries, surplus of population in the rural areas necessitates their transfer, in advanced countries, such a shift becomes necessary because of surplus production in the agricultural sector. In a country like the U.S.A. agricultural production in recent years has increased so fast that the problem is to reduce the surplus production in relation to the demand for it, by shifting agricultural inputs to non-agricultural operations. The fact that when a certain standard of life is reached, higher incomes would lead to increased demand for non-farm products (products of manufac-

---

[24]Baker, C. B., ' Instrumental Goals and Economic Growth,' *Agricultural Adjustment Problems in a Growing Economy*, Ed. by Heady, E. O., and others, Iowa State College Press, 1958, p. 258.

tures) helps the expansion of the non-agricultural sector and its capacity to absorb more labour. But the preference for non-farm products becomes strong only when the bare needs of life (primarily food requirements) are met. If the land-labour ratio is favourable, then these needs can be satisfied even when land is not fully exploited. But in a country where land-labour ratio is adverse, and where the primary requirements of food are barely met, and on top of these there is population pressure, the problem is one of comparison between the rate of increase in population and the rate of increase in farm output. So long as the former is as high as, or higher than the latter, the increased demand for food is chronic. In other words, there is no possibility of a shift in demand to non-farm products. Hence the proportion of people dependent on agriculture is constant or increasing. Assuming that modern technology can be imported at no cost, it is possible to maintain agricultural output with a lesser number of people engaged in the primary sector. But the excess labour cannot be shifted because of inadequate demand for non-farm products. In fact, since capital resources are totally inadequate, it is difficult to bring about any transfer of resources even within agriculture—from low income yielding products like food grains, to high income yielding operations like fisheries, forestry, dairying, livestock farming, etc. The productivity of agricultural labour in the underdeveloped countries of the tropical regions is possibly only just equal to the subsistence minimum of about 400 kilos of grain equivalents per head of farm population per year. And Dr. de Vries feels that unless production per head rises to 600 kilos per year it cannot be possible to set aside pasture land and thus shift to dairy farming or other allied activities.[25]

Scarcity of land and capital resources not only accounts for low productivity but also indirectly explains the persistence of certain social institutions and organizational defects which hinder development of agriculture. Theodore Schultz points out that in an economy where the major part of the income is spent on food, the proportion of rent to national income would be high, that is to say, land's claims on national income will be large in relation to the other factors. If 75 per cent of the income is used for food and $33\frac{1}{3}$ per cent of the cost of food consists of rent, then $\frac{1}{4}$ of the income goes as rent. On the other hand, as it happens in a developed economy, if only 12 per cent of the income is spent on food and 20 per cent of the cost of food is rent, then rent is only 2·5 per cent of national income. The predominance of rent income is likely to lead to the creation of vested interests and distort the structure of agricultural organization in a manner uncongenial to the productive employment of agricultural resources. The problem of land reform is therefore more intricate and of a different nature altogether in the former as against the latter.[26] Continued shortage of capital rubs out the spirit of enterprise of the producers and reduces their capacity and preparedness to take risks.

[25]Quoted in 'The Development of Agricultural Productivity,' Colin, Clark, *The Eastern Economist*, Blue Supplement, April 26, 1957.

[26]*Economic Organization of Agriculture*, McGraw-Hill, New York, 1953, pp. 125–27.

Resistance to change therefore appears as a cultural response to growing economic pressure on limited natural resources. The enjoyment of high rent incomes by the landlords, chronic indebtedness, exhorbitant interest rates and exploitation by middlemen—all these are features of a faulty organization and institutional framework under which the workers cannot feel assured that their extra efforts to increase production will bring them commensurate rewards.

These obstacles to agricultural progress in underdeveloped countries are formidable enough to call forth the maximum effort of any backward nation. However, in the face of the institutional obstacles mentioned above, it is obvious that individual efforts at improvement cannot make any impression, unless the state comes in with the power and resources at its disposal to rectify the defects and reorganize the system. Social attitudes are to be changed; institutional reform has to be brought about by legislation; facilities are to be provided to meet the credit requirements of agriculturists; steps are to be taken to ensure as far as possible stability of incomes: possibilities of improved methods of cultivation and the application of modern techniques are to be demonstrated. All these require enormous financial resources and organizational ability of a high order. Much therefore depends on the attitude of the state to social reform and economic improvement.

The Revival of Interest in Agricultural Development

Since the close of the Second World War, nearly all countries of the world, both developed and underdeveloped, have undertaken ambitious programmes of agricultural investment with a view to build up the agricultural sector of their economies and to increase agricultural production. In so far as there is much difference in the political and economic organization of these countries, in their resources and economic circumstances, there is some variation in their objectives as well as in the methods which they have adopted for implementing their programmes of development. Despite these differences the progress made in the agricultural sector in some countries of eastern Europe including the U.S.S.R., Yugoslavia and Poland which have adopted collectivization, and in the countries of Western Europe which believe in free enterprise, has been remarkable. In the industrial countries, although agricultural progress has not kept pace with industrial progress, and the share of agricultural income in aggregate national output has fallen, agricultural production in absolute terms has increased markedly. Thus between 1950 and 1959, the percentage share of agriculture in gross domestic production declined in the highly industrialized countries of West Europe—Belgium, West Germany and the United Kingdom—from 9 to 7 per cent, 11 to 7 per cent and 6 to 4 per cent respectively; in Denmark it receded from 21 to 17 per cent, in Italy from 29 to 19 per cent and in the Netherlands from 14 to 10 per cent. In Greece and Turkey the decline was small—from 34 to 32 per cent and from 49 to 44 per cent respectively. In all the countries of Europe excepting Ireland, Norway, Portugal and Sweden, the total volume of agricultural production increased substantially. The rise was particularly marked in Greece, Italy, the United Kingdom and Yugoslavia. In the last mentioned country, agricultural output more than doubled between the years 1952–53 and 1959–60. Total farm output in Greece went up by 57 per cent in these eight years, in Italy by 30 per cent and in Yugoslavia by 141 per cent. On the whole, in most of these countries, the gross rate of growth of agricultural output over these years was about 2 to 2·5 per cent per annum.

This improvement in farm output was due to conscious and sustained effort on the part of the people to build up the agricultural sector of their economies. In most of these countries, the primary objective in agricultural policy was the attainment of self-sufficiency in food. The stress laid on increased food production was the effect of a new consciousness about national security in the form of an assured food supply in the eventuality of a war. Not only was attention devoted to increase the output of traditional foodcrops but steps were taken in many countries to grow virtually every kind of foodstuff that enters into the national diets. Recurring balance of payments difficulties also have been responsible for the great importance attached to increasing agricultural output. The objective has been either to earn more foreign exchange by producing and exporting goods which have a ready market in foreign countries, or to conserve foreign exchange by reducing the dependence on imports. A socio-political factor also has operated in the same direction. The growing political influence of the farm populations of the world has been reflected in the strong urge to raise incomes from farming to something comparable to the returns from industry.

Among the measures adopted in these countries to increase agricultural production may be mentioned : (a) Increased use of fertilizers, pesticides and herbicides. Consumption of fertilizers has increased markedly not only in the less developed countries of Europe like Greece, Ireland, Italy, Portugal and Spain but also in the high income countries where they had been already in widespread use before the Second World War. In Denmark, France, West Germany and the United Kingdom, consumption of fertilizers went up by 50 to 90 per cent in the last decade. (b) Mechanization of farming: The extent to which mechanization has been adopted is indicated by the fall in labour inputs in West European agriculture and the significant increase in the use of farm tractors. The fall in labour input since 1950–52 to 1957–59 varies from about 25 per cent in the case of West Germany and Sweden to 4 per cent in the case of Australia. The number of tractors in use increased in the decade by more than four times in Belgium and France, by five times in Western Germany, six times in Finland, and by seven times in Austria. (c) Improvement in seeds and plant strains: The boosting of farm outputs has been due, to a great extent, to the introduction of improved and high yielding varieties of wheat, barley and hybrid maize. (d) Extension services: Much emphasis is laid on agricultural education and advisory services with the result that government expenditure on agricultural research and education has gone up considerably. (e) Apart from these, increased specialization in the raising of farm products and the application of scientific and technical knowledge in improving cattle breeds have helped in the increase in farm output and in the rise in agricultural incomes.

Farm output in the East European countries also—U.S.S.R., Albania, Bulgaria, Czechoslovakia, Hungary, Poland and Romania—has registered an appreciable rise in the latter half of the past decade. Slow growth up to about 1956 has been attributed largely to the upsets created by collectivization of privately owned farms and low investments. Targets for the production of both crop and animal output for the year 1965 have been kept at very high levels and although the progress made in the last few years has been quite satisfactory, the projection of past trends in output does not fully warrant the hope that the targets will be attained. On the other hand, if the West European countries maintain the present trend, it is likely that by 1970 many of the countries will have surpluses in some items of food like cereals, potatoes and eggs while the deficits in others may appreciably dwindle. Since the low income countries of the world are also striving hard to attain self-sufficiency in the matter of foodstuffs, it is likely that in another twenty or twenty-five years price of food articles would come down in relation to other agricultural commodities and non-farm products, unless of course the underdeveloped countries concentrate on industrialization to the extent that they would be importers of food.[27]

Countries of the ECAFE region which are all economically backward, have incorporated detailed programmes of agricultural expansion in their plans of economic development. The share of agriculture in the planned public development expenditure ranges from 8 per cent in China (Mainland) to about 45 per cent in Afghanistan and Pakistan. In the Second Five-Year Plan of India the proportion of expenditure allotted for agriculture was 20 per cent, while in the Third Plan it is 23 per cent.[28] Apart from the general objectives such as economic and social advancement and the achievement of higher per capita incomes, the programmes for agricultural development in these countries have the following major objectives. Nearly all the countries in this group have laid great emphasis on the building up of the agricultural sector with a view to strengthen their balance of payments position. This is understandable in view of their disappointing experience in foreign trade in recent years. The slackening of external demand for their agricultural products, inflationary conditions at home and the need for importing annually large volumes of food have resulted in a chronic balance of payments deficit. Hence the pattern of agricultural development is designed to achieve self-sufficiency in regard to the staple items of food; to produce at home increasing amounts

[27] 'India and Europe—Agriculture,' *The Eastern Economist*, Annual Number, January 5, 1962, New Delhi.

[28] i.e. agriculture, community development and major and minor irrigation.

of other agricultural products which have traditionally been largely imported, such as sugar, fruits, fibres, oil seeds. etc.; to save foreign exchange and also to increase the production and exports of established export crops and devote greater attention to the cultivation of other products for which there is a foreign demand like coffee, canned fruits and sea products. Other objectives are, diversification of agriculture and the broadening of a base of agricultural raw materials for the expansion of domestic manufacturing industries. Diversification has been stressed by countries like Burma, Cambodia and Malaya which are at present depending on one or a few crops as their mainstay of export earnings, and by countries like India, Pakistan and Japan, in order to ensure a varied diet expected or planned to result from higher per capita real incomes.

Primary consideration is given to increase in food output. Thus as regards the staple food crops in this region, Burma fixed a target of 26 per cent increase in the years 1955–60, Ceylon 45 per cent, India 20 per cent, Indonesia 21 per cent, Pakistan 8 per cent, and Philippines 17 per cent. Similar targets have been fixed for other food grains, and industrial raw materials with reference to the income elasticity of demand for these products, internal requirements resulting from population increase and the need for increasing exports. As for means to achieve the targets, programmes are drawn up for extending irrigation, increasing the area under cultivation, and for the adoption of improved methods of cultivation, increased use of fertilizers and provision of credit and marketing facilities to agriculturists; besides, measures have been taken to ensure stable income to agriculturists through a price policy, and land reforms and other organizational changes have been introduced which would provide the incentive for the agriculturists to put forth greater effort in increasing agricultural production. In most of these countries, a good proportion of the total expenditure on agricultural development (ranging from 11·9 per cent in Burma to 64·2 per cent in Pakistan) has been allotted to irrigation which has a direct impact on crop production. India and Nepal show a high rate of investment in community development activities and agricultural extension work, and Japan and China (Taiwan) have laid stress on land development and reclamation. Land reform legislation has been enacted in most of these countries. In Ceylon, the Paddy Lands Act passed early in 1958, gives tenant cultivators of paddy lands inheritable rights to the land they are tilling and protects them against excessive rents and exhorbitant rates of interest on loans. In Pakistan, a sweeping programme of land reform was announced in 1959 which aims at transferring about 3·5 million hectares of land from large land-holders to small cultivators. In India, land reform legislation has been introduced in some states and in January, 1959, the National Congress adopted a resolution on the agrarian organizational pattern, advocating the development of co-operatives and joint farming. In the main, these land reform measures aim at providing security of tenure to the cultivators, consolidating small holdings and eradicating the evils of absentee land ownership.

Despite the comprehensiveness of these measures and the high targets which have been set in the Plans, the achievements cannot on the whole be considered as satisfactory. Although substantial gains in food production have been made, the rate of increase in food output has not kept pace with the rate of increase in population. The dependence of these countries on sources outside the region for their supplies of cereals has increased. The net imports of cereals, mainly wheat, increased from 4·7 million tons in 1955 to 9·4 million or by about 100 per cent in 1956 and 1957 and remained high at about 10 million tons in 1958 and 1959. It has been observed that the pace of implementation of the programmes of development lags behind the Plans. And this deficiency has been attributed to insufficient attention being given to the timely working out of detailed plans, procedural delays particularly those in connection with the granting of financial approval, and insufficient co-ordination of development work at the different rungs of the administrative structure.[29] The lack or inadequacy of statistical data and shortage of skilled personnel for both planning and implementation of the programmes and the defects of the institutions and techniques of planning have also been mentioned as other factors responsible for the slow or unsatisfactory execution of the development schemes.[30] Stress has therefore to be laid on the need for working out appropriate procedures for the co-ordination of development work at different levels, for the sharing of responsibility by administrative officers in charge of the different departments and for setting in the short run, clear limits to the pace of development in certain directions with reference to the scientific knowledge available.

THE EXPERIENCE IN INDIA

There are evidences to show that in the years immediately after the close of the Second World War, agricultural conditions in India deteriorated perceptibly. Over the forty years 1910 to 1950 although gross cropped area increased as a result of double cropping, little new area was brought under cultivation. But since population was increasing rapidly, cultivated land per head declined. The separation of Burma accounted for a reduction in food supplies to the tune of about 1·3 million tons and the partition of the country reduced it further by 0·77 million tons. The deficiency in domestic supplies had to be made good by imports which amounted on the average to 3 million tons of food grains per year in the years 1946 to 1952.[31] The deficit in food grains thus averaged about 6 to 7 per cent of production.[32] The total cost of imported

[29]*Economic Bulletin for Asia and the Far East*, U.N., November, 1957, p. 34.
[30]' Some Aspects of Agricultural Planning in Asia and the Far East,' *Economic Bulletin for Asia and the Far East*, U.N., June, 1960, p. 6.
[31]*First Five-Year Plan*, Planning Commission, Government of India, New Delhi, 1951, p. 175.
[32]According to the Planning Commission however, the proportion would have been a little less, i.e. 5 per cent. *First Five-Year Plan*, p. 176.

grains between 1948 and 1952 amounted to over Rs. 7,500 million, accounting for nearly 60 per cent of the deficit in the country's balance of payments. At the same time, domestic production of food and other agricultural commodities showed little improvement and in some cases actually declined as may be seen from Tables 43 and 44.

Table 43

AGRICULTURAL PRODUCTION IN INDIA: MAJOR COMMODITIES 1947–51

Commodity	Pre-war	1947–48	1948–49	1949–50	1950–51
Cereals—million tons	46·2	43·7	43·3	46·0	41·8
Oil seeds—'000 tons	4,811·0	5,117·0	4,502·0	5,142·0	5,103·0
Cotton lint—'000 bales of 392 lbs.	3,601·0	2,188·0	1,767·0	2,628·0	2,971·0
Jute—'000 bales of 400 lbs.	1,638·0	1,658·0	2,055·0	3,089·0	3,301·0

SOURCE: Rangnekar, D. K., *Poverty and Capital Development in India*, Oxford, India, 1958, p. 39.

It may be observed from Table 43 that of the agricultural commodities jute alone shows a steady improvement over these years. Oil seeds more or less remained stationary, while output of cotton declined. Production of cereals in 1950–51 was less than that of the pre-war level by about 9·5 per cent. On the whole, production of food grains in the five years 1947–52 was well below pre-war levels. It goes without saying that per capita consumption of food which was below estimated requirements, even before the war would have fallen lower still in the post-war years. Apart from seasonal factors, the failure of the agricultural sector even to maintain the earlier standards was due to the fact that cultivation was extended to marginal lands, and more important, the investment in agriculture was very meagre—new investment averaging, not more than Rs. 700 million a year including multi-purpose projects. Since agricultural population in these years was about 250 million, and the extent of cultivated area was about 300 million acres, this works out to Rs. 2·8 per head of agricultural population and Rs. 2·3 per acre of cultivated area.

With the commencement of the era of planned economic development, the Government of India have taken up the cause of agricultural improvement in earnest and have drawn up detailed programmes of investment in agriculture in order to ensure its rapid development. An important point in this connection is the recognition by the government of the important role which agriculture can be made to play in the overall economic expansion of the country. It is felt that the success of the whole plan of economic development " will vitally depend on the results achieved in making the most advantageous use of the land and labour resources engaged in agriculture ".[33] The plan of agricultural

[33]*First Five-Year Plan*, Planning Commission, Government of India, New Delhi, 1951, p. 153.

31

expansion has been designed not only with a view to increase considerably the output of food products as well as industrial raw materials, but also to mobilize and harness the man-power and other resources, to bring about a re-awakening in the minds of the rural masses, instil a spirit of enterprise and co-operation in them, to remove social and institutional obstacles to economic growth, and in short to revitalize the rural sector of the economy so that it would be able to contribute its maximum to the economic development of the country. Thus the plan of development pertaining to agriculture is not purely an economic one but much more comprehensive, including in its scope the institutional and social aspects of the agrarian problem.

Public outlay on agriculture and community development in the decade 1950–51 to 1960–61 covering the first two Five-Year Plans aggregated to Rs. 8,210 million or 12·5 per cent of the total investment outlay in this period. The Third Five-Year Plan envisages an expenditure of Rs. 10,680 million which is 14 per cent of the aggregate investment of Rs. 75,000 million. In all the three Plans considerable emphasis is laid on increasing food output as well as industrial raw materials. The First and Second Plans fixed a target of 14 per cent and 15 per cent increase respectively in food grains while the Third Plan estimates food output to rise by 31·6 per cent over the five years 1960–61 to 1965–66. Higher targets have been set in the Third Plan in respect of industrial materials, particularly cotton and jute in view of the need for building up the industries and making the country less dependent on imports for these materials. It is mentioned that " with the growth of the economy and increase in domestic demands as well as the need to step up exports, success in increasing the production of commercial crops is as vital as increase in the production of food grains ".[34].

From the point of view of improvement in production, the progress made in agriculture in the first ten years of planned development is not unsatisfactory. The index number of agricultural production (with base 1949–50=100) went up from 95·6 points in 1950–51 to 139·1 in 1960–61. This represents an increase of about 45·5 per cent over the ten years or an annual average rise of 4·6 per cent. Improvement in agricultural output was of the order of 17 per cent in the First Plan period and 16 per cent in the Second Plan years. The slightly lesser increase in the latter period was due chiefly to the fact that in two years 1957–58 and 1959–60, the seasons were unfavourable and agricultural output was adversely affected. The details regarding the production of individual commodities are given in Table 44.

Extension in the area under cultivation accounts for about half the increase in agricultural production. The total area under cultivation was 150·7 million hectares in 1958–59 against 131·9 million hectares in 1950–51 which means an extension in gross area sown of 18·8 million hectares. Deducting the increase due to double cropping—6·6 million hectares—the increase in the net area sown was 12·2 million hectares. Part of the improvement in production was

[34]*Third Five-Year Plan*, Planning Commission, Government of India, New Delhi, 1961, p. 302.

Table 44

AGRICULTURAL PRODUCTION IN INDIA: 1949–50 TO 1960–61

Commodity			1949–50	1950–51	1955–56	1956–57	1957–58	1958–59 (a)	1959–60 (b)	1960–61 (c)
Rice	million tons		23·7	20·9	27·1	28·6	24·9	30·4	29·3	32·0
Wheat	,,	,,	6·6	6·6	8·6	9·3	7·7	9·8	9·7	10·0
All cereals	,,	,,	48·4	43·7	54·9	57·4	53·0	62·6	60·5	64·0
Pulses	,,	,,	9·2	8·5	10·9	11·4	9·5	12·9	11·2	12·0
Food grains, cereals and pulses	,,	,,	57·6	52·2	65·8	68·8	62·5	75·5	71·7	76·0
Oil seeds	,,	,,	5·1	5·1	5·6	6·3	6·1	6·9	6·4	7·1
Sugarcane (gur)	,,	,,	4·9	5·6	6·0	6·8	6·9	7·1	7·6	8·0
Cotton	,,	bales	2·6	2·9	4·0	4·7	4·7	4·7	3·8	5·1
Jute	,,	,,	3·1	3·3	4·2	4·3	4·1	5·2	4·6	4·0
All commodities index number			100·0	95·6	116·8	124·0	114·6	132·3	127·2	135·0

SOURCE: *Third Five-Year Plan*, Planning Commission, Government of India, New Delhi, 1961, p. 302.

(a) Partially revised estimates; (b) Final estimates; (c) Provisional.

due to the improvement in yield per unit area; and this was made possible by the adoption of new methods and intensive cultivation, extension of irrigation facilities, introduction of new crops, increased use of fertilizers and insecticides, improvement of animal husbandry, etc.

The question now arises as to how far the agricultural progress that has been made since planning started, has contributed to the general economic development of the country. In an underdeveloped country like India with its characteristic features of an ill-organized agricultural and industrial sector, over-population and lack of capital, agriculture can contribute to economic growth only if food supply is increased considerably, so that the domestic requirements are met satisfactorily; if more industrial materials are produced so that imports of these goods can be reduced or stopped; if productivity and agricultural income per head rises sufficiently high, so that there can be a transfer of population from agriculture and capital formation can be accelerated; and lastly, if there is a general awakening among the rural masses.

Although there has been some improvement in the output of food grains, planned development for a decade has not brought about the much needed self-sufficiency in food. On the basis of a per capita daily consumption of food of 13·67 ounces, the Planning Commission in 1950 estimated the food requirements of the country at the end of the First Plan period at 52·4 million tons; and if there was to be any improvement in per capita levels of consumption, the overall requirement was to go up correspondingly. Thus at 14 ounces per head, total requirement in 1956 was estimated at 53·7 million tons, and at

16 ounces per head, supply would have to rise to 61·4 million tons. Thanks to favourable seasons output of food grains went up from 54 million tons in 1949–50 to 68·8 million tons in 1953–54, but later receded to 64·8 million tons in 1955–56. Even the latter lower figure was about 3 million tons above the target laid down in the Plan. Nevertheless, in view of the rapid increase in population, larger production could not bring about self-sufficiency in food; and government imports of food over the five years 1951–55 amounted to more than 12 million tons. Assuming an annual population growth rate of 1·25 per cent, and keeping in view the projected increase of 17·8 per cent in the per capita national income over five years and the target of making available 18·3 ounces of food grains per day per adult unit by 1960–61, as against 17 ounces a day in 1955–56, the Second Five-Year Plan fixed a limit of additional production of food grains in 1960–61 of 10 million tons. Thus the target of total production to be attained at the end of the Plan was fixed at 75 million tons. This was however, revised later. In 1957, the Food Grains Enquiry Committee estimated, on the basis of a 2 per cent annual rate of growth of population and an increase in national income of 25 per cent, a total demand for food grains of 79 million tons. The Planning Commission therefore revised its estimated total demand for food grains (including human consumption, demand for seed and feed and waste) upwards to 80·4 million tons. However, the actual production in 1960–61 was only 76 million tons, and food imports over the five years of the Second Plan aggregated to about 12·7 million tons.

This continuing dependence on imports in spite of the fact that the target in the First Plan and the original target in the Second Plan have been fulfilled in the periods to which they relate, suggests that the estimates of food requirements tended to fall short of the actual requirements. This is due to under-estimation of population growth rate, as well as of the expansion in demand arising out of economic improvement. Thus in view of the large additions to numbers made in each year, the Food Grains Enquiry Committee of 1957 estimated that an increase in consumption by half the population by one ounce more of cereals per capita per day would put up the total requirements by over 2 million tons.[35] This would mean that the total import requirements would be not 6 million tons as originally envisaged in the Second Plan but 10 million tons. Apart from population growth, various other factors are to be taken into account in estimating food requirements in a growing economy. Demand for food is a function of not only increase in population but also of rise in incomes, the pattern of distribution of incomes, income and price elasticity of demand, change in the habits of food consumption, terms of trade between agricultural and industrial products, etc. If population growth rate is high, income elasticity of demand for food is great, price elasticity of demand is low, and terms of trade adverse to farm products, there will be greater need for food than if the variables move differently. The significance of each of these factors has to be assessed in detail. Thus, since

[35]Report, p. 40.

when per capita income rises there is likely to be a shift from poor quality to better food, it is necessary to calculate the income elasticity of demand of different articles of food. Consumption of cereals per capita in urban areas is slightly less than in rural areas, and hence increase in demand for food arising from different rates of population growth in urban and rural areas is to be separately considered. Variations in the prices of food articles also affect demand. Generally, the price elasticity of demand for food is less than that for non-food articles. Lastly, the terms of trade between agricultural and non-agricultural products also influence the demand for food. If the terms of trade are favourable to farm products, that is, if prices of food articles rise to a greater extent than non-food articles, the consumption of farm products would be somewhat less and the volume of consumption of non-farm products would be some what greater than if there were no changes in relative prices.[36]

Considering these aspects of the problem, the Ford Foundation Team in its Report on India's food problem pointed out in April, 1959 that India would face a severe crisis in her development unless the rate of increase in food production was tripled and total production reached 110 million by 1965–66. According to these experts, if food production increased only at the existing rates, the gap between the supplies and the target will be 28 million tons by 1965–66. The Third Five-Year Plan envisages a rise in food grains output to 100 million tons in 1965–66 representing an increase of about 32 per cent over the level at the commencement of the Plan. The total available supply of food grains in 1960–61 including imports was about 78 million tons. If population increases by 10 per cent in the Third Plan period, the requirements of food would go up by about 8 million tons. It is estimated that income over the five years would increase by 34 per cent. If income elasticity of demand for food is assumed to be 0·7, income increase would necessitate an addition to food grains supply of the order of 23 million tons. Roughly then, supply would have to increase by 31 millions or reach the aggregate of about 110 million tons. This is higher than the target set in the Third Five-Year Plan. In order to attain this aggregate amount of food supply, the present rate of increase in output per year has to be substantially raised. And to the extent sufficient effort is not put forth, the gap between domestic supply and demand will remain and imports will continue, eating into the scarce foreign exchange resources of the country. Looking back at the actuals reached up to 1960-61, in the matter of domestic food production one cannot be very optimistic. The fact is that unless this drain is stopped, economic progress will have to be slow and halting. It may therefore be said that in respect of augmenting food supply, agriculture in India has not contributed to economic growth. On the other hand, deficiency in domestic supplies has operated as a drag on economic expansion.

Turning to industrial raw materials, we find that the achievement in

[36]Coale, A. J. and E. M. Hoover, *Population Growth and Economic Development in Low Income Countries*, Oxford, India, 1959, p. 128,

production so far is not encouraging. The output of both cotton and jute in 1960–61 failed to reach the targets. Thus against the estimated production of 5·5 million bales of cotton and 5 million bales of jute, the actual output in 1960–61 was 5·1 million bales and 4 million bales respectively. Over the five years, of the Second Plan the output of both averaged about 4·5 million bales each per year. The deficiency in domestic supplies has on the one hand adversely affected manufactures and on the other, necessitated large imports. The production of cotton textiles (cloth) increased from 4,658 million metres in 1955 to 4,862 million metres in 1957 but declined in subsequent years and was 4,616 million metres in 1960. Production of jute textiles (hessian and sacking) was 992,000 metric tons in 1955 and with some increase in 1956 and 1958, declined to 980,000 metric tons in 1960. The decline in the production of both cotton and jute was particularly sharp since 1958–59 and consequently imports rose from Rs. 283·5 million in 1958–59 in the case of raw cotton to Rs. 817·4 million in 1960–61, while in the case of raw jute, imports rose from Rs. 26·5 million to Rs. 76·4 million.

Since the scope for extension of the area under cultivation is limited in India (and even where it is possible, it would mean extension to marginal lands), increase in farm output has to depend largely on greater productivity per unit area as well as per worker. The contribution of agriculture to national savings and investment depends directly on productivity and level of consumption. In the last few years, the average yield of major crops per unit area has shown some improvement, but the progress made in India in this respect does not compare favourably with that in the Western countries. Taking all the major agricultural products, the rate of increase in yields per hectare in India has been about 1·7 per cent per annum as compared with 2 to 2·5 per cent in the majority of European countries.[37] Between 1949–53 and 1957–61 the yield per unit area of food crops improved, but commercial crops show only slight increases while in the case of some oil seeds and tobacco there is a decline. But as regards productivity of labour in the agricultural sector, there is little evidence to indicate improvement. In fact, superfluity of labour in relation to complementary resources in the rural areas rules out the possibility of any substantial rise in output per head. According to the findings of the Second All-India Agricultural Labour Enquiry (1956–57), agricultural labour constitutes 12 per cent of India's population and their per capita income declined from Rs. 104 in 1950–51 to Rs. 99·4 in 1956–57. The average per capita income for the economy as a whole in these years was Rs. 265·2 and Rs. 291·5 respectively. In other words, while the national per capita income increased by 10 per cent, per capita agricultural income declined by 5 per cent. It is therefore not possible to expect any net increase in rural savings. Nor has there been any marked change in the occupational pattern in India. And the observation made by the Planning Commission in

[37] *The Eastern Economist*, Annual Number, January 5, 1962, New Delhi, p. 114.

1956 still holds good. The fact that agriculture and allied pursuits continue to absorb about 70 per cent of the working force " means that the secondary and tertiary sectors have not grown rapidly enough to make an impact on the primary sector; nor has the primary sector itself thrown up surpluses which would create conditions favourable for expansion elsewhere " [38]

Mention may be made also of the fact that a decade of planned economic effort has not made any appreciable impact on the rural masses; besides, the technique of planning adopted in the rural sector as well as in the non-agricultural sector and the implementation of the programmes of development have not been without serious shortcomings. Referring to the achievements under planning in the rural sector, the Planning Commission has pointed out that both in the extension of irrigation works and in their use there have been avoidable delays, and greater benefit might have accrued to agriculture if the works had been taken up and executed more speedily. Similarly, the production of fertilizers in the first two Plan periods was not up to expectations and sufficient progress was not made in such lines as the adoption and popularization of improved seeds, use of organic and green manures, soil conservation, etc. Insufficient advancement in these directions has been attributed to administrative delays and failings, and lack of co-operation and participation of the agriculturists.[39]

POSSIBLE LINES OF IMPROVEMENT

What then are the ways of making agriculture contribute to economic development in a country like India? At the outset it should be stated that economic progress, whether it is in industry or in agriculture, depends on the availability of enterprising leaders. In an authoritarian economy this leadership is taken over by the state, but in a free enterprise economy, entrepreneurial skill and business initiative have to be forthcoming from the people; and where they are lacking, government policy should aim at creating circumstances favourable to the development of enterprise. Youngson points out that the remarkable progress of British agriculture in the 18th century was due largely to the emergence of large-scale land ownership. Although the enclosure movement, a favourable rise in wheat prices, and the closer contact with the outside world were factors conducive to the development of agriculture at this stage in British economic history, yet what mattered most was the availability of men with enterprise and financial resources who took up the agricultural business not as a way of life but as a means to gain social distinction. City men and manufacturers who had engaged themselves in trade had the means and an attitude towards land ownership which was commercial rather than feudal.[40]

[38] *The Second Five-Year Plan*, Planning Commission, Government of India, New Delhi, 1956, p. 12.
[39] *Third Five-Year Plan*, Planning Commission, Government of India, New Delhi, 1961, p. 303.
[40] Youngson, A. J., *Possibilities of Economic Progress*, Cambridge, 1959, pp. 119–24.

As a contrast, in contemporary underdeveloped countries a characteristic feature of the rural sector is the woeful scarcity of such men. The agricultural sector does not attract savings from outside, but instead, there is a flight of what little capital and what little talents that are available in the countryside to the urban centres. Writing about the Mediterranean countries, Professor Balogh mentions that in the tribal land holdings in Spain and Morocco to Iraq, Persia, etc. absence of enterprising land lords is conspicuous. The large landholder has little interest in improving the land, and investment is concentrated on crops or animals needing relatively little supervision and enabling the holder to absent himself for the maximum of time.[41] This is mostly true of the underdeveloped countries in the other parts of the world.

Undoubtedly, this attitude is due to a large extent to longstanding social and political factors. But if this is one of the causes of agricultural backwardness, it is necessary to bring about a change in the social system so that it would not permit the continuance of such a state of affairs. Two methods suggest themselves—first, abolition of absentee land ownership and introduction of peasant farming, and second, the creation of opportunities and incentives that would help the bigger land owners to become interested in agriculture and enable them to show enterprise in taking up agriculture as a business. Land reform measures which have been set on foot of late in many underdeveloped countries such as India, are directed towards the first alternative. But the progress of land reforms is slow and halting (unless when government is invested with or has assumed for itself dictatorial powers) and as such threatens to do more harm than good. Land reforms can be successful and help increased production only if they are comprehensive and thorough, implemented quickly and effectively, and what is more important, if they are of a sweeping nature, involving either transfer of land ownership to the state, or as in the case of India, introduction of co-operative farming which requires at least in the initial stages, considerable amount of organization and supervision to be done by the state. Obviously, such a policy can be successful only if the administration is highly efficient and the state is strong and capable of supplying in full measure the entrepreneurship that is required. Thus in Japan since the recent land reforms, the government's role in promoting agricultural productivity increased considerably because of the disappearance of the landlords who once undertook the responsibility for land improvement. However, even when successfully implemented, land reforms need not necessarily promote production. It is possible that to the extent land reform involves an assurance of minimum income and security of tenure, it may make people lazy. Moreover, in over-populated countries where land-labour ratio is low, that is, in countries which do not have enough land to satisfy the community's land hunger, land reforms cannot be considered as the ultimate measure in improving agriculture. The recent breaking up of the land in Yugoslavia did not help productivity. Hence

[41]Balogh, T., 'Agricultural and Economic Development—Linked Public Works,' *Oxford Economic Papers*, February, 1961, p. 29.

collectivization was resorted to, but collectivization also failed because there were too many people on too little land.[42] A mere change in ownership as Prof. Hoselitz points out, cannot lead to increased production if the size of the farm as an operative unit remains unchanged. A large extent of land may be transferred from an absentee landlord to an owner-cultivator. But if the unit of operation remains small, that is, if the pattern of cultivation is the same, then no great benefit can be expected from such transfer. In other words, productivity resulting from land reforms depends on whether or not such reforms result in a change in technology.[43] Nor should the fact be forgotten that land reforms can afford security of tenure only to the tenant, and do not solve the problem of the large number of landless labourers whose effort and work count in agricultural production as much as the enterprise of the land-owner. This would mean that in a country like India, where there is considerable under-employment in agriculture, land reform by itself will mean very little.

Attention should also be drawn to the fact that to the extent there is slackness in the implementation of land reforms, and to the extent government fails to take up the role of the enterprising landlord when once the reforms are effected, it is possible that far from increasing production, such measures would, by disrupting the existing pattern, (even when that pattern happens to be defective) affect productive effort adversely. In many countries, land reforms are undertaken more in the interests of social justice than of economic development as such. And influenced by political considerations, governments may enact programmes which they are unable to implement. The Tenancy Act in India is a case in point. In India, attempts of the government to regulate rents and to prevent the eviction of tenants have not been all successful. The slow progress in the implementation of land reforms in the country has been ascribed to the lack of faith and half-heartedness on the part of those who are responsible for implementation, and also to loopholes in the legislation which have been taken advantage of by the landlords. On the other hand, the piece-meal nature of the reforms and the long gap between the announcement of intention and actual legislation, have led to considerable social disruption in the villages. Fixation of land ceilings and other restrictions have led even well intentioned large land owners to lose the interest they had in agriculture.[44] In reality, much of the progress in agriculture has to depend on the enterprise of such people and hence in adopting measures of land reform, it is worthwhile to give full consideration to the possibility of such reforms dampening the enthusiasm of those landlords who are genuinely interested in the promotion of agriculture. The fact is that what may appear to be an act of social justice

[42]Bicanic, Rudolf, Discussion on Land Reforms. Problems of Economic growth. Report of a Seminar held in Tokyo; Office for Asian Affairs, Delhi, 1960, pp. 153–54.

[43]Hoselitz, Bert F., *ibid.*, p. 157.

[44]The Union Minister for Agriculture recently expressed the view that agrarian reform had generally done harm in many places. *The Hindu*, Madras, February 15, 1963.

may not always be the best from the point of view of economic development. If positive measures to induce the big farmers to put forth their maximum efforts are not possible, it would be advisable at least to avoid negative measures which would smother out even the little enterprise there is. It has also to be borne in mind that the major part of capital formation in the villages has to come from the bigger landlords. Their liquidation would mean that this source of savings is closed up. A recent investigation into capital formation in Uttar Pradesh in India reveals that capital formation is higher in the Block areas and in the case of larger holdings owned by larger income earners.[45]

A second means of promoting agricultural development is to bring about closer contact between the rural areas and the urbanized centres, between agriculture and industries. It is necessary that the spirit of business should be made to flow into agriculture if it is to be rejuvenated. As an economy progresses, villages are opened up to the impact of the towns and agriculture gets commercialized. This is important for the progress of both agriculture and industry, and it is proper that in a scheme of planned development this process is accelerated. There is considerable disparity in the standards of agricultural development not only between different countries, but also between different regions in the same country. Prof. Schultz points out that those areas in a country which are industrialized and urbanized become the spearheads of economic advancement and stimulate progress in the neighbouring regions. The absence of industrialized regions in the low income countries may therefore be regarded as one of the reasons for their agricultural backwardness. Hence diversification of industries and the scattered development of centres of economic growth would help agricultural progress in the underdeveloped countries.[46] A similar view is held by Prof. W. H. Nicholls. On the basis of research conducted recently in the Vanderbilt University, he makes the observation that " the labour, capital and product markets facing agriculture are relatively more efficient in local areas which have enjoyed considerable industrial urban development than in similar nearby areas which have not ". The development of urban centres gives a fillip to agricultural expansion in the surrounding regions by raising the cost of labour and thereby indirectly raising its productivity, by making available financial and capital resources and also by providing an expanding market for the products of the rural areas and thus creating an incentive on the part of the farmers to produce more. The conclusion is therefore drawn that industrial urban development offers the major hope for solving the problem of low agricultural productivity once the prior problems of an adequate food supply have been met; that, if it is not inconsistent with fundamental economies of location and scale, the more widely dispersed such industrial urban development, the more generally can agricultural productivity be increased; and that particularly for those areas which lack the attributes

[45]*Economic Bulletin for Asia and the Far East*, U.N., September, 1961, pp. 29–43.

[46]Schultz, T. W., *Economic Organisation of Agriculture*. McGraw-Hill, New York, 1953, pp. 279–300.

required for sound industrialization, public policy must provide for facilitating farm labour and farm capital mobility at rates far in excess of those which can be expected under complete laissez faire.[47]

This is a convincing plea for the diversification of industries in economically backward countries. Instead of concentrating large industrial projects in areas which are already advanced industrially, it would be a wise policy to draw up schemes for the starting of small industries in rural areas which have natural advantages for developing into towns. In a vast country like India where there are considerable regional differences. and where means of communications are better developed than in many other low income countries, this would be both necessary and feasible. The ideal principle that can be adopted in this connection is to integrate new industries with a rehabilitated agriculture. There is great scope in many of the underdeveloped countries for the processing of many agricultural products—sugar refining, production of canned food, manufacture of soaps, leather goods, cosmetics, etc. It would not be difficult in the case of such industries to adapt technology to local environments and resources so as to make the best use of the existing factor supply position. The Government of India have recently set on foot a scheme of this kind. In April, 1962, the Rural Industries Planning Committee was constituted with the purpose of working out a scheme for the intensive development of small industries in rural areas. The scheme drawn up by the Committee envisages the development of small industries of different kinds including village industries and especially of processing industries based on agriculture. The selection of industries is based on a careful survey of the needs, resources and possibilities of the area and with reference to the resources of material and skill which are locally available or could be easily developed in a short period.[48] However, if the thesis that urbanization helps in agricultural expansion of the surrounding regions is correct, the importance of building up urban centres in the regions where industries are started, should also be kept in view. Development of financial agencies and means of communication and the provision of facilities for the marketing of the products and employment of labour should form part of the scheme. In the present context in India, such a project of starting indus-

[47]Professor Nicholl's conclusions are based on the investigations of Anthony M. Tangs in the South Carolina, Georgia Piedmont region 'and of himself in the Upper East Tennessee Valley covering the years 1850–1950. See *American Economic Review, Papers and Proceedings*, May, 1960, p. 629, and ' Industrialization, Factor Markets and Agricultural Development,' *Journal of Political Economy*, August, 1961, pp. 319–40; also, Ruttan, W. Veron, ' The Potential in Rural Industrialization and Local Economic Development,' in *Agricultural Adjustment Problems in a Growing Economy*, Ed. by E. O. Heady and others, Iowa State College Press, 1958, pp. 186–92. In India the Rural Credit Survey Committee mention that the situations favourable for capital formation in the country appear to be either in regions or districts in which a generally high level of economic activity was attained or in districts or localities where owing to state initiative or otherwise, developmental activity in particular directions had been stimulated. *The All India Rural Credit Survey Report*, Vol. I, Part I, 1953, Reserve Bank of India, Bombay, pp. 728–29.

[48]*Indian Finance*, Calcutta, July 21, 1962, p. 109.

tries in rural areas would be advantageous, in so far as their capital needs will be limited and they are not likely to involve any expenditure of foreign exchange. Apart from this, the implementation of a comprehensive scheme involving not only starting of small industries but also urbanization would reduce the problem of seasonal unemployment, result in the production of new commodities, raise the level of incomes in rural areas, develop the skill, enterprise and intelligence of rural workers and create an interest in them for material well being and advancement. This sort of ' grass roots industrialization ',[49] may well pave the way for industrialization on a bigger scale.

In the ultimate analysis, the agricultural problem in a big underdeveloped country like India is essentially one of moving the millions. In one sense, the vast number of under-employed is practically the sole hidden asset of most underdeveloped countries. Economic growth depends on mobilizing this reserve and making as good an use as possible of this resource in building up the economy. Shortage of complementary resources in the form of capital is quite often mentioned as responsible for the state of under-employment. But as has been pointed out elsewhere in this book[50] the availability of opportunities of using man-power even without the assistance of any large amount of additional capital, makes this argument tenuous and weak. The desire for economic betterment should be created not only in the minds of big farmers, but should also be instilled in the mass of workers. Long years of poverty, ill health and exploitation may account for the apathy and listlessness of the rural masses. But unless this negative attitude to the problems of life is changed, no economic progress is possible. Absence of initiative and enterprise is reflected in the villagers continuing the same old methods of cultivation and depending on old types of implements and tools which their forefathers devised and handled. It is worth observing that addition to capital stock has to be measured not only in terms of number of equipments but also in terms of their quality. Investment in the form of an additional plough or spade if it is the duplication of an existing type can contribute only a little to aggregate production; but the same amount of money if used intelligently in fabricating an equipment of a newer type, better designed, easier to handle and more effective in use, would represent not only additional capital, but additional capital that would have a greater beneficial effect on production. It is such small changes that help in raising the efficiency and income-earning capacity of the individual cultivator. Obviously, such developments cannot be expected in a class of people who do not have the urge to improve.

The need for such an awakening has been increasingly felt in all the underdeveloped countries of the world today. In India, the National Extension Service and Community Development Projects have been started with a view to arouse this spirit among the villagers and to train them in co-operative effort.

[49]Aries, Robert S., ' Technical Co-operation with Underdeveloped Countries,' *Eastern Economist Pamphlets*, New Delhi, 1956, pp. 46–61.
[50]Chapter V, p. 176.

These programmes have given the villagers new helpers—the village level worker, the extension officers, the social education officer and the Block Development Officer—and above them a series of grades of officers in the States and at the Centre with a Minister at the top. To multiply the government staff in this manner would not lead to a rise in agricultural production unless there is an adequate response from the people for whom the schemes are intended; and that response would not be forthcoming unless the government agents working among them have the zeal, the enthusiasm, the drive and understanding of men and things. Such a spirit unfortunately, is quite often lacking and the officers, especially in the lower grades, plod on in the routine way as insignificant parts of a complicated machinery. The fact is that measures of socio-economic improvement like Co-operation and Community Development Projects are conceived from above and imposed on those below.

It is not therefore surprising that such well conceived measures fail to take roots in the rural social set up characterized by attitudes unfavourable to sustained effort. There is no denying the fact that in a situation like this, unless the governments take up the initiative, the obstacles cannot be got over. The loading of the government with additional responsibilities may thus seem justified. But what has to be stressed here is that when such a stupendous task is undertaken by the government, the success or failure of the scheme depends largely on the administration on which the responsibility of implementation devolves. If the administrative system is not efficient and the personnel is lacking in enthusiasm, the achievements can never be hoped to equal the cost. To a large extent, the very slow progress of co-operation in the last half a century or so and the fact that the Community Development scheme has not made much headway in spite of the laudable motives with which it was launched about a decade ago, have to be attributed to the human factor. Attempts to remodel the agricultural sector of the economy through the usual stereotyped measures, such as introduction of better methods of cultivation, better selection of seeds, popularizing the use of pesticides and fertilizers, introducing new tools and equipment, etc. assume the existence of an alert and quickly responsive rural community. But in the present economic and social set-up, unless the masses are stirred into activity these measures cannot achieve any significant results. More important than improving and remodelling the plough is the improving of the man behind the plough.

Chapter XV

INSTABILITY IN ECONOMIC GROWTH

IT IS a commonly observed fact in economic history that the national income of the advanced capitalist countries has not increased at a steady rate, but has grown by fits and starts. While various factors such as natural resources, enterprise and skill of the people, entrepreneurial talents, efficiency of government and administration have contributed to the growth of income, there have been at work certain forces peculiar to the free enterprise economic system which have held down progress at certain times and pushed up the rate of advance at other times. In the U.S.A., U.K. and countries of West Europe, economic as well as non-economic factors like agricultural development, founding of colonies, wars and extensive investment opportunities have ushered in long phases of economic growth covering a period of half a century or more. Thus in the U.S.A. three long waves of growth have been identified. The rapid economic expansion in that country between 1786 and 1842 was caused by a wave of innovations in cotton textiles, coal and iron, the construction of canals and road building and the wide-spread use of the steam engine. The second phase covering the years 1842–1898 was marked by increased railroad building activity and the development of the steel industry. The third period of growth, 1898–1953, was helped by the process of electrification, and the growth of the automobile and chemical industries. It may be presumed that in some of the contemporary underdeveloped countries, attainment of political independence, and their awakening to the need for rapid economic advancement, combined with the increasing interest taken by government in fostering economic growth have set in motion a long phase of economic expansion. However, in those countries which have passed through these long waves of progress and which have attained a pre-eminent position today, the periods of long-term growth have been punctuated by fluctuations and instability. In fact, cyclical fluctuation with a more-or-less regular periodicity have been a characteristic feature of their growth; hence, any proper explanation of the growth process should take into account both these aspects, namely, instability and long-term progress.

Such an examination is particularly relevant to the low income countries of today which are progressing under a system of private enterprise. We have to examine whether these economies are susceptible to such fluctuations; and if they are relatively free, why they are so; whether industrialization and increased investment activity would make the economies more unstable;

and whether any relaxation of their present ambitious programmes of investment would bring in a down trend. But before we examine the position and
problems of underdeveloped countries, it would be advantageous to review
briefly the recent explanations of instability in economic growth.

The periodic occurrence of booms and depressions engaged the attention
of the early economists. Leaving aside the theories which attributed business
fluctuations to extraneous natural forces—such as those of W.S. Jevons and
Henry Moore—most of the early explanations of economic instability were in
terms of over-investment in relation to the absorptive capacity of the economy.
It is usual to classify these theories differently as, under-consumption, monetary,
psychological theories, etc. but all these theories have stressed the fact that
instability arises because demand for goods and services sometimes fails to
keep pace with the rate of investment and increase in productive capacity.
And the difference in emphasis which these writers laid on the various aspects
of over-investment is the main basis of the classification of their theories.
According to some, over-investment was facilitated by the monetary mechanism,
especially expansion of credit; others considered over-investment to be caused
by non-monetary factors. Thus Schumpeter emphasized the role of entrepreneurs and their attitude to and outlook on business conditions as responsible
for over-expansion of productive capacity. Yet others attributed over-investment to purely psychological factors.

Hawtrey and Hayek laid stress on the role of money and credit in causing
business fluctuations. According to Hawtrey changes in money flow, the
expansion of credit and the lowering of interest rates brought about by the
central bank's policy, operate as an incentive for middlemen to build up inventories. This would result in increased investment in producers goods and rise
in prices. The straining of the credit mechanism would necessitate restrictive
credit policy which would bring in a decline in prices and a depression in
economic activity. Hayek distinguished between lower and higher stages of
production, the former representing production of consumer goods and the
latter investment goods. So long as savings are voluntary, a decrease in consumption and increase in savings would offset the increase in investment. But
easier credit policy and expansion of money supply would facilitate increased
investment in anticipation of savings. Inflation would result in forced savings
in the economy but the balance is tilted in favour of investment goods. Over-
investment causes decline in profits, rise in interest rates and brings about the
down turn. The process of contraction brought about in this manner would
end when once again borrowing becomes profitable. Baranowsky pointed out
that economic instability was characteristic of an exchange or money economy.
He argued that it was the money mechanism that helped in the transmission
of the forces of downtrend arising in any one of the sectors of the economy out
of over-production, to the other sectors. Arthur Spiethoff emphasized the
imbalance between materials and durable goods producing industries on the
one hand, and the consumer goods industries on the other, as a causal factor

in economic fluctuations. The primary impact of expansion is felt in the former category of industries. The relative shortage of consumer goods raises their prices initially. But in course of time, expansion of the investment sectors causes increased supply of consumer goods and precipitates a decline in their prices. When these prices have fallen sufficiently low, and the costs of production also have come down, it facilitates increased investment in the durable goods producing industries. The Swedish economist Gustav Cassel also assigned to over-investment in relation to savings, the key role in business fluctuations. Excess investment increases the supply of consumption goods which brings down their prices. Larger spendings on consumer goods reduce savings, raise interest rates and prevent investment from being maintained at a high level. The collapse of investment brings about downturn. According to D. H. Robertson, the fact that many investments are indivisible and involve a long gestation period, makes it difficult to adjust investment to the requirements and absorptive capacity of the economy. The possibility of over-investment because of this uncertainty is strengthened by monetary factors. Hobson and the under-consumptionists attributed to deficiency in consumption the occurrence of business cycles. In the opinion of these writers, the growing disparity in the distribution of incomes in a capitalistic economy has a depressing effect on the levels of consumption. The result is over-saving and the failure of consumption demand to absorb the increased output resulting from larger investments in the economy.

Since the basic factor responsible for fall in prices, profits and decline in the level of economic activity which characterize the downward phase and depression of a business cycle and the reverse trends in the upward phase and boom is the inadequacy or excess of demand in relation to supply, the stress which the above mentioned writers laid on investment is understandable. However, a deeper and more satisfactory analysis of the forces that operate in the course of cyclical fluctuations had to wait until the appearance of Keynesian Economics. The Keynesian analysis of under-employment equilibrium is essentially static, and Keynes did not put forward any complete theory of the business cycle. But his penetrating observations regarding the forces that determine the level of national income and employment, and the new concepts and tools of analysis which he introduced, have helped in a better understanding of the ills of a free enterprise capitalist economy and in the formulation of theories and the building of models of cyclical fluctuations and growth.

The Keynesian concepts of multiplier and accelerator form the basis of the modern theories of business fluctuations. At any point of time the aggregate income of an economy is equal to total consumption plus investment. Under conditions of full employment there is stability so long as the proportion between consumption output and investment output is the same as the proportion in which the community decides to divide its income between consumption and saving. Such a coincidence is however exceptional. In a free enterprise economy there can be equality between the two only if the motivation for savings and for investment comes from the same parties, that is, if private individuals as well as the business sector save with a view to investing.[1] If such a motivation is lacking as it normally happens, there is discrepancy between saving and investment which creates conditions of instability. If there is full employment in the investment sector but savings exceed investment, then the receipts of the entrepreneurs will decline and reduce the level of savings to that of investment. If unemployment starts in the consumption sector it would affect stability in the investment sector also. On the other hand, if investment exceeds savings under conditions of full employment, instability would take the form of inflation.

An increase in investment raises the level of income through the operation of the multiplier, the value of which depends on the marginal propensity to consume. The speed with which the increase in income is brought about depends on the value of the multiplier and the size of the increment in investment. But since the marginal propensity to consume is normally less than one, the increase in income brought about by the multiplier effect gradually declines and becomes zero. Thus if initial increase in investment, ΔI, is 100 and propensity to consume is 0·5, income increases in the following manner: $[1 + \frac{1}{2} + (\frac{1}{2}^2) + \ldots (\frac{1}{2}^n)]\Delta I$ to 200. If the additional investment of 100 is made in successive periods income steadily rises to 200 and remains at that level even when the additional investment is continued because during that time the level of savings also slowly rises to reach a new equilibrium level of 50 per cent, so that beyond that point of time further rise in income is not possible unless the rate of investment is further increased. However, the increase in income results not only from the multiplier directly, but also through the accelerator operating indirectly. A given increase in income calls forth further investment which in turn pushes up income. The total effect on income of a given increase in investment is the product of the combined action of the multiplier and accelerator. An increase in income in a given period raises both investment and consumption in a given proportion. Hence total investment and consumption is this increase brought about by increase in income and the previously existing amounts of consumption and investment. Thus income at a point of time $Y_t = C_t + I_t$. If a represents the proportion of the increase in income spent on consumption, and b represents the proportion of income spent on investment, total income in t, (Y_t), is made up of $a(Y_t - 1 - Y_0) + C_0$ and $b(Y_t - 1 - Y_0) + I_0$, i.e. $Y_t = (a+b) (Y_t - 1 - Y_0) + C_0 + I_0$. Numerically, if marginal propensity to consume is 0·6 and marginal propensity to invest is 0·15, the value of the accelerator-multiplier or super multiplier is $\frac{1}{1 - ·6 + ·15} = \frac{1}{\frac{1}{4}} = 4$. So long as the marginal propensity to consume and marginal propensity to invest are less than one, income will not rise or fall below certain levels. The increment in income as well as decrement in income

[1]Salant, Walter A., ' Saving. Investment and Stability.' *American Economic Review*, May, 1956, Proceedings Number, p. 93.

resulting from an increase or decline in investment will become progressively less and become zero. At the upper limit, savings rise and become equal to investment and at the lower limit, investment declines and becomes equal to savings.

The interaction of the multiplier and accelerator would thus lead to a cumulative upward or downward movement. However in actual fact, the effect on income of a net increase in investment is felt only after a time lag. Increase in investment in period one, raises income in period two, while the change in income in period two raises the level of investment in period three. The introduction of this time lag brings about cyclical fluctuations in the movement of income. Thus if additional expenditure in period one is 1, the marginal propensity to consume is 0·5, and the value of the accelerator is 1, i.e. an additional consumption of 1, calls forth an additional investment of 1, then aggregate income reaches 2·50 in period 3, declines to 1·875 in period 7, rises to 2·03125 in period 11 and remains around 2 after that. And Professor Samuelson has shown[2] that by changing the values of the multiplier and accelerator, considerable variations in the income effect can be observed. If high values are given to these (say, marginal propensity to consume 0·8 and accelerator 4·0) aggregate income expands explosively. With other values, cycles of considerable amplitude are generated.

It is thus seen that the operation of the multiplier and accelerator, provided they assume certain values, is capable of generating cyclical fluctuations. However such an explanation is not satisfactory because the model would show only that the mechanism of an advanced free enterprise economy is such that fluctuations would take place within certain limits and around a certain size of income and level of employment. To the extent that it fails to explain the phenomenon of economic growth in combination with cyclical fluctuations which characterise it, the analysis is essentially static.

On the basis of the interplay of accelerator and multiplier Harrod and Domar have analyzed the forces of instability in modern capitalist economies. Their models draw attention to the fact that the path of equilibrium in a dynamic process of growth is highly slippery; and deviation from it would set in operation, forces which would not help the economy to get back to the position of stability but would make it deviate further and further from the equilibrium path. Basically, stable rate of growth is one in which the rate of growth of output capacity is matched by a corresponding increase in effective demand. According to Harrod, savings are a function of income at a point of time while investment is a function of the increase in income. Given the value of the capital co-efficient, it is easy to know the extent to which income would increase because of a given rise in investment. Putting it the other way, a given increase in income necessitates a certain rate of increase in investment. So long as savings rise at a rate which is equal to the rate of increase in investment, there

[2]For the numerical illustration see, Samuelson, Paul A., *Readings in Business Cycle Theory* Blakiston, 1944, p. 266.

will be stability in the economy. But since rise in investment increases incomes, the stable growth of the latter calls for a steady increase in investment and savings. However expansion cannot continue indefinitely because of natural limitations such as population, resources, etc. When this limit is reached the rate of increase in investment cannot be maintained. But since this is necessary in order to maintain a steady growth of income, a fall in the rate of investment would bring down the rate of growth of income also and initiate a process of downward movement.[3] Domar arrives at the same conclusion.[4] He concentrates on the fact that an act of investment results at the same time in an increase in output capacity as well as in an increase in income. There can be stability in growth only when the rise in the level of effective demand brought about by increase in income is just matched by the growth of capacity output. Instability is thus explained in terms of the disparity between capital supply and the indirect demand for capital or the full utilization of capital resources. The supply of capital or increase in it is dependent on the rate of investment and the demand for capital comes from the level of income in the country. But the two are inter-dependent because investment increases income. Hence there will be stable growth if the rate of investment is such that the additional income generated is just enough to take care of the increased productive capacity resulting from increased investment. An excess of productive capacity over income generated, or demand, would bring about fall in prices and profits and a consequent decline in investment which would further lower demand and thus precipitate a cumulative downturn, while an excess of income over productive capacity will have the opposite effect. Thus in a capitalistic economy which is growing, a stable rate of growth can be maintained only by steadily increasing investment.

From this summary statement of Harrod's and Domar's account of economic instability it is clear that they arrived at basically the same conclusions although there is some difference in their approach to the problem. While Harrod attributes cumulative increase or decrease in income to the expectations of entrepreneurs regarding the prospects of investment in relation to the actual rate of growth, Domar emphasizes the role of disparity between spending power or income and the capacity of output in conditions of instability. In either case,

[3]A recent writer points out that the instability in Harrod's model is exaggerated. If his assumptions are relaxed so as to make them more realistic, the instability in the growth process will be less than made out of by Harrod. As against the assumption of Harrod, savings may change appreciably when income changes. While induced investment increases with increase in incomes, autonomous investment which is important, may move in such a manner as to offset the effects of induced investment. Lastly, the entrepreneur's decisions regarding investment are based not merely on the rate of increase of income in the past, but also on the future prospects as to whether the rise would be temporary or permanent. Neville, J. N., 'The Stability of Warranted Growth,' *Economic Record*, December, 1960, pp. 479–90.

[4]'Capital Expansion, Rate of Growth and Employment,' *Econometrica*, April, 1946, pp. 137–47. 'Expansion and Employment,' *The American Economic Review*, March, 1947, pp. 34–55. A brief account of the Harrod-Domar models of economic growth is given in Chapter II, pp. 45–51.

the tendency is for the economy to go further and further away from equilibrium when once it gets out of the track. While this is an adequate explanation of the inherent instability of a capitalist economy, it is obvious that the analysis is of little relevance to underdeveloped countries where entrepreneurial decisions are not so significant a factor in the determination of income as they are in advanced countries and where unemployment and decline in demand result not from excess capital capacity, but from excess labour supply and the scarcity of capital. The fact is that both Harrod and Domar had in mind present day advanced capitalist economies in their analysis of the problems of stable growth. This is explicitly stated by Harrod.[5] The relevance of these models to the advanced economies is obvious from the fact that capital is the main determinant of output in such countries with the workers attached to it. An increase in capital stock (or investment), has more familiar income effects (multiplier) than labour. Besides, idle capital inhibits further investment while the effects of unemployment of labour on the growth of the labour force are diffused, complex and usually lagged.[6] But apart from its inapplicability to underdeveloped countries, another limitation of the Harrod-Domar models is that the whole argument is based on the assumption of a rigid production function. In so far as there is flexibility in the production function, it would be possible to adapt methods of production to the actual resources position; if so, the consequences indicated in the model would not inevitably follow.[7]

It should further be observed that these models of growth are concerned primarily with the cumulative forces that lead to over-expansion or contraction of an economy because of disparity between savings and investment. Although Harrod speaks of a limit to the uptrend set by the natural rate of growth or the shortages of resources which would bring about a downtrend, and the requirements of basic investment which fix a lower limit, yet no theory of cyclical fluctuations can be deduced from the models. In other words, these models of growth explain the factors which make an economy stable or unstable in the process of growth and do not indicate the manner in which the long term uptrend in any economy is punctuated by periods of depression and expansion. There is no fusing of the forces that are responsible for both growth and fluctuations. What is required is a theory which in explaining the occurrence of cyclical fluctuations in income and employment, explains growth as well. A satisfactory theory of business fluctuations should explain not only the occurrence of cycles, but also their occurrence as part of the pattern of economic growth. Kaldor points out that the earlier models of trade cycle were static in the sense that they treated the fluctuations as movements around a stationary equilibrium. A proper theory of economic develop-

[5]Harrod, R. F., *Towards a Dynamic Economics*, Macmillan, London, 1954, p. 20.
[6]Domar, Evsey, in the *Quarterly Journal of Economics*, November, 1953, pp. 559–60.
[7]Pilvin, Harold, 'Full Capacity Vs Full Employment Growth,' *Quarterly Journal of Economics*, November, 1953, pp. 545–52. For a brief account of Mrs. Robinson's attempt to incorporate labour supply as a determinant of stability or instability see Chapter II, pp. 56–57.

ment according to him should be capable of deriving both trend and fluctuations as the resultant of the same set of influences.[8] Economic progress has been possible in spite of severe fluctuations because with every boom the economy reaches higher and higher levels, and capital formation in each successive boom period has far exceeded the net capital depletion in depression period. Hence the need of a type of analysis " which places long run tendencies in the centre and works the problem of business cycles into that theme " [9]

HICKS' MODEL OF THE TRADE CYCLE

Hicks' model of the trade cycle represents an important step towards integrating a theory of cyclical fluctuations with the factors of economic expansion. He bases his model on the concept of the saving investment relation, the acceleration principle and Harrod's notion of the cycle as a problem of an expanding economy. The process of expansion is explained in terms of the multiplier and accelerator which operate with a time lag. A distinction is drawn between autonomous investment and induced investment—the latter is a function of changes in the level of output and the former a function of the current levels of output. Under autonomous investment Hicks includes " public investment, investment which occurs in direct response to inventions and much of the ' long range ' investment (as Harrod calls it) which is only expected to pay for itself over a long period ".[10] Consumption function and investment function are both assumed to be constant. In the upswing of the cycle income rises as a result of the combined action of the multiplier and accelerator. The upper turning point of income is determined by the availability of resources like population, technology, capital stock, etc. The process of expansion hits against this ceiling and turns down or in some cases when the interaction of the multiplier and accelerator is not strong enough, the downtrend starts even before the ceiling is reached. The decline in investment in the downswing also operates cumulatively but the decline cannot continue indefinitely because of the lower limit which depends on the fact that gross investment cannot fall below zero, i.e. " disinvestment can be no larger than a failure to offset depreciation and the amount of capital stocks used up".[11] At the lower point, some basic investment for replacing inventories and equipment becomes necessary; the autonomous investment asserts itself at this stage and is higher than the amount of disinvestment. The increment of net investment causes an upturn of aggregate income. The magnified additions to consumption and income again take the economy along an upward phase.

Some of the assumptions on which the Hicksian theory of trade cycle is based have come in for a great deal of criticism. Firstly, it is pointed out that a

[8]Kaldor, N., *Essays on Economic Stability and Growth*, Duckworth, London, 1960, p. 194.
[9]Fellner, William, *Trend and Cycles in Economic Activity*, Henry Holt, New York, 1956, p. vi.
[10]Hicks, J. R., *A Contribution to the Theory of the Trade Cycle*, Oxford, 1950, p. 59.
[11]Lee, Maurice W., *Economic Fluctuations*, Richard Irwin, 1955, p. 413.

constant accelerator and multiplier assumed in the model is not realistic. A constant accelerator implies that the ratio of investment to an increase in output remains unaltered throughout the business cycle. The accelerator can be constant only if we assume that the output-capital ratio is determined by technical factors and cannot change. In reality, additional investment depends not only on the increase in output but also on other factors like the profitability of investment, availability of finance, the expectations of entrepreneurs, various indivisibilities in factor resources and investment and so on. In the course of an upswing or downswing the composition of investment undergoes marked changes. Normally, short term investments become attractive towards the ceiling of a cycle and long term investments become attractive as the downturn proceeds. Recent statistical findings relating to the behaviour of the accelerator have on the whole been, according to Eckaus,[12] unfavourable to the principle. He cites the investigations on the subject made by Simon Kuznets[13] and J. Tinbergen,[14] in support of this statement and stresses the need for taking into account the expectations of the entrepreneurs also in assigning a value to the accelerator. According to him a high value of the accelerator arising from a given increase in output alone may be offset by the unfavourable attitude or expectations of the entrepreneurs with the result that an element of stability or instability will be introduced into the system by forces other than the behaviour of the accelerator. Arthur Smithies questions the usefulness of the accelerator as an explanation of investment during either the upswing or downswing,[15] and Prof. Erik Lundberg speaks of the " curse of constant parameters in the mathematical and econometric systems "[16] and stresses the need for abandoning the assumptions of constancy in the accelerator if any realistic approach is to be made to the understanding of business cycle problems.

What is said about the accelerator applies also to the assumption of a constant value of the multiplier. It is not correct to assume that the relationship between savings and aggregate income is independent of the factors which influence the rate of investment.[17] In a period of boom and also in the upward phase of the cycle, larger profits of entrepreneurs bring about larger savings and reinvestment and the proportion of income saved will tend to rise with increase in incomes. The large variation in the total savings ratio due to the sharply fluctuating profits in the national income is borne out by empirical evidence. It thus

[12]Eckaus, R. S., ' The Acceleration Principle Reconsidered,' *Quarterly Journal of Economics*, May, 1953, p. 219.

[13]Kuznets, Simon, ' Relation between Capital Goods and Finished Products in the Business Cycle,' *Economic Essays in honour of W. C. Mitchell*, New York, 1935, pp. 211–67.

[14]Tinbergen, J., ' Statistical Evidence on the Acceleration Principle,' *Economica*, May, 1938, pp. 164–76.

[15]Smithies, A., ' Economic Fluctuations and Growth,' *Econometrica*, January, 1957, p. 5.

[16]Lundberg, Erik, ' The Stability of Economic Growth,' *International Economic Papers*, No. 8, 1958, p. 58.

[17]Duesenberry, J. B., *Business Cycles and Economic Growth*, McGraw-Hill, New York, 1958 pp. 44–46.

INSTABILITY IN ECONOMIC GROWTH

follows that if the accelerator and the multiplier are not constant as assumed by Hicks, they would not be able to produce the cycles in the manner indicated by him. In his model of business cycles Duesenberry gives low values to both the multiplier and accelerator. He feels that a 1 $ increase in income (capital stock being constant) will not raise investment to a greater extent than what will be saved out of the additional income. And this according to him is likely to be $ 0·25. Further, considering the fact that the marginal efficiency of capital falls as income increases, while the marginal cost of funds rises, the amount of additional investment caused by a given increase in income, would also be much lower than usually assumed. If low values are given to the accelerator and multiplier, the instability in the economic system will be less and both booms and depressions will be less pronounced, but would persist for a longer period.[18] Accordingly, the causes for fluctuations would have to be found in factors other than the automatic or endogenous forces of the system.

A second criticism of Hicks' model relates to the use of the floor and the ceiling which keep fluctuations within an upper and lower limit. Doubt is expressed as to whether depressions are brought about by resource limitations. At any rate, the upper limit does not adequately explain the onset of depression. It may play a part in checking growth but not in causing depressions. Duesenberry points out[19] that an examination of the 1953–54 recession in America does not show that ceilings can effectively cause depressions. Shortages of resources are not likely to cause a very large or sudden drop in investment. As an illustration, the causes of major depressions in the U.S.A. in the half century period of 1873 to 1921 are mentioned which do not include shortage of resources. Thus the decline in railroad construction in 1873 and 1883 brought on a severe depression in the first year and a mild one in 1883–85. Gold crisis and monetary and credit crisis of 1893 and 1907 were responsible for the downturns in these years while collapse of the speculative boom based on a wage price spiral accounted for the depression of 1920–21. Quite commonly, depression as has been admitted by Hicks himself, starts even before full employment of resources is reached. As Harrod remarks[20] this may be due to the temporary rise in the propensity to save above its normal level as a result of profit inflation. Decreasing mobility of labour, and shortages of specific types of capital as well as psychological factors manifesting themselves in the form of scepticism of businessmen at the top of the boom as to whether full utilization of increased capital factors would be possible, are other contributory factors which terminate boom before full employment ceiling is reached. It is also remarked that the maximum possible advance at full employment is less than that achieved during the movement towards full employment. This

[18]Duesenberry, J. B., *Business Cycles and Economic Growth*, McGraw-Hill, New York, 1958 pp. 197–98.

[19]Duesenberry, J. B., *ibid.*, pp. 278–82.

[20]Harrod, R. F., 'Domar and Dynamic Economics,' *Economic Journal*, September, 1959, pp. 460–62.

would mean that forces that help in the downtrend become active before the economy touches the limit of its resources. In fairness to Hicks it should however, be added that he was aware of this possibility and observed that these may be cases of ' weak cycles ' in which the endogenous forces of accelerator and multiplier are not strong enough to push income up to the level of the ceiling and as a result downturn may start before this point is reached.

The floor or the lower limit comes into play because there is a maximum possible rate of disinvestment in fixed equipment which prevents the downward movement from accelerating beyond a certain speed. Autonomous investment at the lower limit exerts an upward pressure which is stronger than the downward pressure of disinvestment, but the explanation of the lower turning point based on this principle is not convincing. And Harrod doubts whether autonomous investment is likely to be advancing at the bottom of the slump. Perhaps there is greater possibility that a depression would retard rather than encourage autonomous investment. In his study of American business cycles in the 19th century, Rendigs Fels points out that revival was not due to the wearing out of excess capacity and revival did not wait till induced investment was reduced to zero. Obviously, in some long term investments, such as the railways, the operation of these forces would necessarily take a much long time. In actual fact in many instances, expansion got up steam in spite of the existence of excess capacity. On the other hand, recovery can be due to the fact that different firms recede at different rates during the depression and some may even expand. In some firms disinvestment can be brought about quickly and in others slowly, with the result that before the bottom of the depression is touched, some firms would have disencumbered themselves of any redundancy of capital and would have started making fresh investments which sets in motion the forces of recovery.[21]

Critics of Hicks' theory also doubt whether a hard and fast line of distinction can be drawn between what are called autonomous investment and induced investment. In the short period every investment is autonomous and in the long period much of autonomous investment becomes induced. Induced investment is influenced by the rate at which production increases. But such investments need not necessarily follow immediately the improvement in output conditions. Thus investment in machinery and inventories is of the induced kind, but it is postponable and may be postponed and concentrated in certain phases of the cycle and as such would appear to have no relation to short term changes in production. It is also possible that of the same investment, as for example, in machinery, a part of the investment may be induced and a part may be of the autonomous kind. The usefulness and significance of this dichotomy is therefore questioned in empirical investigation as well as in the formulation of any theory.[22]

[21]Harrod, R. F., ' Notes on Trade Cycle Theory,' *Economic Journal*, June, 1951, pp. 266–67.
[22]Lundberg, Erik, ' The Stability of Economic Growth,' *International Economic Papers*, No. 8, 958, p. 60.

But more relevant for the present purpose is the consideration whether the theory of the trade cycle as formulated by Hicks succeeds in explaining cyclical fluctuations as part of and involved in the growth process. The operation of the accelerator and multiplier and the constraints set by natural resources and autonomous investment, produce the model of a cycle which appears attractive as a theoretical construction. But although Hicks set out with the prime objective of combining trends with cycles, yet no satisfactory explanation is made of how the forces which account for fluctuations also account for economic expansion. The accelerator by itself is weak to generate forces of growth. Hence those factors which are really behind expansion like technology, population growth, exploitation of natural resources, etc. are brought in in the form of autonomous investment. But the adding on of autonomous investment to induced investment in this manner contributes little to our understanding of the problem.[23] And Kaldor draws attention to the point that factors like technological development and population growth cannot by themselves bring about increased investment. In addition to the factors mentioned above, this depends on the attitudes and expectations of the entrepreneurs and unless the role of entrepreneurial expectations is brought into the picture, no complete impression can be had of the growth process.[24]

Recent theories of trade cycles which seek to explain cyclical fluctuations as part of or involved in the process of growth of a capitalist economy fall into two broad categories: (1) Endogenous models which attribute regular fluctuations that are neither explosive nor damped, to inherent forces brought into play by the peculiar behaviour of functions like savings and investment and (2) Exogenous models which consider that the inherent factors which account for fluctuations can produce only damped cycles but that in the actual world the influence of external factors aggravate the forces of instability and make the cycles persistent and sharp. The nature and magnitude of these external shocks determine the amplitude and duration of the fluctuations. Both these, however, rely on factors like population growth, technological development, entrepreneurial expectations etc. to explain economic growth. These external factors are superimposed on the models of business cycles so as to generate forces of growth along with that of instability.

THE ENDOGENOUS MODELS OF BUSINESS FLUCTUATIONS

Endogenous models of trade cycles are based on two important assumptions: firstly change in investment is influenced by current levels of income rather than by changes in the levels of income. In other words, the response of investment to variations of income depends not so much on the rate of increase or decrease in incomes as on the absolute levels of income at which the change

[23]Duesenberry, J. B., *Business Cycles and Economic Growth*, McGraw-Hill, New York, 1958, pp. 46–48.

[24]Kaldor, N., *Essays on Economic Stability and Growth*, Duckworth, London, 1960, p. 208.

takes place.[25] Secondly, apart from the influence of income levels, investment is also affected by the marginal productivity of the existing stock of capital and the level of profits.

Richard Goodwin, M. Kalecki and N. Kaldor explain cyclical fluctuations in incomes and economic activity in terms of the behaviour of certain important variables in the system. There is therefore a close similarity in the models of these writers. Kaldor's model of the trade cycle brings out clearly the basic assumptions underlying this family of theories and the operation of the forces that bring about fluctuations. He assumes that both the savings and investment functions are non-linear, i.e. the proportion of savings and investment to income does not remain constant at all levels of economic activity. At very high levels of income or economic activity, the investment curve gets flattened out because at that stage higher costs of construction and increasing difficulty of borrowing considerably restrict or slow down investment activity. At low levels of activity also investment is bound to be small because of the emergence of surplus capacity and the low levels of profits. However, investment at this level will not be zero because some amount of investment will at any rate be undertaken for long period development purposes which is independent of current activity. Thus the typical investment curve showing changes in investment at different levels of activity will be S shaped with both ends flattened out. On the other hand, the savings curve behaves in just the opposite manner. The decline in savings at very low levels of economic activity will be steep because when income is low, savings will be reduced drastically in order to maintain minimum levels of consumption, while in periods of high activity, savings would rise rapidly because of large profits and the transfer of incomes to people with high propensity to save. Savings curve will be therefore of an inverted S shape with both ends rising or falling sharply. Kaldor in his model of the trade cycle explains the phenomenon with non-linear savings and investment curves but the argument holds good even when one of these variables is assumed to be linear. It would be easier to illustrate the model with a non-linear investment function and a linear savings function as given on p. 507.

Of the three points of intersection of the S and I curves A, B, and C, point C represents an unstable position because above C investment exceeds savings so that if the level of activity exceeds C it will not return to C but move further and further away from it in the upward direction; on the other hand, if the level of activity falls below C, it would further move in the downward direction because below the point C, investment is less than savings. But the position at the points A and B are stable in so far as any departure from these points in either direction would force activity to return to the original position. Above A and B savings exceed investment, and below them investment exceeds savings. Hence a movement above or below A and B cannot be maintained.

However, the points A and B are stable only in the short period. This is so

[25]Tsiang, S. C., ' Accelerator Theory of the Firm and the Business Cycle,' *Quarterly Journal of Economics*, August, 1951, pp. 325–41.

because if the economy remains at these levels for some time, both S and I curves would shift their position for reasons mentioned above, namely, the tendency for savings to increase and investment to taper off at high levels, so that the S curve shifts further up and the I curve down while at the lower point A, after a time, the I curve moves up and the S curve declines further. This shifting of the two curves forces the level of activity to move up or down, thus bringing about a cyclical fluctuation. Thus at a high level of activity when because of limited fresh investment opportunities and shortage of resources investment slackens, and S rises because of increasing profits, the two curves would move in opposite directions making B a point of tangency (B_1). B_1 is unstable because

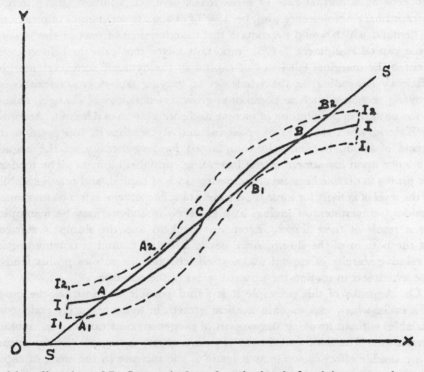

in either direction of B_1 S exceeds I, so that the level of activity comes down to the point A_1. But at the lower point the investment curve shifts upward and savings fall sharply so that a new point of tangency is reached at A_2. This point again is unstable in the upward direction because both below and above this point I exceeds S, so that the level of activity can only move up and reach B_2. Investment curve again falls and the process of decline and rise in the level of economic activity is repeated. It should be noted that in the above illustration S is assumed to be linear and not shifting. But with the S curve shifting in either direction at very high and very low levels of activity and with a non-linear shape which is more realistic, the process of expansion and contraction becomes more automatic.

As has been indicated above, theories of business cycles which attempt to explain the phenomenon of fluctuations in terms of inherent forces of instability are based on an important characteristic of the economic system namely the tendency for the rate of profits to decline with expansion in the stock of capital. This acts as a disincentive to further accumulation of capital and investment, and thus contributes to instability. In his model of the trade cycle Kalecki attaches great significance to the dampening effect of accumulated capital stocks at the top of the boom. The net addition to the stock of capital in a given period of time is the effect of gross additions made in the previous period minus depreciation and obsolescence. Obsolescence is ordinary when it proceeds as a normal rate of gross investment. In addition, there may be extraordinary obsolescence also, because of change in techniques of production or demand which would necessitate the abandonment of part or the whole of some capital equipment.[26] One important factor that calls forth fresh investment is the marginal efficiency of capital in the dynamic sense, i.e. marginal efficiency depending on the whole set of varying factors characteristic of a growing economy, such as population growth, technological changes, changes in the pattern of distribution of income and composition of demand. According to Kalecki when the level of economic activity reaches its top position in a period of boom, it cannot be maintained for long because of the negative influence upon investment of the increasing capital equipment. The tendency for profits to decline because of increasing stock of capital, and relative stability in the level of activity for some time, have a tangible adverse effect on investment. Besides, reinvestment of savings at high levels of activity may be incomplete. As a result of these forces, investment slackens and the slump is started.[27] At the bottom of the slump, since depreciation of capital is not made good, a relative scarcity of capital makes itself felt, and the rate of profits tends to rise which sets in motion the upward trend of the economy.

On the basis of this principle it is found possible to construct the model, of a cycle which can explain cyclical growth in terms of purely endogenous variables without invoking the support of exogenous constraints or autonomous investment. The basic constituent of such a theory is the fact that investment has a double effect in so far as it leads to the increase in the stock of capital which would have a depressive effect n further investment and therefore on further rise in income and also an opposite effect because it causes an increase in demand via increase in income. In other words, to the extent fresh investment raises the level of income and demand, it has an expansionary effect on income and activity but at the same time in so far as it adds to the stock of capital, it reduces the marginal efficiency of capital, lowers the rate of profits and thereby exerts a dampening effect on further investment and rise in

[26]Smithies, Arthur, 'Economic Fluctuations and Growth', *Econometrica*, January, 1957, p. 21.

[27]Kalecki, M., *Theory of Economic Dynamics*, Rinehart, New York, 1954, pp. 125–26. Kalecki however, recognizes the importance of shortages of equipment and labour also in bringing about a decline in investment. *ibid.*, p. 127.

incomes. The behaviour of income therefore depends on the relative pulls of these two opposing forces in the economy.

Hence the basic condition necessary for stable growth is that the rate of growth of capacity for producing output should be equal to the rate of increase in demand for output. As has been shown by Domar, the same factor, namely, investment is responsible for increasing output as well as in causing an increase in demand for output. The level of investment depends positively upon the previous period's income and negatively on the stock of capital in the previous period. In other words, investment is an increasing function of previous period's income and a decreasing function of previous period's capital stock. And it follows that investment would be increasing so long as the positive effect of income expansion is greater than the negative effect of capital accumulation. Investment brings about a change in income or effective demand through the usual multiplier. Starting from a position of equilibrium, there would be stability if the change in investment expressed as a proportion of the previous period's income is the same as the change in income, also expressed as a proportion of the income of the previous period. This would mean that stable growth or expansion is possible if, given a decrease or increase in demand, a corresponding change is brought about on the investment side. Any excess or deficiency in investment would raise or lower income cumulatively. But because of the effect of accumulating capital stock, the behaviour of investment will be such as to bring about an automatic reversal of the process of growth or decline in income. Thus when capital stock is inadequate, a rise in demand will accelerate investment and would lead to a rise in both income and capital stock. When the capital stock has increased and become excessive, its depressing effect on investment would exceed the accelerating effect of increasing income on investment, and thus bring down the rate of investment. After a stage, lower levels of investment would have brought down both income (or demand) as also capital stock available in the economy. When excess capacity is completely rundown, it would no longer have any depressing effect on investment. On the other hand, the need for maintaining basic capital equipment intact, would revive investment activity and raise the level of demand and move the economy upward until capital stock becomes once again excessive and exerts a downward pressure on investment. This explanation of cyclical fluctuations it is claimed, satisfies the requirements of growth also in so far as in every upward phase the level of income is raised and the economy gets used to the employment of larger capital equipment and to higher levels of production.[28] In other words, the point at which capital stock becomes excessive in relation to income and output, is steadily pushed forward.

Despite its theoretical attractiveness, the explanation of cyclical fluctuations in terms of variations in internal factors like savings and investment has come in for a good deal of criticism. Models of this kind are based on certain simpli-

[28]Kurihara, Kenneth K., 'An Endogenous Model of Cyclical Growth,' *Oxford Economic Papers*, October, 1960, pp. 243–46.

fied assumptions regarding the behaviour of the parameters, which are far from realistic. There is no uniformity in the pattern of different business cycles; each has a particular pattern in respect of timing, amplitude and duration, influenced by particular circumstances and as such generalization is not possible. Duesenberry remarks " the observed ' cycles ' cannot be accounted for by a mechanism which tends to produce the same sequence of events over and over again. The observed cycles differ not only in detail but also in the basic causal mechanisms behind them unless we describe that mechanism in the broadest and most general terms ".[29] Statistical economists are sceptical about the inherent power of purely economic factors to generate cycles and have also questioned whether there is a regular periodicity at all of cycles. And it appears that this question whether there is any regularity or not about business cycles can never be satisfactorily answered because present day economic policy seems to have succeeded in a large measure in controlling such fluctuations, so that the chances of booms and depressions to work themselves out are progressively becoming less and less.[30] Nor have the findings and conclusions of the endogenous theorists been satisfactorily confirmed by historical evidence. What has been stated in criticism of Hicks' model of the trade cycle, namely, that it depends on high values being assigned to the accelerator and multiplier is applicable to all endogenous models of this kind. To these factors should be added the consideration that the various lags in the system, in dividend payments, in investment decisions, in construction, in housing demand, etc. would further moderate the forces of instability. Not only is the pressure upward or downward of these forces not so great as often times assumed, but they take a much longer time to operate and to make themselves felt. All these points lead to the conclusion that the capitalist economic system in actual fact is much more stable than a simple multiplier accelerator model would suggest.

THE EXOGENOUS THEORY OF CYCLICAL FLUCTUATIONS

Difficulties like this have led to the view that the causes for cyclical fluctuations have to be found outside the system which occur at random and are erratic and cannot therefore be assigned a proper place in any theoretical model. The idea that the cyclical fluctuations in advanced capitalist economies may be due to erratic and uncorrelated shocks was first suggested by Ragnar Frisch in 1933.[31] In recent years, writings of economists like Fellner and Duesenberry[32]

---

[29]Duesenberry, J. B., *Business Cycles and Economic Growth*, McGraw-Hill, New York, 1958, p. 334.

[30]Robinson, J., *The Accumulation of Capital*, Macmillan, London, 1956, p. 212.

[31]Frisch, Ragnar, ' Propagation and Impulse Problems in Dynamic Economics,' *Economic Essays in honour of Gustav Cassel*, London, 1933, pp. 171-205.

[32]Duesenberry, J. B., *Business Cycles and Economic Growth*, McGraw-Hill, New York, 1958; Fellner, W., *Trends and Cycles in Economic Activity*, Henry Holt, New York, 1956; Adelman, Irma, ' Business Cycles, Endogenous or Stochastic,' *Economic Journal*, December. 1960, pp. 784-96.

reveal a return to and further elaboration of this point of view. The factors which these writers emphasize as those which make for economic expansion and contraction are of such a nature as to preclude them from being incorporated into any systematic model. Nevertheless, they are important from the point of view of cyclical fluctuations and their impact on the economic system is to be properly assessed. In general, two aspects of these exogenous theories stand out clearly. Firstly, they ascribe to certain structural or institutional factors the characteristic instability of the capitalist system. Secondly, they assume that although the capitalist system is unstable, endogenous factors by themselves are incapable of generating cyclical fluctuations of the nature and order observed in actual fact. It is the occurrence of external shocks that cause periodic rise and fall in incomes and levels of activity.

Stable growth is possible only if the technological and organizational improvements that are required are brought about without any friction. In other words, improvements are to be adapted to the availability of resources. Structural rigidities or institutional factors may stand in the way of mobilizing the resources and in adapting them to the requirements of the economy and thus hamper economic growth or make for instability. Thus the proper regulation of money supply and the credit mechanism is essential to ensure stability in income growth. This would mean that the credit system should be flexible enough to be adjusted to the requirements of reasonable price stability. According to this view, certain structural changes that took place in the American economy in the first quarter of the 20th century reduced the stability of the system and this was the reason why the depression of the 1930s was more severe than the earlier ones. For instance, the emergence of oligopolies represents a change in the market structure of the economy which has an aggravating effect on instability. This is because oligopolists have a greater incentive than the monopolists to replace equipment more quickly, to reduce costs and to improve their products; the fact that they have a lower risk discount and greater willingness to borrow than monopolists is conducive to greater capital intensity. The growing significance of investment in housing is another structural change that has affected investment activity. Investment in house construction generates cycles of its own which may sharpen the general cyclical fluctuations or dampen them. Apart from these, changes in the propensity to consume, dividend policy of business corporations, availability of credit, technological improvements, etc. all have an influence on general economic conditions and may pave the way for business cycles of different patterns and intensity. Among the structural factors that affected the stability of the American economy in the first quarter of the 20th century, the more significant were the decline in the importance of the growing sectors of the economy, slackening in investment activity in house construction, the decline in the rate of growth of population and the fact that the stock market crash of 1929 was different from the previous financial panics in so far as it had a more direct impact on consumption.

Structural changes would make an economy vulnerable to cyclical fluctuations but they may not produce directly or set in motion forces of instability of a cyclical type. This role, in exogenous theories is assigned to erratic or random stocks such as technological changes, political events which affect expectations of businessmen, changes in tastes, arbitrary changes in monetary and/or fiscal policy, shortages of capital goods or labour, security market speculation, etc. It may be due to the over-expansion of a particular industry or industries which would draw resources from other industries or sectors, raise prices and profits and further increase investment. The boom conditions then may spread to other industries as well, and when investment has been carried to extreme heights, rise in costs and the awareness on the part of entrepreneurs of over-investment and anticipated fall in profits would bring about a rapid decline in investment as well as incomes; over-optimism gives place to over-pessimism and precipitates depression. Revival according to this view is possible because of relative stability in consumption level, rise in the working force and possibilities of fresh innovations and of profits in other lines. Fall in costs and in interest rates because of the piling up of money with lending institutions provides additional incentives for fresh investments.[33] According to Duesenberry the upward movement in income and level of activity can be interrupted by the events listed above, which would prevent income from rising further and thereby cause capital stock to become relatively excessive, or shift the investment demand function downward in which case also income would fall. Either way, capital stock becomes too much in relation to income so that investment would decline bringing down income also in the usual cumulative manner. The downtrend may be accelerated by adverse expectations and declining security prices. Eventually, the investment demand function will shift upward when the original causes that brought about the decline are eliminated. And the revival may lead on to another boom if another set of favourable shocks appear. Fellner who has laid much stress on structural factors and institutional rigidities as factors of instability, feels that at the top of the expansion process, resource rigidities and the problem of reallocation of resources bring to a halt the uptrend. Thus the over-expansion of the capital goods sector in relation to the consumer goods sector necessitates a reallocation of resources which may not take place smoothly. Failure of the monetary mechanism to get adjusted to the new demand conditions may be an additional factor contributing to the downtrend. Revival according to him becomes possible when the structure of production gets rearranged. He believes that there is a latent demand for goods and services at profitable rates which may be submerged temporarily in a period of rapid change upward or downward but after a time when the mobility of resources is restored and structural changes are effected, this latent demand would assert itself and necessitate fresh investments.[34]

[33]Rostow, W. W., *The Process of Economic Growth*, Oxford, London, 1953, pp. 115–18.
[34]Fellner, William, *Trends and Cycles in Economic Activity*, Henry Holt, New York, 1956, pp. 304–06.

As has been observed already, the bringing in of qualitative factors, while giving a greater realistic colour to the analysis of business cycles, takes away the neatness which characterizes the endogenous theoretical models. The importance of the exogenous explanation consists in the fact that it is a corrective to the unrealistic assumptions underlying the endogenous theory. It is also worth noting that neither of these classes of theories is of the pure type. We have seen that even in those models which explain fluctuations in terms of fundamental factors like savings and investment, external causes like scarcity of resources at full employment are brought in to explain the upper limit, while the so-called exogenous theories depend upon the basic or minimum requirement of goods and services to explain the lower limit and upper turning point.

The defect with the mathematical endogenous models is that in making assumptions regarding the behaviour of the fundamental parameters, they assume away the realities of the situation. It is certainly incorrect to think that trends and cycles which are affected by economic as well as non-economic forces can be fitted into a theoretical scheme which requires quantitative assessment of the variables. To proceed on the basis that since by mathematically assigning certain values to the multiplier and accelerator, cycles of the required amplitude can be produced and hence those values are correct which simulate fluctuations of the pattern that is true to reality, amounts to sacrificing realism to theoretical perfection. By trying to fit the facts of economic life into the straight jacket of a mathematical formula, little is done to help in a clear understanding of the true nature of the factors underlying instability and causing cyclical fluctuations or in formulating policies that would control instability successfully.

FLUCTUATIONS AND LONG TERM GROWTH TRENDS

This inadequacy of the mathematical models is particularly pronounced in the matter of explaining trends. In taking up for analysis cyclical fluctuations and economic growth together, so as to find out the set of causal factors which account for both, attention is to be focussed on the fact that growth in income can occur along with fluctuations only if with every successive boom and depression both the tops of the boom and the bottom of depression reach higher and higher levels. This means that we have to examine the factors responsible for carrying booms to steadily increasing heights and the factors which prevent a depression from falling to as low a depth as the preceding one.

In this, the approach of the exogenous models seems to be helpful. In the absence of a rising trend, cyclical fluctuations would move round a stationary level. This however, is not what actually happens. Hence, the trend factors have to be introduced *ad hoc* and superimposed on the stationary model. These factors are therefore of a supplementary nature, are independent of the pure cycle theory and cannot be derived from it.[35] There are three basic factors which account for the uptrend. These are growth of population, improvement in technology and the role of the entrepreneur. In over-populated countries it may be questioned whether further growth in numbers would help economic advancement. But the fact is that although in such a situation a lower rate of growth of population or even a decline in it would accelerate economic progress, yet the very fact that population is growing, necessitates increased capital formation and output even if the existing standard of life is just to be maintained. Expressed differently, population growth implies (when per capita output is to be maintained) growth of aggregate output as well as of capital stock. At the same time, depletion of capital is likely to be less in depression when population is growing than when it is stationary or declining. If it is assumed that full employment output is attained in boom periods, the very fact that population is increasing, means that the level of full employment output will be rising with every successive boom. A growing population also necessitates increase in the required total capital stock. This means higher investment which would prolong the boom and shorten the period of slump.

Fellner points out that he basic problem involved in economic growth as the classical economists had shown, is to arrest the force of the Law of Diminishing Returns which otherwise would bring in the stationary state. This is only another way of saying that unless the productivity of the different factors of production is increased by means of technological development, the economy will get stagnated. In all advanced countries of the world, technological advancement has proceeded steadily over the centuries and this has been one of the basic reasons for their growth. It is true that progress in technology slackens in periods of depression but the trend is obviously upward so that the new technology that is devised and put into use when there is a high level of business activity, is of a better and more improved type than the technology in the previous boom. To technological advancement should be added improvements in organizational skill as an important factor accounting for the uptrend in the economy.

However, technological advancement while it fosters capital formation and economic growth, requires as a pre-condition, large investments in order to create the circumstances favourable to progress in technology. Herein lies the role of the entrepreneur in the free enterprise capitalist economy. The level of investment primarily depends on the expectations of businessmen regarding future demand and prospects of profits. From one point of view, all investment is an attempt to modify the existing capital stock in the direction of that which is appropriate not only to the current situation but also to what is expected in the future.[36] In other words, if an investment is to be undertaken,

[35]Pasinetti, Luigi, ' Cyclical Fluctuations and Economic Growth,' *Oxford Economic Papers*, June, 1960, p. 229.

[36]Gordon, R. A., ' Investment Behaviour and Business Cycles,' *Review of Economics and Statistics*, February, 1955, pp. 25–26.

there must be investment opportunities which of course depend on the growth of national income, on the possibilities of making a new product and putting it into the market, and also on the need for changing the composition of the stock of capital because of the emergence of new techniques of production. The entrepreneur is one who is capable of realizing and seizing the opportunities of profitable investment and who is responsible for making innovations in the business and commercial fields of activity. Innovations help economic growth in so far as they involve the application of improved methods of technology and an increase in the labour force. Since innovations and adoption of improved technology involve large financial investments, the effect would be an increase in output as well as a rise in the level of effective demand.

Writers like Kaldor, Kalecki and Goodwin emphasize the key role played by the entrepreneur in bringing about economic growth as well as cyclical fluctuations. The real cause of economic progress according to Kaldor is to be found in human attitudes to risk taking and money making. The upswing may take the economy up to the full employment level at which physical shortages deter further rise. But human ingenuity and enterprise often succeed in pushing up this ceiling further. Shortages of capital and other bottlenecks call into play the enterprise and skill of the true entrepreneurs who through innovations, adoption of improved technology, and through reallocation of resources find out ways of getting over the obstacles. In this process they raise the productive capacity of the economy and help it to reach higher levels of activity in each successive boom. And the very fact that a higher plateau is reached in a boom keeps the economy from falling into as low depths of depression as previously, with the result that the next upturn starts from a higher level. In this manner, the activity of entrepreneurs is largely responsible for bringing about the secular uptrend in an economy.

But if entrepreneurial activity in a capitalist economy is one of the major factors that help growth, it is also responsible for fluctuations in economic activity. Businessmen's attitudes and expectations affect the levels of investment. If they are reckless and quick to take risks there is likelihood of over-investment and over-expansion. On the other hand, if they are timid and conservative and are pessimistic regarding the prospects of business, they precipitate a downturn. In so far as innovations, technological development and investment opportunities open the way for increasing investment, any limitations in these agencies would bring about the reverse process. In view of the various social, technical and economic obstacles to invention and innovation, innovational investment also tends to be irregular.[37] The reduction in the pace of innovations will naturally have a deterrent effect on investment activity and may well be the initial cause to set the economy on its downward path. The exhaustion of investment opportunities at the top of a boom is assigned an important role in the downturn in Schumpeter's theory of business

[37]Hamberg, D., ' Investment and Saving in a Growing Economy,' *The Review of Economics and Statistics*, May. 1955, p. 199.

cycles. It is possible that if innovation continues strong, the expansion may be prolonged even if monetary stringency or full employment stands in the way. But in the course of the boom, innovation itself gets weakened because the available opportunities for making innovations get depleted. The very fact that there is a slackening in the rate of increase of output would squeeze out the incentive for making innovations. Furthermore, although innovational investment has a tendency to be postponed if general business conditions are not favourable, and get concentrated usually in boom periods, yet there is considerable disparity in the matter of such investment as between different industries. This disequilibrium arises from the fact that opportunities for innovation are different for different industries. Those industries which have benefited by innovations and technological advance are able to stand well the keen competition which ensues when there is relative narrowing of the market for output, while old firms lose business and are competed out of existence. Competition also brings about a rise in costs and fall in profits and leads to the liquidation of old and weak firms which bring down with them the better established ones also. Thus even as innovation and entrepreneurial activity help in taking the economy on the upward path, the slackening of the same forces brings about the downtrend.[38]

Given the basic factors responsible for economic growth as well as for instability, namely growth of population, technological development and entrepreneurial activity, we have to see the manner in which these factors help the economy to maintain its uptrend in the face of fluctuations. One obvious explanation is the improvement in labour productivity resulting from technological advance. Scientific progress which is continuous makes it possible to utilize resources more and more efficiently. During every boom, the new capital goods produced embody the latest improvements which increase the productivity per head of labour. And as the supply of labour itself increases with growth of population, the aggregate output goes up from boom to boom. Secondly, the obstacles to further expansion which confront the entrepreneur in boom periods, namely shortage of capital, labour and other resources, necessitate the adoption of new methods of production involving reallocation of resources and also the improvement in the resource position itself. Thus capital stock may be augmented, productivity per unit of capital may be raised, the quality of labour may be improved by better technical training, education and better organization, and social overheads may be expanded. In this way, the bottlenecks of production are ever widened so that in each boom period there is possibility of reaching the target of production of the previous boom more easily and surpassing it. Mrs. Robinson points out that if such widening of bottlenecks is not possible in a boom, fresh investment may not be made but new plants will be set up representing replacements. As a result, while net investments will be low, gross investments will be high. Since

[38]Fels, Rendigs, ' The Theory of Business Cycles,' *Quarterly Journal of Economics*, February, 1952, pp. 25–42.

net investment per annum is less, a longer time passes before excess capacity appears and the boom will last longer.

According to Mrs. Robinson, the behaviour of wages and prices in boom and depression periods also helps in the attainment of higher levels of income. In the downswing and when slump. is reached, prices fall more sharply than money wages and as a result, real wages will tend to be high. Thus employment of more labour is not attractive to the entrepreneur and idle capacity tends to increase. Since the output capacity increases in each boom period, the decline in the succeeding slump when it is of the same absolute magnitude as the preceding one brings about a greater volume of idle capacity in the consumption goods sector and a higher level of real wages. To the extent the disparity between wages and prices increases the losses of entrepreneurs, it would be in their interests to see that output does not run down so far, that is, idle capacity does not increase too much; as a result the low level equilibrium is reached at a higher rate of output. This would mean that competition makes it necessary that some of the additional capacity that has come into existence since the last slump, is utilized during the depression. Hence revival starts at a higher level of output.[39]

Another explanation for the long term trend in income in the upward direction over successive business cycles is given in terms of the ratchet effect of consumption and profits. Modigliani and Duesenberry have shown that consumption expenditure at any point of time is determined by the highest level attained previously. This would mean that if income decreases in one period, consumption expenditure does not fall, but tends to adhere as much as possible to the highest point reached before. The assumption here is, that when once consumption reaches a high level, the tendency for people is to consider it as the normal and standard one, so that they find it difficult to lower the level even when income does not warrant the maintenance of such a high level. Arthur Smithies is of the view that this stickiness of consumption expenditure is true of other forms of outlays and income. Thus the level of profits and investment by businessmen, and government expenditure are also influenced by this ratchet effect. The profit expectation of entrepreneurs is affected by the high levels attained in previous prosperity periods so that they cannot easily adjust themselves to the low levels in depression. Investment decisions are also influenced in this manner because businessmen estimate whether capacity is excessive or deficient with reference to the output which they regard as normal rather than to what it is in depression. This would mean that depletion of capital stock would not be allowed to go to extremes in slump because the decline in demand in the depression would not convince the businessmen that capital capacity is excessive in relation to long term demand. Rather they would be inclined to maintain capital at that level which was appropriate when demand was higher. The combined influence of the stickiness of consumption expenditure, profit levels and investment outlay

[39]Robinson, J., *The Accumulation of Capital*, Macmillan, London, 1956, p. 214.

would therefore prevent aggregate spending from falling in slump periods to the extent to which it declined in the preceding downturn. It thus follows that successive upswings starting from higher and higher levels of slump would push the economy to greater and greater heights in the following booms. Added to this factor are the basic ingredients of long term growth, namely, increasing population, technological development and innovations which make booms more and more pronounced and lengthened.

RELEVANCE OF BUSINESS CYCLE THEORIES TO UNDERDEVELOPED ECONOMIES

How far are these theories of business fluctuations relevant to underdeveloped countries? Do these theories provide us the means to understand better the conditions of instability in these countries? Or does the disparity in the standards of economic development reached by the low income countries as compared with the advanced ones call for a different explanation of instability in the former?

It may at the outset be stated that even in the advanced capitalist economies of today business cycles have lost much of their intensity and have given place to fits of mild recessions at certain times and increased levels of economic activity at other times. And this change has been brought about by a number of factors. Firstly, our knowledge of the functioning of the economic mechanism has increased vastly. There is today a much clearer perception of the role of key factors like consumption, investment and saving in the determination of aggregate income and levels of activity. Statistical data relating to these variables are more perfect and accurate. Studies relating to consumer behaviour and reaction to variations in income, the effects of public expenditure and borrowing and of the monetary and fiscal policy of the state, growth of population and changes in the age composition of population and the economic significance of variations in the distribution of income, all these have furnished a good stock of information which makes it possible to forecast more accurately the behaviour of the national economy in response to variations in these factors. This improved knowledge has undoubtedly helped in taking successful measures to prevent the occurrence of crisis or control them effectively when the first symptoms become known. Secondly, the economies of most countries have been increasingly planned and regulated. The rigidity of planning differs vastly between various countries according to their political systems and ideology, but even in free enterprise countries, the fact that government is interfering more and more in economic affairs with a view to ensure a stable rate of growth cannot be disputed. Restrictions on foreign trade, exchange rate manipulations, control and regulation of public expenditure, monetary policy and fiscal policy are some of the more important methods which aim at the objective of bringing about external and internal stability. The ideal breeding ground for business fluctuations is a highly industrialized free enterprise economy in whose affairs the government interferes little. In these days of economic planning such an ideal ground no longer exists.

Economic growth has also been attended with the emergence of a great number of built-in automatic stabilizers in the economy, which are capable of taking in the shocks incidental to economic growth and thereby immunizing the economy from major fluctuations. Mention may here be made of increased taxation and the mounting weight of budgetary expenditures. This would mean that a large portion of the national income is released as well as absorbed through government activity. In this sector, adjustment between outlay and income is easier than in the private sector where co-ordination in investment and expenditure policy is obviously difficult. Furthermore, the technique of controlling cyclical fluctuations through budgetary policy has been considerably improved upon in recent years. Apart from the fact that taxation and public expenditure can be designed with a view to control booms and depressions, the tendency for the receipts of certain taxes as for example, income-tax, to vary with variations in income, and the similar automatic adjustment of certain items of public expenditure to economic conditions have introduced a great element of stability in the modern economy. Even in the private sector, there is greater possibility of reducing the disparity between savings and investment because of the changes in the relative significance of different methods of financing. Higher corporate savings and increasing reliance of big business firms on self-financing of investment have strengthened the automatic stabilizers in this part of the national economy. With changes in the volume of investment becoming more closely associated with the volume of business saving, it has been possible to maintain a better balance between these two crucial forces which affect stability.

Fourthly, in recent years the level of investment in most of the countries, both developed and underdeveloped, has been maintained quite high. This upward trend has been more or less continuous with the result that even when symptoms of recession have appeared, forces of depression have not been able to make themselves really felt. Long term public investment has continued to lay claim to a considerably larger share of the national income than it was some twenty years ago. Although there was the fear of a possibility of depression in the after-war years in the U.S.A., no serious downtrend materialized thanks to accumulated investment needs, recurring export surpluses and high defence expenditure.[40] Lastly, it has been pointed out that developed economies have accumulated a large capital stock, so that any additions made to it form only a negligible proportion and their effect on the course of income would only be of a marginal nature. It would therefore appear that violent fluctuations of the type which occurred in the 19th century and in the 1930s in advanced countries like the United Kingdom and the U.S.A. have become probably a thing of the past. Sharp cyclical fluctuations of earlier years have

[40]Lundberg, Erik, ' The Stability of Economic Growth,' *International Economic Papers*, No. 8, 1958, p. 54.

not only been toned down to conditions of instability, but techniques are being evolved to control and eradicate even the remaining elements of fluctuations.

Economic fluctuations of the type and intensity which have occurred in advanced countries have not confronted the low income countries. Tinbergen notes that the structural characteristics of an economy have much to do with the type of business cycles which it generates. Of particular importance are the marginal propensity to consume and invest, the lag between income and consumption, the tendency towards speculation and the life time of capital goods. Even among developed economics, those which are more or less closed to external influences, like Germany and Japan in the interwar years, develop cycles of their own, which do not conform to the pattern of business fluctuations in other countries. It is obvious that in economies which are rigidly controlled and planned like that of Soviet Russia, any great disparity between outlay and demand or savings and investment is not likely to arise, and as such they are relatively free from instability of the nature common in free enterprise economies before the Second World War. Regarding the significance of structural differences, it is suggested that the short period of the American Cycle (the Kitchin) may be due to the shortness of the lag between income and expenditure in that country. It is also possible that the reduction in the average period of the business cycle in the U.S.A. in the course of the 19th century may be accounted for by the reduction in the average life time of machinery employed in production in that period.[41]

According to Simon Kuznets an economy should have four characteristics if business cycles are to occur. Firstly, it should have reached a high level in technical arts so that mankind can control natural calamities. Development of technical arts creates chances for instability in so far as it requires large investments in durable capital. Secondly, there should be the dominance of business enterprise as a unit of economic organization. In other words, a large proportion of the country's economic activity is to be guided by the pecuniary calculus and a search for profits by business enterprises resulting in increased competition among these enterprises. Thirdly, there should be a relatively free and peaceful state of economic relation among national units. This is necessary because only on this assumption can purely economic factors which generate instability be isolated and identified. Armed conflicts, wars and the threat of war would distort the economy and create conditions of instability, but these are not economic factors. Fourthly, the economy should be a diversified one and not a one-industry economy.[42] In brief, business cycles occur in economies which are industrialized and advanced and are of the capitalist, free enterprise type in which government's role is more or less passive.

Wesley C. Mitchell has shown that business cycles can occur only in those communities which have a distinctively modern type of economic organization

[41]Tinbergen, J. and J. J. Polak, *The Dynamics of Business Cycles*, Chicago, 1955, pp. 230–31.
[42]Kuznets, Simon, *Economic Change*, Norton, New York, 1955, pp. 125–32.

and in which economic activities have taken on the form of making and spending money. The evolution of a modern exchange economy is marked by the development of markets and big business firms, change in the form of business organizations, growth of joint stock corporations, emergence of organized financial institutions and money and investment markets. It is the development of these institutions which facilitates large-scale borrowing and the making of free and independent decisions with regard to investment; promotes exchange within the country as well as with other nations and also fosters a high degree of specialization in economic activities. Such developments while ensuring economic progress increase at the same time, the uncertainties and miscalculations in the matter of savings and investment and thereby make the economy more unstable. In support of this view, Professor Mitchell quotes Dr. Scott's study of British business records from the middle of the 16th century to 1720[43] and Dr. William Thorp's description of English crises from 1793 to 1925.[44] Dr. Scott's findings show that early economic crises in England were connected with natural calamities like famines and plague, and also with civil wars and high-handed acts of government. These obviously were merely periodic economic calamities and did not in any way partake of the nature of business cycles. In Dr. Thorp's study which relates to a later period, disasters of a non-business origin recede into the background and greater prominence is assumed by economic factors as agents of cyclical fluctuations. It is also seen in the annals prepared by the latter scholar, that in countries which were not economically advanced at the time he wrote, like China, India, Brazil, South Africa and Russia, the vicissitudes of economic life were not of a business character. However, even in these countries, those sectors of the economy which were open to the foreign markets, the export sector, were influenced by cyclical fluctuations occuring in advanced countries. It is therefore clear that unless an economy has developed to a certain stage it would not generate or experience cyclical fluctuations. Even in advanced countries, the impact of cycles is not uniformly felt in all the sectors; the better organized and leading industries like manufacturing, railroads, mining and construction work are most seriously affected by depression, while agriculture and retailing which are characterized by small scale organization and by the prominence of non-commercial aims feel the influence least.[45]

Some of the low income countries have made rapid economic progress in recent years and are on the way towards the attainment of the status of developed economies. Economic development in these countries has been attended with the emergence of the characteristics of a business economy according to Mitchell's interpretation of the term. Since the close of the Second World

[43]Scott, W. R., *The Constitution and Finance of English, Scottish and Irish Joint Stock Companies to 1720*, Vol. I, Cambridge, 1912.

[44]Thorp, W. L., *Business Annals*, National Bureau of Economic Research, 1926. Both quoted in Mitchell, Wesley C., *Business Cycles*, NBER, New York, 1927.

[45]Mitchell, Wesley C., *Business Cycles*, NBER, New York, 1927, p. 88.

War, the movement of these economics has been on the whole upward with temporary slackening of the rate of progress in certain years. Such setbacks have not induced any major recession, mostly because of the fact that investment in both the public and private sectors has been kept up at a high tempo. Large development expenditures by governments, deficit financing and ambitious industrialization programmes seem to have started a long phase of economic advancement in the contemporary underdeveloped countries. Inflationary pressures and high levels of effective demand and relative scarcity of consumer goods are symptomatic of the upward phase of a business cycle. This uptrend is likely to be continued for long because of the great interest taken by governments in bringing about rapid economic progress. So long as there is no slackening of the investment activity, this uptrend would persist and there is little chance of any depression or slump in the normal course of events. This has been the experience not only of underdeveloped countries like India but also of countries which are fairly well advanced like Sweden, Italy and Japan. Thus the slackening of business activity in the U.S.A. in 1948–49 did not affect Sweden. The recession after the Korean Boom in 1951 took the form of only a slight decline in the average annual rate of growth of national income. Similarly in Italy since 1947, the annual rate of growth of income has been 3·2 per cent while in the U.S.A. it has been 2·6 per cent. When industrial production fell by 5·9 per cent in the U.S.A. in 1949, there was no decline in Italy. The rate of growth of Gross National Product in Japan in 1948–49 was 4 per cent, but between 1952–54 and 1958–60 it was as high as 8·2 per cent. In all these three countries, governments' economic and fiscal policy and large investment expenditures in the public sector reduced instability and accelerated economic growth.[46]

The agricultural sector is susceptible to fluctuations of its own, and hence it may be expected that underdeveloped economies in which agriculture predominates would experience fluctuations of a pattern peculiar to themselves. It is also plausible to argue that the periodicity of output trends in the agricultural sector would influence the industrial sector as well. Such an influence may arise from the fact that the industrial sector has to depend for raw materials on agriculture and also because agriculture is responsible for more than half the aggregate income of these countries so that variations in output and price of agricultural commodities would directly affect the size and distribution of income of the country. It would thus appear that an increase in the supply of agricultural commodities owing to climatic factors or other reasons, if it results in a fall in prices, would be beneficial to industries which would increase their investments and expand; similarly, a rise in agricultural income would raise the level of effective demand in the economy and would have a general

[46]Lundberg, Erik, ' Stability Problems in the Scandinavian Countries in the Post-war Period,' Hildebrand, George H., ' Growth and Stability in the Post-war Italian Economy,' Tsuru, Shigeto, ' Growth and Stability of the Post-war Japanese Economy,' *The American Economic Review*, May, 1961, Papers and Proceedings.

exhilarating effect. Also, increased production of foodgrains and industrial raw materials would have a stimulating effect on industries engaged in the handling, stocking, transportation and sales of agricultural commodities.

Primarily then, the influence of agricultural conditions on general economic activity is great in low income countries because agriculture constitutes the major sector and is responsible for a large part of the national product. Yet, what happens in actual fact cannot be determined easily. It is pointed out that the low ratio of the costs of raw materials to total costs of industrial production reduces the influence of primary production on industries. In other words, a decrease in the price of raw materials does not sufficiently increase the margin of profits in the industrial sector. Furthermore, a fall in the price of industrial materials if it is likely to turn out to be temporary, would not be much of an incentive either to industries using the raw materials or to enterprises which are concerned with intermediary dealings, the transporting and otherwise handling of these commodities. However, it is likely that agricultural surpluses which occur periodically with a certain degree of regularity would foster investment in inventories of agricultural produce. If banks and other financial institutions help to finance such operations, the inventory accumulation habit is promoted so that in a period of boom in agriculture there is likely to be a rise in total monetary demand stemming from this activity. The reverse happens in periods of poor crops when there will be running down of inventories of foodgrains and industrial materials causing a decline in investments on a fairly extensive scale. In this manner cycles in agricultural production may have some effect in stimulating or discouraging general investment activity and may produce general minor cyclical fluctuations in the economy.[47]

Obviously, the effect of agricultural fluctuations on the general stability of the economy depends on the standard of development attained by the country. In particular, the effect of agricultural cycles depends largely on the degree of elasticity of output as well as of demand. Normally, it may be presumed that if agricultural income falls, it would affect adversely those industries supplying the needs of the farm population and would be beneficial to those meeting the requirements of the non-agricultural population. But to what extent agricultural income will be affected by variations in output depends on the degree of elasticity of demand for agricultural produce. Thus if elasticity of demand is great, any increase in production need not bring in a serious decline in prices and agricultural incomes. It should be remembered that income elasticity of demand of the producer for farm output is high in underdeveloped countries. It is likely therefore that when prices rise, the supply curve would turn backward as a result of the farm population consuming more of the output and releasing less for the market. On the other hand, in an industrial country since the elasticity of demand for food grains is low, a good harvest and increased supply of farm products would bring about a redistribution of real income which would have slightly deflationary effects. But in so far as agricultural

[47]Hamberg, D., *Business Cycles*, Macmillan, New York, 1951, pp. 280–91.

income is a small proportion of aggregate income in the developed countries, the over-all effect would be quite negligible. Besides, in advanced industrial countries like the U.S.A., government policies to stabilize agricultural prices and incomes have considerably reduced the chances of instability in the agricultural sector spreading to the other sectors and causing a general fluctuation.

It may therefore be said that although agriculture is not capable of generating any general cyclical fluctuations in industrial countries, it is undoubtedly a source of instability in underdeveloped countries. However, our knowledge relating to the role of the primary goods producing sector in this matter is limited. Studies of economic fluctuations have been done only against the background of industrial countries like England, Germany, France, the U.S.A., etc. But as Professor Simon Kuznets observes, it is necessary for a proper understanding of cyclical fluctuations to extend the study to the mercantilist period in Europe and also to countries which are economically backward and whose economic structure is altogether different from that of the industrial, high income countries.[48] It is reasonable to presume that in the developed countries at an early stage of their economic evolution, when agriculture was an important source of total income, the role of the agricultural sector in general instability was correspondingly great. A recent analysis of business cycles in the U.S.A. in the latter part of the 19th century (1865-1897) when there occurred six business cycles, shows that crop conditions exerted a powerful stimulus to recovery on three occasions. In 1879 and 1897 although the upturn had started before favourable crop conditions emerged, the latter gave a strong push to an expansion which might otherwise have been weak and slow.[49] And James Wilson, the English economist wrote in 1839 that price changes of wheat brought about by variations in output produced a constantly recurring cycle of production and prices and that agricultural cycles generated in this manner had important repercussions on other sectors of the economy also.[50]

Within the agricultural sector, the different crops experience cyclical phases of rise and decline in prices and income according to varying patterns. Thus apart from the wellknown Hog cycles which cover a period of three to four years, Tinbergen has noted cycles in coffee prices of about sixteen years in which prices and output vary in opposite directions, short cycles of about two years in cotton, and building cycles of sixteen years. In India, systematic minor fluctuations of three to four years and major cycles of about seven or eight years have been observed in agricultural production.[51] Cyclical fluctuations in the rural

[48]Kuznets, Simon, *Economic Change*, Norton, New York, 1955, pp. 142-43.

[49]Fels, Rendigs, *American Business Cycles, 1865-1897*, Chapel Hill, 1959, p. 220.

[50]Link, Robert G., *English Theories of Economic Fluctuations 1815-1848*, Columbia, 1959, pp. 104-05.

[51]Khan, Nasir Ahmad, *Problems of Growth of an Underdeveloped Economy*, Asia Publishing House, Bombay, 1961, pp. 55-78.

sector in India in the inter-war years illustrate the extent to which such changes can affect the general stability of an underdeveloped economy. Among particular crops, the periodicity of wheat and rice is seven to eight years, and of cotton, jute and oil seeds, eleven to twelve years; while in the case of industrial production, cotton and jute manufactures, pig iron, cement and paper—the period is roughly ten to eleven years. On the whole, the output variations of most of the food grains conform to the pattern of rice and wheat, but as regards industrial raw materials, the periodicity is similar to that of manufactures. Data relating to the inter-war years reveal two important points. In the first place, agricultural prices especially that of food grains moved in the reverse direction to output. Secondly, the wholesale prices of all commodities, agricultural as well as manufactured, show trends which are little in conformity with the trends in the prices of food grains. The pattern in production and prices in respect of rice and jute in India in the inter-war years is summarized below.

Years	Production Increase + Decrease −	Years	Change in price Increase + Decrease −
1918–22	—	1917–18	+
1922–24	+	1919–23	—
1924–29	—	1923–27	+
1929–33	+	1928–33	—
1933–37	—	1934–39	+

It may be seen that the periods in which production went up or down fit in more or less with the periods in which prices changed in the opposite direction. On the other hand, wholesale prices rose steadily from 1915 to 1920, (prices nearly doubled in these years) declined from 202 points in 1920 (Index number of wholesale prices Calcutta—Base, July, 1914=100) to 87 in 1933, and rose gradually to 108 in 1939 or by about 22 per cent. Movement in general prices reflects broadly the general business conditions, and in industrial countries like the United Kingdom and the U.S.A. conforms on the whole to the variations in business and economic conditions. The trends in production and prices of food grains in India between 1918 and 1939 would justify the inference that variations in prices were due to changes in output and not vice versa. It is not plausible to explain that changes in prices brought about changes in output, because response in agricultural production to variations in prices cannot be quick and marked as the data above would indicate, especially in a country like India where climatic conditions are still the deciding factor in agricultural output. The lack of correlation between agricultural prices and general prices makes it clear that the former did not in any way influence the latter. In other words, the cyclical fluctuations in prices and output in the rural sector moved in a pattern of its own, different from the general pattern of price trends in the country.

Apart from agricultural conditions at home, one important source of instability in many underdeveloped countries is external trade. Particularly in those primary producing countries which get a good part of their incomes out of exports of agricultural commodities and industrial raw materials, changes in levels of income and activity are mainly the effect of their contact with the economically advanced countries. Business cycles are transmitted from the richer industrial countries to low income countries via foreign trade. Obviously, the extent to which instability of this kind is caused in underdeveloped countries depends on the nature of the commodities which they export and the position of the importing countries in international trade. Thus if the demand for the underdeveloped country's exports is income elastic in the importing countries, and the supply of these commodities is relatively inelastic, instability will be greater in the exporting country when there is fluctuation in the income of the importing country. This is particularly relevant to low income countries which are exporting raw materials to advanced countries like the U.S.A. Because of the difference in the elasticity factors on the demand and supply side, terms of trade change against the exporting economy in a time of depression in the importing country. This affects export earnings and therefore the national income of the former countries. The larger the proportion of export earnings to national income, the greater obviously will be the effect on the economy concerned. As transmitters of external instability, industrial raw materials which are used for the production of capital goods are more powerful than agricultural goods. And this is clearly due to the fact that the demand for capital goods shows considerable variations over the different phases of a business cycle. The vulnerability of primary producers in this matter is well illustrated by the findings of a recent United Nations study of instability in the export markets of forty-seven underdeveloped countries in the years 1900–1950.[52]

Fluctuations in the value of Indian exports in the last ten years have been mild and in view of the fact that the value of exports forms only a small proportion—less than six per cent—of national product, the effect of exports on national income has been negligible. However, business conditions in foreign countries have much influenced the trend in our exports. As may be seen from Table 45 recessionary conditions in the U.S.A. in 1953 and 1957 caused an appreciable decline in Indian exports. Moreover, the relative immunity of national income from external instability seems to be a feature of only recent years. A study of economic fluctuations in India during the inter-war years[53] shows that in this period variation in export earnings was the main cause of fluctua-

[52]*Instability in Export Markets of Underdeveloped Countries*, U.N., 1952, pp. 3–7; see also Chapter XI, pp. 375 and 376 of the present volume.
[53]Rao, J. C., *A Study of Economic Fluctuations in India during the Inter-War Years, 1921–38*. Thesis submitted for the Ph.D. of the University of Bombay, 1961.

Table 45

NATIONAL INCOME AND VALUE OF EXPORTS IN INDIA 1951–61
(In Million Rupees)

Year	Value of Exports	National Income at Current Prices
1951–52	7,330	99,700
1952–53	5,770	98,200
1953–54	5,310	1,04,800
1954–55	5,930	96,100
1955–56	6,090	99,800
1956–57	6,200	1,13,100
1957–58	5,910	1,13,900
1958–59	5,590	1,26,000
1959–60	6,440	1,29,400*
1960–61	6,450	1,42,000†

*Revised; †Preliminary.

SOURCE: *Reports on Currency and Finance*, Reserve Bank of India, Bombay, and *Third Five-Year Plan*, Government of India, New Delhi.

tions in money incomes in the country. While 33 per cent of the food output in the country was marketed, the proportion in respect of commercial crops was 90 per cent. And of this a good part was exported. Hence their domestic prices were closely linked to international prices. The author of this study finds that while spurts in exports accounted for the revival in each of the three cycles in this period, the upper turning points coincided with sharp declines in the level of exports and he concludes that fluctuations in economic activity in India were dominated by export variations and were thus mainly exogenous in character.

It thus appears that trends in agricultural output and prices in the low income countries though they may be of a cyclical nature, get submerged in the instability caused by external factors. But even if the economy is a closed one, it is not likely that cyclical fluctuations arising in the agricultural sector would be able to start cumulative forces in the downward or upward direction in the economy as a whole. This is clearly because in these countries the industrial sector is also weak through which alone such magnifying effect can follow. Favourable climatic conditions would produce a bumper crop output. Assuming that a good part of increased production is brought into the market, it does not follow that money income of the agricultural class would increase to any substantial extent, because increase in the quantity marketed will be offset by decrease in price per unit of output. It is likely that demand from the industrial sector for both industrial raw materials and food grains would rise and prevent prices from falling as low as it otherwise would in the absence of an elastic demand. But a favourable effect like this depends on the size and absorptive capacity of the non-agricultural sector. On the other hand, when agricultural output falls, any appreciable price rise is prevented to the extent the industrial sector uses up stocked raw materials or resorts to importing of these goods. The result is that though prices rise to some extent, the rise will not be sufficient to offset the fall in production. Thus in the absence of a large and expanding industrial sector, the agricultural sector is deprived of maximum benefit in a period of good harvest, while in a bad season it is not saved from the adverse effect of a decline in output on its incomes.

The rise or fall in income in any sector of the economy can generate cumulative forces only via investment activity. It is here that the significance of a well developed industrial and business sector responsible for large investment outlays and savings becomes manifest. In an economy where capital goods are produced at home, an initial rise in income may necessitate increased investment in capital goods production with the result that income would rise in a cumulative fashion. The reverse happens in depression. Import of capital goods therefore constitutes a source of leakage in the flow of investment. This obviously is the reason why in underdeveloped countries fluctuations in the primary sector do not develop into general cycles. But whether manufactured at home or imported, an addition to the stock of capital goods represents capital formation; and a pre-condition for such outlays is that income increases sufficiently so that businessmen feel it worthwhile to increase investment in producer goods. If in boom periods more imports of machinery and capital goods are made, it is an indication that the initial increase in income is adequate enough to stimulate capital formation. However, facts relating to cyclical trends in India in the inter-war years show no such uniform relationship. Although during the cycle of 1928–33 import of capital goods varied with cyclical phases, this is not true of the cycle of 1921–26. The peak of this cycle was reached about the beginning of 1925. But throughout these five years or so, the import of capital goods declined, indicating that there was no capital formation in the economy. On the other hand when export earnings decline, domestic investment slackens.

Although underdeveloped countries are free from cyclical fluctuations of the amplitude and severity common in advanced countries because of the very fact that they are underdeveloped, yet the instability imported into these countries through their trade relations with advanced countries is vicious enough to seriously hamper their economic progress. The fluctuation in income brought about by changes in external demand for the products of these countries represents the direct effect of external instability. But in addition there is an indirect pressure exerted by this factor in the form of an adverse effect on domestic investment and utilization of productive capacity. Decline in export earnings lowers the level of domestic investment not only because income is decreased, but also because underdeveloped countries are depending on advanced countries for their capital equipment. To the extent their export earnings decline, their capacity to import these goods for investment purposes is reduced. Fall in the external offtake of some of the products of these countries brings about compulsory under-utilization of their major scarce factor, namely, capital goods. It is observed that in Latin America, the product per unit of capital fell sharply during the world crisis of the 1930s and rose again during the subsequent recovery. Similarly, the slight decline in economic activity in the years immediately before the Second World War brought about by fall in external demand, resulted in an under-utilization of capacity and a decline in the ratio of output to capital.[54] This underlines the need on the part of low income countries to have as their objectives in their programmes of development, not only the raising of aggregate and per capita incomes, but also the alleviating of the consequences of external instability as far as possible. One way of achieving this end is to adopt a compensatory fiscal policy involving the reduction of investments which have large import components in a period when export earnings contract, and increasing other investments with a low import co-efficient such as building construction. The deferred investments can be accelerated when the adverse phase of external factors has passed. In favourable periods when external resources are available to the extent required, the country may launch upon such programmes of investment which would transform the structure of its economy and facilitate future economic growth. Obviously, a regulated flow of international capital to fit in with the requirements of the capital importing country would be an additional important means of ensuring steady economic growth unimpaired by external instability.

We have already seen that in the post-war years in both developed and under-developed countries, the forces of instability have been held in check to a considerable extent by the large investment programmes undertaken in the private sector and also by governments. Such investment outlays which are largely deficit financed, maintain a high level of effective demand in the economy so that even when symptoms of recession occur, they are got over quickly. In most of the underdeveloped countries, demand has been running continuously at such high levels that external recessions show their effect only in the form of a temporary slackening in the rate of growth of their incomes. So long as the tempo of investment is maintained, the chances of a recession arising are considerably reduced. The question therefore arises whether it would be possible to keep up the rate of increase in investment continuously. In theory, a decline in the rate of investment would reduce incomes cumulatively and bring in a depression. It is even possible that the slackening of investment in one or a few sectors of the economy would have an adverse repercussion on other sectors and initiate a general downtrend. Thus a shift in government investment from one sector in which the capital-output ratio is high to another or other sectors where the capital-output relationship is different, many bring about a decline in prices and recessionary conditions. Or, the policy of the

[54]*Analyses and Projections of Economic Development, an Introduction to The Technique of Programming*, U.N., 1955, pp. 16–17.

government in respect of the private sector may bring about a fall in investment in particular lines in that sector. Inflation resulting from excess investment may bring about serious distortion of the distribution pattern and thereby cause a decline in demand for particular categories of goods and services. The only way of avoiding internal instability of this kind is to maintain a balance between savings and investment so as to keep inflationary pressures within bounds. It may however be hoped that with better understanding of the functioning of a free enterprise economy and of modern techniques of monetary and fiscal policy with which we are becoming increasingly conversant, it would be possible to keep the forces of instability under control.

Chapter XVI

THE ROLE OF GOVERNMENT

Two DISTINCT features are observable in the economic development of low income countries in recent years: one is the increasing role assumed by the state in initiating and fostering economic growth; the other is the adoption of planned programmes of development in nearly all the underdeveloped countries of the world. These trends naturally raise the following questions. What are the circumstances that led to and justify the interference of the state in economic activities ? Why has planning for development become necessary ? And how far has government's increasing interest in economic development and economic planning helped in the rapid progress of contemporary underdeveloped economies ? The present and the following chapters attempt to answer these questions in the order in which they have been stated.

THE NATURE OF GOVERNMENT INTERVENTION

Government activity in the economic sphere has increased both in advanced as well as underdeveloped economies. Obviously in socialist countries where the means of production are owned by the state. the state's role in the economic affairs of the country has become nearly all-comprehensive. But even in developed free enterprise countries, governments have taken at one stage or another, deliberate action to expand the technological and material bases of their economies. In a country like the U.S.A. which stands today as a classic example of free enterprise, nearly $\frac{4}{5}$ of the total output is produced by private enterprise; the great bulk of the national income is spent by individuals with comparatively little restriction; there is a great deal of freedom in the making of economic decisions and in the choice of occupations; the bulk of the property of all kinds is owned by individuals and there is also a great degree of freedom for workers. Nevertheless government's intervention in economic life has been necessitated in the interests of maintaining stability. As Steiner points out, in the past, social and economic equilibrium were sought to be reached by free market mechanism; but now through the inter-working of collective public action and individual action in the market place. The Federal Government of the U.S.A. prescribes rules of economic behaviour covering more and more economic activities in the country. It has extended its ownership and operation of productive facilities as well as its area of business management. Apart from this, the government takes interest in the direct and indirect control of prices, determines the distribution of goods and services in the economic system and by its monetary, fiscal and credit policies, influences powerfully the economic activity in the country. The growing influence of the government in economic life has naturally resulted in an increase in the proportion of national income which is re-routed through budgetary action.[1]

But, broadly speaking, while in the advanced free enterprise economies government's activity is mostly of a restrictive nature, in the low income countries of today, it is more of an assistive nature. The extent of government's influence in economic affairs is indicated by: (1) the claim of the public sector on the national wealth or resources such as man-power, and the stock of real capital; (2) the proportion of national income which is contributed by the public sector in the form of wages of all government employees and the profits of public corporations and also the share of national income absorbed by the state through taxation and borrowing; (3) the share of the public sector in the spending of the national income is also a good indicator of the relative importance of state activity in economic life. Statistical data relating to most of these items are meagre in underdeveloped countries and as such, these criteria have not much value in assessing the magnitude of influence exerted by governments in economic affairs. However, data showing the trend of income from public administration and defence in some countries of East Asia indicate the increase in the state's economic activity in the last few years. The proportion of income from public administration and defence constituted 7·6 per cent of total income in Burma in 1950 and rose to 10·6 per cent in 1958. In Cambodia the rise was from 6·5 per cent in 1951 to 12·7 per cent in 1957 and in Ceylon from 8·1 to 11·6 per cent in the same period. In India, Pakistan, Philippines and Thailand these percentages moved up from 4·5 to 5·9 per cent, 4·8 to 7·0 per cent, 6·5 to 7·9 per cent and 4·4 to 5·4 per cent respectively, between the years 1950 and 1958.[2]

Between 1950 and 1958, the proportion of government expenditure to gross national expenditure increased in the underdeveloped countries of East Asia from about 13 per cent to about 21 per cent.[3] There is however, considerable disparity in the rate of increase in this proportion. It is obvious that government's spending and hence the scope of government's influence in economic affairs depends on various factors like the economic ideology of the country, the scope and initiative of the private sector, the administrative efficiency of the government and its ability to mobilize resources, the type of investments required and the urgency for them, the attitude of the people and their co-operation and political security or insecurity at home and abroad. Thus as an

[1]Steiner, George A., *Government's Role in Economic Life*, McGraw-Hill, New York, 1953, pp. 236–41.

[2]*Economic Survey of Asia and the Far East*, U.N., 1960, p. 57.

[3]Includes the following countries—Burma, Ceylon, China (Mainland), India, Indonesia, Korea (Southern), Pakistan, Philippines, Thailand. *Economic Survey of Asia and the Far East*, U.N., 1960, p. 56, Table 17.

extreme case may be mentioned mainland China, where if the expenditure on ' co-operative ' and joint state private sectors is also included, the proportion of government expenditure to gross national expenditure would have increased to as much as 97·0 per cent in 1957. Among the other countries the rise is small in the case of Philippines, Indonesia and Thailand while in Burma the proportion nearly doubled; in Ceylon, India and Pakistan the rise was about 75 per cent.

It is important to observe that much of this rise in government expenditure was due to the increasing interest taken by governments in economic development. A review of the rapidly rising public outlay on developmental schemes in recent years in some of the Asian countries brings to light three important aspects of the trend: firstly, investment outlay of the government as a proportion of the national product has increased; secondly, the share of public investment in aggregate national investment has gone up, that is to say, the ratio of public investment to private investment has steadily risen; thirdly, government investment expenditure as a proportion of total government expenditure has also increased. This is shown in Table 46.

Table 46

SHARE OF PUBLIC INVESTMENT IN ECAFE COUNTRIES 1950–58

Country	Public Investment					
	as per cent of Gross National Product		as per cent of national investment		as per cent of total government expenditure	
	1950	1958	1950	1958	1950	1958
Afghanistan	...	...	...	...	41	46 (1956)
Burma	3·5	10·4	34	48	23	37
Ceylon	6·3	8·4	72	70	33	33
China (Mainland)	2·4	17·1	...	100	15	52
Federation of Malaya	1·9	3·3 (1957)	38	28	13	24
India	2·7	7·1	60	71	29	43
Indonesia	2·7 (1951)	1·7	28	37	17 (1951)	9
Japan	8·8	11·0	54	41	37	42
Pakistan	1·7	4·8	...	...	17	31
Philippines	3·2	2·1	44	26	29	18
Thailand	2·1	3·2	...	...	20	23

SOURCE: Abstracted from Tables 24 and 25 in *Economic Survey of Asia and the Far East*, U.N., 1960, pp. 71 and 72.

On the whole, in most of these countries, government investment as a ratio of GNP has gone up. But excepting China, where there has been a spectacular rise from 2·4 per cent of GNP in 1950 to 17·1 per cent in 1958 and a steady increase from 2·7 per cent to 7·1 per cent in India, the rates of the other countries show considerable fluctuations. Over the years the percentage of government investment to GNP averaged about 10 per cent in Japan, 2·7 per cent in Philippines, 7 per cent in Ceylon and about 9 per cent in Burma. Excepting China, where the structure and organization of the government is distinct from the rest of the countries, in India alone is it possible to observe a deliberate drive to increase public investment with a view to bring about rapid economic development of the country. Between 1950 and 1957 there was almost a three-fold growth (at constant prices) of the net capital formation out of the budgetary resources of the Central and state governments in India. Public investment on development projects in the First Plan amounted to Rs. 15·6 billion, and increased to Rs. 36·5 billion in the Second Five-Year Plan period, representing a rise from about 3 per cent of national income to a little less than 6 per cent. Public investment in the Third Five-Year Plan is estimated at Rs. 63 billion.

Not only has public investment as a share of gross national product gone up, but there has also been an increase in the proportion of government investment to aggregate investment of the economy. The elimination of private investment in China resulted in the state becoming responsible for 100 per cent of the total investment in 1958. There has been substantial increase in this ratio in the other countries of the region. Government investment formed 46 per cent of total investment in India in the years 1951–56 but rose to 54 per cent in the Second Plan period and is expected to go up to 60 per cent in the Third Plan. Between 1950 and 1958, this proportion rose from 34 to 48 per cent in Burma, and from 28 to 37 per cent in Indonesia. In Ceylon, there is a slight fall from 72 to 70 per cent while in Japan and Philippines there is a marked decrease from 54 to 41 per cent and from 44 to 26 per cent respectively. The trend in this ratio reflects broadly the role assumed by the respective governments in economic development and the scope of expansion allowed for private investment. It is worth noting that there is an appreciable difference in this respect between the advanced capitalist economies and the less developed countries. Thus in 1950, in the United Kingdom, out of the total national product, 3 per cent went into capital formation in the public sector and 14 per cent in the private sector. In Denmark it was 4·3 and 20·6 per cent, in Finland 5·2 and 25·2 per cent, in France 1·2 and 11·2 per cent and in New Zealand 7·7 and 18·2 per cent. In general, while in the Western industrial countries, public investment formed between one-fifth and two-fifth of total national investment, in Asia it ranged from about one-fourth to over two-third. The larger and increasing proportion of public investment to total national investment in the newly developing countries is understandable in view of the fact

Economic Survey of Asia and the Far East, U.N., 1960, p. 71.

that growth in these countries is not a spontaneous but an engineered one, and in which the nature of investment required for promoting growth is such that an acceleration in the rate of investment in the initial stages at least, has to be brought about by state enterprise.

As a proportion of total government outlay also, public investment has tended to increase. Investment expenditure formed 29 per cent of aggregate outlay of the government in India in 1950; it rose to 43 per cent in 1958. On the whole in the Asian countries, the share of investment in total government expenditure varied between 20 and 40 per cent. Owing to budgetary and other difficulties, government investment outlay in Indonesia came down from 17 per cent in 1951 to 9 per cent in 1958. But in the other countries where the proportion is low as in the Philippines and Thailand, the explanation is to be found in the fact that these countries share the outlook that " the private sector could be relied upon to bring about a more efficient utilisation of national resources than the public sector ".[5]

CAUSES FOR THE EXPANSION OF GOVERNMENT'S ROLE

Many factors have helped this trend. Even in countries which have long been the stronghold of free enterprise, experience has shown that the basic assumptions underlying the laissez faire principle do not hold good in practice and as such an increasing dilution of this ideal has been found necessary to make the capitalist free enterprise system workable. The tendency towards the formation of monopolistic organizations under the free enterprise system, the unpreparedness and reluctance on the part of private entrepreneurs to make investments in schemes of collective value, the lack of attention to the long run problems of the economy and too much concentration on the immediate prospects of profits, the absence of integration among the various sectors of the economy and the possibility of adverse economic results arising from uncoordinated economic decisions, constitute the major defects of the private enterprise system.[6] In general, these deficiencies of private enterprise manifest themselves in the form of a discrepancy between the point at which the marginal social benefit of an economic policy or decision approximates its marginal social cost and the point at which the marginal private benefit of such policy approximates its marginal private cost.[7] In other words, economic decisions of private entrepreneurs relating to investment in particular directions or on the scale of operations, while bringing about the maximum net returns from the point of view of the individual investor, need not necessarily maximize social benefit.

[5]ibid., p. 73.

[6]Finer, Herman, 'The Role of Government,' *Economic Development: Principles and Patterns*, Williamson, H. F. and J. A. Buttrick, Eds., New York, 1954, p. 369.

[7]Spengler, Joseph J., 'The Social Structure, the State and Economic Growth,' *Economic Growth: Brazil, India, Japan*, Kuznets, Simon, Wilbert E. Moore and Joseph J. Spengler, Eds., Duke, 1955, p. 371.

The depression of the 1930s brought to the fore the inherent instability of the capitalist economic system and Keynes' writings in the latter years of that decade focussed attention on the need for state interference in investment activities to compensate for the deficiency of investment in the private sector and as a means to promote stability in the capitalist system. More recently, the outbreak of the Second World War and the increasing role thrust upon governments in directing and regulating the economy brought into relief the capacity of the state in organizing economic activity in an efficient manner when circumstances demanded it. It should also be observed that the efficiency of the administrative machinery has steadily improved over the years so that modern governments are capable of tackling much more complicated problems than could have been thought of a hundred years ago. As Hanson observes, the extent to which government will be permitted to widen its scope of activity in a democratic set-up depends on the issue whether the state is competent enough to carry out the functions assigned to it. According to him, Adam Smith and the other early economists adhered to laissez faire largely because the governments of their day were notoriously inefficient and corrupt.[3] Since the techniques of administration have improved vastly, governments have become more and more confident to take upon themselves added responsibilities in the economic as well as in the political sphere.

But while in advanced economies government interventionism emerged as a therapeutic to capitalist crises, in the underdeveloped countries the state has increased its economic powers because of the exigencies of underdevelopment. After the close of the Second World War, many small countries which had for long been colonies or dependencies of the major powers of the West, regained their political freedom. In South-East Asia, twelve countries and territories Burma, Cambodia, Ceylon, Federation of Malaya, India, Indonesia, Korea, Laos, Pakistan, Philippines, Singapore and Viet-Nam—attained independent political status. Political liberation opened the eyes of the many small nations to the wide gulf between the standards of economic development attained by them and by the advanced nations of the West, and strong nationalist feelings, once directed to the attainment of political liberty were now concentrated on the problem of securing economic liberty as well. The spirit of economic nationalism and the imbibing of the social philosophy of the welfare state by the intelligentsia of these countries favoured the conferment of the necessary powers on the government to enable it to bring about social and economic changes. The governments of these countries have therefore assumed the role of the entrepreneur and have directed attention to the problems of reorganization of agriculture, development of basic industries and the provision of economic and social overheads which are the basic prerequisites of economic growth.

The main justification for the increasing role of the government in economic activities in contemporary low income countries, has therefore to be found in

[3]Hanson, A. H., *Public Enterprise and Economic Development*, Routledge and Kegan Paul, London, 1959, p. 203,

the fact that the economic circumstances in these countries are such as to require the government to do certain things which were done by private entrepreneurs in the present day advanced economies at a corresponding stage in their economic evolution. The various obstacles to economic growth which the underdeveloped countries face have been discussed at some length in the earlier chapters of this volume. We have here to recapitulate and summarize some of these points in order to focus attention on what the state can do to overcome them.

Even in the developed economies state interference becomes necessary in a period of shortage and scarcity as in war. Scarcity of resources is a chronic feature of underdeveloped economies and the disadvantages of state management and control of the economy are tolerated in view of the offsetting effects of such activity against the wastages inherent in the free enterprise mechanism. Such wastages appear to be of minor significance when the resources are abundant, but not so when they are meagre. This explains why collectivism has appeared attractive to underdeveloped countries and why it first developed in such countries.[9] The scarcity of resources combined with various social and economic rigidities makes spontaneous growth impossible in the low income countries. Thus in underdeveloped countries, the conscious direction of economic affairs by government agencies is, as Arthur Lewis points out, at the same time much more necessary and much more difficult to execute than in advanced countries.[10]

Despite its limitations, the fact that private enterprise contributed significantly to the economic development of the Western powers in the 18th and 19th centuries is beyond dispute. The spontaneous nature of growth in these countries was due to the emergence of a wealthy and industrious entrepreneurial class. The building up of a solid base of pre-industrial wealth in the Western countries through foreign trade, colonial expansion and slave trade, and large returns from foreign investments helped the development of technology and promoted industrialization. The accumulation of large profits and reinvestments ensured rapid economic growth without much assistance from the state. But the position of present day pre-industrial countries is very much different. Production in these countries is lopsided, with undue predominance of agriculture and a very narrow industrial sector. Low incomes and savings, the low level of technology, and the lack of enterprise, constitute a vicious circle in economic life. Political dependency and foreign exploitation for long, have sapped the resources of the economy and the spirit of the people and their desire for economic improvement. The type of industrial development and the improvement in means of communication that took place under colonial regime did not help in the accumulation of industrial wealth. Current profits have tended to be dissipated in conspicuous consumption and the investment

[9]Mendes-France, Pierre, and Gabriel Ardant, *Economics of Action*, Heinemann, London, 1955, p. 200.

[10]Lewis, Arthur, *The Principles of Economic Planning*, Allen and Unwin, London, 1949, p. 121.

habits that have developed are of a nature, not helpful to rapid economic development. Savings are diverted into investment in real estate and in commercial and speculative ventures. The community combines a low propensity to save with an even smaller willingness to invest in productive enterprises. The profits earned by the foreign capitalists by their investments in extractive industries went to the metropolitan powers. On the other hand, the competition of imported machine products prevented the development of domestic industries and the formation of capital from pre-industrial manufacturing.

The fact that political revolution has preceded economic revolution in the underdeveloped countries has presented another difficulty in capital accumulation. The share of labour has started to increase before the industrial revolution was completed. There is certainly justification for the adoption of measures which would bring about social and economic equality and ensure public co-operation in productive effort. In developed countries the adoption of welfare state policy has reduced inequalities, but coming at a stage when industrialization had highly advanced and national per capita incomes had risen markedly, egalitarian measures only strengthened the economic system and conduced to stability and greater effort. But in the initial period of rapid industrialization, inequalities continued and such inequalities constituted a source of large industrial savings, wages being low, and facilitated rapid capital accumulation. In contrast to this, in the underdeveloped countries of today, egalitarian measures would only result in the equitable distribution of poverty. To be really beneficial such measures have to be preceded by accumulation of wealth.[11] Only then, can better distribution be expected to achieve the economic objective of increased productive effort. This problem can be solved only if government directs its attention on both the fronts—namely, economic development and accumulation of capital on the one hand, and better distribution of wealth and incomes on the other.

Not only is a large effort required in the underdeveloped countries to generate the forces of growth, but there is also a great urgency about it. These economies have stagnated for long owing to political and social factors and the disparity between their economic position and that of high income countries is rapidly widening further. This is due to the fact that technological improvements which have advanced far in the latter and which constitute one of the major factors responsible for their rapid growth, are making faster progress in recent years. Apart from this, a sense of great urgency has been brought about by the demographic factor. Rapid growth in numbers and increasing pressure of population have made it necessary that the underdeveloped countries of today develop their economies quickly even in order to maintain their existing low standards of life. It has been pointed out by many economists that this population barrier can be broken and the process of growth can be initiated only if large investments on a wide front are made. Such a big push is possible only if the govern-

[11]Myrdal, Gunnar, *Economic Theory and Underdeveloped Regions*, Vora, Bombay, 1958, p. 53.

ment makes an effort. Unless capital formation is stepped up from the present low level of 6 per cent or so in many backward economies to 15 per cent or more of the national income, and unless the per capita availability of capital is considerably augmented, no way out of the vicious circle of poverty and stagnation can be found. Any improvement in economic and national welfare is possible only through rapid industrialization which appears to be the best way to close the ' scissors ' of resources and numbers.[12] In the present economic set-up, this consummation which is devoutly to be wished for, cannot be realized unless the state steps in and throws its weight into the business of economic betterment. There is also the great need for investments in overheads to provide the ground work on which the economy has to be built up. But this again, requires huge initial investments. The lumpiness of such investments, their long periods of gestation and the indirect routes of payoff, make them unattractive from the point of view of private enterprise. Hence in most of the underdeveloped countries the state has concentrated on the task of providing such primary requirements.

Since the social and economic circumstances that prevail in the underdeveloped countries of today are different from those in the Western industrial countries in the 18th and 19th centuries, it is not possible to expect much from the private entrepreneur. In this sense, the emphasis on the role of the private entrepreneur as the key factor responsible for economic development would appear much exaggerated and also irrelevant to contemporary circumstances. Today, the state in the low income countries has to be both an innovator and adapter.[13] It is sometimes held that the higher is the degree of economic backwardness, the greater is the role of the government. This idea springs from the feeling among the people in underdeveloped countries that public action alone can achieve certain economic ends, and that the government can better transfer established technology and forms of organization from advanced countries to the backward ones. Certainly, in so far as underdeveloped countries are late comers in the field of industrialization, it would be an easier task for the state to adapt the technology that have been tried and tested in advanced countries to the needs and resources of the poorly endowed countries. This would mean that a simpler apparatus of the state is sufficient to achieve good results from adaptation. But it should be remembered that an important point

[12]Aubrey, Henry G., ' The Role of the State in Economic Development,' *The American Economic Review*, 1951, p. 266.

[13]However, H. W. Singer is sceptical about the outcome of such a development. The assumption of the entrepreneur's role according to him, diverts government from its normal duties; it throws an enormous burden on the quality of administration which itself is dependent on economic development; also when in underdeveloped countries government substitutes private entrepreneurship, the result is likely to be an extreme form of nationalism. This results in clinging to traditional institutions, reluctance to adopt new technology and adherence to traditional and outmoded methods of production, lavish expenditure on armies, embassies, etc. He cites the example of government outlay on Khadi in India. ' Obstacles to Economic Development,' *Social Research*. Vol. 20, 1953, No. 1 Spring, p. 21. But this seems to be an exaggerated fear.

in favour of state's entry in the economic field is its competence to bear the responsibilities which are involved. The ability of the state to influence the results of economic activity springs from the fact that government in a modern economy is the largest consumer, spender and saver besides being a large resource owner and innovator. Because of its economic might, it can affect the flow of resources and their utilization in a manner that is conducive to social benefit which is not likely to be attained by the activity of private entrepreneurs.

In fine then, the state is justified in taking an increasing part in economic development because of the peculiar circumstances prevailing in the economically backward countries. Long periods of stagnation, social rigidities, lack of capital resources, the inertia of the people and absence of enterprise, the pressure of population, the need for making large initial investments in economic and social overheads and the urgency of the problem, the need to telescope a hundred years progress into a decade, all these call for state intervention in the matter of economic development. The consequence of assigning such a key role to the state would be the expansion of the nationalized sector in the economy. This however need not necessarily involve the progressive elimination of the private sector. If efficiently directed and administered, public investment would become the " strategic lever of economic development of underdeveloped countries,"[14] and the public sector would be the driving force of development of the whole national economy. By providing new employment opportunities, generating new incomes, creating additional demand and by bringing about an expansion of the domestic market, the growth of public investment would help both directly and indirectly the expansion of the private sector as well, and the overall growth of the economy.

HOW FAR CAN THE STATE GO?

Given the importance of public investment in economically backward countries, the question arises as to how far the state should go in this direction. Although all underdeveloped countries have realized the need for, and importance of government's active participation in economic development, there is considerable variation in their views regarding the area of the state's economic activity. At one extreme stand countries like China and some small nations of Eastern Europe, where economic activities have been more or less completely nationalized. Means of production are owned mostly by the state and the sphere of private enterprise has been severely narrowed down so that it has become a mere appendage of the national economy. Savings and investment are the responsibility of the state, and the volume and distribution or direction of investment and the distribution of the national product are determined and carried through by the agency of the state. On the other hand, in the Philippines and in most of the countries of South America, private enterprise is still

[14]Lange, Oskar, *Essays on Economic Planning*, Asia Publishing House, Bombay, 1960, p. 35.

strong and retains a dominant sway in the national economy. In these countries, the state's function is of an assistive nature; it is responsible for providing the basic overhead facilities and giving financial and other assistance to private enterprise. In India since the adoption of planning in 1951 the public sector has steadily expanded. In Indonesia, in the early schemes of economic development, an important role was assigned to the state and public investment constituted 2·7 per cent of GNP in 1951. Ceylon has vascillated between public and private enterprise as is illustrated by the vicissitudes of the plywood industry. This industry was taken over from the private sector by the government, but state undertaking proved a failure and the industry was handed back to private enterprise. But there was no perceptible progress of the industry either in the private or in the public sector.

Whether there should be all-out state interference in economic affairs, or whether government should adopt a go slow policy, depends primarily on the social and political ideology of the community and also on the economic circumstances of the country. The latter would include the administrative efficiency of the government and its capacity to carry the people with it in its schemes of economic expansion and also the nature of investment required. The capacity of the government to achieve the goals set in its programmes of development depends on factors which reflect how advanced the society and its economy are, such as the quality of the bureaucracy and the type of institutions available for tackling the problems of development; it also depends on the degree to which the goals are compatible with those subscribed to by the population.[15] The type of investment required is also a decisive factor in determining the scope of state activity. Obviously, if growth can be initiated only by providing the economic infrastructure, the state has to undertake the construction of roads and railways, development of hydro-electric schemes, etc. Where however, these are already established, and the private sector is alert and efficient enough to make use of the opportunities for expansion, the government can considerably limit the scope of its developmental functions. Most of the underdeveloped countries have a form of mixed economy in which, while the public sector has assumed the responsibility for developing particular industries and for providing overhead facilities, there is ample scope for the activity of the private sector also. In such a controlled economy, the government's intervention aims " not only at preserving the capitalist management of property but also at leaving the individual a field for free action. In principle, the management of an enterprise remains fiee, but the state through a number of measures modifies the conditions in which it is run. These measures are based on the criterion of usefulness instead of on that of profit. The state decides on the usefulness of such and such imports. It provides foreign exchange only for the expenditure which it considers as most useful and penalizes by

[15]Spengler, J. J., ' The Social Structure, the State and Economic Growth,' *Economic Growth: Brazil, India, Japan*, Kuznets Simon, Wilbert E. Moore and J. J. Spengler, Eds., Duke, Durham, N. C., 1955, p. 370.

means of taxation the production of articles regarded as superfluous, if not actually harmful; it fixes certain prices, profit margins, etc."[16]

It is therefore unwise to make any definite statement as to the extent to which state control should be increased in order to bring about rapid economic growth. If we leave out of account the social and other implications of a fully controlled authoritarian economy, it may be found that in respect of the economic results that can be achieved, a totalitarian state is more successful than a liberal state; and this because of the fact that the former is capable of disregarding the feelings, tastes and values of the underlying population and of removing the social and institutional obstacles to growth with less hesitation and fuss than can a liberal state.[17] According to Oskar Lange the nationalized sector since it plays a key role, has necessarily to expand. In the present context, the economic ills of underdeveloped countries can be remedied and they may be set well on the way of economic progress only if the public sector expands rapidly and brings about state socialism. If the scope of the nationalized sector is restricted and it is prevented from progressive expansion, the result would be the emergence of monopoly capitalism as in the United Kingdom and the U.S.A. The low income countries may regard state capitalism as a progressive phenomenon on the whole. But state capitalism though it may initiate the economic progress of an underdeveloped country, cannot sustain such progress for a long period. It becomes reduced to a subsidiary of private capitalism. Lange feels that in the long run, the economic progress of an underdeveloped country can be maintained only by the development of the economic foundations of a socialist society. This conclusion however, is unconvincing. In view of the wide variations in economic conditions even among the low income countries, differences in the social attitudes and cultural patterns of the people, and the disparity in the standards of administration, it would be unwise to lay down any axiomatic rule that rapid economic development is possible only under a particular type of economic organization and political system. The fact is that rapid economic development has taken place under sharply contrasting types of organization. It may nevertheless, be added that when once government has taken the decision to step into the field of economic development, it has to continue its support for long. Experience in some of the underdeveloped countries has disproved the notion that when once the initial step is taken by the state, private enterprise would take care of the rest. Thus Hanson points out that even in the South American countries which are strongly biased towards private enterprise, it needed a rate of public investment of between 30 and 40 per cent of national income to sustain the economic progress of the post-war years. Further, when in 1953 public investment was reduced as part of the measures to economize in public expenditure, there was no increase but actually a decrease in private investment. Clearly,

[16]Mendes-France, Pierre and Gabriel Ardant, *Economics and Action*, Heinemann, London, 1955, pp. 201–02.

[17]Spengler, J. J., *ibid.*, p. 373.

whether private enterprise would easily take over from the state and maintain the trends of economic activity is determined by and large, by the inherent strength of the private sector, its economic and social structure and the national traditions and social attitudes of the community.[18]

GOVERNMENTAL MEASURES TO PROMOTE ECONOMIC GROWTH

The various measures which modern governments have adopted in order to influence the economic life of the community and to foster economic development can be classified as direct and indirect. The latter includes monetary and fiscal policy, control and regulation of foreign trade and foreign exchange. In addition to the traditional techniques of monetary control like the discount rate and open market operations which the central bank adopts in order to regulate the general level of economic activity through control of credit and volume of money supply, new techniques have become popular in recent years which are of greater use and significance in the matter of economic development. The techniques of varying reserve requirements of commercial banks and selective credit controls are becoming more and more common in all countries which have a sound central banking system. Apart from using the monetary methods, the state can regulate economic activity through its budgetary and public debt policy. Distribution of public expenditure and methods of taxation and public borrowing programmes affect private consumption, savings and investment. Taxation has been made use of for increasing domestic savings by restricting consumption, for preventing investment in undesired channels and for directing investment into those lines which promote the country's economic growth and also as a means to secure better distribution of wealth and incomes. Similarly, the technique of deficit financing helps in raising the level of investment through forced savings. And fiscal policy can be designed with a view to control foreign trade, promote exports, regulate the importation of luxury articles and to conserve foreign exchange. By the regulation of foreign exchange and exchange control, the state aims at maintaining the external balance of the economy and at ensuring the discriminative use of foreign resources for development purposes.

Direct services of the state which help economic development can be classified as follows: (1) Provision of economic and social overhead facilities; (2) Bringing about institutional and organizational changes ; (3) Augmenting the supply and increasing the mobility of the factors of production and (4) Direct participation in industrialization and help to private industries.

1. *Economic and Social Overhead Facilities*

In order to ensure an accelerated rate of growth. the provision of economic

[18]Hanson, A. H., *Public Enterprise and Economic Development*, Routledge and Kegan Paul. London. 1959. pp. 23 & 24.

and social overhead capital and services is essential. Economic overhead capital or economic infrastructure includes investment in transport (railways, roads, harbours, air fields), communication, electric power, irrigation, land reclamation, etc. Expansion of social overhead capital involves expenditure on education, health, housing and various other welfare schemes. The availability of adequate overhead facilities brings about external economies to other industries, lowers their capital co-efficients and by thus improving the efficiency of general investment, makes possible a more rapid rate of economic growth. Most of the modern underdeveloped countries do not have an adequate supply of these facilities and since private enterprise would not normally venture into these fields, governments have started large investment programmes to fill this gap. Investments in irrigation and agriculture have taken the first place in the development plans of Ceylon and Cambodia while transport and communication are given great prominence in Burma, India and Nepal.

The proportion of investment on infrastructure to total public investment in some of the countries of South and East Asia is shown in Table 47.

Table 47

DISTRIBUTION OF PUBLIC INVESTMENT IN SOUTH AND
EAST ASIAN COUNTRIES 1950—59
(Per cent of total investment)

Country	(1) Transport and Communications	(2) Construction	(3) Energy	(4) Health and Education	Total 1 to 4	Industry	Agriculture	Others
Burma	30	16	15	5	66	16	15	3
Ceylon	22	13	8	11	54	3	35	8
China (Mainland)	15	3	...	6	24	51*	9	16
India	32	...	8	16	56	13	29	2
Philippines	40	3	...	15	58	6	22	14
Thailand	43	9	8	12	72	4	19	5

*Industry and construction.
SOURCE: *Economic Survey of Asia and the Far East*, U.N., 1960, p. 75, Table 27.

It is seen from Table 47 that in all the countries in the list excepting China, the volume of public investment on economic and social overheads—transport and communications, construction, energy, health and education—constitutes well over 50 per cent of the total public investment; in Thailand it is as high as 72 per cent and in Burma 66 per cent. In both these countries, transport and communications account for a large portion of total public investment. On health and education, the ratio of public investment is 15 per cent in India, while in Burma it is only 5 per cent. The large investment in

China on industries and construction (51 per cent) explains the small proportion on economic and social overheads.

2. *Institutional Changes*

Among institutional changes that can be brought about by the state may be mentioned, land reforms and reform of inheritance and tenancy laws, which are necessary for establishing security of tenure; organization of companies and large and small enterprises; regulation of competition and control of monopolies to ensure better methods of production and avoidance of wastage of resources; setting up of producers' and consumers' co-operatives; promoting leadership in villages through community projects and village reconstruction schemes; facilitating better mobility of labour and raising the standards of social morality and character of the community. These measures directly help economic growth by bringing about better organization of production and also by building up non-material or intangible capital which is as important to productive effort as physical capital. Many of these improvements have taken place spontaneously or through private and individual efforts in developed countries, but in backward economies these changes have not only to be effected quickly but also have to be brought about by revolutionizing the modes of conduct and behaviour of the population and its social attitudes which have shaped into an unhealthy pattern over long years of economic stagnation. The state has, besides, to assume responsibility in the matter of bringing about better relationship between capital and labour. By means of social and labour legislation and proper regulation of private business, the state can assist in reducing the chances of friction between management and labour, create in labour a sense of responsibility for increasing output and minimize losses of production through strikes and lockouts.

One important method of fostering economic expansion through government activity is the promotion of markets. The extent of domestic markets depends on the level of income of the buyers, the proportion of expenditure on particular products, and the size of the country and its population. Various institutional factors and the limited degree of monetization restrict the size of the markets in an underdeveloped country. Here also the state can play an effective part by removing the institutional obstacles. Governments can widen financial activity by organizing suitable institutions like the capital market. Thus by establishing the credit communal in Belgium, the government helped the small and medium sized communes to mobilize their savings and canalize them into profitable investment. Governments can also change the size of an existing market by opening new means of communications. Expanding the size of the markets ensures more stable prices and facilitates the growth of firms to their optimum size through healthy competition. It is also possible for governments to modify the way and manner in which a market functions by influencing supply or demand. Thus the level of demand can be raised by providing consu-

35

mer credit facilities, while by enforcing a minimum wage for labour, the supply conditions in the factor market can be altered. In addition to these direct methods of organizing and developing markets, governments can, by promoting industrialization and by raising the level of income and employment, indirectly assist in the expansion of markets.[19] In so far as in free enterprise and mixed economies markets remain the ' steering gear ' of economic activity, the development of this institution would give specific direction to the economy and encourage investment activity.

3. *Increasing the Supply and Mobility of Factors of Production*

As we have seen in the earlier chapters, the basic problem of underdeveloped countries is the shortage of necessary resources and their relative immobility. There is an acute scarcity of capital and also an inadequate supply of entrepreneurial skill. While labour in general is excessive in relation to the complementary resources, skilled labour is lacking, and this has constituted a serious obstacle to industrialization. Scarcity of entrepreneurship is indicated by the existence of investment opportunities that remain unexploited. To a large extent, this is symptomatic of the general backwardness of the economy. Much improvement is possible in this direction if government can create the necessary environment and pre-conditions for entrepreneurial growth. The educational system is the appropriate instrument for the extension of literacy and the imparting of necessary skills and knowledge. The establishment of large-scale production units by the state provides opportunities for the development of managerial and entrepreneurial skill. Apart from this, the state can take steps to give special protection and encouragement to small entrepreneurs, and if necessary, secure the services of foreign entrepreneurs in the initial stages of development. Although the role of foreigners in the managerial structure has been the subject of much severe criticism, the fact cannot be denied that in countries where lack of entrepreneurship is an important deterrent to industrial progress, the provision of facilities for the starting of branches of foreign enterprises would help in familiarizing the people with the techniques of management and entrepreneurship. As regards scarcity of technically skilled labour, apart from the promotion of general education, such measures as the starting of industrial training centres, greater emphasis on technical education, vocational school system and improving mobility of labour through furnishing information about employment opportunities, opening of employment exchanges, etc. would be helpful. It should however be remembered that the scarcity of both entrepreneurship and skilled labour is as much the cause as the effect of industrial backwardness. Industrial development provides facilities for training in industrial leadership as well as opportunities for the growth of skilled labour force. In other words, programmes of industrialization

[19]DeLaVinelle, Louis Duquesne, ' Economic Policy as an Instrument of Progress, ' *International Social Science Bulletin*, UNESCO, Vol. VI, No. 2, 1954, pp. 265–66.

and general economic development undertaken or sponsored by governments may be considered as the proper and effective means of solving the problem of scarcity of skilled labour and entrepreneurial talents.

That dearth of capital and financial resources is the major problem in underdeveloped countries is an obvious fact and the governments of these countries have taken steps towards augmenting these resources by import of foreign capital as well as by the better mobilization and more careful utilization of the domestic resources. In many of the underdeveloped countries, the lack of organized financial institutions has stood in the way of the proper mobilization of even the meagre savings that are available. Even where governments are reluctant to enter the industrial field, and prefer to leave a wide scope for private enterprise, it is found to be both justifiable and necessary to help private enterprise through the provision of more satisfactory financial facilities. Thus in those low income countries of today in which private enterprise is allowed to predominate, the state's activity is mostly concentrated on the organization and development of financial agencies and credit institutions which would meet the needs of private business. Extensive loans have been given by the governments of China (Taiwan), Japan, Southern Korea, the Philippines and other countries for rehabilitating their industries in the post-war years. The Indian government has granted substantial loans to the private sector especially to the iron and steel industry. To promote exports and to facilitate the imports of capital goods and raw materials for the development of domestic industries, export and import credit arrangements have been made by governments by the establishment of export banks and by operating insurance schemes to cover various export risks. Besides, special arrangements have been made for providing financial and credit assistance to small-scale industries. The Industrial Finance Corporation is becoming increasingly popular in the underdeveloped countries of South America and Asia as an agency to meet the long term and medium term financial requirements of industries. Since the creation of corporations of this type has been necessitated by the lack of adequate institutional facilities such as those available in the advanced countries, the operation of these agencies has to be governed by sound commercial principles. Nevertheless, in so far as the purpose of such institutions is to help economic development, they would have to be discriminatory in their assistance, favouring particularly those industries which are essential for the rapid economic development of the country, but which fail to secure funds from the banks and the public in the normal course. Similarly, regulation of private investment through control of capital issues is of use in ensuring investment of scarce capital resources in enterprises which are not merely profitable from the point of view of the entrepreneur but also contribute to the over-all economic development of the country.

4. Direct Participation in Industrialization

While in some of the underdeveloped countries governments have relied on private enterprise for the building up of industries and have restrained themselves to the role of providing financial and other assistance, in others, the state has adopted a more ambitious policy involving direct participation in the industrial field. This has led to the nationalization of basic industries and to the assignment of spheres of industrial activity for the private and public sectors. Besides, government also assumes the role of the entrepreneur in starting new industries and in giving a lead to private enterprise. Extension of government's activity in the industrial sphere has the objective of not only initiating the process of industrial growth but also preventing the emergence of big monopolistic organizations and concentration of wealth. In some countries like India the area of the state's activity in the industrial sector has progressively increased. On the other hand, in others governments start the industries and set them going and then hand them over to the private sector.

When in the 18th and 19th centuries, some of the present day economically advanced nations experienced the first phase of their industrial growth, the governments' role in economic life was on the whole restricted within narrow confines. In the early days of British industrialization the principle of laissez faire predominated. It has been pointed out that " the rise of the new industrial and commercial bourgeoisie actually led to a freeing of economic enterprise from old government restrictions ".[20] The industrial development and the growth of trade and transport that took place in the country was due almost entirely to private enterprise and initiative. The government of the U.S.A. in a corresponding stage of that country's economic development took up a less neutral attitude and gave some form of assistance to private enterprise, but that help was restricted to providing settlers and railroads with land, establishing land grant colleges, developing roads and harbours and fostering some industries through protective tariffs and subsidies.[21] In contrast are the communist countries like Soviet Russia and China where private enterprise is regarded as fundamentally anti-social and as such could be given only a temporary and progressively narrowing role in economic development. The major objective of the state's economic policy is rapid economic development and this is sought to be attained by a complete control over the productive resources of the economy, by directing investment into planned channels and by undertaking the distribution of the end product, all done in accordance with comprehensive economic plans. To this category would belong the East European countries also which have come within the orbit of the Soviet system of government. Complete control of the economy by the state and the adoption of authoritarian methods of planning and development have brought about impressive results in production in these countries.

The other countries fall between these extremes. In some of the underdeveloped countries like the Philippines in South-East Asia, and Chile and Mexico in South America, governments are reluctant to enter the industrial

[20] & [21]Meir, Gerald M., and Robert E. Baldwin, *Economic Development—Theory, History and Policy*. Asian Students' Edition, Asia Publishing House, Bombay, 1960, p. 361.

field and consider that the state could best help industrialization by leaving free scope for private enterprise but at the same time offering them financial and technical assistance. The high rate of growth in national output registered in Mexico (10 per cent in 1955–56) was due mainly to private enterprise. Government gave assistance to private industry in the form of tariff protection, and tax exemption and also by constructing public works and by providing communal facilities like transport, irrigation and electricity supply. It has also provided financial facilities to private business through the organization of mixed corporations financed by both private and public agencies similar to the ' Fomentos ' in other parts of Latin America. These mixed corporations have helped financing heavy industry as well as river valley development in the country. But the state's participation in the manufacturing industry has been much limited. The Mexican government brought out the Salte Plan in 1950 for the economic development of the country over a period of five or six years but has abstained from any direct investment in the industrial sector. Apart from the nationalization of the petroleum industry in 1938 for political reasons and the assumption of public ownership of railways in 1937, there was no other instance of nationalization in that country during this period. A similar attitude was taken by the government of Brazil. According to the International Bank Mission's calculations, the Nacional Financiera or the Investment Bank of Brazil made a net contribution to the industrial sector of the economy between 1946 and 1950 of no more than 9·6 per cent of the financial requirements. On the other hand, public investment was concentrated on irrigation projects which accounted for as much as 95 per cent of the total public investment in agriculture between 1939 and 1946.[22]

Governments in some other cases have thought it fit to take the initial steps in industrialization by starting new industries so as to show the way to private enterprise. The idea is to leave such government undertakings to the private sector when industrialization has gained sufficient momentum. This has been found successful in countries which have large resources and which have an enterprising class of industrialists to take over from government. Thus in Germany in the first half of the 19th century, government took the initiative in industrialization in the form of direct participation in iron and coal production, in exploration and technological experimentation, in fostering technical education and in the development of applied science and research with a view to build a sound foundation for the industrial growth of the country. In course of time, efficient technology had become standardized and known throughout the private sector which was able to seize the opportunity and build up quickly on the foundations laid by the state. In Australia, economic growth was fostered by a healthy competition between the private and public sectors. In the course of industrial development the private sector gained strength enough to exert pressure on the state to provide the conditions suitable to the growth

[22]Hanson, A. H., *Public Enterprise and Economic Development*, Routledge and Kegan Paul, London, 1959, pp. 132–45.

of free enterprise. The government of Switzerland adopted on the whole a policy of economic and political neutrality in relation to industry; nevertheless it helped private industry to flourish at home and to expand by opening up markets for the rural industries in foreign countries. In Canada, basic development policies were laid down by the state and although in implementing these policies the initiative was exercised by the government, the private sector was given scope enough to secure a large share of the industrial expansion during the 19th century. In all these cases, governments without taking any important part in actual investment in industries, gave assistance as well as guidance, assumed the initial risks and showed the way to private enterprise. But obviously, the extent to which help of this nature can be fully utilized by the economy depends on the material and human resources of the country. The sequence of economic development taking place in this manner under the fostering care of the government has been divided into three phases by Bert Hoselitz: first, a solidarity phase compassing the period of unification, integration, etc., in which political stability and an organized form of government are established; second, the goal attainment phase, including the period of state direction for constructing the economic and non-economic infrastructure necessary for the economy to grow and third, an adaptation phase, during which private enterprise develops and adjusts itself to the political set up, enlarges its growth potentialities, and acquires sufficient strength to expand further along independent lines. Although this is the normal and logical trend when government's objective is to build up a strong economy based on private enterprise, yet in the course of this process owing to political factors or the failure on the part of private enterprise to make good use of the opportunities, the different stages may get prolonged or distorted.[23]

In Japan, this approach of the state towards industrial development has been found to be most successful. With the establishment of a strong central government under the Meiji leadership in the latter half of the 19th century, the state took up for itself the task of spearheading the industrialization process. In the initial stages the government played fully the entrepreneurial role and its activity covered every variety of enterprise. Apart from constructing and operating the railways, and developing the means of communication, the state opened new coal mines, started agricultural experiment stations and established iron foundries, shipyards and machine shops. In order to support and encourage the textile industry, foreign equipment was imported by government and foreign experts were brought down to mechanize and improve silk reeling and cotton spinning. The state set up model factories for the manufacturing of cement, glass and paper. Many local industries were reorganized and new industries of the Western style were started by government initiative. Initial risks were borne by the state, the way was prepared for technical advance, and private ventures were encouraged and patronized and enabled to follow on the heels

[23]Ranis, Gustav, ' Some Case Studies of Economic Development and Hoselitz's General Theoretical Schema: A Comment,' *Kyklos*, Vol. XIII, Fasc. 2, pp. 277–81.

of the state.[24] In course of time as private business started taking over from the government, the latter retreated from the entrepreneurial advance which it had made in the early years. However, at this stage, government continued to provide all facilities for the private big business (Zaibatsu) to expand. The state's educational reforms, encouragement of Western learning and science, its money, credit and fiscal policies, the establishment of quasi-public banks which facilitated mobilization of domestic savings, government's help to technological research and adaptation, the important land tax reform of 1873 which replaced the old feudal dues by a money tax, government's foreign trade and tariff policies, the adoption of a definite policy of industrial protection at the close of the century, reorganization of agriculture and measures to protect labour and ensure better industrial relationship, all these helped rapid economic growth. The big business became virtual partners of the state in its policy of economic advancement and acquired considerable political influence, prestige and authority. This trend continued till the late 1930s when the Great Depression and the exigencies of the Sino-Japanese War necessitated a reversal of the policy and extensive control of the economy by the state. But by that time the economy had been transformed and the country emerged as one of the leading industrial nations of the world. Thus in Japan also, the process of industrial growth was initiated by the state by playing the part of the entrepreneur, while later development and expansion may be described as predominantly one of private ownership and market competition.

As Lockwood points out, much of this rapid progress was due to the character and talents of the people. That government initiative alone will not bring about rapid industrial advancement is illustrated by the experience of Turkey. The political and social changes brought about under Ataturk in the 1920s were expected to help economic development of the country. But early attempts at encouraging private enterprise failed about the 1930s. Hence emphasis came to be placed on the public sector not on ideological grounds but out of need. The Iz Bank founded in 1924 by Ataturk on the lines of an Industrial and Finance Corporation expanded quickly and by the 1930s it controlled many industrial concerns. By then, there was a deliberate shift to state enter- prise. A Five-Year Plan for economic development was announced in 1934 and a new state organization—the Sumer Bank—a state enterprise of the public corporation type, was placed in charge of planning and development. But little planned development resulted. Agriculture was ignored and the bad planning and ill-advised location of iron and steel industries proved a costly venture. Subsequently, the Eti Bank was organized and entrusted with the responsibility of running the nationalized mines. It was authorized to trade in minerals and mineral equipment, to exploit mines and oil fields, to generate and distribute electricity and to provide all kinds of banking services. Attempts

[24]Lockwood, William W., 'The State and Economic Enterprise in Japan, 1868–1938,' *Economic Growth : Brazil, India, Japan*, Kuznets, Simon and others, Eds.. Duke, Durham, N.C., 1955, pp. 537–602.

were also made to improve agriculture by providing credit facilities through the Agency of the Agricultural Bank (founded in 1888) and also by means of guaranteed prices for agricultural products. On the whole, over the years 1929–1938, industry and agriculture developed very largely through state enterprise. Factory production doubled and the share of industry and construction in the national income rose from 13 per cent to 16 per cent. However, with the coming into power of the Democratic Party in 1950, private enterprise was revived and it has since then grown more rapidly than public enterprise. But this shift in emphasis seems to be premature; private enterprise has not shown itself strong enough to build up the industrial structure of the economy. What had been accomplished under state control and regulation before 1938 has not helped in generating the forces of growth in the economy.

It would thus appear that the success of state's initiative in the industrial field depends largely on the economic and social circumstances of the country and the quality of the human resources available. It also leads to the conclusion that in underdeveloped countries when once government has stepped in as the entrepreneur, it is good if its responsibility is continued until the economy reaches a stage when growth can be maintained without much government support. A proper assessment is to be made of the relative potentialities and capacity of either sectors, and the state may hand over to the private sector the task of building up the economy only when a strong foundation is laid, and only when it becomes certain that the rate of growth can be maintained at a high level by private enterprise. Viewed in this light, the principle adopted by the government of India in its development policy of providing opportunities to the private sector so that it can grow as the economy expands, seems to be the appropriate one. The industrial policy resolution of the government adopted in 1948 made it clear that state participation in industry and the conditions in which private enterprise should be allowed to operate were to be judged with reference to the two objectives, namely, increase in production and national wealth and more equitable distribution of wealth and income. Government's attempt to achieve these objectives through its programmes of planned economic development has resulted in the progressive expansion of the public sector since 1951. Since there is an important difference between the types of investments in the public and private sectors it is not possible to assess the relative performance of the two. Much of public investment is on social and economic overheads and the development of basic industries while private investment is concentrated on manufactures and the production of consumption goods. But there can be no doubt that public investment in the last ten years or so has considerably added to the fixed capital of the country and has increased its potentiality for rapid growth.

It is however, incorrect to assume that the expansion of the public sector would progressively and inevitably lead to state socialism in India. Two points may be mentioned in support of this view. Firstly, planning is democratic in this country, and the economic development that is taking place is within the frame-work of political democracy. Economic advancement and egalitarian policies would strengthen the base of democracy and not destroy it. Secondly, the border line between the public and private sectors has been kept quite flexible. In fact in recent years, the state has given opportunities to private enterprise to extend its scope. Concessions granted to the fertilizer industry, and in the matter of manufacture of synthetic rubber and the starting of joint ventures in the steel industry with foreign capital, illustrate this point. Nor is it fair to think that when once an industry is nationalized it would continue indefinitely in the public sector. It is in fact possible to envisage a process in which while on the one side new activities are taken over by the state, on the other there is a gradual relaxation or surrendering of government control. In a democratic state there is no reason why an industry which has been nationalized cannot be denationalized when circumstances warrant such a policy. Moreover as Hanson points out, the amount of state enterprise is not an index of governmental intervention in economic life. Sweden is not less socialistic than Britain because she has fewer nationalized industries. Techniques and policies relating to development may undergo modifications as a result of experience.[25]

LIMITATIONS OF GOVERNMENT ENTERPRISE

From what has been stated in the preceding few pages about the role of government in economic development, it would be clear that the state can contribute importantly to the economic advancement of the low income countries. But it remains to add that there are certain obvious limitations to the expansion of government enterprise. In comparison with private enterprise, state undertakings need not necessarily be superior. The assumption of more and more economic responsibilities by the state adds to the burden and cost of administration. The administrative mechanism grows unwieldy, the public service swells rapidly, and the demand for the services of skilled people tends to outrun supply. When this happens it would be difficult to maintain the quality of the administrative service. Less efficient and less talented people would have to be taken in, and as such some amount of dilution is likely to occur. Besides, as the government undertakes to do more and more in the economic field, new offices are created, the number of controls and regulations is increased, and with that, chances of corruption and graft rise in proportion. This is to be specially guarded against in underdeveloped countries where the standard of public morality is not of a high order. Government is usually subject to various political pressures, which are likely to distort its objectivity and affect its ability to concentrate on the really important economic undertakings. There is the further danger that the state in its over-enthusiasm to get things done, may grow less tolerant of individual enterprise, with the result that private

[25]Hanson, A. H., *Public Enterprise and Economic Development*, Routledge and Kegan Paul, London, 1959, pp. 16–18.

initiative may be strangled out altogether. Lastly, with the functions of the government increasing, there is the possibility of the state assuming dictatorial powers. The state may then conscript labour for employment in public works, raise taxation to exhorbitantly high levels or accelerate capital formation to the extent of seriously lowering general consumption standards. The safeguard against this danger lies in the attitude of the people and the strength of their faith in democratic ideals. An enlightened democracy can see to it that the government takes the people into its confidence, explains to the electorate what it undertakes to do, consults them at important stages in the execution of programmes of development and enlists their co-operation in government undertakings. If this is possible, state sponsored economic development need not be a threat to democracy or private enterprise.

Chapter XVII

PLANNING FOR ECONOMIC DEVELOPMENT

THE ADOPTION of economic planning by developed as well as underdeveloped countries in recent years has involved a great deal of state interference in economic life. Economic planning is " essentially a way of organising and utilising resources to maximum advantage in terms of defined social ends. The two main constituents of the concept of planning are (i) a system of ends to be pursued and (ii) knowledge as to available resources and their optimum allocation."[1] H. D. Dickinson defines economic planning as " the making of major economic decisions—what and how much is to be produced and to whom it is to be allocated by the conscious decision of a determinate authority, on the basis of a comprehensive survey of the economic system as a whole ".[2] Thus if the objective is to increase the national and per capita output without unduly straining the economy or causing any chronic imbalances, economic planning would involve a correct assessment of the resources available, charting out a programme of economic utilization of the resources so that each unit of resource is used in the most efficient manner possible, the allocation of resources among different lines of investment so that optimum over-all results are obtained and also the adoption of ways and methods to ensure that the increased output is shared by the different sections of the community in an equitable manner. Obviously, to prepare and carry out such a programme of action, a central agency is required which would be able to co-ordinate the various units of production and assume responsibility for the efficient allocation and employment of the resources. Thus planning directly involves state interference, so that the greater the degree of planning in an economy, the wider and more comprehensive becomes the scope of government activity. In this sense, an economic plan may be viewed as a " programme for the strategy of a national government in applying a system of state interference with the play of market forces, thereby conditioning them in such a way as to give an upward push to the social process ".[3]

WHY PLANNING HAS BECOME INCREASINGLY POPULAR

Various factors contributed to the adoption of economic planning in nearly

[1]*First Five-Year Plan*, Government of India, New Delhi, 1951, p. 7.
[2]Dickinson, H. D., *Economics of Socialism*, Oxford, London, 1939, p. 41.
[3]Myrdal, G., *Economic Theory and Underdeveloped Regions*, Vora, Bombay, 1958, p. 91.

all countries of the world in the last three decades. In the first place, some of the basic defects of capitalism and free enterprise have drawn attention to the fact that unless a free enterprise economy is regulated and controlled, it would not ensure stable economic growth or maximize social welfare. In other words, free enterprise economy has to be planned and guided by the agency of the government in order to attain the best results. Secondly, the experience gained by modern governments in the economic field during the world wars increased the popularity of economic planning. The need for mobilizing vast national resources for war, controls on civilian consumption, and foreign trade, the allocation of resources and the adoption of measures to cut down waste and to ensure the economic utilization of available resources, gave considerable experience to government agencies in the techniques of economic planning. It is obvious that where resources are limited and the demand for the resources is large, planned distribution and utilization of resources is a matter of necessity. Large-scale destruction of industries and capital assets in the war shattered completely the economies of the belligerent countries and when war ended, they were faced with the huge task of reconstructing and rehabilitating their economies. To convert the economies to a peace time basis, to rehabilitate the refugees, to build up capital assets and to utilize properly the foreign aid that became available, it was found necessary for the governments to lay down efficient lines of action and programmes of reconstruction. Thus the Monnet Plan in France introduced in 1946–47 aimed primarily at repairing the huge damages caused by the war and reconstructing the economy. The same motive and purpose actuated the launching of planned programmes of development in the East European countries—Poland, Czechoslovakia and Hungary. A third important factor which attracted attention to economic planning was the remarkable achievements of Nazi Germany and Soviet Russia. Economic planning in the former country had the major objective of making the country militarily strong.   The First Four-Year Plan launched by the Nazi Party in May 1933 was directed to the remedying of unemployment in the country through a comprehensive scheme of public works, while keeping wages at depression levels. It was eminently successful. In two years time, the number of people employed increased from 11·5 to 16·5 million and unemployed decreased from 6 million to 2 million. The Second Four-Year Plan started in September 1936, had two main objectives, rearmament and economic self-sufficiency. Both agricultural and industrial output increased, the latter to a much greater extent than the former; over full employment was reached and the building up of war industries, roads and railways and elaborate fortifications made Germany the most powerful military nation in Europe. Although the ultimate objective of planning was the building up of military strength, and although spontaneous public co-operation was lacking, planning was conspicuously efficient in Germany and it revealed what could be achieved by planning if it is properly organized and executed. Similarly, the remarkable progress of

Soviet Russia since the close of the First World War, under a system of rigid and well thought out programmes of action on authoritarian lines has been an eye opener to the potentialities of economic planning for development. Fourthly, the emergence of most of the underdeveloped countries after the Second World War from their long colonial status into free political status and their keen desire to develop themselves quickly has necessitated both state intervention as well as planning for development. It may also be added, that the change in the ideology of the people, their growing social consciousness and the realization of the social and economic evils of maldistribution of income and wealth have drawn attention to the need for directing economic growth in a manner that would bring about not only increased production but would ensure more equitable distribution of the larger output; egalitarian measures have therefore been called for, and regulation of the economic mechanism has become necessary to ensure social justice and equality. The stress laid on this factor in the Five-Year Plans of India is illustrative of the change in economic and social ideology. The statements relating to the objectives of planning indicate in clear terms that economic planning is needed as much for bringing about rapid development as for translating the ideals of social justice and equality into practice.

CORRECTIVE AND DEVELOPMENT PLANNING

There is a basic difference in the objective of planning between developed free enterprise economies and the low income countries which function within a democratic frame-work. Planning in the first attempts to free the economy of the evils of unrestricted competition and seeks to ensure a stable rate of growth. The emphasis here is more on stability, whereas in underdeveloped countries the primary objective is accelerating the pace of growth. In the former, planning is of the corrective type; in the latter it is of the developmental type. The series of measures adopted by the advanced, free enterprise economies in the 1930s introduced a considerable element of planning, direction and guidance in their economic system. As we have seen, in Germany the National Socialists directed their attention to the eradication of unemployment through planned regulation of the market and planned control of prices and wages. The Blum experiment in France in 1936–37 although not successful, meant actually the adoption of a scheme of economic planning for the future with the intention of setting aright the imbalance in the economy caused by the economic crisis. But the most important attempt in this line was the adoption of the New Deal in the U.S.A. under the Roosevelt regime in 1933. The series of measures under this scheme aimed at stabilizing the national economy through a planned programme of action covering all the important sectors of the economy. Corrective economic planning of this nature has come to stay in this country which at one time was the best representative of an unplanned economy. The United States Employment Act of 1946 is a good example of the nature and scope of planning in an advanced capitalist economy. The idea underlying this scheme is to counteract the forces of depression as well as inflation through directing and guiding private enterprise. Deflation is sought to be controlled by raising the propensity to consume through redistribution of incomes, by wage policy and social security measures, provision of easy credit facilities, urbanization and other means which would raise the level of spending; and also by promoting investment through reduction of taxation, lowering of interest rates, control of wages and various price support measures. Inflationary trends are attempted to be held in check through reversal of this policy, which would involve the imposing of taxes on consumption to reduce consumer spending, and increasing savings by the public as well as by the state by having surplus budgets, and by discouraging private investment through taxation, interest rate and wage policy. What is significant to observe in all these measures of corrective planning is that government restrains itself from too much interference in the economic life of the community, but at the same time takes steps to guide and regulate private enterprise in such manner that the forces of instability do not get out of control.

Planning of this nature is inadequate to meet the requirements of underdeveloped countries. In these countries there is an urgent and great need for a thorough shaking up of the social and institutional rigidities so as to liberate the forces of incentive and enthusiasm for a better and richer life. This is one of the reasons why both state intervention and planning are necessary in economically backward countries. Apart from this, the fact that the underdeveloped countries are poor, itself calls for planned development. Poverty necessitates and justifies state interference. Moreover, the evils of gross inequalities in the distribution of income and wealth have a greater anti-social effect and are far less tolerable in underdeveloped countries than in developed countries. Hence the emphasis laid in the programmes of planned development in the former countries on the need for removal of social injustice and concentration of income and wealth. The fact that a country is economically very poor, makes it imperative that wastage of economic resources arising from the operation of the free forces of a competitive economic system should have to be avoided. This aspect of the need for planning arises from the fact that in a free market economy, since investment is made on the basis of individual decisions and since a pattern of investment which obtains at a particular point of time influences price behaviour in future, a correct forecasting of future trend in prices or the profitableness of different investments cannot be made. This lack of knowledge creates an additional uncertainty in economic activity and hampers growth. Besides there is a social loss involved in wrong investments resulting from uncoordinated decisions of private entrepreneurs. Firstly, the shifting of the resources from investments which have already been made to new and desirable lines of investments takes time. Secondly, price change may not be a correct indicator in this matter. In a free enterprise economy, a changed allocation becomes necessary because of the price indicator which shows that the previous investment decision was wrong. But the nature of the price change itself is influenced by the previous investment; hence if the previous investment was wrong, the variation in price would be an unreliable guide to proper investment decisions. Economic planning reduces the chances of such social loss resulting from uncoordinated investment decisions.[4]

THE NATURE OF DEVELOPMENTAL PLANNING

The basic factors underlying developmental planning are the forecasting of the future demands and the possibilities and scope of expansion, assessment of existing resources and the allocation of the resources in a manner that will help attainment of these objectives. It involves five important stages. Firstly, surveying of national resources in order to estimate their cost and to envisage the alternative courses of action; secondly, taking a general decision between these alternatives; thirdly, drawing up the programme of action; fourthly, executing the programme and fifthly, adjusting it to changed circumstances. The last mentioned point draws attention to the fact that the plan should be flexible enough to bring about changes when circumstances demand such changes.[5] The most important feature of planning for development is that it injects the time factor and the problem of change into the centre of economic analysis. It links up the present resources position with future development possibilities; its success therefore depends on the forethought and vision that are brought into it.[6] This aspect of planning underlines the need for having a short range as well as a long range plan. Thus the long term plan would lay down the broad pattern and direction of future development; the short term plan—of about four to seven years—outlines the targets and programmes to be implemented within that period, and the annual plans would be the breakdown of short term plans into one year periods to facilitate annual budgeting and implementation.[7] Long term or perspective planning is necessary to have a general idea of the nature of the progress that is possible within the resources available to the economy. It should indicate broadly the lines of progress, while short term and annual plans are necessary to give more definiteness to the actual progress to be attained in different lines in specific periods of time. Unless such definite targets are set for attainment in fixed periods, there will not be any incentive for effort. Besides, it makes it possible to bring about a proper balancing between the financial and real resources available and the investment requirements of the economy.

Economic development implies the expansion of the different productive

[4]Dobb, Maurice, *An Essay on Economic Growth and Planning*, Routledge and Kegan Paul, London, 1960, pp. 6 & 7.

[5]Hanson, A. H., *Public Enterprise and Economic Development*, Routledge and Kegan Paul, London, 1959, p. 111.

[6]Elliot, John E., ' Economic Planning Reconsidered,' *Quarterly Journal of Economics*, February, 1958, p. 67.

[7]*Economic Bulletin for Asia and the Far East*, U.N., December, 1951, p. 28.

units of an economy so that the output of each sector or unit increases. Increased production involves larger investment in different lines of production, greater use of materials of production and higher levels of employment. Thus as output is increased, money income also rises. However, since there is the likelihood of different sectors or different units of production expanding in varying degrees (or contracting in some cases), the composition of output as well as the pattern of income distribution among the different income earners of the community changes. Hence one of the important conditions of stability in economic development is the maintaining of a balance between demand for the various commodities and services that are produced and the supply of these goods and services. In other words so far as internal demand and domestic output are concerned, a programme of economic development can be considered as harmonious only if the distribution of investment among the various industries is in exact balance with the distribution of the increased income among the various goods demanded. Otherwise, there will be instability in particular sectors. Such a situation can be avoided if planning for the different sectors of the economy is based on a satisfactory demand analysis.

A second requisite of scientific planning is the fixing of priorities for the different projects of development. This is obviously necessary in view of the scarcity of resources in relation to the needs of development. The over-all targets of output have to be determined with reference to the resources available in the economy. And an intelligent utilization of resources helps to attain the targets with less strain on the economy than would be possible otherwise. The major objective is of course to increase production as much as possible, but given the resources, it is important to choose not only those lines of advancement which are most conducive to over-all economic growth and discriminate between the different projects, giving greater importance to those which are of strategic importance and which are suitable for development from the point of view of the natural resources position and the needs of the economy, but also to assign lower priorities or leave out altogether other projects which do not satisfy the above conditions. Prof. Tinbergen points out that in the underdeveloped countries, a frequent handicap to the selection of the best projects is the conflicting claims for the priority of different projects made by the different departments or ministries. The only way of avoiding undue importance being given to certain types of projects is for the national planning agency to take steps to reduce this conflict and bring about greater co-ordination between the various departments or claimants. According to him while the choice of the projects is to be made primarily with reference to the availability of scarce resources such as capital, land or foreign currency, it would be well advised if three principles are borne in mind in this connection; firstly, the selection of investment projects is not to be divorced from other decisions; secondly, an investment programme must fit into the production programme of the country as a whole; and thirdly, the programme should be composed of such projects as would make the maximum contribution to the country's welfare. Apart, from these, the fact that successful planning should aim at generating the forces of growth within the economic system demands that in the selection of projects due consideration is to be given to the question whether a project would lead to increased or lower savings.[8]

Equally important as the assignment of priorities to the different projects is the securing of an over-all balance between the different industries. Each industry and each unit of production in an economy is closely interrelated to the others through demand as well as supply. Each industry requires for its operation the outputs of other industries while its output forms the input of other industries. Hence the expansion of any particular industry is possible only if the output of some other industries is also increased; at the same time increased output of the first enables the expansion of others. Looking at the problem from the demand side, it is clear that increased production of any commodity is not justifiable unless there is expansion of other industries which require more of the output of the former to maintain their higher levels of production. This interrelationship between industries makes it important that schemes of investment in particular projects are drawn up on the basis of a full knowledge of the repercussions of that investment on other industries. In this sense " scientific planning means co-ordinating every thing in one simultaneous (and integrated) piece of analysis and doing it on some optimum basis. It is solving the whole nexus as one simultaneous problem where everything determines everything else."[9] The inter-industry or input-output table in which industries are listed as producers in rows, and as consumers or purchasers in columns, provides a master chart depicting the interdependence of the various units and as such, provides the tools which enable the planner to find out the optimum solution in the matter of allocation of investment. When the final targets of production are fixed with reference to the resources available and prospective demand, it is possible to calculate the extent to which investment is to be increased, and the scale of operations raised in the different industries on the basis of the technical co-efficients or co-efficients of production of each industry. Since the input-output and consumption relations of existing industries are known by experience, it is not necessary to calculate a priori an entirely new system of relations in order to balance the detailed processes in an economy. It is enough if the required changes are introduced in the relations already existing, so that the optimum pattern of investment can be found by successive approximation.[10] With the elaboration and the refinement of the input-output tables, modern techniques of economic planning have become more scientific and systematic. A great deal of forecasting of trends in future demand and output is essential for investment planning. The efficiency of planning which is indicated by the extent to which demand of all sorts is balanced against output, directly depends on the correctness of these estimates.

[8]Tinbergen, J., *The Design of Development*, Johns Hopkins, Baltimore, 1958, pp. 29–37.

[9]Frisch, Ragnar, *Planning for India*, Asia Publishing House, Bombay, 1960, p. 2.

[10]Lange, Oskar, *Essays on Economic Planning*, Asia Publishing House, Bombay, 1960, p. 6.

36

The inter-industry tables are greatly helpful in this direction. In fact the extent to which this method is made use of in drafting plans for economic development is indicative of the standard of proficiency of a nation in its planning activity.

AUTHORITARIAN AND DEMOCRATIC PLANNING

Planning of the type mentioned above necessarily involves greater state interference in economic affairs. Government is the only centralized agency which can draw up and implement a national plan for economic development covering all sectors and industries of the state. Since scientific and efficient planning requires a system of programming based on inter-industry analysis, it follows that the more comprehensive and systematic the planning is, the greater will be the role of the government. Planning then tends to become rigid and authoritarian. The obvious advantage of such a method of development planning is that it is more comprehensive and more efficient than when it is of the flexible or democratic type. In the latter, planning is practically confined to the official sector, but an attempt is made to regulate and guide activity outside the government's area through indirect means. It is based on a system of free enterprise and the government only seeks to influence economic and investment decisions by playing upon investment incentives of the entrepreneurs via fiscal or monetary policy, but does not control or regulate the operation of the economy directly. This applies to the total amount or rate of investment, its distribution between economic sectors and the technical forms in which investment is embodied.[11]

Authoritarian or socialist planning appeals to the poor and underdeveloped countries of the world because of its scientific nature and its efficiency. Even when the methods employed in the different stages of economic planning involve considerable restriction of individual freedom, the fact that the targets are attained in the specified time and according to schedule, has earned great popularity for this technique of planning in countries which are in dire and urgent need of improving their economic standards and in which understandably enough, prime consideration is given to rapid increase in output. In fact, the stress laid on national economic self-sufficiency and on industrialization provides an explanation for the appeal of authoritarian planning to poor countries. Besides, in the low income countries, the difficulty of matching domestic savings with public investment requirements because of the inability of the population to produce the necessary savings voluntarily, favours authoritarian methods in so far as under such methods the required savings are brought about inevitably by the state's economic activity. Even when the methods involve hardship, the very fact that the savings are realized in some manner so as to avoid any defaulting or short fall in investment programmes

[11]Dobb, Maurice, *An Essay on Economic Growth and Planning*, Routledge and Kegan Paul, London, 1960, p. 2.

makes the authoritarian methods tolerable. The burden is borne patiently because of the assured results. A significant cut in the rate of investment in underdeveloped countries will not find favour with the community, but at the same time, in view of the many difficulties, it is not possible to rely much on voluntary savings. For these reasons, increasing state activity and authoritarian planning tend to be tolerated and in a way even welcomed.

In actual fact however, the sort of planning that is adopted in the under-developed countries of today is not, in all cases, of the rigid authoritarian type, but ranges all the way from the relatively limited planning of an essentially private or mixed enterprise economy, to the comprehensive, all-embracing planning of a totalitarian economic system. It is in fact difficult to find either among the developed or underdeveloped countries a system of economic planning which conforms entirely to any pure type. Thus even in Russia which stands as an example of socialist planning, small proprietors do exist, while in the U.S.A. which takes its place at the other extreme, there is a large public sector. Moreover in most of the free enterprise economies, there has been a progressive expansion of government's economic activities; while in the 19th century the British government spent less than 10 per cent of the national income, in many of the European countries at present, the state is responsible for the spending of more than 20 per cent of the national income. In general, it may be said that the extent of state interference and the nature of planning which would be found effective depend on the economic and social circumstances of the country concerned. In the earlier stages of development, future possibilities are not clear; statistical information is inadequate and the resources available are not correctly known. Detailed programming of economic development is therefore not possible and hence planning has to be flexible and general. Secondly, the state's role in planned development depends to a great extent on the degree of initiative, enterprise and activity forthcoming from the private sector. In this sense, limited planning of the indicative type in France may be not only justifiable but may be considered as best suited to developed countries whose economies have been built up over the years by private enterprise. Thirdly, the general attitude of the people with regard to government measures—whether they are willing to co-operate with the government, their public spiritedness, their preparedness to entrust to government more and more economic functions—and the efficiency of the administration also affect the nature and type of planning. Lastly, the particular problems that a country has to face in its initial stages of development influence the scope of economic planning. The prevalence of structural rigidities and other bottlenecks which hamper increased productive activity such as capital shortage, scarcity of foreign currency or skilled labour and transport difficulties, requires that the objective of planned development should be first, the removal of these obstacles to growth by the adoption of specific remedial measures, and the postponement of systematic and comprehensive planning until the ground is prepared for it.

However, in countries where the people attach any importance to democratic values of life, public co-operation and voluntary effort which are essential for accelerating economic growth can be aroused only if planning is democratic, and the community at large is enabled to take part in the formulation and execution of the plan and made to feel that the plan is of the people and for the people. Excessive centralization tends to discourage individual effort, particularly so when the workers are accustomed to disciplined and supervised work. In countries where people lack individual initiative and enterprise and look up to the state for leadership, the very fact that the state imposes itself on their economic destinies would perpetuate their alertlessness and passivity. Hence the United Nations experts on planning emphasize the importance of ensuring that " the political and economic planning mechanism provide the fullest scope, at each stage for individual and local participation . . . the preparation of plans and the determination of goals should be affected by a process of building up from local and regional proposals ". [12] There is in fact scope for economic planning under varying conditions of public ownership or control of industry. That ' unplanned socialism ' and ' planned capitalism ' are not self-contradictory terms has been shown by recent experiences in planning and nationalization in the Scandinavian countries and in England. In a ' mixed economy ' where a public sector of industry coexists with an organized and developed private sector, there is scope for the spontaneous development of private enterprise as well as for direction and regulation by the state. Thus in France since 1945 while planning is done on advanced inter-industry lines, the execution of the programmes is left mostly in the hands of private enterprise. The French method of planning is purely indicative. Its essence lies in the fact that all those concerned with carrying out the plan are associated with the process of drawing it up so that they become willing collaborators in seeing that its targets are achieved. The French system of planning involves the drafting of programmes of development by the technocrats in consultation with industry on the basis of estimated rates of economic growth likely to be achieved without disturbing the balance of payments. After this is done, industrialists and trade unions are invited through some twenty-five modernization commissions to work out the consequences for their own sectors. The state reinforces the drive towards these targets by a series of financial and fiscal incentives to private industry. [13] It would therefore appear that in a country where private enterprise is strong, and where a private sector in industry is well developed, much can be gained if planning allows ample scope to this sector and keeps the public sector within certain

[12]Frankel, Herbet S., ' United Nations Primer for Economic Development,' *Quarterly Journal of Economics*, August, 1952, p. 311.

[13]Castle, Barbara, ' Planning: The French Way,' *The Hindu*, Madras, October 20, 1961. The author however adds that though the mere setting of targets by the state gives a stimulus to private industry, much depends on the mood of the economy. If " the impetus to growth is interrupted, ' indicative ' planning proves inadequate ".

defined limits. Economic planning in this sense would aim at directing and regulating economic growth and at building up the economy on the contribution of both the sectors; it would be a means of guidance and regulation as well as of co-ordinating the different productive units of the economy.

It is worth adding that whatever be the type of planning—whether rigid and authoritarian or flexible and democratic—the techniques involved are to a great extent common for both. Scientific planning is based on certain patterns and principles which are not affected by the political frame-work within which the economic system operates. Thus the general principles of economic planning, namely the fixing of physical targets of output in different industries, their co-ordination by input, output and consumption balances, the problem of utilization of scarce resources, and the balancing between the physical and financial allocation of resources and between output and demand, hold good for any economy. It is, however, in the matter of financing of the plans and in the offering of incentives and in the administrative procedure involved in the formulation and execution of the plan that differences arise. This would mean that there is scope for the adoption of certain proved techniques of planning in a mixed economy possibly to the same extent as in another one with a different organizational set up. However, planning creates some additional problems in the former. In an economy where all the means of production are owned by the state, and the agencies of production as well as distribution are controlled by the government, and where the level of consumption is determined with reference to the output available, planning is relatively easy. Since the whole scheme is centralized, there is a greater degree of exactness about the outcome of different investment decisions. Hence the state finds it relatively easy to draw up schemes of investment allocations and production targets with reference to over-all objectives. The different production units fit in easily in the total system, and the possibility of any imbalance arising between demand and output is limited. On the other hand, in a mixed economy, such rigid control is not possible. While the state can indicate the lines along which the private sector can progress, and set the targets also, it can only through incentives stimulate private enterprise to the effort required. Much therefore depends upon the attitude and co-operative spirit of the private sector. The great problem of economic planning in mixed economies is thus one of co-ordination between the two sectors. Since in a mixed economy reliance is placed on the private sector to achieve the desired improvements in production, best use has to be made of private motivation and incentives. On the other hand, if there is to be planning in fact as well as in theory, it is necessary to ensure that private economic activities do not conflict with the public targets. To secure these objectives attention has to be directed to the maintenance of a sound balance between controls and incentives. The basic difference in the art of economic planning between authoritarian and free enterprise economies is that in the latter the policy should have to be more indirect; it has to be more subtle and use finer instruments of implementation,

Programming in the latter has therefore to be more elaborate. In short, the problem of planning in free enterprise economies is much complex and demands for its solution the best talents and brains.

CONDITIONS FOR SUCCESSFUL PLANNING

The successful implementation of a plan for economic development depends largely on the circumstances and conditions prevailing in a country. In the first place, the government should be strong and efficient and the economic organization of the country should be sound. Since planning requires efficient centralized direction, it is obvious that a weak and unstable central government cannot formulate or carry out efficiently any comprehensive national programme of economic development. However, economic circumstances in some of the underdeveloped countries require a certain amount of decentralization. The vastness of some of these countries, regional diversity in resources and problems, inadequate means of communication, low educational standards of the people and immobility of labour call for special attention being devoted to particular areas. In the drafting of the plan as well as in its implementation, the special problems and requirements of different regions are to be taken into account. It is therefore possible that the actual execution of particular projects in the plan in a large country may differ from what is formulated in the plan. These differences have to be tolerated to some extent, and the necessary adjustments are to be made so long as such alterations do not affect the major objectives and tone of the general plan. But decentralization should not be carried too far. The distribution of planning functions among a number of overlapping and competing bodies as in the Philippines would seriously impair the attainment of the objectives of the plan. Co-ordination of the individual ministries and departments in implementing the plan programmes is also essential. Otherwise, relaxation of control and the giving of free scope for the different sections of administration would lead to the unhealthy vying of different units with one another as it happened in Ceylon. The final responsibility for the execution of the plan must be centralized and the central government should be strong and efficient enough to direct and co-ordinate the work of the various executive agencies and semi-autonomous bodies. Professor Stone recommends a specific co-ordination agency headed by a full time official who " should be viewed for economic development purposes as an arm of the chief Executive " [14]

The second requirement for successful planning is the existence of certain well-defined objectives. That makes planning purposive, helps in the greater concentration of national effort towards the attainment of the objectives and gives direction and meaning to the various steps taken in that line. In Soviet Russia, vigorous industrialization and rapid building up of the economy so as

[14]Quoted in Hanson, A. H., *Public Enterprise and Economic Development*, Routledge and Kegan Paul, London, 1959, p. 113.

to surpass the achievements of capitalist economies have been repeatedly mentioned as the keynote of planning and the sustained effort of the nation is directed to that end by interpreting the programme of action as a national war on the economic front. Much of the success of economic planning in Nazi Germany was due to the singleness of purpose with which the resources of the country were mobilized and utilized for freeing the economy from the evils of depression and making the country militarily strong and invincible. In fact, planning is not possible unless there is an objective before the nation, and the more clearly defined and more realistic the objective, the greater are the chances of success.

Public co-operation is essential for successful planning especially when planning is democratic. One means of evoking the enthusiasm of the people and their co-operative spirit is by proving that the fruits of their efforts accrue to themselves without any great delay. People in a village are normally prepared to work hard and put forth great effort on road construction, sinking of wells or repairing of irrigation tanks in their own village because they know that they themselves would benefit by their activity. Another requisite is the feeling of the people that the benefits of economic development would be shared by all in as equitable a manner as possible. Governmental measures which give an assurance to the people that economic advancement would reduce the disparity in income and wealth are a sure means of evoking the latent enthusiasm of the workers. In this sense, the announcement by the Government of India of the social objectives of planning—viz. establishment of social justice and economic equality and the distribution of the increased production resulting from economic progress equitably to all—satisfies not only the egalitarian ideals of the community, but also has an important economic significance in that the announcement of such ideals, and what is more important, the translation of these ideals into practice would secure the co-operation of the people and enlist their support for planned development. Prof. Lange observes that " as a general principle, successful planning for economic development must imply the abolition—or at least neutralization—of such concentrations of private economic power as would block the realization of the plan ".[15]

To a considerable extent, efficiency of planning depends on whether the formulation of the plan is based on accurate data. Adequate statistical data are of prime importance not only in the drafting of a realistic plan, but also needed in the course of its implementation. Periodic checking up of the progress of the plan and the revisions that may be called for in view of current developments would not be possible unless the data available for the planning authority are exhaustive and correct. Accurate statistical information is required to fix up priorities in investment programmes and for bringing about inter-industry co-ordination. Statistical details of price changes, employment, foreign trade conditions, foreign trade earnings and foreign exchange requirements, are essential for correct budgeting and also for helping the evaluation of programmes

[15]Lange, Oskar, *Essays on Economic Planning*, Asia Publishing House, Bombay, 1960, p. 22.

and revision of targets. In short, statistics form the basis on which a development plan has to be formulated. Without it planning tends to become a mere guess work. Attention has been drawn by the United Nations experts to the serious gap in the statistical data available in the underdeveloped countries, and they have laid great stress on the need for setting up Central Statistical Organizations which should be responsible for the collection, co-ordination and standardization of statistics. The Central Statistical Organization is to be in close touch with the planning staff of the government so that it can be aware of the specific needs for data for planning purposes.[16]

A sound administrative mechanism is a *sine qua non* for effective planning. In fact, most of the conditions above mentioned are implied in or covered by administrative efficiency. According to Prof. Kapp: " Public administration is strategic in the sense that it influences and determines the success of the entire development plan and that it is susceptible to deliberate social control and change ".[17] A competent planning agency is needed for formulating, implementing and reformulating the plan. Such an agency has to make important political and administrative decisions and as such it should comprise persons who are not only experts in the field of planning but also have sufficient administrative skill and experience. A good system of administration is needed not only in the initial stages of planning but also to tackle many problems that may crop up in the course of carrying out the plan. In a planned economy various kinds of controls have to be imposed, financial, monetary and credit controls, control of capital issues, foreign trade, foreign exchange, etc. This cannot be done satisfactorily unless the administrative system of the country is competent and efficient. Apart from these, planning may involve the organization and running of private enterprises and also necessitate legislative measures for bringing about social and economic reforms such as land reforms, company law, etc.

Many of the above-mentioned conditions are lacking in most of the underdeveloped countries and planning for development becomes a more complicated affair because of their great poverty and lack of resources. Another obstacle to efficient planning in these countries is that they have imbibed a new social ideology rather too early. The adoption of democratic forms of government and universal franchise have conferred on the people a great amount of political rights. The sudden rise in their political status before they became mature enough to realize their responsibilities and duties as citizens has led to an over-emphasis of their rights and claims. This has stood in the way of generating and mobilizing savings as effectively as could be done under a different system or under the same system of government with people having different social attitudes. There is therefore a tendency for democracy to get diluted and to give way to some form of dictatorship or guided

[16]*Economic Bulletin for Asia and the Far East*, U.N., November, 1955, pp. 63-70.

[17]Kapp, William K., ' Economic Development, National Planning and Public Administration,' *Kyklos*, Vol. XIII, 1960, Fasc. 2, p. 173.

democracy. The acute pressure of population in some of these countries constitutes an additional serious socio-economic problem, the satisfactory solution of which calls for administrative efficiency and leadership of a high order. But the state in many cases is not competent and the administrative system far from efficient. Lack of statistical data and absence of centralized agencies to collect statistical information and the paucity of qualified planners account for haphazard planning, inadequate implementation of plans and incomplete co-ordination between the different agencies of planned development. In many of the underdeveloped countries, the administration is not efficient enough even to carry out the basic functions of government. Attempts to make use of such a defective mechanism for purposes of planned development results only in muddled planning.

Among the underdeveloped countries India has on the whole, a fairly efficient administrative mechanism. But recent experience of planning in the country has brought into relief the incapacity of the administrative machinery to bear the tasks of planning. The deficiency of the administrative mechanism in India has three aspects. In the first place, the present system of administration was designed in the days of colonialism strictly for revenue collection and the administration of justice. The administrative personnel therefore served primarily as collectors of revenue, keepers of records, policemen and in some cases as magistrates in criminal cases. Organizing development effort and executing plans of economic improvement are a new experience. Excessive bureaucratization and centralization, lack of adequate supervision and absence of provision for assigning accountability for particular actions and tasks on the different incumbents in the rungs of the official heirarchy, have resulted in divided responsibility and in a situation in which everybody is responsible for everything before anything is done. A second aspect of the situation is the rapid addition of rules and standing orders to the old ones with the result that administrative procedure has become complicated and cumbersome causing considerable delay and vexation. Failure to take decisions quickly by officers in charge of such departments as irrigation and public works, results quite often in serious and avoidable losses and hampers development efforts. Recently, the Resources and Economy Committee set up by the Government of Mysore found the astonishing fact that exclusive of the time covered by cabinet consideration, it took normally 272·2 days on the average for a file to be processed in the Secretariat. *The Hindu* of Madras remarks that the cost of such administrative delays and lapses " mounts with each passing year as the government tend to penetrate more and more into even the sphere of industrial production where speed and efficiency are vital for competitive survival. The debacle of the Rourkela steel plant was recently traced as much to rolls of red tape as to technical difficulties ".[18] Thirdly, there is the human factor. The fact that the administrative machinery was designed for purposes other than economic development, explains not only the incapacity of the

[18] *The Hindu,* Madras, September 18 and 19, 1962.

administrative mechanism to cope with the new problems arising out of the development activities of the state, but also the unhelpful attitude of executive officers to the underlying rural population. The authoritarian indifference, callousness, and lack of any human concern for the local interests of illiterate peasants and villagers which characterize the average executive officers, help only in destroying the little enthusiasm that the rural folk may have for achieving economic improvement. This is true of even the village co-operative societies which have been set up with the ostensible purpose of helping the rural community and serving as agencies to foster a spirit of hard work and co-operative effort. Instances are common of members leaving the societies disgusted with the sort of attention and service they get at the hands of the officers and agents who do not know the rules and regulations pertaining to the subject of their administration and who have neither the ability nor the willingness to understand the problems and difficulties of the villagers.

The urgent and important need of underdeveloped countries therefore appears to be the reforming of the administrative machinery. Economic underdevelopment in these countries is reflected in underdeveloped administration. Investment in the reform of administration would bring about in an indirect way larger returns than what such investments in industries would yield. A sound and efficient system of administration would help in the better organization and management of public enterprises and public investment schemes and better mobilization and utilization of savings; it would also bring about favourable changes in the attitudes of people. To quote Professor William Kapp " the so called marginal social productivity of additional investments may be greatest in the field of administrative reforms. Adequate investments in such reforms if properly conceived and carried out, may finally break the monotonous constancy of most ratios between input and output which have marked the stationary backwardness of the underdeveloped world ".[19]

DEVELOPMENT PLANS IN UNDERDEVELOPED COUNTRIES

The above-mentioned limitations have however not deterred most of the underdeveloped countries from adopting planning as the means to step up their rates of economic growth. A few of them have already had about a decade of experience in planned development while in most of them the first plans are still in progress. On page 571 are given the names of the South-East Asian countries which have introduced planned programmes of economic expansion and the periods to which their respective Plans relate.[20]

Development Plans have been adopted by the South American countries also. About two years after the end of the Second World War, the small

[19]Kapp, William K., ' Economic Development, National Planning and Public Administration.' *Kyklos*, Vol. XIII 1960, Fasc. 2, p. 200.

[20]*Economic Bulletin for Asia and the Far East*, U.N., December, 1958 and December, 1961.

Country	Plan period	Title
Afghanistan	1956–57—1960–61	Five-Year Plan
Burma	1952–53—1959–60	Eight-Year Development Programme
”	1961–62—1964–65	Second Four-Year Plan
Cambodia	1959 —1964	Five-Year Plan
Ceylon	1947–48—1952–53	First Six-Year Plan
”	1954–55—1959–60	Second Six-Year Plan
”	1957 —1968	The Ten-Year Plan
China (Mainland)	1953 —1957	First Five-Year Plan
” ”	1958 —1962	Second Five-Year Plan
Federation of Malaya	1956 —1960	Five-Year Capital Expenditure Plan
” ”	1961 —1965	Second Five-Year Plan
India	1951–52—1955–56	First Five-Year Plan
”	1956–57—1960–61	Second Five-Year Plan
”	1961–62—1965–66	Third Five-Year Plan
Indonesia	1956–60	Five-Year Development Plan
”	1961–69	Eight-Year Plan
Iran	1955–56—1961–62	Seven-Year Plan
”	1962–63—1966–67	Five-Year Plan
Japan	1953–54—1959–60	Seven-Year Plan
”	1955–56—1961–62	Modified Seven-Year Plan
”	1961–62—1970–71	New Long-range Economic Plan
Nepal	1956–57—1960–61	Five-Year Plan
Pakistan	1955–56—1959–60	First Five-Year Plan
”	1960–61—1964–65	Second Five-Year Plan
Philippines	1957–61	Five-Year Economic and Social Development Programme
”	1959–60—1961–62	Three-Year Programme of Economic and Social Development
Thailand	1961–66	Six-Year Development Plan

countries of Eastern Europe, Czechoslovakia, Poland, Hungary, Romania, Bulgaria and Yugoslavia, started their short period programmes of reconstruction which were officially completed about 1948–49. Since then most of them have adopted Five-Year Development Plans. In Bulgaria the First Plan which was to run till the end of 1953 was officially completed in 1952 when the Second Plan was adopted. This was succeeded by a three-year plan in 1958. Yugoslavia has adopted annual plans.

In the early post-war years, the primary concern of these countries was the rehabilitation or reconstruction of their economies which had been shattered severely by World War II or by internal political disturbances. Thus in the case of the East European countries, there were reconstruction plans between the years 1946 and 1949. In 1949–52 China concentrated her attention on rehabilitating her economy, which had been seriously ravaged by the civil war. Similarly in India although the idea of economic planning was put forth even during the course of the Second World War, internal disturbances resulting from the partition of the country in 1947 and the various new economic problems arising on the wake of it, necessitated the adoption of reconstruction measures before planning on a full scale was started. This was true of Burma and some other East Asian countries as well. Regular planning for economic development thus started only about the beginning of the second half of the century.

As is natural, the major objective of economic planning is the acceleration of economic growth. But in most cases, the objectives have not been properly defined and are mostly vague. Broadly speaking, a distinction may be made between qualitative and quantitative objectives. The former is general and has no time limit and would include such aims as the establishment of a socialistic pattern of society, reduction of inequalities in income distribution, laying of a basis for self-sustained growth, rehabilitation or diversification of the economy, maintaining or strengthening the balance of payments position, etc.; while to the category of quantitative objectives would belong, increasing the level of national income or per capita income, raising the level of employment, etc. These latter objectives can be expressed in quantitative terms for both the long and the short run. The income increase—both aggregate and per capita—envisaged in the plans of some of the Asian countries is shown in Table 48.

Table 48

PLANNED ANNUAL RATE OF INCREASE IN NATIONAL AND PER CAPITA INCOME
(Compound rate of increase)

Country	Plan Period	National Income Rise per cent	Per capita Income Rise per cent
Burma	1961–62—1964–65	5·9	3·6
Cambodia	1959–64	5·0	2·0
Ceylon	1957–68	5·9	2·9
China (Taiwan)	1957–68	7·4	3·7
Federation of Malaya	1960–65	4·1	0·8
India	1961–62—1965–66	6·0	3·8
Indonesia	1961–69	3·7	1·4
Iran	1962–63—1966–67	6·0	3·5
Japan	1961–62—1970–71	7·2	6·3
Pakistan	1960–61—1964–65	3·7	1·8
Philippines	1959–60—1961–62	5·9	2·8
Thailand	1961–66	5·0	3·0

SOURCE: *Economic Bulletin for Asia and the Far East*, U.N., December, 1961, p. 4, Table 1.

The considerable disparity between annual percentage increase in national income and increase in per capita income in some countries reflects, of course, the high rate of increase in population. A per capita rise of income of 3 per cent per year should be considered quite high in comparison with the rates attained even in quite advanced countries. Among the countries listed above, Japan has a planned rate of increase in per capita income of 5 to 7 per cent per annum during 1955–56 to 1961–62 while the rate in Malaya is below one per cent for the period 1960–65. Burma, China (Taiwan), India and Iran have a comparatively high rate—3·5 to 3·8 per cent envisaged in their current plan periods. In the other countries the rate is between 1·5 and 3 per cent. The high rate of 3·6 per cent for Burma has to be explained by the absence of any population pressure in the country. According to the Eight-Year Development Plan of Burma, Gross National Product was to rise from Kyats 3,900 million in 1951–52 to Kyats 7,000 million in 1959–60 or by 70 per cent. This would mean a rise in per capita income of 69 per cent, i.e. from K. 201 to K. 340 and per capita consumption by 54 per cent. Planned development in Indonesia is expected to bring about an increase in national income by 95 per cent and per capita income by 40 per cent in 1975 as compared with 1955. The current development plan of Ceylon aims at bringing about a higher rate of expansion of productive capacity than population growth. In India, accordding to the Third Five-Year Plan, national income is to rise by over 30 per cent between 1961–62 and 1965–66 and per capita income by 17 per cent (i.e. from Rs. 330 to Rs. 385).

The principal objective of the development plans of Japan is to provide " full employment by accomplishing persistently the maximum rate of economic growth consistent with economic stability ". The emphasis on employment is natural in countries where population pressure is great. Thus the Ten-Year Plan of Ceylon and the First Four-Year Plan of Singapore both emphasized as the major objective, the achievement of a higher level of employment. Higher levels of employment have been stressed in the plans of Pakistan and India also. In fact, the stress laid on the different objectives depends largely on the circumstances and problems of the country concerned. Thus the idea of rehabilitation is mainly to be found in the plan of Burma and to a lesser extent in that of Indonesia. In the Philippines where about 80 per cent of the exports consist of four commodities—sugar, copra, abaca and timber—the major theme of the plan is diversification of the economy and changing its structure so that there will be more dependence on internal diversified production, and less dependence on a few basic products. The Development Plans in most of the countries aim at saving or earning of foreign exchange, but this objective is particularly stressed in the plans of Afghanistan, Burma, Indonesia, Pakistan and the Philippines. In the last two countries as well as in Japan, export promotion is a prominent feature of the plans.

Planned development has involved a sharp step up in the rate of investment from the pre-plan averages in all the countries, and in most of these the rate of investment has progressively increased with successive plans. As has been observed in the previous chapter, the contribution of the public sector to this acceleration of investment has varied from country to country. And corresponding to the differences in the relative significance of the public and private sectors, there is variation in the composition of investment also. Normally, a tendency to lay great emphasis on heavy and capital goods industries is observable in the socialist economies. Thus in the First Development Plans of East European countries 40 to 50 per cent of the total investment was devoted to industries. And of the investment in industries, producers goods industries absorbed 80 to 90 per cent. Transport and communications accounted for between 15 and 25 per cent while to agriculture was assigned about 8 to 12 per cent of total investment. The distribution of investment in the First Five-Year Plan of China (1953 to 1957) was as follows: industry 40·9 per cent, cultural, educational and public health facilities 18·6 per cent, transport and communications 11·7 per cent, agriculture, water resources and forests 8·0 per cent. Top priority was given to heavy industries on the score that they provide the foundation for future development, while light industries were assigned a low investment priority since they had idle capacity. The Second Five-Year Plan of Mainland China envisaged a doubling of the gross volume of industrial output, including both modern industry and handicrafts, between 1957 and 1962, while the gross value of agricultural output was planned to increase by about 35 per cent. The proportion of the gross value of producer goods to total gross value of industrial output was to increase from 38 per cent in 1957 to 50 per cent in 1962.

Among the other countries, much emphasis is placed on heavy industries in the plans of Japan, India and Pakistan. Heavy industry looms large in the investment programme of Japan because it has been assumed that the demand for Japanese-made capital goods would be increasing sharply in the neighbouring, less developed countries. Thus while industrial production was expected to rise by 60·5 per cent between 1956 and 1962, production in the chemical industry was to go up by 89 per cent, metal industry by 81 per cent and machinery industry by 76 per cent. As a consequence of the greater emphasis laid on producer goods, the ratio between heavy industries and light industries changed from 59 : 41 in 1956 to 66 : 34 in 1962.[21] A similar trend is observable in the Development Plans of India and Pakistan also.

Investment in agriculture varies considerably as may be seen from Table 49.

It should be observed that the figures given in the Table are estimates contained in the Plans. Actuals have differed mostly in the downward direction. As may be expected, agriculture is assigned a low priority in those countries in which industries are given a high priority. Thus in the first Development Plans of East European countries, agricultural investment was only 8 to 12 per cent of total investment while in the Chinese First Plan, agriculture, water resources and forests together accounted for only 8 per cent. However, recent experiences in many of the underdeveloped countries of adverse balance of

[21] *Economic Bulletin for Asia and the Far East*, U.N., December, 1958, p. 15.

Table 49

PROPORTION OF PUBLIC INVESTMENT IN AGRICULTURE* IN SOME ECAFE COUNTRIES AS GIVEN IN THE PLANS

(Proportion to total investment expressed as per cent)

Country	Plan Period	Proportion to Total Investment (per cent)
Burma	1961–62—1964–65	27
Ceylon	1960–68	30
Federation of Malaya	1961–65	37
India	1961–62—1965–66	24
Indonesia	1956–60	32
Pakistan	1960–61—1964–65	43
Philippines	1960–62	31
Singapore	1961–64	10
Thailand	1961–66	42
Viet Nam (South)	1957–61	43

*Includes agriculture, irrigation, forestry and fishery; in some countries it includes Community Development also.

SOURCE: *Economic Bulletin for Asia and the Far East*, December, 1961.

payments, shortage of industrial raw materials, inadequacy of food supplies and inflationary pressures in the economy have drawn attention to the imbalance between agriculture and industries caused by over-investment in industry or neglect of agriculture. As a result, some improvement in the allocation of investment in favour of agriculture is noticeable in the recent Plans.

Since the major objective of economic planning in underdeveloped countries is rapid economic growth, it is relevant to consider how far planning has helped to accelerate economic progress in the low income countries. However, it is difficult to give any satisfactory answer to this question. For one thing, what is due exclusively to planning cannot be known because we do not know what would have been the fate of the economy in the absence of planning. Among the underdeveloped regions, high rates of growth have been registered in countries where there is centralized planning as in Mainland China as well as in others where planning is more or less of an indicative nature as in some of the South American countries. In the last ten years or so, the rate of growth of income in the low income countries has been on the whole higher than it was before. But we cannot say how much of this acceleration was due to the adoption of planned programmes of development and how much was due to other factors. There is no disputing the fact that the securing of political freedom after centuries of dependence has aroused in the masses a sort of development consciousness. The economic progress in recent years has to be attributed partly at least to this change in the attitudes of the people. Secondly, it is possible to estimate the contribution of planning to economic growth only if other conditions such as seasonal factors and political circumstances remain constant. It is unfair to compare the economic achievements of a country with political stability and enjoying an uninterrupted succession of favourable seasons with that of another in which these conditions are absent. Rise in income in the former may be due more to the favourable circumstances than to the fact that it has adopted a plan for economic development. Equally important as political stability and favourable seasons are external factors, particularly the nature of demand for the country's exports. It would thus mean that if the factors above-mentioned are unfavourable, economic planning is not given a fair chance, and any judgment about its success or failure would be of limited value. Thirdly, it is difficult to measure the effects of economic planning. Mere rise in national or per capita income is not a correct indicator of the extent to which a country has benefited by a national plan of development. Planned outlays on economic or social infrastructure do not add to income immediately, but are nevertheless of the greatest importance in providing the basic facilities that would help future growth. Similarly fundamental structural changes would have taken place in the economy; institutional rigidities would have been removed and the social attitudes would have been revolutionized; all these factors augment considerably the potentialities of the economy to grow rapidly. But these are changes of a qualitative nature and cannot be measured. We have therefore to depend on other indicators which are quantitatively assessable such as changes in national income and per capita income, levels of employment, volume of exports and imports, agricultural and industrial output, etc. in order to have an idea of the trend of an economy. These are obviously rough indicators and do not give a complete picture of the nature of transformation that takes place in an economy.

Fairly high levels of income growth have been attained by some under-developed countries in the last few years. A recent study of planned development in the countries of Asia and the Far East made by the Economic Commission of the United Nations for this region has made available the data given in Table 50. Among the countries listed, Japan alone has succeeded in maintaining an actual increase in income above the planned income targets. The annual per capita income growth of over 8 per cent attained in the years 1955–56 to 1959–60, compares favourably with the rates reached in the highly advanced countries of the world. It should however be remembered that Japan cannot be grouped with the underdeveloped countries, and much of the increase in income in these years is due to the fact that she had already attained a high stage of industrialization. In recent years, there has been a remarkable improvement in productivity helped by rapid technological advance and the shift of workers from agriculture to manufacturing industries. Development of the machinery industry has had both forward and backward linkage

Table 50

PLANNED AND ACTUAL RATE OF INCREASE IN NATIONAL AND PER CAPITA INCOME IN SOME COUNTRIES OF ASIA AND THE FAR EAST

Country	Annual Planned increase (per cent) Period	National income	Per capita income	Annual Actual increase (per cent) Period	National income	Per capita income
Burma	1952–53—			1950–51—		
	1959–60	7·4	6·2	1959–60	4·7	3·5
Ceylon	1959—1968	5·9	2·9	1950—1959	3·5	1·0
China (Mainland)	1953—1957	...	...	1950—1957	11·8	...
	1951–52—			1951–52—		
	1955–56	2·1	0·9	1955—56	3·4	1·6
India	1956–57—			1956–57—		
	1960–61	4·6	3·3	1960–61	3·7	1·5
Indonesia	1956—1960	3·0	1·3	1956—1959	2·1	—0·6
Japan	1953–54—			1953–54—		
	1959–60	4·5	3·7	1959–60	7·8	6·7
	1955–56—			1955–56—		
	1961–62	6·5	5·7	1959–60	9·2	8·2
Pakistan	1955–56—			1955–56—		
	1959–60	2·8	1·4	1959–60	2·1	0·2
Philippines	1956–57—			1956—1959	5·0	1·8
	1960–61	6·0	...			
Thailand	1961—1966	6·0	3·0	1951—1959	4·7	1·8

SOURCE: *Economic Bulletin for Asia and the Far East*, U.N., December, 1961, adapted from Table 8, page 19.

effects, that is to say, it has helped the growth and expansion of both a large number of ancillary industries as well as other industries concerned with the manufacture of end products like plastics, rubber products, paints, etc. In contrast to Japan the less developed countries of the region make a poor showing although in some like Mainland China and India, the results attained have been quite satisfactory. In China net material product during 1950–57 increased at the high annual rate of about 12 per cent. China's growth rate in these years was in fact higher than that reached by the U.S.S.R. in the early stages of industrialization. However, in the Second Plan period in China, the production of consumer goods and agricultural commodities was lower than what was expected. Although in 1958–59 bumper harvests were reported, in 1960, there was a serious shortage of grains and raw materials which necessitated a drastic revision of the targets downwards as well as large imports of food and raw cotton in 1961. In India, during the First Five-Year Plan period, national income increased by 18 per cent as against a target of 12 per cent. This was due mainly to the marked progress in agricultural production which was much above expectations. But

37

in the Second Five-Year Plan, against a target of 25 per cent increase, the actual increase in national income was only 20 per cent. Over the decade 1951–60, although aggregate national product increased by 42 per cent, income per head rose by only 16 per cent. In Pakistan and Burma, many adverse circumstances seriously affected execution of the programmes of development. The short fall in the implementation of the First Plan in Pakistan was due to the failure of the agricultural sector because of adverse weather conditions which resulted in heavy import of food grains, and deterioration in the terms of trade and consequent decline in foreign exchange earnings; also, unexpectedly large increase in non-developmental expenditures and sharp rise in prices, shortage of key personnel, equipment and materials, and ineffective co-ordination between government agencies, dislocated planning and prevented the attainment of the targets. The extent to which adverse external circumstances can hamper planning is well illustrated by the experience of Burma. Against a target of 7·4 per cent increase in national income and 6·2 per cent in per capita income set in the Eight-Year Plan, the actual achievement was 4·7 and 3·5 per cent respectively. About 1955, gross domestic product barely surpassed the pre-war level, while per capita output and consumption were 17 per cent and 14 per cent below the pre-war level. The main reason for this decline was the adverse turn in the world market for rice, Burma's chief export commodity. The actual export proceeds from rice were only half of the plan estimates. Excessive emphasis on the development of basic facilities like transport and power raised the capital-output ratio of the economy, necessitated large imports of materials and equipment and caused a severe strain on the resources and balance of payments position of the country. By 1955, the Eight-Year Plan had been virtually abandoned and was superseded by the First Four-Year Plan (1956–57—1959–60) which " emphasized the objective of reducing instability, strengthening the base of the economy, and stressed the importance of foreign exchange earning and saving and a low capital-output ratio or new quick yielding projects ".[22]

Economic development brings about certain structural changes particularly a change in the relative proportions of the various constituents of the national product. A rise in the proportion of non-agricultural output to total output and a corresponding fall in the proportion of agricultural output go usually with economic advancement. Between 1950 and 1959 in Japan, the contribution of agriculture to net domestic product decreased from 25·9 to 16·5 per cent while that of manufacturing increased from 24·8 to 27·0 per cent. The increase under transport and communication, ownership of dwellings and public administration and defence was much more appreciable. Among the other countries, it is interesting to find that in those which have a poor record in the matter of increase in income, structural changes have been quite significant. Thus while in India the contribution of agriculture, forestry and fishing declined from 51·2 per cent in 1950 to 48·0 per cent in 1959, and manufacturing

[22]*Economic Bulletin for Asia and the Far East*, U.N., December, 1961, p. 23.

and construction rose slightly from 15·3 to 16·8 per cent, in Burma the decline in agriculture was from 46·4 to 42·5 per cent between 1951 and 1959, and the rise in manufacturing from 10·3 to 14·1 per cent. Similarly, in Pakistan the contribution of agriculture to net domestic product decreased from 60·8 per cent in 1950 to 55·1 per cent in 1959 while the share of manufacturing output went up appreciably from 7·2 to 12·4 per cent. Nevertheless, the agricultural sector continues to be very large in most countries of the region. In 1959 the agricultural sector was responsible for slightly over 55 per cent of the domestic product in Indonesia and Pakistan and 40–50 per cent in Burma, Cambodia, Ceylon, India and Thailand. According to Professor Kuznets, the proportion of agricultural output to total output is on the average 25 per cent for the world medium income countries and 46 per cent for the low income countries. Viewed against this classification, it is clear that most countries of South and East Asia occupy a position well at the bottom of the low income group.

Underdeveloped countries have had only a short experience in planning, and it is unfair to make any assessment of the effectiveness of planning in generating growth on the basis of achievements so far made. To some extent the meagreness of the results attained, has to be attributed to the fact that in many countries full attention could not be devoted to planned efforts because of political disturbances, adverse external circumstances and inflationary conditions at home. Nor can it be said that planning has been carried out on efficient lines in the other countries which were relatively free from such difficulties. Administrative deficiency, lack of statistical data and inadequacy of trained personnel and experience, explain to a large extent the vague and haphazard manner in which plans were formulated and the half-hearted manner in which they were implemented.[23] In some instances there has been over-ambitiousness in fixing investment and production targets. In others, over-investment in certain sectors has caused imbalances in the economy. Investment in social overheads has in some countries exceeded the absorptive capacity of the economy. In most cases there is lack of adequate provision to ensure co-ordination between the various agencies responsible for implementing the programmes in the plan. Another serious gap in planning is the lack of attention to demand projections and inter-industry relations. However, in the

[23]Thus with reference to the poor results attained in some Middle Eastern and South American countries, Hanson gives the following reasons: inadequate and incorrect statistics in Turkey and the Arab states; absence of economic studies in Colombia; lack of clarity of objectives in Argentina; organizational defects such as division of monetary authority between five different agencies in Brazil; no financial co-ordination in Puerto Rico; lack of inter-agency co-ordination in Argentina; in Panama, lack of a Plan because of non co-operation of ministries—Hanson, A. H., *Public Enterprise and Economic Development*, Routledge and Kegan Paul, London, 1959, pp. 108–10. The deficiencies of planning in some of the British colonies have been brought out in a recent article by Douglas Dosser. Among these may be mentioned, the lack of co-ordination between individual sector plans, faulty allocation of investment and the lack of understanding of the effects of an expansion of any particular sector on the other sectors through the supply and demand side. Dosser, Douglas, ' The Formulation of Development Plans in the British Colonies,' *Economic Journal*, June. 1959, pp. 255–66.

final analysis the fact emerges that for planning to be successful, the country should have attained a certain minimum standard in economic development. In an economy which is really backward, with a large non-monetized sector, lacking in basic facilities and financial institutions and with an inefficient administrative machinery, the initial attempt should not be planning for development but for rehabilitation, reconstruction and reorganization. Planning for economic development can take roots and fructify only when the ground is properly laid for the economy to grow.

Chapter XVIII

PLANNED ECONOMIC PROGRESS IN INDIA

A BRIEF review of planned economic progress in India in the last ten years or so would help to illustrate the possibilities and scope of planning in a typical underdeveloped economy. The experience of India is of special significance because planning in the country has had an uninterrupted progress over more than a decade. Since the partition of the country in 1947 until the recent clash with China, the Indian Union has been free from any serious political or social disturbances. Her administrative system, although not very satisfactory judged by Western standards, is yet more efficient than that of many other underdeveloped countries. Further, in contrast to countries like Burma, Malaya or Ceylon, the economy of India is not export-oriented. Export earnings of the country form only about six per cent of the national income and as such, external demand factors or fluctuations in world markets have not seriously affected the trend of income in the country. The course of economic planning has in fact had a fair trial in the country. It is therefore relevant to examine how far economic planning has helped to generate the forces of growth in the country.

OBJECTIVES OF PLANNING

Planning in India has three important objectives. The first is an appreciable increase in national income. The First Five-Year Plan, 1951–52—1955–56, envisaged national income, which was estimated at Rs. 90 billion in the first year of the Plan, to rise to Rs. 100 billion at the end of it, that is, by 11 per cent. The Second Plan 1956–57—1960–61 fixed a target of income increase by 25 per cent over the five years. A similar increase of 5 per cent or more per year is indicated in the Third Five-Year Plan, 1961–62—1965–66. This improvement in national income would involve the attainment of self sufficiency in food grains and increased agricultural production and also expansion of basic industries like steel, chemicals, fuel and power and the establishment of machine-building capacity, so that the requirements of further industrialization can be met out of the country's own resources.[1] The second objective, is the expansion of employment opportunities and the utilization of the man-power resources of the country to the fullest extent possible. Thirdly, in conformity with the Directive Principles of State Policy enunciated in Articles 36 to 51

[1]*Third Five-Year Plan*, Planning Commission, Government of India, New Delhi, 1961, p. 48.

of the Constitution of India, planned development aims at establishing progressively greater equality of opportunity and reduction of disparities in income and wealth and a more even distribution of economic power. It is stressed that the operation of the economic system should not result in the concentration of wealth and the means of production in the hands of a few to the detriment of the community at large. The positive aspect of this purpose of planned development is indicated in the Second Plan which states that the task before an underdeveloped country is not merely to get better results within the existing framework of economic and social institutions, but to mould and refashion these so that they contribute effectively to the realization of wider and deeper social values. Accordingly, the goal of a socialistic pattern of society is outlined in the Second Plan in which " the basic criterion for determining the lines of advancement must not be private profit but social gain ".[2]

These three objectives are closely inter-related. Higher levels of income can be attained through increased agricultural and industrial production by making full use of the natural and human resources available. And the establishment of a better social order is necessary to enlist the co-operation of the masses and prompt them to greater personal effort without which increased production would not be possible.

PATTERN OF INVESTMENT

The attainment of the first two objectives depends largely on the extent to which savings are generated and mobilized and the manner in which the savings are invested. In this respect, two important trends are observable. In the first place. the state has assumed an important role in development activity. Secondly, as regards the pattern or composition of investment, increasing emphasis is laid on the development of heavy or capital goods industries in order to accelerate growth and also to make the country self-sufficient in the matter of capital equipment and machinery. Although the Industrial Policy Resolution of 1948 emphasized clearly the responsibility of the government in promoting industrial development and envisaged an increasingly active role for the public sector, yet the planning authorities in 1951 did not consider an expansion of the public sector either necessary or desirable. The state's responsibility for developing key industries such as iron and steel, heavy chemical and heavy electrical industries was asserted; nevertheless, in the initial stages of development the state was to concentrate on the provision of basic services like power and transportation, and progress in the industrial field was assumed to depend to a great extent on private effort and investment.

But there is a significant change in emphasis in the Second Plan. The revised Industrial Policy Statement of the Government, of April 1956, stated that in view of the adoption of the socialist pattern of society as the national objective " all industries of basic and strategic importance or in the nature of

[2] *Second Five-Year Plan,* Planning Commission, Government of India, New Delhi, 1956, p. 22.

public utility services should be in the public sector. Other industries which are essential and require investment on a scale which only the state could provide have also to be in the public sector. The state has therefore to assume direct responsibility for the future development of industries over a wide area." The Second Plan accordingly envisaged a large expansion of public enterprise in the sphere of heavy industries, oil exploration and coal. In its own sphere the private sector was to be left unhampered, but government policy in respect of industries should aim at influencing private decisions " through fiscal measures, through licensing and to the extent necessary through direct physical allocations so as to promote and to facilitate the realization of the targets proposed ".[3] Further emphasis on the responsibility of the state in the development of " those industries which will make the economy self-sustaining such as steel, machine building and the manufacture of producer goods and reduce as rapidly as possible the need for external assistance to purchase these goods and also permit a broadening of the export base " is laid in the Third Five-Year Plan.[4] Stressing the importance of basic industries in accelerating economic growth, the Third Plan states, " An expanding public sector engaged specially in developing basic industries and producing large surpluses for development will itself be one of the most important factors determining the rate at which the economy can grow ".[5] The growing emphasis on the development of heavy industries and the assumption of an increasing role in this matter by the state are reflected in the investment allocation figures in Table 51.

It may be seen from Table 51 that investment in the public sector as a proportion of total investment in the economy increased from 46 per cent in the First Plan to 54 per cent in the Second Plan and is expected to rise to more than 60 per cent in the Third Plan period. Looking at it from another point of view, government investment increased by 134 per cent between the First and Second Plan years and would go up by 72 per cent between the Second and Third Plans, while the corresponding rates of increase in private sector investment are 70 per cent and 32 per cent respectively. The increase in public sector outlay has been concentrated mostly on industries and minerals. The rise under these two heads is particularly marked in the Second Plan period. The absolute amount spent by the government on industries and minerals went up from Rs. 740 million in the First Plan to Rs. 9,000 million in the Second Plan representing an increase by more than twelve times while between the Second and Third Plans it is expected to rise by about 69 per cent. These two items absorbed 4 per cent of total public outlay in 1951–56 and 20 per cent in the Second Plan period and is expected to reach the same proportion of one-fifth of total outlay in the Third Plan. The proportion of public outlay on power has remained more or less constant in the three Plans

[3] *Second Five-Year Plan*, Planning Commission, Government of India, New Delhi, 1956, p. 28.
[4] *Third Five-Year Plan*, Planning Commission, Government of India, New Delhi, 1961, p. 64.
[5] *ibid.* p. 50.

Table 51

DISTRIBUTION OF OUTLAY IN THE THREE FIVE-YEAR PLANS
(Rupees millions)

	First Plan (actuals)		Second Plan (actuals)		Third Plan	
	Expenditure	Per cent	Expenditure	Per cent	Expenditure	Per cent
Investment in Public Sector	15,600	46	36,500	54	63,000	60·6
Investment in Private Sector	18,000	54	31,0C0	46	41,000	39·4
Total investment	33,600	100	67,500	100	104,000	100·0
Outlay in the Public Sector:						
(a) Agriculture and Community Development	2,910	15	5,300	11	10,680	14
(b) Major and Medium irrigation	3,100	16	4,200	9	6,500	9
(c) Power	2,600	13	4,450	10	10,120	13
(d) Village and Small industries	430	2	1,750	4	2,640	4
(e) Industries and Minerals	740	4	9,000	20	15,200	20
(f) Transport and Communications	5,230	27	13,000	28	14,860	20
(g) Social Services and Miscellaneous	4,590	23	8,300	18	15,000*	20
Total	19,600	100	46,000	100	75,000	100

*Including inventories of Rs. 2,000 million.
SOURCE: *Third Five-Year Plan.*

(13 per cent in the First Plan, 10 per cent in the Second Plan and 13 per cent in the Third Plan) while the outlay on transport and communications receded from 27 per cent and 28 per cent in the first two Plans to 20 per cent in the Third Plan and that on Social Services and Miscellaneous declined from 23 per cent in the First to 18 and 17 per cent in the Second and Third Plans. The public outlay on agriculture and community development decreased from 15 per cent in 1951–56 to 11 per cent in 1956–61 and rises to 14 per cent in 1961–66.

Comparing the distribution of public investment in India's Third Plan with that in the current Plans of some other countries of Asia and the Far East—Burma, Ceylon, Malaya, Indonesia, Nepal, Pakistan, Philippines, Thailand and Viet Nam (South)—we find that public investment in agriculture is less than one-fourth of the total investment only in India and the Philippines (24 per cent and 22 per cent respectively). The proportion of government investment expenditure on industry and mining are the highest in Ceylon (32 per cent) and India (30 per cent). But in the former country, the share of agriculture in public investment is substantially higher than that in India. Most of the countries mentioned above are devoting a large proportion of expenditure on transport and communications. In Burma and Thailand, nearly half the investment is on this head. It should however be mentioned that India compared with the other countries has a better system of transport and communications. In most of them the provision of these basic overhead facilities and the organization of agriculture on efficient lines are an essential prerequisite for introducing any scheme of planned development.

The justification for devoting a large proportion of public investment to heavy, machine-building industries in India, as has been repeatedly stressed by the development plans, is that such industries are necessary for developing other industries like manufacture of consumption goods and that they are the source of large external economies and are essential for activizing the growth potentialities of the economy. An additional point mentioned in their favour is that by developing them, a large saving in foreign exchange requirements can be effected. That such basic industries would increase general productive efficiency and help in accelerating economic development is an accepted fact. According to Professor Chenery's estimates, the growth elasticity of all industry is 1·36, transport and communications 1·29, other services 1·07 and primary production 0·49.[6] It would therefore appear that the emphasis laid on the public sector and on heavy industry in India was actuated more by practical needs than by ideological considerations. But it may be pointed out that undue emphasis on investments of this nature may create serious imbalances in the economy which would hamper growth. The threat to industrialization caused by the recent decline in agricultural output in China which necessitated a modification of the Stalinist technique of development involving emphasis on investment goods industries, reliance on capital intensive technology and relative neglect of investment in agriculture is an illustration of this point.

PLANNED DEVELOPMENT AND ECONOMIC GROWTH

How far has planned development in India for a decade or more helped in generating the forces of self-sustained growth? The success or failure of any scheme of planning for economic development should be judged not with reference to the attainment or otherwise of the short term production targets in individual sectors of the economy, but with reference to the extent to which structural changes—changes in the organization of the economy and in the patterns of income creation and income distribution—have taken place, and the extent to which the dormant forces of growth have been released and activated. It is relevant at this stage to recall to our mind what Rostow pointed out as indicators of economic transformation—emergence of leading sectors, the marked rise in the rate of savings and investment, institutional and organizational changes and changes in the social attitudes and motivations of the people.[7]

[6]Chenery, H. B., ' Patterns of Industrial Growth,' *The American Economic Review*, September, 1960, pp. 634–35.

[7]*See* Chapter II, pp. 63–77

These factors are a good explanation of the manner in which economic development took place in some of the free enterprise economies of the world in the 18th and 19th centuries—Britain, Germany and the U.S.A. But in view of the changed political and economic circumstances in which the present-day low income countries are developing, the relative significance of the different conditions of growth as laid down by Rostow requires some reassessment. In an economy like India of today, in which economic development is planned, and in which public sector investment is as great as or greater than private sector investment, and where public investment is concentrated on economic infrastructure and basic industries, it is clear that in initiating the process of growth the state would have to play as important a part as private entrepreneurs played in the 19th century. The importance of the conditions that ensure a free flow of loanable funds is certainly as great in planned and mixed economies as in free enterprise economies but they take on a different form and aspect in the former. While in the free enterprise economies in their early stages of development, banking and financial institutions and the capital market developed spontaneously out of the needs of private entrepreneurs and by their own enterprise and initiative, in a country like India the provision of financial facilities has to be organized by the state. In other words, the state plays an important part not only in the utilization of savings but also in the mobilization and canalization of such savings. At the same time, the increasing interest taken by the state in the development of transport and communications and in the starting of capital goods and basic industries may be expected to spark off the transformation into self-sustained growth in an underdeveloped economy.

Hence the question how far planned economic development in India in the last decade has taken the country towards the stage of self-sustained growth has to be answered mostly in terms of what the state has achieved. As Rostow himself has indicated, the commencement of the era of planning may be considered as an event which has ushered in the transformation stage. The attainment of political freedom, the acquiring of international status as a free nation and the awakening of the masses to the need for building up the economy may be considered as the non-economic forces which have initiated this process of transformation. And this process would continue until the stage of self-sustained growth is reached. Effective planning and development along proper lines would shorten this period of transformation and bring nearer the next stage of development when economic growth becomes automatic and normal. In this sense, the success or failure of planned development in the country has to be judged with reference to the following three considerations :

(a) Whether per capita income has increased substantially so that larger savings are available in the economy and the investment rate has risen appreciably.

(b) Whether social attitudes have changed in a manner conducive to economic progress; in other words, whether the achievement so far made has aroused in the minds of the people a desire to make further improvements, and widened their vision of the possibilities of development, whether it has awakened mass enthusiasm and support for development.

(c) Whether public investment for the provision of economic infra-structure and the development of basic industries has furnished a sound foundation for rapidly building up the superstructure.

The 10 per cent rate of investment, the attainment of which according to Rostow marks the transition to self-sustained growth, should not be interpreted too narrowly. It is certainly wrong to assume that an economy will be wallowing in stagnation so long as its rate of investment is below this level and when once this point is reached, the all important transformation takes place. What is significant about the minimum rate of investment to be reached is that this rate should be high enough to ensure such a rate of growth of income that would help further increase in investment. In view of the lack of statistical data going as far back as the pre-take off stage of the developed economies, it is not possible to make any definite statement as to the extent to which the present low rate of investment in underdeveloped economies is to be raised in order to bring about the take off. Rostow illustrates his statement with investment data relating to Sweden and Canada in the last three or four decades of the 19th century. However in some contemporary underdeveloped countries we find that investment rate is equal to or exceeds the rate of 10 to 15 per cent of national income attained in the Western developed countries. In some of the South American countries, the rate of investment as a proportion of net national product very much exceeded 10 per cent in the early 1950s. In Burma, gross investment in 1956–57 to 1959–60 was 18·7 per cent; in China (Taiwan) it was 22·1 per cent in 1952–59. The ratio averaged 16 to 20 per cent in Japan in the years 1913–39 when her growth rate was high. In reality, the extent to which a given rate of investment would help in increasing income and accelerating savings and capital formation depends upon the efficiency of investment, that is, the capital-output ratio and also the rate of growth of population. But since the economic and non-economic conditions prevailing in the present-day developed countries in their early stages of growth, were different from that of modern low income countries, it is difficult to have any precise notion of the level of investment that would ensure self-sustained growth. Economic development in the Western countries in the 19th century was brought about by private enterprise. Increased production of certain manufactured consumption goods and the emergence of some leading sectors of the economy facilitated the establishment and development of other industries. But the nature of economic development in the underdeveloped countries of today is different. In these countries investment in the initial stages has to be on economic and social overheads and on heavy industries which involve large initial capital outlay. Further, the rate of growth of population is very much higher than what it was in the Western countries in the 19th century.

For these reasons, the minimum rate indicated by Rostow has to be raised considerably. Roughly we may say that a rise in the rate of net investment to about 15 or 18 per cent of the net national product is necessary if an under-developed country of the present day is to approach the stage of self-sustained growth.

Viewed against this requirement, the achievement of India in the past few years is far from satisfactory. The national income of India at 1960-61 prices increased from Rs. 102·4 billion at the beginning of the First Plan to Rs. 121·3 billion in 1955–56 and to Rs. 145·0 billion in 1960–61.[8] Over the decade covered by the first two plans, 1950–51 to 1960–61, national income increased by 42 per cent, but since population increased by 21 per cent in these ten years, the improvement in per capita income was meagre. It went up from Rs. 284 in 1950–51 to Rs. 306 in 1955–56 and to Rs. 330 in 1960–61, that is, per capita income increased by only 16 per cent. The annual compound rate of increase in national income and per capita income has been very low in India as compared with other underdeveloped countries. The relative position of India is seen from Table 52.

Table 52

INCREASE IN NATIONAL AND PER CAPITA INCOME
IN SOME COUNTRIES OF ASIA AND THE FAR EAST 1950–60
(Compound rate of increase at constant prices)

Country	Period	Increase in National Income (per cent)	Increase in Per Capita Income (per cent)
Burma	1950–51—1959–60	4·7	3·5
Cambodia	1951—59	4·0	1·5
Ceylon	1950—59	3·5	1·0
China (Mainland)	1950—57	11·8	...
India	1950–51—1960–61	3·6	1·6
Indonesia	1951—59	3·6	1·6
Japan	1955–56—1959–60	9·2	8·2
Pakistan	1950–51—1959–60	2·0	0·2
Philippines	1950—59	5·8	2·6
Thailand	1951—59	4·7	1·8

SOURCE: *Economic Bulletin for Asia and the Far East*, U.N., December. 1961, p. 19, Table 8.

In the ten years 1950–51 to 1960–61, the rate of per capita income increase in India was much below the rate attained in Japan and was lower

[8]The national income of India at current prices is estimated at Rs. 146·3 billion for 1961–62 ; the revised estimate for 1960–61 is Rs. 144·6 billion.

than that of other underdeveloped countries like Burma, Philippines and Thailand.

Corresponding to the meagre increase in per capita income, the savings and investment level also failed to move up to any appreciable extent. In the five years of the First Plan, savings increased from about 5 per cent of national income to about 7 per cent and at the end of the Second Plan it rose slightly to 8·5 per cent, which was 3 per cent less than the rate expected to be achieved. Total tax revenue of the Union and State governments amounted to 7 per cent of national income in 1950–51; in 1960–61 it increased to only 9 per cent. Investment at the end of the Second Plan reached the target of about 11 per cent of the national income but this could not have been attained without the massive foreign aid which amounted to as much as 3 per cent of national income. To some extent the poor show of savings was due to the deterioration of the effectiveness of investment and the failure of the state to mop up a good proportion of the increased incomes of the wealthier classes. Investment resulted in a proportionately lesser increase in income in the Second Plan years than in the First. Increased agricultural production, combined with the better utilization of existing capacity brought down the capital-output ratio in the years 1951–56 to 2 : 1 against an anticipated ratio of 3 : 1. On the other hand, in the Second Plan period, a capital-output ratio of 2·3 : 1 was assumed but the actual turned out to be higher (3·3 : 1). Looked at in another way, as compared with the First Plan, total investment just about doubled in the Second Plan in absolute terms and the rate of investment increased from about 7 per cent to about 11 per cent of national income, but increase in national income in the latter period was only slightly higher than in the First Plan years (20 per cent as against 18 per cent). Obviously, much of the rise in the ratio of capital to output was due to the greater emphasis on heavy industries in the Second Plan. Nevertheless, the unimpressive results in income creation can be fully explained only if other factors like wastes in investment expenditure and the failure to utilize fully the capital created in the process are taken into account. The failure in savings is all the more disappointing when viewed in the light of the fact that much of the increase in income was concentrated in a few hands who belonged already to the highest income groups. Hence the question arises whether there was not failure to fully mobilize the savings potential provided by the higher incomes of particular classes of income earners. The fact is that while the consumption level of the masses of the society including the so-called middle class fixed income earners has not improved, there are ample evidences indicating indulgence in conspicuous consumption by the richer few. The increased production of luxury articles like refrigerators, air conditioners, automobiles, quality furniture, electrical appliances, etc. by the private sector is not a sign of the rise in the general standard of living of the community, but indicative of the increasing demand for these products coming from the richer classes who have benefited by the redistribution of purchasing power brought about by inflation. Much of the resources which could have been saved and invested is thus frittered away.[9] In brief, planned development in India in the first decade of planning did not help in raising the savings margin to anywhere near the level necessary to bring about accelerated growth.

The next question to be considered is whether planned development has brought about the changes in social attitudes that are conducive to economic growth. An analysis of changes in human behaviour, attitudes and motivation or of modifications in social customs and pattern of living is clearly beyond the scope of a study in Economics. A quantitative assessment of such variations is difficult. Nevertheless in so far as an improvement in this direction is set as one of the major objectives of planned development in India, to be attained through public investment in social welfare measures and by means of an egalitarian tax and public expenditure policy, it would be possible to infer indirectly from government outlays on this head, the nature and degree of change that has taken place. It may also be added that successful execution of the programmes of development, particularly those which affect directly the immediate interests of the community, goes a long way towards enlisting the co-operation and support of the masses. Negatively, it means that to the extent public development expenditure has failed to show clear results, it has failed to arouse popular enthusiasm.

In view of the vastness of the country, the size of its population and its rapid rate of increase, the very low standards of health and literacy, the social rigidities and the adverse influence of custom and tradition, and the general apathy of the masses, public outlays on social services and welfare schemes under the first two Plans has to be considered as inadequate. Social services accounted for 23 per cent of the First Plan outlay, but the proportion declined to 18 per cent in the Second Plan and in the Third Plan the provision made under this head is only 17 per cent of the total outlay. It has also to be remembered that in the years 1951–1961, the actual expenditure under this head was much less than the planned amount. In the reappraisal of the Second Plan in 1958 in which the aggregate expenditure on the Plan was sought to be readjusted to the resources position, the outlay on social services and transport was lowered. Planned efforts over a decade succeeded in raising the percentage

[9]Gosh, Alak, *Indian Economy: its Nature and Problems*, 6th edition, World Press, Calcutta, 1962, p. 93. In this respect there is a sharp contrast between India and China. The rate of domestic savings in China is much higher than in India and this has been due largely to stricter measures of mobilizing savings. Cinema attendance and passenger travel have increased considerably in India much more than in China, and that from an initially higher level. Besides the ratio of output to investment is higher in China. In heavy industry, the capital-output ratio is 6 : 1 in India while it is 3 : 1 in China. Although much of this difference is due to the more important role of government in the latter country, yet even within the democratic framework, India can adopt certain measures like increased rural taxation, prevention of tax evasion, etc. which would increase the savings available for investment and accelerate economic progress— Malenbaum, Wilfred, ' India and China: Contrasts in Development Performance.' *The American Economic Review*, June, 1959, pp. 285–309.

of students enrolled in schools in the age group 6 to 11 years from 42·6 to 61·1 only. The All-India Educational Survey undertaken in 1957–59 pointed out that for the country as a whole in 1957 about 29 per cent of rural habitations and about 17 per cent of the rural population were not served by any school.[10] Outlay on public health, increased from Rs. 1,400 million in the First Plan to Rs. 2,250 million in the Second, and is estimated at Rs. 3,418 million in the Third Plan. This again falls short of the great needs of the economy. The increase in the number of hospitals and dispensaries from 8,600 in 1950–51 to 12,600 in 1960–61 and of beds from 113,000 to 185,600, is obviously very inadequate in a country with a population of 439 million, in which the average expectation of life of 40 years is among the lowest in the world, and where one out of ten children born, dies before completing one year of life. Bauer draws attention to the fact that the expenditure on education in the Second Plan is between one-third and two-fifth of that on large and medium industries in the public sector, and that development expenditure on elementary education is about half the cost of each of the three steel plants planned in the public sector.[11] The expenditure on elementary education increased by only Rs. 20 million in the Second Plan over the First, from Rs. 850 million to Rs. 870 million. The inadequacy of trained teachers and their very low incomes and status and the extreme measures taken to economize on educational facilities leave no doubt about the neglect of this important sector of the economy. In this connection, the great emphasis which Japan placed on educational investments in the early years of her industrial development, and the fact that China started in this field from a lower level than India but has marched ahead of the latter, contain an important lesson.[12] The unimpressive performance of the Community Development projects and the halting manner in which land reform measures have progressed are other indications of the fact that social reconstruction has not been given the serious attention which it deserves.

Although repeated stress has been made in all the plans about the social objectives of bringing about economic equality and better distribution of the benefits of economic improvement among all classes of people, this objective still remains a distant ideal. Statements have been made over and over again in public documents about reducing disparities in income and wealth through taxation, control of monopolies, fixation of land ceilings and minimum wages, better treatment of labour, granting of subsidies, etc. However, inflation and rise in capital values have only accentuated inequalities. The increase in agricultural and industrial production has not improved social well-being or reformed social structure, while community development has benefited only a minority. Thanks to a steady rise in prices, the lower middle classes have

[10]*Third Five-Year Plan*, Planning Commission, Government of India, New Delhi, 1961, p. 574.
[11]Bauer, P. T., *Indian Economic Policy and Development*, Allen & Unwin, London, 1961, pp. 51-52.
[12]Nurkse, R., ' Reflections on India's Development Plan,' *Quarterly Journal of Economics*, May, 1957, p. 198 and Malenbaum, Wilfred, ' India and China—Contrasts in Development Performance,' *The American Economic Review*, June, 1959, p. 297.

now lower real incomes, and the industrial workers have barely maintained the pre-war level of real wages. Growing influence of industrial magnates in national economic decisions, increasing corruption in public life and the discount at which social values are held, make one feel that there is less economic democracy today than there was ten years ago.[13] It is estimated that as much as 30 per cent of the increase in total income during the decade covered by the first two Five-Year Plans accrued to the higher income groups. The result is that the bulk of the population do not feel that they have benefited in any obvious way from the economic development of ten years.[14] There has therefore been no social reawakening and the enthusiasm of the people has not been aroused. That in the initial stages of planned effort in an underdeveloped country like India which has stagnated for long, there is need for a great measure of austerity is understandable. A realistic note in this matter was struck by the First Five-Year Plan which stated that only a negligible rise in the levels of consumption could be expected over the first two Plans and that any appreciable rise in consumption could be expected only from about 1970.[15] But the fact is that in a backward economy where the consumption levels are miserably low, where planned development is taking place within a democratic framework, and where social ideals of justice and equality are loudly proclaimed, the average consumer expects some improvement in his lot as a result of all the ambitious investment schemes and would be left with a sense of frustration when his hopes are not realized at least in some measure. Far from evoking his enthusiasm, this failure to raise consumption standards would only estrange his feelings and deprive him of what little faith he might have had in government schemes of economic expansion. The average intake of food in the country is still below accepted nutritional standards, and the consumption of cloth per head which rose from 9·2 yards in 1950–51 to 15·5 yards in 1955–56 has remained constant since then and is only around the pre-war level. Housing is woefully deficient and about a half of the population of India has on an average only Rs. 13 per month per head to spend on consumer goods. It is therefore not surprising that labour productivity has not improved. Nor is sufficient attention devoted in the Plans to increase the wages of labour and its productive efficiency. It is revealing to find that in the Chinese development plans, while great emphasis is laid on heavy industries, still due attention is given to improving the productivity of labour, wage level and also the supply of consumption goods, especially food, and to raising the standards of life of the masses. The Polish Second Development Plan aimed at raising labour productivity by 50 to 60 per cent and raising workers' wages by 40 per cent,

[13]Gyanchand, ' Social Premises of Planning in India,' *Asian Studies*, Bombay, February, 1962, pp. 31–32.

[14]Raj, K. N., ' Some Features of the Economic Growth of the Last Decade in India,' *The Economic Weekly*, Annual Number, Bombay, February 4, 1961, p. 271.

[15]*First Five-Year Plan*, (People's edition) Planning Commission, Government of India, New Delhi, 1951, p. 15.

and achieved considerable success in that direction.[16] According to the United Nations *Economic Survey of Asia and the Far East, 1961*, the productivity of industrial labour in China rose by 52 per cent between 1952 and 1957.

Public co-operation in planned effort at economic development depends to a great extent on the degree of success attained in achieving the targets which in turn is determined by the efficiency of planning techniques. Here again, the performance of economic planning in India has not been such as to create popular confidence and elicit the support of the masses. Particularly significant is the failure to reduce the magnitude of unemployment or secure self-sufficiency in food. While the implementation of certain development schemes and the starting and expansion of industries have increased employment opportunities, the volume of unemployment has also increased. The Second Plan estimated that the proportion of agricultural labour force would come down from about 70 per cent of the total to 60 per cent or so by 1975–76. But for this to happen, something like a four-fold increase in the numbers engaged in mining and factory establishments has to be brought about.[17] At the commencement of the Second Plan, the backlog of unemployment was estimated at 5·3 million persons. It was expected that in the course of 1956 to 1961 labour force would increase by about 10 million which, it was hoped, would be absorbed by the new employment opportunities created in the course of the five years. But in actual fact employment in the Second Plan period increased by only 6·5 million so that the number of unemployed at the end of the Second Plan should have increased to about 9 million. According to the Third Plan, the addition to the labour force because of growth of population in the five years covered by it would be about 17 million. If this is added to the backlog of 9 million, the total employment that would have to be provided in the Third Plan period would be of the order of 26 million. But the Third Plan hopes to create new employment for only about 15 million persons. This would mean that unemployment in the country would have increased by about 50 per cent at the end of the Third Plan as compared with the position at the end of the Second Plan. To this has to be added the problem of the under-employed whose number is reckoned at about 15 to 18 million. In view of this situation the employment target of about 15 million set in the Third Plan is very much below the minimum needed even to maintain the present unsatisfactory level of employment. The economic effect of an increase in the number seeking work at a much faster rate than increase in employment opportunities, is that it would aggravate inequality and will reduce the volume and effectiveness of investment.[18] The planning authorities and the government are certainly aware of the seriousness of this problem, but the measures adopted to ease the problem appear unsatisfactory. Professor Nurkse pointed out in 1957 that

[16]Ghosh, Alak, *New Horizons in Planning*, World Press, Calcutta, 1960, p. 141.

[17]*Second Five-Year Plan*, Planning Commission, Government of India, New Delhi, 1956, p. 14.

[18]Balogh, T., 'Equity and Efficiency: the Problem of Optimal Investment in a Frame Work of Underdevelopment,' *Oxford Economic Papers*, February, 1962, pp. 26–27.

38

the technique of encouraging cottage industries and light consumer goods industries like handloom, oil pressing, etc. through direct and indirect subsidies, quotas and prohibitions on factory products, would adversely affect factory industry, create vested interests and only shift the locus of disguised unemployment from the agricultural sector to the cottage industries sector.[19] Also, the attempt to spread out employment geographically, by giving preference to backward areas would necessitate ancillary investment in transport, housing, etc. and thereby reduce the efficiency of total investment.[20]

The failure to increase domestic food production to a sufficient extent so as to attain self-sufficiency has. been mentioned in an earlier chapter.[21] Before the commencement of the First Plan, the country was importing on the average about 3 million tons of food grains annually to meet domestic consumption requirements. The growth of population at a rate of 2·25 per cent per year would itself have created an additional demand of about 0·8 million tons per year. Over the five years of the First Plan, food production increased by 26 per cent, but in the Second Plan period, the increase was only 15 per cent. Moreover, the output of food grains has fluctuated considerably from year to year as the figures in Table 53 would show. Although agricultural production improved by about 31 per cent between 1949–50 and 1958–59, agricultural productivity deteriorated over the first three years of the First Plan, improved haltingly in the next five years and showed an appreciable rise in 1958–59. On the whole in this decade, improvement in agricultural productivity was slow and unsteady.

Table 53

OUTPUT OF FOOD GRAINS IN INDIA 1950–60

(*In million tons*)

Year	Output	Year	Output	Year	Output
1949–50	57·6	1955–56	65·8	1958–59	75·5 (a)
1950–51	52·2	1956–57	68·8	1959–60	71·7 (b)
		1957–58	62·5	1960–61	76·0 (c)

(a) Partially revised estimates. (b) Final estimates. (c) Provisional.

SOURCE: *Third Five-Year Plan*, Planning Commission, Government of India, p. 302.

The encouraging results obtained in the First Plan period in food production was due partly to a run of favourable seasons. But this should not lead to any underestimation of the steps taken by the government to improve agricultural conditions. It may be said that had the interest in agriculture been maintained in the Second Plan years, the performance at the food front in the latter half

[19]Nurkse, R., ' Reflections on India's Economic Development Plan,' *Quarterly Journal of Economics*, May, 1957, pp. 194–95.
[20]Balogh, T., *ibid.*, p. 30.
[21]Chapter XIV, pp. 483–485.

of the last decade might have been much better than what it actually was. The urgent need for stepping up agricultural production seems to be recognized in the Third Plan, in which the allotment of public outlay on agriculture and community development is double that made in the Second Plan, although as a proportion of aggregate outlay the rise is modest—from 11 per cent to 14 per cent. This is a welcome feature but past experience makes it clear that planned development in the ten years 1951–61 has not succeeded in effecting the break through on the agricultural front which is of basic importance in ensuring rapid growth of the economy.

It is clear that the failure to translate the egalitarian ideals into practice, the unsatisfactory manner in which the problem of unemployment has been handled, and the very limited success in the direction of attaining self-sufficiency in food should provide an explanation, at least partially, for the lack of popular enthusiasm and support for schemes of economic development. They are also indicative of defects in the formulation and implementation of development projects. Recent studies of planned development in India have brought to light two major deficiencies—one is general, relating to the over-all conception of planning, the other relates to the technique.

An important criticism of planning in India is that the principle of un-balanced development which seems to underly the Second and Third Plans, might be suitable for a country like Russia where the land-labour ratio is high, but not for India with an entirely different factor supply situation, and in which development is sought to be attained in a different political and organiza-tional set up. While the allocation of large investment expenditure on the heavy and capital goods sector may be justified under certain special circum-stances, the assumption that the growth of income depends largely on the magnitude of investment expenditure seems to be mistaken. Investment decisions may be wrong, or the implementation of investment policies may be defective, or the enforcement of controls and the attempt to drain away the savings into the public sector through taxation may have an adverse effect on the growth of the private sector. As a result, the increase in income may fall considerably short of the expected targets. On the other hand, an increase in income even without any addition to investment is conceivable when the existing stock of capital and other resources are better utilized, and better organization of labour improves productivity. The argument that a bold and largely-conceived plan, one in which impressive targets are set and high outlays are envisaged is a wise one, in that it would arouse local enthusiasm and attract a large inflow of foreign capital is unconvincing. A more modest plan, well drafted and properly executed, and which achieves its targets in the time and manner envisaged, is more likely to elicit public co-operation than one which leaves a wide gap between objectives and attainments. Cer-tainly, as has been remarked by Bauer, "grandiose plans cannot mobilize resources which do not exist ".[22]

[22]Bauer, P. T., *Indian Economic Policy and Development*, Allen and Unwin, London, 1961, p. 99.

38a

The technique of planning in India is criticized on the ground that the approach is mostly from the supply side. The availability of resources is first assessed, then the target is set for individual items of production and the allocation of investment is made on the basis of the capital-output ratio. In fact too much reliance seems to be placed on this relationship, the practical value of which in the context of an underdeveloped economy where statistical information is inadequate and unsatisfactory, is highly doubtful. A plan for development based on the assumption that if capital-output ratio is 2·3 : 1 and desired income increase is Rs. 26,800 million, investment should be Rs. 62,000 million—which is the logic behind the investment target in the Second Five-Year Plan—seems to be at best a crude method. Proper and scientific planning requires that the demand side is also to be taken into account, and the output or supply of intermediate products is determined with reference to final requirements. In other words, investment allocation should be made not only on the basis of resources available which ensure a given volume of output in different lines of production, but also on the basis of requirements of different categories of goods or the final demand for them arising in the different sectors. As Malenbaum puts it: " A series of output targets does not constitute a development plan. The specific production goals must be related on the one hand to the required stock of capital and the inputs of a flow of goods and services, and on the other, to the supply of technical and managerial skills. Information on this might permit an assessment of whether the targets could be attained."[23] Prof. Mahalanobis' model of planning for India[24] which formed the basis of the Second Five-Year Plan and which made an attempt at using a modified form of the inter-industry technique is criticized as being incomplete, in so far as it does not make use of any calculation of the final demand for consumption goods. In this model the supply of each group of consumer goods is determined only from the considerations of supply conditions quite independently of the possible level of demand for them.[25] In this respect the Third Plan does not mark any improvement. In its critical appraisal of India's Third plan, the World Bank Mission headed by Mr. Robert Sandove pointed out that the Third Plan is weak in its detailed phasing of projects and programmes. The first defect according to the Mission is the lack of technical planning and preparation which has resulted in much less than optimum benefits being obtained from the capital invested, especially in steel, petroleum and fertilizers. Secondly, the present macninery to co-ordinate the investment programmes of the different ministries is not as effective as it should be. According to Prof. Reddaway " there is little or no logic in the whole apparatus

[23]Malenbaum, Wilfred, ' India and China—Development Contrasts,' *Journal of Political Economy*, February, 1956, p. 12.

[24]' The Approach of Operational Research to Planning in India,' *Sankhya*, Calcutta, December, 1955, pp. 3–62.

[25]Komiyo, Ryutaro, ' A Note on Prof. Mahalanobis' Model of Indian Economic Planning,' *The Review of Economics and Statistics*, February, 1959, p. 29.

of Indian Planning. The numerous production targets are nearly all for semi-manufactures and capital goods and are not really related to the objective of giving Indian consumers a better standard of living; rather they represent nothing more than the projected development of industries which the Planners think that a modern state ought to possess."[26]

The stresses and strains which the Indian economy experienced when it was midway through the Second Plan are an obvious indication of the deficiencies in planning. Foreign exchange budgeting has all along remained one of the weakest spots in Indian planning. Faulty estimate of foreign exchange requirements and availability, has led to frequent changes in import and export policy and seriously hampered the timely completion of investment schemes in both the public and private sectors. According to the World Bank Mission referred to above, the worst limitation to the successful implementation of the Third Plan is foreign exchange. Balance of payments difficulties have led to a large build-up of projects waiting for foreign exchange allocations. Such delays have unfortunate repercussions on the whole economy. As regards internal stability, attempts at stabilization of prices have conspicuously failed. The general wholesale price index rose from 98·1 in 1956 to above 105 in 1957 and 1958 but since then, spurted up to reach the high level of 131·1 in August, 1962. That deficiencies in production, particularly of food have much to do with this rise in prices is clear from the fact that an appreciable fall in the production of food grains and some industrial raw materials in 1957–58 brought about a sharp uptrend in prices in the next year. But it also reflects the lack of a price policy in the country and the failure to maintain a balance between the levels of investment and the resources available. In addition to the obvious adverse economic and social consequences of persistent inflationary conditions a steady and continuous rise in prices creates a feeling in the minds of the people that the administration is incapable of tackling the problem successfully. At any rate, in so far as inflation has an obvious depressive effect on real incomes, the fixed income classes and wage earners are led to think that what is called planned economic development has only helped in lowering the purchasing power of the rupee and in transferring wealth to the already wealthy classes. In such a situation it is idle to expect that the co-operation of the masses would be forthcoming or their enthusiasm in development effort could be aroused.

It now remains to examine to what extent heavy public outlays on basic industries and on economic overheads have helped in preparing the ground for the economy to take off into self-sustained growth. A reference to Table 51 would show that the proportion of public outlay on power, organized industry and minerals, and transport and communications formed 44 per cent of total public outlay on development in the First Plan period and increased to 58 per cent in the Second Plan; it forms 53 per cent in the Third Plan. The

[26]Reddaway, W. B., *The Development of the Indian Economy*, Allen and Unwin, London, 1962, p. 82.

rise is particularly marked in the Second Plan. While public outlay between the First and the Second Plans increased by about 135 per cent, expenditure on the above three items increased more than three-fold. Public outlay envisaged in the Third Plan represents a rise of about 60 per cent over the Second, while outlay on the heads of development mentioned above, is expected to increase by 50 per cent. There has been a commensurate increase in output also. Over the ten years 1950–51 to 1960–61, industrial production increased by 94 per cent; the output of iron and steel rose by 138 per cent and chemicals by 188 per cent, while machinery of all types increased to five times the size at the beginning of this period.

National income according to the Third Plan would rise from about Rs. 145 billion at the end of the Second Plan to about Rs. 190 billion in 1965–66 representing an increase of about 30½ per cent over the income of 1960–61. Among the different sectors contributing to total product, large increases of 237 per cent, 145 per cent and 114 per cent are envisaged for engineering, metal manufacture and power, respectively, while agricultural output would improve by 21 per cent. But since agriculture accounts for nearly half the total income, that sector would contribute to 33 per cent of the total increase of Rs. 45 billion in income. As compared with the position in 1960–61, agricultural output will decline from 47 per cent to 42 per cent of total income in 1965–66 while the share of power, metal manufacture and engineering will increase from 0·4 to 0·6 per cent, 1·1 to 2·0 per cent and 0·7 to 2·5 per cent respectively. Details of the expansion in output of certain industrial goods which are of basic importance for the building up of the economy are given in Table 54.

These figures show that the achievements under certain heads like chemicals and machine tools (graded) were remarkable. Although a stimulus to increased production of capital goods and basic materials was given even in the First Plan, yet the general policy in industrial production in that period was to better utilize existing capital capacity. It was however, in the Second Plan years when primary attention was given to the building up of the industrial base of the economy, that production of capital goods, machinery and chemicals showed a phenomenal rise. And as the Planning Commission claims, industrial advance between 1955–56 and 1960–61 was in keeping with the avowed objective of enabling the economy to reach as soon as possible the stage of self-sustained growth.

That the establishment of a strong base in the form of heavy capital goods industries, and the development of power and transport is a pre-condition for rapid industrialization of the country, is an obvious fact. In reality, the hope for the economy reaching early the stage of self-sustained growth lies to a large extent on the further progress to be attained in this line. In an important recent publication Prof. W. B. Reddaway[27] points out that if a growth rate of income at a compound rate of 5 or 6 per cent per annum is to

[27]Reddaway, W. B., *The Development of the Indian Economy*, Allen and Unwin, London, 1962.

Table 54

TRENDS IN THE PRODUCTION OF INDUSTRIAL GOODS AND MACHINERY 1951—1961

Items of Production	1950–51	1955–56	1960–61 Estimated	1965–66 Targets*	Percentage increase in 1960–61 over 1950–51
1. Power : Electricity					
Installed capacity (million kW.)	2·3†	3·4†	5·7	12·7	148
Generated (million kWh)	6,575†	10,777†	19,850	45,000	202
2. Minerals					
Iron ore (million tons)	3·2	4·3	10·7	30·0	234
Coal (million tons)	32·3	38·4	54·6	97·0	69
3. Large-scale Industries					
Steel ingots (million tons)	1·4	1·7	3·5	9·2	150
Finished steel (million tons)	1·0	1·3	2·2	6·8	120
Aluminium ('000 tons)	3·7	7·3	18·5	80·0	400
Copper ('000 tons)	6·6	7·5	8·9	20·0	35
Cement machinery (value in Rs. million)	...	3·4†	6·0	45·0	...
Sugar machinery (value in Rs. million)	...	1·9	33·0	100·0	...
Industrial boilers (value in Rs. million)	...	...	4·0	250·0	...
Machine tools graded (value in Rs. million)	3·4	7·8	55·0	300·0	1,518
Tractors (number)	...	...	2,000	10,000	...
Electric motors (200 b.H.P. and below '000 H.P.)	100	272	700	2,500	600
4. Chemicals					
Nitrogenous fertilizers ('000 tons of N)	9	79	110	800	1,122
Phosphatic fertilizers ('000 tons of P_2O_5)	9	12	55	400	511
Sulphuric acid ('000 tons)	99	164	363	1,500	267
5. Cement (million tons)	2·7	4·6	8·5	13·0	215
6. Railway Locomotives					
Steam (number)	7	179	295	1,175	3,214
Diesel (number)	...	...	...	434	...
Electric (number)	...	...	...	232	...

*Overall targets for both the public and private sectors.
†Relates to Calendar Year.
SOURCE: *Third Five-Year Plan*, Annexure 1, pp. 77–84.

be attained, it is necessary to increase substantially the supply of the quantities of machinery each year. The value of the total supply of these goods in 1960–61 is estimated at about Rs. 5 billion of which imported machinery and components of machinery account for about a half. The value of machinery required for the process of development would rise to probably Rs. 10 billion in 1965–66 and to Rs. 15 billion in 1970–71. If imports of machinery in these years were restricted to about Rs. 4 billion which is about 20 per cent only less than the value of present total imports, it would mean that production of these goods in India (that is, the Indian element in the total) would have to rise from Rs. 2·5 billion in 1960–61 to Rs. 6 billion in 1965–66 and to Rs. 11 billion in 1970–71. And in order to make production of machinery of this scale possible, it is necessary that development should also be in ' depth ' that is, it would be essential to produce more iron ore, more power and coal and increase railway freight service, etc. These figures look abnormal, but Prof. Reddaway cites the figures relating to the United Kingdom in 1959 and shows that they are quite realistic.

The policy of building up heavy industries, started in the Second Plan period, is to be continued into the Third Plan. The idea behind this policy is that the economy should become self-sufficient in the matter of capital goods and machinery so that the strain on the balance of payments will be eased. Self-sufficiency is not an essential condition of self-sustained growth. A country may be importing necessary goods which it cannot produce, yet it may have a high rate of income growth and can easily meet its import obligations out of its export earnings. The stress is on the ease with which domestic earnings are increased and savings accelerated. However in a country like India, self-sufficiency in respect of capital goods is a requisite for attaining the stage of self-sustained growth. Since exports and imports constitute only a small fraction of total income and there is difficulty in increasing the exports, the wherewithal to bring about self-sustained growth has to be found within the country. This makes increased production of capital goods and machinery and the development of power and transport all the more important. And the prospects in this matter seem quite encouraging. According to Prof. Reddaway's calculations, while Gross National Product would increase by 30 per cent between 1960–61 and 1965–66, imports of goods and services will decline by 4 per cent, and exports of goods and services will increase by 16 per cent. As a proportion of Gross Domestic Product, both imports and exports will fall between these years from 8·1 per cent to 5·9 per cent and from 5·8 to 4·7 per cent respectively. These trends show that the development is towards greater self-sufficiency.[28] In detail, imports as a percentage of domestic supplies will decline in respect of agricultural goods from 3·4 to 1·3 per cent; oil and mining from 23 to 16·2 per cent; engineering goods from 52·8 to 33·7 per cent and other factory products from 9·8 to 5·9 per cent. It is noteworthy that the imports of engineering goods which formed more than half the total domestic supplies in 1960–61 would decline to one-third in 1965–66.

[28]Reddaway, W.B., *The Development of the Indian Economy*, Allen and Unwin, London, 1962, p. 162.

It is thus seen that while the achievements in a decade of planned economic progress in India in the matter of savings and in bringing about the necessary changes in social attitudes have been disappointing, the progress in industrialization and especially in the building up of basic industries constitutes an important redeeming feature.

Estimates have been made as regards the point of time when the Indian economy would be able to take off into self-sustained growth. The Second Five-Year Plan made the projection that investment as a proportion of national income would rise from 7 per cent in 1955–56 to 11 per cent in 1960–61, 14 per cent by 1965–66 and 16 per cent in 1970–71, and would thereafter remain more or less stable. National income would be doubled in 1967–68 and per capita income would be doubled by 1973–74.[29] In view of the fact that the actual rate of growth of population in the last few years was much higher than anticipated, the Third Plan is more modest in its estimates of income growth. According to it, national income would increase from Rs. 190 billion at the end of the Third Plan to about Rs. 250 billion and to Rs. 330–340 billion at the end of the Fourth and Fifth Plans; and per capita income, from around Rs. 330 at the end of 1960–61 to about Rs. 385, Rs. 450 and Rs. 530 in 1966, 1971 and 1976; that is to say, by 1976 per capita income would not be double that of the income in 1960–61, but would represent only a 66 per cent increase. This would necessitate a rise in investment from 11 per cent in 1960–61 to 14–15, 17–18 and 19–20 per cent of national income by the end of the Third, Fourth and Fifth Plans. It is difficult to make any guess about the occurrence of the take-off with reference to the per capita income or even the rate of investment attained. Paul Bareau feels that India is not likely to reach the point of self-generating industrial development in the next ten years but it would take twenty or thirty years more.[30] In a recent study of planned development in East Asian countries in the last decade, the United Nations Economic Commission for Asia and the Far East make the observation that in view of the many well-known obstacles, it is unrealistic to expect that many underdeveloped countries of the region would attain the stage of self-sustained growth within the next twenty years. They point out that since domestic savings are very meagre, in this critical period of twenty years, " a foreign aid generated take-off which is to lead to a self-sustained growth becomes a necessity ".[31]

Estimates of this kind have to be, by and large, merely a matter of faith. It does not seem correct to assume that when the investment rate reaches a certain level at a particular period of time, the economy would shake itself off the tentacles of economic backwardness and usher itself into an era of accelerated growth. The process of economic transformation is strenuous and

[29]*Second Five-Year Plan*, Planning Commission, Government of India, New Delhi, 1956, pp. 10–11.

[30]Bareau, Paul, ' India's Third Plan,' *The Banker*, February, 1961, p. 93.

[31]*Economic Bulletin for Asia and the Far East*, December, 1961, p. 25.

may be quite long drawn. Nor is there any assurance that when once a high
rate of investment and income growth is attained there would not be any falling
back. All that can be said is, that when the basic factors that conduce to a
high growth rate are set, i.e. economic overheads are provided, and structural,
organizational and institutional changes are brought about, there is an opportunity for the economy to lift itself up from the state of stagnation, so that the
very process of growth would alter the pattern of savings and composition of
income and other circumstances in a manner that would make further growth
easier. The brief analysis of the experience of India in planned development in
the last few years shows that no great improvement has been brought about
in certain vital factors, like savings and social attitudes, but that considerable
progress has been made in the direction of providing the economic infrastructure and the building up of basic industries which would help accelerated
growth. While Rostow laid stress on the leading sectors of the economy and
the role of the entrepreneurs in initiating the process of growth, he did not
ignore the fact that heavy investment activity by the state such as for rearmament or modernization of the army as in Germany and Japan would set in
motion the forces of economic expansion. In this sense, the entrepreneurial
role assumed by the government in India and the large investment outlays in
the public sector may well be the element which would trigger off the forces
of growth. Undoubtedly, in the increased activity which is taking place in
the private sector, public investment outlays played a significant part by
contributing directly to the provision of necessary overheads and indirectly by
stimulating demand. Large government spendings on heavy industries have
raised the capital-output ratio and strained the resources of the country. But
this is the inevitable result of the nature of the development that is taking place,
when an attempt is being made to bring about an economic revolution in a
much shorter time than it took for the present-day developed countries in their
early stages of growth. Increased concentration on basic industries has led
to a relative excess of overheads and under-utilization of capacity in some lines
of activity, but it only means that as economic activity in both the private and
public sectors gains momentum, and the growth of income brings about a
rise in the level of demand, the added capital equipment would be better and
fully utilized, so that efficiency of investment would increase and the capital-
output ratio would fall. Thus the stage when this phase of industrialization—
that is building up heavy capital goods industries—tapers off, will be the stage
when self-sustained growth would become possible.[32] Savings in the economy
will be enlarged and further rise in investment would become easier. It is
not too much to hope that this increase in the rate of growth of income and

---

[32]This of course does not mean a permanent relaxation of investment effort in capital goods.
It only means that the present tempo of activity in this line will slacken so that capital equipment
would get used up fully, but it would be followed by successive phases of greater concentration
on the capital goods sector and increased utilization of capital. This in fact is the characteristic
of growth.

investment would help to bring about the changes in institutions and social attitudes which are now lagging behind. Economic change and social change would then favourably react upon each other and growth would become cumulative.

INDEX